Theoretical Advancement in Social Impacts Assessment of Tourism Research

This book provides the reader with a fresh perspective on the use of theory in the body of research centred on social impacts of tourism. Theory is advanced in three primary forms within this volume. Some apply novel frameworks (e.g., theory of interaction ritual; degrowth paradigm; and mere exposure theory) to contexts involving destination residents. Others consider various uniquely complemented theoretical frameworks (e.g., social exchange theory and affect theory of exchange; Weber's theory of rationality and Foucauldian constructs; and emotional solidarity and cognitive appraisal theory). Still others develop theoretical frameworks (e.g., influence of presumed influence model, elaboration likelihood model, and social exchange theory; tourist–resident social contact; quality of life; and socio-ecological systems theory and chaos theory) for others to potentially consider and test. The chapters in this edited volume contribute to the evolving advancement of theoretical applications within the research area of social impacts of tourism.

This book will be of great interest to all upper-level students and researchers in tourism, planning and related fields. The chapters in this volume were originally published as a special issue of *Journal of Sustainable Tourism*.

Kyle Maurice Woosnam is Professor of Parks, Recreation and Tourism Management at the Warnell School of Forestry & Natural Resources, University of Georgia, USA. He is also Senior Research Fellow at the School of Tourism and Hospitality Management, University of Johannesburg, South Africa.

Manuel Alector Ribeiro is an Associate Professor in Tourism Management at the School of Hospitality and Tourism Management, University of Surrey, UK. He is also Senior Research Fellow at the School of Tourism and Hospitality Management, University of Johannesburg, South Africa; and an integrated member of the Research Centre for Tourism, Sustainability and Well-being (Cinturs) at the Faculty of Economics, University of Algarve, Portugal.

Theoretical Advancement in Social Impacts Assessment of Tourism Research

Edited by
Kyle Maurice Woosnam
and Manuel Alector Ribeiro

LONDON AND NEW YORK

First published 2024
by Routledge
4 Park Square, Milton Park, Abingdon, Oxon OX14 4RN

and by Routledge
605 Third Avenue, New York, NY 10158

Routledge is an imprint of the Taylor & Francis Group, an informa business

Introduction © 2024 Kyle Maurice Woosnam and Manuel Alector Ribeiro
Chapters 1–13 © 2024 Taylor & Francis

All rights reserved. No part of this book may be reprinted or reproduced or utilised in any form or by any electronic, mechanical, or other means, now known or hereafter invented, including photocopying and recording, or in any information storage or retrieval system, without permission in writing from the publishers.

Trademark notice: Product or corporate names may be trademarks or registered trademarks, and are used only for identification and explanation without intent to infringe.

British Library Cataloguing in Publication Data
A catalogue record for this book is available from the British Library

ISBN13: 978-1-032-53696-5 (hbk)
ISBN13: 978-1-032-53699-6 (pbk)
ISBN13: 978-1-003-41319-6 (ebk)

DOI: 10.4324/9781003413196

Typeset in Myriad Pro
by Newgen Publishing UK

Publisher's Note
The publisher accepts responsibility for any inconsistencies that may have arisen during the conversion of this book from journal articles to book chapters, namely the inclusion of journal terminology.

Disclaimer
Every effort has been made to contact copyright holders for their permission to reprint material in this book. The publishers would be grateful to hear from any copyright holder who is not here acknowledged and will undertake to rectify any errors or omissions in future editions of this book.

Contents

Citation Information vii
Notes on Contributors ix

Introduction: advancing theory within social impacts of tourism research 1
Kyle Maurice Woosnam and Manuel Alector Ribeiro

1 Towards a better tourist-host relationship: the role of social contact between tourists' perceived cultural distance and travel attitude 15
Daisy X. F. Fan, Hanqin Qiu, Carson L. Jenkins and Chloe Lau

2 Complementing theories to explain emotional solidarity 40
Emrullah Erul, Kyle Maurice Woosnam, Manuel Alector Ribeiro and John Salazar

3 The importance of collaboration and emotional solidarity in residents' support for sustainable urban tourism: case study Ho Chi Minh City 56
Hung Nguyen Phuc and Huan Minh Nguyen

4 Hapless victims or empowered citizens? Understanding residents' attitudes towards Airbnb using Weber's Theory of Rationality and Foucauldian concepts 76
Makarand Mody, Kyle Maurice Woosnam, Courtney Suess and Tarik Dogru

5 Empowerment of women through cultural tourism: perspectives of Hui minority embroiderers in Ningxia, China 99
Ming Ming Su, Geoffrey Wall, Jianfu Ma, Marcello Notarianni and Sangui Wang

6 Effects of social media on residents' attitudes to tourism: conceptual framework and research propositions 121
Robin Nunkoo, Dogan Gursoy and Yogesh K. Dwivedi

7 Re-theorizing social emotions in tourism: applying the theory of interaction ritual in tourism research 138
Dongoh Joo, Heetae Cho, Kyle Maurice Woosnam and Courtney Suess

8 Understanding the tourist-resident relationship through social contact: progressing the development of social contact in tourism   154
Daisy X. F. Fan

9 It's time to act! Understanding online resistance against tourism development projects   173
Philipp K. Wegerer and Monica Nadegger

10 Conceptualizing peer-to-peer accommodations as disruptions in the urban tourism system   190
Emily Yeager, B. Bynum Boley and Cari Goetcheus

11 Support for tourism: the roles of attitudes, subjective wellbeing, and emotional solidarity   206
Ian E. Munanura, Mark D. Needham, Kreg Lindberg, Chad Kooistra and Ladan Ghahramani

12 Indigenous residents, tourism knowledge exchange and situated perceptions of tourism   222
Tramy Ngo and Tien Pham

13 Exploring how perceived tourism impacts evolve over time (2009–2019) in an era of uncertainty: economic crisis, host-guest interactions, and Airbnb   240
Dimitrios Stylidis and Matina Terzidou

Index   264

Citation Information

The following chapters were originally published in the *Journal of Sustainable Tourism*, volume 31, issue 2 (2023). When citing this material, please use the original page numbering for each article, as follows:

Chapter 1
Towards a better tourist-host relationship: the role of social contact between tourists' perceived cultural distance and travel attitude
Daisy X. F. Fan, Hanqin Qiu, Carson L. Jenkins and Chloe Lau
Journal of Sustainable Tourism, volume 31, issue 2 (2023), pp. 204–228

Chapter 2
Complementing theories to explain emotional solidarity
Emrullah Erul, Kyle Maurice Woosnam, Manuel Alector Ribeiro and John Salazar
Journal of Sustainable Tourism, volume 31, issue 2 (2023), pp. 229–244

Chapter 3
The importance of collaboration and emotional solidarity in residents' support for sustainable urban tourism: case study Ho Chi Minh City
Hung Nguyen Phuc and Huan Minh Nguyen
Journal of Sustainable Tourism, volume 31, issue 2 (2023), pp. 245–264

Chapter 4
Hapless victims or empowered citizens? Understanding residents' attitudes towards Airbnb using Weber's Theory of Rationality and Foucauldian concepts
Makarand Mody, Kyle Maurice Woosnam, Courtney Suess and Tarik Dogru
Journal of Sustainable Tourism, volume 31, issue 2 (2023), pp. 284–306

Chapter 5
Empowerment of women through cultural tourism: perspectives of Hui minority embroiderers in Ningxia, China
Ming Ming Su, Geoffrey Wall, Jianfu Ma, Marcello Notarianni and Sangui Wang
Journal of Sustainable Tourism, volume 31, issue 2 (2023), pp. 307–328

Chapter 6
Effects of social media on residents' attitudes to tourism: conceptual framework and research propositions
Robin Nunkoo, Dogan Gursoy and Yogesh K. Dwivedi
Journal of Sustainable Tourism, volume 31, issue 2 (2023), pp. 350–366

Chapter 7
Re-theorizing social emotions in tourism: applying the theory of interaction ritual in tourism research
Dongoh Joo, Heetae Cho, Kyle Maurice Woosnam and Courtney Suess
Journal of Sustainable Tourism, volume 31, issue 2 (2023), pp. 367–382

Chapter 8
Understanding the tourist-resident relationship through social contact: progressing the development of social contact in tourism
Daisy X. F. Fan
Journal of Sustainable Tourism, volume 31, issue 2 (2023), pp. 406–424

Chapter 9
It's time to act! Understanding online resistance against tourism development projects
Philipp K. Wegerer and Monica Nadegger
Journal of Sustainable Tourism, volume 31, issue 2 (2023), pp. 425–441

Chapter 10
Conceptualizing peer-to-peer accommodations as disruptions in the urban tourism system
Emily Yeager, B. Bynum Boley and Cari Goetcheus
Journal of Sustainable Tourism, volume 31, issue 2 (2023), pp. 504–519

Chapter 11
Support for tourism: the roles of attitudes, subjective wellbeing, and emotional solidarity
Ian E. Munanura, Mark D. Needham, Kreg Lindberg, Chad Kooistra and Ladan Ghahramani
Journal of Sustainable Tourism, volume 31, issue 2 (2023), pp. 581–596

Chapter 12
Indigenous residents, tourism knowledge exchange and situated perceptions of tourism
Tramy Ngo and Tien Pham
Journal of Sustainable Tourism, volume 31, issue 2 (2023), pp. 597–614

Chapter 13
Exploring how perceived tourism impacts evolve over time (2009–2019) in an era of uncertainty: economic crisis, host-guest interactions, and Airbnb
Dimitrios Stylidis and Matina Terzidou
Journal of Sustainable Tourism, volume 31, issue 2 (2023), pp. 615–638

For any permission-related enquiries please visit:
www.tandfonline.com/page/help/permis

Notes on Contributors

B. Bynum Boley, Department of Parks, Recreation & Tourism Management in the Warnell School of Forestry, University of Georgia, Athens, GA, USA.

Heetae Cho, Department of Physical Education and Sports Science, Nanyang Technological University, Singapore, Singapore.

Tarik Dogru, Dedman School of Hospitality Administration, Florida State University, Tallahassee, FL, USA.

Yogesh K. Dwivedi, School of Management, Swansea University Bay Campus, Swansea, UK.

Emrullah Erul, Department of Tourism Management, Faculty of Tourism, Izmir Katip Çelebi University, Izmir, Turkey.

Daisy X. F. Fan, Department of People and Organisations, Faculty of Management, Bournemouth University, Poole, Dorset, UK.

Ladan Ghahramani, Global Marketing Services, Travel Oregon, Portland, OR, USA.

Cari Goetcheus, Landscape Architect, Historic Preservation Program in the College of Environment + Design, University of Georgia, Athens, GA, USA.

Dogan Gursoy, Carson College of Business, Washington State University, Pullman, WA, USA.

Carson L. Jenkins, Hospitality and Tourism Management, University of Strathclyde, Glasgow, UK.

Dongoh Joo, Sport, Outdoor Recreation, and Tourism Management Program, University of Tennessee at Chattanooga, Chattanooga, TN, USA.

Chad Kooistra, Department of Forest and Rangeland Stewardship, Colorado State University, Fort Collins, CO, USA.

Chloe Lau, School of Hotel and Tourism Management, The Hong Kong Polytechnic University, TST East, Kowloon, Hong Kong.

Kreg Lindberg, Department of Forest Ecosystems and Society, Oregon State University-Cascades, OR, USA.

Jianfu Ma, North Minzu University, Ningxia Hui Autonomous Region, Yinchuan, China.

Makarand Mody, School of Hospitality Administration, Boston University, Boston, MA, USA.

Ian E. Munanura, Department of Forest Ecosystems and Society, Oregon State University, Corvallis, OR, USA.

Monica Nadegger, Department of Tourism and Leisure Business, Management Center Innsbruck, Innsbruck, Austria.

Mark D. Needham, Department of Forest Ecosystems and Society, Oregon State University, Corvallis, OR, USA.

Tramy Ngo, Yorke Peninsula Council, Maitland, South Australia, Australia; Dong Nai Technology University, Vietnam.

Huan Minh Nguyen, Faculty of Trade and Tourism, Industrial University of Hochiminh City, Vietnam.

Hung Nguyen Phuc, Faculty of Trade and Tourism, Industrial University of Hochiminh City, Vietnam.

Marcello Notarianni, Tourism Consultant, Madrid, Spain.

Robin Nunkoo, Department of Management, University of Mauritius, Reduit, Mauritius; School of Tourism and Hospitality, University of Johannesburg, South Africa; Griffith University, Gold Coast, Australia; Copenhagen Business School, University of Copenhagen, Denmark.

Tien Pham, Griffith Institute for Tourism, Griffith University, Nathan, Australia.

Hanqin Qiu, College of Tourism and Service Management Nankai University, Tianjin, China.

Manuel Alector Ribeiro, School of Hospitality and Tourism Management, University of Surrey, UK; School of Tourism and Hospitality Management, University of Johannesburg, Auckland Park, South Africa; and Research Centre for Tourism, Sustainability and Well-being (Cinturs), University of Algarve, Faro, Portugal.

John Salazar, Department of Agricultural & Applied Economics, College of Agricultural & Environmental Sciences, University of Georgia, Athens, GA, USA.

Dimitrios Stylidis, Marketing Branding & Tourism, Middlesex University, London, UK.

Ming Ming Su, School of Environment and Natural Resources; China Anti-Poverty Research Institute, Renmin University of China, Beijing, China.

Courtney Suess, Department of Recreation, Park and Tourism Sciences, Texas A&M University, College Station, TX, USA.

Matina Terzidou, Marketing Branding & Tourism, Middlesex University, London, UK.

Geoffrey Wall, Department of Geography and Environmental Management, Faculty of Environment, University of Waterloo, Ontario, Canada.

Sangui Wang, China Anti-Poverty Research Institute; School of Agricultural Economics and Rural Development, Renmin University of China, Beijing, China.

Philipp K. Wegerer, Department of Tourism and Leisure Business, Management Center Innsbruck, Innsbruck, Austria.

Kyle Maurice Woosnam, Warnell School of Forestry & Natural Resources, University of Georgia, Athens, GA, USA and School of Tourism and Hospitality Management, University of Johannesburg, Auckland Park, South Africa.

Emily Yeager, Department of Recreation Sciences, East Carolina University, Greenville, NC, USA.

Introduction: Advancing theory within social impacts of tourism research

Kyle Maurice Woosnam and Manuel Alector Ribeiro

Introduction

The mark of most evolving fields growing out of parent disciplines is a continued advancement in theoretical application. Such advancements serve as the "lifeblood" of efforts that continue to "push the envelope" and ensure we contribute the most substantive research possible. Moving into the fifth decade of research concerning the social impacts of tourism, we find ourselves at a pivotal juncture. Arguably, the question to ponder is not, "do we need to advance theoretically our field forward" but rather, "how do we do it?" An introspective examination of our past and present will help us to chart a path forward.

Though we now accept tourism impacts research to encompass inextricably linked social, cultural, environmental, political, and economic aspects, that has not always been the case. The initial push by impacts researchers focused heavily on economics (Deery, Jago, & Fredline, 2012), with social, cultural, and environmental impacts considered secondarily. Over time, we have seen the pendulum swing in the opposite direction, due in part to multiple factors. Not the least of these is the realization that financial gain from tourism is not the sole endgame of destinations and their residents (Nunkoo & Gursoy, 2019). This has paved the way for a more widespread acknowledgment of the inextricable link between various impact forms (Mason, 2016). Additionally, we are seeing fewer studies focusing on destinations where tourism is a new discovery. As a result, economic gain does not seem as paramount as the social-cultural, environmental, and political impacts of tourism, especially given COVID-19 and global matters of justice, war, and climate change. Finally, we are witnessing a greater appreciation for sustainability (considering the triple-bottom-line) in tourism across society, industry, and the academy (Ruhanen, Moyle, & Moyle, 2019). This is evidenced in the burgeoning impact and popularity of the *Journal of Sustainable Tourism* within the field. As we find ourselves in a time of COVID-19 pandemic recovery and great uncertainty due to climate change, natural disaster, war/armed conflicts and terrorism, and political and racial divides, no time is better than now to realize the growing need to advance our theoretical development in our social impacts of tourism research.

The evolution of social impacts of tourism research is marked by five key developmental stages (Figure 1). Though Deery et al. (2012) highlight some of these stages, we adapted their approach by reorganizing and reclassifying their proposed stages and adding a newly developing stage. The groundwork was initially laid for social impacts research through the definition of key concepts, typologies, and conceptual model development, heavily focused on residents' attitudes. In this first stage, works by Doxey (1975), Rothman (1978), Butler (1980), and Mathieson and Wall (1982) highlight the heterogeneous perspectives of destination residents in responding to tourism. In essence, these works are considered seminal by many studying social impacts of tourism.

Figure 1. Social impacts of tourism research development stages (as adapted from Deery, Jago, and Fredline, 2012).

The second stage in the evolution of social impacts of tourism research marked the beginning of more case study–based, atheoretical, and empirical inquiries. This stage was characterized by an increased focus on understanding the diverse experiences and perspectives of residents in various destinations. Researchers during this period sought to gather empirical evidence on the specific impacts of tourism development on local communities, as well as the factors shaping residents' attitudes and perceptions. Several key developments took place during this stage: (i) *Diverse methodological approaches*: Researchers employed a range of quantitative and qualitative methodologies to explore residents' attitudes and perceptions, such as surveys, interviews, and observational studies (Kendall & Var, 1984; Long, Perdue, & Allen, 1990; Pizam, 1978). These methods provided rich data that helped to uncover the complex and context-specific nature of tourism impact studies. (ii) *Geographical expansion*: Studies in this stage extended beyond the traditional Western tourism destinations and began to encompass a broader range of geographic areas, including developing countries and emerging tourism markets (Akis, Peristianis, & Warner, 1996; Liu & Var, 1986). This expansion allowed researchers to explore the unique social and cultural contexts in which tourism development takes place and to identify similarities and differences in residents' attitudes across various settings and over time (Ahmed, 1986; Johnson, Snepenger, & Akis, 1994; Liu, Sheldon, & Var, 1986). Some notable studies from this stage include Belisle and Hoy (1980), who examined the socio-cultural impacts of tourism in a small Mexican town; Farrell (1979) examines the distinctions between "Western" and "Pacific" perspectives on the topic, as well as the differences between "island" and "continental" approaches when it comes to understanding the perceived environmental consequences of tourism. Lui et al. (1987) identified variations in how residents of Hawaii and North Wales, compared to those in Turkey, perceive the estimated physical effects of tourism. (iii) *Focus on specific impacts*: The second stage saw an increased focus on examining specific social and cultural impacts of tourism, such as the influence of tourism on community identity, social cohesion, cultural preservation, and intergroup relations. Researchers during this period aimed to provide a more nuanced understanding of how tourism development can affect different aspects of community life and social relations. Seminal works at this phase include Evans-Pritchard (1989), who explored the influence of tourism on social relations and cultural practices in a Spanish village; Liu and Var (1986), who investigated the role of various factors in shaping residents' attitudes toward tourism in a Hawaiian community; (iv) *Identification of predictor variables*: Researchers in this stage sought to identify factors that predict residents' attitudes toward tourism development, such as demographic characteristics, length of residence, and proximity to tourist attractions (Haralambopoulos & Pizam, 1996; Jurowski, Uysal, & Williams, 1997). These variables are parts of studies developed by Perdue, Long, and Allen (1990), who conducted a comparative analysis of residents' attitudes in two U.S. tourism destinations; and Milman and Pizam (1988), who assessed the social impacts of tourism in an urban context in Florida. These studies aimed to uncover patterns and trends in residents' attitudes and to inform more targeted and effective tourism planning and management strategies.

The second stage of social impacts of tourism research laid the foundation for more theoretically grounded and contextually sensitive studies in subsequent stages (Deery et al., 2012). The empirical evidence gathered during this period helped to reveal the complexities of tourism impacts and underscore the need for more sophisticated and integrated theoretical frameworks to explain the diverse experiences and attitudes of residents in different tourism destinations (Nunkoo, Smith, & Ramkissoon, 2013; Woosnam & Ribeiro, 2023).

The third stage is characterized by scale design, development, and testing measures of residents' attitudes. This stage represents a more nuanced effort in theory development within residents' attitudes research. The focus during this stage was to develop standardized, multidimensional, and reliable measurement tools that could capture the complex and context-specific nature of residents' attitudes toward tourism development (Woosnam & Ribeiro, 2023). During this period Lankford and Howard (1994) are credited with developing the first multidimensional scale, known as the Tourism Impact Attitude Scale (TIAS), to measure residents' perceptions of tourism development. TIAS was designed to measure residents' perceptions of tourism development. Some researchers argued that the TIAS did not capture a more holistic perspective of residents' attitudes in terms of sustainability (Ap & Crompton, 1998). In response, Ap and Crompton (1998) developed another general scale that encompassed residents' attitudes toward perceived tourism impacts in the way of social, economic, and environmental aspects. This scale aimed to provide a more comprehensive understanding of residents' attitudes by considering the triple-bottom-line approach to sustainable tourism development. Other researchers also contributed to the development of new scales for measuring residents' attitudes during this period. Examples include Andereck et al.'s (2005) who developed the tourism development impact scale, which focused on the perceived positive and negative impacts of tourism, and Ko and Stewart (2002) refined the perceived positive and negative tourism impact scales, which examined residents' perceptions of both the benefits and costs of tourism development. These scales aimed to further refine the measurement of residents' attitudes and to address the methodological limitations of earlier scales. Alongside the development of new scales, researchers also sought to validate and refine existing scales through empirical testing in various settings (Vargas-Sánchez, Porras-Bueno, & Plaza-Mejía, 2011; Nunkoo & Ramkissoon, 2011). These efforts aimed to enhance the reliability and validity of the scales, as well as to ensure their applicability and relevance in different tourism contexts.

The third stage of social impacts of tourism research contributed significantly to the advancement of theory development and the standardization of measurement tools for assessing residents' attitudes. The scales developed during this stage have provided researchers with robust instruments to explore the complex and multifaceted nature of residents' attitudes toward tourism development, thus enabling more rigorous and comparable studies across various destinations and contexts.

The fourth stage of social impact of tourism research emphasizes further scale development, refinement, and increased application of theoretical frameworks. This period witnesses a shift toward examining the social impacts of tourism within the context of sustainability, reflecting the growing awareness of the need for sustainable tourism practices. During this stage, researchers developed new scales to assess residents' attitudes toward sustainable tourism development. Choi and Sirakaya (2005) created the Sustainable Tourism Attitude Scale (SUS-TAS), aiming to measure residents' support for sustainable tourism practices. This scale was later validated in cross-cultural contexts (Sirakaya-Turk, 2007; Sirakaya-Turk, Ekinci, & Kaya, 2008), shortened, and transformed into a more parsimonious scale while retaining its original seven dimensions (Ribeiro, Pinto, Silva, & Woosnam, 2018; Sirakaya & Gursoy, 2013; Yu, Chancellor & Cole, 2011; Zhang, Cole, & Chancellor, 2015). Meanwhile, Woosnam and Norman (2010) introduced the Emotional Solidarity Scale (ESS), focusing on understanding how residents' interactions and relationships with tourists influence their perspectives on tourism development. These scales highlight the increasing importance of incorporating sustainability principles in social impact studies. This stage is also marked by more extensive application of theoretical frameworks, such as the social exchange theory (SET), which posits that residents' attitudes toward tourism development are shaped by the perceived benefits and costs of their interactions with tourists and the industry (Ap, 1992). Researchers increasingly applied this theory to explain residents' attitudes in various contexts, leading to a better understanding of the factors driving support or opposition to tourism development. Studies employing SET include Andereck et al. (2005), Choi and Murray (2010), Jurowski and Gursoy (2004), McGehee and Andereck (2004), Ribeiro et al. (2017), and Gursoy et al. (2017), among others.

The fourth stage of social impact of tourism research has significantly contributed to the advancement of the field by refining measurement tools and deepening the theoretical understanding of residents' attitudes toward tourism development. By focusing on sustainability and applying established theoretical frameworks, this stage has laid the groundwork for more nuanced and context-sensitive analyses of the social impacts of tourism, leading to more informed tourism planning and management strategies.

Over the past decade, we have transitioned into the most recent stage of social impact of tourism research, characterized by further development and testing of theoretical models. This shift has been reinforced by the top four tourism journals, which either explicitly or implicitly call for theoretical application as a criterion for publishing. This stage has seen a considerable increase in the use of advanced statistical techniques, such as structural equation modeling, to investigate complex relationships in tourism research and facilitate theory building and theory testing (Boley et al., 2014; Látková & Vogt, 2012; Nunkoo & Ramkissoon, 2012). During this stage, research has also started to treat social impacts of tourism as an antecedent of various outcome variables. For example, Munanura et al. (2023) and Phuc and Nguyen (2023) explored the relationship between social impacts and emotional solidarity, while Tilaki et al. (2021) and Woosnam et al. (2023) examined the effects of social impacts on residents' receptiveness toward tourists during the COVID-19 pandemic. Other studies have investigated the influence of social impacts on pro-tourism behavioral support (Erul, Woosnam, & McIntosh, 2020; Ribeiro et al., 2017). This stage reflects a more comprehensive and sophisticated approach to understanding the social impacts of tourism, with researchers increasingly drawing on established theories and innovative methodologies to unravel the complex relationships among various factors (Erul & Woosnam, 2022; Erul, Woosnam, Ribeiro & Salazar, 2023; Liang, Luo, & Bao, 2021; Maruyama, Ribeiro, & Woosnam, 2023). This deeper understanding is crucial for informing tourism planning and management strategies, as it provides insights into the mechanisms through which residents' attitudes toward tourism development are shaped and the consequences of these attitudes for destination sustainability.

In a nutshell, the most recent stage of social impact of tourism research has made significant strides in advancing the field by building on earlier achievements, incorporating advanced statistical techniques, and exploring new outcome variables and theories. As a result, our understanding of the complex relationships between residents' attitudes, social impacts, and tourism development has become more nuanced and context-sensitive, paving the way for more informed and sustainable tourism planning and management.

To chart a path forward for theoretical advancement of the social impacts of tourism research, this work aims to accomplish numerous endeavors. Firstly, we will explore the historical development of theoretical advancements in this field, tracing the progression from the late 1970s to the present day. This analysis will enable us to understand how the field has evolved and identify the key milestones that have shaped the current state of research on the social impacts of tourism. Following this, we will showcase the valued contributions of the chapters included in this volume, highlighting their significance and relevance to the broader field of social impact research. By examining these chapters, we aim to demonstrate the diverse range of topics and theoretical frameworks employed by researchers in this area, thereby offering a comprehensive understanding of the current state of knowledge and the diverse perspectives that inform the study of social impacts of tourism research. Finally, in closing this introductory chapter, we will outline several avenues for future research. These recommendations will be aimed at addressing current gaps in literature, promoting the integration of novel theoretical perspectives, and encouraging researchers to explore new theoretical approaches in their investigations. By providing these suggestions, we hope to inspire the next generation of researchers to continue advancing our theoretical understanding of the social impacts of tourism research and contribute to the development of more sustainable tourism practices.

Highlighting theoretical advancements in assessing social impacts of tourism: A shift toward a more comprehensive approach

For the better part of two decades (1984–2003), research centered on social impacts of tourism primarily lacked theoretical grounding, driven by imminent problems faced by industry practitioners (Gursoy & Nunkoo, 2019; Nunkoo et al., 2013). Although studies on social impacts of tourism have struggled with theoretical application, Ward and Berno (2011) argue that most of the works employing theoretical perspectives have centered around SET. This was echoed in the works by Gursoy et al. (2019), Nunkoo et al. (2013), Nunkoo (2016), and Hadinejad et al. (2019). SET posits that individuals' attitudes toward tourism and their subsequent level of support for its development are influenced by their evaluations of the outcomes of tourism for themselves and their communities (Ward & Berno, 2011). However, this approach has faced criticism from researchers such as Joo et al. (2023) and Maruyama, Keith, and Woosnam (2019), who argue that SET reduces the relationship between residents and tourists to a primarily financial exchange, overlooking the importance of social interactions and relationships between the parties involved. Furthermore, since SET does not provide a testable model, it is often considered in conjunction with other theoretical frameworks (Ward & Berno, 2011). Recent studies have adopted this approach, integrating SET with other theories to provide a more comprehensive understanding of the social impacts of tourism (Chang, 2021; Erul et al., 2023; Ouyang, Gursoy, & Sharma, 2017; Ribeiro et al., 2017; Yeager et al., 2020). As research on social impacts of tourism continues to evolve, there is a growing need for the development and application of more comprehensive theoretical frameworks that can better account for the complex relationships and interactions between residents and tourists. This shift toward more inclusive approaches will ultimately contribute to a deeper theoretical understanding of the social impacts of tourism, providing valuable insights for practitioners and policymakers in the development of more inclusive and sustainable tourism industry.

Although SET has been widely used in social impacts of tourism research, other theoretical frameworks have also been applied, albeit to a lesser extent. One such framework is the social representations theory (SRT), which has been employed by a few tourism researchers (Monterrubio & Andriotis, 2014; Moscardo, 2011; Sarr, Sène-Harper, & Gonzalez-Hernandez, 2021), building upon Moscovici's (1984) initial work. The theories of reasoned action (TRA) and planned behavior (TPB) are two additional frameworks that have gained some interest in recent years for explaining residents' attitudes toward tourism impacts. These theories, originally popular for understanding the antecedents of visitors' or tourists' behaviors, have been increasingly employed by researchers due to their established testable models, particularly when exploring residents' pro-tourism behaviors (Erul et al., 2020; Erul & Woosnam 2022; Nunkoo & Ramkissoon, 2010; Ribeiro et al., 2017; Wu & Chen, 2018). Emotional solidarity theory, which stems from Durkheim's ([1915] 1995) work and focuses on how residents' interactions and relationships with tourists explain the social impacts of tourism, has also attracted growing attention in the literature (Joo et al., 2021; Munanura et al., 2023; Phuc & Nguyen, 2023; Woosnam, 2012). Additionally, Weber's theory of formal and substantive rationality is gaining traction, particularly when considering residents' empowerment through tourism (Boley et al., 2014; Gannon, Rasoolimanesh, & Taheri, 2021; Mody et al., 2023; Strzelecka, Boley, & Strzelecka, 2017; Yeager et al., 2020). This theory helps researchers understand the balance between rational decision-making processes and the underlying values and beliefs that shape residents' perspectives on tourism development. While SET remains a predominant framework in social impacts of tourism research, other theories have been applied to provide a more comprehensive understanding of residents' attitudes and behaviors. These alternative theoretical frameworks contribute to the development of a richer, more nuanced understanding of the social impacts of tourism, ultimately benefiting tourism planning and management.

Hadinejad et al. (2019) identified several theories that have received limited attention in the context of social impacts of tourism research over the past decade. These include the bottom-up spillover theory (Eslami et al., 2019; Suess et al., 2021), social dilemma theory (Zheng, Liang, & Ritchie, 2020), social identity theory (Chiang et al., 2017; Nunkoo & Gursoy, 2012; Palmer, Koenig-Lewis, & Jones, 2013), intergroup contact theory (Joo et al., 2018), and integrated threat theory (Monterrubio, 2016; Ward & Berno, 2011). Two key observations can be made from this work. First, most of the research using these theories has been conducted within the last decade, indicating that the field is gradually expanding and embracing a wider range of theoretical perspectives. Second, these theories reflect a growing recognition that residents' perspectives on the social impacts of tourism are influenced, to some extent, by their interactions and relationships with tourists, rather than solely focusing on the resulting tourism development. This shift in focus acknowledges the complex, multifaceted nature of residents' experiences and attitudes toward tourism and its social impacts. By considering these less frequently applied theories, researchers can develop a more comprehensive understanding of the social impacts of tourism and offer more targeted, effective recommendations for tourism planning and management. Additionally, this broader theoretical approach helps to capture the diverse perspectives of residents and tourists, thereby contributing to more inclusive, sustainable tourism development strategies.

While there have been some advancements in the theoretical application in the field of social impacts of tourism research, it remains hindered by a lack of theoretical development and testing. As highlighted by Hadinejad et al. (2019) in their review of articles published between 2011 and 2017 in leading tourism journals (i.e., *Journal of Sustainable Tourism*, *Journal of Travel Research*, *Tourism Management*, and *Annals of Tourism Research*), 44.5% of the articles were atheoretical in nature. This represents progress compared to the 54.3% of atheoretical articles between 1984 and 2010 (Nunkoo et al., 2013); however, a more significant focus on theoretical application is necessary to further advance this area of research. As a field, we must strive for improvement. Considering our current review of theoretical applications in social impacts of tourism research, we encourage readers to consult the works by Gursoy and Nunkoo (2019), Hadinejad et al. (2019), and Nunkoo et al. (2013) for a more comprehensive and robust review. These studies emphasize the importance of integrating theory into social impacts of tourism research to foster a deeper understanding of the complex relationships and factors that influence residents' perceptions and attitudes toward tourism. By prioritizing theoretical development and testing, researchers can contribute to the advancement of the field, ultimately leading to more effective and sustainable tourism development.

Structure of the book

As we emphasize the importance of theoretical advancements in social impacts of tourism research, it is worth noting that the 13 chapters in this book demonstrate significant progress in this domain. These chapters address a variety of topics, including relationships between community residents and tourists, social impacts and residents' perspectives, residents' empowerment, and overtourism. Here, we discuss each aspect in turn.

Resident–tourist relationships

The work by Fan and colleagues speaks to the relationships with a focus on Allport's (1954) contact theory. Not only does Fan et al. (2023) incorporate a mixed methods approach (which should be more prevalent in extant work), but it highlights tourists' perspectives of the interaction with residents and how that shapes attitudes about the destination. Fan et al. (2023) demonstrate that perceived cultural distance and social contact with residents (for which the authors develop a new scale encompassing social- and service-oriented contact and quality of contact) are salient constructs in determining tourists' attitudes about the destination. We see this work as extremely timely given how distance and contact are at the forefront of travelers' minds following the COVID-19 pandemic. Considering value co-creation and co-destruction, Fan (2023) delivers a conceptual work that highlights four relationships rooted in social contact between residents and tourists: scripted relationship (favorable for residents/unfavorable for tourists); co-creating (favorable for both); co-destructing (unfavorable for both); and egotistical (unfavorable for residents/favorable for tourists). The research agenda she lays out building on this typology will no doubt foster even more timely research centered on destination interactions.

The emotional solidarity theory is also advanced within this issue (Erul et al., 2023; Joo et al., 2023; Munanura et al., 2023; Phuc & Nguyen, 2023). Considering SET in tandem with the affect theory of exchange, Erul et al. (2023) demonstrates how Turkish residents' perspectives of existing tourism explained support for future tourism development (69% of the variance), which in turn, predicts emotional solidarity with tourists (25–80% of variance across the three dimensions). Closely related, Munanura et al. (2023) tests a structural model (using constructs developed from the cognitive appraisal theory and social exchange theory) to determine antecedents to Oregon (U.S.) residents' support for tourism. What the authors found was that 78% of the variance in support for tourism was accounted for through perceived impacts (i.e., environmental and community), expected change in subjective well-being, and emotional solidarity with tourists. Two other works within this issue develop emotional solidarity theory by testing models whereby the emotional solidarity construct acts as a mediator between beliefs or values and residents' attitudinal support for tourism. In Vietnam, Phuc and Nguyen (2023) show us that residents' values, perceptions of tourism collaboration, and emotional solidarity with tourists all uniquely explain attitudinal support for tourism development. According to the conceptual work by Joo et al. (2023), what may contribute even further to our knowledge of emotional solidarity are interaction rituals (through the interaction ritual theory). Religious tourism contexts would seem to be the most ideal environment in which to test such relationships (Joo & Woosnam, 2020; Kamath et al., 2022).

Social impacts and residents' attitudes

Four chapters within this volume advance research concerning social impacts and residents' attitudes about tourism in general. Two chapters are conceptual in nature. Given the increasing dependence on social media, Nunkoo, Gursoy, and Dwivedi's (2023) work is timely as it pulls together analytical perspectives of the information society, elaboration likelihood model, influence of presumed influence model, and SET. A causal chain framework encompassing aspects of social media exposure and influence (e.g., own media exposure, personal exposure, presumed influence, and influence of presumed influence) among destination residents is linked to 25 propositions ripe for future researchers to test through modelling (see Figure 1 in their chapter). The final conceptual chapter by Yeager, Boley, and Goetcheus (2023) proposes a theoretical framework, drawing from socio-ecological systems and chaos theories, for future researchers to test. This framework emphasizes that the density, location, and pace of growth of peer-to-peer accommodations are crucial factors in determining when destinations reach their social carrying capacity.

The remaining two chapters pertaining to social impacts' present findings from empirical research. Stylidis and Terzidou (2023) report findings from a longitudinal study among residents of Greece to see how perceptions of impacts have changed across three-time horizons (between 2009 and 2019). The authors found that (through application of the mere exposure theory) residents' perceptions are fluid and have likely changed in part due to the preponderance of peer-to-peer accommodations within the destination. This adds credence to notions raised by Yeager et al (2023). Ngo and Pham (2023) present descriptive findings from their study (in Vietnam) concerning residents' attitudes about tourism. The distinctiveness of this work stems from its inclusive approach to incorporating often-overlooked study participants and utilizing diffusion and adult learning theories as the foundational basis for the research. Ngo and Pham (2023) capture the voices of indigenous residents through a phenomenological qualitative design, concerning perspectives of tourism impacts. In essence, understanding such voice is a step in the direction toward empowering residents to actively participate in planning for sustainable tourism.

Residents' empowerment and overtourism

Three works within this book capture advancements made in research on residents' empowerment through tourism. Su et al. (2023) take us to China to learn more about how embroidery tourism has provided women with greater economic stability. Through qualitative means, findings speak back to the three primary dimensions (i.e., psychological, social, and political) of residents' empowerment through tourism (Scheyvens, 1999) but also consider educational and economic empowerment. It is from these three traditional dimensions of empowerment (along with positive and negative perceptions of tourism impacts, trust in political decision-making, and quality of life) that Mody et al. (2023) explain residents' support for peer-to-peer accommodations using Weber's Theory of Rationality and Foucauldian concepts. The final chapter within this area of research covering overtourism, by Wegerer and Nadegger (2023), utilizes netnographical analysis to investigate activists' justification for posting degrowth discourse on social media platforms. As such, protection of the natural environment and disinterest of capitalism within the Austrian Alps were salient drivers. Consequently, activist rationales tend to criticize the growth imperative of capitalism broadly rather than directly addressing the project and its proponents.

Moving forward

Based on the review of pertinent work in the initial portion of this chapter and the additional chapters in this book, a host of future research opportunities exist—none of which are in any order of importance. Let us first start with one of the most obvious. It is safe to say that though the COVID-19 pandemic is quickly becoming a thing of the past in many countries, future health epidemics and pandemics will likely be part of our lives for the unforeseen future. How we travel and how we impact/are impacting others around us will need to be considered more conscientiously. It is nearly impossible to conceive of the social impacts of tourism without realizing the sheer presence of tourists (even unseen by residents) is now considered an impact. It is true that all the research comprised in the 13 chapters was undertaken prior to the pandemic. That said, as researchers, we should constantly be asking ourselves, "How can our research designs and how are our study findings informed in the midst of recovering from the pandemic?" Now more than ever, we should start to emphasize the role of empathy in our research, as residents and as tourists, for one another (Woosnam et al., 2018). Additionally, we might consider presenting residents with hypothetical situations to consider in determining acceptable levels of tourists and under what conditions? This would most certainly be helpful for destinations considering greatest sustainability while trying to attract tourists to return. We might also begin to ask tourists about their willingness to return and under what conditions (see Torres, Ridderstaat, & Wei, 2021).

This segues nicely into an evolving need to concurrently incorporate perspectives of both residents and tourists when engaging in social impacts of tourism research. Nearly one-third of the chapters in this book focused on the relationship between the parties, providing greater credence to the notion that host and guest are inextricably linked (Stylidis, 2022; Woosnam, 2013). Work that continues to operationalize measures of social contact and the contact theory between residents and tourists (building on the work of Fan, 2023 and Fan et al., 2023) will be most timely. With more research focusing on emotional solidarity between residents and tourists (in this book and elsewhere), greater work is needed to examine additional outcomes of the construct beyond attitudinal measures. For instance, how does emotional solidarity prompt an individual's likelihood to behave in a certain way (behavioral support or withdrawal) (Erul et al., 2020) or better yet, actual behavior. Future research should also shift slightly to consider the construct from tourists' perspectives (like the work by Woosnam and Aleshinloye, 2013). Finally, the original emotional solidarity theoretical framework should be used in tandem with complementary theories (e.g., cognitive appraisal theory, interaction ritual theory, mere exposure theory, social exchange theory, theory of formal and substantive rationality, TRA and TPB, etc.).

While we are discussing the subject of social impact outcomes, researchers should consider effects of overtourism and peer-to-peer accommodations since the two are so prevalent in the current tourism literature but also seem to be highly linked, especially in urban destinations (Celata & Romano, 2022). In this book alone, six of the 13 chapters focused on one of these two topics. Here again, we suggest that future researchers should examine outcomes of residents' perceptions of overtourism and peer-to-peer accommodations such as intentions to act, such as compromised relations between residents and tourists (Cheung & Li, 2019), protest and resistance (Smith, Sziva, & Olt, 2019), support of degrowth (Wegerer & Nadegger, 2023), and civic engagement (Torres, 2021). Of course, residents' empowerment may also factor into perceptions of overtourism and peer-to-peer accommodations (given its noted use within this issue). For instance, empowerment through tourism may, in essence, act as a moderator within some future models.

Future testable models need to be driven by theoretical frameworks to further advance our field and address the concerns stated by multiple authors regarding limited theoretical development and testing (Gursoy & Nunkoo, 2019; Hadinejad et al., 2019; Nunkoo et al., 2013). Furthermore, proposed models should include outcome variables measuring either behavioral intentions or actual behavior. This approach will help to ensure greater actionable research with strong practical implications.

Where we can really see the practical implications of our research on social impacts of tourism is by undertaking studies that focus specifically on the United Nation's sustainable development goals (SDGs) (UNWTO, 2017). Though Scheyvens (2018) and Bramwell et al. (2017) argue that too few tourism scholars engage in pressing global issues, we need to approach our work in social impacts of tourism with the understanding that though our work may occur in distinct communities, it has global implications. No time is better than now to realize that global concerns highlighted within the SDGs (e.g., poverty, hunger, well-being, clean water and sanitation, decent work and economic growth, sustainable cities, and communities, etc.) are compounded by the COVID-19 pandemic as fewer individuals can or desire to travel just as destinations are resistant or fearful of allowing visitors to their communities. We implore researchers to engage in research that will address the SDGs, most specifically those focused on alleviating poverty (SDG 1), fostering good health and well-being (SDG 3), providing decent work and economic growth (SDG 8), ensuring cities and communities are sustainable (SDG 11), encouraging responsible consumption and production (SDG 12), and alleviating climate change (SDG 13). Together, in solidarity and synergistic efforts, we can advance our field while making a difference in the world, one destination at a time.

References

Allport, G. W. (1954). *The nature of prejudice*. Addison-Wesley.
Ahmed, S. A. (1986). Understanding residents' reaction to tourism marketing strategies. *Journal of Travel Research*, 25(2), 13–18.
Akis, S., Peristianis, N., & Warner, J. (1996). Residents' attitudes to tourism development: The case of Cyprus. *Tourism Management*, 17(7), 481–494. https://doi.org/10.1016/s0261-5177(96)00066-0
Andereck, K. L., Valentine, K. M., Knopf, R. C., & Vogt, C. A. (2005). Residents' perceptions of community tourism impacts. *Annals of Tourism Research*, 32(4), 1056–1076.
Ap, J. (1992). Residents' perceptions on tourism impacts. *Annals of Tourism Research*, 19(4), 665–690.
Ap, J., & Crompton, J. L. (1998). Developing and testing a tourism impact scale. *Journal of Travel Research*, 37(2), 120–130.
Belisle, F. J., & Hoy, D. R. (1980). The perceived impact of tourism by residents a case study in Santa Marta, Colombia. *Annals of Tourism Research*, 7(1), 83–101.
Boley, B. B., McGehee, N. G., Perdue, R. R., & Long, P. (2014). Empowerment and resident attitudes toward tourism: Strengthening the theoretical foundation through a Weberian lens. *Annals of Tourism Research*, 49, 33–50.
Bramwell, B., Higham, J., Lane, B., & Miller, G. (2017). Twenty-five years of sustainable tourism and the *Journal of Sustainable Tourism*: Looking back and moving forward. *Journal of Sustainable Tourism*, 25(1), 1–9.
Butler, R. W. (1980). The concept of a tourist area cycle of evolution: Implications for management of resources. *Canadian Geographer*, 24(1), 5–12.
Celata, F., & Romano, A. (2022). Overtourism and online short-term rental platforms in Italian cities. *Journal of Sustainable Tourism*, https://doi.org/10.1080/09669582.2020.1788568
Chang, K. C. (2021). The affecting tourism development attitudes based on the social exchange theory and the social network theory. *Asia Pacific Journal of Tourism Research*, 26(2), 167–182.
Cheung, K. S., & Li, L. H. (2019). Understanding visitor–resident relations in overtourism: Developing resilience for sustainable tourism. *Journal of Sustainable Tourism*, 27(8), 1197–1216.
Chiang, L., Xu, A., Kim, J., Tang, L., & Manthiou, A. (2017). Investigating festivals and events as social gatherings: The application of social identity theory. *Journal of Travel & Tourism Marketing*, 34(6), 779–792.
Choi, H. C., & Murray, I. (2010). Resident attitudes toward sustainable community tourism. *Journal of Sustainable Tourism*, 18(4), 575–594.
Choi, H. S. C., & Sirakaya, E. (2005). Measuring residents' attitude toward sustainable tourism: Development of sustainable tourism attitude scale. *Journal of Travel Research*, 43(4), 380–394.
Deery, M., Jago, L., & Fredline, L. (2012). Rethinking social impacts of tourism research: A new research agenda. *Tourism Management*, 33(1), 64–73.
Doxey, G. V. (1975). A causation theory of visitor-resident irritants, methodology, and research inferences. *Sixth annual conference proceedings of the Travel Research Association*, San Diego, CA: Travel and Tourism Research Association, 195–198.
Durkheim, E. ([1915] 1995). *The elementary forms of the religious life*. New York: Free Press.

Erul, E., & Woosnam, K. M. (2022). Explaining residents' behavioral support for tourism through two theoretical frameworks. *Journal of Travel Research*, *61*(2), 362–377. https://doi.org/10.1177/0047287520987619

Erul, E., Woosnam, K. M., & McIntosh, W. A. (2020). Considering emotional solidarity and the theory of planned behavior in explaining behavioral intentions to support tourism development. *Journal of Sustainable Tourism*, *28*(8), 1158–1173.

Erul, E., Woosnam, K. M., Ribeiro, M. A., & Salazar, J. (2023). Complementing theories to explain emotional solidarity. *Journal of Sustainable Tourism*, *1*(2), 229–244. https://doi.org/10.1080/09669582.2020.1800718

Eslami, S., Khalifah, Z., Mardani, A., Streimikiene, D., & Han, H. (2019). Community attachment, tourism impacts, quality of life and residents' support for sustainable tourism development. *Journal of Travel & Tourism Marketing*, *36*(9), 1061–1079.

Evans-Pritchard, D. (1989). How "they" see "us": Native American images of tourists. *Annals of Tourism Research*, *16*(1), 89–105.

Fan, D. X. (2023). Understanding the tourist-resident relationship through social contact: progressing the development of social contact in tourism. *Journal of Sustainable Tourism*, *31*(2), 406–424.

Farrell, B. H. (1979). Tourism's Human Conflicts. *Annals of Tourism Research*, *6*, 122–136.

Fan, D. X., Qiu, H., Jenkins, C. L., & Lau, C. (2023). Towards a better tourist-host relationship: the role of social contact between tourists' perceived cultural distance and travel attitude. *Journal of Sustainable Tourism*, https://doi.org/10.1080/09669582.2020.1783275

Fredline, E., & Faulkner, B. (2000). Host community reactions: A cluster analysis. *Annals of Tourism Research*, *27*(3), 763–784.

Gannon, M., Rasoolimanesh, S. M., & Taheri, B. (2021). Assessing the mediating role of residents' perceptions toward tourism development. *Journal of Travel Research*, *60*(1), 149–171.

Gursoy, D., & Nunkoo, R. (Eds.) (2019). *The Routledge handbook of tourism impacts: Theoretical and applied perspectives*. Routledge.

Gursoy, D., Ouyang, Z., Nunkoo, R., & Wei, W. (2019). Residents' impact perceptions of and attitudes towards tourism development: A meta-analysis. *Journal of Hospitality Marketing & Management*, *28*(3), 306–333.

Gursoy, D., Yolal, M., Ribeiro, M. A., & Panosso Netto, A. (2017). Impact of trust on local residents' mega-event perceptions and their support. *Journal of Travel Research*, *56*(3), 393–406.

Hadinejad, A., Moyle, B. D., Scott, N., Kralj, A., & Nunkoo, R. (2019). Residents' attitudes to tourism: A review. *Tourism Review*, *74*(2), 150–165.

Haralambopoulos, N., & Pizam, A. (1996). Perceived impacts of tourism: The case of samos. *Annals of Tourism Research*, *23*(3), 503–526.

Johnson, J. D., Snepenger, D. J., & Akis, S. (1994). Residents' perceptions of tourism development. *Annals of Tourism Research*, *21*(3), 629–642.

Joo, D., Cho, H., Woosnam, K. M., & Suess, C. (2023). Re-theorizing social emotions in tourism: Applying the theory of interaction ritual in tourism research. *Journal of Sustainable Tourism*, *31*(2), 367–382.

Joo, D., Tasci, A. D., Woosnam, K. M., Maruyama, N. U., Hollas, C. R., & Aleshinloye, K. D. (2018). Residents' attitude towards domestic tourists explained by contact, emotional solidarity and social distance. *Tourism Management*, *64*, 245–257.

Joo, D., & Woosnam, K. M. (2020). Measuring tourists' emotional solidarity with one another—A modification of the emotional solidarity scale. *Journal of Travel Research*, *59*(7), 1186–1203.

Joo, D., Xu, W., Lee, J., Lee, C. K., & Woosnam, K. M. (2021). Residents' perceived risk, emotional solidarity, and support for tourism amidst the COVID-19 pandemic. *Journal of Destination Marketing & Management*, *19*, 100553.

Jurowski, C., & Gursoy, D. (2004). Distance effects on residents' attitudes toward tourism. *Annals of Tourism Research*, *31*(2), 296–312.

Jurowski, C., Uysal, M., & Williams, D. R. (1997). A theoretical analysis of host community resident reactions to tourism. *Journal of Travel Research*, *36*(2), 3–11. https://doi.org/10.1177/004728759703600202

Kamath, V., Ribeiro, M. A., Woosnam, K. M., Mallya, J., & Kamath, G. (2022). Determinants of visitors' loyalty to religious sacred event places: A multigroup measurement invariance model. *Journal of Travel Research*, *62*(1), 176–196.

Kendall, K. W., & Var, T. (1984). The perceived impacts of tourism: The state of the art. School of Travel Industry Management, University of Hawaii at Manoa.

Ko, D.-W., & Stewart, W. P. (2002). A structural equation model of residents' attitudes for tourism development. *Tourism Management*, *23*(5), 521–530. https://doi.org/10.1016/S0261-5177(02)00006-7

Lankford, S. V., & Howard, D. R. (1994). Developing a tourism impact attitude scale. *Annals of Tourism Research*, *21*(1), 121–139.

Látková, P., & Vogt, C. A. (2012). Residents' attitudes toward existing and future tourism development in rural communities. *Journal of Travel Research*, *51*(1), 50–67.

Liang, Z., Luo, H., & Bao, J. (2021). A longitudinal study of residents' attitudes toward tourism development. *Current Issues in Tourism*, *24*(3), 3309–3323.

Liu, J. C., Sheldon, P. J., & Var, T. R. D. A. (1986). A cross-national approach to determining resident perception of the impact of tourism on the environment. In *Tourism services marketing: advances in theory and practice* (pgs. 129–151). Special conference series, volume II, 1986. Academy of Marketing Science, University of Miami.

Liu, J. C., Sheldon, P. J., & Var, T. (1987). Resident perception of the environmental impacts of tourism. *Annals of Tourism Research*, *14*(1), 17–37. https://doi.org/10.1016/0160-7383(87)90045-4

Liu, J. C., & Var, T. (1986). Resident attitudes toward tourism impacts in Hawaii. *Annals of Tourism Research, 13*(2), 193–214.

Long, P. T., Perdue, R. R., & Allen, L. (1990). Rural resident tourism perceptions and attitudes by community level of tourism. *Journal of Travel Research, 28*(3), 3–9.

Maruyama, N. U., Keith, S. J., & Woosnam, K. M. (2019). Incorporating emotion into social exchange: Considering distinct resident groups' attitudes towards ethnic neighborhood tourism in Osaka, Japan. *Journal of Sustainable Tourism, 27*(8), 1125-1141.

Maruyama, N. U., Ribeiro, M. A., & Woosnam, K. M. (2023). The effect of minority residents' attitudes and emotional solidarity on ethnic neighborhood tourism: A multigroup invariance analysis. *Journal of Sustainable Tourism, 31*(2), 383–405.

Mason, P. (2016). *Tourism impacts, planning and management* (3rd Ed.). Routledge.

Mathieson, A., & Wall, G. (1982). *Tourism: Economic, physical and social impacts*. Longman.

McGehee, N. G., & Andereck, K. L. (2004). Factors predicting rural residents' support of tourism. *Journal of Travel Research, 43*(2), 131–140.

Milman, A., & Pizam, A. (1988). Social impacts of tourism on central Florida. *Annals of Tourism Research, 15*(2), 191–204.

Mody, M., Woosnam, K. M., Suess, C., & Dogru, T. (2023). Hapless victims or empowered citizens? Understanding residents' attitudes towards Airbnb using Weber's Theory of Rationality and Foucauldian concepts. *Journal of Sustainable Tourism, 31*(2), 284–306.

Monterrubio, C. (2016). The impact of spring break behaviour: An integrated threat theory analysis of residents' prejudice. *Tourism Management, 54*, 418–427.

Monterrubio, J. C., & Andriotis, K. (2014). Social representations and community attitudes towards spring breakers. *Tourism Geographies, 16*(2), 288–302.

Moscardo, G. (2011). Exploring social representations of tourism planning: Issues for governance. *Journal of Sustainable Tourism, 19*(4–5), 423–436.

Moscovici, S. (1984). The phenomenon of social representations. In R. Farr & S. Moscovici (Eds.) *Social representations* (pgs. 3–70). Cambridge University Press.

Munanura, I. E., Needham, M. D., Lindberg, K., Kooistra, C., & Ghahramani, L. (2023). Support for tourism: The roles of attitudes, subjective wellbeing, and emotional solidarity. *Journal of Sustainable Tourism, 31*(2), 581-596. https://doi.org/10.1080/09669582.2021.1901104

Ngo, T., & Pham, T. (2023). Indigenous residents, tourism knowledge exchange and situated perceptions of tourism. *Journal of Sustainable Tourism, 31*(2), 597–614. https://doi.org/10.1080/09669582.2021.1920967

Nunkoo, R. (2016). Toward a more comprehensive use of social exchange theory to study residents' attitudes to tourism. *Procedia Economics and Finance, 39*, 588–596.

Nunkoo, R., & Gursoy, D. (2012). Residents' support for tourism: An identity perspective. *Annals of Tourism Research, 39*(1), 243–268.

Nunkoo, R., & Gursoy, D. (2019). Introduction to tourism impacts. In R. Nunkoo and D. Gursoy (Eds.) *The Routledge handbook of tourism impacts: Theoretical and applied perspectives* (pgs. 1–20). Routledge.

Nunkoo, R., Gursoy, D., & Dwivedi, Y. K. (2023). Effects of social media on residents' attitudes to tourism: Conceptual framework and research propositions. *Journal of Sustainable Tourism, 31*(2), 350-366.

Nunkoo, R., & Ramkissoon, H. (2010). Gendered theory of planned behavior and residents' support for tourism. *Current Issues in Tourism, 13*(6), 525–540.

Nunkoo, R., & Ramkissoon, H. (2011). Developing a community support model for tourism. *Annals of Tourism Research, 38*(3), 964–988. https://doi.org/10.1016/j.annals.2011.01.017

Nunkoo, R., & Ramkissoon, H. (2012). Power, trust, social exchange and community support. *Annals of Tourism Research, 39*(2), 997–1023.

Nunkoo, R., Smith, S. L., & Ramkissoon, H. (2013). Residents' attitudes to tourism: A longitudinal study of 140 articles from 1984 to 2010. *Journal of Sustainable Tourism, 21*(1), 5–25.

Ouyang, Z., Gursoy, D., & Sharma, B. (2017). Role of trust, emotions and event attachment on residents' attitudes toward tourism. *Tourism Management, 63*, 426–438.

Palmer, A., Koenig-Lewis, N., & Jones, L. E. M. (2013). The effects of residents' social identity and involvement on their advocacy of incoming tourism. *Tourism Management, 38*, 142–151.

Perdue, R. R., Long, P. T., & Allen, L. (1990). Resident support for tourism development. *Annals of Tourism Research, 17*(4), 586–599.

Phuc, H. N., & Nguyen, H. M. (2023). The importance of collaboration and emotional solidarity in residents' support for sustainable urban tourism: Case study Ho Chi Minh City. *Journal of Sustainable Tourism, 31*(2), 245–264.

Pizam, A. (1978). Tourism's impacts: The social costs to the destination community as perceived by its residents. *Journal of Travel Research, 16*(4), 8–12.

Ribeiro, M. A., Pinto, P., Silva, J. A., & Woosnam, K. M. (2018). Examining the predictive validity of SUS-TAS with maximum parsimony in developing island countries. *Journal of Sustainable Tourism, 26*(3), 379–398.

Ribeiro, M. A., Pinto, P., Silva, J. A., & Woosnam, K. M. (2017). Residents' attitudes and the adoption of pro-tourism behaviours: The case of developing island countries. *Tourism Management, 61*, 523–537.

Rothman, R. A. (1978). Residents and transients: Community reaction to seasonal visitors. *Journal of Travel Research*, *16*(3), 8–13.
Ruhanen, L., Moyle, C. L., & Moyle, B. (2019). New directions in sustainable tourism research. *Tourism Review*, *74*(2), 138–149.
Sarr, B., Sène-Harper, A., & Gonzalez-Hernandez, M. M. (2021). Tourism, social representations and empowerment of rural communities at Langue de Barbarie National Park, Senegal. *Journal of Sustainable Tourism*, *29*(8), 1383–1402.
Scheyvens, R. (1999). Ecotourism and the empowerment of local communities. *Tourism Management*, *20*(2), 245–249.
Scheyvens, R. (2018). Linking tourism to the sustainable development goals: A geographical perspective. *Tourism Geographies*, *20*(2), 341–342.
Sirakaya-Turk, E. (2007). Concurrent validity of the sustainable tourism attitude scale. *Annals of Tourism Research*, *34*(4), 1081–1084.
Sirakaya-Turk, E., Ekinci, Y., & Kaya, A. G. (2008). An examination of the validity of SUS-TAS in cross-cultures. *Journal of Travel Research*, *46*(4), 414–421.
Sirakaya-Turk, E., & Gursoy, D. (2013). Predictive validity of SUSTAS. *Tourism Analysis*, 18(5), 601–605.
Smith, M. K., Sziva, I. P., & Olt, G. (2019). Overtourism and resident resistance in Budapest. *Tourism Planning & Development*, *16*(4), 376–392.
Strzelecka, M., Boley, B. B., & Strzelecka, C. (2017). Empowerment and resident support for tourism in rural Central and Eastern Europe (CEE): The case of Pomerania, Poland. *Journal of Sustainable Tourism*, *25*(4), 554–572.
Stylidis, D. (2022). Exploring resident–tourist interaction and its impact on tourists' destination image. *Journal of Travel Research*, https://doi.org/10.1177/0047287520969861
Stylidis, D., & Terzidou, M. (2023). Exploring how perceived tourism impacts evolve over time (2009–2019) in an era of uncertainty: Economic crisis, host-guest interactions, and Airbnb. *Journal of Sustainable Tourism*, https://doi.org/10.1080/09669582.2021.1939707
Su, M. M., Wall, G., Ma, J., Notarianni, M., & Wang, S. (2023). Empowerment of women through cultural tourism: Perspectives of Hui minority embroiderers in Ningxia, China. *Journal of Sustainable Tourism*, *31*(2), 307–328.
Suess, C., Woosnam, K. M., Mody, M., Dogru, T., & Sirakaya Turk, E. (2021). Understanding how residents' emotional solidarity with Airbnb visitors influences perceptions of their impact on a community: The moderating role of prior experience staying at an Airbnb. *Journal of Travel Research*, *60*(5), 1039–1060.
Tilaki, M. J. M., Abooali, G., Marzbali, M. H., & Samat, N. (2021). Vendors' attitudes and perceptions towards international tourists in the Malaysia Night Market: Does the COVID-19 outbreak matter? *Sustainability*, *13*(3), 1553.
Torres, R. M. (2021). The empty boxes of Venice: Overtourism—conflicts, politicisation and activism. In C. Ba, S. Frank, C. Müller, A.L. Raschke, K. Wellner, & A. Zecher (Eds.) *The power of new urban tourism* (pgs. 147–160). Routledge.
Torres, E. N., Ridderstaat, J., & Wei, W. (2021). Negative affectivity and people's return intentions to hospitality and tourism activities: The early stages of COVID-19. *Journal of Hospitality and Tourism Management*, *49*, 89–100.
UNWTO. (2017). *Tourism and the sustainable development goals—Journey to 2030*. Retrieved on 1 January 2022 from www.e-unwto.org/doi/epdf/10.18111/9789284419401
Vargas-Sánchez, A., Porras-Bueno, N., & de los Ángeles Plaza-Mejía, M. (2011). Explaining residents' attitudes to tourism: Is a universal model possible? *Annals of Tourism Research*, *38*(2), 460–480.
Ward, C., & Berno, T. (2011). Beyond social exchange theory: Attitudes toward tourists. *Annals of Tourism Research*, *38*(4), 1556–1569.
Wegerer, P. K., & Nadegger, M. (2023). It's time to act! Understanding online resistance against tourism development projects. *Journal of Sustainable Tourism*, *31*(2), 425–441.
Woosnam, K. M. (2012). Using emotional solidarity to explain residents' attitudes about tourism and tourism development. *Journal of Travel Research*, *51*(3), 315–327.
Woosnam, K. M. (2013). Modifying the IOS scale among tourists. *Annals of Tourism Research*, *42*, 431–434.
Woosnam, K. M., & Aleshinloye, K. D. (2013). Can tourists experience emotional solidarity with residents? Testing Durkheim's model from a new perspective. *Journal of Travel Research*, *52*(4), 494–505.
Woosnam, K. M., Draper, J., Jiang, J. K., Aleshinloye, K. D., & Erul, E. (2018). Applying self-perception theory to explain residents' attitudes about tourism development through travel histories. *Tourism Management*, *64*, 357–368.
Woosnam, K. M., Joo, D., Ribeiro, M. A., Johnson Gaither, C., Sánchez, J. J., & Brooks, R. (2023). Rural residents' social distance with tourists: An affective interpretation. *Current Issues in Tourism*, 1–15. https://doi.org/10.1080/13683500.2023.2191836
Woosnam, K. M., & Norman, W. C. (2010). Measuring residents' emotional solidarity with tourists: Scale development of Durkheim's theoretical constructs. *Journal of Travel Research*, *49*(3), 365–380.
Woosnam, K. M., & Ribeiro, M. A. (2023). Methodological and theoretical advancements in social impacts of tourism research. *Journal of Sustainable Tourism*, *31*(2), 187–203. https://doi.org/10.1080/09669582.2022.2046011
Wu, S. T., & Chen, Y. S. (2018). Local intentions to participate in ecotourism development in Taiwan's Atayal communities. *Journal of Tourism and Cultural Change*, *16*(1), 75–96.
Yeager, E., Boley, B. B., & Goetcheus, J. (2023). Conceptualizing peer-to-peer accommodations as disruptions in the urban tourism system. *Journal of Sustainable Tourism*, *31*(2), 504–519.
Yeager, E. P., Boley, B. B., Woosnam, K. M., & Green, G. T. (2020). Modeling residents' attitudes toward short-term vacation rentals. *Journal of Travel Research*, *59*(6), 955–974.

Yu, C.-P., Chancellor, C., & Cole, S. (2011). Measuring residents' attitudes toward sustainable tourism: A reexamination of the sustainable tourism attitude scale. *Journal of Travel Research*, 50(1), 57–63.

Zhang, Y., Cole, S. T., & Chancellor, C. H. (2015). Facilitation of the SUS-TAS application with parsimony, predictive validity, and global interpretation examination. *Journal of Travel Research*, 54(6), 744–757.

Zheng, D., Liang, Z., & Ritchie, B. W. (2020). Residents' social dilemma in sustainable heritage tourism: The role of social emotion, efficacy beliefs and temporal concerns. *Journal of Sustainable Tourism*, 28(11), 1782–1804.

Towards a better tourist-host relationship: the role of social contact between tourists' perceived cultural distance and travel attitude

Daisy X. F. Fan, Hanqin Qiu, Carson L. Jenkins and Chloe Lau

ABSTRACT
The ambiguous effect of cultural distance on travel attitude and tourist behaviours has long been debated, but its implications are vital to the success of achieving a sustainable tourist-host relationship. The study explored the direct and indirect effects of perceived cultural distance on travel attitude by adopting a mixed-methods approach and introducing a multi-dimensional perspective regarding the tourists' social contact with the local. The mediating role of tourist-host social contact was also confirmed. The study found that the relationship between perceived cultural distance and travel attitude is "contact elastic". Results empirically support the co-existence of the paradoxical effects of cultural distance on travel attitude. Implications are provided to policy-makers, practitioners and local communities regarding achieving a sustainable tourist-host bond.

Introduction

Tourism brings people from diverse cultural backgrounds into contact with each other, and such communication builds a mutual appreciation of their viewpoints, which leads to understanding, respect and liking each other (Allport, 1979; Fulbright, 1976). However, cultural shock engendered from interactions with the hosts may generate uncertainty and panic, which may lead to negative perception towards the destination (Goeldner & Ritchie, 2008; Lepp & Gibson, 2003; Ward et al., 2003). Cohen (1972) highlighted that the communication gap, such as language, can intensify the isolation of the mass tourist from the host society. The incoherence in the literature leaves the relationship between perceived cultural distance and travel attitude a mystery and calls for empirical investigation of this contradiction from diverse perspectives.

Culture is a key component to understand and unveil the intricate intergroup relationship. Considering Cohen's (1972) and Jaakson's (2004) tourist bubble, social separation acts like a bubble, creating a protective wall for tourists in the host communities (Smith, 1989; Ward et al., 2005). Within this wall, tourists travel with their original culture, perceive things through their cultural lens and behave with their cultural standards and judgments in mind. Though abundant studies have explored the concept of culture and cultural distance (Caulkins 1999; Hofstede et al., 2010; Triandis, 1994), a convincing explanation of the dynamic cultural effects on tourists' behaviours and perceptions are still absent.

The social contact between tourists and residents can influence tourists' positive perception of their destinations and the residents by boosting mutual understanding, eliminating bias and stereotypes and enhancing intergroup relations (Allport, 1979; Binder et al., 2009; Kawakami et al., 2000; Kirillova, Lehto, & Cai, 2015; Pettigrew, 1998). By contrast, social contact can lead to negative perception by increasing intergroup tension, hostility and suspicion between tourists and hosts (Bochner, 1982; Pizam et al., 2000). Although tourist-host social contact has strong predictive power on tourists' perception towards their trips, a limited number of studies have investigated the tourist-host social contact's effect on tourists' travel attitude (Fan et al., 2017). Less attention has been paid to its role in interpreting the relationship between tourists' perceived cultural distance and travel attitude. In addition, as stated by Tasci (2009) and Joo et al. (2018), the directional relationships between distance and tourist behaviours, including tourist-host interactions and visit intentions, can be a "chicken and the egg" situation or a case of concurrently existing human phenomena. Cultural distance and social contact hence tend to influence and reinforce each other concurrently. However, most of the existing studies investigating the relationship between cultural distance and social contact put cultural distance as an outcome of social contact (Aleshinloye et al., 2020; Joo et al., 2018; Yilmaz & Tasci, 2015). The effect of tourists' perceived cultural distance on their social interactions with the local people in the destination is largely overlooked.

This study investigates from a tourist perspective and aims to bridge the abovementioned research gaps by exploring how tourists' perceived cultural distance and social contact with the host can influence their travel attitude towards a destination. The specific research objectives are 1) to explore the direct relationships among perceived cultural distance, tourist-host social contact and travel attitude and 2) to examine the mediating effect of tourist-host social contact in the relationship between perceived cultural distance and travel attitude by building on those direct relationships.

Theoretical background

Cultural distance and travel attitude

Culture holds a broad range of interpretations, including knowledge, belief, custom and habits that influence individuals' ways of selecting, understanding, processing and using the information they receive (Triandis, 1994). Cultural distance is defined as the extent to which the culture of the original region differs from the culture of the host region (Goeldner & Ritchie, 2008). Cultural distance represents the differences among groups of people who perform activities and perceive the world differently (Potter, 1989).

As culture holds a wide range of understanding, different scholars may have a different understanding of their studies, and the measurement of cultural distance varies accordingly in different research topics and settings. For example, Hofstede's cultural dimensions theory provides a framework with six value dimensions for measuring national culture, including power distance, individualism–collectivism, masculinity–femininity, uncertainty–avoidance, long-term orientation and indulgence–restraint (Hofstede et al., 2010). Hofstede's cultural dimensions are widely applied in tourism research in relation to tourism demand (Ahn & McKercher, 2015; Fan et al., 2017), choice of destination (Esiyok et al., 2017) and acculturation process (Mazanec et al., 2015). Grid-group cultural theory claims that people can be classified into four major social types, namely, individualists, fatalists, hierarchists and egalitarians (Caulkins 1999; Douglas 1982; Li et al. 2015). For cultural differences from the perspective of tourists, Wei et al. (1989) stated that elements, such as accommodation, food and level of hygiene could lead to cultural conflicts that generate varying perceptions of what constitutes appropriate behaviour. In addition, Reisinger and Turner (1998a, 1998b, 2002a, 2002b) reported that cultural values, rules of social behaviour, perceptions, social (tourist–host) interaction and satisfaction are essential dimensions that reflect the cultural differences between Western hosts and Asian tourists. Fan, Zhang, Jenkins, et al. (2017) developed a three-dimensional measurement scale of perceived cultural distance from a tourist's perspective. The measurements of perceived cultural distance include cultural retention, behavioural and social characteristics. This set of measurements captures tourists' perceived cultural distance encountered in travel, rather than measurements generated or adopted from other disciplines. Similarly, Lee et al. (2018) identified social environment, personal relationship, living arrangements and verbal communication as four dimensions of mainland Chinese tourists' perceived cultural distance when traveling to Taiwan.

Attitude represents individuals' tendency to evaluate symbol, object or perspective of the world favourably or unfavourably (Ajzen, 1991; Mayo & Jarvis, 1981). Attitude has also caught considerable attention from scholars. Attitude is a reliable indicator of how people act given a set of conditions in different styles of life. In the context of tourism, travel attitude is the predisposition or feeling towards a travel destination or service, and is based on multiple-perceived product attributes (Hsu & Huang, 2012; Moutinho, 1987). Attitude can be multi-dimensional. Rosenberg et al. (1960) proposed the three components in attitude, namely, cognitive, affective and behavioural (Mayo & Jarvis, 1981). The cognitive component refers to beliefs based on tangible evidence perceived as fact by an individual at a given time spot. Affective component is the emotional judgment an individual makes towards an object. The behavioural component describes the tendency to respond favourably or unfavourably to a certain object. Furthermore, the single-dimensional attitude has been adopted predominantly in tourism research. Most tourism studies believed that attitude is a single-dimensional construct that represents the affect for or against a psychological object, event or situation (Bagozzi & Burnkrant, 1979). This assumption is implemented in the Theory of Reasoned Action (TRA) (Fishbein & Ajzen, 1975) and the Theory of Planned Behaviour (TPB) (Ajzen, 1988), which are fundamental theories for ample research in different disciplines, including tourism (Hsu et al., 2006; Lam & Hsu, 2006).

Cultural distance is reported to have negative and positive effects on travel attitude in different studies. From a distance decay perspective, cultural distance may affect tourists' inclination to travel to a certain destination negatively. The negative effect of cultural distance is found on international tourist flows (Liu et al., 2018; Yang et al., 2019). People sought differences and changes when travelling to the extent that differences and changes remain non-threatening (Cohen, 1979). Goeldner and Ritchie (2008) concluded that the larger the cultural distance between the tourist origin country and the destination, the greater the resistance to travel to that destination.

Moreover, cultural differences in areas, such as food, language, cleanliness, the pace of life, recreation, the standard of living, humour, intimacy and privacy etiquettes are often associated with stress, even though the travel purpose is for relaxation or sight-seeing (Leung et al., 2013; Martin et al., 2017; Spradley & Phillips, 1972). Ng et al. (2007) adopted five different cultural distance measures and argued that the greater the perceived cultural similarity of a foreign destination to Australia, the more likely for Australians to visit a destination. Therefore, people will have a positive attitude towards others with similar cultures (Moufakkir, 2011). All the research suggests the greater the cultural distance between a destination and a tourist's home country, the more negative the tourist would feel towards the destination.

This argument has been challenged by studies in tourist motivation. Travel motivation has been examined as a good predictor for travel attitude in various research contexts (Ajzen, 1991; Hsu et al., 2010; Hung & Petrick, 2011). In travel motivation studies, cultural novelty-seeking/discovery is one of the highly ranked items that inspire tourists to travel (Beard & Ragheb, 1983; Crompton, 1979; Dewar et al., 2001; Hsu et al., 2010; Ragheb & Beard, 1982; Ryan & Glendon, 1998) and has a significantly positive effect on tourists' attitude towards a destination (Hsu et al.,

2010). In that case, cultural distance rather than cultural similarity can arouse tourists' positive travel attitude. A destination's cultural features are also associated with destination choice (McKercher & Cros, 2003). McKercher and Chow (2001) argued that the greater the cultural difference, the more likely that tourists would participate in cultural activities and the more important cultural attributes are in their destination decision-making process.

According to existing literature, this study aims to test such relationship in the social contact context. Therefore, Hypothesis 1 can be derived as follows:

> **H1a**: Perceived cultural distance is positively related to travel attitude.

> **H1b**: Perceived cultural distance is negatively related to travel attitude.

Tourist-host social contact and travel attitude

Cross-cultural social contact is the contact between individuals from different cultural contexts (Cusher & Brislin, 1996; Yu & Lee, 2014). Tourist-host social contact is perceived as a unique type of cross-cultural contact due to tourists' short and well-structured time, purposes of travel and poor adaptation to the local community (Barthes, 1973; Pearce, 1982).

The concept of social contact has been explored and measured from different perspectives. Activities (Mo, Howard & Havitz, 1993; Reisinger & Turner, 2002a, 2002b; Rothman, 1978) and frequency (Woosnam & Aleshinloye, 2013) of social contact were applied as the only measurements of social contact. Other research considered multiple dimensions to measure the social contact experience. For instance, Huang and Hsu (2010) examined the activity, frequency, influence, valence, intensity, power and symmetry of customer-to-customer interaction on cruises. Fan, Zhang, Jenkins, et al. (2017) developed a tourist-host social contact scale from a tourist viewpoint. The measurements included three dimensions, namely, social- and service-oriented contact and quality of contact. Items in social- and service-oriented contact measured the quantity of social contact and each contact activity was rated by the degree of frequency a tourist had with hosts, from a range of "never" to "very frequently". This scale considers the quantity (i.e. social- and service-oriented contact activities) and quality aspects of contact. The quantity of contact is categorised into social- and service-oriented aspects, which could distinguish various effects from different contacts. In addition, considering activity and its corresponding frequency together allows a precise way to evaluate the effect caused by individual activity.

Existing literature has explored the effects of social contact on tourists' travel attitude; however, no agreement has been achieved. As a conventional understanding, contacts between two parties can bring a positive attitude towards each other. Allport's (1979) contact theory proposed that contacts may offer ways to minimise stereotyping and discrimination between two culturally different regions under certain conditions, such as with common goals, equal status and sanctioned support (Joo et al., 2018; Yu & Lee, 2014). Contact theory in social psychology provides a general idea of the outcome of international encounters. In the context of tourist and host relationship studies, social contact between the two groups enhances positive attitudes and mutual understanding toward each other (Amir & Ben-Air, 1985; Carneiro & Eusébio, 2015; Pearce, 1982; Pizam et al., 2000). For instance, the social contact has a significant effect on the resident's perceptions of the effects of tourism on the quality of life (Carneiro et al., 2018; Carneiro & Eusébio, 2015) and the attitude towards tourists (Joo et al., 2018). For tourists, the contact with the local can lead to a positive travel experience in the destination (Li & Liu, 2020). Compared with long-lasting kinds of contact, contact between groups through tourism will need to accumulate, diversify, and deepen to achieve a positive change in intergroup attitudes and behaviour (Yilmaz & Tasci, 2015). The same attitude towards the hosts can be spread to their attitude towards the travel destination (Fan, Zhang, Jenkins, & Tavitiyaman, 2017; Pearce, 1982; Pizam et al., 2000).

The above popular belief has been challenged by empirical studies, which argue that intergroup contact does not necessarily reduce intergroup tension, prejudice, hostility and discriminatory behaviour (Anastasopoulos, 1992; Milman et al., 1990; Pizam et al., 1991). The contact results depend heavily on the contact conditions between the two sides as concluded previously in contact theory (Pizam, 1996; Thyne et al., 2006). The negative effect may result from the unique nature of social contact in tourism. During the relatively short time of visit, the limited and shallow contacts between two culturally different parties may induce communication difficulties and increase tension, hostility and suspicion (Nyaupane et al., 2015). For instance, cross-cultural voluntourism is argued to reinforce negative perceptions between tourists and local recipients, as many voluntourists consider local recipients as "inferior" or "less-able" (Sin, 2009; Woosnam & Lee, 2011). Under such context, the greater the social contact, the more likely the negative attitude will be triggered towards the hosts and the destination.

To address the contradictory relationship between tourist-host social contact and travel attitude as indicated in the literature, Hypothesis 2 is established as follows:

> **H2a**: Tourist-host social contact is positively related to travel attitude.

> **H2b**: Tourist-host social contact is negatively related to travel attitude.

Perceived cultural distance and tourist-host social contact

Tourists undoubtedly constitute the largest group of cross-cultural experiencers. The effects of cultural attributes on tourist-host contact depend largely on the degree of cultural similarity and difference between contact participants (Levine, 1977). Cultural similarity leads to mutual understanding, sense of familiarity and social interaction among individuals (Brewer & Campbell, 1976; Feather, 1980; Lin et al., 2019). A positive relationship is found between culture similarity and socialisation (Siehl & Martin, 1985). Meanwhile, cultural dissimilarity distorts the meanings of the behaviour (Triandis, 1977), results in communication difficulties and emotional detachment (Fan, Zhang, Jenkins, & Tavitiyaman, 2017), as well as inefficient social contact (Robinson & Nemetz, 1988). In that case, future interaction may even be lost (Fan, Zhang, Jenkins, et al., 2017; Kamal & Maruyama, 1990).

Based on the existing literature, Hypothesis 3 is proposed as follows:

> **H3**: Perceived cultural distance is negatively related to tourist-host social contact.

Mediating role of social contact

Considering the relationship between perceived cultural distance and social contact, and that between social contact and travel attitude, social contact may serve as the mediator between perceived cultural distance and travel attitude. In one circumstance, perceived cultural distance has a negative effect on travel attitude by restricting effective interactions with the locals. Tourists travelling to a destination with large perceived cultural distance are encapsulated by their culture and tend to have limited interactions with the hosts because of communication obstacles or psychological uncertainty (Cohen, 1972; Fan, Zhang, Jenkins, et al., 2017). In that case, tourists do not obtain the chance to understand the locals, which would lead to a negative travel attitude. According to staged authenticity (Cohen, 2007; MacCannell, 1973), perceived cultural distance can ensure that tourists engage in well-designed and non-threatened contacts with well-trained destination representatives, such as service staff. The trained staff can prevent tourists from encountering disappointing, misunderstood and unexpected contacts with the hosts induced by the cultural shock. As a result, tourists may generate positive travel attitude. To demonstrate this relationship, Hypothesis 4 is proposed as follows:

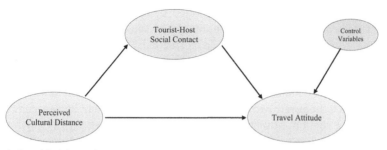

Figure 1. Theoretical model of the study.
* Significant path at the 0.05 level.
** Significant path at the 0.01 level.
*** Significant path at the 0.001 level.

H4: Tourist-host social contact mediates the relationship between perceived cultural distance and travel attitude.

Upon the formation of all the hypotheses, the theoretical model of this study is established and shown in Figure 1.

Methodology

Research context

This study selected Hong Kong tourists travelling to mainland China as the research context, based on the remarkable tourist flow, cultural bond, differences, and residential contact between the two regions. The 100 years of colonisation by the UK and separation from mainland China has made Hong Kong and mainland China ethnically similar but ideologically different regions. The cultural, historical and political connections, as well as differences between the two regions, have gained considerable attention in academic and non-academic domains. Moreover, several recent incidents in Hong Kong, such as the 2014 Umbrella Revolution and 2019 protests, reflect the urgency and practicality of understanding the relationship between Hong Kong and mainland China. With the high tourist flow in both directions, contacts between tourists and hosts at the individual level can be massive and important to the relationship between the two regions. The urgent need for understanding the role social contact plays in achieving a sustainable relationship between tourists and hosts makes this an ideal case for the current study.

Questionnaire and interview protocol development

The mixed-methods approach was used to achieve a set of research objectives from different perspectives. The quantitative approach was applied to examine statistically the structural model proposed by research objectives 1 and 2. The complicity of the model and the sensitivity of the cultural distance and social interactions between Hong Kong tourists and mainland Chinese hosts places the mechanism of how the social contact moderates the relationship between cultural distance and travel attitude beyond statistical indices. Therefore, the qualitative approach was used to understand further the underlying reasons for those proposed relationships.

In the quantitative approach, a survey was carried out to test statistically the hypotheses and the structure of the proposed model. Before the questionnaire design, the measurement instruments for the three constructs were selected and justified. In this study, the measurements of perceived cultural distance and tourist-host social contact were adopted from Fan, Zhang, Jenkins, et al.'s (2017b) work, which was a mixed-methods study and shared the same research context as the current one, i.e., Hong Kong tourists travelling to mainland China. The measurements of travel attitude were adopted and further consolidated from a series of attitude studies (Han et al., 2010; Hsu et al., 2010; Lam & Hsu, 2006; Sparks & Pan, 2009; Wang & Ritchie, 2012).

Besides perceived cultural distance and tourist-host social contact, several variables relating to travel patterns and experiences needed to be controlled in this model because of the potential effects on travel attitude (Poon & Huang, 2017). Travel patterns, such as length of stay, frequency of travel and travel mode (individual or package tour travellers) may affect tourists' perceptions and behaviours during their trips (Chen et al., 2016; Sung et al., 2001; Thrane, 2016; Zhang & Lam, 1999). Moreover, in the current research context, which is Hong Kong tourists travelling to mainland China, respondents' immigration background tended to have a strong effect on their cultural perceptions and their social behaviours in the destinations because of the considerable number of immigrants from mainland China to Hong Kong. People who have immigration background from mainland China may have a better understanding of the culture of the destination and a stronger connection to the destinations than Hong Kong tourists who have no such background (Shen et al., 2017; Ye et al., 2014). Therefore, length of stay, frequency of travel, travel mode and immigration generation are set as the control variables for the current model.

The questionnaire included four parts. The first part comprised screening questions that aimed to select the qualified respondents for the current study. In this study, respondents should be Hong Kong permanent residents and have travelled to mainland China for leisure purposes in the last two years. The second part contained trip-related questions, which aimed to seek respondents' travel patterns and personal experiences. The third part included 41 five-point Likert-type scale questions measuring the three constructs in the proposed framework. The last part of the questionnaire was for the demographic questions. Questions were set to obtain the profile and social characteristics of the respondents. The original questionnaire is provided in Appendix 1. The questionnaire was originally designed in English. For convenient distribution to Hong Kong residents, the questionnaire was translated into traditional Chinese by back-translation technique.

After obtaining the quantitative result, semi-structured in-depth interviews were conducted to collect the tourists' insights regarding the rationale of the quantitative results. The qualified respondents for the current interview are permanent Hong Kong residents who have travelled to mainland China for leisure purposes in the past two years. Questions were designed to reflect the different concepts and relationships proposed in the conceptual model. First, to warm up interviewees to the topic, they were asked on their travel experiences to mainland China. Second, after the warmup, interviewees were requested to evoke any memories of perceived cultural distance and social interactions with the locals they may have encountered during their travel. Third, interviewees were asked to share their overall attitude towards the trip with examples. To correspond to specific relationships in question, informants were then asked if they experienced any impact of perceived cultural distance on tourist-host social contact and travel attitude. If yes, they were asked how they thought the effect might work. Lastly, questions were also asked regarding the effects of tourist-host social contact on travel attitude. Respondents' demographic data, including age, gender, education, occupation, personal monthly income and marital status, were collected at the end.

Sampling and data collection

In terms of the survey, Shanghai, Beijing, Hangzhou and Chongqing, were the top four destination cities for Hong Kong overnight travellers to Mainland China between 2012 and 2016 and were selected to as data collection spots for quota sampling purpose (CNTA, 2017). Considering a large number of migrants in Hong Kong are from Guangdong and Fujian provinces in mainland China, cities in the two provinces were excluded from this study to avoid potential cultural similarity issue. According to the market share of the top four destination cities, the quota of Shanghai and Beijing was set to 250 and 150, respectively, whereas Hangzhou and Chongqing were 100 each. The proposed sample of 600 was large enough to run the model with a reliable and valid outcome (Hair et al., 2010). The research team collected data from October 2015 to February 2016 in the departure hall of the airport in each selected city, during low and high seasons. As a result, 660 valid samples were collected from Shanghai (250), Beijing (155), Hangzhou (145) and Chongqing (110).

A total of 22 semi-structured interviews were conducted to permanent Hong Kong residents with travel experience to mainland China for leisure purposes in the last two years. Convenience sampling was applied. The interviews were carried out using the interviewees' native language and each interview lasted for 26 to 88 minutes. New interviewees were not invited when the information collected was saturated. The transcripts were translated into English with the assistance to two professional language editors specialising in Cantonese and English.

Data analysis

Partial least squares structural equation modelling (PLS-SEM) was selected to estimate the models. PLS-SEM has advantages in dealing with complex models (i.e. three mediating hypotheses testing) and formative relationships (i.e. second-order structure) (Hair et al., 2011; Henseler et al., 2016). Samples with missing values were deleted due to the requirements of PLS-SEM. Thus, 635 valid responses were retained. For the measurement model, confirmatory factor analysis (CFA) was performed to confirm the dimensionality and structure of each factor. Reliability and validity were also tested. In the structural model, SEM was conducted to examine the relationships in the model. Bootstrapping, which is a resampling method, was used to examine the significance of the mediation effects. Bootstrapping involves repeatedly randomly sampling observations with replacement from the data set to compute the desired statistic in each resample. Computing over bootstrap resamples provide an approximation of the sampling distribution of the statistic of interest. Based on the computed sample mean and standard deviation, t-statistics can be calculated to determine the significance of the mediating effect.

Textual data derived from the transcripts were interpreted and analysed with thematic analysis, which focused on exploring themes within data and emphasised the rich description of the data set (Daly et al., 1997). Thematic analysis engages a process of categorising and grouping textual data to explore the emerging meaning relevant to the current two research objectives (Braun & Clarke, 2006). Software NVivo 11 was applied to code the transcripts technically. Considering the principles, during coding, meaningful units in participants' transcripts were captured and utilised to formulate key themes regarding the tourists' perceptions towards the concepts and their interrelationships as proposed in the model. Therefore, two themes covering both direct and indirect relationships are proposed in the research model. Within the direct relationship, the three sub themes included the relationship between cultural distance and travel attitude, tourist-host social contact and travel attitude as well as cultural distance and tourist-host social contact. Investigator triangulation was also applied to ensure the trustworthiness of the qualitative result (Lincoln & Guba, 1985). All authors regularly conducted intra-team communication and coding structure comparison during data analysis to ensure accuracy and credibility of the results. Inter-rater reliability was used to check the interrater agreement scoring of all the themes across all raters. As a result, the index was 87%, which was deemed satisfactory (Tran & Ralston, 2006).

Findings

Quantitative data analysis

Respondents' demographic information and travel patterns are indicated in Table 1. Among the 635 respondents, 56.98% were male. Respondents accounting for 34.13% were in the age group

Table 1. Demographics of Samples (n = 635).

Demographics	%	Demographics	%
Gender		**Marital status**	
Male	56.98	Single	32.32
Female	43.02	Married with child(ren)	52.80
Age		Married without child(ren)	13.76
18–24	10.53	Others	1.12
25–34	23.92	**Relation to the tourism industry**	
35–44	27.11	Yes	7.09
45–64	34.13	No	85.67
65 or above	4.31	Not applicable	7.24
Education		**Background of living in mainland China before**	
Primary or below	0.95	Yes	31.26
Secondary school	14.74	No	68.74
Diploma/Certificate	14.90	**Which immigrant generation are you?**	
Sub-degree course	3.01	First	12.91
Bachelor or above	66.40	Second	38.90
Monthly household income (HKD)		Third and above	17.01
0–9,999	0.34	I do not know	8.82
10,000–19,999	7.91	Not applicable	22.36
20,000–29,999	7.74	**Mode of tour**	
30,000–39,999	11.95	Individual travelers	79.37
40,000–49,999	9.09	Package tour	20.63
50,000–59,999	12.46	**Travel times**	
60,000 or above	36.20	1–3 times	23.46
Not applicable	14.31	4–6 times	20.63
Occupation		7–9 times	10.87
Managers and administrators	32.91	10–19 times	13.23
Professionals	29.41	20 times or more	31.81
Associate professionals	3.82	**Length of stay**	
Clerks	7.00	1–2 days	11.34
Service workers and shop sales workers	3.97	3–5 days	64.25
Craft and related workers	2.23	6–8 days	15.75
Plant and machine operators and assemblers	0.48	9 days or more	8.66
Elementary occupations	0.79		
Retired	6.04		
Students	7.79		
Not applicable	5.56		

of 45 to 64 years old, followed by 35 to 44 (27.11%) and 25 to 34 (23.92%). Two-thirds of the respondents held a bachelor's degree or above, and one-third of them had a monthly household income of 60,000 HKD or above. The majority (85.67%) worked in non-tourism related industries. Around 33% of respondents categorised themselves as managers or administrators, and 30% as professionals. Over half (52.8%) were married with child(ren).

In terms of the respondents' connections to the tourist destination, 31.26% lived in mainland China. Moreover, 12.91% were the first generation to immigrate to Hong Kong and 38.9% immigrated to Hong Kong following their parental generation. Regarding their current trips to mainland China, the majority travelled individually (79.37%) and stayed for three to five days (64.25%). In their lifetime, close to one third were frequent travellers who visited mainland China for more than 20 times and 23.46% travelled to mainland China up to three times. The demographic information of respondents was compared with a survey of Hong Kong travellers to mainland China conducted by the Hong Kong Census and Statistics Department (2015) to ensure the representativeness of the sample. The comparison revealed the two samples had similar proportions regarding gender, age and mode of tours, which indicates good representativeness of the sample.

Measurement model. Before any other statistical tests, the descriptive statistics of the 41 items, including mean, standard deviation, kurtosis and skewness values are presented in Appendix 2. The reliability and validity of PLS-SEM are not subject to the distribution of the data and thus, the results of the current study would be unbiased. In the measurement model, CFA was conducted to evaluate the adequacy of the measurements. In this model, as perceived cultural distance included sub-constructs, the current measurement model should be confirmed by the second-order CFA. One of the main objectives of this study was to examine the mediating role of tourist-host social contact, and thus, three dimensions were considered individually to obtain their separate mediating effects. Four items were deleted due to low factor loadings of below 0.4. These items were "People in mainland China and Hong Kong have different cuisines" and "People in mainland China and Hong Kong have different views on restrictions of freedom" from Perceived Cultural Distance construct and "Interaction with the service personnel during tours (e.g. tour guides, bus drivers)" and "Interaction with the locals during leisure activities" from the tourist-host social contact construct. Factor loadings for the remaining 37 items equalled to or exceeded 0.695. Table 2 indicates the results of reliability and validity tests of the measurement model, as requested for the CFA model reporting (Assaker, Huang & Hallak, 2012; Rasoolimanesh et al., 2017). In PLS, the reliability was examined by the composite reliability and $\rho_A s$. The composite reliabilities were all above 0.810 and the $\rho_A s$ were all above 0.659, indicating an acceptable reliability level (Bagozzi & Kimmel, 1995). Construct validity was examined by convergent and discriminant validity. Convergent validity was examined by the value of AVE for each construct. The results showed that all AVEs were beyond the threshold of 0.5, thereby meeting the ideal AVE for a well-developed construct (i.e. equal to or above 0.5) (Hair et al., 2010). Hence, convergent validity was established (Aleshinloye et al., 2020; Hair et al., 2010). The differences between constructs were examined using discriminant validity (Byrne, 2010), which monitors the external dissimilarity among factors (Hung & Petrick, 2011). Discriminant validity was assessed by the heterotrait-monotrait ratio of correlations (HTMT). As shown in Table 3, all the HTMTs were significantly less than the unit at 5% significant level, with all HTMTs between the two constructs below 0.9, thereby representing a satisfactory validity level (Fan et al., 2020; Henseler et al., 2016).

Structural model. Table 4 shows the results of the path analysis and hypotheses testing in the structural model. The first essential criterion for assessing a PLS structural equation model is R^2. R^2 measures the relationship of a latent variable's explained variance to its total variance by the exogenous latent variables in the model (Assaker et al., 2012). The R^2 of the structural model was 0.442 and the adjusted R^2 was 0.435, which indicated a good explanatory power of this model. Among all the seven paths, six paths were significant, indicating significant effects from the exogenous constructs to their corresponding endogenous constructs. In particular, perceived cultural distance had positive effect on travel attitude (coefficient = 0.067, p = 0.037) service-oriented contact had positive effect on travel attitude (coefficient = 0.091, p = 0.038) quality of contact had a strongly positive effect on travel attitude (coefficient = 0.628, p = 0.000). Perceived cultural distance positively affected social-oriented contact (coefficient = 0.092, p = 0.020) and service-oriented contact (coefficient = 0.155, p = 0.000), but negatively affected the quality of contact (coefficient = -0.128, p = 0.002). Social-oriented contact had no significant effect on travel attitude (coefficient = 0.002, p = 0.968). Therefore, H1a was fully supported and H2a and H3 were partially supported.

Regarding the mediating effect of tourist-host social contact in the structural model, the bootstrapping method was used to examine the existence of the mediation. As presented in Table 5, the direct effect of perceived cultural distance on travel attitude was significant and positive (coefficient = 0.067, p = 0.029). The indirect effects mediated by tourist-host social contact varied across different contacts. The indirect effect mediated by social-oriented contact was not significant (coefficient = 0.000, p = 0.951) and the one mediated by service-oriented contact was positive (coefficient = 0.014, p = 0.016). On the contrary, the mediating effect of quality of contact was reported to be negative (coefficient = -0.080, p = 0.001). In that case, the overall indirect effect by tourist-host social contact was negative (coefficient = -0.066, p = 0.011) and the total effect between the constructs of perceived cultural distance and travel attitude was not significant. Therefore, H4 was supported.

Table 2. Results of the measurement model (n = 635).

Constructs and Items	Standardized factor loading	Composite reliability	rho A	Average variance extracted (AVE)
Perceived cultural distance (PCD)				
Cultural retention (CR)		0.810	0.659	0.587
People in mainland China and Hong Kong have different traditional customs.	0.803			
People in mainland China and Hong Kong have differences in terms of richness of traditional customs.	0.782			
People in mainland China and Hong Kong have a different sense of culture retention.	0.710			
Behavioural characteristics (BC)		0.829	0.703	0.619
People in mainland China and Hong Kong are different at the civilization level.	0.813			
People in mainland China and Hong Kong have different privacy protection.	0.787			
People in mainland China and Hong Kong have different hygiene standards.	0.758			
Social characteristics (SC)		0.891	0.818	0.804
People in mainland China and Hong Kong are different in their way of communication.	0.930			
People in mainland China and Hong Kong are different in their way of making friends.	0.862			
Social-oriented contact (social OC)		0.917	0.903	0.612
Interaction with the locals when travelling together (showing around)	0.832			
Interaction with the locals in participating performance	0.818			
Interaction with the locals by exchanging gifts	0.808			
Interaction with the locals by experiencing their customs	0.799			
Interaction with the locals by enquiring or receiving help from them	0.777			
Interaction with the locals when there is a conflict	0.721			
Interaction with the locals by visiting their homes	0.712			
Service-oriented contact (service OC)		0.906	0.875	0.658
Interaction with the service personnel while dining	0.879			
Interaction with the service personnel while shopping	0.848			
Interaction with the service personnel in accommodation	0.812			
Interaction with the locals during leisure activities	0.775			
Interaction with the service personnel in transportation	0.734			
Quality of contact (QC)		0.881	0.836	0.599
Friendly	0.834			
Harmonious	0.830			
Intense	0.768			
Equal	0.734			
Cooperative	0.695			
Travel attitude (TA)		0.956	0.950	0.644
favourable	0.849			
Good	0.842			
Satisfying	0.831			
worthwhile	0.821			
Right	0.820			
fascinating	0.814			
Fun	0.809			
Exciting	0.797			
Arousing	0.783			
Positive	0.774			
Desirable	0.744			
Enjoyable	0.739			

Table 3. Results of the Heterotrait-Monotrait ratio of correlations (HTMT).

	Travel attitude	Behavioural characteristics	Cultural retention	Quality of contact	Social characteristics	Service-oriented contact	Social-oriented contact
Travel attitude	–						
Behavioural characteristics	0.062	–					
Cultural retention	0.095	0.623	–				
Quality of contact	0.728	0.177	0.093	–			
Social characteristics	0.051	0.565	0.581	0.155	–		
Service-Oriented contact	0.283	0.244	0.113	0.284	0.103	–	
Social-oriented contact	0.205	0.188	0.062	0.241	0.055	0.688	–

Note: All the HTMTs are significantly less than the unit at 5% significant level.

Table 4. Results of the path analysis and hypotheses testing.

Hypotheses Path	Construct	Path	Construct	Coefficient	P	Results
H1a and H1b	Perceived cultural distance	→	Travel attitude	0.067	0.037	H1a Supported
H2a and H2b	Social-oriented contact	→	Travel attitude	0.002	0.968	H2a Partially
	Service-oriented contact	→	Travel attitude	0.091	0.038	Supported
	Quality of contact	→	Travel attitude	0.628	0.000	
H3	Perceived cultural distance	→	Social-oriented contact	0.092	0.020	Partially
	Perceived cultural distance	→	Service-oriented contact	0.155	0.000	Supported
	Perceived cultural distance	→	Quality of contact	−0.128	0.002	

Upon the completion of hypotheses assessment, a structural model with path coefficients and significant levels was drawn accordingly and presented in Figure 2. The figure indicated that the control variables, namely, length of stay, frequency of travel, travel mode and immigration generation, did not have significant effects on travel attitude.

Qualitative data analysis

Interview transcripts were analysed to explore the relationship among perceived cultural distance, tourist-host social contact and travel attitude, and to supplement interpretive evidence for the model.

First, interviewees were asked on the effects of cultural distance on their social contact with the locals. Results revealed that perceived cultural distance can negatively affect the quality of contact, which led to an unpleasant contact experience. Most of the mentioned cultural distance was related to behavioural and social norms. As reported by Informant 10, *"Especially in some attractions, people are used to jumping the queue. This behaviour always creates quarrels with the locals"* (Informant 10, female, 30–39, clerk).

Some of the places are less developed compared with Hong Kong. People have a weak sense of hygiene. Seeing some men just pee on the side of the road is uncomfortable and do not need to be mentioned to the kids. I think it is just that area lacks proper education support (Informant 5, female, 20–29, professional). "I saw people spit everywhere …." (Informant 11, female, 40–49, clerk).

However, differences in culture can also encourage social interactions between the tourists and hosts. Informants claimed they were amazed and attracted by the different lifestyles, traditional culture and socialisation practices in the destination and would like to interact with the locals to explore.

People from the north are so different from us. They are more hospitable, warm-hearted and honest. I like to go to their local communities to explore more about their life. I visited the Beihai Park in Beijing once and found some senior people were writing on the ground with the water-inked Chinese brush pen. We never see that in Hong Kong. Those senior people noticed and chatted with us. They asked for our names and wrote our names with the water-inked Chinese brush pen for us, which was very impressive to us. They were very friendly and nice …. I think this city is very internationalised and tolerant to people from other places. (Informant 2, female, 30–39, hunting for jobs)

Second, in terms of the effects of social contact on tourists' travel attitude, results generally indicated a positive association between the two. More contacts with the locals could provide more opportunities for the tourists to cultivate a favourable and positive attitude towards the trip. As indicated by Informant 6,

We stayed in a guest house and the house owner made our journey! As we would like to hire a car at the very last minute, no car was left. The owner was so kind as to give us a ride, no, it was a journey. He drove us around the small town and then down to the beach. I was so surprised that he seemed to know everyone. He introduced many different things to do here and we were so lucky as we did not make any travel plan. That trip was unforgettable (Informant 6, female, 40–49, professional).

I love to go to the local street markets, buying food and chatting with people when travelling. I can know what the local people are like, what they eat, and how they communicate with each

Table 5. Mediating effects in the structural model.

Hypothesis Path	Construct	Path	Construct	Direct effect	Indirect effect		Total effect	Result
H4	Perceived Cultural Distance	→	Travel Attitude	0.067 (0.029)	Social-oriented contact	0.000 (0.951)		
					Service-oriented contact	0.014 (0.016)		
					Quality of contact	−0.080 (0.001)	−0.066 (0.011)	0.001 (0.978)	Supported

Note: Figures in parenthesis are p values.

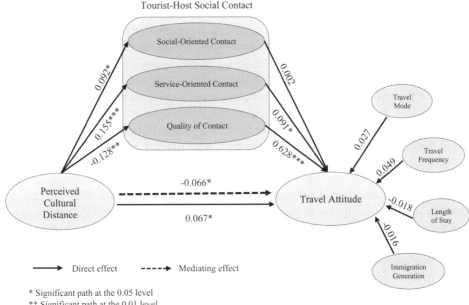

Figure 2. Final structural model with standardized path coefficients.

other. That is the best place that you can get to know the local without any commercial cosmetics. (Informant 20, male, 50–59, early retirement)

Lastly, the mediating role of social contact in the relationship between perceived cultural distance and travel attitude was evident but showed contrary effects between quantity and quality of social contact. On the one hand, perceived cultural distance can lead to positive travel attitude by encouraging tourists' participation in various social contact in a destination.

"Experiencing different cultures is the main reason that I travel. I go to the local parks, try the authentic food and bargain in small shops. I get to know the local culture by chatting with people there. Then I find my trip very exciting". (Informant 20, male, 50–59, early retirement)

On the other hand, tourists who perceive large cultural distance with the hosts reported negative travel attitude towards the destination by generating a negative attitude towards the contact experiences with the hosts.

One can easily get disappointed by the huge cultural shock. At least it is the case for myself. When you have a close experience with the so-called local thing, for example, loudly shouting at each other in a restaurant, unexpected (close) personal distance and ways of expression, I feel uncomfortable. Sometimes I prefer to travel within a small group of my people, so I can have my familiar environment with me and don't get shocked. (Informant 19, female, 60–69, retirement)

Discussion and implications

Considering indirect effects could offer alternative means to understand a relationship and provide insights to a broad body of knowledge due to the complex nature of tourist perceptions and behaviours. The current study explored the direct effect of perceived cultural distance on tourists' travel attitude and considered the mediating effect of tourist-host social contact in this relationship.

Perceived cultural distance and tourist-host social contact

Based on the data, perceived cultural distance has a negative effect on the quality of contact, but had a negative effect on the quantity of contact. According to the literature, differences in the cultural background may distort the meanings of expression and cause a decline in the efficiency and quality of interaction (Kamal & Maruyama, 1990). The larger the cultural distance between the tourists and the hosts, the more negative the tourists perceive their contact experiences (i.e. hostile, superficial, clashing, unequal and competitive in quality of contact) with their hosts. However, cultural distance may lead to more contacts in terms of quantity between tourists and hosts regardless of the types of contact, which seems to be contrary to the literature (Fan, Zhang, Jenkins, et al., 2017; Kamal & Maruyama, 1990; Robinson & Nemetz, 1988).

Interpretations can be derived from the literature and interviews. For the positive effect of quantity of contact because of cultural novelty seeking, tourists from a different cultural background would have the desire to explore the destination and the local culture by interacting with the hosts (McKercher & Chow, 2001; McKercher & Cros, 2003). The larger the cultural distance, the more the tourists are motivated to interact with the locals (Fan, Zhang, Jenkins, et al., 2017). In that case, the tourists tend to contact a variety of local people for social and service purposes to know more about the destination. However, the more contact the tourists have, the more negative feelings are likely to be generated because of miscommunication and meaning distortion induced by the cultural difference (Fan, Zhang, Jenkins, et al., 2017; Kamal & Maruyama, 1990). To conclude, cultural distance enables tourists to contact as much as they like with the hosts, but the overall contact quality with the hosts is constrained by the cultural distance (Levine, 1977). The overlooking of the dimensionality of social contact from previous literature may lead to a simple and unstable homogeneity in different individual cases. Considering the quality and quantity aspects of social contact enables researchers to differentiate the opposite effects from different aspects.

Tourist-host social contact to travel attitude

In terms of the relationship between the tourist-host social contact and the travel attitude, the current study generally supported the positive association between the two constructs. The study extended Allport's (1979) contact theory to the tourism context and further examined the importance of contact conditions proposed in Allport's theory, which were largely overlooked by previous studies examining the outcomes of contacts. The result showed consistency with Allport's (1979) contact theory, which emphasises that intergroup contact can produce positive effect if such contact is under certain conditions, such as equal status, common goals, cooperation and personal interactions. Tourism, being described as a great force for peace and understanding, can provide an equal, cooperative, pleasant and personal environment, which may naturally nurture positive intergroup connections.

Concerning different dimensions of social contact, the quality of contact is reported to have a salient effect on travel attitude. The strong effect may result from the nature of this concept. Fan et al. (2017b) stated that tourists subjectively evaluate the quality of contact and travel attitude. Positive perception towards the contacts with the hosts may directly link to positive perception towards a destination. The affective association may overshadow tourists' objective judgment towards the two concepts (Huang & Hsu, 2010). Regarding the quantity of contact, the service-oriented contact was positively related to tourists' travel attitude, whereas the social-oriented contact did not show any significant effect on travel attitude. In the service-oriented contact, tourists' contact points are mostly the representatives of the tourist sectors (Cohen, 1972; MacCannell, 2018), including hotel service staff, tour guides, restaurants service staff and taxi drivers, as disclosed in the interviews. Such kinds of interactions result in relatively shallow contacts. Nonetheless, the contacts can be helpful and useful for tourists' trips in the short run and may leave a positive impression for the tourists due to the favourable nature (Zatori et al., 2018).

Mediating role of tourist-host social contact

As the most profound finding of the current study, the tourist-host social contact was found to be a mediator of the relationship between perceived cultural distance and travel attitude. Interestingly, by adopting the three dimensions to measure the abstract concept of tourist-host social contact, different dimensions of tourist-host social contact played different roles in mediating the relationship. By participating in social contact in a destination, the positive effect of perceived cultural distance on travel attitude was significantly enhanced. However, due to the salient effect of quality of contact on travel attitude, tourists who perceived large cultural distance with the hosts may have negative travel attitude towards the destination by generating negative attitude towards the contact experiences with the hosts. Therefore, the overall mediating effect of tourist-host social contact turned out to be negative.

As stated at the beginning of this paper, considering social contact may provide supplemental ways to understand the ambiguous relationship between cultural distance and travel attitude. When considering the direct effect per se, cultural distance positively affected tourists' travel attitude at a weak level. However, events that occurred beyond the direct relationship but eventually reflected on this relationship may not be as simple as the linear assumptions proposed in the literature. Social contact, together with many other potentially influencing factors, delivers an indirect effect, which may further reinforce or weaken the original effect. In this model, tourist-host social contact is reported to mediate negatively the relationship between perceived cultural distance and travel attitude. This negative effect further results from a positive mediating role of the quantity of contact (service-oriented social contact) and the negative mediating role of quality of contact. Due to the inconsistency between the direct and indirect effects, the total effect in this model between perceived cultural distance and travel attitude was positive but not significant. As can be deduced, social contact is merely one behaviour out of many others that can mediate the effect of cultural distance and travel attitude. Considering other attributes may lead to a different total effect between the two constructs.

In response to the fundamental research question, "how does perceived cultural distance influence travel attitude?", suggestions can be drawn as follows. Perceived cultural distance influences tourist's travel attitude in diverse ways and can directly and positively affect travel attitude. Meanwhile, the perceived cultural distance may deliver a positive effect on travel attitude by participating in service-oriented social contact. However, perceived cultural distance can negatively affect tourists' travel attitude by generating negative contact experience with the hosts.

Associating the findings of the current study with the existing literature, this study provided empirical support for the previous argument. In particular, scholars who held the belief that contacts between two parties with large cultural distances may lead to a negative attitude deemed that differences in cultural background induced cultural shock, perceptions of risk (Lepp & Gibson, 2003), communication problems (Pearce, 1982) and many other negative emotions due to the cultural uncertainty (Goeldner & Ritchie, 2008; Ng et al., 2007). The mediating role of quality of social contact in this model explains the underlying negative relationship between perceived cultural distance and travel attitude. Perceived cultural distance arouses tourist' motivation of novelty seeking, which may lead to positive travel attitude towards a destination (Hsu et al., 2010; Hung & Petrick, 2011; Zatori et al., 2018). This statement is empirically supported by the mediator of the quantity of social contact. As reported in the findings, tourists are attracted by cultural differences in a destination and tended to contact a variety of residents to explore the local lifestyle, customs and other cultural attractions. The wide-ranging contact with the hosts, especially through service staff, enables tourists to be capsulised in a "well-designed" and "staged" experience (MacCannell, 2018). By such kind of "proper" exploration, tourists' hold positive travel attitude towards the destination. To conclude, although the two arguments appeared contradictory, they captured diverse effects of perceived cultural distance on travel attitude via two different approaches and hence led to distinct consequences.

Considering the concept of tourist bubble, as described by Cohen (1972) and Jaakson (2004), social and cultural separation is like an environmental bubble, which creates a protective wall for the tourists from the host society. Such kind of bubble can influence tourists' travel experiences, perceptions and their attitudes towards the destinations. The current study concurred with the literature and further developed the concept by specifying the roles that different aspects of social contact play in the relationship. As shown in this study, social contact-mediated the relationship between perceived cultural distance and travel attitude positively and negatively. In that case, remaining in the cultural bubble may not necessarily lead to a negative attitude and decapsulating oneself out of the bubble may not guarantee a positive outcome. The result heavily depends on the variety and extent of the contact with the hosts in a destination.

Theoretical contributions and practical implications

This study is the first to introduce the tourist-host social contact into the debate of the relationship between perceived cultural distance and travel attitude and explained this relationship by considering direct and indirect effects. Previous studies have described predominantly the role of perceived cultural distance as either positive or negative. The incoherence has been challenged by different individual works but no convincing results have been achieved. The most insightful finding of this study is the confirmation of the relationship between perceived cultural distance and travel attitude as "contact elastic". The current study verified the simultaneous existence of positive and negative mediating effects of social contact. The relationship between perceived cultural distance and travel attitude depended largely on the different mediating roles of social contact, which served as a rubber band in the middle. To summarise, the quantity of contact may enhance the positive effect of perceived cultural distance on tourists' travel attitude, whereas the quality of contact may result in the negative effect of perceived cultural distance towards tourists' travel attitude. The study offered empirical support to paradoxical arguments and expanded the existing body of knowledge by introducing indirect effects to the arguable relationship.

The study examined the role of tourist-host social contact as outcome and antecedent. Perceived cultural distance has diverse effects on different dimensions of tourist-host social contact. Not limited to the tourism realm, the co-existence of contrary effects of perceived cultural distance on social contact and the dynamic role of social contact in mediating the relationship between cultural distance and attitude may also help in understanding human beings' socialisation process and cultural determinism.

The study has certain implications for the government, operators and host societies. From the government's viewpoint, in addition to the economic benefits, tourism is expected to induce positive attitudes between tourists and hosts. Based on the discussion elaborated above, the effect of perceived cultural distance on tourists' travel attitude was determined heavily by the trade-off between the quantity and the quality of the contact with the hosts. Thus, this relationship should be utilised with caution given that the contact with the local hosts may not necessarily lead to the positive attitude and isolating oneself from interacting with the locals may not guarantee a negative outcome. Opportunities can be created for wide-ranging interactions, especially for service purposes, to achieve a sustainable relationship between tourists and hosts with different cultural backgrounds. Resident volunteers can be tapped in attractions and city centres to provide guidance and translations, join the service staff in different service outlets and participate in interactive cultural performances and festivals. While enjoying the advantages of the quantity of social contact, efforts should also be exerted, such as offering professional training to the service staff on a regular basis to minimise the negative effect of perceived cultural distance on the quality of social contact, leading to negative travel attitude.

In a tourism destination, actions can be taken to improve the tourist-host relationship and maintain the sustained growth of tourism development. For example, the support of local communities is a vital component to the successful maintenance of a good relationship with the tourists (Tasci & Severt, 2017). The government can consider improving the residents' awareness of tourism through continuous tourism education (Malihah & Setiyorini, 2014; Thyne et al., 2018). Such kind of education informs the hosts on the benefits of tourism and the behavioural and perceptional differences that residents may experience because of their different cultural backgrounds. With a tolerant and hospitable host environment, the sustainable tourist-host relationship can be nurtured naturally. Moreover, service-oriented social contact plays an important role in enhancing positive travel attitude, and thus, service staff training in service quality, handling cultural distance and expression of hospitality should be carried out by corresponding operators to ensure a pleasant experience for the tourists. From a tourist's viewpoint, familiarisation of the destination's lifestyle, behavioural patterns and communication culture before departure can facilitate their enjoyable encounter with the hosts during their stay, leading to a positive attitude towards the destination.

With many countries and territories now recognising tourism as a substantial development option and one with considerable economic benefits, governments are often reluctant to place limitations on inbound tourism numbers. Many long-standing issues in the tourism literature, such as carrying capacity, limit growth, and social and environmental concerns are subordinated to economic considerations. However, tourism remains a non-essential purchase, which is substituted easily for other products and services or within the tourism destination choice spectrum. Moreover, tourist spots have many potential competing destinations. For this reason, governments and tourism destinations should consider the social relationship between residents and tourists. Ignoring concerns of residents on the volume or nature of tourist activities can ferment ill-feeling and antipathy towards tourism and tourists, causing them to reach the stage where tourists choose alternative destinations with consequent economic effects.

Conclusion and limitations

The present study examined empirically the relationships among perceived cultural distance, tourist-host social contact and travel attitude by adopting a mixed-methods approach and developing a multi-dimensional social contact between tourists and hosts. Building on those direct relationships, the study investigated further the mediating effect of different dimensions of social contact between perceived cultural distance and travel attitude. The results indicated that perceived cultural distance can affect tourists' travel attitude directly and indirectly. A larger perceived cultural distance can lead directly to a more favourable travel attitude. Meanwhile, perceived cultural distance can affect tourists' travel attitude positively by involving more tourist participation in a variety of contacts with the hosts, especially with tourism contact points. However, the perceived cultural distance may generate negative quality of contact and such kind of unfavourable emotions may lead to negative travel attitude. The findings confirmed theoretically the direct and indirect effects of perceived cultural distance on travel attitude and identified for the first time the mediating effect of tourist-host social contact in this relationship. The study offered a new outlook to explain the ambiguous viewpoints on the effect of cultural distance on travel attitude. The study also provided practical suggestions for destination policymakers, tourism practitioners and local communities regarding how to handle the "contact elastic" relationship to maintain a favourable and sustainable tourist-host bond.

As with other studies, this study needs to be considered with the following limitations. First, the research context for the current study was between Hong Kong and mainland China, which has a small and supplementary cultural distance. In that case, results obtained from this cultural context may vary from cases with large and intolerable cultural differences. Second, the tourist-host social contact adopted in this study referred to the general mass tourists with broad and diverse travel interests and patterns. Different markets of tourism, for instance, voluntourism, ecotourism, cultural tourism and B-Leisure (Business + Leisure) tourism may generate different contact patterns and quality. In that case, their effects on the relationship between perceived cultural distance and travel attitude may differ. Taking this study as the starting point, future studies could explore the proposed cultural distance-social contact-travel attitude relationship in cross-country cultural contexts to examine the applicability of this model. Furthermore, because of the different contact parties and patterns, different niche markets should undergo specialised investigation to explore any nuanced findings in different market segments. Finally, other potential outcomes caused by cultural distance and social contacts between tourists and hosts, such as travel experience, destination immersion and perceived destination image can be integrated into the current model to explore broader social-cultural effects.

Disclosure statement

No potential conflict of interest was reported by the author(s).

ORCID

Daisy X. F. Fan http://orcid.org/0000-0002-5247-8394
Hanqin Qiu http://orcid.org/0000-0001-5632-7545
Chloe Lau http://orcid.org/0000-0003-2895-2073

References

Ahn, M. J., & McKercher, B. (2015). The effect of cultural distance on tourism: A study of international visitors to Hong Kong. *Asia Pacific Journal of Tourism Research*, *20*(1), 94–113. https://doi.org/10.1080/10941665.2013.866586
Ajzen, I. (1988). *Attitude, personality and behavior*. Open University Press.
Ajzen, I. (1991). The theory of planned behavior. *Organizational Behavior and Human Decision Processes*, *50*(2), 179–211. https://doi.org/10.1016/0749-5978(91)90020-T
Aleshinloye, K. D., Fu, X., Ribeiro, M. A., Woosnam, K. M., & Tasci, A. D. (2020). The influence of place attachment on social distance: Examining mediating effects of emotional solidarity and the moderating role of interaction. *Journal of Travel Research*, *59*(5), 828–849. https://doi.org/10.1177/0047287519863883

Allport, G. W. (1979). *The nature of prejudice*. Addison-Wesley Pub.

Amir, Y., & Ben-Ari, R. (1985). International tourism, ethnic contact, and attitude change. *Journal of Social Issues*, *41*(3), 105–115. https://doi.org/10.1111/j.1540-4560.1985.tb01131.x

Anastasopoulos, P. G. (1992). Tourism and attitude change: Greek tourists visiting Turkey. *Annals of Tourism Research*, *19*(4), 629–642. https://doi.org/10.1016/0160-7383(92)90058-W

Assaker, G., Huang, S., & Hallak, R. (2012). Applications of partial least squares structural equation modeling in tourism research: A methodological review. *Tourism Analysis*, *17*(5), 679–686. https://doi.org/10.3727/108354212X13485873914128

Bagozzi, R. P., & Burnkrant, R. E. (1979). Attitude measurement and behavior change: A reconsideration of attitude organization and its relationship to behavior. *Advances in Consumer Research*, *6*, 295–302.

Bagozzi, R. P., & Kimmel, S. K. (1995). A comparison of leading theories for the prediction of goal directed behaviours. *British Journal of Social Psychology*, *34*(4), 437–461. https://doi.org/10.1111/j.2044-8309.1995.tb01076.x

Barthes, R. (1973). *Mythologies*. Paladin.

Beard, J. G., & Ragheb, M. G. (1983). Measuring leisure motivation. *Journal of Leisure Research*, *15*(3), 219–228. https://doi.org/10.1080/00222216.1983.11969557

Binder, J., Zagefka, H., Brown, R., Funke, F., Kessler, T., Mummendey, A., Maquil, A., Demoulin, S., & Leyens, J.-P. (2009). Does contact reduce prejudice or does prejudice reduce contact? A longitudinal test of the contact hypothesis among majority and minority groups in three European countries. *Journal of Personality and Social Psychology*, *96*(4), 843–856. https://doi.org/10.1037/a0013470

Bochner, S. (1982). The Social Psychology of Cross-Cultural Relations. In Stephen Bochner (Eds.), *Cultures in contact: Studies in cross-cultural interaction* (pp. 5–29). Pergamon.

Braun, V., & Clarke, V. (2006). Using qualitative analysis in psychology. *Qualitative Research in Psychology*, *3*(2), 77–101. https://doi.org/10.1191/1478088706qp063oa

Brewer, M. B., & Campbell, D. T. (1976). *Ethnocentrism and intergroup attitudes: East African evidence*. Sage.

Byrne, B. (2010). *Structural equation modeling with AMOS: Basic concepts*. Applications, and programming (2nd ed.). Taylor & Francis.

Carneiro, M. J., & Eusébio, C. (2015). Host-tourist interaction and impact of tourism on residents' Quality of. *Life. Tourism & Management Studies*, *11*(1), 25–34.

Carneiro, M. J., Eusébio, C., & Caldeira, A. (2018). The influence of social contact in residents' perceptions of the tourism impact on their quality of life: A structural equation model. *Journal of Quality Assurance in Hospitality & Tourism*, *19*(1), 1–30. https://doi.org/10.1080/1528008X.2017.1314798

Caulkins, D. D. (1999). Is Mary Douglas's grid/group analysis useful for cross-cultural research? *Cross-Cultural Research*, *33*(1), 108–128. https://doi.org/10.1177/106939719903300107

Chen, Y., Schuckert, M., Song, H., & Chon, K. (2016). Why can package tours hurt tourists? Evidence from China's tourism demand in Hong Kong. *Journal of Travel Research*, *55*(4), 427–439. https://doi.org/10.1177/0047287515612597

China National Tourism Administration of P.R.C. (2017). *The yearbook of China Tourism Statistics 2016*. China Travel and Tourism Press.

Cohen, E. (1972). Toward a sociology of international tourism. *Social Research*, *39*(1), 164–182.

Cohen, E. (1979). A phenomenology of tourist experiences. *Sociology*, *13*(2), 179–201. https://doi.org/10.1177/003803857901300203

Cohen, E. (2007). Authenticity' in tourism studies: Aprés la lutte. *Tourism Recreation Research*, *32*(2), 75–82. https://doi.org/10.1080/02508281.2007.11081279

Crompton, J. L. (1979). Motivations for pleasure vacation. *Annals of Tourism Research*, *6*(4), 408–424. https://doi.org/10.1016/0160-7383(79)90004-5

Cusher, K. & Brislin, (1996). *Intercultural interactions: A practical guide*. Sage.

Daly, J., Kellehear, A., & Gliksman, M. (1997). *The public health researcher: A methodological guide*. Oxford University Press.

Dewar, K., Meyer, D., & Li, W. M. (2001). Harbin, lanterns of ice, sculptures of snow. *Tourism Management*, *22*(5), 523–532. https://doi.org/10.1016/S0261-5177(01)00007-3

Douglas, M. (1982). *In the active voice*. London.

Esiyok, B., Çakar, M., & Kurtulmuşoğlu, F. B. (2017). The effect of cultural distance on medical tourism. *Journal of Destination Marketing & Management*, *6*(1), 66–75. https://doi.org/10.1016/j.jdmm.2016.03.001

Fan, D. X., Hsu, C. H., & Lin, B. (2020). Tourists' experiential value co-creation through online social contacts: Customer-dominant logic perspective. *Journal of Business Research*, *108*, 163–173. https://doi.org/10.1016/j.jbusres.2019.11.008

Fan, D. X., Zhang, H. Q., Jenkins, C. L., & Lin, P. M. (2017). Does tourist–host social contact reduce perceived cultural distance? *Journal of Travel Research*, *56*(8), 998–1010. https://doi.org/10.1177/0047287517696979

Fan, D. X., Zhang, H. Q., Jenkins, C. L., & Tavitiyaman, P. (2017). Tourist typology in social contact: An addition to existing theories. *Tourism Management*, *60*, 357–366. https://doi.org/10.1016/j.tourman.2016.12.021

Fan, D. X., Liu, A., & Qiu, R. T. (2017). The impact of the culture distance on tourism demand–an econometric method from a global perspective [Paper presentation]. In: Advances in Tourism Marketing Conferences 2017 Proceedings, 6–9 September 2017, Casablanca, Morocco.

Feather, N. (1980). Similarity of value systems within the same nation: Evidence from Australia and Papua New Guinea. *Australian Journal of Psychology*, *32*(1), 17–30. https://doi.org/10.1080/00049538008254669

Fishbein, M. A., & Ajzen, I. (1975). *Belief, attitude, intention and behavior: An introduction to theory and research*. Addison-Wesley.

Fulbright, J. W. (1976). The most significant and important activity I have been privileged to engage in during my years in the Senate. *The Annals of the American Academy of Political and Social Science*, *424*(1), 1–5. https://doi.org/10.1177/000271627642400102

Goeldner, C. R., & Ritchie, J. R. (2008). *Tourism: Principles, practices, philosophies*. John Wiley & Sons. Inc. Retrieved 15 October 2013, from http://www.myilibrary.com?ID=176679

Hair, J. F., Black, W., Babin, B., & Anderson, R. (2010). *Multivariate data analysis*. Prentice-Hall.

Hair, J. F., Ringle, C. M., & Sarstedt, M. (2011). PLS-SEM: Indeed a silver bullet. *Journal of Marketing Theory and Practice*, *19*(2), 139–152. https://doi.org/10.2753/MTP1069-6679190202

Han, H., Hsu, L. T., & Sheu, C. (2010). Application of the theory of planned behavior to green hotel choice: Testing the effect of environmental friendly activities. *Tourism Management*, *31*(3), 325–334. https://doi.org/10.1016/j.tourman.2009.03.013

Henseler, J., Hubona, G., & Ray, P. A. (2016). Using PLS path modeling in new technology research: Updated guidelines. *Industrial Management & Data Systems*, *116*(1), 2–20. https://doi.org/10.1108/IMDS-09-2015-0382

Hofstede, G., Hofstede, G. J., & Minkov, M. (2010). *Cultures and organizations: Software of the mind* (Revised and expanded 3rd ed.). McGraw-Hill.

Hong Kong Census and Statistics Department (2015). Socio-economic Characteristics and Consumption Expenditure of Hong Kong Residents Making Personal Travel to the Mainland of China, 2014. Retrieved July 11, 2017, from Hong Kong Special Administrative Region Web site: http://www.statistics.gov.hk/pub/B71511FB2015XXXXB0100.pdf

Hsu, C. H. C., & Cai, L., Li, M. (2010). Expectation, motivation, and attitude: A tourist behavioral model. *Journal of Travel Research*, *49*(3), 282–296. https://doi.org/10.1177/0047287509349266

Hsu, C. H., & Huang, S. (2012). An extension of the theory of planned behavior model for tourists. *Journal of Hospitality & Tourism Research*, *36*(3), 390–417. https://doi.org/10.1177/1096348010390817

Hsu, C. H. C., Kang, S. K., & Lam, T. (2006). Reference group influences among Chinese travelers. *Journal of Travel Research*, *44*(4), 474–484. https://doi.org/10.1177/0047287505282951

Huang, J., & Hsu, C. H. (2010). The impact of customer-to-customer interaction on cruise experience and vacation satisfaction. *Journal of Travel Research*, *49*(1), 79–92. https://doi.org/10.1177/0047287509336466

Hung, K. L., & Petrick, J. F. (2011). Why do you cruise? Exploring the motivations for taking cruise holidays and the construction of a cruising motivation scale. *Tourism Management*, *32*(2), 386–393. https://doi.org/10.1016/j.tourman.2010.03.008

Jaakson, R. (2004). Beyond the tourist bubble?: Cruiseship passengers in port. *Annals of Tourism Research*, *31*(1), 44–60. https://doi.org/10.1016/j.annals.2003.08.003

Joo, D., Tasci, A. D. A., Woosnam, K. M., Maruyama, N. U., Hollas, C. R., & Aleshinloye, K. D. (2018). Residents' attitude towards domestic tourists explained by contact, emotional solidarity and social distance. *Tourism Management*, *64*, 245–257. https://doi.org/10.1016/j.tourman.2017.08.012

Kamal, A., & Maruyama, G. (1990). Cross-cultural contact and attitudes of Qatari students in the United States. *International Journal of Intercultural Relations*, *14*(2), 123–134. https://doi.org/10.1016/0147-1767(90)90001-D

Kawakami, K., Dovidio, J. F., Moll, J., Hermsen, S., & Russin, A. (2000). Just say no (to stereotyping): Effects of training in the negation of stereotypic associations on stereotype activation. *Journal of Personality and Social Psychology*, *78*(5), 871–888. https://doi.org/10.1037/0022-3514.78.5.871

Kirillova, K., Lehto, X., & Cai, L. (2015). Volunteer tourism and intercultural sensitivity: The role of interaction with host communities. *Journal of Travel & Tourism Marketing*, *32*(4), 382–400. https://doi.org/10.1080/10548408.2014.897300

Lam, T., & Hsu, C. H. C. (2006). Predicting behavioral intention of choosing a travel destination. *Tourism Management*, *27*(4), 589–599. https://doi.org/10.1016/j.tourman.2005.02.003

Lee, C. H., Chen, H. S., Liou, G. B., Tsai, B. K., & Hsieh, C. M. (2018). Evaluating international tourists' perceptions on cultural distance and recreation demand. *Sustainability*, *10*(12), 4360. https://doi.org/10.3390/su10124360

Lepp, A., & Gibson, H. (2003). Tourist roles, perceived risk and international tourism. *Annals of Tourism Research*, *30*(3), 606–624. https://doi.org/10.1016/S0160-7383(03)00024-0

Leung, D., Woo, G. J., & Ly, T. P. (2013). The effects of physical and cultural distance on tourist satisfaction: A case study of local-based airlines, public transportation, and government services in Hong Kong. *Journal of China Tourism Research*, *9*(2), 218–242. https://doi.org/10.1080/19388160.2013.784572

Levine, D. N. (1977). Simmel at a distance: On the history and systematics of the sociology of the stranger. *Sociological Focus*, *10*(1), 15–29. https://doi.org/10.1080/00380237.1977.10570274

Li, Y. Q., & Liu, C. H. (2020). Impact of cultural contact on satisfaction and attachment: Mediating roles of creative experiences and cultural memories. *Journal of Hospitality Marketing & Management*, 29(2), 221–245. https://doi.org/10.1080/19368623.2019.1611516

Lincoln, Y. S., & Guba, E. G. (1985). *Naturalistic inquiry*. Sage Publications.

Lin, P. M., Fan, D. X., Zhang, H. Q., & Lau, C. (2019). Spend less and experience more: Understanding tourists' social contact in the Airbnb context. *International Journal of Hospitality Management*, 83, 65–73. https://doi.org/10.1016/j.ijhm.2019.04.007

Liu, H., Li, X. R., Cárdenas, D. A., & Yang, Y. (2018). Perceived cultural distance and international destination choice: The role of destination familiarity, geographic distance, and cultural motivation. *Journal of Destination Marketing & Management*, 9, 300–309. https://doi.org/10.1016/j.jdmm.2018.03.002

Li, M., Zhang, H., Xiao, H., & Chen, Y. (2015). A grid-group analysis of tourism motivation. *International Journal of Tourism Research*, 17(1), 35–44. https://doi.org/10.1002/jtr.1963

MacCannell, D. (1973). Staged authenticity: Arrangements of social space in tourist settings. *American Journal of Sociology*, 79(3), 589–603. https://doi.org/10.1086/225585

MacCannell, D. (2018). Staged authenticity: Arrangements of social space in tourist settings. In: S. B. Gmelch, & A. Kaul (Ed.), *Tourists and tourism: A reader*. Waveland Press.

Malihah, E., & Setiyorini, H. P. D. (2014, October). Tourism education and edu-tourism development: Sustainable tourism development perspective in education. In 1st International seminar on tourism (ISOT)– Eco-resort and destination sustainability: planning, impact, and development, 1–7. Bandung, Indonesia.

Martin, B. A., Jin, H. S., & Trang, N. V. (2017). The entitled tourist: The influence of psychological entitlement and cultural distance on tourist judgments in a hotel context. *Journal of Travel & Tourism Marketing*, 34(1), 99–112. https://doi.org/10.1080/10548408.2015.1130112

Mayo, E. J., & Jarvis, L. P. (1981). *The psychology of leisure travel: Effective marketing and selling of travel services*. CBI Publishing Company Inc.

Mazanec, J. A., Crotts, J. C., Gursoy, D., & Lu, L. (2015). Homogeneity versus heterogeneity of cultural values: An item-response theoretical approach applying Hofstede's cultural dimensions in a single nation. *Tourism Management*, 48, 299–304. https://doi.org/10.1016/j.tourman.2014.11.011

Mckercher, B., & Chow, B. (2001). Cultural distance and participation in cultural tourism. *Pacific Tourism Review*, 5(1), 23–32.

Mckercher, B., & Cros, H. D. (2003). Testing a cultural tourism typology. *International Journal of Tourism Research*, 5(1), 45–58. https://doi.org/10.1002/jtr.417

Milman, A., Reichel, A., & Pizam, A. (1990). The impact of tourism on ethnic attitudes: The Israeli-Egyptian case. *Journal of Travel Research*, 29(2), 45–49. https://doi.org/10.1177/004728759002900207

Mo, C. M., Howard, D. R., & Havitz, M. E. (1993). Testing an international tourist role typology. *Annals of Tourism Research*, 20(2), 319–335. https://doi.org/10.1016/0160-7383(93)90058-B

Moufakkir, O. (2011). The role of cultural distance in mediating the host gaze. *Tourist Studies*, 11(1), 73–89. https://doi.org/10.1177/1468797611412065

Moutinho, L. (1987). Consumer behaviour in tourism. *European Journal of Marketing*, 21(10), 5–44. https://doi.org/10.1108/EUM0000000004718

Ng, S. I., Lee, J. A., & Soutar, G. N. (2007). Tourists' intention to visit a country: The impact of cultural distance. *Tourism Management*, 28(6), 1497–1506. https://doi.org/10.1016/j.tourman.2006.11.005

Nyaupane, G. P., Timothy, D. J., & Poudel, S. (2015). Understanding tourists in religious destinations: A social distance perspective. *Tourism Management*, 48, 343–353. https://doi.org/10.1016/j.tourman.2014.12.009

Pearce, P. L. (1982). Tourists and their hosts: Some social and psychological effects of inter-cultural contact. In S. Bochner (Ed.), *Cultures in contact: Studies in cross-cultural interaction* (p. 199). Pergamon Press Ltd.

Pettigrew, T. F. (1998). Intergroup contact theory. *Annual Review of Psychology*, 49(1), 65–85. https://doi.org/10.1146/annurev.psych.49.1.65

Pizam, A. (1996). Does tourism promote peace and understanding between unfriendly nations? In A. Pizam and Y. Mansfeld (Eds.), *Tourism. Crime and international security issues* (pp. 203–213). Wiley.

Pizam, A., Jafari, J., & Milman, A. (1991). Influence of tourism on attitudes: US students visiting USSR. *Tourism Management*, 12(1), 47–54. https://doi.org/10.1016/0261-5177(91)90028-R

Pizam, A., Uriely, N., & Reichel, A. (2000). The intensity of tourist-host social relationship and its effects on satisfaction and change of attitudes: The case of working tourists in Israel. *Tourism Management*, 21(4), 395–406. https://doi.org/10.1016/S0261-5177(99)00085-0

Poon, K. Y., & Huang, W. J. (2017). Past experience, traveler personality and tripographics on intention to use Airbnb. *International Journal of Contemporary Hospitality Management*, 29(9), 2425–2443. https://doi.org/10.1108/IJCHM-10-2016-0599

Potter, C. C. (1989). What is culture: And can it be useful for organisational change agents. *Leadership & Organization Development Journal*, 10(3), 17–24. https://doi.org/10.1108/EUM0000000001136

Ragheb, M. G., & Beard, J. G. (1982). Measuring leisure attitudes. *Journal of Leisure Research*, 14(2), 155–162. https://doi.org/10.1080/00222216.1982.11969512

Rasoolimanesh, S. M., Ringle, C. M., Jaafar, M., & Ramayah, T. (2017). Urban vs. rural destinations: Residents' perceptions, community participation and support for tourism development. *Tourism Management*, 60, 147–158. https://doi.org/10.1016/j.tourman.2016.11.019

Reisinger, Y., & Turner, L. (1998a). Cross-cultural differences in tourism: A strategy for tourism marketers. *Journal of Travel & Tourism Marketing*, 7(4), 79–106. https://doi.org/10.1300/J073v07n04_05

Reisinger, Y., & Turner, L. (1998b). Cultural differences between Mandarin-speaking tourists and Australian hosts and their impact on cross-cultural tourist-host interaction. *Journal of Business Research*, 42(2), 175–187. https://doi.org/10.1016/S0148-2963(97)00107-0

Reisinger, Y., & Turner, L. W. (2002a). Cultural differences between Asian tourist markets and Australian hosts, Part 1. *Journal of Travel Research*, 40(3), 295–315. https://doi.org/10.1177/0047287502040003008

Reisinger, Y., & Turner, L. W. (2002b). Cultural differences between Asian tourist markets and Australian hosts, Part 2. *Journal of Travel Research*, 40(4), 385–395. https://doi.org/10.1177/0047287502040004004

Robinson, G., & Nemetz, L. (1988). *Cross-cultural understanding*. Prentice-Hall.

Rosenberg, M. J., Hovland, C. I., McGuire, W. J., Abelson, R. P., & Brehm, J. W. (1960). *Attitude organization and change*. Yale University Press.

Rothman, R. A. (1978). Residents and transients: Community reaction to seasonal visitors. *Journal of Travel Research*, 16(3), 8–13. https://doi.org/10.1177/004728757801600303

Ryan, C., & Glendon, I. (1998). Application of leisure motivation scale to tourism. *Annals of Tourism Research*, 25(1), 169–184. https://doi.org/10.1016/S0160-7383(97)00066-2

Shen, H., Luo, J., & Zhao, A. (2017). The sustainable tourism development in Hong Kong: An analysis of Hong Kong residents' attitude towards Mainland Chinese tourist. *Journal of Quality Assurance in Hospitality & Tourism*, 18(1), 45–68. https://doi.org/10.1080/1528008X.2016.1167650

Siehl, C., & Martin, J. (1985). *Measuring organizational culture*. University of Southern California, Center for Effective Organizations Paper, G 85-11. University of Southern California.

Sin, H. L. (2009). Volunteer tourism: "Involve me and I will learn? *Annals of Tourism Research*, 36(3), 480–501. https://doi.org/10.1016/j.annals.2009.03.001

Smith, V. L. (1989). *Hosts and guests: The anthropology of tourism*. University of Pennsylvania Press.

Sparks, B., & Pan, G. W. (2009). Chinese outbound tourists: Understanding their attitudes, constraints and use of information sources. *Tourism Management*, 30(4), 483–494. https://doi.org/10.1016/j.tourman.2008.10.014

Spradley, J. P., & Phillips, M. (1972). Culture and stress: A quantitative analysis. *American Anthropologist*, 74(3), 518–529. https://doi.org/10.1525/aa.1972.74.3.02a00190

Sung, H. H., Morrison, A. M., Hong, G. S., & O'Leary, J. T. (2001). The effects of household and trip characteristics on trip types: A consumer behavioral approach for segmenting the US domestic leisure travel market. *Journal of Hospitality & Tourism Research*, 25(1), 46–68. https://doi.org/10.1177/109634800102500105

Tasci, A. D. A. (2009). Social distance: The missing link in the loop of movies, destination image, and tourist behavior? *Journal of Travel Research*, 47(4), 494–507. https://doi.org/10.1177/0047287508326534

Tasci, A. D. A., & Severt, D. (2017). A triple lens measurement of host–guest perceptions for sustainable gaze in tourism. *Journal of Sustainable Tourism*, 25(6), 711–731. https://doi.org/10.1080/09669582.2016.1225746

Thrane, C. (2016). The determinants of Norwegians' summer tourism expenditure: Foreign and domestic trips. *Tourism Economics*, 22(1), 31–46. https://doi.org/10.5367/te.2014.0417

Thyne, M., Lawson, R., & Todd, S. (2006). The use of conjoint analysis to assess the impact of the cross-cultural exchange between hosts and guests. *Tourism Management*, 27(2), 201–213. https://doi.org/10.1016/j.tourman.2004.09.003

Thyne, M., Watkins, L., & Yoshida, M. (2018). Resident perceptions of tourism: The role of social distance. *International Journal of Tourism Research*, 20(2), 256–266. https://doi.org/10.1002/jtr.2179

Tran, X., & Ralston, L. (2006). Tourist preferences influence of unconscious needs. *Annals of Tourism Research*, 33(2), 424–441. https://doi.org/10.1016/j.annals.2005.10.014

Triandis, H. C. (1977). Subjective culture and interpersonal relations across cultures. *Annals of the New York Academy of Sciences*, 285(1 Issues in Cro), 418–434. *Issues in Cross-Cultural Research*, https://doi.org/10.1111/j.1749-6632.1977.tb29370.x

Triandis, H. C. (1994). *Culture and social behavior*. McGraw-Hill.

Wang, J., & Ritchie, B. W. (2012). Understanding accommodation managers' crisis planning intention: An application of the theory of planned behaviour. *Tourism Management*, 33(5), 1057–1067. https://doi.org/10.1016/j.tourman.2011.12.006

Ward, C., Bochner, S., & Furnham, A. (2005). *The psychology of culture shock*. Routledge.

Wei, L., Crompton, J. L., & Reid, L. M. (1989). Cultural conflicts: Experiences of US visitors to China. *Tourism Management*, 10(4), 322–332. https://doi.org/10.1016/0261-5177(89)90011-3

Woosnam, K. M., & Aleshinloye, K. D. (2013). Can tourists experience emotional solidarity with residents? Testing Durkheim's model from a new perspective. *Journal of Travel Research*, 52(4), 494–505. https://doi.org/10.1177/0047287512467701

Woosnam, K. M., & Lee, Y. J. (2011). Applying social distance to voluntourism research. *Annals of Tourism Research*, 38(1), 309–313. https://doi.org/10.1016/j.annals.2010.06.003

Yang, Y., Liu, H., & Li, X. (2019). The world is flatter? Examining the relationship between cultural distance and international tourist flows. *Journal of Travel Research*, *58*(2), 224–240. https://doi.org/10.1177/0047287517748780

Ye, B., Zhang, H. Q., Shen, H. J., & Goh, C. (2014). Does social identity affect residents' attitude toward tourism development? An evidence from the relaxation of the Individual Visit Scheme. *International Journal of Contemporary Hospitality Management*, *26*(6), 907–929. https://doi.org/10.1108/IJCHM-01-2013-0041

Yilmaz, S. S., & Tasci, A. D. (2015). Circumstantial impact of contact on social distance. *Journal of Tourism and Cultural Change*, *13*(2), 115–131. https://doi.org/10.1080/14766825.2014.896921

Yu, J. Y., & Lee, T. J. (2014). Impact of tourists' intercultural interactions. *Journal of Travel Research*, *53*(2), 225–238. https://doi.org/10.1177/0047287513496467

Zatori, A., Smith, M. K., & Puczko, L. (2018). Experience-involvement, memorability and authenticity: The service provider's effect on tourist experience. *Tourism Management*, *67*, 111–126. https://doi.org/10.1016/j.tourman.2017.12.013

Zhang, H. Q., & Lam, T. (1999). An analysis of Mainland Chinese visitors' motivations to visit Hong Kong. *Tourism Management*, *20*(5), 587–594. https://doi.org/10.1016/S0261-5177(99)00028-X

Complementing theories to explain emotional solidarity

Emrullah Erul, Kyle Maurice Woosnam, Manuel Alector Ribeiro ⓘ and John Salazar

ABSTRACT
The purpose of this paper is to test the effect of residents' attitudes concerning tourism development on support for future tourism development, and ultimately whether such a relationship explains a sense of solidarity with tourists. To do this, a theoretical model was developed and tested based on the social exchange theory and affect theory of exchange. Residents of Antalya, Turkey ($N = 660$) comprised the sample from which data were collected. Structural equation modelling results demonstrated that residents' attitudes explained 69% of the variance in support for future tourism development, and in turn, this support explained between 25% and 80% of the variance in factors comprising residents' emotional solidarity with tourists. Findings provide support for the complementary use of the two theories. To round out the paper, implications, limitations and future research are offered.

Introduction

The tourism industry offers economic benefits, growth, and opportunities not only for businesses seeking profits but also for individuals desiring employment and improved standards of living. Unfortunately, negative social and environmental effects can potentially result from industry initiatives. While benefits (i.e. diversifying the economy and providing jobs), have been noted within the literature, proactive planning must be in place that encompasses the assessment of residents' perceptions of existing and potential tourism development. Such efforts will contribute to mitigating negative tourism impacts (e.g. erosion of local natural and cultural amenities, rising costs and land values, as well as crowding) (Gursoy et al., 2017a; Hall & Lew, 2009; Zuo et al., 2017).

Previous studies claim that disregarding residents' wishes and needs may lead to hostility between residents and tourists (Kwon & Vogt, 2010; Woosnam & Erul, 2017). Similarly, "If residents fear tourism, their resistance and hostility can destroy the local industry's potential" (Murphy, 1985, p. 153). These perspectives have indicated that understanding residents' opinions and perceptions regarding tourism development are crucial in developing tourism resources and garnering support for the industry (Gursoy et al., 2017a; Nunkoo & Gursoy, 2017; Ribeiro et al., 2017; Stylidis et al., 2014; Woosnam & Erul, 2017; Zuo et al., 2017).

Turkey, with its rapid growth in tourist arrivals, is home to numerous destinations that could gain from considering residents' perspectives of the existing tourism and future development potentials. According to the Turkey Ministry of Culture and Tourism (TMCT) annual reports (2019), international tourist arrivals in the country have increased from 16.3 million in 2002 to 39.5 million in 2018. Likewise, tourism earnings have ballooned from TRY₺82.8 billion to TRY₺ 114.2 billion over the period 2012–2018 (Statista, 2019). In addition to this, Turkey is ranked eighth among the top ten most-visited countries by reaching approximately 38 million international visitors in 2017 (UNWTO, 2018). Many of these visitors have selected Antalya in the southwestern part of Turkey on the Mediterranean Sea, which is evidenced by the fact that the city hosted 9 million international tourists in 2018 (TMCT, 2019). Considering such growth in visitor numbers, tourism planners in Antalya need to be cognizant of the consequences of tourism and proactively plan for tourism in such ways that the industry further embraces sustainable development.

In efforts to proactively plan for sustainable tourism, many researchers have considered the social exchange theory (hereafter abbreviated as SET) to assess residents' perspectives of the industry and its accompanying development (see Kang & Lee, 2018; Nunkoo & Gursoy, 2012; Rasoolimanesh et al., 2015; Zuo et al., 2017). In fact, previous scholars have been able to explain the relationship between tourism impacts and future support for tourism development considering the SET framework (Gursoy et al., 2017a; Gursoy et al., 2017a; Nunkoo & Gursoy, 2017; Ribeiro et al., 2017; Stylidis et al., 2014). As some would attest, SET is one of the most widely-used theories within the travel and tourism literature (Kang & Lee, 2018; Nunkoo, 2016; Ribeiro et al., 2017; Stylidis et al., 2014).

However, the theory is not without its limitations. Some scholars (Ward & Berno, 2011; Woosnam & Norman, 2010; Woosnam et al., 2009) have stated that the theoretical perspective has the potential to reduce relationships between residents and tourists to economic exchanges, perpetuating the idea that interactions between the parties are largely superficial (Wall & Mathieson, 2006). This approach shortchanges the social relationship between locals and destination visitors. As such, Woosnam (2011) and Ward and Berno (2011) purport that utilizing complimentary theoretical frameworks in addition to the social exchange theory may help to more accurately explain residents' support for tourism development within their communities by considering relationships with tourists that exist beyond those rooted in economic terms. The affect theory of exchange originally developed from the early workings of Lawler (2001) and complements the SET by including emotions as a function of the exchange. In other words, Lawler (2001) expanded the SET to deal with emotions and solidarity which demonstrates how exchange creates emotions and strengthen social ties (i.e. emotional solidarity). In light of these arguments, this paper has two main purposes: 1) to initially consider the role residents' perceptions of existing tourism impacts play in explaining future support for tourism development based on the social exchange theory and 2) to examine if residents' support for future tourism development serves to explain a greater degree of variance in the relationship they possess with tourists (through the emotional solidarity scale) based on the affect theory of exchange.

Literature review

Residents' attitudes about tourism development

Research focusing on residents' attitudes about existing tourism development, perceptions of tourism impacts, and support for tourism development has been ongoing for more than four decades (García et al., 2015; Gursoy et al., 2017a; 2017b; Kang & Lee, 2018; Nunkoo & Gursoy, 2017; Rasoolimanesh et al., 2017; Ribeiro et al., 2017; Stylidis et al., 2014; Woosnam & Erul, 2017;

Zuo et al., 2017). While findings surrounding these aspects of research are varied and, in some regards, mixed, one consistent finding is prevalent: community support and the inclusion of local residents throughout the planning process serve as significant determinants of successful sustainable tourism (Nunkoo & Gursoy, 2017; Woosnam et al., 2018a; Zuo et al., 2017). In a similar vein, residents' attitudes and their perceptions of tourism impacts are key factors for successful tourism because such individuals are directly affected or influenced by tourism and its consequences (Hall & Lew, 2009; Murphy, 1985; Rasoolimanesh et al., 2017). Implicit in this work is that residents and their perspectives play a crucial role in assessing existing tourism impacts as well as their support for future tourism development (Gursoy et al., 2017a; Rasoolimanesh et al., 2015).

Overall, previous scholars found that if residents perceive impacts of tourism in a positive perspective, they are more willing to support additional and/or further tourism development (García et al., 2015; Gursoy et al., 2017a; Ribeiro et al., 2017) but residents who perceive more costs than benefits will likely have greater opposition towards tourism development (Gursoy et al., 2017b; Kang & Lee, 2018; Nunkoo & Gursoy, 2012). To sum up, residents are vital stakeholders in forging successful sustainable tourism within destinations. Considering their opinions and needs (i.e. including them in tourism planning and listening to concerns) not only garners residents' support for tourism developments but also mitigates the potential for perceived negative impacts over time.

Social exchange theory

According to the social exchange theory (SET), Homans (1961) emphasized that relationships between individuals are forged by a subjective benefit-cost analysis, taking into consideration alternative scenarios. SET can be defined as, "A general sociological theory concerned with understanding the exchange of resources between individuals and groups in an interaction situation" (Ap, 1992, p. 668). The more positive the outcome of exchanges between individuals, the more likely they will remain in the relationship; on the other hand, the less positive the outcome of exchanges between individuals, the more likely they will exit the relationship or desire a change.

SET has been championed within the travel and tourism literature to explain why residents either favor or disapprove of tourism within their community based on perceived benefits or costs, perceptions of the positive or negative impacts, and trust (Gursoy et al., 2017a; 2017b; Kang & Lee, 2018; Nunkoo & Gursoy, 2012; 2017; Nunkoo & Ramkissoon, 2012; Ribeiro et al., 2017; Wang & Pfister, 2008; Zuo et al., 2017). This has been evidenced through the seminal work by Lankford and Howard (1994), which highlights the distinct factors of the Tourism Impact Scale (TIAS), attitudinal support for tourism development and contributions to community, employed by Wang and Pfister (2008) and Woosnam (2012). In a similar vein, Gursoy et al. (2017b) found that while residents' who perceived benefits from tourism had more positive attitudes about tourism and optimistic views concerning future tourism development, residents' who perceived more costs tended to have more negative attitudes about tourism and more pessimistic opinions about future tourism development in their community. A host of work has provided evidence revealing that the potential benefits from an exchange can contribute to positive attitudes concerning tourism and even allow individuals to be more tolerant of negative tourism impacts (Kwon & Vogt, 2010; Nunkoo & Gursoy, 2012; Nunkoo & Ramkissoon, 2012).

The social exchange theory was utilized in this study to explain why and under what situations local residents would have positive attitudes toward tourism and would support future tourism development. Furthermore, findings will be explained considering and developing this framework. This theory claims that residents who perceive positive impacts of tourism, especially from an economic perspective, would support tourism development and would have positive attitudes toward existing and future tourism development (García et al., 2015; Gursoy et al., 2017a; Nunkoo & Ramkissoon, 2012). Thus, we hypothesize that:

Hypothesis$_{1a}$ (H$_{1a}$): Residents' *attitudinal support for tourism development* will significantly predict their attitudes about future tourism development in Antalya.

Hypothesis$_{1b}$ (H$_{1b}$): Residents' *attitudinal contributions to community* will significantly predict their attitudes about future tourism development in Antalya.

Affect theory of exchange and emotional solidarity research in tourism

Ward and Berno (2011) considered the contact hypothesis and integrated threat theory in tandem with SET to predict residents' attitudes toward tourism. Similarly, Nunkoo and Gursoy (2017) created a model to determine residents' political trust and their support for tourism under the application of SET, institutional theory of political trust, and cultural theory of political trust. Finally, Ribeiro et al. (2017) used the theory of reasoned action along with SET to determine residents' perception about tourism and their pro-tourism behavior. The current paper takes a similar approach in utilizing the affect theory of exchange (including emotions as a function of the exchange) as a complementary framework to SET in an effort to explain locals' support for future tourism development within Antalya, and ultimately, how that support contributes to a sense of solidarity residents perceive with tourists.

The most common definition of the affect theory of exchange is "when exchanges occur successfully, actors experience an emotional uplift (a "high"), and when exchanges do not occur successfully, they experience emotional downs" (Lawler, 2001, p. 322). According to the affect theory of exchanges, Lawler proposed that exchange is a joint activity and as the degree of exchange activity increases, some degree of emotions or feeling would appear. In other words, the relation between the actors and perceptions and/or feelings of sharing activity can be influenced depending on the exchange. In this study, the relationship or solidarity between residents and tourists are dependent upon residents' attitudes toward tourism development. The current study claims that as the degree of support for tourism development increases, residents' solidarity with tourists will also increase.

Emotional solidarity research to date in tourism has focused either exclusively on residents' perspectives of the construct with tourists (e.g. Suess et al., 2020; Woosnam, 2011; Woosnam et al., 2018b; Woosnam et al., 2017; Woosnam & Norman, 2010; Woosnam et al., 2009) or on tourists' perspectives of the construct with residents (e.g. Juric et al., 2020; Ribeiro et al., 2018; Simpson & Simpson, 2017; Woosnam et al., 2018c; Woosnam et al., 2015). Following this, the Emotional Solidarity Scale has been used as the outcome of other constructs such as shared beliefs, shared behavior, and interaction (Woosnam, 2011; Woosnam et al., 2009), as well as the predictor of additional measures including support for tourism development (Hasani et al., 2016; Woosnam, 2012), festival impact and support for festival development (Li & Wan, 2017), tourists' satisfaction and destination loyalty (Ribeiro et al., 2018), social distance (Joo et al., 2018), and perceived safety (Simpson & Simpson, 2017 Woosnam et al., 2015). To date, research concerning emotional solidarity (as measured by the ESS), as a predictor of support for tourism development is growing. For example, Woosnam (2012) first used the ESS and its factors (i.e. welcoming nature, sympathetic understanding, and emotional closeness) to predict residents' perceived impacts of tourism (as measured through the Tourism Impact Attitude Scale or TIAS). This was followed by the work of Hasani et al. (2016) that demonstrated a similar relationship (i.e. ESS predicting resident attitudes and support for tourism) holds in the context of rural tourism in Malaysia. In another Asian context, Li and Wan (2017) provided evidence that the ESS significantly explained Macao residents' perceptions of positive festival impacts as well as of support for such events. Most recently, Lai and Hitchcock (2017) found that the three ESS factors

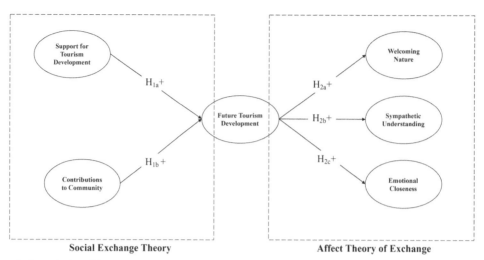

Figure 1. Conceptual model.

explained distinct aspects of perceived tourism impacts in Macau, with welcoming nature and sympathetic understanding serving as better predictors than emotional closeness.

While these studies speak to the relationship between solidarity and residents' support for tourism development, none of the ESS studies focused on how support of tourism development can serve as a predictor of ESS factors (i.e. welcoming nature, sympathetic understanding, and emotional closeness) instead of being predicted. In other words, residents' support for future tourism development has not been considered a precursor to explaining residents' emotional solidarity with tourists. As mentioned at the opening of this paper, Ward and Berno (2011) have suggested that multiple theoretical frameworks (i.e. social exchange theory along with other frameworks) should be considered. Therefore, this study will use the affect theory of exchange along with SET to test the effect of resident attitudes about tourism development (TIAS) on support for future tourism development (FTD), and ultimately whether this support for future tourism development can explain solidarity with tourists (see Figure 1). Therefore, it is hypothesized that:

Hypothesis$_{2a}$ (H$_{2a}$): Residents' attitudes about future tourism development will significantly predict their degree of *welcoming nature* with such tourists in Antalya.

Hypothesis$_{2b}$ (H$_{2b}$): Residents' attitudes about future tourism development will significantly predict their degree of *sympathetic understanding* with such tourists in Antalya.

Hypothesis$_{2c}$ (H$_{2c}$): Residents' attitudes about future tourism development will significantly predict their degree of *emotional closeness* with such tourists in Antalya.

Study methods

Study site

Turkey tourism generated TRY₺359.2 (US$98.4 billion) (approximately 11.6% of Turkey's GDP) and employed approximately 2 million jobs (7.4% of total employment) in 2017 alone (World Travel and Tourism Council, 2018). By 2028, tourism will support 2.7 million jobs in Turkey (World Travel and Tourism Council, 2018). According to the Turkey Ministry of Culture and Tourism 2019 reports, the rate of change for foreign tourist arrivals in Turkey has increased by 21.8% from 2017 to 2018. Over the last five years, Turkey has attracted on average, 33 million international visitors each year (TMCT, 2019). With such figures, it is easy to see the importance of tourism to the Turkish economy.

Arguably, nowhere is tourism more important in Turkey than in Antalya. Located in southwestern Turkey along the Mediterranean coast, Antalya is considered the country's leading tourism destination. The weather, coastal environment, historical and cultural assets, along with high-quality tourism facilities contribute to its growing appeal. According to the Turkish Statistical Institute reports, slightly more than 2 million residents live in Antalya (TSI, 2017). With Belek, Kemer, Side-Manavgat, Alanya, and Kas¸ tourism centers, Antalya and its residents host more than 10 million international tourists each year (TSI, 2017). According to the TMCT reports in 2019, Antalya ranked second in 2018 with 12.4 million foreign visitors after Istanbul.

Sampling and data collection

The current study was undertaken in Antalya among local residents (i.e. heads of household or business owners), who were at least 18 years of age. Data were collected by using a cluster sampling strategy (i.e. the author visited every fourth home or business on the street in four selected districts: Antalya city center, Serik, Kemer, and Manavgat). Individuals were contacted at their homes or places of business and asked if they were willing to participate in the survey. If they agreed, they were provided a self-administered questionnaire to be completed and collected by one of the authors the same day.

Of the 950 residents contacted by a researcher, 223 declined (an acceptance rate of 76.5%). The research team distributed 727 surveys, with 660 residents completing the on-site self-administered questionnaire (a completion rate of 90%); yielding an effective response rate of 69%. The response rates for the four selected districts ranged from between 68% to 71% (i.e. Antalya city center ($n = 160$) and Serik ($n = 165$) are 68% and Kemer ($n = 165$) and Manavgat ($n = 170$) are 71%).

Survey instrument

This study focused on three primary measures (asked on a 5-point Likert scale, where 1 = strongly disagree; 5 = strongly agree) for Antalya residents. The first of the scales was the Tourism Impact Attitude Scale (hereafter abbreviated as TIAS) used to measure perceptions of existing impacts. TIAS has most recently been utilized by Woosnam (2012), though formulated by Lankford and Howard (1994). Previous researchers (see Wang & Pfister, 2008; Woosnam, 2012) found that TIAS has two distinctive factors: *support for tourism development* and *contributions to the community*. Five items for each of the factors were used for data collection. The second measure was a unidimensional scale with seven items (Doh, 2006) to measure residents' perceptions of future tourism development (hereafter abbreviated FTD). Based on the work of Woosnam and Norman (2010), the 10-item Emotional Solidarity Scale or ESS was used in the final section of the questionnaire. Three distinct factors have comprised the ESS in previous work: *welcoming nature*, *emotional closeness*, and *sympathetic understanding*. The instrument for data collection was originally designed in English and translated into Turkish following a back-translation procedure (Brislin, 1970). Furthermore, the lead researcher was fluent in both Turkish and English to assist in this translation process.

Demographic profile

Table 1 indicates that a majority of the sample was comprised of men (62%) as well as married individuals (56%). Slightly more than half of the sample participants held at least an undergraduate degree (52%) and was employed in a tourism-related position (51%). Overall, the sample was

Table 1. Descriptive summary of Antalya respondents.

Variable	N	%
Gender ($n = 660$)		
Male	408	61.8
Female	252	38.2
Age ($n = 660$, Median = 30-39 years of age)		
18–29	271	41.1
30–39	176	26.7
40–49	164	24.8
50–59	46	7.0
60 and over	3	0.5
Marital status ($n = 660$)		
Married	367	55.6
Single	277	42.0
Divorced or separated	10	1.5
Widowed	6	0.9
Level of education ($n = 660$, Median = undergraduate degree)		
Less than high school	46	7.0
High school	177	26.8
Technical or vocational school	71	10.8
Undergraduate degree 343	52.0	
Graduate degree	23	3.5
Employment status ($n = 660$)		
Tourism-related employment	337	51.1
Not tourism-related employment	191	28.9
Student	104	15.8
Homemaker	19	2.9
Retired or unemployed	9	1.4
Annual household income ($n = 660$, Median = Less than 36,000 Turkish Lira[a])		
Less than 36,000 Turkish Lira	435	65.9
36,000–72,000 Turkish Lira	184	27.9
More than 72,000 Turkish Lira	41	6.2

[a]At the time data were collected for this study, two Turkish Lira was approximately the equivalent of US$1.

fairly young with 68% of individuals falling between the ages of 18 and 39. A large portion (65.9%) of residents' annual income level was less than TRY₺36,000.

Results

Measurement and structural models

Since our data were collected via a single data source, common method bias (CMB) may represents a threat to our data (Jordan & Troth, 2020; Spector, 2006). To assess the CMB, we conducted a Harman's one-factor test where all 20 items used for testing the proposed model were loaded onto an unrotated single exploratory factor analysis (EFA) (Podsakoff et al., 2003). The results indicated that no single factor accounted for more than 18.13% of the variance among our variables. Consequently, CMB is absent and highly unlikely to represent any threat in this study. Furthermore, because measured variables in structural equation modelling (SEM) may be affected by non-normal distribution (West et al., 1995), we evaluated the normality of our data by checking the values of both skewness and kurtosis. The results of these two measures of distributions, provided by AMOS output, were below 3.0 and 7.0 respectively (Ribeiro et al., 2018; West et al., 1995), providing evidence of the normality underlying the Maximum Likelihood estimation of SEM and the appropriateness of data collected in Antalya, Turkey.

Prior to examining the role perceived tourism impacts may play in explaining support for future tourism development, and ultimately explain emotional solidarity (from the structural model), a measurement model (using confirmatory factor analysis) was formulated using IBM AMOS version 24. The use of co-variance structural equation modeling (CB-SEM) to assess the CFA and structural relationships is supported by the normally of the data and the sample size

Table 2. Measurement model results.

Constructs and Indicators	Factor Loadings	t-value	Composite Reliability	AVE
Sympathetic understanding (SU)			0.80	0.75
I identify with Antalya visitors.	0.82	N/A[a]		
I have a lot in common with Antalya visitors.	0.68	16.86***		
I feel affection toward Antalya visitors	0.76	18.94***		
Welcoming nature (WN)			0.70	0.73
I feel the community benefits from having visitors in Antalya.	0.71	N/A[a]		
I am proud to have visitors come to Antalya.	0.75	17.29***		
Emotional closeness (EC)			0.84	0.85
I have made friends with some Antalya visitors.	0.82	N/A[a]		
I feel close to some visitors I have met in Antalya.	0.88	20.62***		
Support for tourism development (STD)			0.91	0.84
I believe that tourism should be actively encouraged in Antalya.	0.82	N/A[a]		
I support tourism and want to see it remain important in Antalya.	0.90	29.41***		
I support new tourism facilities that will attract new visitors to Antalya.	0.86	21.92***		
Antalya should support the promotion of tourism.	0.81	20.44***		
Contributions to community (CTC)			0.76	0.71
The tourism sector provides many desirable employment opportunities for Antalya residents.	0.73	N/A[a]		
The quality of life in Antalya has improved because of tourism development in the area.	0.78	16.32***		
I have more recreational opportunities (place to go and things to do) because of tourism in Antalya.	0.63	14.08***		
Future tourism development (FTD)			0.86	0.72
Overall, the benefits of tourism development in Antalya will outweigh its costs.	0.64	N/A[a]		
In general, new tourism development should be actively encouraged in Antalya.	0.78	16.49***		
Tourism looks like the best way to help my community's economy in the future.	0.63	13.82***		
Tourism should play a vital role in the future of Antalya	0.73	15.63***		
I support new tourism development in Antalya.	0.79	16.67***		
Tourism development in my community will benefit me or some member of my family.	0.72	15.48***		

[a]In AMOS, one loading has to be fixed to 1; hence, t-value cannot be calculated for this item.
[b]Scale: All items were asked on a 5-pt scale where 1 = strongly disagree and 5 = strongly agree.
Note: ***$p < 0.001$ level (one-tailed); CR = composite reliability; AVE = average variance extracted.

was large enough to run SEM (Hair et al., 2017). Yet, this study uses CB-SEM to develop a new theoretical framework by analyzing two well-established theories (SET and ATE) in tandem to explain emotional solidarity (Hair et al., 2017). By using CB-SEM, this measurement model helps to examine the factor structure of construct items and must be established before considering the structural paths between latent measures (Kline, 2015). Knowing that prior findings have demonstrated a two-factor structure for the TIAS (i.e. *support for tourism development* or STD) and *contributions to community* or CTC), a single factor for FTD, and a three-factor structure for the ESS (i.e. *welcoming nature, emotional closeness*, and *sympathetic understanding*), each of the six factors were added (using IBM AMOS 24) to subsequent models (along with the inclusion of cross-loaders and error covariances). Table 2 indicates that all factor structures were consistent with previous findings in the tourism literature.

It should be noted that those items not retained for the final CFA (and the structural model) were eliminated due to cross-loadings (Tabachnick & Fidell, 2013), high error covariances

Table 3. Fit indices of measurement and structural models.

Fit indices[a]	CMIN(χ^2)	df	p-value	χ^2/df	IFI	TLI	CFI	RMSEA
Measurement model	345.969	152	0.000	2.276	0.973	0.966	0.973	0.04
Structural model	369.709	158	0.000	2.340	0.971	0.965	0.971	0.04

aCMIN: Chi-square; df: Degrees of freedom; p-value: Probability level; IFI: Incremental Fit Index; TLI: Tucker-Lewis index; CFI: Comparative fit index; RMSEA: Root mean square error of approximation.

(Byrne, 2016), or low AVE scores (Byrne, 2016; Hair et al., 2018). Overall, seven items (i.e. one *sympathetic understanding* item, two *welcoming nature* items, one *support for tourism development* item, two *contributions to community* items, and one FTD item) were removed from the final CFA due to one of these situations. From the CFA results, both the TIAS and ESS demonstrated high composite reliabilities and average variance extracted AVE for corresponding factors. While the composite reliabilities should be at least 0.70, AVEs should be 0.50 or higher (Hu & Bentler, 1998; Woosnam, 2012). Reliabilities for the six factors ranged from 0.70 to 0.91 (i.e. TIAS *support for tourism development* was 0.91 and TIAS *contributions to community* was 0.76; ESS *welcoming nature* was 0.70, ESS *emotional closeness* was 0.84, ESS *sympathetic understanding* was 0.80, and FTD was 0.86). AVE scores ranged from 0.71 to 0.85 (see Table 2).

Based on the measurement model results, incremental model fit indices (i.e. Incremental Fit Index (IFI), Tucker-Lewis index (TLI) and Comparative fit index (CFI)) all were in excess of 0.95, and the absolute model fit indices (e.g. Root mean square error of approximation hereafter abbreviated as RMSEA) was lower than 0.05, indicating very good model fit (Hair et al., 2018; Hu & Bentler, 1998; Woosnam, 2012). More specifically, the CFA model fit was: $\chi^2(152) = 345.97$, $p < 0.001$, RMSEA = 0.039, IFI = 0.973, TLI = 0.966, and CFI = 0.973 (see Table 3). All of the 20 items within the measurement model had standardized factor loading values in excess of 0.50, which according to Hair et al. (2018) suggestion, is acceptable (see Table 3).

In addition to examining the internal consistency of each factor (i.e. through CR estimates), measures of construct validity were also assessed. Discriminant validity is the extent to which the constructs differ from one another. We examined discriminant validity by using two approaches. First, we used the recommendation that the AVE for each factor should be greater than the squared factor correlations using the method recommended by Fornell and Larcker (1981). As presented in Table 4 (below diagonal), such was the case in all but two instances (AVE of *welcoming nature* and FTD was less than squared factor correlations between the two factors). Second, we followed the suggestion put forth by Henseler et al. (2015) to use the heterotrait–monotrait ratio (HTMT) as a superior way of assessing discriminant validity. Following the Henseler et al. (2015) recommendation to use a more liberal threshold value of 0.9, Table 4 (above diagonal) shows that all HTMT ratio in this study were lower than the cut-off of HTMT$_{90}$ providing support for discriminant validity of the constructs. However, welcoming nature and future tourism development failed to achieve the discriminate validity by using the Fornell-Lacker approach, the measurement was achieved when applying a HTMT$_{90}$ method. Although, both welcoming nature and future tourism development are conceptually different, they might be difficult to be distinguished empirically in all tourism research contexts (Henseler et al., 2015). Convergent validity was also confirmed based on significant t-values associated with each factor loading and AVEs in excess of 0.50 (Hair et al., 2018).

Following the establishment of the measurement model, a structural path model was assessed to address each formulated hypothesis within Figure 1. Similar to the measurement model, results indicated that the structural model fit the data very well: $\chi^2(158) = 369.71$, $p < 0.001$, RMSEA = 0.04, IFI = 0.971, TLI = 0.965, and CFI = 0.971. In assessing the particular paths between TIAS factors and FTD, support for tourism ($\beta = 0.50$, $p < 0.001$) and contributions to community ($\beta = 0.44$, $p < 0.001$) were both significant within the model (See Table 5). The squared multiple correlation (R^2_{SMC}) was 0.69, indicating that the two TIAS factors uniquely explained 69% of the variance in residents' support for future tourism development. Similarly,

Table 4. Discriminant validity: Fornell-Larcker Criterion and Heterotrait–Monotrait (HTMT) ratio.

Measures	Mean	SD	EC	STD	CTC	WN	SU	FTD
Emotional closeness (EC)	3.43	1.12	**0.85**	0.43	0.19	0.46	0.72	0.53
Support for tourism development (STD)	4.47	0.77	0.42	**0.84**	0.57	0.68	0.33	0.72
Contributions to community (CTC)	3.88	0.87	0.44	0.56	**0.71**	0.76	0.45	0.70
Welcoming nature (WN)	4.01	0.92	0.63	0.69	0.74	**0.73**	0.68	0.87
Sympathetic understanding (SU)	3.02	0.99	0.71	0.32	0.41	0.66	**0.75**	0.51
Future tourism development (FTD)	3.97	0.77	0.54	0.74	0.69	0.87	0.50	**0.72**

Note: The bold diagonal elements represent average variance extracted.
Above diagonal elements are the Heterotrait–Monotrait (HTMT) ratio; off-diagonal are the correlations between factors based on the Fornell-Larker Criterion.
All items were asked on a 5-point scale where 1 = strongly disagree and 5 = strongly agree.

Table 5. Hypothesized relationships between constructs and observed relationships from the structural model.

Hypothesized relationship	B	Beta (β)	t-value	Supported?
H_{1a}: Support for tourism development → Future tourism development (FTD)	0.45	0.50	10.24***	Yes
H_{1b}: Contributions to community → Future tourism development (FTD)	0.41	0.44	8.75 ***	Yes
H_{2a}: Future tourism development → Welcoming nature (WN)	1.00	0.90	14.07***	Yes
H_{2b}: Future tourism development → Sympathetic understanding (SU)	0.74	0.50	10.11***	Yes
H_{2c}: Future tourism development → Emotional closeness (EC)	0.83	0.55	10.84***	Yes

Note: ***$p < 0.001$.
R^2_{SMC}: FTD = 0.69; WN = 0.80; SU = 0.25; EC = 0.30.

the paths between FTD and ESS factors, welcoming nature (β = 0.90, $p < 0.001$), emotional closeness (β = 0.83, $p < 0.001$), and sympathetic understanding (β = 0.74, $p < 0.001$) were all significantly explained through residents' degree of support for future tourism development (see Table 5). The squared multiple correlations (R^2_{SMC}) were: 0.80 (for welcoming nature); 0.30 (for emotional closeness); and 0.25 (for sympathetic understanding). In other words, support for future tourism development explained between 25% and 80% of the variance in the three ESS factors. As shown in Table 5, all five hypotheses were supported.

Conclusion

Discussion

The primary purpose of this study was to determine: 1) if residents' existing attitudes concerning tourism plays a significant role in explaining their support for future tourism development and 2) if that support for future development in turn could contribute to the explanation of residents' perceived solidarity with tourists. In so doing, both the social exchange theory and affect theory of exchange were considered in tandem (following Ward and Berno (2011) suggestion).

Each of the TIAS factors significantly predicted the FTD factor (see Table 5). The first TIAS factor, *support for tourism development* as well as the second TIAS factor, *contributions to community* were significant. In other words, when people are aware of the importance of existing tourism and tourism development, they are likely to perceive positive impacts of existing tourism (i.e. *support for tourism development* and *contributions to community* factors), which is likely to positively influence their attitudes about supporting future tourism development. The path model results confirmed previous studies' findings examining the relationship between impacts of existing tourism and support for future tourism development (Doh, 2006; García et al., 2015; Gursoy et al., 2017a; Nunkoo & Ramkissoon, 2012; Ribeiro et al., 2017). The study concluded that the positive perceptions of existing tourism and tourism development have a strong impact (as demonstrated by the unique effect size of each contributing TIAS factor) on support for subsequent tourism development. This result is consistent with the social exchange theory in that residents who saw tourism as a positive activity are more likely to support additional or future development (García et al., 2015; Nunkoo & Ramkissoon, 2012).

Support for future tourism development was considered a predictor of residents' perceived solidarity with tourists. All three ESS factors (i.e. *welcoming nature, sympathetic understanding,* and *emotional closeness*) were significantly predicted by the FTD factor (see Table 5). The relationship between FTD and *welcoming nature* was the most significant path within the model, explaining 80% of the variance in the factor. In other words, the level of support for future tourism explains a high degree of variance in residents welcoming tourists into their community. Taken collectively with the other two squared multiple correlation results for sympathetic understanding and emotional closeness, and it can be said that support for future tourism development is a precursor for residents' emotional solidarity with tourists. Previous studies (Nunkoo & Gursoy, 2017; Ribeiro et al., 2017; Ward & Berno, 2011; Woosnam, 2011) claim that SET is not adequate by itself to explain residents' attitudes about tourism and their intimate relationship with tourists. Findings of the current study validate this claim and provide support for the continued utilization of additional theories in tandem with the social exchange theory.

To date, while a few works (Li & Wan, 2017; Woosnam, 2011; Woosnam et al., 2009) have considered the ESS as the outcome of some other measures (e.g. community attachment, shared beliefs, shared behavior, and interaction), most of the ESS studies (see Hasani et al., 2016; Li & Wan, 2017; Ribeiro et al., 2018; Simpson & Simpson, 2017; Woosnam, 2012; Woosnam et al., 2015) have utilized the ESS as a predictor of some other measure (e.g. TIAS factors, support for tourism, and perceived safety). Overall, previous scholars highlight the growing functionality of the ESS in explaining outcome variables especially support for tourism developments. Such results reveal just how important the perceived relationship is between residents of and tourists to a particular destination, demonstrating how residents' perceptions of the relationship with tourists aid in explaining the former's degree of support for future tourism. However, the current study claims that ESS is a significant outcome of residents' support under the application of affect theory of exchange. Ultimately, tourism means more than the economic impact on a community, which potentially highlights residents' desire to interact and engage in cultural exchanges with future tourists.

Implications

In order to understand resident attitudes regarding their support for future tourism development and their emotional solidarity with tourists, the current study makes a number of theoretical and practical contributions. Findings provide support for extending and complementing the SET framework with the inclusion of the affect theory of exchange—an ideal Ward and Berno (2011) encouraged. As such, results provide evidence that support for future tourism development can be influenced by residents' perceived positive impacts of tourism, and their support for future tourism explain residents' emotional solidarity with residents.

To date, no work has demonstrated such a link (i.e. residents' support for tourism a predictor of their solidarity) either within the residents' attitudes of tourism literature or that surrounding emotional solidarity. Ultimately, this work shows that support for future tourism is based on perceived positive impacts of tourism (e.g. the financial transactions or economic exchanges that occur between residents and tourists) that explained by the social exchange theory. In addition to this, residents' support for tourism development determine the interpersonal relationships that exist between representatives of each group (explained by the affect theory of exchange).

This work contributes to the growing work focusing on support for tourism and its accompanying development (see Gursoy et al., 2017; Nunkoo & Gursoy, 2012; 2017; Woosnam, 2012). As Lawler (2001) has purported, that when the exchange between individuals (e.g. residents and tourists) is positive (i.e. when each receive benefits from the exchange) actors will experience high emotions, feelings or solidarities. Our study reflects this and provides greater credence and empirical support for connecting perceptions of existing impacts, support for future tourism development, and ultimately, perceived emotional solidarity with tourists. Additional work should consider potential moderators of the relationship between impacts and future support for tourism, such as level of interaction with tourists (Woosnam & Norman, 2010), perceived personal benefits from tourism impacts (Wang & Pfister, 2008), degree of dependence on tourism or perceptions of social equity or justice (Jamal & Camargo, 2014). In so doing, more variance can potentially be explained in the outcome variable.

In addition, this study has several practical implications for policymakers, planners, government officials, and managers in Antalya as managers plan for sustainable tourism in the city. First, policymakers, government officials, managers, and planners should consider the role that residents' support for future tourism developments plays in positive perceptions of the relationships with tourists. Promotional campaigns can convey personal testimonies of residents as to how they perceive tourists and what that means for future interactions. Moreover, residents must be involved in each stage of the tourism development process: planning, implementing, and monitoring. Residents should be afforded forums to voice concerns regarding tourism and actively participate in decisions made concerning tourism planning and management.

Beyond these planning strategies, policymakers and government officials should consider opportunities that will contribute to increased levels of support for tourism. As our results indicate, existing perceptions of the benefits of tourism go far to explain the support of future tourism which in turn would help foster greater degrees of positive relationships with tourists. Tourism education campaigns targeting local residents regarding the benefits of tourism would be one means by which to facilitate residents' positive perceptions of the tourism impacts.

In addition to these, our results indicated that as residents become more supportive, the degree of their solidarity towards tourist increases. Briefly, residents' support for tourism development has the potential to contribute to positive interactions with tourists. Ways in which this can be accomplished is through increasing the number of festivals and events that allow for greater perceived impacts of tourism that results in supporting further tourism development, which can serve to ultimately increase positive exchanges between residents and tourists. This would be in line with more sustainable tourism development (Li & Wan, 2017), further aiding in the facilitation of positive social, cultural, and economic exchanges among locals and visitors.

Limitations and future research recommendations

This study is not without its limitations. The first of which is the sample representativeness; only four districts were included in the sample of Antalya residents. As revealed in Table 1, two demographic characteristics call into question this representativeness—respondents' median age is fairly low and a high percentage of individuals were employed within the tourism industry. While the four districts were randomly selected, due to temporal constraints, collecting data in additional areas was not undertaken. It is recommended that work linking TIAS, FTD and ESS should be done in additional locations so as to further validate our findings.

Despite demonstrating high reliabilities, employment of model constructs revealed some discriminant validity concerns. As shown in Table 4, the squared factor correlations between *welcoming nature* and FTD was greater than the average variance extracted for either construct when the Fornell-Larcker method was used. Though we removed two initial items from *welcoming nature* (due to cross-loading issues), an alternative approach would have been to remove the construct from the structural model entirely. The reason this was not done was to maintain the factor integrity of the ESS by including all three of its factors within the structural model. Should issues like this arise in subsequent work, we recommend utilizing the newly modified ESS that was developed by Joo and Woosnam (2019) which includes two distinct factors—communality and fairness.

Additionally, only two estimates of construct validity (i.e. convergent and discriminant) were assessed. Focusing on additional types of validity such as criterion or predictive should be a focus for future studies. As Churchill (1979) conceded, such advanced validities are difficult to demonstrate but given the extensive body of research focusing on tourism impacts and emotional solidarity, one can make a case for potential outcome variables from the two antecedents used in this study. From this research, it is clear the TIAS is an important scale in explaining support for tourism development and perceived tourism impacts; however, measures speaking to cultural impacts and additional negative social impacts (i.e. crowding, congestion, etc.) are excluded from the scale. Ultimately, one should undertake research that would include additional items to the TIAS in an effort to capture a more robust assessment of residents' attitudes concerning tourism (while perhaps allowing for greater usability of the scale in a diversity of contexts). This would also aid in determining if such additions can potentially increase reliabilities and even contribute to a greater degree of variance explained in the construct and its accompanying dimensions (Woosnam, 2012).

Attitudes are not static; they can change often and for many reasons (Woosnam & Erul, 2017). Future research focusing on the relationships between TIAS, FTD, and ESS in Antalya should involve data collected at different points in time to gain a longitudinal perspective of how attitudes progress. In such research, the time of year or even year may serve as a variable that can explain a magnitude of change in attitudes. Of course, in considering ESS, it would worthwhile to consider how such solidarity comes about and changes as a result of residents' support for tourism development. Qualitative methods would be suitable to capture the process by which this solidarity develops.

Residents' emotional solidarity with tourists was an outcome of future support for tourism development, subsequent research should consider antecedents of solidarity such as shared beliefs, shared behaviors, and with interaction with tourists (Woosnam & Norman, 2010), and place attachment (Aleshinloye et al., 2020; Patwardhan et al., 2020; Woosnam et al., 2018c). These precursor constructs to emotional solidarity were not included within the questionnaire (nor the model) but would likely contribute to a greater degree of solidarity or feelings toward tourists as demonstrated in previous work. Work that extends this model should also consider controlling for potential confounding variables such as tourism-related employment or degree of dependence on the tourism industry. Such measures have been shown to influence support for tourism development (Chuang, 2010). Finally, while this work sought to respond to Ward and Berno (2011) charge of incorporating additional theory in tandem with SET, the two frameworks should not be considered the only two theories that can explain future support for tourism and their solidarity with tourists. Other potential theories that may serve worthwhile to consider are the contact hypothesis, the social identity theory, intimacy theory, and social representations theory, to name a few.

Disclosure statement

No potential conflict of interest was reported by the author(s).

ORCID

Manuel Alector Ribeiro http://orcid.org/0000-0003-4484-1082

References

Aleshinloye, K. D., Fu, X., Ribeiro, M. A., Woosnam, K. M., & Tasci, A. D. (2020). The influence of place attachment on social distance: Examining mediating effects of emotional solidarity and the moderating role of interaction. *Journal of Travel Research*, 59(5), 828–849. https://doi.org/10.1177/0047287519863883

Ap, J. (1992). Residents' perceptions: On tourism impacts. *Annals of Tourism Research*, 19(4), 665–690. https://doi.org/10.1016/0160-7383(92)90060-3

Brislin, R. W. (1970). Back-translation for cross-cultural research. *Journal of Cross-Cultural Psychology*, 1(3), 185–216. https://doi.org/10.1177/135910457000100301

Byrne, B. M. (2016). *Structural equation modeling with AMOS: Basic concepts, applications, and programming*. Routledge.

Chuang, S. T. (2010). Rural tourism: Perspectives from social exchange theory. *Social Behavior and Personality: An International Journal*, 38(10), 1313–1322. https://doi.org/10.2224/sbp.2010.38.10.1313

Churchill, G. A. Jr, (1979). A paradigm for developing better measures of marketing constructs. *Journal of Marketing Research*, 16(1), 64–73. https://doi.org/10.1177/002224377901600110

Doh, M. (2006). *Change through tourism: Resident perceptions of tourism development* (Unpublished Doctoral Dissertation), Texas A&M University, College Station, TX.

Fornell, C., & Larker, D. (1981). Structural equation modeling and regression: Guidelines for research practice. *Journal of Marketing Research*, 18(1), 39–50.

García, F. A., Vázquez, A. B., & Macías, R. C. (2015). Resident's attitudes towards the impacts of tourism. *Tourism Management Perspectives*, 13, 33–40.

Gursoy, D., Milito, M. C., & Nunkoo, R. (2017a). Residents' support for a mega-event: The case of the 2014 FIFA World Cup, Natal, Brazil. *Journal of Destination Marketing & Management*, 6(4), 344–352. https://doi.org/10.1016/j.jdmm.2017.09.003

Gursoy, D., Yolal, M., Ribeiro, M. A., & Panosso-Netto, A. (2017b). Impact of trust on local residents' mega-event perceptions and their support. *Journal of Travel Research*, 56(3), 393–406. https://doi.org/10.1177/0047287516643415

Hair, J. F., Black, W. C., Babin, B. J., & Anderson, R. E. (2018). *Multivariate data analysis* (8th Ed.). Cengage.

Hair, J. F., Hult, G. T. M., Ringle, C., & Sarstedt, M. (2017). *A primer on partial least squares structural equation modeling (PLS-SEM)* (2nd ed.). Sage Publications.

Hall, C. M., & Lew, A. A. (2009). *Understanding and managing tourism impacts: An integrated approach*. Routledge.

Hasani, A., Moghavvemi, S., & Hamzah, A. (2016). The impact of emotional solidarity on residents' attitude and tourism development. *Plos One*, 11(6), e0157624https://doi.org/10.1371/journal.pone.0157624

Henseler, J., Ringle, C. M., & Sarstedt, M. (2015). A new criterion for assessing discriminant validity in variance-based structural equation modeling. *Journal of the Academy of Marketing Science*, 43 (1), 115–135. https://doi.org/10.1007/s11747-014-0403-8

Homans, G. (1961). *Social behavior: Its elementary forms*. Harcourt, Brace & World.

Hu, L. T., & Bentler, P. M. (1998). Fit indices in covariance structure modeling: Sensitivity to underparameterized model misspecification. *Psychological Methods*, 3(4), 424–453. https://doi.org/10.1037/1082-989X.3.4.424

Jamal, T., & Camargo, B. A. (2014). Sustainable tourism, justice and an ethic of care: Toward the just destination. *Journal of Sustainable Tourism, 22*(1), 11–30. https://doi.org/10.1080/09669582.2013.786084

Joo, D., & Woosnam, K. M. (2019). Measuring tourists' emotional solidarity with one another—A modification of the emotional solidarity scale. *Journal of Travel Research, 59*(7), 1186–1203. 004728751987850. https://doi.org/10.1177/0047287519878503

Joo, D., Tasci, A. D., Woosnam, K. M., Maruyama, N. U., Hollas, C. R., & Aleshinloye, K. D. (2018). Residents' attitude towards domestic tourists explained by contact, emotional solidarity and social distance. *Tourism Management, 64*, 245–257. https://doi.org/10.1016/j.tourman.2017.08.012

Jordan, P. J., & Troth, A. C. (2020). Common method bias in applied settings: The dilemma of researching in organizations. *Australian Journal of Management, 45*(1), 3–14. https://doi.org/10.1177/0312896219871976

Juric, J., Lindenmeier, J., & Arnold, C. (2020). Do emotional solidarity factors mediate the effect of personality traits on the inclination to use nonmonetary peer-to-peer accommodation networks? *Journal of Travel Research*, 0047287519895127.

Kang, S. K., & Lee, J. (2018). Support of marijuana tourism in Colorado: A residents' perspective using social exchange theory. *Journal of Destination Marketing & Management, 9*, 310–319. https://doi.org/10.1016/j.jdmm.2018.03.003

Kline, R. B. (2015). *Principles and practice of structural equation modeling*. Guilford Publications.

Kwon, J., & Vogt, C. A. (2010). Identifying the role of cognitive, affective, and behavioral components in understanding residents' attitudes toward place marketing. *Journal of Travel Research, 49*(4), 423–435. https://doi.org/10.1177/0047287509346857

Lai, I. K. W., & Hitchcock, M. (2017). Local reactions to mass tourism and community tourism development in Macau. *Journal of Sustainable Tourism, 25*(4), 451–470. https://doi.org/10.1080/09669582.2016.1221413

Lankford, S. V., & Howard, D. R. (1994). Developing a tourism impact attitude scale. *Annals of Tourism Research, 21*(1), 121–139. https://doi.org/10.1016/0160-7383(94)90008-6

Lawler, E. J. (2001). An affect theory of social exchange. *American Journal of Sociology, 107*(2), 321–352. https://doi.org/10.1086/324071

Li, X., & Wan, Y. K. P. (2017). Residents' support for festivals: Integration of emotional solidarity. *Journal of Sustainable Tourism, 25*(4), 517–535. https://doi.org/10.1080/09669582.2016.1224889

Murphy, P. E. (1985). *Tourism: A community approach*. Methuen.

Nunkoo, R. (2016). Toward a more comprehensive use of social exchange theory to study residents' attitudes to tourism. *Procedia Economics and Finance, 39*, 588–596. https://doi.org/10.1016/S2212-5671(16)30303-3

Nunkoo, R., & Gursoy, D. (2012). Residents' support for tourism: An identity perspective. *Annals of Tourism Research, 39*(1), 243–268. https://doi.org/10.1016/j.annals.2011.05.006

Nunkoo, R., & Gursoy, D. (2017). Political trust and residents' support for alternative and mass tourism: An improved structural model. *Tourism Geographies, 19*(3), 318–339. https://doi.org/10.1080/14616688.2016.1196239

Nunkoo, R., & Ramkissoon, H. (2012). Power, trust, social exchange and community support. *Annals of Tourism Research, 39*(2), 997–1023. https://doi.org/10.1016/j.annals.2011.11.017

Patwardhan, V., Ribeiro, M. A., Payini, V., Woosnam, K. M., Mallya, J., & Gopalakrishnan, P. (2020). Visitors' place attachment and destination loyalty: Examining the roles of emotional solidarity and perceived safety. *Journal of Travel Research, 59*(1), 3–21. https://doi.org/10.1177/0047287518824157

Podsakoff, P. M., MacKenzie, S. B., Lee, J.-Y., & Podsakoff, N. P. (2003). Common method biases in behavioral research: A critical review of the literature and recommended remedies. *The Journal of Applied Psychology, 88*(5), 879–903. https://doi.org/10.1037/0021-9010.88.5.879

Rasoolimanesh, S. M., Jaafar, M., Kock, N., & Ramayah, T. (2015). A revised framework of social exchange theory to investigate the factors influencing residents' perceptions. *Tourism Management Perspectives, 16*, 335–345. https://doi.org/10.1016/j.tmp.2015.10.001

Rasoolimanesh, S. M., Ringle, C. M., Jaafar, M., & Ramayah, T. (2017). Urban vs. rural destinations: Residents' perceptions, community participation and support for tourism development. *Tourism Management, 60*, 147–158. https://doi.org/10.1016/j.tourman.2016.11.019

Ribeiro, M. A., Pinto, P., Silva, J. A., & Woosnam, K. M. (2017). Residents' attitudes and the adoption of pro-tourism behaviours: The case of developing island countries. *Tourism Management, 61*, 523–537. https://doi.org/10.1016/j.tourman.2017.03.004

Ribeiro, M. A., Pinto, P., Silva, J. A., & Woosnam, K. M. (2018). Examining the predictive validity of SUS-TAS with maximum parsimony in developing Island countries. *Journal of Sustainable Tourism, 26*(3), 379–398. https://doi.org/10.1080/09669582.2017.1355918

Ribeiro, M. A., Woosnam, K. M., Pinto, P., & Silva, J. A. (2018). Tourists' destination loyalty through emotional solidarity with residents: An integrative moderated mediation model. *Journal of Travel Research, 57*(3), 279–295. https://doi.org/10.1177/0047287517699089

Simpson, J. J., & Simpson, P. M. (2017). Emotional solidarity with destination security forces. *Journal of Travel Research, 56*(7), 927–940. https://doi.org/10.1177/0047287516675063

Spector, P. E. (2006). Method variance in organizational research: Truth or urban legend? *Organizational Research Methods*, *9*(2), 221-232. https://doi.org/10.1177/1094428105284955

Statista. (2019). *International tourism spending in Turkey*. Retrieved February 15, 2018 from https://www.statista.com/statistics/398467/international-tourism-spending-in-turkey/

Stylidis, D., Biran, A., Sit, J., & Szivas, E. M. (2014). Residents' support for tourism development: The role of residents' place image and perceived tourism impacts. *Tourism Management*, *45*, 260-274. https://doi.org/10.1016/j.tourman.2014.05.006

Suess, C., Woosnam, K. M., & Erul, E. (2020). Stranger-danger? Understanding the moderating effects of children in the household on non-hosting residents' emotional solidarity with Airbnb visitors, feeling safe, and support for Airbnb. *Tourism Management*, *77*, 103952. https://doi.org/10.1016/j.tourman.2019.103952

Tabachnick, B. G., & Fidell, L. S. (2013). *Using multivariate statistics* (6th Ed.). Allyn and Bacon.

Turkey Ministry of Culture and Tourism. (2019). Tourism statistics, foreign travelers. Retrieved February 15, 2018 from http://www.kultur.gov.tr/EN-153018/number-of-arriving-departing-visitors-foreigners-and-ci-.html

Turkish Statistical Institute. (2017). Population Statistics. Retrieved February 21, 2019 from http://www.turkstat.gov.tr/UstMenu.do?metod=temelist

United Nations World Tourism Organizations (UNWTO). (2018). *Tourism Statistics, Foreign Travelers in 2018*. Retrieved February 15, 2018 from http://marketintelligence.unwto.org/publication/unwto-tourism-highlights-2018

Wall, G., & Mathieson, A. (2006). *Tourism: Change, impacts, and opportunities*. Pearson Education.

Wang, Y., & Pfister, R. E. (2008). Residents' attitudes toward tourism and perceived personal benefits in a rural community. *Journal of Travel Research*, *47*(1), 84-93. https://doi.org/10.1177/0047287507312402

Ward, C., & Berno, T. (2011). Beyond social exchange theory: Attitudes toward tourists. *Annals of Tourism Research*, *38*(4), 1556-1569. https://doi.org/10.1016/j.annals.2011.02.005

West, S. G., Finch, J. F., & Curran, P. J. (1995). Structural equation models with nonnormal variables: Problems and remedies. In R. H. Hoyle (Ed.), *Structural equation modeling: Concepts, issues, and applications* (pp. 56-75). Sage Publications, Inc.

Woosnam, K. M. (2011). Comparing residents' and tourists' emotional solidarity with one another: An extension of Durkheim's model. *Journal of Travel Research*, *50*(6), 615-626. https://doi.org/10.1177/0047287510382299

Woosnam, K. M. (2012). Using emotional solidarity to explain residents' attitudes about tourism development. *Journal of Travel Research*, *51*(3), 315-327. https://doi.org/10.1177/0047287511410351

Woosnam, K. M., & Erul, E. (2017). Residents' perceived impacts of all-inclusive resorts in Antalya. *Tourism Planning & Development*, *14*(1), 65-86. https://doi.org/10.1080/21568316.2016.1183515

Woosnam, K. M., & Norman, W. C. (2010). Measuring residents' emotional solidarity with tourists: Scale development of Durkheim's theoretical constructs. *Journal of Travel Research*, *49*(3), 365-380. https://doi.org/10.1177/0047287509346858

Woosnam, K. M., Aleshinloye, K. D., Ribeiro, M. A., Stylidis, D., Jiang, J., & Erul, E. (2018b). Social determinants of place attachment at a World Heritage Site. *Tourism Management*, *67*, 139-146. https://doi.org/10.1016/j.tourman.2018.01.012

Woosnam, K. M., Aleshinloye, K. D., Strzelecka, M., & Erul, E. (2018c). The role of place attachment in developing emotional solidarity with non-hosting residents. *Journal of Hospitality & Tourism Research*, *42*(7), 1058-1066. https://doi.org/10.1177/1096348016671396

Woosnam, K. M., Draper, J., Jiang, J. K., Aleshinloye, K. D., & Erul, E. (2018a). Applying self-perception theory to explain residents' attitudes about tourism development through travel histories. *Tourism Management*, *64*, 357-368. https://doi.org/10.1016/j.tourman.2017.09.015

Woosnam, K. M., Erul, E., & Ribeiro, M. A. (2017). Heterogeneous community perspectives of emotional solidarity with tourists: Considering Antalya, Turkey. *International Journal of Tourism Research*, *19*(6), 639-647. https://doi.org/10.1002/jtr.2136

Woosnam, K. M., Norman, W. C., & Ying, T. (2009). Exploring the theoretical framework of emotional solidarity between residents and tourists. *Journal of Travel Research*, *48*(2), 245-258. https://doi.org/10.1177/0047287509332334

Woosnam, K. M., Shafer, C. S., Scott, D., & Timothy, D. J. (2015). Tourists' perceived safety through emotional solidarity with non-hosting residents in two Mexico-United States border regions. *Tourism Management*, *46*, 263-273. https://doi.org/10.1016/j.tourman.2014.06.022

World Travel and Tourism Council. (2018). *Travel & Tourism Economic Impact 2018, Turkey*. Retrieved February 21, 2019, from https://www.wttc.org/-/media/files/reports/economic-impact-research/countries-2018/turkey2018.pdf

Zuo, B., Gursoy, D., & Wall, G. (2017). Residents' support for red tourism in China: The moderating effect of central government. *Annals of Tourism Research*, *64*, 51-63. https://doi.org/10.1016/j.annals.2017.03.001

The importance of collaboration and emotional solidarity in residents' support for sustainable urban tourism: case study Ho Chi Minh City

Hung Nguyen Phuc and Huan Minh Nguyen

ABSTRACT
Some sustainable tourism development studies address support issues for local communities as well as brand destination factors, but to date there has not been rigorous scrutiny of support for varieties of tourism in the urban context. The purpose of the study is to assess residents' views and support for sustainable tourism development in urban destinations. A quantitative and cultural methodology is used in this study with the participation of 451 residents in three large communities in Ho Chi Minh City, Vietnam. The study finds that: (1) the measure of communities' support is determined by residents' perceptions, residents' perception of value, collaboration and emotional solidarity with their community; (2) there is a relationship between collaboration and emotional solidarity in the context of sustainable development. Thus, the paper carefully considers the two significant factors of collaboration and emotional solidarity in assessing influences upon residents' support for sustainable tourism development. The findings provide more useful evidence for planning and managing sustainable development as well as in marketing strategies in other areas of tourism, such as industry infrastructure and transportation links, quality of hospitality and service facilities and archeological effort to develop urban travel offerings of historical interest.

Introduction

Tourism has been considered as an essential development driver in many countries because it brings several economic, socio-cultural benefits. These benefits may include reducing poverty rates in traditional communities (Tasci et al., 2014), generating more jobs for local residents and promoting the consumption of local products (Lee, 2013), boosting business activities in rural areas, improving infrastructure (Ji et al., 2015), increasing local residents' incomes and promoting acculturation effectively (Mathew & Sreejesh, 2017; Gursoy et al., 2015). Therefore, raising the awareness of the gains available for local people through tourism development is crucial (Choi & Murray, 2010). Local residents play an essential role in the overall development of community and therefore, in sustainable tourism development (Mihalic, 2016). Sustainable tourism becomes a preferred initiative in developing local communities. Thus, extending sustainable tourism will influence many aspects of the tourism sector, which includes the expansion of existing businesses and development of new enterprises. (Hanafiah et al., 2016).

By definition, sustainable tourism development requires the involvement and support of different stakeholders, such as tourists, local people, local businesses and government (D'Mello et al., 2016). Positive perceptions and support from these groups, especially from local residents, have a significant influence on planning and tourism development (Lee, 2013; Lundberg, 2015). This is positive because residents can usually provide the best quality services and most effectively maintain quality at tourist destinations (Woo et al., 2015). Research has found there is an organic relationship between residents' perceptions of value and sustainable tourism development (Lundberg, 2015; Woo et al., 2018). Therefore, by studying local perceptions of benefits, in terms of economic, cultural-social, environmental values and sustainable quality of life, we can better understand and effectively evaluate sustainable tourism development in specific locations.

There have been several studies conducted in this direction (Wight, 1993). However, only a few have investigated the impacts of emotional solidarity on the development of sustainable urban tourism. Emotional solidarity is expressed through local attitudes and perceptions towards tourists, and have been shown to be influenced by personal factors and individual perceptions (Woosnam, 2012). In addition to residents, the participation of other stakeholders in the collaborative development of sustainable tourism was found to be especially important in urban destinations, as shown in the work of Liu et al. (2017). The historical functions of local communities were transformed and the analysis of the interaction between tourism and community life became increasingly important (Liu et al., 2017).

To fill a gap identified in these studies, this research aims to evaluate the impact of local residents' perceptions, collaboration and emotional solidarity upon their support for sustainable urban tourism. Moreover, the paper will study mechanisms engaging residents in support for sustainable tourism and in collaborative interactions with relevant stakeholders. To illustrate the applicability of the approach, the study will focus on residents living in Ho Chi Minh City (HCMC), the fastest growing and most populated city in Vietnam, contributing 22% of national GDP (People's Committee of Ho Chi Minh City, 2019). A prominent political, historical, economic, cultural and scientific centre, its population was 8,561,608 in 2018 and is expected to increase to 13.8 million by 2025. Service provision is one of the most important industries in the strong growth of HCMC (Truong, 2013) and, tourism is a fast-growing sector, making HCMC the centre of national tourism. Specifically, HCMC ranks as one of the must-visit and most attractive places in Asia, receiving over 7 million international visitors per year (Truong, 2013). For various reasons, sustaining the development of urban tourism in HCMC is critical.

Literature reviews

Residents' tourism perceptions

Local residents play important roles in sustainable community development because they directly interact with tourists, helping to provide unforgettable experiences. Thus, Lee and Hsieh (2016) claims that positive perceptions become extremely important in building tourism development and planning for tourism sector management. In addition, community support for development significantly contributes to economic and social advances, environment protection and the improvement of living standards. Resident support helps to effectively monitor and plan tourism activities to improve positive perceptions of tourism development. Therefore, getting to know the attitudes of residents about tourism development projects is crucial (Dyer et al., 2007). The satisfaction of local residents helps to form a base for sustainable development and is one of the key indicators to measure individuals' support (Nicholas et al., 2009; Woo et al. 2015). When local residents have positive perceptions of tourism activities, they tend to offer more support for further tourism development (Erul et al., 2020; Siu et al., 2013). Sharma and Gursoy (2015) pointed out that support is maintained and developed in the future if there are evident personal benefits in tourism for community residents. In particular, the level of support from residents is highly dependent on their awareness and commitment as this determines the stability and sustainability of tourism development (Gursoy et al., 2010).

Collaboration

Collaboration is found to be important in promoting community development, especially in the field of tourism (Vogt et al., 2016). In an ideal sustainable development system, local authorities, investors, tourism business organizations and residents would gather together and collaborate to create sustainable development and benefits (Li & Hunter, 2015). Improved community awareness will facilitate greater support and more sustainable tourism development (Anda & Temmen, 2014); thus, to ensure sustainable development, it is necessary to create favorable conditions for stakeholders to participate actively, and for all parties to discuss common issues.

Belletti et al. (2017) claimed that support from travel agencies, local authorities and tourists also play an essential role in the sustainable development of tourism. Thanks to support and collaboration among stakeholders, tourism is effectively enhanced by local communities and travel agencies (Goodwin, 2016). Close collaboration creates a positive effect and in turn, greater impacts upon community support (Domínguez-Gómez & González-Gómez, 2017). Nunkoo et al. (2013) found that collaboration between local residents and other stakeholders significantly affects tourism development. As such, this paper investigates the following first hypothesis.

Hypothesis 1: Collaboration between local residents and other stakeholders positively influences residents' support for sustainable tourism development.

Emotional solidarity

Emotional solidarity is defined as an intergroup emotional investment, and use of this as a concept refers to attachments to be explained in terms of an emotional character which varies in intensity according to the frequency and the nature of the interaction. Different intensities of emotional solidarity are modified by factors such as residents' length of residence (Woosnam et al., 2014), residents' community attachment (Li & Wan, 2017) tourists' destination loyalty (Patwardhan et al., 2020) and tourists' attachment and travel distance to a destination (Joo et al., 2017). Thus, emotional solidarity is assessed as a degree of intimacy between individuals that affects perceptions of residents and tourists (Woosnam, 2011). This has a significant impact upon collaboration among stakeholders in the development of local community because it can increase likelihood of active participation and collaboration to create a better community (Ritchie & Rigano, 2007). It is also found that individual personality and positive attitudes in local residents towards tourists are useful measures of emotional solidarity because different personality results in different reactions to tourists and the development of tourism (Lin et al., 2014; Moghavvemi et al., 2017). Moreover, residents' perceived values can be assessed with the emotional solidarity scale consisting of three basic dimensions, including a welcoming nature, emotional closeness, and a sympathetic understanding (Woosnam & Norman, 2010). As Woosnam (2012) found, emotional solidarity significantly predicted residents' support for tourism development. Thus, this paper investigates the following second hypothesis.

Hypothesis 2: Residents emotional solidarity with tourists positively influences the former's support for sustainable tourism development

Residents' perception of value regarding sustainable development

Several studies have found positive and negative attitudes toward sustainable tourism development among residents in urban and rural areas. If its benefits outweigh costs, residents tend almost always to have a positive perception of tourism development and vice versa (Haobin Ye

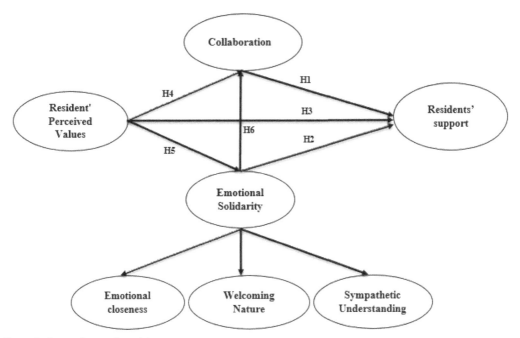

Figure 1. Proposed research model.

et al., 2014; Rasoolimanesh et al., 2015). Specifically, the benefits typically include: increase in household income, standard of living, job creation and revenue to the local tax agency (But & Ap, 2017; McDowall & Choi, 2010). In addition, the development of local business networks, preservation of historic sites (Andereck et al., 2005), community interest, conservation of resources and public services (Lankford & Howard, 1994), survival of traditional arts and handicraft products (McGehee et al., 2002) all support the development of positive perceptions and attraction to developing tourism, which can increase public investment and funding for environmental protection (McKinley, 2017).

Therefore, to have community support, projects in tourism development must show local residents that the projects bring more benefits than costs, and more positive outcomes than negative impacts (Lee, 2013). The residents, of course, need to be informed and to connect their existing information with new details with which they are presented for new projects to be supported. The support of residents seems foundational for community development (Lee, 2013) because investors must show their social responsibility and social justice compliance in considering the needs of residents (Tolkach & King, 2015). Thus, the following third hypothesis is investigated in this paper.

Hypothesis 3: Residents' perceived value of tourism positively influences their support for sustainable tourism development.

Effects of residents' perceived value upon collaboration and emotional solidarity

Effects of residents' perceived value on collaboration

Residents' perceived value is considered an important criterion to evaluate the effectiveness of collaboration in sustainable development because collaboration requires close links among different parties in the community (Gursoy et al., 2002; Jaafar et al., 2015). For example, tourists tend to be reluctant to visit places where they are not welcomed or poorly treated (Diedrich & García-Buades, 2009); therefore, good collaboration between residents and tourists will almost always result in mutual benefits. Once tourism is developed, both residents and tourists can enjoy good

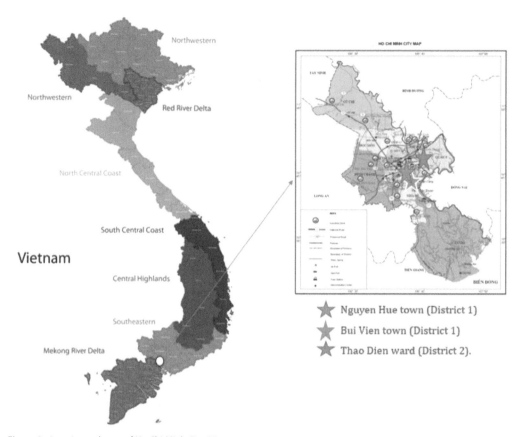

Figure 2. Location and map of Ho Chi Minh City, Vietnam.

infrastructure, urban development, service systems and entertainment (Carlisle et al., 2016). Thus, the following fourth hypothesis is investigated in this paper.

Hypothesis 4: Residents' favourable valuations of sustainability in turn positively influences collaboration

Effects of residents' perceived value to emotional solidarity

If residents' perceived value is positive, emotional solidarity will be also be positively promoted. Improvements in emotional solidarity will result in a greater positive perceptions and stronger participation among local residents, tourists and the public sector (Lai & Hitchcock, 2017; Liao & Chern, 2015; Li & Wan, 2017; Woosnam, 2011; Woosnam & Norman, 2010). Yet, despite observed mutual effects, the relationship between collaboration among stakeholders and emotional solidarity is still untested. Thus, this study will also examine the following fifth and sixth hypotheses (Figure 1).

Hypothesis 5: Residents' perceived value of tourism positively influences their emotional solidarity with tourists.

Hypothesis 6: Residents emotional solidarity with tourists positively influences collaboration.

Research procedure

Research space

Our survey was conducted in mid-December 2018–January 2019. As shown in Figure 2, Ho Chi Minh City conveniently borders with many provinces in the southwestern and southeastern regions of Vietnam, creating favorable conditions for the development of the economic and tourism sectors. We conducted our survey in three of the most crowded communities located at (1)

Nguyen Hue town (District 1); (2) Bui Vien town (District 1); and (3) Thao Dien ward (District 2). Approval from local authorities in each location was obtained for our surveys. These three communities were selected in this study to ensure wide coverage in respondents' evaluation as they are affected by HCMC tourism development; and specifically because many tourism activities take place in these areas, so they obviously affect the lives of local residents.

The areas chosen for data collection were representative of spaces across the city. Nguyen Hue town (District 1) is the city's major commercial center, with theater, historical sites and entertainment venues, offering high quality services and a variety of tourism products. Thus, it is usually considered an attractive destination for almost every international tourist. Meanwhile, Bui Vien town consists many famous hotels, restaurants and entertainment services, and attracts many tourists to nighttime entertainment activities; with a variety of services and products suitable for different tourists visiting HCMC. Likewise, the Thao Dien ward (District 2) provides good quality of life such as villas, an entertainment center, modern infrastructure and travel convenience; thus, many tourists love to stay there.

Data collection

A self-completed 5-point Likert scale questionnaire was used in this study. Its contents focused upon the perceptions of local residents on four key aspects, including: (1) perceived values (five items) adapted from Lee and Back (2006) and Lee et al. (2010); (2) collaboration (eight items) taken from Kapera (2018); (3) emotional solidarity with emotional closeness (four items), welcoming nature (four items), and sympathetic understanding (three items) adapted from Woosnam and Norman (2010); (4) residents' support for sustainable tourism development (four items) taken from Rasoolimanesh and Jaafar (2016) and Wang and Pfister (2008).

Twenty students at xxx University voluntarily helped the authors to deliver the printed questionnaires to appropriate participants and then collect their responses. The students were divided into three groups, including: seven students surveying in Nguyen Hue town, eight in Bui Vien town, and five in Thao Dien Ward. The students took professional training with the authors on how to effectively approach residents who currently live, work or do business in the targeted communities. After completing a questionnaire, each participant was offered a small notebook as a token of appreciation for their participation.

Data analysis

In this study, the investigated scales were first tested for their reliability using Cronbach's Alpha coefficients. A scale is considered reliable if Cronbach's Alpha coefficient exceeds 0.7 and its corrected total-item correlation of each item is greater than 0.3 (Nunnally & Bernstein, 1994). Then, the reliable scales were further analyzed with Exploratory Factor Analysis (EFA) which requires: (1) eigenvalues ≥ 1; (2) Total variance explained $\geq 50\%$; (3) KMO ≥ 0.5; (4) Sig. coefficient of the KMO test ≥ 0.05; (5) Factor loadings of all observed variables are ≥ 0.5; and (6) Weight difference between the loadings of two factors > 0.3 (Hair et al., 2009).

Next, the data were analyzed with Confirmatory Factor Analysis (CFA) to further confirm the results obtained from EFA. Finally, Structural Equation Modeling (SEM) was used to test the proposed model which is considered appropriate if the significance value of Chi-square test is no more than 5%; CMIN/df ≤ 2 (but in some cases, CMIN/df ≤ 3 is also acceptable); and GFI, TLI, CFI ≥ 0.9. Besides these criteria, recent researchers suggest that GFI should be greater than 0.8, RMSEA ≤ 0.08, composite reliability> 0.6, and the extracted variance > 0.5 (Hair et al., 2009).

Table 1. Profile of respondents.

Characteristics		Frequency	%
Gender	Male	167	37
	Female	284	63
Age group	20-29	125	27.7
	30-39	148	32.8
	40-49	98	21.7
	>50	80	17.8
Length of residence (Years)	< 5 years	45	10
	5-10 years	78	17.3
	11-20 years	125	27.7
	21-30 years	87	19.3
	31-40 years	81	18
	>41 years	35	7.7
Level of Education	Postgraduate	84	18.6
	Undergraduate/Graduate	304	67.4
	Secondary	36	8.0
	Primary	19	4.2
	None	8	1,8
Occupation	Employee	98	21.7
	Housewife	45	10
	Student	85	18.8
	Retired	40	8,7
	Service industry	110	24.4
	Business	73	16.4
Income (VND/ month)	VND5Mil and below	89	19.7
	VND6Mil- VND12Mil	125	27.1
	VND12Mil- VND20Mil	140	31
	VND20Mil- VND29Mil	85	18.8
	Above VND30Mil	12	3.4

Note: Exchange rate is about 23,000VND/USD.

Empirical results

Descriptive statistics

In this study, a total of 465 questionnaires were delivered and 458 collected. Among them, seven were invalid; thus, only 451 questionnaires were available for analysis and the valid response rate was 96.98%. The results revealed gender difference among respondents, with 37% being men and 63% being women. Within age groups, the group accounting for the highest proportion of responses were between 30-39 years of age. Most respondents were residents who have lived in the community for 11-20 years. Their main professions are office workers, staff working in the service industry and students in which the level of training was mainly undergraduate/graduate. In terms of income, the respondents earned from VND12Mil - VND20Mil. These demographics are shown in Table 1.

Scale reliability tests

Table 2 presents the results of the scale reliability tests in which Cronbach's Alpha coefficients of the scales were all greater than 0.7 and their corrected item-total correlations were all greater than 0.3. The scales are therefore appropriate and acceptable.

Exploratory factor analysis

The results of EFA are briefly shown in Table 3, which shows that the analysis result of four different factors was 52.877%. When evaluating the results of the factors, the value of each item is greater than 0.4 which is suitable for EFA (Hair et al., 2009). The results of Cronbach's alpha values of factors show that all values are satisfactory and meet the condition of being greater than

Table 2. Scale reliability test results.

Observed variables	Scale mean if item deleted	Scale variance if item deleted	Corrected- item total correlation	Cronbach's Alpha if item deleted
Residents' Perceived value (PS): Cronbach's Alpha = 0.829				
PS1	16.09	9.675	0.621	0.800
PS2	16.34	8.360	0.622	0.798
PS3	16.36	8.309	0.639	0.792
PS4	16.04	9.804	0.636	0.798
PS5	16.42	8.226	0.664	0.784
Collaboration (CO): Cronbach's Alpha = 0.852				
CO1	20.19	8.059	0.451	0.863
CO2	20.11	7.168	0.739	0.807
CO4	20.10	7.661	0.607	0.833
CO5	20.14	7.271	0.697	0.816
CO6	20.11	7.407	0.720	0.812
CO7	20.12	7.648	0.628	0.829
Emotional closeness (EC) Cronbach's Alpha = 0.934				
EC1	13.08	4.768	0.823	0.921
EC2	13.14	4.751	0.860	0.909
EC3	13.17	4.725	0.863	0.907
EC4	13.06	4.916	0.831	0.918
Welcoming Nature (WN) Cronbach's Alpha = 0.901				
WN1	12.60	5.926	0.713	0.894
WN2	12.63	5.187	0.826	0.854
WN3	12.60	5.494	0.817	0.857
WN4	12.60	5.707	0.760	0.878
Sympathetic Understanding (SU) Cronbach's Alpha = 0.914				
SU1	8.28	2.084	0.834	0.870
SU2	8.23	2.119	0.832	0.872
SU3	8.22	2.018	0.815	0.887
Residents' Support for Sustainable Tourism Development (RS) = 0.826				
RS1	12.05	3.056	0.655	0.779
RS2	12.06	2.869	0.661	0.779
RS3	11.95	3.202	0.662	0.777
RS4	11.98	3.329	0.639	0.788

0.6 (Nunnally & Bernstein, 1994). Core items fully reflect the content of the factors. All of these factors were used to assess the level of perception of local residents that impacts support for sustainable tourism development. Most factor loading values were greater than 0.6, and significant at $p < 0.001$ (Fidell et al., 2013). However, two collaboration items were removed due to low loadings. This study model was appropriate looking at KMO = 0.857; Chi-Square = 2670.29; df = 91; and Sig = 0.000.

Similarly, Table 4 shows the results of EFA for emotional solidarity. The results show that the total variance is 65.873%. The Cronbach's Alpha values of the three factors show that all values were satisfactory and met the condition of being greater than 0.6 (Nunnally & Bernstein, 1994). As with the EFA, core items fully reflected the content of the factors. The overall mean is 4.1. These three factors are transformed into a mean score that is used as an indicator for the underlying structure as "emotional solidarity (ES)" with the subsequent multivariate analysis (Chen & Phou, 2013; Hair et al., 2009). This study model is totally appropriate for examining the KMO = 0.934; Chi-Square = 4504.260; df = 55, and Sig = 0.000

Confirmatory factor analysis

Table 5 presents the combined results of factors related to the perceptions of local residents and factors affecting residents' support for sustainable tourism development. The relevant values are Cronbach's Alpha, CR and AVE. Therefore, the values mentioned are totally appropriate and satisfy the pre-defined requirements.

Table 3. Exploratory factor analysis result.

Factors/items	Factor loading	Eigenvalue	% Of variance explained	Cronbach's alpha	Overall mean
Residents' Perceived Value (PS)		2.560	15.003	0.829	4.063
PS4	0.733				4.27
PS5	0.726				3.90
PS1	0.704				4.22
PS3	0.701				3.97
PS2	0.691				3.95
Collaboration(CO)		4.579	29.476	0.863	4.038
CO2	0.790				4.05
CO5	0.788				4.01
CO6	0.779				4.04
CO7	0.708				4.03
CO4	0.671				4.06
Residents' Support for Sustainable Tourism Development (RS)		1.795	9.574	0.826	4.003
RS3	0.802				4.06
RS1	0.734				3.96
RS4	0.713				4.04
RS2	0.707				3.95
KMO					0.857
Bartlett's Test	Chi-Square				2670.29
	df				91
	Sig.				0.000

Notes: *p < 0.001.

Table 4. Exploratory factor analysis of Emotional Solidarity result.

Factors/items	Factor loading	Eigenvalue	% Of variance explained	Cronbach's alpha	Overall mean
ES		7.246	62.484	0.947	4.241
EC4	0.841				4.42
EC3	0.821				4.31
EC2	0.819				4.34
WN3	0.798				4.20
WN2	0.786				4.18
EC1	0.785				4.40
SU2	0.782				4.14
WN1	0.770				4.21
WN4	0.765				4.21
SU1	0.765				4.09
SU3	0.759				4.14
KMO					0.934
Bartlett's Test	Chi-Square				4504.260
	df				55
	Sig.				0.00

*p < 0.001.

Figure 3 demonstrates the results of the CFA model with the aim of re-confirming the relevance of the research model compared to the data collected. Specific results are shown through: Chi-square = 730.623; df = 265; p-value = 0.000; CMIN/df = 2.757 < 3; GFI = 0.884, TLI = 0.926; CFI = 0.935; RMSEA = 0.062, which are satisfactory to the required criteria.

Figure 3 also confirms the one-way relationship meeting conditions related to convergence value and unique value. In addition, discriminant validity was used to evaluate AVE values with the squared correlations between coupling structures. All the AVE estimates were higher than the squared inter-construct correlations. These structures are considered to be different from other factors (Fornell & Larcker, 1981; Hair et al., 2009). The results are shown in Table 6.

Table 5. Confirmatory factor analysis.

Term	Scale	No. of Reliability test	Reliability test Cronbach's Alpha	Composite	Average Variance extracted
Respondents' support for the development of sustainable tourism in urban destinations in Ho Chi Minh City, Vietnam	ES	11	0.947	0.941	0.596
	PS	5	0.829	0.836	0.506
	CO	5	0.863	0.864	0.561
	RS	4	0.826	0.828	0.547

Structural equation modelling

Tests for model goodness of fit and hypotheses

Figure 4 briefly shows the results of SEM analysis of the suitability of the study data. With the values of Chi-square = 730.623; df = 265; p-values = 0.000, CMIN/df = 2.757 < 3; GFI = 0.883; TLI = 0.926; CFI = 0.932; RMSEA = 0.062, the proposed model is considered satisfactory to the required criteria. Thus, it can be affirmed that the research model is reliable.

Hypotheses tests using SEM model

Table 7 confirms the significance of the study hypotheses, indicating that the six hypotheses established are all significant with p-values less than 0.05; thus, all of the hypotheses (H1, H2, H3, H4, H5, and H6) are supported by the data.

Discussions and managerial implications

Discussion

This research examines the perceptions of local residents engaging in and supporting sustainable tourism development by analyzing their positive and negative perceptions. Additionally, we also analyze the impacts of residents' perceived values, collaboration and emotional solidarity as a factor in residents' support for sustainable tourism development. In the proposed model, collaboration and emotional solidarity are considered new factors particularly important to sustainable tourism development in current urban areas and directly affecting participation in tourism development for local residents. The relationships investigated in this study were presented in six hypotheses. This study aims at providing practical evidence of the involvement of local residents in sustainable tourism development.

Strong relationships were found between collaboration, emotional solidarity, residents' perceived values and residents' support for sustainable tourism development. Collaboration ($\beta = 0.291$, $p < 0.001$), emotional solidarity ($\beta = 0.113$, $p = 0.021$), residents' perceived values ($\beta = 0.305$, $p < 0.001$) all positively and significantly explained residents' support for sustainable tourism development. In addition, the findings of the study indicate that collaboration and emotional solidarity are important factors for the participation of residents in tourism development, building cooperative relationships among stakeholders to create effective systems of participation in tourism development. This finding is consistent with previous studies indicating the importance collaboration between residents and the government in decision-making (Borlido, 2016). In order to establish a common rule that can be applied to a wide range of stakeholders including local authorities, tourism organizations, travel agencies and other tourism-related services, communities of participating organizations, such as education institutions and local media organizations, will contribute to enhancing community participation and support in tourism development (Rastegar et al., 2017).

More specifically, our findings indicate that emotional solidarity has a great influence upon the support of residents for sustainable development. The results are consistent with prior

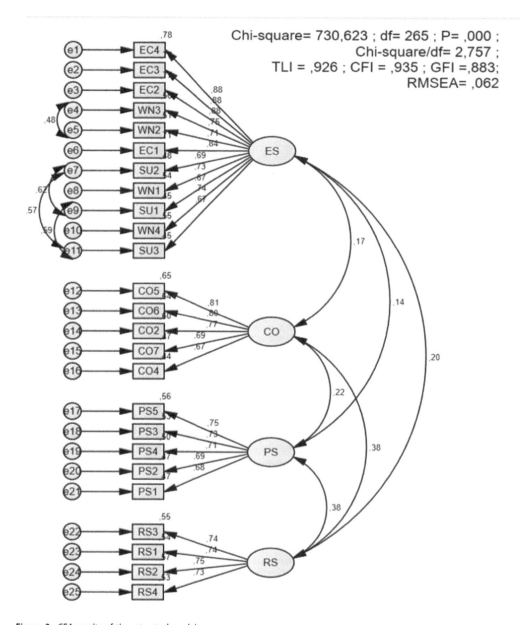

Figure 3. CFA results of the saturated model.

Table 6. Correlation matrix.

Constructs	Residents' Perceived Value	Emotional Solidarity	Collaboration	Resident Support
Residents' Perceived Value	0.711[a]			
Emotional Solidarity	0.136[b]	0.772		
Collaboration	0.217	0.171	0.749	
Resident Support	0.383	0.204	0.377	0.739

Notes: [a]Average variance extracted;.
[b]Inter-construct squared correlations.

studies that suggest residents will actively participate in community development to ensure their benefits (Lai & Hitchcock, 2017; Li & Wan, 2017). Such factors as emotional closeness, a welcoming nature and sympathetic understanding will contribute positively to building the image of the

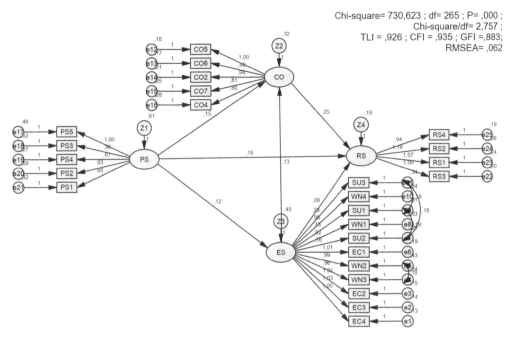

Figure 4. Standardized SEM model.

Table 7. Coefficients from SEM Model.

Hypothesized relationship				Coefficient	Standardized Coefficient	S.E	C.R.	P	Conclusion
H1	CO	→	RS	0.245	0.291	0.045	5.393	***	Supported
H2	ES	→	RS	0.083	0.113	0.036	2.311	0.021	Supported
H3	PS	→	RS	0.193	0.305	0.035	5.491	***	Supported
H4	PS	→	CO	0.149	0.197	0.041	3.614	***	Supported
H5	PS	→	ES	0.118	0.136	0.045	2.614	0.009	Supported
H6	ES	→	CO	0.126	0.144	0.044	2.844	0.004	Supported

Note: ***p < 0.01.

community in tourists' perceptions and thus resulting in developments in the tourism industry. This emphasizes structural relationships between the images residents and tourists hold about destinations, that in turn have positive impacts upon support for the development of tourism (Stylidis et al., 2014). The study suggests positive and consistent findings compared to previous assessments, establishing a significant relationship between residents' perceived values and residents' support for sustainable tourism development (Lee, 2013; Stylidis et al., 2014). Previous studies have also shown economic, cultural-social and environmental impacts of perceived values, which are considered factors that influence community support (Prayag et al., 2013).

Table 6 demonstrated that a relationship exists between residents' perception of value and collaboration. The results indicate that residents' perception of value has a positive and significant impact on collaboration ($\beta = 0.197$, $p < 0.001$). This demonstrates that residents' perception of values and benefits affect the participation and cooperation of many stakeholders, including organizations such as tourism organizations, travel agencies, local organizations, tourists, etc. Many studies have shown that can exist between different stakeholders in sustainable tourism development, such as between local government and stakeholders, and which will hinder the development of tourism (Niezgoda & Czernek, 2014). Conflicts of interest and purposes will affect the common goals of sustainable development; for example, residents prioritize enhancing benefits in the development of their locality (Mika, 2015). Therefore, the interests of parties involved in tourism development should be balanced, and communication policies should be developed to increase the exchange of information between local authorities and local communities (Borlido, 2016; De Pourcq et al., 2017).

This study has also shown that there is a positive and significant impact of residents' perceived value on emotional solidarity ($\beta = 0.136$, $p = 0.009$). When residents are aware of the values and benefits of participating in sustainable tourism development communities, a spirit of emotional solidarity shall be built. Emotional solidarity consists of three basic dimensions: emotional closeness, a welcoming nature and sympathetic understandings that have great impacts upon the perceptions and attitudes of residents, therefore, once residents are aware of the said values and benefits, this will have a positive impact on emotional closeness. Where there is a relationship between residents and tourists in the development of tourism, because residents realize values and benefits they may get from tourism, they will form a positive perception of emotional solidarity in sustainable tourism development. These results are consistent with those of earlier studies suggesting that there is a relation between the level of perception and emotional solidarity in the impact on tourism (Moghavvemi et al., 2017).

Moreover, this research also indicates the impact of emotional solidarity on collaboration. The findings indicate that emotional solidarity has a positive and significant effect on collaboration ($\beta = 0.144$; $p = 0.004$). Many stakeholders collaborate in implementing tourism development activities to ensure the interests of stakeholders in the direct relationship between the residents of the community and tourists (Woosnam, 2011; Woosnam & Norman, 2010). As such, factors such as welcoming nature and sympathetic understanding play an important role in showing the perceptions of residents. When residents have positive attitudes, such attitudes shall affect collaboration and efforts to build connections between many stakeholders for achieving the common goals of the residents' community (Woolf et al., 2016). The results are consistent with previous evaluations suggesting that emotional solidarity is primarily responsible for contributing to positive perceptions of tourism and tourism development among residents, thus building the cooperation to realize the common goal of community development (Woolf et al., 2016). In tourism development, each stakeholder can play a different role in creating a unified entity in which emotional solidarity plays a role connecting and affecting other stakeholders so that they can collaborate and support each other to create a sustainable development environment.

Implications

This study investigates the impacts of residents' perceptions on their support for sustainable tourism development in urban destinations in HCMC. Academically, the study has the following fundamental contributions:

First, this study overcomes the shortcomings in previous studies on sustainable tourism development in examining different dimensions of the context of market performance. Therefore, these research findings can contribute to the assessment and considerations of market orientations for building a sustainable development environment. As mentioned in previous studies, it is important to understand market trends in order to develop specific strategies for sustainable tourism development (Ely, 2013; Kavoura & Bitsani, 2013; Milman, 2015; Orbasli, 2013). Additionally, this research also contributes to the literature reflected in the impacts of residents' perceptions of sustainable tourism development through the viewpoints of tourists and local authorities.

Second, the study also makes relevant contributions in identifying factors affecting support by local residents. Previous studies have examined the impacts of perception of values and benefits of residents on their participation, but they failed to include the context of sustainable development in urban areas. Thus, this study sheds light on such impacts for sustainable tourism development (Basu, 2003; Lee, 2013). In addition, this research also contributes a positive understanding of the relation between perceived values, benefits and support of residents in sustainable development with different factors thus contributing to the literature on sustainable tourism development.

Third, this study has shown that three factors directly influence the participation of residents. These are: perception of values, collaboration, and emotional solidarity. These factors have been verified through a survey model that shows that the link between these factors is the foundation for sustainable tourism development. In addition, while previous studies focused primarily on the perception of benefits for residents as the most important factor impacting upon support, this study contributes to the literature new assessments related to collaboration and emotional solidarity. Very few scholars have studied these factors in the context of sustainable tourism development in urban destinations. In addition, this study also indicates new findings: there is a link between collaboration and emotional solidarity in which emotional solidarity includes the emotional closeness, welcoming nature and sympathetic understanding that has such positive effect upon collaboration (Borlido, 2016; Kapera, 2017).

The study also makes practical contributions to tourism management in urban destinations. The results highlight the impact of residents' perception of value, collaboration and emotional solidarity as factors in residents' support for sustainable tourism development in urban destinations, namely HCMC, Vietnam. Therefore, local authorities should raise local residents' awareness to attract their support to ensure sustainable development through solutions such as propagandizing, education and training in order to impact positive perceptions of residents in the strategy of developing tourism in the community.

In addition, the findings of the study have implications for and may contribute to the promotion of related fields such as archeology, market management, social planning and development in general. Investment planning strategies in local tourism need to include surveys and evaluations in order to understand the perceptions of residents before making investments. The study appreciates the role of resident perceptions in sustainable development, so it can be considered a criterion for sustainable development. Consequently, it is necessary to have periodical consultation with residents to understand attitudes and perceptions in the decision-making process (Stylidis et al., 2014; Vargas-Sánchez et al.,2014). This strategy will reduce conflicts or negative aspects in sustainable development (Chhabra, 2010). The research results also provide values for local service providers and tourism operators, such as supporting the recruitment of local residents, improved infrastructure, and local community support (Bennett & Dearden, 2014). The purpose is to distribute the benefits appropriately according to the goal of sustainable development (Sebele, 2010; Stylidis et al.,2014). These solutions will help residents trust development and thus support businesses in advantageous ways during development processes. For example, travel agencies can advertise tourism products among local residents, promoting river culture, showing traditional costumes or appreciating local cuisine.

Limitations and research directions

The study was conducted in only three communities in HCMC; thus the sample fails to have good representative characteristics for all tourism activities in the urban destinations of HCMC. Consequently, future studies should be done on a broader scale with larger communities to ensure wider coverage and scale. In addition, the study fails to further identify specific perceived values among varieties of residents, so subsequent studies should have a distribution of perceived benefits and values such as economic, social-cultural, environmental, etc.

It is also suggested that future research direction requires a periodic assessment of residents' perceptions because the nature of perception is that it is easily influenced or easily changed by external factors. Future research may be done at each stage of a development cycle to improve effectiveness. Another interesting question is where future research could specify types of tourism such as cultural tourism, rural tourism and ecotourism to determine the degree to which sustainability is suitable within distinct destinations.

Disclosure statement

No potential conflict of interest was reported by the authors.

References

Li, Y., & Hunter, C. (2015). Community involvement for sustainable heritage tourism: A conceptual model. *Journal of Cultural Heritage Management and Sustainable Development*, 5(3), 248–262. https://doi.org/10.1108/JCHMSD-08-2014-0027

Anda, M., & Temmen, J. (2014). Smart metering for residential energy efficiency: The use of community based social marketing for behavioural change and smart grid introduction. *Renewable Energy*, 67, 119–127. https://doi.org/10.1016/j.renene.2013.11.020

Andereck, K. L., Valentine, K. M., Knopf, R. C., & Vogt, C. A. (2005). Residents' perceptions of community tourism impacts. *Annals of Tourism Research*, 32(4), 1056–1076. https://doi.org/10.1016/j.annals.2005.03.001

Basu, P. K. (2003). Is sustainable tourism development possible? Broad issues concerning Australia and Papua New Guinea. Tourism and economic development: Case studies from the Indian Ocean region, 140–149

Belletti, G., Marescotti, A., & Touzard, J. M. (2017). Geographical indications, public goods, and sustainable development: The roles of actors' strategies and public policies. *World Development*, 98, 45–57. https://doi.org/10.1016/j.worlddev.2015.05.004

Bennett, N. J., & Dearden, P. (2014). Why local people do not support conservation: Community perceptions of marine protected area livelihood impacts, governance and management in Thailand. *Marine Policy*, 44, 107–116. https://doi.org/10.1016/j.marpol.2013.08.017

Borlido, T. (2016). Law, social capital and tourism at Peneda-Gerês: An exploratory analysis of the leadership and decision-making processes. *Dos Algarves: A Multidisciplinary e-Journal*, 28(28), 29–44. https://doi.org/10.18089/DAMeJ.2016.28.1.3

But, J. W. P., & Ap, J. (2017). The impacts of casino tourism development on Macao residents' livelihood. *Worldwide Hospitality and Tourism Themes*, 9(3), 260–273. https://doi.org/10.1108/WHATT-02-2017-0011

Carlisle, S., Johansen, A., & Kunc, M. (2016). Strategic foresight for (coastal) urban tourism market complexity: The case of Bournemouth. *Tourism Management*, 54, 81–95. https://doi.org/10.1016/j.tourman.2015.10.005

Chen, C. F., & Phou, S. (2013). A closer look at destination: Image, personality, relationship and loyalty. *Tourism Management*, 36, 269–278. https://doi.org/10.1016/j.tourman.2012.11.015

Chhabra, D. (2010). Host community attitudes toward tourism development: The triggered tourism life cycle perspective. *Tourism Analysis*, 15(4), 471–484. https://doi.org/10.3727/108354210X12864727453340

Choi, H. C., & Murray, I. (2010). Resident attitudes toward sustainable community tourism. *Journal of Sustainable Tourism*, 18(4), 575–594. https://doi.org/10.1080/09669580903524852

De Pourcq, K., Thomas, E., Arts, B., Vranckx, A., Léon-Sicard, T., & Van Damme, P. (2017). Understanding and resolving conflict between local communities and conservation authorities in Colombia. *World Development*, 93, 125–135. https://doi.org/10.1016/j.worlddev.2016.12.026

Diedrich, A., & García-Buades, E. (2009). Local perceptions of tourism as indicators of destination decline. *Tourism Management*, 30(4), 512–521. https://doi.org/10.1016/j.tourman.2008.10.009

D'Mello, C., Chang, L. C., Pillai, S. K. B., Kamat, K., Zimmermann, F. M., & Weiermair, K. (2016). Comparison of multistakeholder perception of tourism sustainability in Goa. *International Journal of Hospitality & Tourism Systems*, 9(2).

Domínguez-Gómez, J. A., & González-Gómez, T. (2017). Analysing stakeholders' perceptions of golf-course-based tourism: A proposal for developing sustainable tourism projects. *Tourism Management*, 63, 135–143. https://doi.org/10.1016/j.tourman.2017.05.015

Dyer, P., Gursoy, D., Sharma, B., & Carter, J. (2007). Structural modeling of resident perceptions of tourism and associated development on the Sunshine Coast. *Tourism Management*, *28*(2), 409–422. https://doi.org/10.1016/j.tourman.2006.04.002

Ely, P. A. (2013). Selling Mexico: Marketing and tourism values. *Tourism Management Perspectives*, *8*, 80–89. https://doi.org/10.1016/j.tmp.2013.07.003

Erul, E., Woosnam, K. M., & McIntosh, W. A. (2020). Considering emotional solidarity and the theory of planned behavior in explaining behavioral intentions to support tourism development. *Journal of Sustainable Tourism*, *28*(8), 1158–1173. https://doi.org/10.1080/09669582.2020.1726935

Fidell, S., Tabachnick, B., Mestre, V., & Fidell, L. (2013). Aircraft noise-induced awakenings are more reasonably predicted from relative than from absolute sound exposure levels. *The Journal of the Acoustical Society of America*, *134*(5), 3645–3653. https://doi.org/10.1121/1.4823838

Fornell, C., & Larcker, D. F. (1981). Structural equation models with unobservable variables and measurement error: Algebra and statistics.

Goodwin, H. (2016). *Responsible tourism: Using tourism for sustainable development*. Goodfellow Publishers Ltd.

Gursoy, D., Chi, C. G., & Dyer, P. (2010). Locals' attitudes toward mass and alternative tourism: The case of Sunshine Coast. *Journal of Travel Research*, *49*(3), 381–394. https://doi.org/10.1177/0047287509346853

Gursoy, D., Jurowski, C., & Uysal, M. (2002). Resident attitudes: A structural modeling approach. *Annals of Tourism Research*, *29*(1), 79–105. https://doi.org/10.1016/S0160-7383(01)00028-7

Hair, J. F., Black, W. C., Babin, B. J., Anderson, R. E., & Tatham, R. L. (2009). *Análise multivariada de dados*. Bookman Editora.

Hanafiah, M. H., Azman, I., Jamaluddin, M. R., & Aminuddin, N. (2016). Responsible tourism practices and quality of Life: Perspective of Langkawi island communities. *Procedia - Social and Behavioral Sciences*, *222*, 406–413. https://doi.org/10.1016/j.sbspro.2016.05.194

Haobin Ye, B., Qiu Zhang, H., Huawen Shen, J., & Goh, C. (2014). Does social identity affect residents' attitude toward tourism development? An evidence from the relaxation of the Individual Visit Scheme. *International Journal of Contemporary Hospitality Management*, *26*(6), 907–929. https://doi.org/10.1108/IJCHM-01-2013-0041

Jaafar, M., Noor, S. M., & Rasoolimanesh, S. M. (2015). Perception of young local residents toward sustainable conservation programmes: A case study of the Lenggong World Cultural Heritage Site. *Tourism Management*, *48*, 154–163. https://doi.org/10.1016/j.tourman.2014.10.018

Ji, M., Li, M., & King, B. (2015). The Impacts of China's new free-trade zones on Hong Kong tourism. *Journal of Destination Marketing & Management*, *4*(4), 203–205.

Joo, D., Woosnam, K. M., Shafer, C. S., Scott, D., & An, S. (2017). Considering Tobler's first law of geography in a tourism context. *Tourism Management*, *62*, 350–359. https://doi.org/10.1016/j.tourman.2017.03.021

Kapera, I. (2018). Sustainable tourism development efforts by local governments in Poland. *Sustainable Cities and Society*, *40*, 581–588. https://doi.org/10.1016/j.scs.2018.05.001

Kavoura, A., & Bitsani, E. (2013). Managing the world heritage site of the Acropolis. *International Journal of Culture, Tourism and Hospitality Research*, *7*(1), 58–67. https://doi.org/10.1108/17506181311301363

Lai, I. K. W., & Hitchcock, M. (2017). Local reactions to mass tourism and community tourism development in Macau. *Journal of Sustainable Tourism*, *25*(4), 451–470. https://doi.org/10.1080/09669582.2016.1221413

Lankford, S. V., & Howard, D. R. (1994). Developing a tourism impact attitude scale. *Annals of Tourism Research*, *21*(1), 121–139. https://doi.org/10.1016/0160-7383(94)90008-6

Lee, T. H. (2013). Influence analysis of community resident support for sustainable tourism development. *Tourism Management*, *34*, 37–46. https://doi.org/10.1016/j.tourman.2012.03.007

Lee, C. K., & Back, K. J. (2006). Examining structural relationships among perceived impact, benefit, and support for casino development based on 4 year longitudinal data. *Tourism Management*, *27*(3), 466–480. https://doi.org/10.1016/j.tourman.2004.11.009

Lee, T. H., & Hsieh, H. P. (2016). Indicators of sustainable tourism: A case study from a Taiwan's wetland. *Ecological Indicators*, *67*, 779–787. https://doi.org/10.1016/j.ecolind.2016.03.023

Lee, C. K., Kang, S. K., Long, P., & Reisinger, Y. (2010). Residents' perceptions of casino impacts: A comparative study. *Tourism Management*, *31*(2), 189–201. https://doi.org/10.1016/j.tourman.2009.02.011

Liao, Y. T., & Chern, S. G. (2015). Strategic ecocity development in urban–rural fringes: Analyzing Wulai District. *Sustainable Cities and Society*, *19*, 98–108. https://doi.org/10.1016/j.scs.2015.07.014

Lin, Y., Kerstetter, D., Nawijn, J., & Mitas, O. (2014). Changes in emotions and their interactions with personality in a vacation context. *Tourism Management*, *40*, 416–424. https://doi.org/10.1016/j.tourman.2013.07.013

Liu, J., Nijkamp, P., Huang, X., & Lin, D. (2017). Urban livability and tourism development in China: Analysis of sustainable development by means of spatial panel data. *Habitat International*, *68*, 99–107. https://doi.org/10.1016/j.habitatint.2017.02.005

Li, X., & Wan, Y. K. P. (2017). Residents' support for festivals: Integration of emotional solidarity. *Journal of Sustainable Tourism*, *25*(4), 517–535. https://doi.org/10.1080/09669582.2016.1224889

Lundberg, E. (2015). The level of tourism development and resident attitudes: A comparative case study of coastal destinations. *Scandinavian Journal of Hospitality and Tourism, 15*(3), 266–294. https://doi.org/10.1080/15022250.2015.1005335

Mathew, P. V., & Sreejesh, S. (2017). Impact of responsible tourism on destination sustainability and quality of life of community in tourism destinations. *Journal of Hospitality and Tourism Management, 31*, 83–89. https://doi.org/10.1016/j.jhtm.2016.10.001

McDowall, S., & Choi, Y. (2010). Thailand's destination image through the eyes of its citizens. *International Journal of Hospitality & Tourism Administration, 11*(3), 255–274.

McGehee, N. G., Andereck, K. L., & Vogt, C. A. (2002, June). An examination of factors influencing resident attitudes toward tourism in twelve Arizona communities. In *Proceedings of the 33rd Annual Travel and Tourism Research Association Conference*, Arlington, VA.

McKinley, D. C., Miller-Rushing, A. J., Ballard, H. L., Bonney, R., Brown, H., Cook-Patton, S. C., Evans, D. M., French, R. A., Parrish, J. K., Phillips, T. B., Ryan, S. F., Shanley, L. A., Shirk, J. L., Stepenuck, K. F., Weltzin, J. F., Wiggins, A., Boyle, O. D., Briggs, R. D., Chapin, S. F., … Soukup, M. A. (2017). Citizen science can improve conservation science, natural resource management, and environmental protection. *Biological Conservation, 208*, 15–28. https://doi.org/10.1016/j.biocon.2016.05.015

Mihalic, T. (2016). Sustainable-responsible tourism discourse–Towards 'responsustable'tourism. *Journal of Cleaner Production, 111*, 461–470. https://doi.org/10.1016/j.jclepro.2014.12.062

Mika, M. (2015). Sustainable tourism: A critique of the academic feasibility of the concept. *Turyzm/Tourism, 25*(1), 9–17. https://doi.org/10.2478/tour-2014-0015

Milman, O. (2015). Australia bans hunting'trophies' from lions entering or leaving the country. *The Guardian*, 13.

Moghavvemi, S., Woosnam, K. M., Paramanathan, T., Musa, G., & Hamzah, A. (2017). The effect of residents' personality, emotional solidarity, and community commitment on support for tourism development. *Tourism Management, 63*, 242–254. https://doi.org/10.1016/j.tourman.2017.06.021

Nicholas, L. N., Thapa, B., & Ko, Y. J. (2009). Residents'perspectives of a world heritage site: The pitons management area, St. Lucia. *Annals of Tourism Research, 36*(3), 390–412. https://doi.org/10.1016/j.annals.2009.03.005

Niezgoda, A., & Czernek, K. (2014). Stake holders' relations hips in the sustainable development of tourist destinations. *Zeszyty Naukowe Uniwersytetu Szczecińskiego Ekonomiczne Problemy Turystyki, 4*(28), 39–52.

Nunkoo, R., Smith, S. L., & Ramkissoon, H. (2013). Residents' attitudes to tourism: A longitudinal study of 140 articles from 1984 to 2010. *Journal of Sustainable Tourism, 21*(1), 5–25. https://doi.org/10.1080/09669582.2012.673621

Nunnally, J. C., & Bernstein, I. H. (1994). *Psychometric theory (McGraw-Hill series in psychology)* (Vol. 3). McGraw-Hill.

Orbaşli, A. (2013). Archaeological site management and local development. *Conservation and Management of Archaeological Sites, 15*(3–4), 237–253. https://doi.org/10.1179/1350503314Z.00000000059

Patwardhan, V., Ribeiro, M. A., Payini, V., Woosnam, K. M., Mallya, J., & Gopalakrishnan, P. (2020). Visitors' place attachment and destination loyalty: Examining the roles of emotional solidarity and perceived safety. *Journal of Travel Research, 59*(1), 3–21. https://doi.org/10.1177/0047287518824157

People's Committee of Ho Chi Minh City. (2019). *Report on the implementation of economic, social on Ho Chi Minh City in 2018*. Report of People's Committee of Ho Chi Minh City (Vietnamese).

Prayag, G., Hosany, S., & Odeh, K. (2013). The role of tourists' emotional experiences and satisfaction in understanding behavioral intentions. *Journal of Destination Marketing & Management, 2*(2), 118–127.

Rasoolimanesh, S. M., & Jaafar, M. (2016). Community participation toward tourism development and conservation program in rural world heritage sites. In *Tourism-from empirical research towards practical application*. InTech.

Rasoolimanesh, S. M., Jaafar, M., Kock, N., & Ramayah, T. (2015). A revised framework of social exchange theory to investigate the factors influencing residents' perceptions. *Tourism Management Perspectives, 16*, 335–345. https://doi.org/10.1016/j.tmp.2015.10.001

Rastegar, M., Hatami, H., & Mirjafari, R. (2017). Role of social capital in improving the quality of life and social justice in Mashhad. *Sustainable Cities and Society, 34*, 109–113. https://doi.org/10.1016/j.scs.2017.05.024

Ritchie, S. M., & Rigano, D. L. (2007). Solidarity through collaborative research. *International Journal of Qualitative Studies in Education, 20*(2), 129–150. https://doi.org/10.1080/09518390601159610

Sebele, L. S. (2010). Community-based tourism ventures, benefits and challenges: Khama rhino sanctuary trust, central district. *Tourism Management, 31*(1), 136–146. https://doi.org/10.1016/j.tourman.2009.01.005

Sharma, B., & Gursoy, D. (2015). An examination of changes in residents' perceptions of tourism impacts over time: The impact of residents' socio-demographic characteristics. *Asia Pacific Journal of Tourism Research, 20*(12), 1332–1352. https://doi.org/10.1080/10941665.2014.982665

Siu, G., Lee, L. Y., & Leung, D. (2013). Residents' perceptions toward the "Chinese tourists' wave" in Hong Kong: An exploratory study. *Asia Pacific Journal of Tourism Research, 18*(5), 446–463. https://doi.org/10.1080/10941665.2012.665062

Stylidis, D., Biran, A., Sit, J., & Szivas, E. M. (2014). Residents' support for tourism development: The role of residents' place image and perceived tourism impacts. *Tourism Management, 45*, 260–274. https://doi.org/10.1016/j.tourman.2014.05.006

Tasci, D. A. A., Croes, R., & Bartels Villanueva, J. (2014). Rise and fall of community-based tourism–facilitators, inhibitors and outcomes. *Worldwide Hospitality and Tourism Themes*, *6*(3), 261–276.

Tolkach, D., & King, B. (2015). Strengthening community-based tourism in a new resource-based island nation: Why and how? *Tourism Management*, *48*, 386–398. https://doi.org/10.1016/j.tourman.2014.12.013

Truong, V. D. (2013). Tourism policy development in Vietnam: A pro-poor perspective. *Journal of Policy Research in Tourism, Leisure and Events*, *5*(1), 28–45. https://doi.org/10.1080/19407963.2012.760224

Vargas-Sánchez, A., Porras-Bueno, N., & de los Ángeles Plaza-Mejía, M. (2014). Residents' attitude to tourism and seasonality. *Journal of Travel Research*, *53*(5), 581–596. https://doi.org/10.1177/0047287513506295

Vogt, C., Jordan, E., Grewe, N., & Kruger, L. (2016). Collaborative tourism planning and subjective well-being in a small island destination. *Journal of Destination Marketing & Management*, *5*(1), 36–43.

Wang, Y., & Pfister, R. E. (2008). Residents' attitudes toward tourism and perceived personal benefits in a rural community. *Journal of Travel Research*, *47*(1), 84–93. https://doi.org/10.1177/0047287507312402

Wight, P. A. (1993). Sustainable ecotourism: Balancing economic, environmental and social goals within an ethical framework. *Journal of Tourism Studies*, *4*(2), 54–66.

Woo, E., Kim, H., & Uysal, M. (2015). Life satisfaction and support for tourism development. *Annals of Tourism Research*, *50*, 84–97. https://doi.org/10.1016/j.annals.2014.11.001

Woolf, S. H., Zimmerman, E., Haley, A., & Krist, A. H. (2016). Authentic engagement of patients and communities can transform research, practice, and policy. *Health Affairs*, *35*(4), 590–594. https://doi.org/10.1377/hlthaff.2015.1512

Woosnam, K. M. (2011). Testing a model of Durkheim's theory of emotional solidarity among residents of a tourism community. *Journal of Travel Research*, *50*(5), 546–558. https://doi.org/10.1177/0047287510379163

Woosnam, K. M. (2012). Using emotional solidarity to explain residents' attitudes about tourism and tourism development. *Journal of Travel Research*, *51*(3), 315–327. https://doi.org/10.1177/0047287511410351

Woosnam, K. M., Aleshinloye, K. D., Van Winkle, C. M., & Qian, W. (2014). Applying and expanding the theoretical framework of emotional solidarity in a festival context. *Event Management*, *18*(2), 141–151. https://doi.org/10.3727/152599514X13947236947428

Woosnam, K. M., & Norman, W. C. (2010). Measuring residents' emotional solidarity with tourists: Scale development of Durkheim's theoretical constructs. *Journal of Travel Research*, *49*(3), 365–380. https://doi.org/10.1177/0047287509346858

Woo, E., Uysal, M., & Sirgy, M. J. (2018). Tourism impact and stakeholders' quality of life. *Journal of Hospitality & Tourism Research*, *42*(2), 260–286.

Appendix A. Supplementary data

TABLE A1. Survey instruments and factor loadings of the items.

Constructs	Number of items	Measure items	Sources
Residents' Perceived Value (PS)	5	PS1. The sustainable tourism development of this community has benefited me PS2. The sustainable tourism development of this community has benefited all local residents. PS3. The sustainable tourism development of this community has increased employment opportunities in this region. PS4. The sustainable tourism development of this community has increased individual incomes in this region. PS5. The sustainable tourism development of this community has increased investments in the region.	(Lee & Back, 2006 and Lee et al. (2010).)
Collaboration (CO)	8	CO1. I think there should be good collaboration between government agencies in the development of tourism of the city. CO2. I think that there should be good collaboration between local governments in the development of the city tourism CO3. I think there should be good collaboration between tourism organizations in the development of tourism of the city CO4. I think there should be good collaboration between related organizations in the development of tourism of the city CO5. I think there should be good collaboration between the businesses in developing the city's tourism CO6. I think there should be good collaboration between the media organizations in the development of tourism of the city CO7. I think there should be good collaboration among local residents in the development of tourism of the city CO8. I think there should be good collaboration n among tourists in the development of tourism of the city	Kapera, I. (2018)
Emotional closeness (EC)	4	EC1. I feel close to some tourists I met in this area/community EC2. I have made friends with some tourists in this area/community EC3. I enjoy interacting with tourists EC4. My interactions with tourists are positive and useful	Woosnam and Norman (2010)
Welcoming Nature (WN)	4	WN1. I am proud to have tourists in this area/community WN2. I feel the community benefits from having tourists in this area WN3. I appreciate tourists for the contribution they make to the local economy WN4. I treat tourists well in this area/community	Woosnam and Norman (2010)
Sympathetic Understanding (SU)	3	SU1. I have a lot in common with the tourists in this area/community	Woosnam and Norman (2010)

(*continued*)

TABLE A1. Continued.

Constructs	Number of items	Measure items	Sources
		SU2. I feel affection towards tourists in this area/community	
		SU3. I understand tourists in this area/community	
Support for Sustainable Tourism Development (RS)	4	RS1. I believe that tourism should be actively encouraged in my community	(Rasoolimanesh & Jaafar, 2016; Wang & Pfister, 2008).
		RS2. I support tourism and would like to see it becomes an important part of my community	
		RS3. The local authorities and state government should support the promotion of tourism.	
		RS4. Long-term planning by city officials can control the negative impacts of tourism on the environment	

Hapless victims or empowered citizens? Understanding residents' attitudes towards Airbnb using Weber's Theory of Rationality and Foucauldian concepts

Makarand Mody, Kyle Maurice Woosnam, Courtney Suess and Tarik Dogru

ABSTRACT

Airbnb has been criticized about its negative impacts on residents' quality of life. Yet, extant research on the topic is limited, both in volume and theoretical and empirical efficacy. In light of the need to advance theory-driven research on resident attitudes in tourism, the present study develops and tests an innovative theoretical framework that combines the tenets of Weber's Theory of Rationality and Foucauldian concepts of power, knowledge, and governmentality, to examine non-hosting residents' attitudes towards Airbnb. Findings show that, contrary to popular discourse, non-hosting residents who do not directly participate in Airbnb perceive higher positive than negative impacts. A higher level of psychological, social, and political empowerment—a manifestation of Weber's substantive rationality and the Foucauldian concept of power—both directly and indirectly impacted non-hosting residents' support for Airbnb, while their knowledge of Airbnb and the potential for personal benefits—a manifestation of Weber's formal rationality—had significant direct effects on their levels of Airbnb support. Interestingly, trust in political decision-making—a facet of Foucault's concept of governmentality—did not impact residents' support for Airbnb either directly or indirectly, indicating that the prospect of better governance is not a pre-requisite for residents to support the homesharing phenomenon. Moderation testing along three demographic and three situational moderators reveals differences among sub-groups of residents, and contributes to a theoretically- and empirically-rigorous nomological framework of residents' attitudes towards Airbnb, which can be used by researchers to examine the dynamics of other types of tourism development. For practitioners, including sharing economy platforms, hosts, and policy makers, our findings emphasize the need for strategies that enhance non-hosting residents' sense of agency vis-à-vis the sharing economy as critical to garnering their support.

Introduction

The rapid growth of the sharing economy has been accompanied by an increase in research output on the phenomenon, with Airbnb—as the largest provider of peer-to-peer (P2P) accommodation in the world—arguably being its most prominent posterchild (Dann et al., 2019). While researchers have examined a variety of topics pertaining to Airbnb (Guttentag, 2019), its impact on residents has emerged as a more recent area of research interest (Jordan & Moore, 2018). More specifically, Airbnb and other similar short-term vacation rentals (STVRs) are often portrayed as having negative impacts on residential communities, both in academic research (Yeager et al., 2020), and in popular media (Mody, Suess, & Dogru et al., 2019), with stories largely emphasizing Airbnb's negative impacts on residents' quality of life (QOL) (Shankman, 2017). In fact, the American Hotel and Lodging Association (AH&LA) has used Airbnb's negative socio-economic impacts on residents as one of the key pillars for lobbying against the company (Elliott, 2016).

It is undeniable that residents' perspectives are critical in planning and managing for the sustainable development of any form of tourism (Ribeiro et al., 2018a). Airbnb is no exception to this assertion; its long-term sustainability as a provider of P2P accommodation hinges on its ability to contribute to the sustainable development of the destinations in which it operates. This requires that the perspectives of residents in these destinations—both those who host on the platform, and, more importantly, those who do not (hereafter referred to as *non-hosting residents*)—are considered to inform strategic and policy decisions that strengthen the positive and mitigate the negative socio-economic impacts of the sharing economy.

While some recent progress has been made to understand resident attitudes towards Airbnb and other STVRs, extant research on this issue has been limited in its theoretical, methodological, and/or geographical scope. In particular, we are yet to comprehensively understand—either theoretically and empirically—the perspectives of arguably the largest stakeholder group associated with the sharing phenomenon, non-hosting residents, leaving a critical unattended gap in sharing economy literature and practice. In light of these limitations, the objective of the present study is to develop and test an innovative theoretical framework that combines the tenets of Weber's Theory of Rationality and Foucauldian concepts of power, knowledge, and governmentality, to examine non-hosting residents' attitudes towards Airbnb. The salience of this theoretical framework is emphasized by Yeager et al. (2020), who highlight that the contentious process associated with Airbnb's development in some communities occurs "particularly if nonhost residents perceive a lack of agency in supporting or declining the growth of STVRs" (p. 1).

Using an alternative-model comparison procedure, and a representative sample from the United States, our findings support the perspective that residents are not hapless victims of Airbnb's negative externalities, as is often portrayed in academic and media discourse. In fact, the average non-hosting resident perceived that Airbnb has greater positive impacts on their neighborhoods than it has negative impacts. Moreover, we found that a higher level of psychological, social, and political empowerment—a manifestation of Weber's substantive rationality and the Foucauldian concept of power—both directly and indirectly impacted non-hosting residents' support for Airbnb, while their knowledge of Airbnb and the potential for personal benefits—a manifestation of Weber's formal rationality— had significant direct effects on their levels of Airbnb support. Interestingly, trust in political decision-making—a facet of Foucault's concept of governmentality—did not impact residents' support for Airbnb either directly or indirectly, indicating that the prospect of better governance is not a pre-requisite for residents to support the homesharing phenomenon. Instead, the symbiotic relationship between residents' empowerment pertaining to Airbnb development in their neighborhoods and their knowledge of Airbnb drive a higher perception of its positive impacts and support for the phenomenon. We further tested the superior Weberian and Foucauldian-derived model across different subgroups of non-host residents, differentiated by important demographic (i.e., age, gender, and income) and situational moderators (i.e., own vs. rent, length of residence in the community, and previous Airbnb experience as a guest). Our results thus contribute to a theoretically- and empirically-rigorous nomological framework of residents' attitudes towards Airbnb. While developed in the context of the sharing economy, our framework can be applied by future researchers to comprehensively examine the dynamics of other types of tourism development—both the nascent and the more established. From a practitioner standpoint, our study offers strategies surrounding the critical issue of agency among the important stakeholder group of non-hosting residents.

Literature review

Research on resident attitudes towards tourism

The literature on resident attitudes towards tourism is extensive, "has reached a stage of active scholarship in theory development followed by empirical testing" (Nunkoo et al., 2013, p. 5). Residents are an important group of stakeholders whose lives are impacted by tourism development; thus, understanding their perceptions is viewed as a pre-requisite to effective community participation in tourism planning. Researchers in this area have used a variety of theoretical perspectives to examine resident attitudes. Social exchange theory (SET) is arguably the most prominent, and examines residents' attitudes towards and support for tourism (or lack thereof) as a manifestation of their evaluations of the benefits and costs resulting from tourism development. To a lesser extent, researchers have used alternative theoretical frameworks such as social representation theory, institutional theory, and bottom-up spillover theory to examine resident attitudes (Hadinejad et al., 2019). For example, Khazaei et al. (2015) draw on stakeholder theory in the management field to explore the engagement of the fringe stakeholder group of first-generation immigrants in tourism planning, advocating for "a more inclusive approach to community engagement, reflecting increased diversity and change in host communities" (p. 1049). While these alternative frameworks provide new and interesting insights that are not captured by overly-rational orientation of SET, researcher engagement with them is limited (Hadinejad et al., 2019). Research on resident attitudes towards Airbnb (and/or the sharing economy) offers similar theoretical and empirical shortcomings, which are discussed below and which the present study aims to overcome.

Research on resident attitudes concerning Airbnb/STVRs

Research focusing on Airbnb has exponentially increased in the last five years, notably marked by changing policies within destination planning, competition with the traditional lodging sector (Dogru et al., 2019), and the growing utilization of peer-to-peer (P2P) accommodations. In reviewing the burgeoning research on Airbnb, Guttentag (2019) revealed that the six most common lines of research focused on the P2P company are: Airbnb guests, Airbnb hosts, Airbnb supply and its impact on destinations, Airbnb regulation, Airbnb's impact on the tourism sector, and the Airbnb company overall. That said, the line of research focused on residents' perspectives of Airbnb is recently gaining some steam (Jordan & Moore, 2018). Such study has been motivated, in particular, by stories about Airbnb's contribution to *overtourism* in several destinations (Peltier, 2018), and the tourism-phobia that results from its negative externalities, for example in the case of Barcelona (Ramos & Mundet, 2020). According to Doorn (2019), Airbnb's pursuit of *platform urbanism*—initiatives that seek to impact the materiality, daily lives and governance of cities (Söderström & Mermet, 2020)—have resulted in an institution that aims to co-shape current and future policy debates pertaining to the very fabric of city life and its residents. Thus, the steady increase in considering residents' perspectives is likely due to the growing understanding that when considering impacts of Airbnb, stakeholders are not just hosts and their guests; equally impacted are non-hosting residents (Suess et al., 2020a, 2020b).

Some of the initial qualitative research incorporating non-hosting residents has revealed somewhat mixed findings. Whereas Jordan and Moore (2018) found that residents on Oahu, Hawaii (U.S.) perceived a fairly equal degree of positive and negative impacts (i.e., economic, environmental, and sociocultural), Stergiou and Farmaki (2019) revealed residents in Athens (Greece) predominantly perceived more negative socio-economic and environmental impacts of P2P accommodations. Richards et al. (2019) had similar findings in their research focused on Barcelona residents, indicating that locals felt displaced by tourists (therefore precipitating an anti-tourist sentiment) and that authenticity experiences afforded by P2P accommodations was illusory. In a study of stakeholder perspectives of Airbnb's disruptive impacts on host communities in Queenstown, New Zealand, Cheng et al. (2020) confirmed the complexity of Airbnb growth, "characterised by multiple and conflicting interests, and potential paradoxes in destination management policies". These results are generally consistent with the negative media rhetoric around Airbnb's impacts on destinations and residents' quality of life (Shankman, 2017).

The quantitative work focusing on residents' perspectives of P2P accommodations tends to be less ambiguous. Using the protection motivation theory, Suess et al. (2020a) found that place attachment and economic benefits each uniquely predicted non-hosting residents' emotional solidarity with visitors, which, in turn, explained a sense of feeling safe and ultimately, support for Airbnb (among those with children living in their households). Suess et al. (2020b) also considered both the cognitive appraisal theory and bottom-up spillover theory of subjective well-being to show that non-hosting residents' emotional solidarity with Airbnb guests predicts emotional responses to Airbnb, which influences overall community well-being and personal quality of life (all of which was more pronounced among those with prior experience staying at an Airbnb themselves). Yeager et al. (2020) most recently found that personal economic benefits and empowerment significantly influenced both hosting and non-hosting residents' perceived impacts STVRs and overall support for STVRs in Savannah, Georgia. Sampling residents in Tenerife, Spain, Garau-Vadell et al. (2019) reported that perceptions of the current state of the local economy, the sharing economy overall, and personal economic benefits from P2P all explained residents' perceived impacts of and support for P2P accommodations. Finally, Stienmetz et al. (2019) found that most U.K. residents held neutral opinions of P2P accommodations, with a majority of residents believing such lodging opportunities brought positive economic and negative environmental impacts on quality of life.

Though the research considering residents' perspectives of Airbnb and other STVRs is growing, some notable gaps exist within the extant literature. First, with the exception of Suess et al. (2020a, 2020b), most extant research does not differentiate between the attitudes of host and non-host residents (e.g., Garau-Vadell et al., 2019); thus, it does not present a representative account of the average non-hosting resident, those who are typically highlighted in the media as bearing the brunt of Airbnb's negative externalities. Second, research on this topic tends to be limited in geographical scope, largely focusing on specific, unique destinations (e.g., Jordan & Moore, 2018). Third, from a methodological standpoint, no previous study compared alternative models to evaluate the perspective that provides the strongest theoretical and empirical explanation of resident attitudes towards Airbnb. Finally, the major theoretical framework used in previous research has been that of social exchange theory (SET), which, as Yeager et al. (2020) highlight, "is often criticized for its bias toward inflating the economic costs and benefits of social transactions between visitors and hosts without considering noneconomic factors that may influence residents' support for tourism" (p. 2). Moreover, as Sharpley (2014) pointed out, within the resident perception research, SET is "typically interpreted somewhat simplistically in in the sense that it is argued that, should residents perceive that the costs of tourism (social, economic and/or environmental) outweigh the benefits, then they will have negative perceptions of and withdraw their support for tourism" (p. 45). Other theoretical frameworks, while illuminating, are seldom used. In the present study, we overcome these various limitations by developing and testing an innovative theoretical framework that combines the tenets of Weber's Theory of

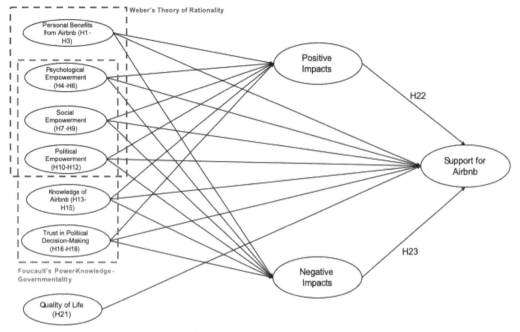

Figure 1. Main model—Weberian and Foucauldian framework.

Rationality and Foucauldian concepts of power, knowledge, and governmentality, to examine the attitudes of U.S. non-hosting residents towards Airbnb. The constructs and relationships offered by these two theories to explain residents attitudes go beyond the overly-rational and simplistic interpretation of SET to account for the wider socio-cultural determinants of residents' attitudes. Moreover, as compared to other theories like social representation, our framework not only captures residents' social construction of their reality vis-à-vis Airbnb ("the what") but also explains how ("the process") that reality is constructed (Sharpley, 2014).

Figure 1 presents the main model that was developed on the basis on this unique theoretical framework; its hypotheses will be explained in the following sections.

Weber's formal and substantive rationality and Airbnb's impacts

One theoretical perspective that has been advanced within the tourism literature (coming from the classical sociologist Max Weber's work) is the theory of formal and substantive rationality. As Yeager et al. (2020) contend, the theory includes both economic and non-economic factors in explaining why residents arrive at the attitudes they do regarding tourism (Boley et al., 2014). In a basic sense, the theory indicates that decisions are made based on the interplay between extrinsic (i.e., formal) motivations and intrinsic (i.e., substantive) motivations. The former is considered when decisions are to be made regarding rational, economic situations (Yeager et al., 2020); the latter is at play when decisions are to be made concerning more deeply-held beliefs, values, or norms (Boley et al., 2014).

Weber's theory has been employed within both the general tourism literature as well as in the context of Airbnb, though the latter, sparingly. One of the first studies to consider the theory was by Boley et al. (2014), whereby the authors found that empowerment through tourism (e.g., psychological, social, and political)—representing Weber's substantive rationality—served to be a better predictor of the positive/negative impacts of tourism and support of tourism than did personal economic benefits from tourism—representing Weber's substantive rationality. Furthermore, both positive and negative impacts significantly explained a substantial degree of variance ($R^2 = 0.51$) in support for tourism. Excluding perceptions of tourism impacts and only considering empowerment and support for tourism, Strzelecka et al. (2017) found that only psychological and social empowerment explained 18% of the variance in support for tourism; once more, personal economic benefit was not significant within the model. Contrary to this, Rasoolimanesh et al. (2017) revealed that economic gain indeed did significantly explain both positive and negative perceptions of tourism. Interestingly enough, only positive perceptions (not negative perceptions) significantly predicted support for tourism development, explaining 39% of the variance in the construct. Zuo et al. (2017) employed somewhat different forms of extrinsic (formal) and intrinsic (substantive) motivations, revealing that perceived benefits and costs significantly predicted residents' support for tourism ($R^2 = 0.45$).

Most recently, Weber's theory of rationality has been employed within the specific context of residents' attitudes towards STVRs (Yeager et al., 2020). What the authors found (in running a model nearly identical to Boley et al., 2014) was that even though personal economic benefits from STVRs significantly explained both positive and negative impacts of STVRs, such benefits did not predict support for STVRs. Additionally, of the nine hypotheses considering the role of the three forms of empowerment on impacts and support, seven were significant (i.e., political empowerment was the weakest dimensional predictor). Overall, Yeager et al. (2020) found that positive and negative impacts of STVRs explained 72% of the variance in support or STVRs. In the present study, since we examine the perspective of non-hosting residents—those who have never hosted on Airbnb—we conceptualize personal benefits as the "potential for personal benefits from Airbnb", i.e., we conceptualize this construct as the extent to which non-hosting residents perceive that they may derive personal benefits from Airbnb in the future.

Based on the preceding presentation of extant empirical research utilizing Weber's theory of formal and substantive rationality (primarily centered on perceived economic benefits and empowerment through tourism), the following hypotheses are advanced in the context of residents' perspectives of Airbnb:

H_1: Personal benefits from Airbnb will significantly increase perceived positive impacts of Airbnb.

H_2: Personal benefits from Airbnb will significantly decrease perceived negative impacts of Airbnb.

H_3: Personal benefits from Airbnb will significantly increase support for Airbnb.

H_4: Psychological empowerment will significantly increase perceived positive impacts of Airbnb.

H_5: Psychological empowerment will significantly decrease perceived negative impacts of Airbnb.

H_6: Psychological empowerment will significantly increase resident support for Airbnb.

H_7: Social empowerment will significantly increase perceived positive impacts of Airbnb.

H_8: Social empowerment will significantly decrease perceived negative impacts of Airbnb.

H_9: Social empowerment will significantly increase resident support for Airbnb.

H_{10}: Political empowerment will significantly increase perceived positive impacts of Airbnb.

H_{11}: Political empowerment will significantly decrease perceived negative impacts of Airbnb.

H_{12}: Political empowerment will significantly increase resident support for Airbnb.

Foucault's power, knowledge, and governmentality and Airbnb's impacts

In addition to being supported by Weber's concept of substantive rationality, Yeager et al. (2020) conceptualization of empowerment as—"a multidimensional, context-dependent, and dynamic process that provides humans, individually or collectively, with greater agency, freedom, and capacity to improve their quality of life as a function of engagement within the phenomenon of tourism" (Aghazamani & Hunt, as cited in Yeager et al., 2020, p. 959)—is representative of Foucault's notion of power as being "omnipresent in all aspects of tourism development" (Yeager et al., 2020, p. 959), and "manifesting itself within the social relationships between the tripartite of tourism actors (tourists, residents, and tourism brokers)" (Boley et al., 2014, p. 34). The introduction of tourism, in any of its forms—in the present case, in the "intrusive form" of Airbnb—has a bearing on the social organization and fabric of the respective communities (Mody & Koslowsky, 2019). In this regard, Foucault's conceptualization of power encourages researchers to examine whether and how the introduction of tourism impacts the "relations of power" from the perspective of different stakeholders.

However, as Wearing and Mcdonald (2002) discuss in their examination of the relationships between tourism intermediaries and communities in Papua New Guinea using a Foucauldian framework, "power and knowledge directly imply one another; there is no power relation without the correlative constitution of a field of knowledge, nor any knowledge that does not presuppose and constitute at the same time power relations" (Foucault, 1977, as cited in Wearing & Mcdonald, 2002, p. 196). Thus, according to Foucauldian theory, there exists a symbiotic relationship between the power in relation to and knowledge of a specific phenomenon, whereby "through our actions (what we say, what we think) we acquire knowledge of reality and thereby influence, consciously or subconsciously, our surroundings, just as we ourselves are influenced by what goes on around us" (Wearing & Mcdonald, 2002, p. 196). In the context of residents' attitudes, Nunkoo and So (2016) identified residents' knowledge of tourism—their understanding of tourism development issues—as central to the sustainability and good governance of the sector. This is because residents who are knowledgeable about tourism are more cognizant of both the benefits and the costs of tourism activity to communities (Andereck et al., 2005). For example, in their study of world heritage destinations, Rasoolimanesh et al. (2017) found that knowledge of tourism did significantly explain both positive and negative perceptions of tourism. Similarly, in the context of STVRs in Majorca, Gutiérrez-Taño et al. (2019) found that the perception of both the benefits and the costs of P2P accommodation rental activity increases if there is a greater knowledge of the activity. Based on these relationships, we hypothesize:

H_{13}: Knowledge of Airbnb will significantly increase perceived positive impacts of Airbnb.

H_{14}: Knowledge of Airbnb will significantly increase perceived negative impacts of Airbnb.

In addition to the relationships between knowledge of a particular tourism activity and its benefits and costs, extant research has also established that knowledgeable residents are also more positive in their support for tourism development. Some of the earlier examinations of this relationship support the role of knowledge of tourism as a pre-requisite to garnering resident support for tourism planning. In one of the earliest such studies, Davis et al. (1988) found that "lovers" of tourism in Florida had a high level of knowledge about tourism, while haters had a low level of knowledge. Such a positive relationship between knowledge and support for tourism is further evidenced in Olya and Gavilyan (2017) study, in which they used fuzzy set Qualitative Comparative Analysis (fsQCA) and complexity theory to conclude that a higher knowledge of tourism lead to higher levels of residents' support for tourism development in Iran. Similarly, Vetitnev and Bobina (2017) found that residents who were more knowledgeable about the Sochi

Games demonstrated more positive attitudes towards hosting them. Based on this previous research, we hypothesize:

> H_{15}: Knowledge of Airbnb will significantly increase resident support for Airbnb.

By developing and testing H_4-H_{15}, our study in the context of Airbnb parallels Wearing et al. (2010) qualitative examination of how the Foucauldian concepts of power and knowledge modulate the perceptions of the benefits and costs that underlie the determination of the sustainability of tourism development in Papua New Guinea. However, there is one additional construct from the Foucauldian framework that is relevant to the present examination of resident attitudes towards Airbnb. As highlighted by Nunkoo and So (2016), knowledge of tourism also refers to the role of local government in industry. This reveals the importance of the concept of governmentality, which according to Foucault, is largely a question of "how people govern themselves and others through the production and reproduction of knowledge" (Wearing & Mcdonald, 2002, p. 197). In their study of tourism in Barcelona, Ramos and Mundet (2020) found that the municipal government's inability to manage tourism effectively strengthened the tourism-phobic sentiment among residents, suggesting that trust in the local government to take the right actions in the interest of residents would have enhanced perceptions of tourism's positive benefits and translated into higher support from residents. In a comparative study of three cities in the U.S., Speier (2017) examined how the local government of Portland adopted a balanced approach to regulating Airbnb that achieved an ideal middle ground between preserving an owner's right to engage in short-term rentals and protecting the nature of the city for all residents. Thus, by protecting non-hosting residents from Airbnb's negative externalities such as nuisances and rising rents, the government's actions inspired a high level of trust among residents, which, in turn, allowed for the sustainable development of Airbnb activity. These relationships between trust in government, as a manifestation of Foucault's governmentality, and residents' perceptions of tourism's positive and negative impacts, and their support for tourism, have been examined in other studies. For example, Nunkoo and So (2016) found that trust in government enhanced residents' perceptions of tourism's positive impacts, while Ouyang et al. (2017) and Gursoy et al. (2017) found that it enhanced residents' perceptions of positive impacts and reduced perceptions of negative impacts surrounding tourism events. Relatedly, Nunkoo and colleagues (Nunkoo et al., 2013; Nunkoo & Gursoy, 2017; Nunkoo & Ramkissoon, 2012) also established a direct positive relationship between trust in government actors and residents' support for tourism. Based on these relationships, we hypothesize:

> H_{16}: Trust in political decision-making will significantly increase perceived positive impacts of Airbnb.
>
> H_{17}: Trust in political decision-making will significantly decrease perceived negative impacts of Airbnb.
>
> H_{18}: Trust in political decision-making will significantly increase resident support for Airbnb.

Airbnb's positive and negative impacts and support for tourism

The final part of our model establishes support for the relationships between the Airbnb's positive and negative impacts, as perceived by residents, and their support for Airbnb, the final dependent variable. These relationships are intuitive in nature: the greater the perception of tourism's positive impacts, the higher residents' support for tourism, while a greater perception of tourism's negative impacts leads to lower resident support. On the basis of the various studies that have validated these relationships across a variety of tourism contexts (e.g., Gursoy et al., 2017; Nunkoo & So, 2016; Suess & Mody, 2016; Uysal et al., 2012, etc.), including in the case of STVRs (Garau-Vadell et al., 2019), we hypothesize:

> H_{19}: Perceived positive impacts of Airbnb will significantly increase resident support for Airbnb.
>
> H_{20}: Perceived negative impacts of Airbnb will significantly decrease resident support for Airbnb.

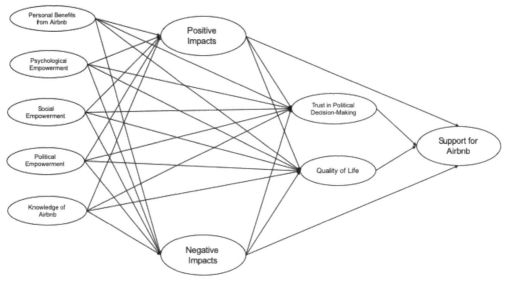

Figure 2. Alternative model.

QOL and support for tourism

Finally, we include the construct of quality of life (QOL) in our combined Weberian and Foucauldian framework. As previously discussed, Airbnb is typically portrayed as having a significant negative impact on residents' QOL in a variety of destinations (Shankman, 2017). However, while commonly accepted as rhetoric, empirical evidence of the impact of QOL on the formation of residents' attitudes towards Airbnb is lacking. In this regard, there are two perspectives that can be adopted to understand the role of QOL in the formation of residents' attitudes. The first perspective establishes QOL as a mediator between residents' perceptions of tourism's positive and negative impacts and their support for tourism development (Kim et al., 2013; Uysal et al., 2016). Thus, if residents perceive higher positive impacts from tourism, it enhances their QOL, while those who perceive higher negative impacts from tourism perceive a reduction in QOL. Furthermore, residents who perceive an increase in QOL will also exhibit greater support for tourism (Nunkoo & Ramkissoon, 2011; Woo et al., 2015). The second perspective questions QOL's mediating role, and argues that residents' perceptions of tourism's impacts may directly contribute to their support for a particular type of tourism, without the intervention of QOL (Nunkoo & So, 2016; Uysal et al., 2012). Thus, in this second perspective, while higher QOL contributes to higher resident support for tourism (Olya & Gavilyan, 2017), it is not impacted by the extent to which residents perceive tourism's positive and negative impacts. In the present context, to determine whether the concepts from our Weberian and Foucauldian framework explain residents' attitudes towards Airbnb, in our main model (Figure 1), we adopt the second perspective and control for the direct effect of QOL by treating it as an antecedent to residents' support for Airbnb. Thus, we hypothesize:

H_{21}: QOL will significantly increase resident support for Airbnb.

Alternative model

We do, however, test the first perspective that suggests a mediating role of QOL, in an alternative model (presented in Figure 2). In addition, the alternative model also adopts a different conceptualization of the concepts of power, knowledge, and governmentality, as established in some previous research that has used Foucauldian theory. For example, according to Nunkoo and Ramkissoon (2012), residents' empowerment is a determinant of their trust in political decision-making, such that the higher the level of residents' power, the more trust they are likely to place in government actors. Pertaining to knowledge, Nunkoo (2015) contends that residents who are more knowledgeable about tourism tend to have higher trust in government to make legitimate and beneficial tourism decisions. Stylidis et al. (2014) similarly emphasize the antecedent roles of resident empowerment and knowledge of tourism in facilitating residents' support "by improving their trust in local authorities and leading to more effective and sustainable development plans" (p. 271). Moreover, these studies also posit that tourism's perceived positive and negative impacts serve as determinants of residents' trust in political-decision making (Zuo et al., 2017). Thus, in contrast with our main conceptualization of the Foucauldian concepts of power, knowledge, and trust as inter-related tripartite antecedents of residents' attitudes (Figure 1), in the alternative model, we test the proposition established in previous research that both QOL and trust in political-decision making play mediating roles in determining residents' attitudes towards Airbnb.

Moderation testing

In addition to testing our main and alternative models developed on the basis of the combined Weberian and Foucauldian framework, we examine the effects of several moderating variables on the proposed relationships of the model that "better explains" the dynamics of residents' attitudes towards Airbnb. Thus, supported by previous research, we examine the hypothesized relationships of the better model across different groups of non-hosting residents based on the demographic moderators of 1) *Age* [millennials vs. older] (Harrill, 2004); 2) *Gender* [male vs. female] (Boley et al., 2017); and 3) *Income* [household income more than $60,000 vs. income less than $60,000] (Wang, 2013); and the situational moderators of 4) *Property ownership* [own vs. rent] (Snaith & Haley, 1999); 5) *Length of residency in the community* [more than eight years vs. less than eight years] (Williams & Lawson, 2001); and 6) *Previous Airbnb experience as guests* [yes (at least one stay) vs. no experience] (Suess et al., 2020b). These moderators were specifically selected based on their salience to the present context of non-hosting residents' attitudes towards Airbnb. While they are often considered when examining tourist perceptions (e.g., Ribeiro et al., 2018b), the study of resident attitudes does not typically include moderating variables. By examining their effects in an exploratory manner (without any specific apriori hypotheses as to their directionality), we contribute to developing a theoretically- and empirically-rigorous nomological framework of residents' attitudes towards Airbnb.

Methodology

Data collection

We collected the sample for the study from the panel provider Qualtrics. Respondents self-selected to be part of both the Qualtrics panel and the present study. To minimize self-selection bias, Qualtrics sends a survey link to its panel members without revealing the subject of the study. Thus, respondents chose whether or not to answer the survey without knowing the topic beforehand, thus mimicking a sampling procedure closer to random selection. Moreover, Qualtrics has panel members respond to periodic refinement questions that enable better targeting, and randomly assigns respondents to a survey that they will likely qualify for based on their responses. This helps further minimize self-selection bias and ensure that non-response is more of a random event versus a systematic event, compared to other sampling platforms (Suess & Mody, 2017).

Table 1. Respondent profile.

Category	n = 525	%
Age		
18-25	89	17.0
26-34	114	21.7
35-54	206	39.2
55-64	77	14.7
65 and over	39	7.4
Gender		
Male	258	49.1
Female	267	50.9
Income		
Less than $15,000	48	9.1
$15,000-$29,999	101	19.2
$30,000-$59,999	163	30.9
$60,000-$89,999	101	19.2
$90,000-$119,999	62	11.7
$1,20,000 or more	50	9.5
Length of residence in community		
Less than 1 year	41	7.8
1-3 years	140	26.7
4-7 years	129	24.6
8-12 years	84	16
More than 12 years	131	25.0
Property ownership		
Own	328	62.4
Rent	197	37.5
Airbnb stays (number of previous experiences as guests)		
0	323	61.5
1	61	11.6
2	50	9.6
3	26	3.0
4 or more	65	12.3

We sampled respondents based on two criteria that define non-hosting residents in the present study: 1) individuals who have never hosted using Airbnb themselves, and 2) have Airbnb activity in their neighborhoods and are aware of this activity. We collected a total of 525 usable responses from individuals who reside in urban, suburban, and rural settings across the U.S. Data collection was completed over a four-day period and respondents were stratified by age, gender, and region within the U.S. to obtain a representative sample. The demographic profile of the respondents (which includes the sample sizes for each of the moderators subsequently tested) is presented in Table 1.

Measurement of constructs

All constructs were measured using 5-point Likert scales that were adapted from the existing literature to the Airbnb context. The three constructs for empowerment—psychological, social, and political—were adapted from Boley et al. (2014) (also used in Yeager et al., 2020); knowledge of Airbnb, trust in political-decision making, and the final dependent construct of support for Airbnb from Nunkoo and So (2016); QOL from Woo et al. (2015); and Airbnb's positive and negative impacts from Dyer et al. (2007) and Nunkoo (2015). The potential for personal benefit scale is similar, in principle, to the personal (economic) benefits scale often used in resident attitude research (e.g., Nunkoo & So 2016; Yeager et al., 2020); however, since our sample comprised non-hosting residents, they have yet to realize any personal (economic) benefits from Airbnb. Thus, this scale was modified to capture their perceived potential benefits from Airbnb. The exact items used to measure the various constructs are not presented (due to word count limits), but are available upon request. For both models, we controlled for the extent of Airbnb development in residents' neighborhoods, using a single-item attitudinal measure of the extent to which

Table 2. Main model (Figure 1): SEM results.

Structural Path	Standardized Estimate	Critical Ratio	p-value
Personal benefits → Positive impacts (H_1)	.024	.47	.633
Personal benefits → Negative impacts (H_2)	-.052	-.58	.562
Personal benefits → Support for Airbnb (H_3)	.136	2.78	.005
Psychological empowerment → Positive impacts (H_4)	.615	7.70	***
Psychological empowerment → Negative impacts (H_5)	-.438	-3.20	.001
Psychological empowerment → Support for Airbnb (H_6)	.479	5.24	***
Social empowerment → Positive impacts (H_7)	.251	3.14	.002
Social empowerment → Negative impacts (H_8)	-.035	-.25	.805
Social empowerment → Support for Airbnb (H_9)	.000	-.002	.998
Political empowerment → Positive impacts (H_{10})	.045	1.27	.206
Political empowerment → Negative impacts (H_{11})	.312	4.68	***
Political empowerment → Support for Airbnb (H_{12})	-.020	-.55	.582
Knowledge of Airbnb → Positive impacts (H_{13})	-.038	-1.07	.283
Knowledge of Airbnb → Negative impacts (H_{14})	.092	1.43	.151
Knowledge of Airbnb → Support for Airbnb (H_{15})	.117	3.22	.001
Trust in political decision-making → Positive impacts (H_{16})	.046	1.73	.083
Trust in political decision-making → Negative impacts (H_{17})	.071	1.48	.137
Trust in political decision-making → Support for Airbnb (H_{18})	-.022	-.83	.406
QOL → Support for Airbnb (H_{19})	-.189	-3.41	***
Extent of Airbnb development → Support for Airbnb	-.054	-2.24	.025
Positive impacts → Support for Airbnb (H_{20})	.288	4.59	***
Negative impacts → Support for Airbnb (H_{21})	-.077	-2.94	.003

***indicates significance at p < .001.

they perceived that there were *too many* Airbnb hosts as neighbors (measured on a 5-point Likert scale). This item was used in a similar manner to the QOL construct, and was expected to decrease residents' support for Airbnb.

Data analysis

Given the main objective of the present study—to develop and test an innovative theoretical framework to examine non-hosting residents' attitudes towards Airbnb, we used the covariance-based Structural Equation Modeling (CB-SEM) procedure. CB-SEM is confirmatory in nature, and thus allows us to test relationships derived from a combined Weberian and Foucauldian framework in an Airbnb context. First, descriptive statistics and distributions were assessed. Second, we conducted a confirmatory factor analysis (CFA) on the constructs used in both the main and alternative models to determine their validity and reliability. In the third stage of analysis, we conducted structural equation modelling (SEM) and subsequently compared the two models using information theory goodness of fit indices, an assessment of path significance, and effect size testing. These three comparisons allowed us to determine which of the two competing models better explained the dynamics of residents' attitudes towards Airbnb. Finally, we examined the effects of the three demographic and three situational moderators on the better model using pairwise parameter comparisons.

Results

CFA results

Since both models comprise the exact same set of constructs (albeit in different structural arrangements), only one set of CFA results applies to both. These results indicated that the CFA model fit the data well (χ^2/df = 1.987, CFI = .934, TLI = .930, SRMR = .043, RMSEA = .043). Cronbach's α ranged from .81 to .96 for all constructs used in the two models, well above the recommended .70 level, indicating high internal consistency between the items measuring the various constructs. All items loaded onto their respective constructs with high and significant

Table 3. Alternative model (Figure 2): SEM results.

Structural Path	Standardized Estimate	Critical Ratio	p-value
Personal benefits → Positive impacts	.036	.71	.466
Personal benefits → Negative impacts	-.038	-.44	.676
Personal benefits → Trust in political-decision making	.000	.005	.998
Personal benefits → QOL	-.048	-.39	.664
Psychological empowerment → Positive impacts	.625	8.83	***
Psychological empowerment → Negative impacts	-.543	-4.18	***
Psychological empowerment → Trust in political-decision making	.121	.78	.458
Psychological empowerment → QOL	.402	2.09	.029
Social empowerment → Positive impacts	.245	3.48	.001
Social empowerment → Negative impacts	.104	.88	.392
Social empowerment → Trust in political-decision making	.086	.68	.491
Social empowerment → QOL	-.769	-5.34	***
Political empowerment → Positive impacts	.054	1.56	.112
Political empowerment → Negative impacts (H_{11})	.263	4.11	***
Political empowerment → Trust in political-decision making	.099	1.50	.132
Political empowerment → QOL	.244	3.42	***
Knowledge of Airbnb → Positive impacts	-.006	-.18	.840
Knowledge of Airbnb → Negative impacts	.041	.58	.595
Knowledge of Airbnb → Trust in political-decision making	-.055	-.90	.354
Knowledge of Airbnb → QOL	.312	4.64	***
Positive impacts → Trust in political-decision making	.208	1.69	.081
Positive impacts → QOL	.103	.77	.447
Positive impacts → Support for Airbnb	.868	18.44	***
Negative impacts → Trust in political-decision making	.079	1.61	.101
Negative impacts → QOL	-.176	-3.44	.001
Negative impacts → Support for Airbnb	-.098	-3.59	***
Trust in political decision-making → Support for Airbnb	-.003	-.11	.912
QOL → Support for Airbnb	-.023	-1.08	.276
Extent of Airbnb development → Support for Airbnb	-.045	-2.02	.032

***indicates significance at p < .001.

(p < .001) standardized factor loadings ranging from .51 to .93, indicating convergent validity. The AVE for each construct was higher than .50, further demonstrating convergent validity. We did, however, encounter a discriminant validity issue, whereby the square root of the AVE for both Airbnb's positive impacts (.771) and support for Airbnb (.832) were less than the bivariate correlation between the two constructs ($\rho = .862$). However, these constructs were adapted from previously validated scales, exhibited significant face validity, and were likely highly correlated due to their positive disposition (residents who view the phenomenon in a positive light are likely to rate highly on both positive impacts and support for Airbnb); thus, we concluded that the models were suitable for subsequent structural estimation.

Multivariate normality

Mardia's multivariate kurtosis coefficient for the data was high (1116.48) and significant (p < .001), indicating multivariate non-normality. However, an examination of the univariate skewness (between −1.285 and .481) and kurtosis (between −1.148 and 2.011) indices for the variables in the two models, as well as the normal quantile-quantile (QQ) plots for these variables, indicated that the data were only marginally non-normal. The maximum likelihood estimation technique has been shown to be fairly robust in these conditions (Bryne, 2010), and was thus utilized for the next stage of SEM.

SEM results: main model (Figure 1)

The structural model indicated an acceptable fit to the data: $\chi2/df = 1.985$; CFI = .934; TLI = .930; SRMR = .043; RMSEA = .044; AIC = 3635.20; BIC = 4364.24). Table 2 presents the parameter estimates for the hypothesized main model. Overall, the results indicate that the constructs derived from the Weberian and Foucauldian framework have significant direct impacts on resident support for Airbnb, as hypothesized, with the exception of governmentality—trust in political-decision making (lack of support for H_{18}). Moreover, only the power-related constructs of psychological empowerment (H_4) and social empowerment (H_7) enhance residents' perceptions of Airbnb's positive impacts. In addition, a higher sense of psychological empowerment reduces perceptions of Airbnb's negative impacts (H_5), while residents who feel more politically empowered perceive greater negative impacts (H_{11}). These results collectively emphasize the importance of psychological empowerment in effecting a positive disposition towards Airbnb. Not only does it enhance perceptions of Airbnb's positive impacts and leads to support for Airbnb, but also alleviates perceptions of negative impacts, indicating the importance of residents feeling a greater sense of control and agency in their relationships vis-à-vis Airbnb in their communities.

SEM results: alternative model (Figure 2)

The structural model for the alternative conceptualization of resident attitudes (Figure 2) indicated an acceptable fit to the data, similar to that for the main model: $\chi2/df = 2.043$; CFI = .930; TLI = .927; SRMR = .046; RMSEA = .046; AIC = 3676.98; BIC = 4449.65). Table 3 presents the parameter estimates for the hypothesized model, which indicate that the relationships that are common to both specifications (main and alternative models) (e.g., psychological empowerment → positive impacts or knowledge → negative impacts) remained largely unchanged, both in directionality and magnitude. The alternative model, however, tested an alternative conceptualization of Foucauldian theory in which governmentality is considered to play a mediating role between Airbnb impacts and resident support, as is QOL, based on previous research on resident attitudes. The results pertaining to these relationships that are unique to the alternative model indicated that none of the relationships pertaining to trust in political-decision making were significant. Moreover, while psychological and political empowerment, and knowledge of Airbnb enhance perceptions of QOL, and Airbnb's perceived negative impacts reduce QOL—all of which are to be expected—social empowerment was found to reduce QOL, a relationship that is theoretically and intuitively inconsistent. Moreover, in this conceptualization, unlike for the main model, QOL did not significantly impact residents' support for Airbnb.

Model comparison

We then compared the main model (Figure 1) with the alternative model (Figure 2) using three non-nested model comparison procedures: information theory goodness of fit indices, an assessment of path significance, and effect size testing. First, since the models are not-nested, a chi-square difference test to compare model fit could not be conducted. Instead, we compared the two models using information theory goodness of fit indices—AIC and BIC, which tend to penalize more complex models (i.e., lower values on these indices are desirable). Despite being less parsimonious (more complex), the main model exhibited lower AIC and BIC values (3635.20 and 4364.24 respectively) than those for the alternative model (3676.98 and 4449.65 respectively), indicating better fit. Second, as discussed above, the proposed mediating roles of governmentality and QOL in the alternative model were not supported. Thus, from an explanatory standpoint, the alternative model did not outperform the main model, which was theoretically more consistent with the tenets of Weberian and Foucauldian theory as applied to the examination of resident attitudes. Finally, we compared the amount of variance explained (squared multiple correlations) in the final dependent construct—support for Airbnb—using Cohen's f^2, a measure of effect size, between the main and alternative models. The main model explained a higher

Table 4. Moderation testing: main model (Figure 1).

Structural Path	Group 1[a] estimate	Group 2[a] estimate	z-score
Age: Millennials (n = 203) vs. Older (n = 322)			
Psychological empowerment → Positive impacts (H_4)	1.053***	.419***	3.11***
Social empowerment → Positive impacts (H_7)	-.114	.430***	3.20***
Gender: Male (n = 258) vs. Female (n = 267)			
Political empowerment → Positive impacts (H_{10})	-.052	.110*	2.03*
Income: Over $60,000 (n = 213) vs. Below $60,000 (n = 312)			
Social empowerment → Support for Airbnb (H_9)	.191*	-.108	2.29*
Political empowerment → Negative impacts (H_{11})	.112	.528***	2.58*
Length of residence: More than eight years (n = 215) vs. Less than eight years (n = 310)			
Political empowerment → Positive impacts (H_{10})	.138***	-.021	-2.04*
Knowledge of Airbnb → Positive impacts (H_{13})	-.177*	.063	2.23*
Previous Airbnb experience: Yes (n = 202) vs. No (n = 323)			
Political empowerment → Positive impacts (H_{10})	.211***	-.020	2.78***

[a]Group 1 refers to the first group presented in the table, for each moderating variable. E.g., for age. Group 1 = Millennials and Group 2 = Older residents.
***significant at $p < .001$.
*significant at $p < .05$.

amount of variance in residents' support for Airbnb ($R^2 = .857$) than the alternative model ($R^2 = .799$), with the difference indicating a large effect size ($f^2 = .4056$). Thus, the theoretical consistency of the main model with Weberian and Foucauldian theory was also reflected in a "better" explanation of residents' attitudes towards Airbnb. Based on these three model comparison criteria, we concluded that the main model was superior to the alternative model, and was retained for the subsequent stage of moderation testing.

Moderation testing: main model (Figure 1)

We tested the effects of the six moderators in the formation of residents' attitudes towards Airbnb: the three demographic moderators of age, gender, and income, and three situational moderators of property ownership, length of residence in the community, and previous experience with Airbnb as guests. We used multiple group moderation and pairwise parameter comparisons to determine whether there were any significant differences between the hypothesized relationships for the various groups created by the six moderators. Prior pairwise parameter comparisons, we tested for and determined that the models were measurement invariant (the results for invariance testing are not presented here due to word count limits). The results of the multiple group comparison are presented in Table 4 (for the purpose of brevity, we only present the relationships that were significantly different between groups).

Moderation testing revealed that there were significant differences between the groups created by all moderators, except for property ownership. Thus, the dynamics of residents' attitudes towards Airbnb were similar whether they owned or rented the property they lived in. In terms of age, we found that for Airbnb's impacts to be perceived more positively, Millennials (i.e., residents between the ages of 18 and 34 years) must feel a higher sense of psychological empowerment, while older residents (i.e., 35 years and above) must feel more socially empowered. In terms of negative impacts, for lower-income residents (below $60,000), a greater sense of political empowerment enhanced Airbnb's perception of negative impacts. While these three results are consistent with the significance and directionality of the findings of the main model (i.e., the findings for H_4, H_7, and H_{11} in the main model), we also found that a greater sense of political empowerment enhanced Airbnb's perceived positive impacts (as hypothesized in H_{10}) for female residents than for males, for those who had stayed in their communities for longer (than eight years), and for those who had previous experience with Airbnb as guests, Similarly, unlike for the main model, we found that the more knowledge long-term residents had about Airbnb, the lesser they perceived its positive impacts on their communities (H_{13}). Finally, for residents with higher income (i.e., over $60,000), a greater sense of social empowerment translated into stronger support for Airbnb. Thus, the results of the moderation testing further support the need to "investigate how political praxis is formed on the foundation of specific power/knowledge relations" (Wearing & Mcdonald, 2002, p. 197), since "power and knowledge directly imply one another" (p. 196), and "power is exercised in relation to the knowledge obtained and recreated" (p. 197).

Discussion and conclusion

In view of the need to advance research on resident attitudes towards tourism, the present study developed and tested an innovative theoretical framework to examine non-hosting residents' attitudes towards Airbnb. By combining Foucault's notions on power, knowledge, and governmentality with Weber's interpretation of formal and substantive rationality, we develop a model that serves as an explanatory tool for non-hosting residents' relationships with Airbnb. Our conceptualization of the relationships between the constructs from these theories was found to be superior to an alternative conceptualization based on extant literature. In so doing, the present study moves past traditional papers that focus on one specific destination, rely on one particular theory, and employ research methods that do not fully leverage the rigor of the chosen methodology and also consider residents as a homogenous group of individuals.

Using a sample of 525 residents from across the U.S., we found that the antecedents derived from Weberian and Foucauldian theory had significant direct impacts on resident support for Airbnb, consistent with the results from Olya and Gavilyan (2017) study of resident support for tourism in Iran. Consistent with Yeager et al. (2020), psychological empowerment was found to be a key driver of Airbnb's positive and negative impacts, and residents' support for Airbnb. Moreover, residents who feel socially empowered also perceive Airbnb to have more positive impacts. Interestingly, contrary to Yeager et al. (2020) (and H_{11}), we found that politically-empowered residents perceived higher negative impacts from Airbnb, while Foucault's notion of governmentality—operationalized as trust in political decision-making—does not appear to play a role in the formation of residents' attitudes to Airbnb; this latter finding is consistent with the results of studies by Gursoy et al. (2017) and Zuo et al. (2017). Thus, while Nunkoo and Gursoy (2016) argue that both citizens' power and their trust in political institutions are vital for a sustainable and democratic tourism planning process, it would appear that politically-empowered citizens, who are likely to have more critical attitudes towards development more generally (Nunkoo & So, 2016), do not necessarily need to have trust in their governments to evaluate tourism's positive and negative impacts and subsequently determine and demonstrate their support for Airbnb development. This assessment is consistent with Ramos and Mundet (2020) study in which they found that politically-empowered residents, who perceived significant negative impacts from tourism in Barcelona, were able to vote out a government that they felt was not taking sufficient action to protect their interests against those of the tourism industry. Moreover, these residents formed community groups that sought to actively regulate tourism's negative impacts on the city, thus demonstrating their lack of support for existing models of tourism and the need for a more sustainable path to tourism development. Similarly, Söderström and Mermet (2020) found that politically-empowered citizens groups in Reykjavik were cognizant of Airbnb's negative effects on their city; however, they were also discerning in that their actions against tourism in Reykjavík primarily targeted the building of new hotels, rather than platforms that were seen as a way of redistributing tourism income to locals. Thus, our findings suggest a narrative contrary to that found in popular discourse highlighting Airbnb's negative impacts on the quality of hapless residents' lives (Shankman, 2017). Instead, we find that residents draw on their substantive rationalities in determining their attitudes towards Airbnb, beyond adopting a purely rational economic perspective (Yeager et al., 2020). In addition to the concepts of empowerment, we found that residents with more knowledge of tourism also indicated higher support for Airbnb, contrary to Gutiérrez-Taño et al. (2019) findings in the context of STVRs in Majorca.

Our interpretation of the Foucauldian concepts of power, knowledge, and trust as interrelated tripartite antecedents of residents' attitudes, also indicated that, in contrast to the alternative conceptualization suggested by some previous studies, QOL, as with governmentality, does not play a mediating role between Airbnb's perceived impacts and resident support for Airbnb. Instead, residents' perceived QOL is a starting point from which the Weberian and Foucauldian concepts are considered in determining resident attitudes. Residents with higher QOL showed lower support for Airbnb ($\beta = -.189$), likely due to fears that their quality of life will be adversely impacted due to Airbnb, as suggested by media rhetoric. However, as Olya and Gavilyan (2017) highlight, "the attributes of other antecedents in the causal recipe" (p. 893) for resident support are important to consider; in the present study, the effects of these other antecedents were largely positive and larger in magnitude than the dampening effect of QOL on resident support. Finally, that the positive effect of Airbnb's perceived positive impacts on resident support ($\beta = .288$) was much higher than the negative effects of Airbnb's negative impacts on resident support ($\beta = -.077$), in combination with the finding that residents perceived significantly higher positive impacts (mean for all items $= 3.59$) than negative impacts (mean for all items $= 2.79$), indicates a largely positive disposition towards Airbnb by non-hosting residents; a disposition that is better explained by our conceptualization of Weber and Foucauldian concepts than that found in extant literature. Our findings have important theoretical and practical implications.

Theoretical contribution

By developing and testing an innovative theoretical framework that combines the tenets of Weber's Theory of Rationality and Foucauldian concepts of power, knowledge, and governmentality to examine non-hosting residents' attitudes towards Airbnb, our study goes beyond the piecemeal adoption of these concepts as in previous research. For example, the dynamics of power in P2P accommodation have indeed been examined, but only in the context of the host-guest relationship (Farmaki & Kaniadakis, 2020). Similarly, Garau-Vadell et al. (2019) study was largely restricted to examining the antecedents that comprise Weber's formal rationality, while Gutiérrez-Taño et al. (2019) considered the role of knowledge without including other antecedents. Yeager et al. (2020) did include both formal and substantive rational antecedents of resident attitudes; however, the latter only comprised the Foucauldian notion of power and not knowledge or governmentality. In effect, the present study combines critical antecedents from these and other previous studies in a conceptualization of a combined Weberian and Foucauldian framework that is salient to explaining residents' attitudes to Airbnb. Moreover, the study overcomes the pitfalls associated with the overly-rational orientation of SET and its bias toward inflating the economic costs and benefits of social transactions between visitors and hosts over noneconomic factors (Hadinejad et al., 2019; Yeager et al., 2020), and examines the determinants of resident perceptions from the wider socio-cultural framework within which they are formed (Sharpley, 2014). Also, while the role of resident QOL in the context of the sharing economy has been much debated, our research is the first to explicitly include this construct in our combined Weberian and Foucauldian framework. Consistent with Olya and Gavilyan (2017) study, we find QOL to be a direct antecedent of resident support for Airbnb, in contrast with its hypothesized mediating role identified in previous research. Finally, in contrast with previous research that has not differentiated between hosting and non-hosting residents (e.g., Garau-Vadell et al., 2019), the present study examines factors that are important to the sustainability of Airbnb in terms of resident support exclusively from the perspective of stakeholders who are impacted by but do not directly participate in the phenomenon; this critical population of non-hosting residents far outnumbers residents that do actively participate in Airbnb. In so doing, we address Yeager et al. (2020) call for inquiry into non-host residents' relationships with STVRs. Here, our use of Foucauldian theory is particularly relevant, as it reveals that in addition to tourists and intermediaries, non-participating residents also have agency in their relationships with Airbnb and tourism development more generally. While developed in the context of the sharing economy, the combined Weberian and Foucauldian framework can be used by researchers to examine the dynamics of other types of tourism development, particularly in contexts where residents' perceived agency vis-à-vis tourism development is threatened and/or important to their participation in the tourism development process.

Practical implications

Our findings have important implications for stakeholders associated with Airbnb and the sharing economy in tourism. The study identifies that for the sharing economy to be truly considered a form of "collaborative consumption", the perspectives of a wide variety of stakeholders, beyond tourists and hosts, must be considered. For Airbnb, the company must look to engage with non-hosting residents in the same manner as it does with its hosting community, by providing both online (e.g., the Community Center for hosts) and offline avenues (e.g., host meetups, for both *Homes* and *Experiences*). The company's advocacy platform—the *Airbnb Citizen* initiative—could be expanded to mobilize residents in addition to its user base (Doorn, 2019) by demonstrating the positive impacts of sharing on neighborhoods and communities more broadly, thus advancing homesharing as a solution for everyone, and not just hosts and guests. The more knowledgeable residents are about Airbnb's impacts—both positive and negative—the greater their support for having such activity in their neighborhoods. Moreover, involving citizens' groups in dialogue—particularly the more active groups and in destinations where Airbnb has been criticized of contributing to overtourism (Peltier, 2018)—will enhance their sense of psychological and social empowerment, both of which are found to be important drivers of Airbnb's perceived impacts and residents' support for the company. Airbnb's recent initiatives for cracking down on "party houses", the verification of all listings on the platform, and an increased willingness to share data with local governments to crack down on illegal sharing activity will bode well in the company's discourse and dialogue with residents more generally. Relatedly, for hosts, adhering to Airbnb's *responsible hosting* policies—particularly those requiring them to be mindful of neighbors (respect and safety), obtaining permissions (ownership and tenancy rules) and following local regulations (taxation, permits, and rent control)—is critical to demonstrating that they are good citizens in the sharing economy, which will further contribute to non-hosting residents' positive attitudes towards the phenomenon.

Destination marketing organizations (DMOs) can play a pivotal role in enabling this dialogue. With resident support, DMOs can leverage the full potential of Airbnb to expand their target markets and attract visitors who would otherwise not have visited. For example, in 2015, the San Francisco Travel Association was one of the first DMOs to announce a destination promotion partnership with Airbnb, leveraging the sharing economy "as a new way of meeting the needs of San Francisco visitors and driving the economic impact of tourism to neighborhoods throughout the city, highlighting local Airbnb hosts who welcome and share their love of San Francisco with visitors every day" ("San Francisco Travel Association partners with Airbnb to meet the needs of visitors," 2015). While not benefitting directly from hosting visitors, non-hosting residents can be made to appreciate the multiplier effects of tourists spending money on businesses and experiences throughout the destination, thus leveraging the formal rationality (perception of personal benefits) associated with Airbnb development. Relatedly, policy makers, particularly those at the level of local government, must recognize that residents who are empowered and have knowledge of P2P accommodation are likely to be more productive partners in their efforts to effectively regulate the phenomenon. While empowered residents can be active as in the case of Barcelona (Ramos & Mundet, 2020), or discerning as in the case of Reykjavik (Söderström & Mermet, 2020), leveraging the Weberian and Foucauldian determinants of resident support can allow local governments to effect *supportive* non-hosting residents, as in the Portland model of Airbnb regulation—residents who appreciate the balance between an owner's right to engage in short-term rentals and the need to protect the nature of the destination for all residents (Speier, 2017). That our findings demonstrate a largely positive disposition towards Airbnb among non-hosting residents bodes well for local governments that are typically seen to struggle with regulating STVRs. Finally, our findings pertaining to the moderating effects of age, gender, income, length of residence in the community, and previous Airbnb experience suggest that local governments must engage with the resident community recognizing that not all residents perceive Airbnb and the sharing economy in the same way; their demographics and situational characteristics impact their disposition towards the phenomenon.

Limitations and future research

It is important to acknowledge certain limitations of the present study, which also present opportunities for future research on this important topic. First, while capturing residents from across the U.S., our results are based on a single cross-sectional sample. Notwithstanding challenges with data collection, future research can adopt a longitudinal approach to modeling residents' attitudes. Such an approach would be consistent with lifecycle models of tourism development, which recognize that residents' attitudes towards tourism are not static and evolve over different stages of tourism development (Uysal et al., 2016). While our study controlled for residents' perceptions of the extent of Airbnb development in their neighborhoods, with the company approaching the shakeout and maturity stages of its business life cycle, and demonstrating a greater proclivity to working with a variety of stakeholders, including local governments, a longitudinal study can capture the modulations of resident support based on concepts from Weberian and Foucauldian theory. Second, while based on a strong theoretical foundation, our model explained a much smaller amount of variance in residents' perceptions of Airbnb's negative impacts ($R^2 = .178$) than it did in the other endogenous constructs, Airbnb's positive impacts ($R^2 = .806$) and support for Airbnb ($R^2 = .854$). Future research can include other non-Weberian and non-Foucauldian antecedents—such as residents' inherent hospitableness (Ribeiro et al., 2017), place attachment (Woosnam et al., 2018), and emotional solidarity (Woosnam, Erul, & Ribeiro et al., 2017)—and can also examine other important outcomes of residents' attitudes such as active opposition to Airbnb (Ramos & Mundet, 2020) or their tax paying behavior (Suess & Mody, 2016). Third, our sample was collected before COVID-19 disrupted the tourism industry. With Airbnb potentially losing a significant portion of its supply in key markets due to the lack of demand (Melendez, 2020), future research can examine whether residents' attitudes towards Airbnb will have significantly changed in a post-COVID world. It is reasonable to hypothesize that given the risk of infection due to COVID-19, residents will be more antagonistic towards visitors in their neighborhoods and will thus demonstrate lower support for Airbnb and other STVRs. Relatedly, researchers must examine whether Airbnb's proactive efforts to support communities during COVID-19—such as providing free or subsidized housing for healthcare professionals, relief workers, and first responders through its *Open Homes* initiative (Harris, 2020), or partnering with DMOs to support domestic travel and local economic growth ("Airbnb Launches Campaign to Support Domestic Travel + Local Economic Growth," 2020)—might lead to more favorable perceptions among residents, both host and non-hosts. Thus, comparing the perspectives of these two sub-groups of residents can provide a more holistic understanding of this critical stakeholder group.

Disclosure statement

No potential conflict of interest was reported by the authors.

References

Airbnb Launches Campaign to Support Domestic Travel+ Local Economic Growth. (2020).
Andereck, K. L., Valentine, K. M., Knopf, R. C., & Vogt, C. A. (2005). Residents' perceptions of community tourism impacts. *Annals of Tourism Research*, *32*(4), 1056–1076. https://doi.org/10.1016/j.annals.2005.03.001
Boley, B. B., Ayscue, E., Maruyama, N., & Woosnam, K. M. (2017). Gender and empowerment : Assessing discrepancies using the resident empowerment through tourism scale. *Journal of Sustainable Tourism*, *25*(1), 113–229. https://doi.org/10.1080/09669582.2016.1177065
Boley, B. B., McGehee, N. G., Perdue, R. R., & Long, P. (2014). Empowerment and resident attitudes toward tourism: Strengthening the theoretical foundation through a Weberian lens. *Annals of Tourism Research*, *49*, 33–50. https://doi.org/10.1016/j.annals.2014.08.005
Bryne, B. (2010). *Structural equation modeling with AMOS: Basic concepts, applications, and programming* (2nd ed.). Routledge.
Cheng, M., Houge Mackenzie, S., & Degarege, G. A. (2020). Airbnb impacts on host communities in a tourism destination: An exploratory study of stakeholder perspectives in Queenstown, New Zealand. *Journal of Sustainable Tourism*, 1–19. https://doi.org/10.1080/09669582.2020.1802469
Dann, D., Teubner, T., & Weinhardt, C. (2019). Poster child and guinea pig – insights from a structured literature review on Airbnb. *International Journal of Contemporary Hospitality Management*, *31*(1), 427–473. https://doi.org/10.1108/IJCHM-03-2018-0186
Davis, D., Allen, J., & Cosenza, R. M. (1988). Segmenting local residents by their attitudes, interests, and opinions toward tourism. *Journal of Travel Research*, *27*(2), 2–8. https://doi.org/10.1177/004728758802700201
Dogru, T., Mody, M., & Suess, C. (2019). Adding evidence to the debate: Quantifying Airbnb's disruptive impact on ten key hotel markets. *Tourism Management*, *72*, 27–38. https://doi.org/10.1016/j.tourman.2018.11.008
Doorn, N. V. (2020). A new institution on the block : On platform urbanism and Airbnb citizenship. *New Media and Society*, *22*(10) 1–19. https://doi.org/10.1177/1461444819884377
Dyer, P., Gursoy, D., Sharma, B., & Carter, J. (2007). Structural modeling of resident perceptions of tourism and associated development on the Sunshine Coast. Tourism *Management*, *28*(2), 409–422. https://doi.org/10.1016/j.tourman.2006.04.002
Elliott, C. (2016). *Airbnb runs "illegal hotels," hotel industry study claims*. Retrieved from Fortune website: http://fortune.com/2016/01/20/airbnb-illegal-hotels-study/
Farmaki, A., Christou, P., & Saveriades, A. (2020, November). A Lefebvrian analysis of Airbnb space. *Annals of Tourism Research*, *80*, 102806. https://doi.org/10.1016/j.annals.2019.102806
Farmaki, A., & Kaniadakis, A. (2020, May). Power dynamics in peer-to-peer accommodation: Insights from Airbnb hosts . *International Journal of Hospitality Management*, *89*, 102571. https://doi.org/10.1016/j.ijhm.2020.102571

Garau-Vadell, J. B., Gutiérrez-Taño, D., & Díaz-Armas, R. (2019). Residents' support for P2P accommodation in mass tourism destinations. *Journal of Travel Research*, *58*(4), 549–565. https://doi.org/10.1177/0047287518767067

Gursoy, D., Yolal, M., Ribeiro, M. A., & Panosso Netto, A. (2017). Impact of trust on local residents' mega-event perceptions and their support. *Journal of Travel Research*, *56*(3), 393–406. https://doi.org/10.1177/0047287516643415

Gutiérrez-Taño, D., Garau-Vadell, J. B., & Díaz-Armas, R. J. (2019). The influence of knowledge on residents' perceptions of the impacts of overtourism in P2P accommodation rental. *Sustainability*, *11*(4), 1043. https://doi.org/10.3390/su11041043

Guttentag, D. (2019). Progress on Airbnb: A literature review. *Journal of Hospitality and Tourism Technology*, *10*(4), 814–844. https://doi.org/10.1108/JHTT-08-2018-0075

Hadinejad, A., D. Moyle, B., Scott, N., Kralj, A., & Nunkoo, R. (2019). Residents' attitudes to tourism: A review Article information. *Tourism Review*, *74*(2), 150–165. https://doi.org/10.1108/TR-01-2018-0003

Harrill, R. (2004). Residents' attitudes toward tourism development: A literature review with implications for tourism planning. *Journal of Planning Literature*, *18*(3), 251–266. https://doi.org/10.1177/0885412203260306

Harris, L. (2020). Airbnb introduces free, reduced housing option for COVID-19 responders. *WCNC*. https://www.wcnc.com/article/news/health/coronavirus/airbnb-introduces-free-reduced-housing-option-for-covid-19-responders/275-79ba462b-2626-4aff-a9e7-31578edb5fc6

Jordan, E. J., & Moore, J. (2018). An in-depth exploration of residents' perceived impacts of transient vacation rentals. *Journal of Travel & Tourism Marketing*, *35*(1), 90–101. https://doi.org/10.1080/10548408.2017.1315844

Khazaei, A., Elliot, S., & Joppe, M. (2015). An application of stakeholder theory to advance community participation in tourism planning: The case for engaging immigrants as fringe stakeholders. *Journal of Sustainable Tourism*, *23*(7), 1049–1062. https://doi.org/10.1080/09669582.2015.1042481

Kim, K., Uysal, M., & Sirgy, M. J. (2013). How does tourism in a community impact the quality of life of community residents? *Tourism Management*, *36*, 527–540. https://doi.org/10.1016/j.tourman.2012.09.005

Melendez, S. (2020). Airbnb's COVID-19 crisis could be a boon for affordable housing. *Fast Company*. https://www.fastcompany.com/90482662/airbnbs-covid-19-crisis-could-be-a-boon-for-affordable-housing

Mody, M., & Koslowsky, K. (2019). Panacea or peril? The implications of Neolocalism as a more intrusive form of tourism. *Boston Hospitality Review*.

Mody, M., Suess, C., & Dogru, T. (2019). Not in my backyard? Is the anti-Airbnb discourse truly warranted? *Annals of Tourism Research*, *74*, 198–203. https://doi.org/10.1016/j.annals.2018.05.004

Nunkoo, R. (2015). Tourism development and trust in local government. *Tourism Management*, *46*, 623–634. https://doi.org/10.1016/j.tourman.2014.08.016

Nunkoo, R., & Gursoy, D. (2016). Rethinking the role of power and trust in tourism planning. *Journal of Hospitality Marketing & Management*, *25*(4), 512–522. https://doi.org/10.1080/19368623.2015.1019170

Nunkoo, R., & Gursoy, D. (2017). Political trust and residents' support for alternative and mass tourism: An improved structural model. *Tourism Geographies*, *19*(3), 318–339. https://doi.org/10.1080/14616688.2016.1196239

Nunkoo, R., & Ramkissoon, H. (2011). Developing a community support model for tourism. *Annals of Tourism Research*, *38*(3), 964–988. https://doi.org/10.1016/j.annals.2011.01.017

Nunkoo, R., & Ramkissoon, H. (2012). Power, trust, social exchange, and community support. *Annals of Tourism Research*, *39*(2), 997–1023. https://doi.org/10.1016/j.annals.2011.11.017

Nunkoo, R., Smith, S. L. J., & Ramkissoon, H. (2013). Residents' attitudes to tourism: A longitudinal study of 140 articles from 1984 to 2010. *Journal of Sustainable Tourism*, *21*(1), 5–25. https://doi.org/10.1080/09669582.2012.673621

Nunkoo, R., & So, K. K. F. (2016). Residents' support for tourism: Testing alternative structural models. *Journal of Travel Research*, *55*(7), 847–861. https://doi.org/10.1177/0047287515592972

Olya, H. G. T., & Gavilyan, Y. (2017). Configurational models to predict residents' support for tourism development. *Journal of Travel Research*, *56*(7), 893–912. https://doi.org/10.1177/0047287516667850

Ouyang, Z., Gursoy, D., & Sharma, B. (2017). Role of trust, emotions and event attachment on residents' attitudes toward tourism. *Tourism Management*, *63*, 426–438. https://doi.org/10.1016/j.tourman.2017.06.026

Peltier, D. (2018). Airbnb launching an effort to address overtourism it helped create. *Skift*. https://skift.com/2018/04/17/airbnb-launching-an-effort-to-address-overtourism-it-helped-create/

Ramos, S. P., & Mundet, L. (2020). Tourism-phobia in Barcelona: Dismantling discursive strategies and power games in the construction of a sustainable tourist city. *Journal of Tourism and Cultural Change*. https://doi.org/10.1080/14766825.2020.1752224

Rasoolimanesh, S. M., Jaafar, M., & Barghi, R. (2017). Effects of motivation, knowledge and perceived power on residents' perceptions: Application of Weber's theory in world heritage site destinations. *International Journal of Tourism Research*, *19*(1), 68–79. https://doi.org/10.1002/jtr.2085

Ribeiro, M. A., Pinto, P., Silva, J. A., & Woosnam, K. (2017). Residents' attitudes and the adoption of pro-tourism behaviours: The case of developing island countries. *Tourism Management*, *61*, 523–537. https://doi.org/10.1016/j.tourman.2017.03.004

Ribeiro, M. A., Pinto, P., Silva, J. A., & Woosnam, K. M. (2018). Examining the predictive validity of SUS-TAS with maximum parsimony in developing island countries. *Journal of Sustainable Tourism*, *26*(3), 379–398. https://doi.org/10.1080/09669582.2017.1355918

Ribeiro, M. A., Woosnam, K. M., Pinto, P., & Silva, J. A. (2018). Tourists' destination loyalty through emotional solidarity with residents : An integrative moderated mediation model. *Journal of Travel Research*, *57*(3), 279–295. https://doi.org/10.1177/0047287517699089

Richards, S., Brown, L., & Dilettuso, A. (2019). The Airbnb phenomenon: The resident's perspective. *International Journal of Tourism Cities*, *6*(1), 8–26. https://doi.org/10.1108/IJTC-06-2019-0084

San Francisco Travel Association partners with Airbnb to meet the needs of visitors. (2015).

Shankman, S. (2017). Documentary: Barcelona and the Trials of 21st Century Overtourism. *Skift*. https://skift.com/2017/08/01/video-barcelona-and-the-trials-of-21st-century-overtourism/

Sharpley, R. (2014). Host perceptions of tourism: A review of the research. *Tourism Management*, *42*, 37–49. https://doi.org/10.1016/j.tourman.2013.10.007

Snaith, T., & Haley, A. (1999). Residents' opinions of tourism development in the historic city of. *Tourism Management*, *20*(5), 595–603. https://doi.org/10.1016/S0261-5177(99)00030-8

Söderström, O., & Mermet, A. (2020). When Airbnb sits in the control room : Platform urbanism as actually existing smart urbanism in Reykjavík. *Frontiers in Sustainable Cities*, *2*, 1–7. https://doi.org/10.3389/frsc.2020.00015

Speier, E. (2017). Embracing Airbnb : How cities can champion private property rights without compromising the health and welfare of the community. *Pepperdine Law Review*, *44*(2), 387–428.

Stergiou, D. P., & Farmaki, A. (2019). Resident perceptions of the impacts of P2P accommodation : Implications for neighbourhoods. *International Journal of Hospitality Management*, . https://doi.org/10.1016/j.ijhm.2019.102411

Stienmetz, J. L., Liu, A., & Tussyadiah, I. P. (2019). *Information and communication technologies in tourism 2012*. Springer. https://doi.org/10.1007/978-3-7091-1142-0

Strzelecka, M., Boley, B. B., & Strzelecka, C. (2017). Empowerment and resident support for tourism in rural Central and Eastern Europe (CEE): The case of Pomerania, Poland. *Journal of Sustainable Tourism*, *25*(4), 554–572. https://doi.org/10.1080/09669582.2016.1224891

Stylidis, D., Biran, A., Sit, J., & Szivas, E. M. (2014). Residents' support for tourism development : The role of residents' place image and perceived tourism impacts. *Tourism Management*, *45*, 260–274. https://doi.org/10.1016/j.tourman.2014.05.006

Suess, C., & Mody, M. (2016). Gaming can be sustainable too! Using Social Representation Theory to examine the moderating effects of tourism diversification on residents' tax paying behavior. *Tourism Management*, *56*, 20–39. https://doi.org/10.1016/j.tourman.2016.03.022

Suess, C., & Mody, M. (2017). Hospitality healthscapes: A conjoint analysis approach to understanding patient responses to hotel-like hospital rooms. *International Journal of Hospitality Management*, *61*, 59–72. https://doi.org/10.1016/j.ijhm.2016.11.004

Suess, C., Woosnam, K. M., & Erul, E. (2020a, February). Stranger-danger ? Understanding the moderating effects of children in the household on non-hosting residents' emotional solidarity with Airbnb visitors, feeling safe, and support for Airbnb. *Tourism Management*, *77*, 103952. https://doi.org/10.1016/j.tourman.2019.103952

Suess, C., Woosnam, K., Mody, M., Dogru, T., & Turk, E. S. (2020b). Understanding how residents' emotional solidarity with airbnb visitors influences perceptions of their impact on a community : The moderating role of prior experience staying at an Airbnb. *Journal of Travel Research*. https://doi.org/10.1177/0047287520921234

Uysal, M., Perdue, R., & Sirgy, M. J. (Eds.). (2012). *Handbook of tourism and quality-of-life research*. Springer.

Uysal, M., Sirgy, M. J., Woo, E., & Lina, H. (2016). Quality of life (QOL) and well-being research in tourism. *Tourism Management*, *53*, 244–261. https://doi.org/10.1016/j.tourman.2015.07.013

Vetitnev, A. M., & Bobina, N. (2017). Residents' perceptions of the 2014 Sochi Olympic Games. *Leisure Studies*, *36*(1), 108–118. https://doi.org/10.1080/02614367.2015.1105857

Wang, S. (2013). Predicting effects of demographics and moderating power of engagement on residents' perceptions of tourism development. *European Journal of Tourism Research*, *6*(2), 170–182.

Wearing, S., & Mcdonald, M. (2002). The development of community-based tourism : Re-thinking the relationship between tour operators and development agents as intermediaries in rural and isolated area communities. *Journal of Sustainable Tourism*, *10*(3) 191–206.

Wearing, S. L., Wearing, M., & Mcdonald, M. (2010). Understanding local power and interactional processes in sustainable tourism: Exploring village–tour operator relations on the Kokoda Track, Papua New Guinea. *Journal of Sustainable Tourism*, *18*(1), 61-76. https://doi.org/10.1080/09669580903071995

Williams, J. R., & Lawson, R. (2001). Community issues and resident opinions of tourism. *Annals of Tourism Research*, *28*(2), 269–290. https://doi.org/10.1016/S0160-7383(00)00030-X https://doi.org/10.1016/S0160-7383(00)00030-X

Woo, E., Kim, H., & Uysal, M. (2015, January). Life satisfaction and support for tourism development. *Annals of Tourism Research*, *50*, 84–97. https://doi.org/10.1016/j.annals.2014.11.001

Woosnam, K. M., Aleshinloye, K. D., Alector, M., Stylidis, D., Jiang, J., & Erul, E. (2018). Social determinants of place attachment at a World Heritage Site. *Tourism Management*, *67*, 139–146. https://doi.org/10.1016/j.tourman.2018.01.012

Woosnam, K. M., Erul, E., & Ribeiro, M. A. (2017). Heterogeneous community perspectives of emotional solidarity with tourists : Considering Antalya, Turkey. *International Journal of Tourism Research*, *19*(6), 639–647. https://doi.org/10.1002/jtr.2136

Yeager, E. P., Boley, B. B., Woosnam, K. M., & Green, G. T. (2020). Modeling residents' attitudes toward short-term vacation rentals. *Journal of Travel Research*, *59*(6), 955–974. https://doi.org/10.1177/0047287519870255

Zuo, B., Gursoy, D., & Wall, G. (2017). Annals of tourism research residents' support for red tourism in China : The moderating effect of central government. *Annals of Tourism Research*, *64*, 51–63. https://doi.org/10.1016/j.annals.2017.03.001

Empowerment of women through cultural tourism: perspectives of Hui minority embroiderers in Ningxia, China

Ming Ming Su, Geoffrey Wall, Jianfu Ma, Marcello Notarianni and Sangui Wang

ABSTRACT
Engagement of vulnerable rural women in the demonstration and practices of cultural heritage for tourism is a strategy that can empower them. Five dimensions of women's empowerment (economic, social, psychological, educational and political) are examined at multiple scales (self, family, community and society) in a Hui ethnic community in Haiyuan County, Ningxia Hui Autonomous Region, northwest of China. This county is nationally recognized for its poverty. Semistructured interviews were undertaken with government officials, management staff of embroidery cooperatives and rural women. It is shown that the involvement of rural Hui women in embroidery tourism has not only advanced them economically but also provided feasible paths for social, psychological, educational and political empowerment to varying degrees. Theoretical contributions and practical implications of the research are then discussed.

Introduction

Intangible cultural heritage, including oral traditions, performing arts, rituals, festive events and arts and crafts that have been transmitted over generations, are widely recognized as a significant resource for cultural heritage tourism (Kim et al., 2019). Integration of intangible cultural heritage into tourism could strengthen the authenticity of tourism offerings and deepen understanding of a destination's culture while generating a variety of benefits for practitioners of such heritage and their communities (Esfehani & Albrecht, 2018; Kim et al., 2019). At the same time, enhancement of the economic and social benefits of such heritage tourism would contribute to poverty reduction and the development of the destination.

Rural women are often practitioners of such intangible cultural heritage and are among the most vulnerable groups in rural societies with lower access to livelihood resources, fewer livelihood choices, lower access to education and lower social status than many urban women and men (Garcia & Pablo, 2017; Handapangoda et al., 2019; Maruyama & Woosnam, 2020; Sha & Ma, 2012; Sun & Liao, 2016). Engagement of rural women in the practices and demonstration of intangible cultural heritage for tourism is a strategy that can perpetuate, and even revive, aspects of local culture, while supporting their social and economic development, raising their status and empowering them (Handapangoda et al., 2019; Sun & Liao, 2016).

Empowerment is a multifaceted and deeply contextual concept with economic, social, psychological, educational and political dimensions (O'Hara & Clement, 2018; Rowlands, 1995; Scheyvens, 1999). These five dimensions exhibit different representations at different scales from the self, family and community to the wider society (Cherayi & Jose, 2016; Kabeer, 2005; O'Hara & Clement, 2018; Scheyvens, 1999). Accordingly, a spatial scale can be applied to the dimensions of empowerment to create a framework for the exploration of empowerment and increase the explanatory power of investigations.

This study focuses on the Hui embroidery of Haiyuan County, which is listed and recognized nationally as a poor county of Ningxia Hui Autonomous Region in Northwest China. Such embroidery has been practiced in Haiyuan County for centuries and is a form of cultural heritage that is deemed to have Hui minority characteristics. Embroidery is a highly gendered practice and the practitioners of Hui embroidery are all women. In order to support local cultural expression and to facilitate poverty reduction, an Intangible Cultural Heritage Incubation Centre (ICHIC) has been established by the county government to support the design, production, training and establishment of paper cutting and embroidery cooperatives as a poverty reduction strategy for rural women. While both paper cuts and embroidery are tangible items, their creations have meanings and significance that are embedded in local culture and, hence, are often considered to be examples of intangible heritage.

Considering Hui embroidery in Haiyuan County as a case study, this article examines how engagement with tourism has affected the practices of cultural heritage and whether and to what extent involvement in Hui embroidery tourism has empowered local women. An empowerment framework with multiple dimensions and scales is proposes and applied. Through examining and assessing influences of cultural heritage participation on women's empowerment in a Chinese context, the study contributes to the theoretical advancement and measurement of women's empowerment, and provides practical implications to enhance the benefits of cultural heritage tourism to women participants.

Literature review

Intangible cultural heritage tourism and women's participation

Tangible forms of cultural heritage, such as buildings, monuments and collections of objects, are complemented by intangible cultural heritage which refers to "traditions or living expressions inherited from our ancestors and passed on to our descendants" (UNESCO, 2020). As defined by UNESCO (2018), intangible cultural heritage includes but is not limited to oral traditions, performing arts, social practices, rituals, festive events, knowledge and skills and traditional craftsmanship. In reality, tangible and intangible heritage are not distinct because the former has meanings and may have other intangible attributes, such as beauty, whereas the latter may have tangible outputs, such as paintings or craft products (Smith & Akagawa, 2009; Smith & Waterton, 2009). In fact, they fit well together and, for example, the efficacy of intangible heritage may be heightened when it occurs in heritage buildings, just as the experience of built structures may be enlivened through the provision of intangible heritage such as music and dance (Smith, 2014; Smith & Akagawa, 2009; Wall & Mathieson, 2006). As argued by Smith (2014), reflecting a moment or a process when cultural and social values and meanings are re/constructed, all heritage is intangible. Embroidery, which is the subject of this article, is both an intangible process that is infused with cultural significance and social meanings, and a tangible heritage product that can be sold and used.

Cultural heritage is of great importance because it celebrates cultural diversity and human creativity, reinforces community identity and continuity and can "help communities and individuals connect with each other" (UNESCO, 2019, 2020). It is dynamic as the forms and meanings of heritage evolve and change from generation to generation in response to the environments in which they are embedded (Kim et al., 2019; UNESCO, 2019). However, the values carried by heritage need to be relevant to and recognized by a community as part of their cultural endowment (Kim et al., 2019; Megeirhi et al., 2020; UNESCO, 2020; Woosnam et al., 2018).

Cultural heritage is widely recognized as a significant resource for heritage tourism (Kim et al., 2019). Integration of cultural heritage into tourism development could strengthen the authenticity of tourism offerings and facilitate a deeper understanding of a destination's culture, thereby enhancing attractiveness and competitiveness (Chhabra et al., 2003; Esfehani & Albrecht, 2018; Gonzalez, 2008; Kim et al., 2019; Xie, 2003). However, it has also been argued that heritage tourism brings changes to the meaning of cultural heritage as it comes to be treated as a commodity for touristic consumption (Chhabra et al., 2003; Garcia & Pablo, 2017; Gonzalez, 2008; Handapangoda et al., 2019; Ryan & Crotts, 1997; Xie, 2003). To ensure authenticity in the process of tourism development, it is strongly advised that the cultural and socio-economic values of heritage should be safeguarded when it is used in tourism (Gonzalez, 2008; Kim et al., 2019; UNESCO, 2019; Xie, 2003). Considering the evolving nature of culture itself, Handapangoda et al. (2019) called for a more open approach to authenticity with the understanding that heritage tourism supports the continuous revival and representation of the past in the present with selection and imagination.

Much intangible cultural heritage has been practiced and transmitted by communities for generations and continuously contributes to their vitality and wellbeing (Kim et al., 2019; UNESCO, 2018, 2019, 2020). It is incomplete if only the material format is presented for the community has played an important role in sustaining the values of such heritage, and this should also be the case in its use for tourism (Kim et al., 2019; UNESCO, 2019). As such, use of cultural heritage for tourism inevitably also generates impacts for local communities, for good and ill (Esfehani & Albrecht, 2018; Kim et al., 2019; Xie, 2003), particularly for the practitioners of such heritage (Kim et al., 2019). A community's intention for the tourism use of cultural heritage should be understood, respected and reflected in the tourism development process (Megeirhi et al., 2020) and community control and benefit acquisition from tourism should be safeguarded (Ryan & Crotts, 1997; Wall & Mathieson, 2006; Yang & Wall, 2009), as residents' perspectives and involvement help to foster greater sustainability and cultural integrity for heritage tourism (Megeirhi et al., 2020; Woosnam et al., 2018).

Traditional crafts and artifacts, such as weaving, carving, embroidery and mask making, are common types of cultural heritage that are widely used in tourism (Garcia & Pablo, 2017; Handapangoda et al., 2019; Long, 2012; Ryan & Crotts, 1997; Sun & Xu, 2018). When modified to showcase local culture and serve as souvenirs for tourists, local arts and crafts become the material embodiment of tourist experience and support cross-cultural understanding and meaning making (Handapangoda et al., 2019; Ryan & Crotts, 1997). Changes in the presentation, the design, the meaning, the techniques and the quality of traditional crafts and artifacts have been widely documented when adapting them to tourist needs (Garcia & Pablo, 2017; Handapangoda et al., 2019; Ryan & Crotts, 1997). For example, in the case of Maori carvings in New Zealand, Ryan and Crotts (1997) documented changes in the use of paint, carving techniques and production mode to reduce the cost to fit tourists' willingness to pay. Changes in the design and product development to suit tourists' tastes and needs for modern daily use have also been widely recognized, such as new designs of Miao and Naxi ethnic embroidery and silver ornaments in south-western China (Long, 2012; Sun & Xu, 2018) and weaving products in Chinchero, Peru (Garcia & Pablo, 2017).

Such changes in heritage practices inevitably precipitate economic, environmental and socio-cultural changes to the local communities, such as reshaping traditional gender roles and social relations (Handapangoda et al., 2019; King & Kongpradit, 2019; Ryan & Crotts, 1997; Trupp & Sirijit, 2017), extending the operation mode from household to community (Garcia & Pablo,

2017), modifying livelihoods and lifestyles of practitioners (Wang, 2019), and result in conflicts between native and non-native practitioners in cultural representation (Sun & Xu, 2018).

Many forms of intangible cultural heritage are highly gendered in their presentation and practices with a high proportion of female participants (Trupp & Sirijit, 2017), particularly for performing arts and traditional crafts-making (Handapangoda et al., 2019; Long, 2012; Pöllänen, 2013; Rogerson, 2000; Ryan & Crotts, 1997; Sun & Xu, 2018; Trupp & Sirijit, 2017; Xie, 2003). Examples discussed in the literature include ethnic minority dancers in China (Xie, 2003; Yang, 2011; Yang & Wall, 2009), female art and craft practitioners in Thailand (King & Kongpradit, 2019; Trupp & Sirijit, 2017) and female dancers elsewhere in Southeast Asia (Wall & Mathieson, 2006). Involvement in the performing arts and craft-making, as a means of participating in tourism, can be significant in the personal and social development of rural women (Rogerson, 2000), not only providing economic benefits (King & Kongpradit, 2019; Trupp & Sirijit, 2017), but also generating rewarding experiences for participants (Pöllänen, 2013). Drawing from a case study in Demark, Prince (2017) argued that engagement of local craft-artists in tourism not only supported their livelihoods but also contributed to the preservation of their artistic integrity and supported their professional ambitions.

Therefore, the involvement of women in the provision of tourism experiences, that are rooted in aspects of their culture, extend beyond economic benefits to encompass social, cultural, physiological and political dimensions (Handapangoda et al., 2019; King & Kongpradit, 2019; Trupp & Sirijit, 2017; Xie, 2003; Yang & Wall, 2009). An understanding of these complexities requires more theoretical and empirical research in different environmental, economic, social and cultural contexts.

A framework for the empowerment of women

Although comprising slightly more than half of the total population globally, women are generally under-represented in most respected activities and positions (Boserup, 1970; Kabeer, 2005; Laszlo et al., 2020; Maruyama & Woosnam, 2020). Gender equality and empowerment of women are among the United Nations' Millennium Development Goals (MDGs) and Sustainable Development Goals (SDGs) (Kabeer, 2005; Malema & Naidoo, 2017; O'Hara & Clement, 2018). Although much progress has been made, obstacles such as gendered violence (Malema & Naidoo, 2017), the feminization of poverty (Bárcena-Martín & Moro-Egido, 2013), biased representation of women (Maruyama & Woosnam, 2020) and low access to education (Cherayi & Jose, 2016) continue to hinder progress in the empowerment of women in much of the world (Bárcena-Martín & Moro-Egido, 2013; Laszlo et al., 2020; Malema & Naidoo, 2017). This is particularly evident in developing countries and for indigenous groups (Boserup, 1970; Kabeer, 2005; Laszlo et al., 2020).

Empowerment is a multifaceted and deeply contextual concept (Arroyo et al., 2019; Boley et al., 2015; Kabeer, 2005; Moswete & Lacey, 2015; Scheyvens, 1999, 2000). It is a process and not just a state or an outcome (Eyben & Napier-Moore, 2009; Malema & Naidoo, 2017; Moswete & Lacey, 2015). Although there is little consensus over an exact definition, it is widely agreed that self-determination, access to opportunities and resources and freedom or the power to make one's own decisions are inherent to the notion of empowerment (Bishop & Bowman, 2014; Eyben & Napier-Moore, 2009; Heimtun & Morgan, 2012; Kabeer, 2005; Moswete & Lacey, 2015; Scheyvens, 1999, 2000; Van Klaveren & Tijdens, 2012).

Empowerment of destination communities has long been considered as a prerequisite for sustainable tourism development (Cole, 2006; Joo et al., 2020; Sofield, 2003). Tourism induced empowerment to individuals and communities has been recorded in different geographical and cultural contexts and from various dimensions, which are not limited to economic, social, cultural, environmental and political aspects (Arroyo et al., 2019; Boley et al., 2015; Heimtun & Morgan, 2012; Maruyama & Woosnam, 2020; Ramos & Prideaux, 2014; Scheyvens, 1999, 2000; Schmidt & Uriely, 2019). The need for such empowerments is particularly prominent in marginal places and to marginalized groups, including women (Joo et al., 2020; Maruyama & Woosnam, 2020).

Due to its complex, dynamic and contextual nature, the measurement of women's empowerment is challenging both in theory and in practice (Bishop & Bowman, 2014; Lombardini & Mccollum, 2018). A number of models have been proposed for analysis of the complex nature of women's empowerment (Boley et al., 2015; Cherayi & Jose, 2016; Eyben & Napier-Moore, 2009; Joo et al., 2020; Kabeer, 2005; Moswete & Lacey, 2015; Scheyvens, 2000). Scheyvens (1999, 2000) classified empowerment into economic, psychological, social and political dimensions, and this conceptualization has been widely adopted to analyze tourism-induced community empowerment (Boley et al., 2015; Cherayi & Jose, 2016; Eyben & Napier-Moore, 2009; Joo et al., 2020; Kabeer, 2005; Moswete & Lacey, 2015; Scheyvens, 2000). Considering that women often have lower access to education compared with men in a variety of contexts and the widely recognized positive impacts of education on the above four aspects of empowerment, educational empowerment is added to the proposed women's empowerment framework (Joo et al., 2020; Kabeer, 2005; Moswete & Lacey, 2015; Sha & Ma, 2012).

Economic empowerment refers to the improvement of women's access to and control over resources for production, such as land and capital, access to employment and entrepreneurial opportunities and economic competence in and outside of home (Cherayi & Jose, 2016; Joo et al., 2020; Kabeer, 2005; Laszlo et al., 2020; Scheyvens, 1999, 2000).

Political empowerment mainly involves political representation, the inclusion of women in positions of power or authority and access to decision making for oneself, one's family, the community and the wider society (Cherayi & Jose, 2016; Joo et al., 2020; Kabeer, 2005; Scheyvens, 1999).

Social empowerment encompasses a complex array of factors, including improved family and social status, social networks and relations, safety in family and society, equality, freedom over marriage, social inclusion and improvements in social institutions (Cherayi & Jose, 2016; Hovorka, 2006; Joo et al., 2020; Jütting & Morrisson, 2005; Scheyvens, 1999, 2000).

Beyond improved access to resources and decision making, it is argued that empowerment "must also include the processes that lead people to perceive themselves as able and entitled to occupy that decision-making space" (Rowlands, 1995, p. 87). Therefore, psychological empowerment, emphasizing the "power within," includes self-confidence, critical consciousness, respect of self and from others, fulfillment, leadership and creativity (Joo et al., 2020; O'Hara & Clement, 2018; Rowlands, 1995; Scheyvens, 1999). A lack of psychological empowerment would hinder the realization of the other empowerment dimensions (O'Hara & Clement, 2018; Rowlands, 1995; Scheyvens, 1999).

Education is proposed as a further dimension of empowerment due to its importance for the other dimensions (Kabeer, 2005; Moswete & Lacey, 2015; Sha & Ma, 2012). Access to education can significantly improve women's cognitive abilities which, in turn, enhances the capacity to reflect and act upon changing conditions, gain access to information and develop new ideas (Kabeer, 2005). Educational empowerment usually includes women's initiation into education; enhanced recognition on the part of the self, family, community and the wider society, of the importance of education to women; improved educational opportunities, including formal education and skill training and capacity improvement (Hovorka, 2006; Joo et al., 2020; Jütting & Morrisson, 2005; Moswete & Lacey, 2015; Scheyvens, 1999; Sha & Ma, 2012; van Klaveren & Tijdens, 2012).

The dimensions of empowerment that have been identified are not independent, but interact and are at times overlapping (Arroyo et al., 2019; Jütting & Morrisson, 2005; Scheyvens, 1999; Stanistreet et al., 2007; van Klaveren & Tijdens, 2012). For example, psychological empowerment might be enhanced by improved education, economic competence, enhanced social status and political enfranchisement (Boserup, 1970; Scheyvens, 1999, 2000). Social empowerment can be achieved with or without economic empowerment (Moswete & Lacey, 2015). Furthermore, the empowerment dimensions exhibit different forms at different scales from the self, family and community to the wider society (Cherayi & Jose, 2016; Kabeer, 2005; O'Hara & Clement, 2018; Scheyvens, 1999). For example, educational empowerment can be seen as a higher educational pursuit for individuals, enhanced education opportunities for women in the family, community and wider society and recognition of the importance and efforts to improve access to education

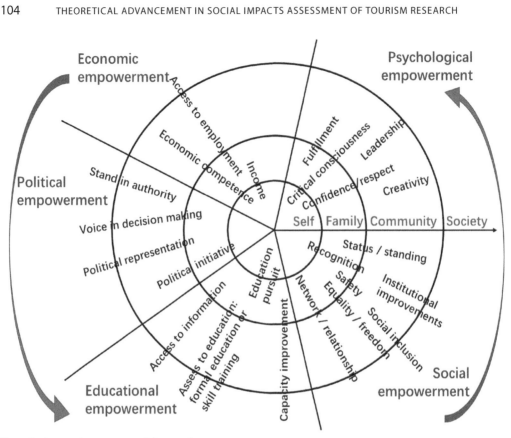

Figure 1. A women's empowerment framework.

for women (Kabeer, 2005; Sha & Ma, 2012). Social empowerment may involve enhancement of women's status in the family, social status improvement in the community and greater recognition in the wider society (Cherayi & Jose, 2016; Sha & Ma, 2012; Sun & Liao, 2016).

Cherayi and Jose (2016), O'Hara and Clement (2018) and Laszlo et al. (2020) analyzed and compared women's empowerment at the individual and household levels in different contexts. Rocha's (1997) ladder of empowerment suggested an empowerment continuum from individual empowerment to collective/community empowerment. The women's empowerment measurement tool published by Oxfam in 2017 provided a three-level framework to measure empowerment of women at personal, relational and environmental levels (Simone et al., 2017). The personal level refers to changes within women themselves, whereas the relational level refers to the relationships and power distribution within a woman's surrounding network as family and community member. The environmental level refers to changes in social norms and attitudes, or political and legislative frameworks in the broader society (Simone et al., 2017). On the basis of above research and to reflect the different representation of women's empowerment at different scales, this study undertakes a systematic analysis through the full scale from the individual, household and community to the wider society levels. In comparison with the three-level measurement of Simone et al. (2017), the separation of empowerment at household and community level permits a better representation of household level empowerment, where women commonly shoulder higher responsibilities in many cultures and societies (Cherayi & Jose, 2016; Laszlo et al., 2020; O'Hara & Clement, 2018; Sha & Ma, 2012; Sun & Liao, 2016).

To further the analysis of the complex structure of women's empowerment, with multiple dimensions and scales, a women's empowerment framework is proposed (Figure 1). The framework integrates five economic, social, psychological, political and educational empowerment dimensions and displays them through four individual, family, community and wider society scales.

Tourism and the empowerment of women

Although the opposite is also true, tourism can empower destination communities, particularly in rural areas or marginal places, in a variety of ways and through multiple impact channels (Arroyo et al., 2019; Boley et al., 2015; Joo et al., 2020; Schmidt & Uriely, 2019; Wall & Mathieson, 2006). Many tourism-associated employment opportunities, particularly in service, catering, accommodation and performance, are highly gendered (Arroyo et al., 2019; Sha & Ma, 2012; Sun and Liao, 2016). Small scale, community-focused or family-run businesses, such as *Nongjiale* rural family hotels in China, have demonstrated substantial benefits to many rural women (Arroyo et al., 2019; Gibson, 2001; Scheyvens, 2000; Sha & Ma, 2012; Su et al., 2019; Sun & Liao, 2016).

Employment opportunities for rural women outside of their homes and traditional roles have generated additional income for women, improving their living standards and reducing their economic dependence on men (Cave & Kilic, 2010; Cherayi & Jose, 2016). In addition to enhanced individual and household economic status, participation in tourism can also improve their social welfare and educational attainment (Arroyo et al., 2019; Duffy et al., 2015; Knight & Cottrell, 2016; Sun & Liao, 2016; Tucker & Boonabaana, 2012). Through interacting with other people and other cultures in tourism, rural women may become more aware of their disadvantaged status in their family and community and, thus, strive for more opportunities outside of their formerly confined domestic space (Arroyo et al., 2019; Cave & Kilic, 2010; Moswete & Lacey, 2015; Sha & Ma, 2012; Sun & Liao, 2016; Zhong, 2010). Previous studies in different cultural contexts have identified that gender roles, and family and societal relationships, are re-negotiated at household and community levels when women participate in tourism employment (Arroyo et al., 2019; Scheyvens, 2000; Sha & Ma, 2012; Sun & Liao, 2016; Tucker & Boonabaana, 2012; Zhong, 2010).

Moreover, through enlarging women's social circle and demonstrating their capabilities beyond the undertaking of domestic chores, tourism participation has the potential to increase women's self-esteem, strengthen their identity and independence and foster initiatives to seek further personal development (Acharya & Halpenny, 2013; Barbieri, et al., 2019; Duffy et al., 2015; Knight & Cottrell, 2016). Political change may be sought to achieve gender equality and enable participation in decision making in their community and in the wider society (Acharya & Halpenny, 2013; Duffy et al., 2015; Joo, et al., 2020).

Although positive consequences of tourism can be identified, negative impacts have also been reported. In many situations, males are privileged in tourism development and women are often confined in low-income and low-skilled jobs that are extensions of their family roles (Arroyo et al., 2019; Çiçek et al., 2017). Rather than increasing freedom, the unequal participation in tourism and unequal benefit distribution from tourism many place additional burdens on women, reinforcing traditional gender ideology and inequality within families (Duffy et al., 2015). There are cases of tourism posting a double-burden on women who are expected to work hard both within and outside of their family setting (Duffy et al., 2015; Sun & Liao, 2016). Tourism employment has been found to disrupt gender roles in family and social structures, weakening family ties in traditional communities, so that positive outcomes from greater involvement in tourism are not assured (Duffy et al., 2015; Van Broeck & Pamukkale, 2001).

Evidence of both positive and negative impacts of tourism involvement on women, particularly in traditional communities, suggests that outcomes are multifaceted and highly contextual (Arroyo et al., 2019; Joo, et al., 2020). Utilizing the empowerment framework that has been introduced above, this article examines and evaluates the empowerment of rural women through tourism.

Ningxia Hui Autonomous Region in the northwest of China has the largest concentration of Hui minority people in the country. Muslim religious and cultural influences emphasize women's household and reproductive responsibilities (Sha & Ma, 2012) and have restricted their ability to take full-time employment outside of the home (Ferguson, 2011; Sha & Ma, 2012; Tucker & Boonabaana, 2012). Using embroidery, an important cultural expression, as a point of entry, this study explores the dynamic relations between heritage, tourism and the empowerment of

Figure 2. Exhibits at the Intangible Cultural Heritage Incubation Centre (ICHIC) (photos by first author, 2017).

women in the Hui minority community. The study furthers theoretical discussions and the measurement of women's empowerment in the tourism context, in particular for a marginalized and conservative society.

Research context and methodology

Haiyuan County Intangible Cultural Heritage Incubation Centre

Haiyuan County in Zhongwei City, Ningxia Hui Autonomous Region (NHAR) in northwest China, is officially recognized nationally as a poor county. Almost all (92%) of the population is rural and 70% are Hui minority. As one of the emerging destinations in China, the overall tourism receipts of Zhongwei City reached 6.01 million Yuan in 2019, about 15% of the overall tourist receipts of NHAR (39.98 million Yuan). Shapotou tourism site, featuring the desert and the Yellow river, is one of the first batch of 5A[1] tourism destinations in China and the most famous one in NHAR. It received more than 1 million tourists in 2019.

Currently, tourism in Haiyuan County is not highly developed and is focused on rural tourism. Although poor, Haiyuan County has rich resources of intangible cultural heritage with Hui characteristics, among which paper cutting and embroidery are the most noteworthy. In recent years, the rich Hui cultural heritage has been considered to be an important resource for creating meaningful tourism experiences in Haiyuan County.

To support the conservation of Hui cultural heritage and ethnic traditions, Haiyuan county government established Haiyuan County Intangible Cultural Heritage Incubation Centre (ICHIC) in 2015 to showcase Hui history. It features and sells embroidery and paper cut products to visitors to Haiyuan County (Figure 2). According to a Haiyuan County government officer and the manager of the incubation center, the incubation centre hosts ten Hui embroidery and paper cutting cooperatives, or micro-firms, which were established and are operated by local Hui women. They are provided with free office and work spaces.

Almost all management staff, employees and participants are rural women, with very few exceptions of men involved in sales and finance. The cooperatives and micro-firms conduct training sessions on embroidery and paper cutting several times each year to rural women in Haiyuan County. Up to the end of 2018, more than 3000 rural women, including about 2600 women from listed poor households, participated in such training. Twelve villages have been developed as "model" embroidery and paper cutting villages. About 1800 listed poor households have been raised out of poverty through engagement in embroidery and paper cutting.

Table 1. List of interviewees.

Type of participants	Interview participants	Age cohort
Local government		
1 Official from the poverty reduction department of Haiyuan County (Male)		
1 Official from the women federation of Haiyuan County (Female)		
Hui embroidery cooperatives		
Cooperative manager	Ms. L	41- to 50-year old
	Ms. T	41- to 50-year old
Women participants	Three participants	20- to 30-year old
	Six participants	31- to 40-year old
	Six participants	41- to 50-year old

Hui embroidery

Embroidery is the art of decorating fabric or other material using needle and thread. It has been practiced throughout China by various ethnic groups for more than 2000 years (Lin, 2005; Zhang, 2006). There are four famous embroidery centres in China: Su Embroidery in Suzhou of Jiangsu Province, Shu Embroidery in Sichuan Province, Xiang Embroidery in Hunan Province and Yue Embroidery in Guangdong Province (Lin, 2005). As an art that is integral to everyday lives, embroidery is predominantly a female pursuit that has been transmitted from mother to daughter over a long period of time (Zhang, 2006). As a symbol of women's intelligence and hard work, skillful practitioners are accorded high respect and admiration (Lin, 2005; Zhang, 2006). As a component of a traditional Chinese woman's life, embroidery is an expression of their moral principles, philosophies, aesthetic ideals, emotions and social life (Lin, 2005; Long, 2012; Zhang, 2006).

Embroidery has been practiced by Hui ethnic minority women in Haiyuan County for centuries, and is known as Hui embroidery (Tang, 2010). The genre is influenced by the Muslim religion, Arabic, Persian and Western Asian cultures and exhibits distinctive artistic presentation, patterns and cultural embedment (Tang, 2010). Traditionally, Hui embroidery features local artistic symbols and religious content for family uses (Tang, 2010).

As expressed by officials of ICHIC and the Women Federation of Haiyuan County, it is expected by the local government that traditional embroidery can be integrated into local tourism offerings, thereby creating employment opportunities for rural women to facilitate poverty reduction, enhance tourists' cultural experiences, preserve local Hui culture and enhance local identity.

Research methods

This research employed a case-study design with qualitative data collected during three field investigations in Haiyuan County during February 2017, October 2017 and May 2018. In order to understand the integration of heritage and tourism on the empowerment of rural women, semi-structured interviews were conducted with officials of the poverty reduction department and the women's federation of the county government, the management staff of two leading embroidery cooperatives and 16 rural women who were engaged in embroidery (Table 1).

As shown in Table 1, the majority of female participants were 30- to 50-year old. All of them were married and originally from Haiyuan County. Their education level was relatively low. Among 19 participants in total, three had senior high school education (including two managers), 11 had junior high school and the rest had primary school education. To ensure the anonymity of interviewees, their names are not revealed.

Interviews with officials of the poverty reduction department and the women's federation of the county government were conducted in the incubation centre. Each interview covered the current status and prospects of Hui embroidery and tourism, and he implications for rural women in Haiyuan County.

The management interviews were carried out individually, face-to-face, at the office of each cooperative and each lasted for about an hour. The development process of the embroidery cooperatives, training of rural women, tourism and Hui embroidery and the impacts on their cooperatives, main constraints and future development prospects were discussed. In particular, the participation of women and changes in their lives was discussed, using the dimensions and scales of the empowerment framework as a guide.

Focus group interviews with embroidery participants were carried out in three groups of four to six participants to make the interviewees more comfortable (Kim et al., 2019). Each focus group interview lasted around 40 min. Personal attitudes, perceptions toward Hui embroidery participation and impacts on their daily life were examined. During focus group interviews, researchers tried to create a casual and comfortable environment, while ensuring that every participant responded to each question. Participant interviewing ceased when no new information was being acquired, indicating that data saturation was reached.

Observations were also made during the fieldwork. Activities in the ICHIC were observed, including the exhibition centre for demonstrating Hui embroidery and paper-cut products, various embroidery cooperatives, the working environment and embroidery being undertaken in the center. Documents were collected, including Haiyuan County basic statistics, Haiyuan County poverty reduction annual reports and annual reports of the women's federation from 2016 to 2018.

Qualitative analysis was carried out for the interview data. Individual interviews and group interviews were noted and transcribed in Chinese. Interview transcripts were then analyzed following the dimensions of the empowerment framework discussed above. Major themes were identified and triangulated with onsite observations and other collected documents. Results were then translated and presented into English.

Findings

Drawing primarily from the government and management interviews, the development status of tourism based on Hui embroidery and the impacts of tourism on women participants in embroidery in Haiyuan County will be discussed first. Then, empowerment of Hui women through tourism participation in embroidery tourism will be examined from economic, educational, social, psychological and political perspectives. In each dimension, differences of women's empowerment will be discussed and compared from individual to societal scales.

Tourism Hui embroidery

Infused with the Hui ethnic culture and tradition as well as influences from Western Asia, Hui embroidery displays rich local character in pattern, design and skills. As conveyed by an ICHIC officer, Hui embroidery is considered to be an important cultural expression of the Hui ethnic minority that can be used in tourism gradually to create rich cultural experiences for tourists and strengthen the cultural identity of the local community.

The managers of both cooperatives that were interviewed had strong personal interests and skills in embroidery that they learned from their mothers. The cooperatives started with small groups of rural women with similar interests in creating embroidery works for family uses in the nearby villages. Supported by the local government's efforts to bolster Hui embroidery and paper cutting and promote their tourism use, both cooperatives moved into the work spaces at ICHIC. High quality Hui embroidery and paper cuts were displayed, interpreted and promoted by ICHIC in their exhibition hall. Gradually, the attention of both tourists and residents was drawn to these examples of Hui heritage and their cultural importance to Haiyuan County. Both managers expressed their pride in their involvement in Hui embroidery and were pleased that,

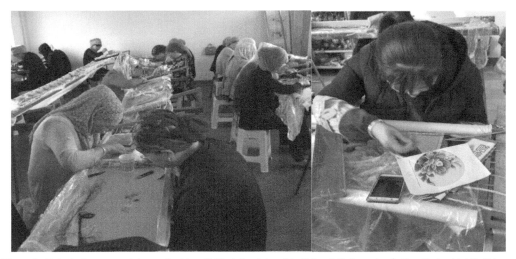

Figure 3. Hui ethnic women doing embroidery (left) at the Intangible Cultural Heritage Incubation Centre (right), Haiyuan County (photographs by the first author, 2017).

with support from government and the development of tourism, they could expand their businesses and have more "sisters" to work for the cooperatives.

Each of the two cooperatives has 30 to 40 regular employees working in ICHIC, who mainly produce large scale products that require high skills, such as silk scarfs and artistic works (Figure 3). The only male employee in Ms L's cooperative is responsible for sales and finance.

In addition to participants working in ICHIC, both cooperatives also recruited rural women through regular training sessions held in nearby villages. According to officials of the ICHIC and the women's federation, such training is supported financially by the local government as an important strategy for poverty reduction of rural women who are free to participate, especially if they are listed as belonging to poor households. When trained participants have acquired the necessary skills, the embroidery cooperatives provide them with raw materials, patterns and designs of products and collect their work regularly, paying for each item. Currently, each interviewed cooperative has about 200 casual participants from nearby villages and usually produce small pieces of embroidery to sell to tourists, such as pendants and shoe insoles, or pieces to be used as part of other products.

According to interviews with the manager of ICHIC and two managers of embroidery cooperatives, tourism use of Hui embroidery has expanded the demand for embroidery products beyond domestic use, such as bed sheets and pillow covers, to products that are suited to tourists' needs and preferences. Some traditional items continue to be popular among tourists, such as blessing bags, pendants and insoles. Some are modified with new patterns and designs to meet tourists' aesthetic preferences, such as traditional Hui head scarves adjusted to neck scarves. Moreover, new products with new designs and modern uses have been developed, such as cups, lipstick cases, wallets, scarves and handbags (Figure 4). In the process of creating new designs and products, both managers and employees contribute their ideas and skills to supplement traditional patterns. As Ms. L, manager of one cooperative, shared with us:

> My sisters in the cooperative all tried hard to think of what we could produce for tourists. We checked many websites. We discuss and try different patterns in the workshop. We also talk with tourists to ICHIC. They give us ideas too. Gradually, we developed many products. For example, hand embroidered silk scarves with flower patterns are very popular among female tourists. It is not an easy process, but very rewarding!

As revealed in interviews, Ms. L expressed that, to increase sales through tourism, with the support of ICHIC, she confirmed collaboration with the Shapotou tourism group, to sell embroidery products at Shapotou. She also established partnerships with local leather and bag producers to make leather or cloth wallets and handbags with embroidery patterns for tourists.

Figure 4. Examples of embroidery artwork and products (Top: embroidery of traditional Chinese painting; Bottom: handbag, slippers, wallet, pendants) (photographs by the first author, 2017).

In summary, our research revealed that involvement with tourism, in both the formal and informal sectors, has increased the demand for and diversity of Hui embroidery products, thereby increasing the participation of women in embroidery production, which is consistent with similar research in other contexts in China and worldwide (Garcia & Pablo, 2017; Handapangoda et al., 2019; Long, 2012; Sun & Xu, 2018). As tourists' demand for embroidery is different than the traditional domestic uses, creativity has been encouraged (Garcia & Pablo, 2017; Long, 2012; Wang, 2019). The embroidery cooperatives and practitioners have been stimulated to create new designs and new products, to establish new collaborations and partnerships, and to try new marketing and sales channels that are suited the tourism market.

Women's empowerment through tourism participation

Drawing upon interviews with Hui embroiderers, the empowerment of women is analyzed using the theoretical framework (Figure 1) consisting of five dimensions and four scales from the individual, family and community to the wider society.

Economic empowerment

Consistent with other studies, tourism has increased the demand for embroidery products and the number of participants (Garcia & Pablo, 2017; Long, 2012; Sun & Xu, 2018; Wang, 2019). The number of rural women producing Hui embroidery for money has greatly increased. They either work in cooperatives in ICHIC or casually at home. All interviewed participants agreed that this resulted in a substantial increase of personal income which had enhanced their family's economic conditions.

Figure 5. Rural women selling embroidered insoles with traditional patterns and local vegetables along the road to a tourist destination (photographs by the first author, 2017).

The flexible working hours and location are well suited to the schedules of rural women who still shoulder traditional household responsibilities. Many interviewees commented that they have relatives and friends who cannot go to the cooperative every day and, therefore, choose to work at home. Even though their income is lower, they appreciate the opportunity to take care of their family and agricultural work, and make extra income in their spare time. Some now sell their products on the roadside close to tourism destinations near their villages (Figure 5).

According to ICHIC statistics, by the end of 2018, more than 3000 rural women made embroidery or paper cuts, supporting substantially their rural families and county level poverty reduction. According to an ICHIC report, 620 families have escaped poverty through participation in embroidery and paper cutting.

At the individual level, salaries are paid based on the quality and quantity of work produced. According to a manager and participant interviews, the average income for long-term employees at embroidery cooperatives is about CNY2700 - CNY2800 (USD 415 − 440) per month, which is higher than the average monthly wage income of CNY 1608.8 (USD 230) in Haiyuan County in the first half of 2019 (HYC, 2019). Casual participants' incomes differ widely due to the circumstances of each participant but are usually around several hundred CNY per month. Income from embroidery substantially enhances the economic competence and independence of rural women who previously did not have any income despite undertaking household chores and agricultural practices. As interviewees stated:

> I am happy that I have an income and do not need to ask for money from my husband. Now I can buy clothes or shoes for myself without asking my husband's permission.
>
> Also, it is more convenient to buy things for my own parents, as it is using my own money.

Educational empowerment

From educational perspectives, similar to cases of Miao and Naxi embroidery (Long, 2012; Sun & Xu, 2018), tourism has enhanced the value, recognition and market demand for Hui embroidery. Training sessions are organized regularly by embroidery cooperatives and supported by ICHIC.

Such training provides educational opportunities for rural women to acquire additional skills that may generate extra income. It is welcomed by rural women and is widely supported by their families. ICHIC also organizes training for existing cooperatives to enhance their professional and business capacities. According to the ICHIC plan and interview results, training has reached about 3000 rural women from 36 villages, including 2600 from listed poor families.

In addition, the research identified that interview participants demonstrated higher pursuit of education and skill training for themselves as involvement in Hui embroidery and tourism made them realize their limitations. As Ms. L said:

> In the past, we used traditional patterns for domestic products or some clients would provide their design. But for tourism products, we need to design and develop by ourselves. It is challenging. We have no education in design or art. That is something we really need to improve. Last year, ICHIC organized a trip to Suzhou to visit Su Embroidery and exchange with their masters. It helped a lot. But I think training in design is necessary for us.

Beyond educational pursuit at the individual level, the importance of support for their children to pursue higher education is also widely recognized by all interviewees. This is extending positive educational impacts to the family level, particularly for the next generation. As one participant shared:

> Education is very important. I just finished middle school. My daughter is now in middle school and her study is good. I told her that she should study hard and go to university. I will support her education.

Social empowerment

Enhanced recognition of the value of Hui embroidery has broadened participants' social circles, contributing to the enhanced status of rural women at a variety of scales (Long, 2012; Sun & Xu, 2018). For the individual, recognition of their own value and their contribution to the family were commonly recognized by interviewees. Even though the status of men in the family is still high, as is traditional in the Hui community (Sha & Ma, 2012), enhanced economic competence and self-recognition underpin noticeable improvements in social standing and freedom at the family level (Sun & Liao, 2016). As one interviewee expressed:

> As I have income as much as my husband, my husband will not comment too much if I buy something he may not like. Sometimes, he asks for my ideas, Haha ….

Interviewees indicated that participation in Hui embroidery is recognized positively as being appropriate and in line with Hui ethnic traditions at the community level. Particularly, as women dominate participation from managers to practitioners, there is a common understanding of traditional Hui culture and respect for women's family responsibilities. This grants women high flexibility in time and location and makes it easier for them to achieve an acceptable balance between work and family commitments. This is much appreciated by participants:

> My family is very supportive to my job here, as it is flexible. If there is something to do at home, I can easily ask for a day off.

> As my kids are going to school in the town centre, I am renting an apartment to accompany my kids in the town center. This job fits me very well. I come to the centre after sending my kids to school every morning. Around noon, I pick up my kids and make lunch at home. After lunch I come back to work. Other jobs do not allow such flexibility. Our manager is very nice to us. If I have to stay at home due to family conditions, I just phone her and tell her the reason. I can make up my work when I have time.

> I am the same, moving to town as my kids go to middle school. I have no other things to do during the day. I enjoy coming here doing embroidery and chatting with fellow sisters.

Even though women still have to maintain their traditional role in the family, the recognition of their ability to contribute to family and society is increasing. The official from the county women's federation commented:

Traditionally in a Hui community, women's social status is low. Women are supposed to take care of families and domestic chores. Therefore, you can see in Ningxia, usually only men migrate to work in cities; most rural women remain in the village. The embroidery and paper cutting cooperatives have given many women an opportunity to earn their own income, develop their career and expand their social circle without leaving home. This is very important to improve their family status and social standing in the community. This is part of our "Women's poverty reduction with skillful hands" action from the provincial to the county level.

Psychological empowerment

At the individual level, all interviewees agree that participation in Hui embroidery has enhanced self-confidence and encouraged positive self-evaluation and recognition of personal ability and value. In addition, respect from family members and tourists or other visitors are pointed out and appreciated by interviewees:

> When I shared my embroidery works with my daughter, she was very impressed and she said, "Mom, you are so talented! Can you teach me embroidery?" I feel very happy and proud to hear that!

> From time to time, there are different types of visitors and reporters coming to our working space to see us doing embroidery. They take many pictures and speak highly of our embroidery works. It is a good recognition of us.

With life no longer fully confined to the family (Sun & Liao, 2016), fellow women working together provide chances to chat, exchange and share ideas and feelings, enhancing their psychological and emotional states.

The two managers interviewed, Ms. L and Ms. T, both demonstrated strong self-confidence and self-recognition during the interviews. They both expressed their feelings of achievements gained from starting and operating a cooperative and, in particular, from bringing many rural women together. Creativity, self-consciousness and self-motivation are important psychological attributes gained through the process of operating a Hui embroidery cooperative. Ms. L said:

> Of course, Hui embroidery opened a door for me! It is a meaningful career. Not only I have benefited from it; many sisters around me have benefited from it! …. If not for Hui embroidery, I would never have had a chance to attend the provincial award ceremony…. Running the cooperative is much more complicated than the embroidery itself. It is not only about a good quality product, but about management, organization, sales and marketing and many other things. I am still learning.

Political empowerment

Interviews with participants reveal that most Hui embroidery participants do not pursue political power or desire to get involved in political decisions. Their attention is still centered on their family and close social networks. Therefore, at the individual level, female participants in Hui embroidery do not exhibit higher political empowerment.

Nevertheless, with the development of Hui embroidery tourism and the growing public recognition of Hui embroidery, women leaders are emerging as represented by Ms. L and Ms. T. Both of them have been accredited with the title "Inheritor of Intangible Cultural Heritage" of Hui embroidery of Ningxia Hui Autonomous Region. Their embroidery has received many awards, has been reported upon by newspapers, and some items are included in the Ningxia Ethnicity Art Museum. Ms. L is also recognized as a "Woman Entrepreneur Star" at the county, city and provincial levels due to her contribution to Hui embroidery and support for local women. Such awards and recognition grant them opportunities to participate in matters at the county level, and sometime at the provincial level, in decision making as county representatives, particularly in areas concerning cultural heritage and rural women through the women's federation department and the poverty reduction department.

Therefore, it can be concluded that the attention accorded to cultural heritage in the form of Hui embroidery and its use as a tourism attraction and product have pushed Hui embroidery, traditionally a female pursuit for family use, into the public agenda and have made it important to the whole ethnic community and the wider society at the provincial level. It has provided opportunities for Hui embroidery participants to make their voices heard in the political decision-making process. Despite small improvements in political empowerment, it is not substantial compared with other four aspects. Faced with more fundamental structural issues, political representation of women is improving slowly at the community and society level in Haiyuan County and Ningxia Hui Autonomous Region.

Discussions

Gendered cultural practices and tourism

Embroidery is traditionally a female practice symbolizing female intelligence and skillful hands (Lin, 2005; Long, 2012; Sun & Xu, 2018; Zhang, 2006) and it reflects the traditional Chinese gender ideology. However, perceptions of Hui ethnic culture and tradition are evolving, and Hui embroidery is now widely considered to be an important cultural expression of the Hui ethnic minority (Sha & Ma, 2012) that can be used in tourism to create rich cultural experiences for tourists and strengthen the identity of the local community (Long, 2012; Sun & Xu, 2018).

The research has identified that involvement in tourism has increased demand and extended the embroidery product line, thus, increasing participation opportunities for rural women by creating paid employment in both formal and informal sectors. This finding is similar to previous research on the use of ethnic embroidery in tourism in China (Long, 2012; Sun & Xu, 2018). With relatively lower requirements in skill and work space than the finer creations, the tourism Hui embroidery product line provides more opportunities for beginners and rural women that cannot work outside home to produce small items and get additional income. In addition, as tourism demand for Hui embroidery products is primarily for small items with modern uses, it calls for new design and product development. Therefore, tourism involvement encourages creativity in the cooperatives and among the practitioners to create new designs, new products and new marketing and sales channels suited to the desires of the tourism industry.

Hui women's empowerment through tourism participation

Research identified that with high flexibility in time and location, engagement in Hui embroidery exhibited high suitability for rural women, who usually shoulder a variety of family responsibilities at home. While ICHIC and its display area have become a tourist attraction and most embroiderers in both the formal and informal sectors will engage with tourists, some can benefit by working from home without necessarily meeting with tourists. They are involved in and benefit from tourism indirectly. Hui embroidery tourism effectively transfers economic benefits from tourism to rural women and their families, which also supports poverty reduction efforts at community and societal scales. This is particularly important for geographically marginalized ethnic areas (Long, 2012; Sun & Xu, 2018). Improvements in education and the social and psychological status of rural women have been observed from individual, family to community and the wider society scales. Despite low recognition of enhanced political awareness among individual participants, political empowerment has been identified for female leaders at the community and societal levels. Emerging women leaders are equipped with recognized skills in intangible cultural heritage and take leadership roles in managing the cooperatives and connecting rural women, and contribute to the maintenance of local culture and traditions, albeit in slightly modified forms.

Practical implications

Several key challenges exist for Hui embroidery tourism development in Haiyuan County. First, Hui embroidery is rooted in the community and practiced through instruction in the family. The practitioners usually do not have systematic training in design, which restricts their product development potential to integrate traditional designs with contemporary aesthetic trends for tourism use. Second, restricted by financial and human resources, Hui embroidery cooperatives do not have the capacity individually to market their products and expand their marketing and sales channels. Nevertheless, Hui embroidery cooperatives are small firms that shoulder high responsibility in poverty reduction. Through providing free training and supplying raw materials in advance for casual participants and guaranteeing to purchase embroidery products from listed poor families, Hui embroidery cooperatives also have to take financial risks.

In response to the above challenges, the following recommendations are proposed. First, to improve design and product development capacity, training sessions and workshops could be organized for management staff and embroidery practitioners, particularly on integrating traditional characteristics with modern artistic trends. Exchanges with other more developed embroidery experts and companies can be organized. In addition, collaborations with educational intuitions can be established, such as the art departments of universities in Ningxia, to initiate programs and activities for students and faculty members to engage in embroidery product design, such as organizing an annual embroidery design competition. Such collaboration will not only provide new ideas in design and product development, to enhance the capacity of current Hui embroidery participants, but also can attract new generations into the Hui embroidery industry to support heritage inheritance.

Second, considering the current needs for professional and technical support and collaboration, a technical centre aiding the ICHIC should be created to foster collaboration and share resources among Hui embroidery and paper cutting cooperatives in ICHIC. The centre could engage in collaborative sales and marketing promotions for all cooperatives, using both traditional and new channels, including popular social media. Such a centre could also provide design and product development services to support cooperatives to enhance the design capacity and improve their in business management skills.

Third, to enhance the financial stability of Hui embroidery cooperatives, poverty reduction funding from the local government could be allocated to cooperatives so that they can better respond to the needs of listed poor families. This would further encourage the actions of cooperatives in poverty reduction. In addition to government financial support, special low interest commercial loans could be negotiated with the support of ICHIC or the local government to support cooperatives.

Study limitations and future research

As a means rather than an end, women's empowerment through tourism is a dynamic, continuous and multifacet process, with understanding and implications evolving with temporal and contextual changes (Eyben & Napier-Moore, 2009; Kabeer, 2005; Malema & Naidoo, 2017; Moswete & Lacey, 2015; Scheyvens, 1999, 2000). The proposed multidimensional and multiscale empowerment framework extends the understanding of women's empowerment and has proven to be useful in evaluating tourism induced empowerment of women in a marginalized society. However, as a highly contested and contextual concept, the discussion of empowerment will continue in other situations. Future studies could apply this framework in other destinations and for different cultural expressions in other cultural and tourism contexts.

This study extends the current discussion on the empowerment of women through tourism. Only the most common dimensions are included in the framework, and other dimensions, such as environmental empowerment emphasizing community's ability to gain power to protect and preserve the surrounding ecosystem (Ramos & Prideaux, 2014) and spiritual empowerment (Heimtun & Morgan, 2012) have not been singled out as distinctive dimensions. This does not mean that such dimensions are irrelevant. Further research can be conducted to focus on elements that are especially important for the target study area to further extend the understanding and measurement of women's empowerment.

Due to restrictions of time and resources, only two main Hui embroidery cooperatives and a limited number of participants working at the ICHIC were interviewed in the research. Future research could reach out to participants working at home in nearby villages to understand their opinions and the changes occurring to their lives. Such research could enhance the understanding of different types of women's empowerment through different types or levels of participation in heritage tourism.

Traditional Hui embroidery has been conveniently integrated into the responsibilities of rural women in Haiyuan County due to its flexibility of time and location. Despite the positive attitude obtained from interview respondents, there is a concern for the "double burden" being imposed on local women beyond traditional domestic responsibilities. Future researchers could conduct interviews with women participants and their family members to assess whether such changes in women's roles have been recognized and to what extent domestic arrangements have been adjusted due to women's engagement in tourism, as has been found in other minority communities in Guizhou Province of China (Sun & Liao, 2016).

In addition, the important role of women leaders has been identified in advancing cultural heritage development and the participation of women in heritage practices and tourism development. In particular, women leaders are exhibiting higher pursuit of political empowerment through tourism and embroidery and have high influence on local women. Further research could focus on how the leadership of women in traditional communities can be encouraged through tourism development linked to the sharing of their cultural heritage.

In focusing upon the changing situation of poor minority women, it should be recognized that their situation is influenced by broad circumstances that are beyond their control. For example, they are required to operate within a culture and governmental power system that impinge on many aspects of their lives and that are difficult to change. Minority women live in societies with structural inequalities that are deeply embedded and more fundamental changes in structural norms may be required to further empower women. It may even be argued that the making of relatively small changes, such as those encapsulated in embroidery and tourism, act to perpetuate the *status quo* to the neglect of more far-reaching societal changes that are required to remove broad constraints that circumscribe situation in which women find themselves. This is an important but much larger topic than heritage tourism. It is an opportunity for further research and, ultimately, actions that modify the ways in which societies operate.

Conclusions

Highly visible expressions of local culture and society have become significant resource in cultural heritage tourism worldwide. Textiles, clothing styles and associated accoutrements have become symbols of societies and are widely used in tourism advertising as markers of "the other," which are worn in performances, displayed in museums and sold as tourism products (Handapangoda et al., 2019; Long, 2012; Ryan & Crotts, 1997; Sun & Xu, 2018; Trupp & Sirijit, 2017). Rural women are important bearers of the underpinning skills and knowledge, yet they are commonly among the most vulnerable stakeholders in rural societies (Long, 2012; Sha & Ma, 2012; Sun & Liao, 2016; Sun & Xu, 2018). Although often poor and of low status, many rural women, especially in ethnic communities, possess skills that are becoming increasingly uncommon in the urban centres from which most tourists emanate (Long, 2012; Sun & Liao, 2016; Sun & Xu, 2018; Wang, 2019). Engaging rural women in the demonstration and practices of their intangible cultural heritage for tourism is a strategy that can be used to maintain and even revive local cultural expressions, while empowering rural women and supporting them and their communities economically (Arroyo et al., 2019; Handapangoda et al., 2019; Long, 2012; Schmidt & Uriely, 2019; Sun & Liao, 2016; Sun & Xu, 2018).

Using Hui embroidery and tourism in Haiyuan County in Ningxia Hui Autonomous Region, China, as a case study, it has been shown that tourism markets are being used to increase the demand and extend the product line of embroidery products (Long, 2012; Sun & Xu, 2018). Thus, the overall participation of women in tourism is increased, both directly and indirectly, and in the formal and informal sectors.

As a dynamic, multifaceted and deeply contextual concept, the measurement of women's empowerment is challenging both in theory and in practice (Arroyo et al., 2019; Bishop & Bowman, 2014; Cole, 2006; Joo et al., 2020; Kabeer, 2005; Lombardini & Mccollum, 2018; Scheyvens, 1999, 2000; Simone et al., 2017). A framework for the assessment of women's empowerment, with five dimensions and four scales, is devised from previous research to guide the investigation of rural women's involvement in Hui embroidery tourism. Such tourism is contributing to economic well-being, and is also providing feasible paths for social, psychological, educational and political empowerment to varying degrees. The women's empowerment framework has proven to be useful in understanding the complexity of women's empowerment and in identifying areas for improvement and can be used to explore other situations.

Note

1. A 5A tourism desintation is the highest level of tourism destinations in the China's government accredation system, which rates tourism desitnstions from A to AAAAA in terms of quality of tourism reserouces, infrastructure, services, management and other criteria.

Acknowledgement

Special thanks to Haiyuan county government and all the interview participants for the support to our research.

Disclosure statement

No potential conflict of interest was reported by the authors.

Funding

This research is supported by the Fundamental Research Funds for the Central Universities, and the Research Funds of Renmin University of China (19XNI004) to Dr. Ming Ming Su.

References

Acharya, B. P., & Halpenny, E. A. (2013). Homestays as an alternative tourism product for sustainable community development: A case study of women-managed tourism product in rural Nepal. *Tourism Planning & Development*, 10(4), 367–387. https://doi.org/10.1080/21568316.2013.779313

Arroyo, C. G., Barbieri, C., Sotomayor, S., & Knollenberg, W. (2019). Cultivating women's empowerment through agritourism: Evidence from Andean communities. *Sustainability*, 11, 3058.

Barbieri, C., Stevenson, K. T., & Knollenberg, W. (2019). Broadening the utilitarian epistemology of agritourism research through children and families. *Current Issues in Tourism*, 22(19), 2333–2336. https://doi.org/10.1080/13683500.2018.1497011

Bárcena-Martín, E., & Moro-Egido, A. I. (2013). Gender and poverty risk in Europe. *Feminist Economics*, 19(2), 69–99.

Bishop, D., & Bowman, K. (2014). Still learning: A critical reflection on three years of measuring women's empowerment in Oxfam. *Gender & Development*, 22(2), 253–269. https://doi.org/10.1080/13552074.2014.920993

Boley, B. B., Maruyama, N., & Woosnam, K. M. (2015). Measuring empowerment in an eastern context: Findings from Japan. *Tourism Management*, 50, 112–122.

Boserup, E. (1970). *Woman's role in economic development*. Allen & Unwin.

Cave, P., & Kilic, S. (2010). The role of women in tourism employment with special reference to Antalya, Turkey. *Journal of Hospitality Marketing & Management*, 19(3), 280–292. https://doi.org/10.1080/19368621003591400

Cherayi, S., & Jose, J. P. (2016). Empowerment and social inclusion of Muslim women: Towards a new conceptual model. *Journal of Rural Studies*, 45, 243–251. https://doi.org/10.1016/j.jrurstud.2016.04.003

Chhabra, D., Healy, R., & Sills, E. (2003). Staged authenticity and heritage tourism. *Annals of Tourism Research*, 30(3), 702–719. https://doi.org/10.1016/S0160-7383(03)00044-6

Chris Ryan, & John Crotts. (1997). Carving and tourism: a maori perspective. *Annals of Tourism Research*, 24(4), 898–918.

Çiçek, D., Zencir, E., & Kozak, N. (2017). Women in Turkish tourism. *Journal of Hospitality and Tourism Management*, 31, 228–234. https://doi.org/10.1016/j.jhtm.2017.03.006

Cole, S. (2006). Cultural tourism, community participation and empowerment. In Melanie Smith & Mike Robinson (Eds.), *Cultural tourism in a changing world: Politics, participation and (re)presentation* (pp.89–103). Channel View Publications.

Duffy, L. N., Kline, C. S., Mowatt, R. A., & Chancellor, H. C. (2015). Women in tourism: Shifting gender ideology in the DR. *Annals of Tourism Research*, 52, 72–86. https://doi.org/10.1016/j.annals.2015.02.017

Esfehani, M. H., & Albrecht, J. N. (2018). Roles of intangible cultural heritage in tourism in natural protected areas. *Journal of Heritage Tourism*, 13(1), 15–29. https://doi.org/10.1080/1743873X.2016.1245735

Eyben, R., & Napier-Moore, R. (2009). Choosing words with care? Shifting meanings of women's empowerment in international development. *Third World Quarterly*, 30(2), 285–300. https://doi.org/10.1080/01436590802681066

Ferguson, L. (2011). Promoting gender equality and empowering women? Tourism and the third Millennium Development Goal. *Current Issues in Tourism*, 14(3), 235–249. https://doi.org/10.1080/13683500.2011.555522

Garcia, & Pablo. (2017). Weaving for tourists in chinchero, peru. *Journal of Material Culture*, 135918351772509.

Gonzalez, M. V. (2008). Intangible heritage tourism and identity. *Tourism Management*, 29, 807–810.

Handapangoda, W. S., Bandara, H. M., & Kumara, U. A. (2019). Exploring tradition in heritage tourism: The experience of Sri Lanka's traditional mask art. *International Journal of Heritage Studies*, 25(4), 415–436. https://doi.org/10.1080/13527258.2018.1481132

Heimtun, B., & Morgan, N. (2012). Proposing paradigm peace: Mixed methods in feminist tourism research. *Tourist Studies*, 12(3), 287–304. https://doi.org/10.1177/1468797612461088

Hovorka, A. J. (2006). Urban agriculture: Addressing practical and strategic gender needs. *Development in Practice*, 16(1), 51–61. https://doi.org/10.1080/09614520500450826

HYC. (2019). *Haiyuan County Government Official Website: Growth of disposable income of urban residents in Haiyuan County in the first half of 2019 8.9%*. Retrieved May 20, 2020 from http://www.hy.gov.cn/xxgk/zfxxgkml/tjxx/tjfx/201907/t20190730_1636286.html

Joo, D., Woosnam, K. M., Strzelecka, M., & Boley, B. B. (2020). Knowledge, empowerment, and action: Testing the empowerment theory in a tourism context. *Journal of Sustainable Tourism*, 28(1), 69–85. https://doi.org/10.1080/09669582.2019.1675673

Jütting, J. P., & Morrisson, C. (2005). Changing social institutions to improve the status of women in developing countries. *SSRN Electronic Journal*. https://ssrn.com/abstract=871445; https://doi.org//10.2139/ssrn.871445

Kabeer, N. (2005). Gender equality and women's empowerment: A critical analysis of the third millennium development goal. *Gender & Development*, 13(1), 13–24. https://doi.org/10.1080/13552070512331332273

Kim, S., Whitford, M., & Arcodia, C. (2019). Development of intangible cultural heritage as a sustainable tourism resource: The intangible cultural heritage practitioners' perspectives. *Journal of Heritage Tourism*, 14(5–6), 422–435. https://doi.org/10.1080/1743873X.2018.1561703

King, R., & Kongpradit, W. (2019). Tourism to a realm of memory: The case of a Thai royal craft. *Journal of Tourism and Cultural Change*, 17(6), 710–724. https://doi.org/10.1080/14766825.2018.1526298

Knight, D. W., & Cottrell, S. P. (2016). Evaluating tourism-linked empowerment in Cuzco. *Annals of Tourism Research*, 56, 32–47. https://doi.org/10.1016/j.annals.2015.11.007

Laszlo, S., Grantham, K., Oskay, E., & Zhang, T. (2020). Grappling with the challenges of measuring women's economic empowerment in intrahousehold settings. *World Development*, 132, 104959. https://doi.org/10.1016/j.worlddev.2020.104959

Lin, X. D. (2005). *Chinese embroidery*. People's Fine Arts Publishing House.

Lombardini, S., & Mccollum, K. (2018). Using internal evaluations to measure organisational impact: A meta-analysis of Oxfam's women's empowerment projects. *Journal of Development Effectiveness*, 10(1), 145–126. https://doi.org/10.1080/19439342.2017.1377750

Long, Y. (2012). The significance and strategy of the development and design of Miao embroidery tourism commodities in Guizhou from the perspective of inheritance and protection. *Guizhou Ethnic Studies*, (05), 59–61. (in Chinese)

Malema, D. R., & Naidoo, S. (2017). The role of community arts and crafts in the empowerment of women living in a rural environment. *World Leisure Journal*, 59(Suppl. 1), 54–60. https://doi.org/10.1080/16078055.2017.1393878

Maruyama, N. U., & Woosnam, K. M. (2020). Representation of "mill girls" at a UNESCO World Heritage Site in Gunma, Japan. *Journal of Sustainable Tourism*, 1–18. https://doi.org/10.1080/09669582.2020.1738443

Megeirhi, H. A., Woosnam, K. M., Ribeiro, M. A., Ramkissoon, H., & Denley, T. J. (2020). Employing a value-belief-norm framework to gauge Carthage residents' intentions to support sustainable cultural heritage tourism. *Journal of Sustainable Tourism*, 28(9), 1351–1370. https://doi.org/10.1080/09669582.2020.1738444

Moswete, N., & Lacey, G. (2015). Women cannot lead: Empowering women through cultural tourism in Botswana. *Journal of Sustainable Tourism*, 23(4), 600–617. https://doi.org/10.1080/09669582.2014.986488

O'Hara, C., & Clement, F. (2018). Power as agency: A critical reflection on the measurement of women's empowerment in the development sector. *World Development*, 106, 111–123.

Pöllänen, S. (2013). The meaning of craft: Craft makers' descriptions of craft as an occupation. *Scandinavian Journal of Occupational Therapy*, 20(3), 217–227. https://doi.org/10.3109/11038128.2012.725182

Prince, S. (2017). Craft-art in the Danish countryside: Reconciling a lifestyle, livelihood and artistic career through rural tourism. *Journal of Tourism and Cultural Change*, 15(4), 339–358. https://doi.org/10.1080/14766825.2016.1154064

Ramos, A. M., & Prideaux, B. (2014). Indigenous ecotourism in the Mayan rainforest of Palenque: Empowerment issues in sustainable development. *Journal of Sustainable Tourism*, 22(3), 461–479. https://doi.org/10.1080/09669582.2013.828730

Rocha, E. M. (1997). A ladder of empowerment. *Journal of Planning Education and Research*, 17(1), 31–44. https://doi.org/10.1177/0739456X9701700104

Rogerson, C. M. (2000). Rural handicraft production in the developing world. *Agrekon*, 39(2), 193–217. https://doi.org/10.1080/03031853.2000.9524938

Rowlands, J. (1995). Empowerment examined. *Development in Practice*, 5(2), 101–107. https://doi.org/10.1080/0961452951000157074

Scheyvens, R. (1999). Ecotourism and the empowerment of local communities. *Tourism Management*, 20(2), 245–249. https://doi.org/10.1016/S0261-5177(98)00069-7

Scheyvens, R. (2000). Promoting women's empowerment through involvement in ecotourism: Experiences from the third world. *Journal of Sustainable Tourism*, 8(3), 232–249. https://doi.org/10.1080/09669580008667360

Schmidt, J., & Uriely, N. (2019). Tourism development and the empowerment of local communities: The case of Mitzpe Ramon, a peripheral town in the Israeli Negev Desert. *Journal of Sustainable Tourism*, 27(6), 805–825. https://doi.org/10.1080/09669582.2018.1515952

Sha, A. X., & Ma, Y. H. (2012). A study on the transformation of women's role in the development of Nongjiale tourism in Hui inhabited areas—Jingyuan County of Ningxia Hui Autonomous Region. *Journal of Northern University for Nationalities (Philosophy and Social Sciences)*, (005), 107–110. (in Chinese).

Simone, L., Kimberly, B., & Rosa, G. (2017). *A 'How To' Guide to Measuring Women's Empowerment: Sharing experience from Oxfam's impact evaluations*. Oxfam GB, Oxfam House.

Smith, L. (2014). *Uses of heritage*. Springer.

Smith, L. & Akagawa, N. (Eds.). (2009). *Intangible heritage*. Routledge.

Smith, L., & Waterton, E. (2009). The envy of the world? Intangible heritage in England. *Brain Research*, 179(2), 385–389.

Sofield, T. H. B. (2003). *Empowerment for sustainable tourism development*. Oxford.

Stanistreet, D., Swami, V., Pope, D., Bambra, C., & Scott-Samuel, A. (2007). Women's empowerment and violent death among women and men in Europe: An ecological study. The *Journal of Men's Health & Gender*, *4*(3), 257–265. https://doi.org/10.1016/j.jmhg.2007.05.003

Su, M. M., Wall, G., Wang, Y. N., & Jin, M. (2019). Livelihood sustainability in a rural tourism destination - Hetu Town, Anhui Province, China. *Tourism Management*, *71*, 272–281. https://doi.org/10.1016/j.tourman.2018.10.019

Sun, J. X., & Liao, J. L. (2016). The influence of tourism participation on the division of labor between the genders in ethnic minority families. *The Ideological Front*, *042*(001), 105–110. (in Chinese)

Sun, J. X., & Xu, Y. X. (2018). Interpretation and reconstruction of intangible cultural heritage for perspectives of culture capitalization: A case study based on Naxi Embroidery. *The Ideological Front*, *3*, 21–27. (in Chinese)

Tang, K. (2010). Haiyuan Hui Embroidery: Integration of the east and west embroidery. *Oriental Collection*, (004), 108–109. (in Chinese)

Trupp, A., & Sirijit, S. (2017). Gendered practices in urban ethnic tourism in Thailand. *Annals of Tourism Research*, *64*, 76–86. https://doi.org/10.1016/j.annals.2017.02.004

Tucker, H., & Boonabaana, B. (2012). A critical analysis of tourism, gender and poverty reduction. *Journal of Sustainable Tourism*, *20*(3), 437–455. https://doi.org/10.1080/09669582.2011.622769

UNESCO. (2018). *Basic texts of the 2003 convention for the safeguarding of the intangible cultural heritage (2018 edition)*. Retrieved May 6, 2020, from https://ich.unesco.org/doc/src/2003_Convention_Basic_Texts-_2018_version-EN.pdf.

UNESCO. (2019). *Living Heritage and Indigenous Peoples*. United Nations Educational, Scientific and Cultural Organization (UNESCO).

UNESCO. (2020). *What is intangible cultural heritage?* Retrieved May 6, 2020 from https://ich.unesco.org/en/what-is-intangible-heritage-00003

Uysal, M., Sirgy, M. J., Woo, E., & Kim, H. L. (2016). Quality of life (QOL) and well-being research in tourism. *Tourism Management*, *53*, 244–261. https://doi.org/10.1016/j.tourman.2015.07.013

Van Broeck, A. M. & Pamukkale. (2001). Turkish Homestay Tourism. In *Hosts and guests revisited: Tourism issues of the 21st century*. Chapter 12; Cognizant Communication Corporation.

Van Klaveren, M., & Tijdens, K. (2012). *Empowering women in work in developing countries*. Palgrave Macmillan.

Wall, G., & Mathieson, A. (2006). *Tourism: Change, impacts, and opportunities*. Pearson Education. Pearson & Prentice Hall.

Wang, X. X. (2019). The livelihood and lifestyle change of Miao nationality's floating silversmith in Southeast Guizhou. *Guizhou Ethnic Studies*, *8*, 52–57. (in Chinese)

Woosnam, K. M., Draper, J., Jiang, J. K., Aleshinloye, K. D., & Erul, E. (2018). Applying self-perception theory to explain residents' attitudes about tourism development through travel histories. *Tourism Management*, *64*, 357–368. https://doi.org/10.1016/j.tourman.2017.09.015

Xie, P. F. (2003). The bamboo-beating dance in Hainan, China: Authenticity and commodification. *Journal of Sustainable Tourism*, *11*(1), 5–16. https://doi.org/10.1080/09669580308667190

Yang, L. (2011). Ethnic tourism and cultural representation. *Annals of Tourism Research*, *38*(2), 561–585. https://doi.org/10.1016/j.annals.2010.10.009

Yang, L., & Wall, G. (2009). Ethnic tourism: A framework and an application. *Tourism Management*, *30*(4), 559–570. https://doi.org/10.1016/j.tourman.2008.09.008

Zhang, D. D. (2006). Embroidery-analysis of Chinese embroidery art. *Culture and Art Research*, (12), 129–134. (in Chinese)

Zhong, J. (2010). A literature review of research on ethnic tourism and minority women's issues in china. *Women Research*, (002), 83–87. (in Chinese)

Effects of social media on residents' attitudes to tourism: conceptual framework and research propositions

Robin Nunkoo, Dogan Gursoy and Yogesh K. Dwivedi

ABSTRACT
The pervasive influence of social media on our lives provides new opportunities to study residents' attitudes to tourism. Even though it is now common for residents to express their opinions and read about tourism development on social media, the consequences of this for their attitudes remain to be understood. This article uses the analytical perspectives of the information society and draws from the elaboration likelihood model, the influence of presumed influence model, and the social exchange theory to develop a causal-chain framework that considers the influence of social media on residents' attitudes to tourism. Twenty-five research propositions emanate from the conceptual framework. The framework examines the direct as well as indirect influence of social media tourism messages on residents' attitudes. It also recognizes users as the receivers and expressers of pro- as well as anti-tourism messages on social media. Our framework is theoretically inclusive, providing a reference to scholars and stimulating new ideas for future research on social media and residents' attitudes. To the best of our knowledge, this is the first study that provides the necessary theoretical foundations and a conceptual framework to study residents' attitudes to tourism in an information era intensified by the growth of social media.

Introduction

Academic discourses on sustainable tourism consider destination communities as the focal point for tourism development and emphasize the importance of addressing their needs and concerns for the success of the industry (Hadinejad et al., 2019; Nunkoo & Gursoy, 2012; Nunkoo & Ramkissoon, 2011). Residents are viewed as one of the most important stakeholders whose endorsement is a prerequisite for the sustainable development of the tourism industry (Ribeiro et al., 2017; Wassler et al., 2019). Thus, research on residents' attitudes has proliferated over the past decades, which utilized a variety of theories with various disciplinary roots (Hadinejad et al.,

2019; Nunkoo et al., 2013; Sharpley, 2014). These theories include social exchange theory (SET, Gursoy et al., 2019; Maruyama et al., 2019; Nunkoo & Gursoy, 2012; Nunkoo & So, 2016; Ribeiro et al., 2017), the social representation theory (Lu et al., 2019; Suess & Mody, 2016; Wassler et al., 2019), the theory of planned behavior (TPB) and theory of reasoned action (TRA, Lepp, 2007; MacKay & Campbell, 2004; Oh & Hsu, 2001), and the tourist area life cycle (Diedrich & García-Buades, 2009; Hunt & Stronza, 2014; Lundberg, 2015).

Studies that utilized these theories have mainly assumed that residents form their attitudes utilizing the information and knowledge they gain thorough various sources. However, the source of such information and knowledge and the cognitive mechanism through which they influence attitudes have not received much attention. Research suggests clearly that an increasing number of individuals rely heavily on social media platforms for gathering information and gaining knowledge about various issues. Furthermore, information disseminated through social media channels is found to have a notable influence on public engagement with various socio-economic, political, and environmental issues (Hansen, 2019), including tourism (Navío-Marco et al., 2018). Thus, the pervasive influence of social media on our lives provides new opportunities to study residents' attitudes to tourism. The rise of social media as a new cultural and social phenomenon of the information society has considerably enhanced people's ability to engage with public affairs and issues, which help them shape their opinions and behaviors, and enabled them to coordinate massive and rapid responses towards those affairs and issues (Baum & Potter, 2019; Hamid et al., 2017; Joshi et al., 2019; McGregor, 2019; Valenzuela, 2013; Valeriani & Vaccari, 2016). For example, using various examples, Gretzel (2017) discusses how social-media has facilitated tourism activism.

Recently, some studies have investigated the influence of media on residents attitudes to tourism, but those studies have focused on traditional news media such as newspapers, that generally function within the framework of the agenda-setting theory (Hao et al., 2019; Lu et al., 2019). Whereas, social media users co-create and curate news for their social networks, attribute their own meanings to information, and express them in a naturalistic manner to others (Balkin, 2004; Bolat, 2019). Consequently, compared to traditional media, social media works in different ways to influence public opinion. Much research on social media in tourism takes a marketing orientation, focusing largely on its influence on travelers' decision-making (e.g. Dolan et al., 2019; Giglio et al., 2019; Jansson, 2018; Liu et al., 2019). The consequences of social media for sustainable tourism have also been discussed in some studies, but their emphasis are on tourists' behaviors, with little considerations given to destination communities (Dickinson et al., 2017; Gössling, 2017; Han et al., 2017).

Receipt and expression of messages and news on social media has concomitant implications for users' attitudes and behaviors (Yoo et al., 2016). However, "there is a dearth of studies that specifically focus on the use of social media by residents" (Uchinaka et al., 2019, p. 138). Even though it is now very common for residents to express their opinions and read about tourism development on social media platforms (Becken, Alaei, Chen, Connolly, & Stantic, 2017; Becken et al., 2019; Ketter & Avraham, 2012; Postma & Schmuecker, 2017), the consequences of this for residents' attitudes to tourism remain to be understood, leaving a major gap in the existing literature. Considering the possible effects of social media on residents' attitudes and behaviors toward tourism, knowledge advancement in this field requires scholars to push the boundaries of existing research by delving into new theoretical perspectives that provide the appropriate constructs, domain, and set of relationships and make accurate predictions. In response to the literature gaps, this article draws from the analytical perspectives of the information society and uses as theoretical bases the elaboration likelihood model (ELM, Petty & Cacioppo, 1986; Sussman & Siegal, 2003), the influence of presumed influence model (IPIM, Gunther & Storey, 2003), and the SET (Ap, 1992) to develop a causal-chain framework that explains the cognitive processes through which information on social media influences residents' attitudes to tourism and their resulting behavioral consequences.

Residents' attitudes to tourism impacts

Residents' attitudes to the positive and negative impacts of tourism is as important as the actual impacts of tourism (McGehee & Anderek, 2004). On the positive side, tourism improves the local economies, creates business, investment and employment opportunities, provides additional income for the government, improves the local infrastructure, enhances the image of a place, provide recreational opportunities, develops the cultural identity, and valorizes local traditions (Gursoy & Rutherford, 2004; Nunkoo & Gursoy, 2012; Nunkoo & Ramkissoon, 2011; Nunkoo & Smith, 2013; Ribeiro et al., 2017; Woosnam et al., 2018). The adverse consequences of tourism are also well documented (Nunkoo et al., 2013; Nunkoo & Ramkissoon, 2010, 2011; Prayag et al., 2013). Tourism destroys the occupational identity of local people, increases costs of living, harms the natural environment and local culture, and contributes to traffic congestion and pollution (Gursoy & Rutherford, 2004; Nunkoo et al., 2010; Nunkoo & Gursoy, 2017; Nunkoo & Ramkissoon, 2011, 2012; Woosnam et al., 2018).

Residents' attitudes in an online information society

The information society provides a broad analytical perspective to study the influence of social media on residents' reactions to tourism in an era where the creation, manipulation, and distribution of information is a significant socio-economic and political activity. Emerged in the 1970s and throughout the 1980s, the information society is characterized by a shift in the economic model of production from an industrial society to an information society and social transformation, driven by information and communication technologies and the availability of information (Bell, 2004; Martin, 1995; Webster, 2006). Rapid advancement of information and communication technologies during the last decade has resulted in the formation of an information society which has systematically transformed the socio-economic and political texture of communities. Despite contentions, Martin's (1995) definition is the probably the most appropriate, as it conceptualizes the information society away from its technological determinism, by considering its socio-economic and political consequences. According to Martin (1995), an information society is

> "… a society in which the quality of life, as well as prospects for social change and economic development, depend increasingly upon information and its exploitation. In such a society, living standards, patterns of work and leisure, the education system and the market place are all influenced markedly by advances in information and knowledge. This is evidenced by the increasing array of information-intensive products and services, communicated through a wide range of media, many electronic in nature" (p. 3).

In contemporary times, the information society is predominantly hosted online, with social media platforms occupying a dominant place. Social media are interactive and computed-mediated technologies that enable the creation and exchange of user generated contents. They include, but are not limited to social networking sites such as Facebook, micro-blogging services such as Twitter, and video and picture sharing sites such as YouTube and Instagram (Kaplan & Haenlein, 2010). Social media usage is the most important online activity, with an anticipated increase in users from 2.65 billion in 2018 to 3.1 billion in 2021. Globally, the social network penetration currently stands as 45%, while North America and East Asia have a penetration rate as high as 70% (Clement, 2019).

Social media facilitates the sharing of user-generated contents, allowing for the democratization of information (Kaplan & Haenlein, 2010; Lund et al., 2018) and making the free expressions of ones opinions at the forefront of policy issues and discourses (Balkin, 2004). Digital platforms such as social media shifts power dynamics in social movements, by allowing marginalized and aggrieved groups to connect together and engage in collective actions in pursing change (Cullinane et al., 2014; Leong et al., 2019; Leong et al., 2015). In this way, social media fosters a 'spiral of empowerment' by breaking the 'spiral of silence' among the public (Lee & Chun, 2016). Although there are some evidences of organized manipulation campaigns on social media by certain groups and individuals who frame public discourses - referred to as 'cyber troops' (Bradshaw & Howard, 2018), social media, if properly utilized and managed, fosters freedom of speech by allowing the ordinary citizens, not just political, social, and economic elites, to participate in the dissemination of ideas. Participation here refers to the creation, growth, and spread of ideas, news and opinions of tourism development by the public, which promote a democratic culture about individual liberty that can foster collective self-governance of tourism development (Balkin, 2004; Black et al., 2011; Shirky, 2011). It is not surprising therefore, that social media platforms have become established spheres for the formation of public opinions (Dahlberg, 2006; McGregor, 2019).

Social media is now an important source of news for the public (Bergström & Jervelycke Belfrage, 2018; Ku et al., 2019; Pentina & Tarafdar, 2014). It has altered the general public's role from passive recipients to active users who take part in the production and dissemination of news (Choi, 2016) - what Burns (2008) refers to as bottom-up news 'produsage'. Social media provides interactive platforms that go beyond geographical and economic boundaries and the ability of users to collaboratively create and curate news, offer transparent and a socially negotiated information characterized by 'multi-perspectivity" (Ku et al., 2019; Pentina & Tarafdar, 2014). Compared to traditional media, social media exposes users to unlimited and diverse types of information, potentially promoting cognitive variety and diversity and facilitate sense-making (Pentina & Tarafdar, 2014). While searching for news on social media can be deliberate, incidental consumption of news is also very common (Boczkowski et al., 2018) and provide online users information they would otherwise not have received (Bergström & Jervelycke Belfrage, 2018).

At the same time, fake news, also known as junk news, deliberately created to mislead the public is also prevalent on social media platforms (Waldrop, 2017) – what Hills (2019) refers to as the 'dark side' of the information society. Fake information can relate to news materials such as those seeking to undermine the contributions of tourism to environmental degradation or climate change on one hand, or exaggerate the adverse socio-economic consequences of the industry, on the other. For example, it is common for tourism operators to engage in greenwashing by using online marketing deceptively to promote their products and services as sustainable, despite their adverse socio-economic and environmental consequences (Rahman et al., 2015; Smith & Font, 2014). Certainly, most of the contents on social media are not related to public issues such as tourism development, just as most of the contents portrayed on television are not news. However, as social media becomes more pervasive in our daily life, available contents are expected to diversify as well (Valenzuela, 2013), with implications for tourism (Fedeli, 2020).

Social media also has implications for the process of public knowledge generation of tourism and consequently, for the contemporary elites who live by this knowledge (Bharati et al., 2015; Robins & Webster, 1999). Lévy (1997) describes the cyberspace as a new knowledge space, distinguished by its open, fluid, and dynamic qualities in contrast to an older knowledge space characterized by linearity, hierarchy, and rigidity of structures. In the new knowledge space, Lévy argues, "communities, discover and construct their own objectives, and come to know themselves as intelligent collectives" (Lévy, 1997, p.197). Social media makes it possible for users to share knowledge, increasing collective intelligence among human groups and providing the basis for a social transformation, if not a social revolution (Lévy, 1997). For local communities, public knowledge of tourism is a source of empowerment and allows them to distinguish between the different components of tourism and to understand how development is organized and managed (Nunkoo, 2015). Collective intelligence, however, may cause societal conflicts between professionals and the general population (Bell, 2004) over public goods and use of community resources for tourism purposes for example (Alipour & Arefipour, 2020; Rigall-I-

Torrent & Fluvià, 2011), which can significantly influence the formation process of residents' attitudes and behaviors toward tourism.

While on the one hand social media promotes public understanding of tourism, on the other, it (re)shapes meanings and societal conventions about tourism development, both influencing how residents (de)construct the tourism phenomenon. In the process of expressing and disseminating their opinions, social media users create meanings that in turn help constitute them as persons and the communities and sub-communities they belong to (Balkin, 2004; Bolat, 2019). Participation leads to the creation of new meanings out of old ones, and when individuals repeat messages and opinions of others, while contributing through comments, their reiteration often carries a different meaning or context. Thus, social media users re-shape meanings and cultural conventions about things (Balkin, 2004), which may alter public understanding of (sustainable) tourism, with consequences for the ways in which residents' perceive tourism development.

Tourism discourses on social media

Social media platforms have become important spaces where public discourses about community issues are generated and circulated (Kou et al., 2017). They play an important role in communicating and building residents' perceptions of complex issues such as sustainable tourism and improving their understanding of the directions of public discourses. Therefore, growing public engagement with social media, along with the demise of traditional media, makes it significant and important to examine its influence on residents' reactions to tourism development. Residents' engagement with social media can come in various forms such as the creation, reading, watching, or sharing of information, opinions, videos or pictures about tourism development over social networks. Social media messages are expressed in a naturalistic manner and are displayed to all users, creating the opportunities for interactions with other users (Mehmet & Simmons, 2018). As Shakeela and Weaver (2012) argue, "technology mediates the resident/tourism encounter and can amplify the voice of all stakeholders" (p. 1342).

There is increasing evidence that residents' use social media to express their opinions about tourism. Jabreel et al. (2017) analyzed 3000 tweets by local residents in 10 European tourism destinations. While residents made mostly positive comments about tourism development in their city, opinions varied across destinations, with some cities receiving more negative tweets from residents than others. Becken et al. (2019) study on the uses of tweets to assess destination sentiment found residents as active tweeters whose opinions on the destination evolved over time. Residents tweeted positively in July and August, which the researchers attributed to increased local pride as a result of the Gold Coast Marathon and lower visitation levels during these months. However, their sentiments turned negative over time as the number of visitors increased. Using comments posted on social media by residents, Shakeela and Weaver (2012) constructed an emotional landscape of their reactions toward a video of a Maldivian service sabotage incident. The study retrieved more than 900 commentaries posted by local residents on social media and classified them as direct reactions (visceral reactions, reflective fight responses, and sentiments) as well as indirect reactions, through cognitive interpretation.

Other studies provide similar evidence of residents' reactions to tourism development on social media (Becken et al., 2017; Kirilenko & Stepchenkova, 2017; Serna et al., 2017). For example, when the Maldivian's tourism authority launched a twitter campaign (#SunnySideofLife) to promote the destination, the tweet was picked-up by local residents to raise awareness of political issues and human right issues at the destination. The hastag was trending on twitter not only because of the positive tweets, but also because of negative tweets about the destination (Siddique, 2012). In other cases, social media applications dedicated specifically to the

Table 1. Examples of tourism discourses on social media.

Social media sites	Country
https://nextdoor.com/	USA
https://www.facebook.com/aretkokinnulaplaz/	Mauritius
https://www.facebook.com/appalfama	Lisbon, Portugal
https://www.facebook.com/Left-Hand-Rotation-290963300240	Lisbon, Portugal
https://twitter.com/antalyacityblog	Antalya, Turkey
https://m.facebook.com/Turnsoutkavoswasreadforyou	Kavos, Greece
@AssBarrisTS	Barcelona, Spain
https://twitter.com/Terraferida	Mallorca, Spain
https://www.gobmallorca.com/	Mallorca, Spain
https://es-es.facebook.com/salvemPortoColom/	Portocolom, Spain
https://twitter.com/mesbarrigirona	Girona, Spain
https://www.facebook.com/Mesbarrigirona/	Girona, Spain
https://twitter.com/hashtag/overtourism	Global
https://twitter.com/toursustainably	Global
https://twitter.com/susttourism	Global
https://twitter.com/Tiredearth	Global
https://www.youtube.com/TiredEarthGroup	Global
https://goodtourismblog.com/	Global
https://twitter.com/sti_travel	Global
https://www.linkedin.com/groups/12088115/	Global
#sustainabletourism	Global

discussions of tourism development issues have been created (Table 1). Some of them are related to tourism issues in specific destinations such as Mauritius, Spain, Greece, and Portugal, others are more global in their orientation.

Theoretical foundation

Elaboration likelihood model

The ELM (Petty & Cacioppo, 1986) has theoretically informed much research on the influence of social media messages on users' attitudes and behaviors (Manca & Fornara, 2019; Zhu et al., 2016). The ELM posits that external information induces attitude change by introducing people with new possibilities, causing them to reexamine prior beliefs and judgments, potentially changing their extant behaviors. As a dual process model, the ELM suggests that attitudes and consequent behavioral changes occur via two routes of persuasion: the central route and the peripheral route, which can be considered as opposing sides of a continuum (Petty & Cacioppo, 1986). The two routes through which attitudinal outcomes are reached differ in at least three distinct ways (Bhattacherjee & Sanford, 2006). First, while the central route processes message-related arguments, the peripheral route processes cues. Second, the central route involves a higher cognitive effort than the peripheral route, requiring the individual to think critically about, carefully examine and scrutinize closely the information. Third, the central route leads to more enduring and stable attitudinal and behavioral changes than the peripheral route (Bhattacherjee & Sanford, 2006).

According to the central route of persuasion, the quality of argument in personally relevant messages has a significant influence on attitude. Petty and Cacioppo (1981, pp. 264–5) conceptualize argument quality as the audience's subjective perception of the arguments in the persuasive message as strong and cogent on the one hand, versus weak and specious on the other. In a resident attitudes context, argument quality may depend on the extent to which social media messages contain relevant scientific information and evidence such as statistics, pictures, and data about environmental and socio-economic conditions that can persuade receivers about the positive/negative impacts of tourism development. When persuasive messages have a low relevance to users, they rely on peripheral cues, which are informational indicators use to assess content other than the content itself (Petty & Cacioppo, 1986). Such cues relate to source credibility, liking for the communicator, and consensus heuristic. For example, social media messages posted by a tourism scientist/expert or a community leader may be considered more credible and persuasive than those posted by non-experts or the common person. Likewise, tourism-related information on which a consensus has been reached among social media users will be more persuasive compared to those where disagreements abound.

The ELM however, does not suggest that the two routes to persuasion lead to different attitudinal and behavioral outcomes. For example, two individuals may form the same attitudes toward tourism development, but their attitude formation may be the result of two entirely different influence routes (argument-based or cue-based). Support for the two routes of persuasion is provided by various studies (Chang et al., 2020; Shi et al., 2018; Wang et al., 2019). For example, in their study on transport behavior, Manca and Fornara, (2019) found that attitude change in individuals concerned with sustainability were influenced by the quality of arguments on the need for travel change, while for those less concerned about sustainability issues, attitudes were influenced by messages presented by an expert source. Tourism information posted on social media usually contains both positive and negative elements about development impacts (Jabreel et al., 2017). These messages are processed by users via the central or the peripheral routes and depending on their contents and personal relevance, they will influence users' attitudes toward the positive and negative impacts of tourism. Thus, the following propositions are developed:

> Proposition 1: Argument quality of personally relevant messages, representing the central route processing, is associated with (a) positive attitudes toward tourism and (b) negative attitudes toward tourism.

> Proposition 2: Peripheral cues such as source credibility, liking for the communicator, and consensus heuristic, representing the peripheral route processing, are associated with (a) positive attitudes toward tourism and (b) negative attitudes toward tourism.

Influence of presumed influence model

While it is true that users change their attitudes and behaviors based on their exposure to personally relevant media messages, theoretical developments over the past two decades suggest that attitude and behavior changes also occurs because of reactions to their anticipation of the influence of a message on others (Gunther & Storey, 2003). This suggests that mass media also exerts indirect and powerful influences on people's attitude (Gunther & Storey, 2003). The construction of messages on social media requires cognitive efforts as users not only consider what they wish to express, but also the way in which such information is perceived by others (Eveland, 2004). After a user has expressed a message on social media, the perceptions of its meaning may be altered through an awareness that other users will read it and comment on it – a process called reasoning, which refers to mental elaboration or collective consideration (Shah et al., 2007).

To this end, drawing on Davison's (1983) notion of third-party effect, Gunther and Storey (2003) developed the IPIM, hypothesizing that individuals estimate the influence of any communicative action on others and as a result, they change their attitudes and behaviors. The IPIM explains attitude change via three stages: first, our exposure to information is the basis on which we make inferences about others exposure to the same content (presumed exposure); second, the presumed exposure of others to information leads to the perception that the content will influence others (presumed influence); and third, the presumed influence on others leads to an alignment of our own attitude to the attitude of others (influence of presumed influence, Gunther and Storey, 2003). The IPIM has been tested empirically across a range of social media context (e.g. Cho et al., 2020; Yoo et al., 2016).

Tourism news content on social media are both anti-tourism and pro-tourism (Gretzel, 2017). For example, #boycotthawaii, which was first spread by supporters' of Donald Trump, was used by local residents to express anti-tourism attitudes to discourage tourists from visiting Hawaii. Anti-tourism movements on social media have also emerged in Europe (e.g. #touristgohome) and were propelled by the use of Facebook and Twitter to generate the interest of mainstream media (Gretzel, 2017). Social media has also expanded the news users' role from passive recipients to active participants in the creation and dissemination of news. Users not only receive messages - referred to as 'news internalizing', but also express their opinions on social media - referred to as 'news externalizing' (Choi, 2016). Therefore, it is important that the IPIM distinguishes between the expression and reception of anti-tourism and pro-tourism messages on social media.

In line with the first stage of the IPIM, the pervasive media influence inference suggests that when users pay attention to a content, they presume that it has a broad reach, and others also pay attention to the same content (Gunther, 1998). As Eveland and McLeod (1999) argue, individuals are naïve social scientists who create theories about media effects on others. Studies on the IPIM provide support for the presumed exposure inference (Stage 1). Ho et al. (2020) showed that public's attention to media messages about nano-enabled food was positively associated with the presumption that others attend to the same messages. Cho et al. (2020) also established a relationship between social media view numbers and presumed exposure of others. Yoo et al. (2016) distinguished between expression and reception of anti-smoking and pro-smoking social media messages and established a significant relationship between respondents' own media exposure and others exposure to similar messages. Therefore, one would expect that the reception and expression of anti-tourism and pro-tourism social media messages will influence the presumption of others' attention to the same messages. Thus:

Proposition 3a: Expression of anti-tourism messages is associated with perceived peer expression of anti-tourism tourism messages.

Proposition 3b: Reception of anti-tourism messages is associated with perceived peer reception of anti-tourism messages.

Proposition 3c: Expression of pro-tourism messages is associated with perceived peer expression of pro-tourism messages.

Proposition 3d: Reception of pro-tourism messages is associated with perceived peer reception of pro-tourism messages.

The second stage of the IPIM relates to presumed influence, which describes people responses to their own perceptions of social norms regarding tourism development. Social norms play a key role in the IPIM (Yoo et al., 2016). Users' perceived influence of media messages on others determines their perceived social norms, as social messages are considered to reflect reality (Eveland & Glynn, 2008). Users consider the media to fulfil an informational role by educating others on the social approval of a certain behavior (Paluck, 2009). Thus, users adjust their perceived social norms according to how they believe social media messages influence others. The relationship between perceived media influence on others and perceived norms (presumed influence) has been established in a variety of settings (e.g. Hong & Kim, 2019; Yang & Zhao, 2018). Some studies distinguished conceptually between the peer expression and reception of positive and negative social media messages and responses to those messages, and found them to have different empirical associations with perceived peer norms (Yoo et al., 2016). Thus:

Proposition 4: (a) Perceived peer expression of anti-tourism messages, (b) perceived peer reception of anti-tourism messages, (c) perceived peer expression of pro-tourism messages, and (d) perceived peer reception of pro-tourism messages are associated with perceived peer norms toward tourism development.

The third stage of the IPIM goes beyond simple perceived influence by examining changes in attitudes and behaviors that result from such perception, a process referred to as the influence of presumed influence. The IPIM suggests that users develop and change their attitude and behaviors based on considerations of normative standards and judgments about what others think (Gunther & Storey, 2003). Social norms are "collective awareness about the preferred, appropriate behaviors among a certain group of people" (Chung & Rimal, 2016, p. 3). Normative influence on attitude and behavior is explained by social conformity, which refers to an individual's willingness to change his own attitudes and behaviors to comply with social norms (Hong & Kim, 2019). Social learning theory posits that individuals diligently monitor their environment to understand the prevalence and acceptability of a certain attitude and behavior (Bandura, 1986). Individuals perceive media representation as a reflection of social boundaries and the (un)acceptability of an idea. Hence, social media users may consider peer expression and reception of tourism messages as the opinions held by other in a community, which shape their perceived norms toward tourism. Studies using the IPIM to assess media influences report an association between perceived peer norms and attitudes and behaviors across a range of context (Ho et al., 2020; Hong & Kim, 2019; Yoo et al., 2016). In tourism, the influence of normative beliefs on attitudes and behaviors is also well acknowledged (e.g. Kim & Hwang, 2020; Meng et al., 2020). Hence:

> Proposition 5: Perceived peer norms about tourism is associated with (a) attitudes to the positive impacts of tourism, (b) attitudes to the negative impacts of tourism, and (c) pro-tourism behavior.

Direct and indirect effects of exposure to social media

Studies using the IPIM have investigated the direct influence of users' exposure to media on their behaviors across a range of settings. For example, Lioa et al. (2016) validated a relationship between respondents' attention to pro-environmental messages in various media outlets and their pro-environmental behavior. Yoo et al. (2016) empirically demonstrated that while the expression and reception anti-smoking messages on social media did not influence smoking intention, they established an association between the expression of pro-smoking messages on intention. Although not based on the IPIM, some tourism studies confirm the effect of media news on residents' attitudes. For example, Lu et al. (2019) and Ritchie et al. (2010) showed that media messages influence residents' support for the Olympic Games. Thus, the following propositions are developed:

> Proposition 6: (a) Expression of anti tourism messages, (b) reception of anti-tourism messages, (c) expression of pro-tourism messages, and (d) reception of pro-tourism messages are associated with pro-tourism behaviors.

The indirect media effects on behavior is a central tenet of the IPIM (Gunther & Storey, 2003). However, such indirect effects does not imply that the direct link between media exposure and behavior is inconsequential, but rather, the IPIM suggests that the indirect media influences have important theoretical and practical implications (Gunther et al., 2006). The indirect effect of media exposure on pro-tourism behavior is implied in our conceptual framework – an indirect effect via presumed influence on others. The IPIM links media exposure to behavioral reactions through cognitive pathways, however, identifying the mediating variables is the most challenging in the application of the model (Gunther et al., 2006; Gunther & Storey, 2003l). Research has identified perceived norms as an important mediating variable between media exposure and behavior. Perceived norms exert powerful influences on individuals, while at the same time, the literature on communication suggests that norms are influenced by exposure to mass media (Gunther et al., 2006). Gunther et al. (2006) found that exposure to pro- and anti-smoking messages indirectly influenced smoking intent through their effects on perceived norms. Yang and Zhao (2018) study reported that the relationship between social media exposure and binge drinking intention is mediated by descriptive norms. Perceived norms also played a mediating role in the relationship between media attention and pro-environmental behavior in Liao et al.

(2016) study. Therefore, we would expect that exposure to tourism messages on social media will influence pro-tourism behavior via perceived norms about tourism development. Hence:

Proposition 7: The relationships between (a) expression of anti-tourism messages, (b) reception of anti-tourism messages, (c) expression of pro-tourism messages, and (d) reception of pro-tourism messages and pro-tourism behavior are mediated by perceived norms about tourism development (not visually shown in Figure 1).

Social exchange theory

Residents' attitudes to the impacts of tourism development has behavioral consequences with implications for sustainability (Bakhsh et al., 2018; Sharpley, 2014). For the tourism industry to develop in a socially compatible way, it is important that local residents support tourism development willingly (Gursoy et al., 2017; Lepp, 2007; Nunkoo, 2015; Ribeiro et al., 2017). Residents' behavior toward tourism is influenced by the extent to which they perceive tourism to result in positive and negative impacts. Such a proposition is supported by both the SET (Ap, 1992) and the TRA (Ajzen & Fishbein, 1977). According to SET, residents will enter in an exchange process with the tourism industry once they have evaluated the positive and negative impacts of the development (Ap, 1992). A similar logic underpin the TRA, which is effective for analyzing non-routine thinking decisions that require deliberations (Ajzen & Fishbein, 1977). Both theories postulate that residents' positive attitudes toward tourism increases their intention to engage in pro-tourism behaviors, while negative attitudes lowers their intention to engage in pro-tourism behaviors (Lepp, 2007; Ribeiro et al., 2017). Thus:

Proposition 8: There is an association between (a) residents' attitudes to the positive impacts of tourism and (b) residents' attitudes to the negative impacts of tourism and their pro-tourism behavior.

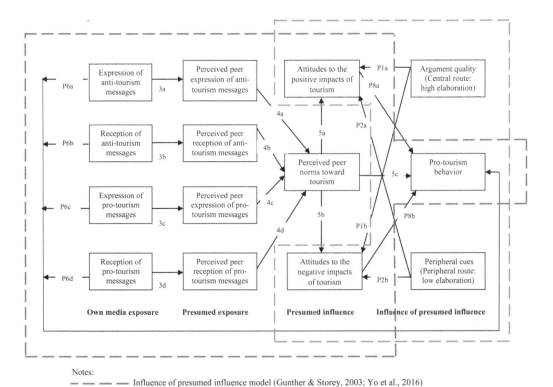

Notes:
– – – Influence of presumed influence model (Gunther & Storey, 2003; Yo et al., 2016)
– – – Elaboration likelihood model (Petty & Cacioppo, 1981); Social exchange theory (Ap, 1992)
The mediating propositions (P7) are not shown, but are implied in the framework.

Figure 1. Conceptual framework of social media influence on residents' attitudes to tourism.

The conceptual framework

Further to the preceding theoretical discussions from the literature, the conceptual framework (Figure 1) is developed based on theoretical premises of the ELM, SET (dotted blue line) and the IPIM (dotted red line). Twenty-five research propositions (including the mediating propositions not visually shown) emanate from the conceptual framework. The framework examines the direct influence of social media tourism messages on residents' attitudes and behavior toward tourism. Theoretical developments over the last two decades suggest that social media also exerts powerful indirect effects (Baek et al., 2019; Gunther & Storey, 2003; Yoo et al., 2016). In line with the IPIM, individuals perceive some influence of a communication on others, and in turn, change their own attitudes and behaviors (Gunther & Storey, 2003). The framework takes this process into account by considering the influence of social media messages on perceived norms toward tourism and the latter's implications for attitudes and behaviors (dotted red line in Figure 1).

The act of receiving and commenting on social media messages has distinct effects on individuals' engagement and involvement in specific issues (Yoo et al., 2006). Thus, the framework distinguishes between message expression and reception effects. The framework also recognizes users as the receivers and expressers of pro- as well as anti-tourism messages on social media platforms. Such a distinction is important theoretically as individuals tend to emphasize negative messages because they lead to more provocative conversations and produce the perception of stronger influence on others – referred to as the negative-influence corollary (Gunther & Mundy, 1993; McLeod et al., 2017). Social media users are more likely to be more concerned with and engaged themselves in messages about the negative impacts of tourism development than positive ones. Furthermore, in response to the criticism of earlier studies (Sharpley, 2014), the framework makes a conceptual distinction between 'residents' attitudes' and 'residents' behavior', on the premise that people's attitudes influence their behavior (Ajzen, 1977, 1991; Steinmetz et al., 2016).

Conclusion

With the rise of an information society predominantly hosted online, social media has a pervasive influence on several aspects of our lives. In the communication and political science literature, the influence of social media on public opinion and behaviors has been a core area of research. However, media effects on residents' attitudes to tourism has not been well investigated (Lu et al., 2019). The few studies on this topic have focused on the influence on traditional news media on residents' attitudes (e.g. Hao et al., 2019; Lu et al., 2019). While traditional news media operate within the agenda-setting framework, social media functions on voluntary contributions by self-selected individuals who co-create, share, report, and distribute news. In addition, social media allows users to curate news for other users by selecting and sharing those worthy of attention (Pentina & Tarafdar, 2014). A proper investigation of the influence of social media therefore requires the use of appropriate concepts and theories that capture its distinctive characteristics while providing a robust theoretical basis for understanding its influence on residents' attitudes to tourism.

Grounded in the broad analytical perspective of the information society, this study develops a conceptual framework of social media influence on residents' attitudes to tourism. The research makes some important theoretical contributions for the literature. The study offers the benefits of conceptual research for theory development (see MacInnis, 2011; Xin et al., 2013; Yadav, 2010). It adopts an interdisciplinary approach, drawing from three different theoretical perspectives to propose a new and logical framework that clarifies the relationships among constructs that have thus far remained unexplored in tourism, rather than testing them empirically. In so doing, the study attempts to "bridge existing theories in interesting ways, link work across disciplines, provide multi-level insights, and broaden the scope of our thinking" (Gilson & Goldberg, 2015, p. 127–128).

To the best of our knowledge, this is the first study that provides the necessary theoretical foundations and a conceptual framework to study residents' attitudes to tourism in an information era intensified by the growth of social media platforms that has substantially changed the ways in which people and communities communicate and interact (Ngai et al., 2015). We welcome researchers to test empirically the proposed conceptual framework and refine it by bringing appropriate modifications of a theoretical nature in the light of empirical evidence. While we advocate an empirical testing of the whole framework to ensure a comprehensive analysis of the influence of social media on attitudes to tourism, researchers can also consider including in their theoretical models a variable that captures residents' exposure to tourism messages on social media. Researchers should also be aware that there are broader social, cultural, economic, and political factors that can influence the process through which social media influence residents' attitudes, however, a discussion of such factors is outside the scope of this article. Although the major limitation of this research is lack of empirical evidence, our framework is theoretically inclusive, providing a reference to scholars and stimulating new ideas for future research on social media and residents' attitudes to tourism.

Disclosure statement

No potential conflict of interest was reported by the authors.

References

Ajzen, I. (1991). The theory of planned behavior. *Organizational Behavior and Human Decision Processes, 50*(2), 179–211.
Ajzen, I., & Fishbein, M. (1977). Attitude-behavior relations: A theoretical analysis and review of empirical research. *Psychological Bulletin, 84*(5), 888–918. https://doi.org/10.1037/0033-2909.84.5.888

Alipour, H., & Arefipour, T. (2019). Rethinking potentials of Co-management for sustainable common pool resources (CPR) and tourism: The case of a Mediterranean island. *Ocean & Coastal Management*, 183:104993.
Ap, J. (1992). Residents' perceptions on tourism impacts. *Annals of tourism Research*, 19(4), 665–690.
Baek, Y. M., Kang, H., & Kim, S. (2019). Fake news should be regulated because it influences both "others" and "me": How and why the influence of presumed influence model should be extended. *Mass Communication and Society*, 22(3), 301–323. https://doi.org/10.1080/15205436.2018.1562076
Bakhsh, J., Potwarka, L. R., Nunkoo, R., & Sunnassee, V. (2018). Residents' support for the Olympic Games: single host-city versus multiple host-city bid arrangements. *Journal of Hospitality Marketing & Management*, 27(5), 544–560.
Balkin, J. M. (2004). Digital speech and democratic culture: A theory of freedom of expression for the information society. *New York University Law Review*, 79, 1–55.
Bandura, A. (1986). *Social foundations of thought and action*. Prentice Hall.
Baum, M. A., & Potter, P. B. (2019). Media, public opinion, and foreign policy in the age of social media. *The Journal of Politics*, 81(2), 747–756. https://doi.org/10.1086/702233
Becken, S., Alaei, A. R., & Wang, Y. (2019). Benefits and pitfalls of using tweets to assess destination sentiment. *Journal of Hospitality and Tourism Technology*, 11(1), 19–34.
Becken, S., Alaei, A. R., Chen, J., Connolly, R., & Stantic, B. (2017). The role of social media in sharing information about the Great Barrier Reef.
Becken, S., Alaei, A. R., Chen, M. J., Connolly, R., & Stantic, B. (2017). *The role of social media in sharing information about the Great Barrier Reef*. Griffith Institute for Tourism, Griffith University.
Bell, D. (2004). Post-industrial society. In F. Webster (ed.), *The information society reader* (pp. 86–102). Routledge.
Bergström, A., & Jervelycke Belfrage, M. (2018). News in social media: incidental consumption and the role of opinion leaders. *Digital Journalism*, 6(5), 583–598. https://doi.org/10.1080/21670811.2018.1423625
Bharati, P., Zhang, W., & Chaudhury, A. (2015). Better knowledge with social media? Exploring the roles of social capital and organizational knowledge management. *Journal of Knowledge Management*, 19(3), 456–475. https://doi.org/10.1108/JKM-11-2014-0467
Bhattacherjee, A., & Sanford, C. (2006). Influence processes for information technology acceptance: An elaboration likelihood model. *MIS Quarterly*, 30:805–825.
Black, L. W., Welser, H. T., Cosley, D., & DeGroot, J. M. (2011). Self-governance through group discussion in Wikipedia: Measuring deliberation in online groups. *Small Group Research*, 42(5), 595–634. https://doi.org/10.1177/1046496411406137
Boczkowski, P. J., Mitchelstein, E., & Matassi, M. (2018). News comes across when I'm in a moment of leisure": Understanding the practices of incidental news consumption on social media. *New Media & Society*, 20(10), 3523–3539.
Bolat, E. (2019). The African new media digital revolution: Some selected cases from Nigeria. In N. D. Taura, E. Bolat, N. O. Madichie (Eds.), *Digital entrepreneurship in Sub-Saharan Africa* (pp. 67–87). Palgrave Macmillan.
Bradshaw, S., & Howard, P. N. (2018). *Challenging truth and trust: A global inventory of organized social media manipulation*. Oxford Internet Institute, University of Oxford. http://comprop.oii.ox.ac.uk/wp-content/uploads/sites/93/2018/07/ct2018.pdf
Chang, H. H., Lu, Y. Y., & Lin, S. C. (2020). An elaboration likelihood model of consumer respond action to facebook second-hand marketplace: Impulsiveness as a moderator. *Information & Management*, 57(2), 103171.
Cho, H., Shen, L., & Peng, L. (2020). Examining and extending the influence of presumed influence hypothesis in social media. *Media Psychology*, 1–23.
Choi, J. (2016). Why do people use news differently on SNSs? An investigation of the role of motivations, media repertoires, and technology cluster on citizens' news related activities. *Computers in Human Behavior*, 54, 249–256.
Chung, A., & Rimal, R. N. (2016). Social norms: A review. *Review of Communication Research*, 4, 1–28.
Clement, J. (2019). Number of social network users worldwide from 2010 to 2021 (in billions). https://www.statista.com/statistics/278414/number-of-worldwide-social-network-users/
Cullinane, N., Donaghey, J., Dundon, T., Hickland, E., & Dobbins, T. (2014). Regulating for mutual gains? Non-union employee representation and the Information and Consultation Directive. *The International Journal of Human Resource Management*, 25(6), 810–828.
Dahlberg, L. (2006). Computer-mediated communication and the public sphere: A critical analysis. *Journal of Computer-Mediated Communication*, 7(1), 0–0.
Davison, W. P. (1983). The third-person effect in communication. *Public Opinion Quarterly*, 47(1), 1–15.
Dickinson, J. E., Filimonau, V., Hibbert, J. F., Cherrett, T., Davies, N., Norgate, S., Speed, C., & Winstanley, C. (2017). Tourism communities and social ties: the role of online and offline tourist social networks in building social capital and sustainable practice. *Journal of Sustainable Tourism*, 25(2), 163–180. https://doi.org/10.1080/09669582.2016.1182538
Diedrich, A., & García-Buades, E. (2009). Local perceptions of tourism as indicators of destination decline. *Tourism Management*, 30(4), 512–521. https://doi.org/10.1016/j.tourman.2008.10.009

Dolan, R., Seo, Y., & Kemper, J. (2019). Complaining practices on social media in tourism: A value co-creation and co-destruction perspective. *Tourism Management, 73*, 35–45. https://doi.org/10.1016/j.tourman.2019.01.017

Eveland, W. P., Jr,., & McLeod, D. M. (1999). The effect of social desirability on perceived media impact: Implications for third-person perceptions. *International Journal of Public Opinion Research, 11*(4), 315–333. https://doi.org/10.1093/ijpor/11.4.315

Eveland, W. P. Jr, (2004). The effect of political discussion in producing informed citizens: The roles of information, motivation, and elaboration. *Political Communication, 21*(2), 177–193.

Eveland, W. P., Glynn, C. J., Donsbach, W., & Traugott, M. W. (2008). *Theories on the perception of social reality*. The SAGE handbook of public opinion research, 155–163.

Fedeli, G. (2020). Fake news' meets tourism: a proposed research agenda. *Annals of Tourism Research, 80*, 102684.

Giglio, S., Bertacchini, F., Bilotta, E., & Pantano, P. (2019). Using social media to identify tourism attractiveness in six Italian cities. *Tourism Management, 72*, 306–312. https://doi.org/10.1016/j.tourman.2018.12.007

Gilson, L. L., & Goldberg, C. B. (2015). Editors' comment: so, what is a conceptual paper? *Group & Organization Management, 40*(2), 127–130. https://doi.org/10.1177/1059601115576425

Gössling, S. (2017). Tourism, information technologies and sustainability: an exploratory review. *Journal of Sustainable Tourism, 25*(7), 1024–1041.

Gretzel, U. (2017). Social media activism in tourism. *Journal of Hospitality and Tourism, 15*(2), 1–14.

Gunther, A. C. (1998). The persuasive press inference: Effects of mass media on perceived public opinion. *Communication Research, 25*, 486–504.

Gunther, A. C., & Mundy, P. (1993). Biased optimism and the third-person effect. *Journalism Quarterly, 70*(1), 58–67. https://doi.org/10.1177/107769909307000107

Gunther, A. C., & Storey, J. D. (2003). The influence of presumed influence. *Journal of Communication, 53*(2), 199–215. https://doi.org/10.1111/j.1460-2466.2003.tb02586.x

Gunther, A. C., Bolt, D., Borzekowski, D. L., Liebhart, J. L., & Dillard, J. P. (2006). Presumed influence on peer norms: How mass media indirectly affect adolescent smoking. *Journal of Communication, 56*(1), 52–68. https://doi.org/10.1111/j.1460-2466.2006.00002.x

Gursoy, D., Milito, M. C., & Nunkoo, R. (2017). Residents' support for a mega-event: The case of the 2014 FIFA World Cup, Natal, Brazil. *Journal of Destination Marketing & Management, 6*(4), 344–352.

Gursoy, D., Ouyang, Z., Nunkoo, R., & Wei, W. (2019). Residents' impact perceptions of and attitudes towards tourism development: A meta-analysis. *Journal of Hospitality Marketing & Management, 28*(3), 306–333.

Gursoy, D., & Rutherford, D. G. (2004). Host attitudes toward tourism: An improved structural model. *Annals of Tourism Research, 31*(3), 495–516.

Hadinejad, A., D. Moyle, B., Scott, N., Kralj, A., & Nunkoo, R. (2019). Residents' attitudes to tourism: a review. *Tourism Review, 74*(2), 150–165. https://doi.org/10.1108/TR-01-2018-0003

Hamid, S., Ijab, M. T., Sulaiman, H., Md. Anwar, R., & Norman, A. A. (2017). Social media for environmental sustainability awareness in higher education. *International Journal of Sustainability in Higher Education, 18*(4), 474–491. https://doi.org/10.1108/IJSHE-01-2015-0010

Hansen, A. (2019). *Environment, media and communication* (2nd ed.). Abingdon, Oxon.

Hao, J. X., Fu, Y., Hsu, C., Li, X., & Chen, N. (2019). Introducing News Media Sentiment Analytics to Residents' Attitudes Research. *Journal of Travel Research*, 0047287519884657.

Hickland, E., Cullinane, N., Dobbins, T., Dundon, T., & Donaghey, J. (2020). Employer silencing in a context of voice regulations: Case studies of non-compliance. *Human Resource Management Journal*.

Hills, T. T. (2019). The dark side of information proliferation. *Perspectives on Psychological Science: A Journal of the Association for Psychological Science, 14*(3), 323–330.

Ho, S. S., Goh, T. J., & Leung, Y. W. (2020). Let's nab fake science news: Predicting scientists' support for interventions using the influence of presumed media influence model. *Journalism*. 1464884920937488.

Ho, S. S., Goh, T. J., Chuah, A. S., Leung, Y. W., Bekalu, M. A., & Viswanath, K. (2020). Past debates, fresh impact on nano-enabled food: A multigroup comparison of presumed media influence model based on spillover effects of attitude toward genetically modified food. *Journal of Communication, 70*(4), 598–621.

Hong, Y., & Kim, S. (2019). Influence of presumed media influence for health prevention: How mass media indirectly promote health prevention behaviors through descriptive norms. *Health Communication*, 1–11.

Hunt, C., & Stronza, A. (2014). Stage-based tourism models and resident attitudes towards tourism in an emerging destination in the developing world. *Journal of Sustainable Tourism, 22*(2), 279–298. https://doi.org/10.1080/09669582.2013.815761

Jabreel, M., Moreno, A., & Huertas, A. (2017). Do local residents and visitors express the same sentiments on destinations through social media?. In R. Schegg & B. Stangl (eds.), *Information and Communication Technologies in Tourism 2017* (pp. 655–668). Springer.

Jansson, A. (2018). Rethinking post-tourism in the age of social media. *Annals of Tourism Research, 69*, 101–110.

Joshi, G. C., Paul, M., Kalita, B. K., Ranga, V., Rawat, J. S., & Rawat, P. S. (2019). Mapping the social landscape through social media. *Journal of Information Science*, 0165551519865487.

Kaplan, A. M., & Haenlein, M. (2010). Users of the world, unite! The challenges and opportunities of Social Media. *Business Horizons*, *53*(1), 59–68. https://doi.org/10.1016/j.bushor.2009.09.003

Ketter, E., & Avraham, E. (2012). The social revolution of place marketing: The growing power of users in social media campaigns. *Place Branding and Public Diplomacy*, *8*(4), 285–294. https://doi.org/10.1057/pb.2012.20

Kim, J. J., & Hwang, J. (2020). Merging the norm activation model and the theory of planned behavior in the context of drone food delivery services: Does the level of product knowledge really matter? *Journal of Hospitality and Tourism Management*, *42*, 1–11. https://doi.org/10.1016/j.jhtm.2019.11.002

Kirilenko, A. P., & Stepchenkova, S. O. (2017). Sochi 2014 Olympics on Twitter: Perspectives of hosts and guests. *Tourism Management*, *63*, 54–65.

Kou, Y., Kow, Y. M., Gui, X., & Cheng, W. (2017). One social movement, two social media sites: A comparative study of public discourses. *Computer Supported Cooperative Work (Cscw))*, *26*(4-6), 807–836. https://doi.org/10.1007/s10606-017-9284-y

Ku, K. Y., Kong, Q., Song, Y., Deng, L., Kang, Y., & Hu, A. (2019). What predicts adolescents' critical thinking about real-life news? The roles of social media news consumption and news media literacy. *Thinking Skills and Creativity*, *33*, 100570. https://doi.org/10.1016/j.tsc.2019.05.004

Lee, M. J., & Chun, J. W. (2016). Reading others' comments and public opinion poll results on social media: Social judgment and spiral of empowerment. *Computers in Human Behavior*, *65*, 479–487. https://doi.org/10.1016/j.chb.2016.09.007

Leong, C., Pan, S. L., Bahri, S., & Fauzi, A. (2019). Social media empowerment in social movements: power activation and power accrual in digital activism. *European Journal of Information Systems*, *28*(2), 173–204. https://doi.org/10.1080/0960085X.2018.1512944

Leong, C. M. L., Pan, S. L., Ractham, P., & Kaewkitipong, L. (2015). ICT-enabled community empowerment in crisis response: Social media in Thailand flooding 2011. *Journal of the Association for Information Systems*, *16*(3), 1.

Lepp, A. (2007). Residents' attitudes towards tourism in Bigodi village. Uganda. *Tourism Management*, *28*(3), 876–885.

Lévy, P. (1997). *Collective intelligence: Mankind's emerging world in cyberspace*. New York: Plenum Trade.

Liao, Y., Ho, S. S., & Yang, X. (2016). Motivators of pro-environmental behavior: Examining the underlying processes in the influence of presumed media influence model. *Science Communication*, *38*(1), 51–73.

Liu, H., Wu, L., & Li, X. (2019). Social media envy: how experience sharing on social networking sites drives millennials' aspirational tourism consumption. *Journal of Travel Research*, *58*(3), 355–369. https://doi.org/10.1177/0047287518761615

Lu, Q., Mihalik, B. J., Heere, B., Meng, F., & Fairchild, A. (2019). Media effect on resident attitudes toward an Olympic bid. *Tourism Management Perspectives*, *29*, 66–75. https://doi.org/10.1016/j.tmp.2018.10.009

Lund, N. F., Cohen, S. A., & Scarles, C. (2018). The power of social media storytelling in destination branding. *Journal of Destination Marketing & Management*, *8*, 271–280.

Lundberg, E. (2015). The level of tourism development and resident attitudes: A comparative case study of coastal destinations. *Scandinavian Journal of Hospitality and Tourism*, *15*(3), 266–294.

MacInnis, D. J. (2011). A framework for conceptual contributions in marketing. *Journal of Marketing*, *75*(4), 136–154.

MacKay, K. J., & Campbell, J. M. (2004). An examination of residents' support for hunting as a tourism product. *Tourism Management*, *25*(4), 443–452. https://doi.org/10.1016/S0261-5177(03)00127-4

Manca, S., & Fornara, F. (2019). Attitude toward sustainable transport as a function of source and argument reliability and anticipated emotions. *Sustainability*, *11*(12), 3288. https://doi.org/10.3390/su11123288

Martin, W. J. (1995). *The global information society*. Aslib Gower.

Maruyama, N. U., Keith, S. J., & Woosnam, K. M. (2019). Incorporating emotion into social exchange: considering distinct resident groups' attitudes towards ethnic neighborhood tourism in Osaka, Japan. *Journal of Sustainable Tourism*, *27*(8), 1125–1117.

McGehee, N. G., & Andereck, K. L. (2004). Factors predicting rural residents' support of tourism. *Journal of Travel Research*, *43*(2), 131–140.

McGregor, S. C. (2019). Social media as public opinion: How journalists use social media to represent public opinion. *Journalism*, *20*(8), 1070–1086.

McLeod, D. M., Wise, D., & Perryman, M. (2017). Thinking about the media: a review of theory and research on media perceptions, media effects perceptions, and their consequences. *Review of Communication Research*, *5*, 35–83.

Mehmet, M., & Simmons, P. (2018). Kangaroo court? An analysis of social media justifications for attitudes to culling. *Environmental Communication*, *12*(3), 370–386. https://doi.org/10.1080/17524032.2016.1220966

Meng, B., Chua, B. L., Ryu, H. B., & Han, H. (2020). Volunteer tourism (VT) traveler behavior: merging norm activation model and theory of planned behavior. *Journal of Sustainable Tourism*, 1–23.

Navío-Marco, J., Ruiz-Gómez, L. M., & Sevilla-Sevilla, C. (2018). Progress in information technology and tourism management: 30 years on and 20 years after the internet-Revisiting Buhalis & Law's landmark study about eTourism. *Tourism Management*, *69*, 460–470.

Ngai, E. W., Tao, S. S., & Moon, K. K. (2015). Social media research: Theories, constructs, and conceptual frameworks. *International Journal of Information Management*, *35*(1), 33–44. https://doi.org/10.1016/j.ijinfomgt.2014.09.004

Nunkoo, R., & Smith, S. L. (2013). Political economy of tourism: Trust in government actors, political support, and their determinants. *Tourism Management*, *36*, 120–132.

Nunkoo, R. (2015). Tourism development and trust in local government. *Tourism Management*, *46*, 623–634.

Nunkoo, R., & Gursoy, D. (2012). Residents' support for tourism: An identity perspective. *Annals of Tourism Research*, *39*(1), 243–268. https://doi.org/10.1016/j.annals.2011.05.006

Nunkoo, R., & Gursoy, D. (2017). Political trust and residents' support for alternative and mass tourism: an improved structural model. *Tourism Geographies*, *19*(3), 318–339. https://doi.org/10.1080/14616688.2016.1196239

Nunkoo, R., & Ramkissoon, H. (2010). Modeling community support for a proposed integrated resort project. *Journal of Sustainable Tourism*, *18*(2), 257–277. https://doi.org/10.1080/09669580903290991

Nunkoo, R., & Ramkissoon, H. (2011). Residents' satisfaction with community attributes and support for tourism. *Journal of Hospitality & Tourism Research*, *35*(2), 171–190.

Nunkoo, R., & Ramkissoon, H. (2012). Power, trust, social exchange and community support. *Annals of Tourism Research*, *39*(2), 997–1023. https://doi.org/10.1016/j.annals.2011.11.017

Nunkoo, R., & So, K. K. F. (2016). Residents' support for tourism: Testing alternative structural models. *Journal of Travel Research*, *55*(7), 847–861. https://doi.org/10.1177/0047287515592972

Nunkoo, R., Gursoy, D., & Juwaheer, T. D. (2010). Island residents' identities and their support for tourism: an integration of two theories. *Journal of Sustainable Tourism*, *18*(5), 675–693. https://doi.org/10.1080/09669581003602341

Nunkoo, R., Smith, S. L., & Ramkissoon, H. (2013). Residents' attitudes to tourism: A longitudinal study of 140 articles from 1984 to 2010. *Journal of Sustainable Tourism*, *21*(1), 5–25.

Oh, H., & Hsu, C. H. (2001). Volitional degrees of gambling behaviors. *Annals of Tourism Research*, *28*(3), 618–637. https://doi.org/10.1016/S0160-7383(00)00066-9

Paluck, E. L. (2009). What's in a norm? Sources and processes of norm change. *Journal of Personality and Social Psychology*, *96*, 594–600. doi:10.1037/a0014688.

Pentina, I., & Tarafdar, M. (2014). From "information" to "knowing": Exploring the role of social media in contemporary news consumption. *Computers in Human Behavior*, *35*, 211–223. https://doi.org/10.1016/j.chb.2014.02.045

Petty, R. E., & Cacioppo, J. T. (1986). The elaboration likelihood model of persuasion. In *Communication and persuasion* (pp. 1–24). Springer.

Petty, R. E., Cacioppo, J. T., & Goldman, R. (1981). Personal involvement as a determinant of argument-based persuasion. *Journal of Personality and Social Psychology*, *41*(5), 847.

Postma, A., & Schmuecker, D. (2017). Understanding and overcoming negative impacts of tourism in city destinations: conceptual model and strategic framework. *Journal of Tourism Futures*, *3*(2), 144–156. https://doi.org/10.1108/JTF-04-2017-0022

Prayag, G., Hosany, S., Nunkoo, R., & Alders, T. (2013). London residents' support for the 2012 Olympic Games: The mediating effect of overall attitude. *Tourism Management*, *36*, 629–640.

Rahman, I., Park, J., & Chi, C. G. Q. (2015). Consequences of "greenwashing" Consumers' reactions to hotels' green initiatives. *International Journal of Contemporary Hospitality Management*, *27*(6), 1054–1081. https://doi.org/10.1108/IJCHM-04-2014-0202

Ribeiro, M. A., Pinto, P., Silva, J. A., & Woosnam, K. M. (2017). Residents' attitudes and the adoption of pro-tourism behaviours: The case of developing island countries. *Tourism Management*, *61*, 523–537. https://doi.org/10.1016/j.tourman.2017.03.004

Rigall-I-Torrent, R., & Fluvià, M. (2011). Managing tourism products and destinations embedding public good components: a hedonic approach. *Tourism Management*, *32*(2), 244–255. https://doi.org/10.1016/j.tourman.2009.12.009

Ritchie, B. W., Shipway, R., & Chien, P. M. (2010). The role of the media in influencing residents' support for the 2012 Olympic Games. *International Journal of Event and Festival Management*, *1*(3), 202–219.

Robins, K., & Webster, F. (1999). *Times of the technoculture*. Routledge.

Serna, A., Gerrikagoitia, J. K., Bernabe, U., & Ruiz, T. (2017). A method to assess sustainable mobility for sustainable tourism: The case of the public bike systems. In In R. Schegg and B. Stangl (eds.), *Information and communication technologies in tourism* (pp. 727–739). Springer.

Shah, D. V., Cho, J., Nah, S., Gotlieb, M. R., Hwang, H., Lee, N.-J., Scholl, R. M., & McLeod, D. M. (2007). Campaign ads, online messaging, and participation: Extending the communication mediation model. *Journal of Communication*, *57*(4), 676–703. https://doi.org/10.1111/j.1460-2466.2007.00363.x

Shakeela, A., & Weaver, D. (2012). Resident reactions to a tourism incident: Mapping a Maldivian Emoscape. *Annals of Tourism Research*, *39*(3), 1337–1358.

Sharpley, R. (2014). Host perceptions of tourism: A review of the research. *Tourism Management*, *42*, 37–49.

Shi, J., Hu, P., Lai, K. K., & Chen, G. (2018). Determinants of users' information dissemination behavior on social networking sites. *Internet Research*, *28*(2), 393–418.

Shirky, C. (2011). The political power of social media: Technology, the public sphere, and political change. *Foreign Affairs*, 90:28–41.

Siddique, H. (2012). Maldives tourism campaign backfires as Twitter shows darker side of island life. https://www.theguardian.com/world/2012/jul/12/maldives-twitter-tourism-campaign-backfires.

Smith, V. L., & Font, X. (2014). Volunteer tourism, greenwashing and understanding responsible marketing using market signalling theory. *Journal of Sustainable Tourism*, *22*(6), 942–963. https://doi.org/10.1080/09669582.2013.871021

Steinmetz, H., Knappstein, M., Ajzen, I., Schmidt, P., & Kabst, R. (2016). How effective are behavior change interventions based on the Theory of Planned Behavior? A three-level meta-analysis. *Zeitschrift Für Psychologie*, *224*(3), 216–233. https://doi.org/10.1027/2151-2604/a000255

Suess, C., & Mody, M. (2016). Gaming can be sustainable too! Using Social Representation Theory to examine the moderating effects of tourism diversification on residents' tax paying behavior. *Tourism Management*, *56*, 20–39.

Sussman, S. W., & Siegal, W. S. (2003). Informational influence in organizations: An integrated approach to knowledge adoption. *Information Systems Research*, *14*(1), 47–65. https://doi.org/10.1287/isre.14.1.47.14767

Uchinaka, S., Yoganathan, V., & Osburg, V. S. (2019). Classifying residents' roles as online place-ambassadors. *Tourism Management*, *71*, 137–150.

Valenzuela, S. (2013). Unpacking the use of social media for protest behavior: The roles of information, opinion expression, and activism. *American Behavioral Scientist*, *57*(7), 920–942.

Valeriani, A., & Vaccari, C. (2016). Accidental exposure to politics on social media as online participation equalizer in Germany, Italy, and the United Kingdom. *New Media & Society*, *18*(9), 1857–1874.

Waldrop, M. M. (2017). News Feature: The genuine problem of fake news. *Proceedings of the National Academy of Sciences of the United States of America*, *114*(48), 12631–12634. https://doi.org/10.1073/pnas.1719005114

Wang, L., Fan, L., & Bae, S. (2019). How to persuade an online gamer to give up cheating? Uniting elaboration likelihood model and signaling theory. *Computers in Human Behavior*, *96*, 149–162. https://doi.org/10.1016/j.chb.2019.02.024

Wassler, P., Nguyen, T. H. H., Mai, L. Q., & Schuckert, M. (2019). Social representations and resident attitudes: A multiple-mixed-method approach. *Annals of Tourism Research*, *78*, 102740. https://doi.org/10.1016/j.annals.2019.06.007

Webster, F. (2006). *Theories of the information society*. Routledge.

Woosnam, K. M., Draper, J., Jiang, J. K., Aleshinloye, K. D., & Erul, E. (2018). Applying self-perception theory to explain residents' attitudes about tourism development through travel histories. *Tourism Management*, *64*, 357–368. https://doi.org/10.1016/j.tourman.2017.09.015

Xin, S., Tribe, J., & Chambers, D. (2013). Conceptual research in tourism. *Annals of Tourism Research*, *41*, 66–88. https://doi.org/10.1016/j.annals.2012.12.003

Yadav, M. S. (2010). The decline of conceptual articles and implications for knowledge development. *Journal of Marketing*, *74*(1), 1–19.

Yang, B., & Zhao, X. (2018). TV, social media, and college Students' Binge Drinking Intentions: Moderated Mediation Models. *Journal of Health Communication*, *23*(1), 61–71. https://doi.org/10.1080/10810730.2017.1411995

Yoo, W., Yang, J., & Cho, E. (2016). How social media influence college students' smoking attitudes and intentions. *Computers in Human Behavior*, *64*, 173–182. https://doi.org/10.1016/j.chb.2016.06.061

Zhu, D. H., Chang, Y. P., & Luo, J. J. (2016). Understanding the influence of C2C communication on purchase decision in online communities from a perspective of information adoption model. *Telematics and Informatics*, *33*(1), 8–16. https://doi.org/10.1016/j.tele.2015.06.001

Re-theorizing social emotions in tourism: applying the theory of interaction ritual in tourism research

Dongoh Joo, Heetae Cho ⓘ, Kyle Maurice Woosnam and Courtney Suess

ABSTRACT
Although social emotions can serve as an effective analytic lens through which to study residents' reactions to tourists and tourism, limited theoretical discussion exists examining how social emotions are related to perceptions or behaviors. Extant literature instead has knitted together empirical support in postulating the relationships among social emotions, perceptions, and behaviors. While such an approach is also considered theoretical in a broad sense, resultant findings can be disjointed across research, making replication more difficult. In response, this article introduces the interaction ritual theory and discusses how the theory can strengthen the theoretical connection between social emotions and other constructs. In so doing, this article suggests that the notions of emotional energy and social marketplace are useful in explaining how residents' perceptions and behaviors change as they respond to tourists and tourism. This article also discusses limitations of the theory and how they can be addressed by considering the theory in tandem with the emotional solidarity theory.

Introduction

Tourism generally entails social interaction between residents and tourists, albeit the interaction might be transient or transactional. A rare exception to this might be a park visitor heading to a wilderness area in search of solitude and without distraction, but even then, the lonesome nature-lover will eventually undergo social encounters as they enter or exit such an environment. Almost every tourism experience, if not all, involves a social component, whether it be superficial interaction with service personnel or rich companionship with fellow tourists. Accordingly, many of the emotions that residents and tourists experience in tourism settings are socially shaped and may even be classified as social emotions.

Unlike physiological or basic emotions, social emotions are influenced by thoughts, feelings, and behaviors of others as experienced, recalled, or anticipated (Hareli & Parkison, 2008). Thereby, social emotions reflect individuals' social concerns or social surroundings (Hareli &

Parkison, 2008). For instance, shame, a social emotion (Leary, 2000), arises when individuals are aware of how their socially undesirable or senseless behaviors will be viewed by others (i.e., social concern) and to avoid feeling ashamed, they will act within social norms. As such, social emotions are not only relational but also function by signaling individuals' proper perceptions and behaviors (Ze'Ev & Oatley, 1996; Hareli & Parkison, 2008) and enhancing social cohesion (Lawler & Thye, 2006).

Given the eminently social nature of tourism and the importance of social emotions in general, there is a keen need for investigating how social emotions shape residents' and tourists' perceptions and behaviors (Buda et al., 2014; Zheng et al., 2020). Resentment (Mckercher, 1993) or pride (Esman, 1984; Weaver & Lawton, 2001) often appear in discussions of how residents feel about the relative material affluence of tourists or the rich cultural and natural heritage in their community. Emotional solidarity (Joo et al., 2018; Joo & Woosnam, 2020; Woosnam et al., 2009) and intimacy (Trauer & Ryan, 2005), which are both socially relational and functional feelings (i.e., social emotions), highlight the positive aspects of the resident-tourist relationship. Romance characterizes social interaction between residents and tourists (e.g., Pruitt & LaFont, 1995), just as fellowship explains social hikers' motivations and behaviors (Lum et al., 2020).

A growing recognition on how social emotions forge residents' reactions to tourism and tourists has come about as well. For a deeper understanding of the intergroup relationship, there is a need to steer away from social exchange or social identity perspectives (Berno & Ward, 2005) to the affective and harmonious side of the resident-tourist relationship (Woosnam et al., 2009). Most notably, emotional solidarity—a prolonged feeling of intimacy or friendship (Woosnam et al., 2009)—is often used to provide such an alternative interpretation of the intergroup relationship. Findings suggest that emotional bonds exist between residents and tourists (Woosnam, 2011; Woosnam & Norman, 2010) which help to formulate positive perceptions (e.g., support for tourism, social distance) (Joo et al., 2018; Joo et al., 2019) and behaviors (e.g., tourist expenditure, revisit intention) (Ribeiro et al., 2017; Woosnam, 2012; Woosnam et al., 2015) regarding tourism.

Despite the recent progression on emotional solidarity, the nature and the influence of other types of social emotions—like shame, guilt, or embarrassment—are largely overlooked in residents' reaction research. This, in part, is attributable to a lack of theoretical advancement. As such, limited use of grand or mid-range theories has explicated how social emotions are connected to perceptions or behaviors within tourism contexts. Grand theories—such as those of Marx, Weber, or Durkheim—help to explain a wide range of social phenomena (Turner & Boyns, 2001). While the abstract and philosophical nature of grand theories may be inappropriate for empirical investigations of complex social phenomena (Mills, 1959), social scientists can benefit from the bird's eye views provided by grand theories (Turner & Boyns, 2001). Mid-range theories are less abstract and more specific, functioning as a bridge between grand theories and empirical settings (Merton, 1968). The social exchange theory (Emerson, 1976) and the social identity theory (Tajfel, 1974) can be viewed as mid-range theories given their levels of abstraction and empiricism.

Grand and mid-range theories help to bring together contextual and specialized findings to form a more structuralized and comprehensive understanding of social phenomena (Turner & Boyns, 2001). It is through such theorizing that empirical findings become more comparable and comprehensible (i.e., "world-revealing" as per White, 1991) and extend predictive utility (i.e., "action-guiding" according to White, 1991) (Brown, 2013). The popularity of the social exchange theory or the social identity theory in residents' reaction research or general tourism research may also be attributable to their relative merits in "world-revealing" and "action-guiding." Regrettably, there is a lack of mid-range theories on how social emotions—or emotions in general—catalyze individuals' perceptions and behaviors pertaining to tourism. Instead, studies often rely on piece-mealed empirical evidence to formulate theoretical frameworks. While such an approach is still valid and theoretical (Smith et al., 2013), residents' reaction research can benefit from utilizing more comprehensive, established, and affective theories (Berno & Ward, 2005).

In response to the scholarly needs, this article introduces Collins (1993) interaction ritual theory and discusses its relevance and utility in understanding the nature of residents' social emotions and their influence on perceptions and behaviors. In so doing, this article also contemplates how the theory can be applied in examining residents' reactions to tourists and tourism. These efforts eventually respond to Buda et al. (2014) call for "an emotional and affectual turn" (p. 112) in tourism research, where "a genuine consideration of emotion in tourism studies, theories, and methodologies" is made (p. 112).

Need for theories on social emotions in tourism

Tourism research has often been criticized for lacking concepts and theories which present a succinct but exhaustive view of the phenomenon (Cohen, 1995; Smith et al., 2013; Taillon & Jamal, 2009), and research on residents' reactions to tourists and tourism is not exonerated from such criticism (Berno & Ward, 2005). While the social exchange theory or the social identity theory are used to elucidate how tourism impacts are perceived by residents and shape their behaviors, these theories neglect the role social emotions may play in the process (d'Hautesserre, 2015; Lawler & Thye, 2006). More importantly, implied in those theories are the views that residents and tourists are segregated and conflicting groups (the social identity theory) whose interaction with one another is primarily driven by economic motives (the social exchange theory). While the emotional solidarity theory is used to refute such conventional assumptions (Joo et al., 2019; Woosnam et al., 2009), the theory also does not provide theoretical ties between social emotions and perceptions or behaviors; instead, its focus is on how the emotion evolves and not how it leads to changes in perceptions or behaviors.

Given the keen importance that social emotions have on resident-tourist relationships (d'Hautesserre, 2015; Lawler & Thye, 1999), such a theoretical void is surprising. This is also problematized in more traditional disciplines (e.g., sociology, economics) where individuals are believed to be rational (i.e., the rational choice theory) (Lawler & Thye, 1999), and as an offshoot of those classic disciplines, the same theoretical void is also witnessed within tourism research. In fact, there are a relatively small number of studies which focus explicitly and primarily on how social emotions relate to other constructs (e.g., perceptions, behaviors) in tourism. For instance, Kaell (2014) and Jacobs (2009) both provided rich qualitative descriptions of fellowship or romance emerging between residents and tourists, but their intentions were to illustrate the phenomena rather than to test relationships. Thus, approaches by Kaell (2014) and Jacobs (2009) were more inductive (e.g., building theories) than deductive (e.g., validating theories), and using an established theory was of little utility and concern in such studies.

Even in deductive and theory-driven research, conceptual frameworks are often guided more by piecemeal evidence than established theories. For instance, Huang and Hsu (2010) based their conceptual framework on individual findings from multiple studies pertaining to the tourist-tourist interaction. A similar approach was undertaken by Ribeiro et al. (2017) as they reviewed how empirical evidence from previous studies justified their hypotheses regarding the relationships among emotional solidarity, satisfaction, and revisit intention. Such an approach is how quantitative studies usually proceed within tourism research; deducing relationships between constructs based on extant empirical findings to justify hypotheses which are then used as building blocks of the conceptual framework (Smith et al., 2013). Indeed, the complex nature of tourism often makes it challenging to find a comprehensive and befitting theory for each research context, and many studies assemble findings and ideas from multiple sources to devise conceptual frameworks tailored to their goals and contexts.

Still, such conceptual frameworks correspond to 'type II theories' as per Smith et al. (2013) and are therefore, theoretically justifiable. According to Smith et al. (2013), a type II theory should have "a concise and coherent statement of relationships about some phenomena" and "generate original and significant hypotheses that can be tested" (p. 882). However, these type II theories are often only equivocally supported (Smith et al., 2013). That is, unlike type I theories (i.e., natural theories) that should not be falsified, there can be multiple type II theories addressing a single social phenomenon, and more importantly, type II theories can fail at times unless the failure is constantly repeated (Smith et al., 2013). In this sense, conceptual frameworks, although they are often specific to each study and thus short-lived (i.e., rarely a single framework is tested twice), also qualify as type II theories.

Regardless, more comprehensive theories from traditional disciplines (e.g., psychology, sociology) are frequently used in tourism research to complement the contextual nature of conceptual frameworks. These grand or mid-range theories are also only type II theories (Smith et al., 2013) but help to set boundaries for conceptual frameworks. That is, each conceptual framework (type II theory) can be bound within more comprehensive grand or mid-range theories (also type II theories). For instance, the theory of planned behavior (Ajzen, 1985) has many variations, but its essence and structure (i.e., attitude, subjective norm, and perceived behavioral control leading to intention and behavior) should remain constant across conceptual frameworks. Otherwise, conceptual frameworks and their results would be increasingly disjointed from one another, making replication overly difficult and findings highly contextual.

Although efforts have been made to establish theories and models concerning resident-tourist relationships, there is a lack of more global theories which connect social emotions to perceptions or behaviors, especially with respect to how residents' social emotions drive their perceptional and behavioral reactions to tourists and tourism. The intergroup contact theory (Allport, 1954) is relevant to how tourism diminishes prejudice but caters to the interaction-perception nexus and neither emotions nor behaviors are explicitly addressed. The emotional solidarity theory (Woosnam et al., 2009) considers a social emotion but lacks clues for how the affective bonds lead to changes in perceptions or behaviors. For this reason, when examining emotional solidarity in tandem with perceptual or behavioral constructs, studies relied on extant empirical findings (i.e., conceptual frameworks) instead of the theory itself (e.g., Li & Wan, 2017; Ribeiro et al., 2017; Woosnam et al., 2015).

Attempts have also been made to expand the social exchange theory by adding emotional elements. The affect theory of social exchange (Lawler, 2001; Lawler & Thye, 2006) posits that negative or positive outcomes from social exchange will elicit corresponding emotions to involved individuals, thereby further shaping their perceptions and behaviors. The theory has been applied to examining how residents react to tourism as well (Zheng et al., 2019). While such theoretical advancement attests to the growing recognition of irrationality in tourism research, the theory maintains the social exchange viewpoint as it is essentially transactional outcomes (e.g., benefits, costs) that dictate the type and the nature of ensuing emotions. Furthermore, the social emotions addressed by Zheng et al. (2019) include happiness and anger which are normally considered basic emotions (Ekman, 1992) that can emerge without social interaction.

In sum, tourism research is in need of a more comprehensive theory linking residents' and tourists' social emotions with their perceptions or behaviors. Without such theories in place, conceptual frameworks may only lead to a contextual and disjointed understanding of how social emotions turn into perceptions and behaviors, failing to form a coherent body of knowledge. Responding to this gap in tourism research, the current article identifies Collins (1993) interaction ritual theory—along with his notion of emotional energy—and implicates its use in strengthening the theoretical link between social emotions and perceptions or behaviors, specifically with respect to residents' reactions to tourists and tourism. According to Collins (1993), emotional energy from social interaction drives perceptional and behavioral reactions to the social interaction. While finding an ultimate solution to testing the theory may require more extensive efforts and technological advancement, this article recommends viable and efficient answers to the issue and ways of strengthening the understanding of residents' social emotions.

Interaction ritual theory

An overview of the theory

Collins (1990, 1993) theory of interaction ritual, along with his notion of emotional energy, can be an effective analytic tool to understand how individuals' social emotions forge their perceptions and behaviors. The theory is rooted in the work of Durkheim (1912), who underscored moral and affective bonds between individuals as the binding force of society. However, unlike Durkheim (1912) who mainly focused on how emotional solidarity emerged, Collins (1988, 1990) emphasized the role that such emotions play in mobilizing society: "What holds a society together – the "glue" of solidarity – and what mobilizes conflict – the energy of mobilized groups – are emotions" (Collins, 1990, pp. 27–28). The emotions, that Collins (1990) refers to here, are in fact social emotions since they emerge from social interaction and undertake the social functioning of mobilizing and holding society together. Thus, Collins (1988) presented a more macro view (i.e., how social emotions relate to other constructs) of social emotions than Durkheim (1912), who concentrated on how affective bonds develop between individuals.

According to Collins (1988, 1990), individuals' interaction with one another follows the process of an interaction ritual, guided by emotional energy. Initially, at least two individuals should direct shared attention on an object or an activity, knowing that each other is doing the same. Such shared attention and mutual awareness then creates what Collins (1990) calls a ritualistic situation or an 'interaction ritual,' where a common mood (e.g., pride, enthusiasm) spreads and accumulates between the individuals. A result of the successful emotional coordination is a sustained feeling of group solidarity between those who participated in the interaction ritual. This long-term outcome, according to Collins (1990), is 'emotional energy.' In brief, a successful interaction ritual (i.e., emotionally charged social interaction) provides individuals with a positive and prolonged feeling of group solidarity (i.e., social emotion) or, in other words, emotional energy (Collins, 1988, 1990).

Individuals usually encounter a series of interaction rituals (i.e., social interaction) that lead to varying degrees of emotional energy. For instance, positive emotional energy (e.g., religious fellowship) from one interaction ritual (e.g., religious meeting) can be invested back into another interaction ritual of the same kind (e.g., additional religious meetings) or activities of supporting or preparing it (e.g., fundraising for the additional religious meetings). This eventually forms a loop of interaction rituals or an 'interactional ritual chain' as Collins (1993) called it, where seemingly independent social experiences are in fact, glued together and propelled, by emotional energy (Figure 1). However, when an interaction ritual (e.g., residents come across arrogant and ignorant tourists) causes negative emotional energy (e.g., resentment), individuals may choose other alternatives (e.g., avoid interacting with tourists, participate in an anti-tourism rally) to the interaction ritual, initiating a new interaction ritual chain.

This migration from one interaction ritual chain to another can be understood as an attempt to "maximize the amount of solidarity they can receive, relative to the costs of producing it" (Collins, 1993, p. 209). That is, individuals seek to maximize emotional rewards (i.e., emotional energy) from each interaction ritual by replacing a less efficient interaction ritual (e.g., encountering sex tourists) with a more rewarding one (e.g., welcoming eco-tourists). Thus, like others who purported the so-called affect theory of social exchange (e.g., Lawler, 2001; Lawler & Thye, 2006), what Collins (1993) conceived of is the social marketplace where emotional energy functions as a currency-equivalent; this can explain why individuals engage in emotional, symbolic, and value-oriented behaviors (e.g., altruistic activities) that run counter to their economic gain. For instance, philanthropists are those motivated by emotional rewards from their altruistic efforts over financial costs and likely to remain in that interaction ritual (i.e., practicing philanthropy) so long as they see it as emotionally rewarding.

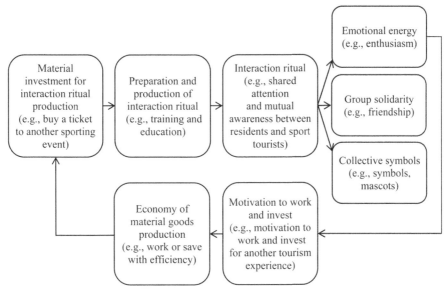

Figure 1. Interaction ritual chain and production of material resources.
Note. The chart is from Collins (1993) with corresponding examples added by the authors.

Individuals face not only a sequence of interaction rituals but also multiple layers of interaction rituals concurrently. For instance, the action of making philanthropic donations can be replaced with other actions (e.g., volunteering) if the individual sees the alternatives as more emotionally beneficial. However, even if the individual decides to continue his/her philanthropic donations, details regarding what, when, where, and how to contribute may change. Thus, a macro-level interaction ritual (i.e., philanthropic behavior) is composed of multiple micro-level interaction rituals (i.e., specific actions or forms of philanthropy) which may also subsume other smaller-scale interaction rituals (i.e., where and when to contribute). Switching between interaction rituals may happen at the micro level as well. Such horizontal (i.e., one interaction ritual to another) or vertical (i.e., from one level to another) switching makes the interaction ritual theory a more comprehensive mid-range theory that provides compelling interpretations of how individuals' perceptions and behaviors are shaped by social emotions in many instances.

In short, theoretical implications of the interaction ritual theory (Collins, 1988, 1990) are twofold. First, expanding on Durkheim (1912), it explains how emotionally successful social interaction leads to positive social emotions (i.e., emotional energy) which then encourage individuals to seek additional experiences of similar kinds or in pursuit of their goal. This knits together multiple interaction rituals, which seem distinctive and disjointed, to form an integral and comprehensive loop where social emotions push individuals from one behavior to another. Secondly, by treating social emotions as a currency equivalent, the theory brings together rationality (i.e., currency) and irrationality (i.e., emotions) so that what appears to be absurd and sentimental can be explained in terms of contemplation and reason. That is, the interaction ritual theory complements the rational choice theory, which by itself has limitations in explaining altruistic, non-calculative, emotion-driven behaviors (Collins, 1993; Lawler & Thye, 1999).

Issues surrounding the empirical use of the theory

Despite Collins (1990, 1993) effort to bring rationality and irrationality together to create a comprehensive and empirically-grounded theory, the interaction ritual theory begs some questions for its relative novelty and utility. First and foremost, the definition of emotional energy, which is central to the theory, remains vague. Although emotional energy is clearly a social emotion given its relational (i.e., shaped socially) and functional (i.e., mobilizes and glues society) aspects, Collins (1990, 1993) did not put forth any formal definition of emotional energy; he merely described it as positive or negative feelings (i.e., psychological drive), existing on a continuum from low to high, where individuals with high emotional energy are likely to be confident or enthusiastic toward interacting with others. Such conceptual ambiguity was also acknowledged by Collins (1990) himself; emotional energy is "[a] general metaphor [that] needs to be unpacked" (p. 39) and "a rather undifferentiated term, that includes various components" (p. 32).

It appears that Collins (1990, 1993) was also fettered by the conceptual fuzziness of emotional energy, as the term was often used in his works with little distinction from emotional solidarity. For instance, describing the interaction ritual theory, Collins (1993) wrote that individuals "move toward the highest *emotional energy* [emphasis added] payoffs they can get relative to their current resource" (p. 213). However, in the same work, he also described individuals' behavior within an interaction ritual chain as follows: "to maximize the amount of *solidarity* [emphasis added] they can receive, relative to the costs of producing it" (Collins, 1993, p. 209). These two statements convey the same idea and indicate that emotional energy and emotional solidarity are interchangeable terms with little distinction. Further supporting the interchangeable relationship and validating emotional energy as a social emotion, Collins (1990) suggested "low emotional energy is a lack of Durkheimian solidarity" (p. 33) which is basically emotional solidarity as referred to in this article.

Regrettably, this definitional ambiguity causes problems in measuring emotional energy and validating the interaction ritual theory. Collins (1990) suggested some possible ways to measure emotional energy, such as analyzing voice, eye-contact, facial expression, and bodily posture and movement. Though inspecting such physiological clues has drawn some scholarly attention (see Scheff, 1990), such an approach usually yields rudimentary data and is not appropriate in capturing social emotions. Some emotions may not develop into observable behaviors, and physiological states may only indicate how strong a feeling is without specifying its nature. Resultingly, physiological signs from basic emotions (e.g., sadness) and social emotions (e.g., shame) may look akin at the surface. Emotional energy, as a social emotion, is a multi-dimensional concept which cannot be measured reliably through unidimensional physiological clues. Acknowledging this, Rössel and Collins (2001) underscored the need for further research on the nature of emotional energy.

Application of the theory in tourism research

The interaction ritual theory can contribute to elucidating how individuals, both residents and tourists, think and behave as their social emotions direct them. First of all, the conditions for an interaction ritual closely resemble a setting for tourism experiences. Touristic activities usually take place in a confined area (i.e., face-to-face setting) where at least two individuals are present. Residents and tourists in a destination share their attention (i.e., shared beliefs) on widely known attractions or activities (i.e., shared behaviors) (Joo & Woosnam, 2020; Woosnam et al., 2009) and often appear in distinctive outfits, appearances, and culture (Wall & Mathieson, 2006). This shared focus and the distinctiveness make residents and tourists aware of one another, thus leading to mutual awareness. Without conscious knowledge, the two groups are in an interaction ritual and may build a common mood which can take on various forms. In a peaceful and friendly atmosphere (e.g., Catholic residents and tourists participating in a Papal Mass in St. Peter's Square), results are likely to be positive and unifying, but for those who were at the scene of the disruptions (e.g., natural disasters or terrorist attacks), the common mood and the emotional energy will most certainly be negative.

As indicated above, individuals may switch between interaction rituals, and residents or tourists are no different, replacing one destination or activity with another based on experienced or anticipated emotional energy. For instance, as alluded to by Sørensen (2003), backpackers are likely to have multiple travel companions throughout their trips and tend to move from one group to another in a brief period of time based on their shared norms and values. In such a case, each backpacker group will be engaging in a common interaction ritual, and positive perceptions and behaviors from its resulting emotional energy can initiate an interaction ritual chain composed of multiple backpacker group experiences. However, there may also be emotional rewards from one destination or activity which are not positive or sufficient. In such an instance, social hikers in Lum et al. (2020) study may abandon the Pacific Crest Trail (a long National Scenic Trail in the western U.S.) and switch to the Appalachian Trail (another long National Scenic Trail in the eastern U.S.), believing it will provide a more emotionally-rewarding interaction ritual. In instances where personal safety may be a factor, a course of action may be not travelling at all.

Despite its potential utility in explaining and predicting individuals' behaviors as they relate to tourism, few studies within the tourism literature have utilized the interaction ritual theory. Zuev and Picard (2015) applied the theory in their study of tourists' experiences in Antarctica. They considered the whole experience as a series of interaction rituals (i.e., smaller events) and analyzed tourists' photos to see how each interaction ritual unfolded. Although this stands as one of few instances where the theory was employed in tourism research, it showed a rather superficial use of the theory. There was a limited discussion of how each interaction ritual in fact embodied mutual awareness and social interaction and how it emanated emotional energy, group solidarity, or ritual symbols among tourists. More importantly, it was unclear how one interaction ritual was followed by another, with emotional energy serving as the fuel.

A more in-depth discussion of the interaction ritual theory with some relevance to tourism was presented by Gordon (2013). In his analysis of North American Major League Baseball park design, Gordon (2013) illustrated how symbols serve as a repository of emotional energy and encourage individuals' participation in nostalgia sport tourism. Although Gordon (2013) acknowledged the usefulness of emotional energy and the social marketplace in understanding individuals' tourism and leisure behaviors, his focus was mostly on how the physical environment heightened emotional energy and not how emotional energy moved individuals from one interaction ritual to another. However, such an influential role of physical settings in bringing individuals together can also be explained by the Durkheim's (1912) notion of *churinga* (i.e., an object of religious significance) and collective effervescence as well.

As such, regardless of its befitting nature in understanding individuals' perceptions or behaviors in tourism settings, the interaction ritual theory is minimally used within tourism research. The existing literature has primarily utilized qualitative research methods and, more importantly, with little consideration on resident-tourist relationships. However, residents' reactions to tourists and tourism can also be understood in terms of interactional rituals, leading to a new theoretical advancement. Residents' reactions deviate across different forms of tourism (Weaver & Lawton, 2013) as well as the number of tourists they face (Doxey, 1975). For instance, sex tourists mostly accompany negative resident reactions, despite the economic benefits, albeit transient, that sex tourists bring to the destination (Ryan & Hall, 2001). On the other hand, religious tourists are generally welcomed by residents (Terzidou et al., 2008; Uriely et al., 2003). Such reactions are often expressed in emotions (e.g., euphoria, apathy, anxiety, irritation, antagonism) as per Doxey (1975).

Even without referring to specific forms of tourism, the advent and growth of the sharing economy has lowered the barrier for resident-tourist interactions and expanded the possibility for social emotions emerging between the two groups (Paulauskaite et al., 2017). A finding indicates that residents who have been Airbnb guests previously are likely to demonstrate higher emotional solidarity with tourists and view tourism as a positive contributor to community well-being and personal quality of life (Suess, Woosnam, & Erul, 2020; Suess, Woosnam, Mody et al., 2020). Emotional solidarity with tourists is associated with residents feeling safer among the presence of tourists in their community and support for Airbnb hosts operating in their neighborhood (Suess et al., 2020). As such, it is possible to regard the resident-Airbnb guest interaction ritual as an important influence on residents' approval or denial of the sharing economy business in local neighborhoods or tourism itself in destinations (i.e., over-tourism).

Based on the assertion that the interaction ritual theory has great potential to help understand how social emotions propel individuals to develop different perceptions of social phenomena and move from one experience to another, research on residents' reactions to tourists and tourism can benefit from quantifying the constructs within the theory (see Figure 1) and testing the relationships between said constructs. Of course, acknowledging potential challenges surrounding this theory application and model testing is imperative.

Validating the interaction ritual theory

Methods of measuring emotions

Validating the interaction ritual theory requires devising ways to measure emotional energy, which sits at the heart of the theory. A healthy degree of discussion exists within the tourism literature regarding how emotions should be measured or tested (Li et al., 2015), but more extensive and up-to-date debates and insights can be found in psychology (Bradley & Lang, 2002; Lang, 1993). Despite differing views on how emotions should be grouped and understood (e.g., basic emotions, multi-dimensional emotions), there are three common ways of capturing emotions: overt behavior, affective language, and physiological clues (Bradley & Lang, 2002).

Emotions, in general, can be manifested via overt behaviors (Lang, 1993). For instance, attacking may be a behavioral manifestation of anger or fear, whereas a sexual approach may reflect love. In a way, this overt behavioral approach resonates with how Collins (1990, 1993) viewed individuals' migration between interaction rituals or bodily movement as signs of positive or negative emotional energy. However, overt behaviors are often less reliable than the other two methods as the evolutionary and socialization process of humans has trained individuals to inhibit, delay, and disguise their behaviors (Bradley & Lang, 2002). Resultingly, overt behaviors are less frequently employed in studying emotions, especially when dealing with complex social emotions like emotional energy.

Of the remaining two approaches, physiological reactions (e.g., heart rate, blood pressure, muscle activity) are favored by psychologists as they can present an uninhibited and uncensored portrayal of emotions (Bradley & Lang, 2002; Li et al., 2015). This approach coincides with Collins (1990) original suggestion of examining voice and eye-contact, but psychologists generally take into account a more extensive range of physiological data (Bradley & Lang, 2002). For instance, electrodermal analysis (EDA) monitors changes in skin, through which arousal (i.e., how strong an emotion is) can be captured. A notable example of EDA utilized in tourism research is Kim and Fesenmaier (2015) study, where tourists' skin conductance was monitored across experiences and between individuals.

Despite the popularity of physiological clues, they often provide an incomplete illustration of emotions (i.e., either valence or arousal but not both) (Wang & Minor, 2008) and, sometimes, it is hard to attribute physiological changes to a single cause (Hopkins & Fletcher, 1994; Poels & Dewitte, 2006). For this reason, in Kim and Fesenmaier (2015) study, follow-up interviews were conducted to interpret EDA data. Furthermore, it should be noted that devices for collecting physiological data can be costly and inappropriate in natural settings (Li et al., 2015; Shoval et al., 2018). For instance, monitoring facial muscles (Poels & Dewitte, 2006) or eye movement (Ravaja, 2004) is done in laboratory settings, which is likely to be a poor fit to tourism research.

The final method is to examine affective language, such as expressive communication (e.g., sounds of contentment, verbal expression) or evaluative reports (i.e., oral or verbal description, self-reported rating) (Bradley & Lang, 2002). Despite its flaws (e.g., errors due to memory distortion, cognitive intervention, or social desirability) (see Li et al., 2015 for further discussion), self-reported rating is accessible, affordable, and convenient to use (Li et al., 2015). Furthermore, given its textual nature, self-reported rating makes it easier to decipher complex emotions and complement other methods of measuring emotions (Bradley & Lang, 2002). Granted that emotional energy is an intricate emotion, whose meaning and nature are yet to be explored, self-reported rating might be a more appropriate method to use.

Emotional solidarity as an indicator of emotional energy

Utilizing self-reported rating requires a scale that is reliable and valid. However, given the conceptual ambiguity associated with emotional energy, there is no scale readily available, and creating such a scale can be a daunting task. Instead, researchers may consider incorporating the interaction ritual theory (Collins, 1990, 1993) in tandem with the emotional solidarity theory (Woosnam et al., 2009), so the interaction ritual theory may be indirectly testable via the Emotional Solidarity Scale (ESS) (Woosnam & Norman, 2010). Although doing so may not be an ultimate solution, it can be an effective means of circumnavigating the conceptual issue associated with emotional energy and the interpretative challenges associated with understanding physiological data.

This approach is built upon the premises that the two theories are comparable to one another but operate in different levels of analysis (i.e., macro and micro). Being rooted in Durkheim's (1912) work, the interaction ritual theory and the emotional solidarity theory equally posit that individuals can develop affective bonds with one another when they share beliefs, behavior, and physical space. Further, both theories underscore the importance of such affective bonds in relationships between individuals. However, as Collins (1990) explained, the interaction ritual theory focuses on the "personal side of having a great deal of Durkheimian ritual solidarity" (p. 32), whereas the emotional solidarity theory retains a more macro view.

That said, emotional energy and emotional solidarity represent the same phenomena (i.e., social emotions) but from two different angles. When it comes to measuring and validating the theories, the ESS allows researchers the ability to undertake quantitative analysis of the emotional solidarity theory, whereas the interaction ritual theory still lacks a scale for emotional energy that is essential to the theory. On the other hand, the interaction ritual theory illustrates how individuals' emotional energy further promotes perceptions and behaviors, whereas such an assumption is not explicated in the emotional solidarity theory but has been explored by researchers (e.g., Ribeiro et al., 2017; Simpson & Simpson, 2017; Woosnam et al., 2015).

These similarities and differences put the two theories in a complementary relationship where one remedies the other's shortcomings (Figure 2). First, the interaction ritual theory provides more solid theoretical grounds for the relationship between individuals' affective bonds and their ensuing perceptions and behaviors. It is evidenced that a positive relationship exists between individuals' emotional solidarity and their behavioral intentions (Simpson & Simpson, 2017; Woosnam et al., 2015). Nevertheless, the evidence has remained mostly empirical, which may only be coincidental and lack solid theoretical grounds. The interaction ritual theory can resolve this issue and reinforce empirical evidence with theoretical grounds, since it theorizes the positive chain between emotional energy and perceptions and behaviors.

On the flipside, the emotional solidarity theory provides a convenient means to operationalize the interaction ritual theory. Even though the interaction ritual theory provides a theoretical connection between individuals' affective bonds and their perceptional or behavioral changes, the theory itself is not empirically testable because it lacks a scale for emotional energy. This issue can be circumvented by considering emotional solidarity as an indicator or proxy of emotional energy, where the latter is measured via the former. Although emotional solidarity may not be identical to emotional energy, they correspond to one another given each refers to collective

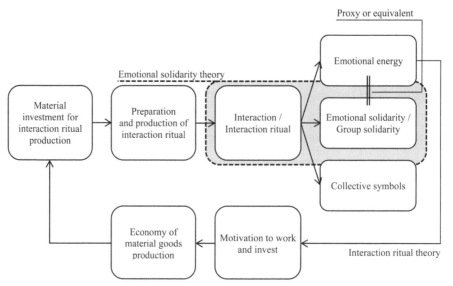

Figure 2. Link between the theories of emotional solidarity and interaction ritual.

and personal aspects of affective bonds (i.e., social emotion) to which Woosnam et al. (2009) referred.

Applying the interaction ritual theory in residents' reaction research

The interaction ritual theory can shed new light on the significance of social emotions in shaping residents' reactions to tourists and tourism. As illustrated earlier, tourism research is often blinded by the social exchange approach and overlooks the influence of social emotions on perceptions and behaviors. As powerful as such economic motivations might be, there has been a growing awareness that social emotions deserve more serious attention in tourism research (Ouyang et al., 2017; Zheng et al., 2019, 2020). Although often neglected, classic concepts and theories regarding tourism also attest to the significance of social emotions. For instance, Doxey's (1975) description of resident attitudes focused on the type of the (social) emotions evoked by varying degrees of tourism development.

Then, how does the interaction ritual theory assist residents' reaction research? On a theoretical level, the interaction ritual theory can operate as a mid-range theory that outlines the relationships among social emotions, perceptions, and behaviors associated with social interaction in tourism settings. Unlike the affect theory of social exchange—which is rather an expansion of the social exchange theory than a new invention—, the interaction ritual theory will highlight the purely emotional aspect of resident-tourist relationships, without being bound by perceived benefits and costs from such relationships. While the social exchange theory is useful to analyze how residents respond to tourism, it is only one of multiple theoretical perspectives, and it is questionable if sufficient effort was made by researchers to seek other explanations when the social exchange theory failed. In that sense, the interaction ritual theory will provide researchers with a new theoretical horizon, helping to foster new theory-driven research. Furthermore, the notion of interaction ritual chain helps to draw the lines that connect various residents' reactions together and seek a comprehensive and longitudinal understanding of the phenomena. That is, the theory not only delineates how social emotions change perceptions and lead behaviors but also suggests what additional outcomes such behaviors will entail. In reality, each behavior is followed by other consequences which then beget additional emotions, perceptions, and behaviors. However, given the predominance of cross-sectional research, researchers—not only those studying tourism—rarely question what would happen after residents approve tourism or tourists express their revisit intentions. While overcoming such an issue requires more than just a new theory, the interaction ritual theory, unlike others, will encourage researchers question what is beyond their findings.

On a more empirical level, there are three tourism settings where the interaction ritual theory can be more tightly applied. According to Collins (1993), an interaction ritual becomes more emotionally charged when there are more individuals—both residents and tourists—participating in it, when the area is more spatially-confined, and when the participatory barrier is higher. Such conditions are usually more pervasive in religious tourism, sport tourism, or event tourism. For instance, Catholic's Papal Masses in Vatican City or Muslim's Hajj rites in Mecca suffice all three conditions that Collins (1993) mentioned. Similarly, sport tourism usually requires entering sporting sites filled with fans who are loyal to certain teams or players (Cho et al., 2020; Gordon, 2013). Event tourism also features similar massive attendance, spatial confinement, and participatory barriers (Woosnam & Aleshinloye, 2018). Especially, when there is greater commonality between residents and tourists, the intergroup relationship can be a major contributor to residents' expectations and experiences related to tourism. For instance, residents around the Camino de Santiago often demonstrate shared attention and mutual awareness with tourists walking the route (Devereux & Carnegie, 2006; Fernández et al., 2016), leading to more emotionally rewarding experiences (i.e., interaction ritual) and comparably positive behaviors for both groups. Li and Wan (2017) and Woosnam and Aleshinloye (2018) also reported a strong correlation between residents' emotional solidarity with festival tourists and their approval of festivals in the community. Small-scale sport tourism—which ensures active participation of both residents and tourists (Fredline, 2005)—is viewed more positively by residents. Indeed, fans of professional or college sports teams are likely to engage in a series of interaction rituals whether they be interacting with residents or tourists, and the positive emotional energy that they get from pre- or post-game festivity tend to uplift how residents think and behave with respect to college football tourists (Cho et al., 2019).

Just like any other theory, the empirical utility of the interaction ritual theory in tourism research depends on the temporal scope of the research and the type of the data available. To see how one social interaction leads to another social interaction (i.e., interaction ritual chain), researchers should follow residents' behaviors. While individuals' behavior at one point in time can be captured effectively via self-reported rating or observation, studying a chain of behaviors across multiple points in time requires a more longitudinal approach which utilizes multiple self-reporting (e.g., experience sampling) or observations. Unfortunately, such longitudinal research usually requires substantial investment of time and effort, making the approach widely advised but rarely employed. Luckily, the technological advancement and the growing use of physiological data collection devices may allow researchers the opportunities to consult and compare multiple types of data. Shoval et al. (2018), in their study of tourists' emotions, demonstrated such a mixed use of EDA, experience sampling, self-administered surveys, and locational data and obtained more multi-dimensional findings in a relatively short period of time, among a small group of individuals. A similar approach can be undertaken to capture residents' emotional energy (physiological data, self-administered surveys), perceptions (self-administered surveys), and behaviors (experience sampling) related to tourism.

Conclusion

Despite the prominence of social emotions in forging residents' and tourists' perceptions and behaviors, there is a relative lack of theories that present a holistic and theoretical view of the relationship. The social exchange theory has been widely popular and effective in explaining individuals' reactions with respect to tourism, but it does not include emotional components.

Likewise, social emotions may only be implicit at best in the social identity theory. Presumably for this reason, studies that looked into relationships between social emotions and other constructs in tourism contexts piecemealed empirical findings to support their hypotheses. While Smith et al. (2013) claimed that such an approach is also considered theoretical, and in fact should be counted as a theory (i.e., type II theory), having a more structured and comprehensive theory to underlie the relationship will provide tourism research with additional depth and breadth. The interaction ritual theory can contribute to theoretical development and testing within tourism research by putting social emotions at the heart of residents' experiences and motivations for tourism experiences.

The interaction ritual theory functions especially well in elucidating social encounters in tourism settings. The facts that tourism is typically confined to a geographical location and residents and tourists are likely to share a set of interests (Woosnam et al., 2009) correspond well to the conditions of an interaction ritual as per Collins (1990). However, what truly sets the theory apart from others is the notion of switching between interaction rituals or, in other words, the social marketplace. That is, individuals face a range of interaction rituals both simultaneously and sequentially and may decide to participate in the interaction ritual that seems most emotionally rewarding. Using the idea, researchers can explain why one form of tourism is more welcomed by residents than others or how residents become emotionally detached from tourists and react hostile to tourism. As Collins (1993) put it, multiple layers of interaction ritual occur simultaneously, ranging from purely individualistic to collective, and allow for versatile application.

Applying the interaction ritual theory in tourism research requires overcoming a couple of challenges. First and foremost, the notion of emotional energy is only vaguely defined and not operationalized. Researchers suggested using physiological clues. While there is increasing use of physiological data in examining emotions, they often provide an incomplete and superficial depiction of social emotions and collection devices can be inaccessible and intrusive on occasions. One viable alternative suggested in this article is to treat emotional solidarity as an indicator of emotional energy, so the interaction ritual theory can be indirectly validated using the scale for emotional solidarity. Such an approach is supported by the fact that both the interaction ritual theory and the emotional solidarity theory are enrooted in Durkheim (1912), and Collins (1993) himself used the term emotional energy and emotional solidarity in an interchangeable manner. Given the ESS has been proven solid in its psychometric properties in tourism research, such an indirect approach may be reasonable.

Finally, it should be noted that the intention of this article was to introduce the interaction ritual theory to tourism research and to call for greater scholarly attention on its potential use and benefits in providing an alternative understanding of residents' reactions to tourism. As Berno and Ward (2005) lamented, being confined to a social exchange perspective, albeit efficient, likely narrows researchers' views and limits their efforts of exploring new possibilities. Emotion does not disregard reason but instead complements it, and examining the emergence and the influence of social emotions is crucial to understanding residents' repulsion against tourists during periods of over-tourism (pre-pandemic) and under-tourism (amid the pandemic). While this answers the call that Berno and Ward (2005) made, what was claimed here should be understood as explorative efforts and not as ultimate solutions or conclusions. Likewise, while religious tourism, sport tourism, and event tourism were illustrated as potential topics for theory application, tourism research should also seek other possibilities where the interaction ritual theory can bring about even more knowledge on the subject.

Acknowledgement

The authors confirm that this study was not funded by any organization and report no potential conflict of interest.

Disclosure statement

No potential conflict of interest was reported by the authors.

ORCID

Heetae Cho http://orcid.org/0000-0002-8927-9743

References

Allport, G. W. (1954). *The nature of prejudice*. Addison Wesley.
Berno, T., & Ward, C. (2005). Innocence abroad: A pocket guide to psychological research on tourism. *The American Psychologist*, *60*(6), 593–600. https://doi.org/10.1037/0003-066X.60.6.593
Bradley, M. M., & Lang, P. J (2002). Measuring emotion: Behavior, feeling, and physiology. In R. D. Lane & L. Nadel (Eds.), *Cognitive neuroscience of emotion* (pp. 242–276).Oxford University Press.
Brown, C. (2013). The poverty of grand theory. *European Journal of International Relations*, *19*(3), 483–497.
Buda, D. M., d'Hauteserre, A. M., & Johnston, L. (2014). Feeling and tourism studies. *Annals of Tourism Research*, *46*, 102–114. https://doi.org/10.1016/j.annals.2014.03.005
Cho, H., Joo, D., Moore, D., & Norman, W. C. (2019). Sport tourists' nostalgia and its effect on attitude and intentions: A multilevel approach. *Tourism Management Perspectives*, *32*, 100563. https://doi.org/10.1016/j.tmp.2019.100563
Cho, H., Joo, D., & Woosnam, K. M. (2020). Cross-cultural validation of the nostalgia scale for sport tourism (NSST): A multilevel approach. *Journal of Hospitality & Tourism Research*, *44*(4), 624–643.
Cohen, E. (1995). Contemporary tourism – Trends and challenges: Sustainable authenticity or contrived post-modernity? In R. Butler & D. Pearce (Eds.), *Change in tourism: People, places, processes* (pp. 12–29). Routledge.
Collins, R. (1988). The Durkheimian tradition in conflict sociology. In J. C. Alexander (Ed.), *Durkheimian sociology: Cultural studies* (pp. 107–128). Cambridge University Press.
Collins, R. (1990). Stratification, emotional energy, and the transient emotions. In T. D. Kemper (Ed.), *Research agendas in the sociology of emotions* (pp. 27–57). State University of New York Press.
Collins, R. (1993). Emotional energy as the common denominator of rational action. *Rationality and Society*, *5*(2), 203–230.
d'Hauteserre, A. M. (2015). Affect theory and the attractivity of destinations. *Annals of Tourism Research*, *55*, 77–89.
Devereux, C., & Carnegie, E. (2006). Pilgrimage: Journeying beyond self. *Tourism Recreation Research*, *31*(1), 47–56. https://doi.org/10.1080/02508281.2006.11081246
Doxey, G. V. (1975). A causation theory of visitor-resident irritants: Methodology and research inferences. In *Travel and Tourism Research Associations Sixth Annual Conference Proceedings* (pp. 195–198).
Durkheim, E. (1912). *The elementary forms of the religious life*. Free Press.
Ekman, P. (1992). Are there basic emotions? *Psychological Review*, *99*(3), 550–553. https://doi.org/10.1037/0033-295x.99.3.550
Esman, M. R. (1984). Tourism as ethnic preservation: The Cajuns of Louisiana. *Annals of Tourism Research*, *11*(3), 451–467.
Fernández, B. M. C., González, R. C. L., & Lopez, L. (2016). Historic city, tourism performance and development: The balance of social behaviours in the city of Santiago de Compostela (Spain). *Tourism and Hospitality Research*, *16*(3), 282–293. https://doi.org/10.1177/1467358415578473
Fredline, E. (2005). Host and guest relations and sport tourism. *Sport in Society*, *8*(2), 263–279.
Gordon, K. O. (2013). Emotion and memory in nostalgia sport tourism: Examining the attraction to postmodern ballparks through an interdisciplinary lens. *Journal of Sport & Tourism*, *18*(3), 217–239.
Hareli, S., & Parkinson, B. (2008). What's social about social emotions? *Journal for the Theory of Social Behaviour*, *38*(2), 131–156. https://doi.org/10.1111/j.1468-5914.2008.00363.x
Hopkins, R., & Fletcher, J. E. (1994). Electrodermal measurement: Particularly effective for forecasting message influence on sales appeal. In A. Lang (Ed.), *Measuring psychological responses to media messages* (pp. 113–132). Lawrence Erlbaum Associates.
Huang, J., & Hsu, C. H. (2010). The impact of customer-to-customer interaction on cruise experience and vacation satisfaction. *Journal of Travel Research*, *49*(1), 79–92. https://doi.org/10.1177/0047287509336466
Jacobs, J. (2009). Have sex will travel: romantic 'sex tourism' and women negotiating modernity in the Sinai. *Gender, Place & Culture*, *16*(1), 43–61.
Joo, D., Cho, H., & Woosnam, K. M. (2019). Exploring tourists' perceptions of tourism impacts. *Tourism Management Perspectives*, *31*, 231–235. https://doi.org/10.1016/j.tmp.2019.05.008

Joo, D., Tasci, A. D., Woosnam, K. M., Maruyama, N. U., Hollas, C. R., & Aleshinloye, K. D. (2018). Residents' attitude towards domestic tourists explained by contact, emotional solidarity and social distance. *Tourism Management*, *64*, 245–257. https://doi.org/10.1016/j.tourman.2017.08.012

Joo, D., & Woosnam, K. M. (2020). Measuring tourists' emotional solidarity with one another—A modification of the emotional solidarity scale. *Journal of Travel Research*, *59*(7), 1186–1203. https://doi.org/10.1177/0047287519878503

Kaell, H. (2014). *Walking where Jesus walked: American Christians and holy land pilgrimage*. NYU Press.

Kim, J., & Fesenmaier, D. R. (2015). Measuring emotions in real time: Implications for tourism experience design. *Journal of Travel Research*, *54*(4), 419–429. https://doi.org/10.1177/0047287514550100

Lang, P. J. (1993). The three-system approach to emotion. In N. Birbaumer & A. Öhman (Eds.), *The organization of emotion* (pp. 18–30). Hogrefe-Huber.

Lawler, E. J. (2001). An affect theory of social exchange. *American Journal of Sociology*, *107*(2), 321–352.

Lawler, E. J., & Thye, S. R. (1999). Bringing emotions into social exchange theory. *Annual Review of Sociology*, *25*(1), 217–244. https://doi.org/10.1146/annurev.soc.25.1.217

Lawler, E. J., & Thye, S. R. (2006). Social exchange theory of emotions. In J. Stets & J. H. Turner (Eds.), *Handbook of the sociology of emotions* (pp. 295–320).Springer.

Leary, M. R. (2000). Affect, cognition, and the social emotions. In J. P. Forgas (Ed.), *Studies in emotion and social interaction, second series. Feeling and thinking: The role of affect in social cognition* (pp. 331–356).Cambridge University Press.

Li, S., Scott, N., & Walters, G. (2015). Current and potential methods for measuring emotion in tourism experiences: A review. *Current Issues in Tourism*, *18*(9), 805–827. https://doi.org/10.1080/13683500.2014.975679

Li, X., & Wan, Y. K. P. (2017). Residents' support for festivals: Integration of emotional solidarity. *Journal of Sustainable Tourism*, *25*(4), 517–535. https://doi.org/10.1080/09669582.2016.1224889

Lum, C. S., Keith, S. J., & Scott, D. (2020). The long-distance hiking social world along the Pacific Crest Trail. *Journal of Leisure Research*, *51*(2), 165–182. https://doi.org/10.1080/00222216.2019.1640095

Mckercher, B. (1993). Some fundamental truths about tourism: Understanding tourism's social and environmental impacts. *Journal of Sustainable Tourism*, *1*(1), 6–16. https://doi.org/10.1080/09669589309450697

Merton, R. K. (1968). *Social theory and social structure*. Simon and Schuster.

Mills, C. W. (1959). *The sociological imagination*. Oxford University Press.

Ouyang, Z., Gursoy, D., & Sharma, B. (2017). Role of trust, emotions and event attachment on residents' attitudes toward tourism. *Tourism Management*, *63*, 426–438. https://doi.org/10.1016/j.tourman.2017.06.026

Paulauskaite, D., Powell, R., Coca-Stefaniak, J. A., & Morrison, A. M. (2017). Living like a local: Authentic tourism experiences and the sharing economy. *International Journal of Tourism Research*, *19*(6), 619–628. https://doi.org/10.1002/jtr.2134

Poels, K., & Dewitte, S. (2006). How to capture the heart? Reviewing 20 years of emotion measurement in advertising. *Journal of Advertising Research*, *46*(1), 18–37. https://doi.org/10.2501/S0021849906060041

Pruitt, D., & LaFont, S. (1995). For love and money: romance tourism in Jamaica. *Annals of Tourism Research*, *22*(2), 422–440. https://doi.org/10.1016/0160-7383(94)00084-0

Ravaja, N. (2004). Contributions of psychophysiology to media research: Review and recommendations. *Media Psychology*, *6*(2), 193–235.

Ribeiro, M. A., Pinto, P., Silva, J. A., & Woosnam, K. M. (2017). Residents' attitudes and the adoption of pro-tourism behaviours: The case of developing island countries. *Tourism Management*, *61*, 523–537. https://doi.org/10.1016/j.tourman.2017.03.004

Rössel, J., & Collins, R. (2001). Conflict theory and interaction rituals: The microfoundations of conflict theory. In J. H. Turner (Ed.), *Handbook of sociological theory* (pp. 509–531). Springer.

Ryan, C., & Hall, C. M. (2001). *Sex tourism: Marginal people and liminalities*. Routledge.

Scheff, T. J. (1990). Socialization of emotions: Pride and shame as causal agents. In T. D. Kemper (Ed.), *Research agendas in the sociology of emotions* (pp. 281–304). State University of New York Press.

Shoval, N., Schvimer, Y., & Tamir, M. (2018). Real-time measurement of tourists' objective and subjective emotions in time and space. *Journal of Travel Research*, *57*(1), 3–16. https://doi.org/10.1177/0047287517691155

Simpson, J. J., & Simpson, P. M. (2017). Emotional solidarity with destination security forces. *Journal of Travel Research*, *56*(7), 927–940. https://doi.org/10.1177/0047287516675063

Smith, S. L., Xiao, H., Nunkoo, R., & Tukamushaba, E. K. (2013). Theory in hospitality, tourism, and leisure studies. *Journal of Hospitality Marketing & Management*, *22*(8), 875–894.

Sørensen, A. (2003). Backpacker ethnography. *Annals of Tourism Research*, *30*(4), 847–867.

Suess, C., Woosnam, K. M., & Erul, E. (2020). Stranger-danger? Understanding the moderating effects of children in the household on non-hosting residents' emotional solidarity with Airbnb visitors, feeling safe, and support for Airbnb. *Tourism Management*, *77*, 103952.

Suess, C., Woosnam, K., Mody, M., Dogru, T., & Sirakaya Turk, E. (2020). Understanding how residents' emotional solidarity with airbnb visitors influences perceptions of their impact on a community: The moderating role of prior experience staying at an Airbnb. *Journal of Travel Research*, 0047287520921234.

Taillon, J., & Jamal, T. (2009). Understanding tourism as an academic community, study, and/or discipline. In D. Papineu (Ed.), *Philosophy* (pp. 4–20). Oxford, UK: Oxford University Press.

Tajfel, H. (1974). Social identity and intergroup behaviour. *Social Science Information*, 13(2), 65–93.

Terzidou, M., Stylidis, D., & Szivas, E. M. (2008). Residents' perceptions of religious tourism and its socio-economic impacts on the island of Tinos. *Tourism and Hospitality Planning & Development*, 5(2), 113–129.

Trauer, B., & Ryan, C. (2005). Destination image, romance and place experience—an application of intimacy theory in tourism. *Tourism Management*, 26(4), 481–491. https://doi.org/10.1016/j.tourman.2004.02.014

Turner, J. H., & Boyns, D. E. (2001). The return of grand theory. In J. H. Turner (Ed.), *Handbook of sociological theory* (pp. 353–378).Springer.

Uriely, N., Israeli, A., & Reichel, A. (2003). Religious identity and residents' attitudes toward heritage tourism development: The case of Nazareth. *Journal of Hospitality & Tourism Research*, 27(1), 69–84.

Wall, G., & Mathieson, A. (2006). *Tourism: change, impacts, and opportunities.* Pearson Education.

Wang, Y. J., & Minor, M. S. (2008). Validity, reliability, and applicability of psychophysiological techniques in marketing research. *Psychology and Marketing*, 25(2), 197–232.

Weaver, D. B., & Lawton, L. J. (2001). Resident perceptions in the urban–rural fringe. *Annals of Tourism Research*, 28(2), 439–458. https://doi.org/10.1016/S0160-7383(00)00052-9

Weaver, D. B., & Lawton, L. J. (2013). Resident perceptions of a contentious tourism event. *Tourism Management*, 37, 165–175. https://doi.org/10.1016/j.tourman.2013.01.017

White, S. K. (1991). *Political theory and postmodernism.* Cambridge University Press.

Woosnam, K. M. (2011). Testing a model of Durkheim's theory of emotional solidarity among residents of a tourism community. *Journal of Travel Research*, 50(5), 546–558.

Woosnam, K. M. (2012). Using emotional solidarity to explain residents' attitudes about tourism and tourism development. *Journal of Travel Research*, 51(3), 315–327.

Woosnam, K. M., & Aleshinloye, K. D. (2018). Residents' emotional solidarity with tourists: Explaining perceived impacts of a cultural heritage festival. *Journal of Hospitality & Tourism Research*, 42(4), 587–605.

Woosnam, K. M., Dudensing, R. M., & Walker, J. R. (2015). How does emotional solidarity factor into visitor spending among birders in the Lower Rio Grande Valley of Texas? *Journal of Travel Research*, 54(5), 645–658. https://doi.org/10.1177/0047287514522884

Woosnam, K. M., & Norman, W. C. (2010). Measuring residents' emotional solidarity with tourists: Scale development of Durkheim's theoretical constructs. *Journal of Travel Research*, 49(3), 365–380. https://doi.org/10.1177/0047287509346858

Woosnam, K. M., Norman, W. C., & Ying, T. (2009). Exploring the theoretical framework of emotional solidarity between residents and tourists. *Journal of Travel Research*, 48(2), 245–258. https://doi.org/10.1177/0047287509332334

Ze'ev, A. B., & Oatley, K. (1996). Development of social emotions and constructive agents. *Behavioral and Brain Sciences*, 19(1), 124–125.

Zheng, D., Liang, Z., & Ritchie, B. W. (2020). Residents' social dilemma in sustainable heritage tourism: the role of social emotion, efficacy beliefs and temporal concerns. *Journal of Sustainable Tourism*, 28(11), 1782–1804.

Zheng, D., Ritchie, B. W., Benckendorff, P. J., & Bao, J. (2019). The role of cognitive appraisal, emotion and commitment in affecting resident support toward tourism performing arts development. *Journal of Sustainable Tourism*, 27(11), 1725–1744. https://doi.org/10.1080/09669582.2019.1662029

Zuev, D., & Picard, D. (2015). Reconstructing the Antarctic tourist interaction ritual chain: visual sociological perspective. *The Polar Journal*, 5(1), 146–169. https://doi.org/10.1080/2154896X.2015.1025495

Understanding the tourist-resident relationship through social contact: progressing the development of social contact in tourism

Daisy X. F. Fan

ABSTRACT
Social contact becomes an essential agenda of tourist-resident relationship research. However, the development of social contact in tourism and how it could influence the tourist-resident relationship is still ambiguous. This conceptual study addresses those research gaps by providing an overview of the current development in tourist-resident social contact; developing a tourist-resident social contact axis to understand different tourist-resident relationship through social contact; and delineating the future research directions of tourist-resident social contact. This research contributes to the theory by clarifying the development of the concept in terms of contact antecedents, contact types and contact impacts, proposing a social contact axis to understand the tourist-resident relationship through four contact scenarios and offering directions to guide the future investigations. Practically, results benefit different stakeholders regarding how to jointly develop a favourable and sustainable tourist-resident relationship.

Introduction

Tourists are surrounded by the social environment when traveling in a destination and the social interactions have become a crucial part of their overall travel experience (Fan et al., 2019). Meanwhile, social contact with tourists can influence residents' wellbeing (Eusébio et al., 2018) and further determine their support level for the tourism development (Tsaur et al., 2018). Practice theory (Echeverri & Skålén, 2011; Yin et al., 2019) suggests that, through various social practices, actors engage with each other to create values. Therefore, social contact becomes an important agenda of tourist-residents relationship research (Choi & Sirakaya, 2005; Maruyama et al., 2017; Yu et al., 2011). Furthermore, a favourable social contact with tourists could boost residents' positive attitude towards the tourists and the tourism development (Carneiro et al., 2018), whereas an irritating contact experience may intensify the destination social conflict, and reduce the social tolerance and acceptance of the destination society (Pizam et al., 2000; Zhang et al., 2017). Therefore, understanding the social contact between tourists and residents is essential in achieving the social sustainability of tourism (Zhang et al., 2017).

Tourism provides a natural occasion connecting different groups of people together, such as tourists, hosts, service providers and authorities. Different types of social contact, such as tourist-resident, tourist-service personnel, tourist-destination marketing organisation, tourist-tourist, and resident-resident interactions (Lovelock & Wirtz, 2004; Pearce, 2005; Rihova et al., 2015; Wu, 2007) could occur in tourism activities and impact on interacting groups. However, due to its uniqueness in contact context, duration and purposes, social contact in tourism distinguishes itself from the general cross-cultural social contact (Pearce, 1982). Given the importance of social contact, tourist-resident social contact is not receiving sufficient attention in tourism academia. Specifically, due to the limited exploratory studies focusing on social contact, the antecedents of contact between tourists and residents are not fully investigated. For long, social contact has been treated as a homogenous concept, so the different types of social contact and their diverse impacts on both participant groups are yet to be specified. Furthermore, though the importance of social contact in tourist-residents relationship is acknowledged, the mechanism of transforming different practices into relationships is still mystery. As the formation of a relation needs the engagement and efforts from both participant groups, a paired investigation regarding the tourists' and residents' contact experiences is urgently needed.

To fulfil those research gaps, this conceptual study is guided by the following objectives: to provide an overview of the current development in tourist-resident social contact; to develop a tourist-resident social contact axis to understand different tourist-resident relationships through social contact; and to delineate the future research directions of tourist-resident social contact. This research contributes to the knowledge by providing a systematic overview of the tourist-resident social contact. The consolidated output provides a refined portrait of this concept and its relationship with other relevant concepts. The tourist-resident contact axis innovatively applies the contact experiences of both groups to interpret the tourist-resident relationship. It also offers a blueprint for researchers who aim to apply social contact in different tourist-resident studies. Practically, results could benefit different stakeholders in destinations, such as destination marketing officers, tour operators and the host communities regarding how to jointly develop a sustainable tourist-resident relationship.

Overview of the tourist-resident social contact research

Definitions and measurements of social contact

In general, social contact is an encounter between two or more individuals and is a building block of society (Wey et al., 2019). By contacting others, people set rules, institutions and systems for living. In tourism, cross-cultural social contact describes the encounter between individuals from different cultural contexts in tourism related activities (Fan et al., 2017a; Yu & Lee, 2014).

The measurement of social contact has gained noticeable attention since early 1970s. Cohen (1972, p177) proposed that "the degree to which and the way they affect each other depend largely on the extent and variety of social contacts the tourists have during their trips". Therefore, the extent of contact, the variety of contact and the impact of contact composed the three aspects of evaluating social contact. Early research adopted the single dimension to measure social contact, such as activity (Rothman, 1978) and frequency of contact (Woosnam & Aleshinloye, 2013). More studies used multiple dimensions to measure a comprehensive experience of social contact. Fan et al. (2017a) by reviewing all relevant measurements of social contact, concluded that, activity, number of contact points, frequency, quality, strength, influence, valence, intensity, power and symmetry were used in different combinations to measure the social contact. In the tourism setting, Fan et al. (2017b) argued that both quantity and quality of social contact should be considered when assessing their impacts on tourists' perceptions.

Antecedents of social contact

Contact activities start with the antecedents of social contact between tourists and residents. As indicated in the hierarchical constraint theory (Crawford et al., 1991), leisure and tourism behaviour constraints posited three categories, namely intrapersonal, interpersonal and structural barriers. Intrapersonal barriers describe individual psychological states and attributes which interact with leisure preferences. Interpersonal barriers are the results of interpersonal interaction or the relationship between individuals' characteristics. Structural barriers refer to those intervening and environmental factors between behaviour preference and actual participation. It is argued that constraints are encountered hierarchically, first at the intrapersonal level, then to the interpersonal level and eventually to the structural level. Applying the categories of hierarchical constraints theory in understanding the antecedents of social contact between tourists and hosts, there are three categories of contact antecedents.

As shown in Figure 1, the first category intrapersonal antecedents represent factors that relates to individuals' own evaluation of the appropriateness, personal skills and psychological features. Personality is reported to be an important determinant for the social interactions between two groups of people (Lin et al., 2019; Plog, 1974). In cross-cultural encounters, language skill is also essential for an effective communication (Lin et al., 2019). From a tourist viewpoint, purpose of travel and personal role in travel determines the degree of contact with the local (Fan et al., 2017a). For example, if tourists travel to explore the destinations' culture and lifestyle, they are more likely to interact with the local to fulfill their expectation and to obtain the desired experience and information. If a tourist is depending on his or her travel partners for all travel plans, information inquiries, and on-site decisions, the tourist may not contact the local very much in person during the travel.

The second category is interpersonal antecedents, which includes the joint preference regarding the social interactions. Tourists who prefer ingroup contact or seek for interpersonal existential authenticity (Wang, 1999) in their travel may not have much interaction with the local (Fan et al., 2017a). Discriminations and stereotypes could also influence the tourist-host social contact from both sides (Tung, 2020; Ye et al., 2013). Allport's (1979) contact theory offers the earliest reference for the tourist-host contact conditions, which proposes that intergroup contact could reduce prejudice between group members under certain conditions, including common goals, intergroup cooperation as well as personal interactions (Fan et al., 2017a).

The last category of contact antecedents is the structural antecedents, describing those environmental conditions or contexts for social contact. Allport's (1979) contact theory specified that equal status and support of authorities were essential to ensure a positive contact outcome. In the tourism context, various situational factors were reported to influence the tourist-host social contact. Traveling in package tour or individually as well as the length of stay could determine the chance of tourist-host encounters (Cohen, 1972). Cultural differences between tourist and resident groups could distort the meaning in communication and inhibit further interactions (Fan et al., 2020). People with serious cultural and political sensitivity, such as historical antagonism, religious hostility, and territory conflict, may not have a positive context for tourist-host social contact (Fan et al., 2017a; Tomljenovic, 2010). Moreover, destination maturity, types of attraction and destination security level could also influence the degree of contact between tourists and hosts (Fan et al., 2017a). For example, well developed and clearly directed destinations can encourage self-serviced travel rather than consulting with the local. Metropolis destinations, compared with socio-cultural and nature-based tourism destinations, generate less social interactions.

Types of social contact

Social contact could occur in different formats. By interacting partners, there are tourist-resident, tourist-service personnel, tourist-destination marketing organisation, tourist-tourist (both ingroup and strangers) interactions (Lovelock & Wirtz, 2004; Pearce, 2005; Rihova et al., 2015; Wu, 2007). In the last few years, the online social contact between tourists and hosts before, during and after trips have gained increasing attention (Jansson, 2007; Neuhofer et al., 2012, 2014). Different online and face-to-face contact preferences as well as combination lead to different travel experiences. Fan et al. (2019) proposed a six-fold tourist typology, namely: disconnected immersive traveller, digital detox traveller, diversionary traveller, dual zone traveller, daily life controller and social media addict. Last, contact can also be categorised by its nature and purposes. Farmaki (2017) stated that there were passive and active forms of contact in travel. Han et al. (2019) proposed three types of social interactions with grounded theory, namely protocol-oriented interaction, help-related interaction, and sociable interaction. Fan et al. (2017b) revealed that social-oriented and service-oriented social contacts performed differently in influencing tourists' perceived cultural distance in travel.

Impacts of social contact

Social contact in tourism brings different impacts to tourists and residents. The impacts of social contact have been well addressed in tourism activities (Bochner, 1982; Cusher & Brislin, 1996; Yu & Lee, 2014) from either a tourist's or a resident's perspective. Figure 1 summarises the impacts of tourist-host social contact. For tourists, depending on the degree and quality of contacts, social contact with the host is reported to help obtain recommendations for the trip and knowledge about the destinations (Fan et al., 2017a). A series of perception changes could also occur, such as recognising cultural differences, changing destination images, increasing the perceived residents' emotional affinity (Aleshinloye et al., 2020), enhancing experience and travel attitude (Fan et al., 2020; Li & Liu, 2020) and developing personal cultural competence (Altinay & Bowen, 2006; Chen et al., 2013; Wei et al., 1989). A deep interaction with residents could lead to further impacts, such as making friends with residents, and changing one's ethnic identity (Cohen, 1972; Moufakkir & Kelly, 2010). Nevertheless, contact without fostering conditions, such as equal status, common goals, intergroup cooperation, support of authorities as well as personal interaction could lead to negative contact outcomes, such as prejudice, anxiety (Berno & Ward, 2005; Maoz, 2006) and intergroup animosity (Saguy et al., 2009). From a resident viewpoint, frequent social contact with the tourists could lead to a positive attitude toward the interactions (Akis et al., 1996), enhance the perceived impacts of tourism on their quality of life (Carneiro et al., 2018; Eusébio et al., 2018), increase the residents' emotional solidarity, reduce the social distance with tourists (Aleshinloye et al., 2020; Joo et al., 2018; Woosnam & Lee, 2011; Yilmaz & Tasci, 2015) and enhance the support for tourism development (Tsaur et al., 2018). On the negative side, too much contact, to the point that residents cannot enjoy their own public resources and environment (Zhang et al., 2017) and are not able to effectively engage in daily activities, may induce the negative effects, resulting in host-guest conflict (Zhang et al., 2017), emotions of burnout, irritation and antagonism as explained by Doxey's (1975) Irridex Model (Joo et al., 2018).

Social contact and the sustainable tourist-resident relationship

Social contact is essential to achieve a sustainable relationship between tourists and hosts with different cultural backgrounds (Fan et al., 2020), however, it is also important to realise that not all kinds of social contacts in all tourism settings could foster positive and favourable tourist-host relationships. Though evidence was shown regarding the general positive and negative patterns of contact, there is a lack of paired analysis illustrating the interrelated and dynamic impacts of tourist-resident social contact. Theoretically, when interpreting the mechanism of social contact, Allport's (1979) contact theory plays a dominating role. A broader and more diverse view is encouraged in explaining the impacts of tourist-host social contact. Therefore, the following section aims to apply the social exchange theory, value co-creation and co-destruction together with contact theory to delineate an overview of tourist-resident relationship with different

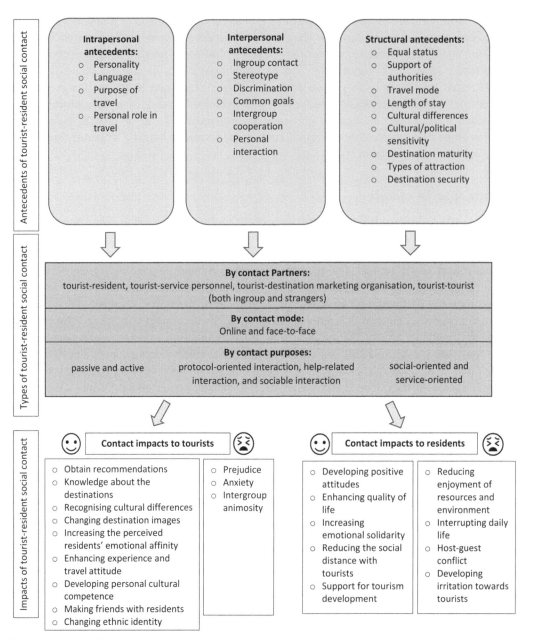

Figure 1. Overview of the tourist-resident social contact development.

contact scenarios presented. A brief introduction of different related theories and concepts is provided prior to the contact-relationship analysis.

Theoretical foundation for analysing the tourist-resident social contact

Social exchange theory and types of residents, tourists and destinations

Tourists' and residents' perceived benefits and costs through social contact play essential roles in determining the tourist-resident relationship. First introduced by Thibaut and Kelley (1959) from the economic theory, social exchange theory emphasises the perceived costs and benefits of a relationship as well as the relationship satisfaction of the participant groups. Exchange is perceived as a social characteristic that occurs during the traveling encounter between the hosts and the tourists (Sutton, 1967). The desire of the hosts in promoting the economic and social development of the destination (Moscardo et al., 2017) is the initiation stage of the exchange, followed by the formation stage where the exchange actually occurs. Transaction evaluation is the third stage, where the hosts assess the benefits and costs from tourism development. At the last stage, two possible outcomes of the exchange exist. If the benefits exceed the costs, the hosts will support the tourism development; otherwise, they may show a negative attitude toward tourism development (Ap, 1992). Such kind of exchange could be social-cultural, environmental, and economic (Jurowski et al., 1997). In the exchange process, comparison is key to provide the standard for all the relationship judgement (Ward & Berno, 2011). Government plays an essential role in determining the social exchange process in a destination through the interplay between trust to the government and the empowerment of the residents in tourism development (Nunkoo & Ramkissoon, 2012). Social exchange theory is widely used in explaining residents' attitude towards local tourism development, however less studies have applied it in understanding tourists' attitude towards tourism and their travel experience (Fan et al., 2019). Moreover, the theory was challenged by its ignorance of different cultural contexts, the complexity of social relations, and the irrational attitude and behaviours (Matatolu, 2019). Social exchange theory is also used together with other well-established theories, such as Doxey's (1975) Irridex Model and Butler's (1980) tourism area life cycle (TALC) to understand residents' attitude and attitude change in tourism development.

Doxey's (1975) Irridex Model proposes that the attitude of residents to tourists and tourism development depends on the varying social, economic, and environmental impacts on the destination. Residents' attitudes can be categorized into four stages, namely, euphoria, apathy, annoyance (irritation), and antagonism. At the initial stage, the hosts are excited at the potential economic and social benefits generated by tourism development. As the destination develops and the number of tourists increases, host attitudes gradually become apathetic, annoyed and, eventually, antagonistic. This model is widely used in addressing residents' attitude issues in cross-culture (e.g. Akis et al., 1996; Fan et al., 2019), cross-border (e.g. Zhang et al., 2018), overtourism (Cheung & Li, 2019), destination marketing (Kwon & Vogt, 2010) and longitudinal settings (Ma et al., 2020). It represents the attitudinal change induced by the tourist-host social contact on the resident side. Some limitations were discussed regarding the assumption and the representation of the Irridex Model. It is argued that the model assumes the attitude homogeneity in a community and therefore the intrinsic factors influencing the community members are largely ignored. Furthermore, the model also overlooks the structural efforts that could be made by the government or tourism organisations to reduce the negative attitude of residents (Cordero, 2008).

According to the degree of social contact in travel, Cohen (1972) characterized tourists into four roles: organized mass tourist, individual mass tourist, the explorer and the drifter. The first two tourist types are further called as institutionalized tourists and the other two are named non-institutionalized tourists. In brief, the organized mass tourists are largely confined to their home environment and habit when traveling. Individual mass tourists carry less home elements than the organized mass tourists, but still within their familiar zones. Different from mass tourists, explorers arrange their trips by their own, and try to avoid those staged attractions in a destination. Though they seek novelty in their trips, they do not entirely immerse themselves in the travel and tend to observe and experience through their own cultural lens and make judgments according to their own standards. Drifters venture further away than the explorers. They make their trips flexible, share the same way of living with the locals and wholly immerse in the host culture.

Another tourist typology which relates to the social contact is Plog's tourist psychographics. Plog (1972) discovered six psychographic groups of tourists, which are dependable, near-dependable, centric-dependable, centric-venturer, near-venturer and venture groups. A traditional tour destination would be appealing first to venturer and last to dependable. In general, venturers first discover a new travel destination and begin to talk about their experience with people around them. Such trend will be followed by near-venturers. Near-venturers' arrivals to the destination bring the development of local tourist facilities. As the destination becomes more popular and mature, the mid-centric tourists will take over the market. The huge increase in number of tourists leads to further development of the destination. When the tourist volume reaches or exceeds the maximum capacity of the destination, it will bring destruction to the destination. Meanwhile, the appeal of the destination gradually passes the magic mid-point in the population curve of tourists, and tourist volume begins to decrease. The tourist market shifts from mid-centric to near-dependable, and finally to dependable tourists.

Last, Butler's (1980) TALC states that, the development of a tourism area normally goes through six stages, namely, the exploration, involvement, development, consolidation, stagnation, and post-stagnation stages. Based on the original TALC, Agarwal (1997, 2002) proposed one more stage, "reorientation," between the stagnation and the post-stagnation stages to represent the dynamic process of restructuring. Zimmermann (1997) revealed the co-existence of multiple cycles of different forms of tourism. As for the post-stagnation stages, there are five more possible situations proposed, including rejuvenation, reduced growth, stabilization, decline and immediate decline (Butler, 1980). However, the last stage in TALC is challenged due to the difficulties to identify and to measure (Getz, 1992). It is argued that the natural or human-induced changes could interrupt the proposed developing trends in TALC and could also result in emergent destinations and industries (Baum, 1998). Moreover, no consensus has been reached regarding the specific reasons that could lead to the decline, stabilization, or rejuvenation of tourism in an area (Fan et al., 2019). Despite the criticism, the TALC model is one of the earliest tourism models originated in the tourism field and has been broadly applied to assess the tourism development and to determine the carrying capacity of destinations (Butler, 2019). TALC is also discussed together with Plog's tourists' typology and Doxey's Irridex Model to comprehensively understand the tourists' psychological change and residents' attitudinal change along with the tourism development (Fan et al., 2019).

Contact theory
When exploring tourists' attitude towards and outcomes of social contact, Allport's (1979) contact theory was broadly used in different studies (Fan et al., 2017a; Farmaki, 2017; Tomljenovic, 2010). Contact theory by Allport (1979) originally offered a way to minimise stereotyping and discrimination between two culturally different regions (Yu & Lee, 2014). It suggests that intergroup contact can reduce prejudice between group members under certain conditions, such as equal status, common goals, intergroup cooperation, and support from authorities. In other words, the impacts of contact depend on the kind of contact, and the situation in which contact occurs. There is also an agreement that under certain unfavourable conditions, contact could generate adverse effects, increase prejudice and distrust rather than leading to mutual respect and liking (Tomljenovic, 2010). Furthermore, unpleasant, involuntary or tension laden contact could promote competition and frustration, such as political conflict (Guo et al., 2006; Kim & Prideaux, 2003; Zhang et al., 2017) and economic recession (Anson, 1999).

Value co-creation and co-destruction
Tourism naturally brings tourists and residents to encounters. The experiences of their encounters may affect their satisfaction, wellbeing, future behaviors (Sharpley, 2014), and lead to mutual benefits or conflicts between the two groups (Bimonte & Punzo, 2011, 2016). Therefore, what kinds of benefits as well as costs could be jointly developed is key to anticipate the contact outcomes. Value co-creation and co-destruction could be useful theories to understand the benefits and costs generated during the tourist-resident social contact. According to the practice theory,

an action is only feasible and understandable in relation to shared practices and that social order is comprised by practices (Echeverri & Skålén, 2011; Foucault, 1977; Giddens, 1984). Practices involve a temporally unfolding and spatially discrete link of behaviours that include practical activities, performances, and representations or talk (Warde, 2005). Practices act as background coping skills that simultaneously limit and enable interactions between different groups (Echeverri & Skålén, 2011). Based on the practice theory, social contact provides a natural occasion allowing the value formation process between tourists and residents. In the tourism encounters, different interactions lead to diverse experiences for both groups, which may further lead to distinct value formations both positively and negatively.

Value is understood as "the consumer's overall assessment of the utility of a product based on perceptions of what is received and what is given" (Zeithaml, 1988, p. 14). The concept of value co-creation emphasises the collaboration between multiple stakeholders to co-create value (Prahalad & Ramaswamy, 2004; Vargo et al., 2020; Vargo & Lusch, 2004) and the core of such co-creation activities is to determine the value that needs to be co-created. There are several logics facilitating the understanding of value. Good-domain (G-D) logic (Cetin et al., 2014) highlights goods-related values from the firm's standpoint and emphasises the value-in-exchange, where value is realised at the point of exchange (Kotler, 1967). Introduced by Vargo and Lusch (2004), the service-domain (S-D) logic emphasises customers' active role in co-creating value and valuable experiences with the service organization, stressing the provider-to-customer co-creation. The S-D logic perceives value as value-in-use, meaning "the value for customers, created by them during their usage of resources" (Grönroos & Gummerus, 2014, p. 209). Comparatively, by putting customers at the centre of the quest, the customer-domain (C-D) logic emphasises the importance of value created within experiences and practices in customers' own social contexts. Thus, the value co-creation from a C-D logic provides a suitable perspective on tourists' value co-creation though social contact with the residents. In the C-D logic and tourism context, value co-creation is identified as "the tourist's co-creation practices and experience that takes place in his or her own social context" (Rihova et al., 2015, p. 358). Similarly, when putting the residents at the centre of the quest and considering the value co-created for the residents, it focuses on the value formatted within experiences and practices in residents' own social contexts. Value co-creation provides collaboration opportunities between different parties in the condition that both could benefit from the activity; willingly participate in the activity; and understand their own and the other party's role as contributors to the process (Gummerus, 2013). Though a few studies have applied value co-creation in the tourist behaviour and experience research (Binkhorst & Den Dekker, 2009; Rihova et al., 2015, 2018), the development of this concept in understanding the relationship between tourists and residents is still scarce (Chen et al., 2020; Lin et al., 2017), especially in investigating the interrelated relationship from both sides simultaneously.

While co-creating values in the tourist-resident social contact, value co-destruction can exist simultaneously (Smith, 2013). Echeverri and Skålén (2011) identified four roles that actors could play in the interaction, including value co-creator, value co-recoverer, value coreducer and value co-destroyer. Though it is evident that not all resources are value-adding but can be value-destroying (Echeverri & Skålén, 2011; Neuhofer, 2016; Yin et al., 2019), the notion of value co-destruction is still seen as implicit compared with value co-creation (Plé & CáCeres, 2010). Value co-destruction is defined as an interactional process between participants that results in a decline in at least one of the participants' wellbeing (Plé & CáCeres, 2010). Value co-destruction can result from accidental or intentional misuse of resources (Plé & CáCeres, 2010). The concept of value co-destruction was applied in the tourism field to understand the tourist experience (Neuhofer, 2016), information and technology use (Dolan et al., 2019; Sthapit & Björk, 2020), service quality (Luo et al., 2019) and sharing economy (Buhalis et al., 2020; Camilleri & Neuhofer, 2017; Yin et al., 2019). For example, Neuhofer (2016) revealed value could be diminished and destroyed in the following three ways when information and communication technology (ICT)

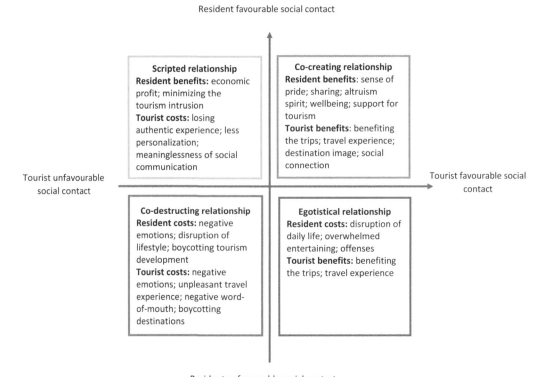

Figure 2. Social contact and tourist-resident relationship axis.

comes into play, namely: barrier to escapism from everyday life and relaxation; interference of 'living' the experience; and pressure and addiction. By exploring different stakeholders in the Airbnb ecosystem, Buhalis et al. (2020) argued that value co-destruction occurred due to uncontrolled and rapid expansion. For guests, co-destruction included expectations not met, overmarketing and safety/security issues, whereas for the residents, the co-destruction was reflected in noise pollution, traffic, crime, inflation etc.

A Tale of four tourist-resident relationships through social contact

Though tourists and residents could generate both benefits and costs during their interactions, such kind of value-formation is not necessarily guaranteeing a mutually beneficial or harmful outcome. Therefore, the tourist-resident relationship can be dynamic and heterogenous. This section aims to delineate four scenarios, illustrating different tourist-resident relationships generated from different types of social contact. As shown in Figure 2, by dividing the social contact into both favourable and unfavourable experiences, this axis presents the four possible tourist-resident relationships through social contact, namely co-creating relationship, egotistical relationship, scripted relationship and co-destructing relationship.

Co-creating relationship

The first scenario is co-creating relationship with the contact being favourable for both groups. Such kind of desirable relationship is a result of co-creation with efforts from both sides, and these efforts result from a mutually recognised benefits from such interactions. The co-creation relationship can be normally found at three stages of destination development in Butler's (1980) TALC, namely exploration, involvement and continuous growing (rejuvenation, reduced growth and stabilization) in post-stagnation stage. In the initial stage of tourism development and facing a small number of tourists, residents are generally welcoming the tourists and exciting about the future tourism development. The social interactions with tourists could also fulfil their sense of pride by sharing and touring, and their altruism spirit to provide quality and interactive experience to tourists (Moyle et al., 2010). It also corresponds to the first stage of euphoria in Doxey's (1975) Irridex Model, where residents are euphoric at the potential economic and social benefits brought by tourism development (Fan et al., 2019). From a tourist viewpoint, this group of tourists could be the venturers and near-venturers in Plog's (1974) tourist psychographic group, while drifters and explorers in Cohen's (1972) tourist typology. The value co-creating contact could also occur in a stabilised and well-maintained destination, where tourists and residents, after periods of imbalanced and extreme relationship adjustment, come to a sustained and positive relationship through social contact. Moreover, to ensure a win-win contact situation, contact theory provides references to foster a favourable contact for both parties. Since equal status, common goals, intergroup cooperation, and support from authorities are necessary conditions for positive contacts to take place, efforts should be made jointly from different stakeholders to ensure the favourable contacts. According to the social exchange theory, the supportive and favourable contact comes from the perceived benefits from both parties. From the tourist side, contacting with the local could bring both short-term and long-term benefits, such as enriching the trip, gaining knowledge about the destination, enhancing the travel experience, changing/reinforcing destination image, changing identity, and establishing social connections (Fan et al., 2017a; Lin et al., 2019). From a resident viewpoint, by interacting with tourists, they could develop a sense of pride as the local, share local knowledge, provide quality experience for tourists, enrich their social capacity and enhance their overall wellbeing (Eusébio et al., 2018; Moyle et al., 2010). Such kind of interactions with tourists also lead to a positive attitude toward the tourism development (Tsaur et al., 2018).

Egotistical relationship
Egotistical tourist-resident relationship occurs when there are imbalanced benefits and costs perceived by both groups. This type of relationship results from a favourable tourist contact experience, however an unfavourable resident contact experience. Due to such imbalanced situation, values could not be co-created as the residents could not reciprocally gain benefits from the contact with tourists. Instead, they perceive costs from the tourism encounters. Therefore, the tourist-residents relationship generated from this kind of social contact is egotistical as it only fulfills the willingness from the tourist's perspective. Such kind of contact situation could be found in the development stage in TALC, where destinations experience a rapid development and a dramatic increase in tourist numbers. As the development going on, residents start to feel overwhelmed at the tourism induced impacts and the interactions are more than they have expected or could cope with. Therefore, the residents enter the apathy stage and start to feel irritated towards the tourists in Doxey's Model. Meanwhile, as the residents' apathetic emotion is still implicit, tourists maintain a passionate attitude towards the destinations and attempt to interact with the local. They can be categorised into the centric-venturers tourists in Plog's typology, and explorers and individual mass tourists in Cohen's (1972) model. Referring to the contact theory, the unhealthy relationship could be an outcome of lacking proper government regulations in terms of tourism development. Monitoring and controlling the volume and quality of tourists can help avoid the uncontrollable situation. Unequal status could also be an important reason behind such situation. For instance, the Dharavi slum in Mumbai became the favourite tourist experience of 2019 in India and even higher than Taj Mahal (Telegraph UK, 2019). Tourists visiting slum tourism destinations mainly want to meet their curiosity and experience the inequality of living conditions. However, residents' negative feelings brought by the tourist gaze, unrespectful inquiries and irresponsible disruption in their daily life could be treated as a

sacrifice to exchange for the tourists' "interactive" and "informative" travel experience. Such kind of imbalanced relationship could be intensified in those interactions between groups of people with historical, cultural and religious differences or even conflicts, for example the rise of dark tourism in the Chernobyl Exclusion Zone in Ukraine and Auschwitz concentration camp in Poland. To respond to the social exchange theory, in this contact process, tourists may obtain different benefits as described in scenario 1, such as earning local information, new knowledge, change or reinforce destination image and experiencing differences. However, as such kind of social contact misses the collaboration from the local, the benefits for the tourists could be limited and superficial (Fan et al., 2017a). For the residents, unfavourable social contact with the tourists could bring costs, such as disruption of daily life, overwhelmed entertaining for tourists, and sometimes, offenses from disrespectable interactions (Joo et al., 2018; Zhang et al., 2017).

Scripted relationship
Alternatively, the third scenario presents another possibility of the imbalanced relationship with happy residents but disappointed tourists. In this relationship, as the tourism number going up, residents become skillful and experienced with receiving tourists, meanwhile, they become apathetic with the tourists with limited excitement, enthusiasm, and hospitality. Tourism gradually become a result of commoditization (Cohen, 1988). However, such kind of standardised tourism social experience could not encourage tourists to co-create values with the host through social contact as they are exhausted with the commercialisation atmosphere and scripted conversions. Tourists are traveling to pursue authenticity, though the representation of it can be diverse, such as objective, constructive and existential (Wang, 1999). In this relationship, local people seek to minimise intrusion by tourists by providing tourism experiences based on "staged authenticity" (Cohen, 1979; MacCannell, 1976). However, tourists travel all the way to the destination for a real authentic experience, but not a staged authenticity. This mismatch results in a negative social contact experience, and this is consistent with the contact theory, which pointed out contact without a common goal could generate unfavourable outcomes (Allport, 1979). Scripted relationship could happen in consolidation and stagnation stages in TALC as the tourist increasing rate starts to be stable or declined. Residents' attitude towards tourism development in this relationship is apathy in Doxey's Irridex Model. Tourists in this relationship belong to the centric-dependable tourists in Plog's model and institutionalised (both organized and individual mass tourists) tourists in Cohen's contact typology. Referring to the social exchange theory, though residents could benefit from such interactions with tourists regarding the economic profit and minimising the tourism intrusion (MacCannell, 1976), tourists tend to lose the authentic experience, personalisation, meaning of social communication in the meanwhile (Chhabra et al., 2003; Cohen & Cohen, 2012; Frochot & Batat, 2013).

Co-destruction relationship
The last relationship in this axis is the co-destruction tourist-resident relationship through social contact. In this process, tourism encounters serve as catalysts for severe intergroup conflicts. Both sides contribute to this holistic and tensive relationship and neither of them get favourable outcomes from such co-destruction. The co-destruction relationship could normally be found among the over-tourism destinations, where the local can no longer bear the negative impacts of tourism development and the unpleasant social interactions with mass tourists. Their daily life has been adversely influenced by the huge number of tourists. Therefore, they participate in this co-destruction to drive away the tourists and to express their dissatisfaction towards the uncontrolled tourism development. Hong Kong and Venice are two typical examples that we could refer to and there are many more in the world. Residents boycott tourists by abusing, bullying, anti-tourism protests and even physical conflicts. Some of the negative contacts are intensified

by the perceived stereotypes, discriminations, cultural differences as well as political sensitivity. Tourists co-destruct the relationship by performing badly in the destinations, such as unethical and illegal behavours (e.g. jumping the queues, destroying the natural environment, and crime) and disrespecting the local cultures and social norms (e.g. speaking loudly, not following the social rules, disrespecting the local religions and breaking the hygiene standard) (Seraphin et al., 2018; Shen et al., 2017; Ye et al., 2013; Zhang et al., 2017). This scenario corresponds to TALC's stagnation and possibly lead to the decline track in the post-stagnation stage if no government/ official interventions are taken place. Residents' attitude towards tourism and tourists are becoming antagonism in Doxey's Irridex Model, whereas tourists are mainly following into the near-dependable and dependable psychocentric categories in Plog's typology and the organised mass tourists in Cohen's typology. Considering the costs brought by the value co-destruction in social contact, residents may develop negative emotions, such as disrespect, offense, inequality, conflict, competition, anger and antagonism (Fan et al., 2020), get disrupted for their lifestyle (Moyle et al., 2010), and boycott further tourism development (Tsaur et al., 2018). Tourists could feel various negative emotions, such as hostility, discrimination and unwelcome, have unpleasant travel experience, spread negative word-of-mouth, and boycott the destinations (Luo & Zhai, 2017).

The above-discussed four tourist-resident relationships delineate four typical outcomes of different social contact encounters in tourism. In different relationships, tourists and residents tend to hold different perceived benefits and costs from the interactions, which determines the outcome of social exchange in this interactive process. It is noticed that tourists and residents could co-create as well as co-destruct values through social contact as long as they have the same or similar goals towards the contact, which is the reciprocal benefits, or alternatively mutual costs. However, tourists and residents are not always holding the similar perceptions towards the contact experience, and this leads to the rest two types of relationships, namely egotistical and scripted relationships. Four relationships do not have a sequence to follow and it is not necessary that one destination should go through all the four stages. Moreover, a destination's relationship type could change over time depending on the ongoing situation and the overall destination development. For example, the egotistical relationship could become the co-destruction relationship if the perceived costs from the residents continue to increase and limited structural intervention are implemented. Similarly, if destinations of scripted relationship could recognise the unsatisfied tourists and make changes accordingly to enhance tourists' experience, they could move to co-creation relationship afterwards. The corresponding categories of destination lifecycle, resident attitude and tourist types in each scenario only represent the typical cases of a destination development and may not be inclusive for every single destination. In addition, as in realty, one destination could have several main tourism markets simultaneously, it is possible that residents could develop different tourist-resident relationships with tourist groups with diverse cultural backgrounds, social distance and political intimacy. Moreover, destinations' developing level (Fan et al., 2017a) and tourists' socio-demographics may also influence the contact outcomes. In that case, several tourist-resident relationships could co-exist in one destination. Therefore, this four-fold tourist-resident relationship through social contact should be understood as dynamic and interrelated, rather than static and dominating.

Progressing the research agenda

Based on the overview of social contact research and the four-fold tourist-resident relationship through social contact, several research directions are proposed to guide the future investigations in social contact.

The diversity of social contact research

Tourist-resident social contact involves the efforts from both parties and the contact can be dynamic and diverse. For instance, as illustrated in Figure 1, tourist-resident social contact can be actualised in both online and face-to-face formats. Though some studies have touched the online social contact realm (Fan et al., 2019, 2020; Jansson, 2007; Kirillova & Wang, 2016; Neuhofer et al., 2014), more efforts should be made to further develop the understanding of the digital connection between the two parties, for example, what kind of technologies could facilitate or inhibit such kind of social interactions, and what kind of online and offline contact combination could maximise the tourist experience in different stages of travel. Furthermore, social contact can hold different purposes and occur in different situations, but existing studies mostly treat tourist-resident social contact as homogenous and ignore the nuanced differences across different types of social contact. For example, social-oriented and service-oriented social contacts between tourists and residents could generate opposite impacts on tourists' travel attitude (Fan et al., 2017b).

Value co-creation vs. co-destruction through social contact

As contact theory (Allport, 1979) suggested, intergroup contact may not necessarily lead to a positive outcome if certain situations are not presented. Existing literature dominantly explored the positive impacts of social contact, however, the negative side of contact is still largely overlooked and in an implicit manner. There is an extensive literature investigating the impacts of both positive and negative intergroup social contacts in social psychology and communication disciplines (Árnadóttir et al., 2018; Graf et al., 2014), however, its application in tourism field is still in its infancy. Considering the importance of understanding the working mechanism of social contact between tourists and residents, it is in urgent need for tourism scholars to conduct relevant studies to address the research gaps. Moreover, as tourist-resident social contact offers a natural occasion for both parties to co-create or alternatively, co-destruct values, more empirical studies are encouraged to unlock such process. It is also noticed from Figure 2 that, there are situations that an imbalanced relationship takes place between tourists and residents. Such kind of imbalanced and unsustainable relationship could potentially lead to an adverse outcome for the two groups if limited regulations, strategies and monitoring systems are carried out. Therefore, more attention should be paid to such kind of tourist-resident relationship.

Taking social contact conditions into consideration

Though a considerable number of studies explored the social contact in the tourism field, limited research has specified the contact conditions in the study design. Contact antecedents can be categorised into intrapersonal, interpersonal and structural aspects, corresponding to different layers of conditions for social contact. Allport (1979) in the contact theory proposed that "intergroup contact can effectively reduce prejudice between group members under certain conditions, such as equal status, common goals, intergroup cooperation, and support from authorities" (Fan et al., 2017a, p. 358), however, those propositions need to be examined by empirical studies. Though some studies have applied cultural differences (Lin et al., 2019) and political sensitivity (Fan et al., 2017a; Guo et al., 2006; Kim & Prideaux, 2003) to interpret their research findings relating to contact, contact conditions are not getting sufficient attention from the tourism academia. Therefore, more contact conditions in different tourist-resident relationship settings should be investigated in either direct or indirect manners (e.g. mediating effect and moderating effect) to reduce the ambiguity of the various contact effects. Furthermore, different research methods can be involved, such as experiment design and longitudinal studies, to capture the dynamic nature of different contact conditions in tourist-resident relationship.

Paired tourist-resident social contact

When it comes to tourist-resident social contact, it always involves two groups of people, namely tourists and residents. However, the majority of the existing studies only employed one group for investigations and ignored the paired and interrelated nature of social contact (Tsaur et al., 2018). Indeed, judging a relationship from merely one participant group may not obtain a holistic and comprehensive view as different participant groups hold different benefits and costs during the social contact. Thus, studies involving two contact participant groups or more can advance in the social contact research agenda. Methodologically, advancing analytical approaches, such as multi-level analysis could be applied to deal with the data collected from paired data sources in different levels (Liu et al., 2020).

Conclusion and limitations

This conceptual research flags the importance of understanding the tourist-resident relationship through social contact. Rich theoretical contributions can be identified. First, this study offers a systematic and comprehensive overview of the tourist-resident social contact based on the existing literature. It outlines the development of the concept in terms of contact antecedents, contact types and contact impacts. Particularly, this overview is the first attempt to categorise different social contact antecedents into intrapersonal, interpersonal and structural levels according to the hierarchical constraint theory (Crawford et al., 1991). Such clustering deepens our understanding of different contact antecedents and clarifies the direct and indirect influences on social contact. Meanwhile, the study also compares the different impacts of social contact on tourists and residents, respectively. Results indicate that social contact could bring in different impacts to tourists and residents in both positive and negative manners. It challenges the traditional goodwill towards contacts and peace, which is, social contact could always bring positive consequences for both contact groups. The dark side of social contact and the contact impacts on residents are spotlighted. Second, by applying the social exchange theory, contact theory, and value co-creation concept, the study proposed a social contact axis to understand the tourist-resident relationship through different contact scenarios. Four types of relationships were identified with different combinations of tourists and residents contact experiences, namely co-creating, egotistical, scripted and co-destructing relationships. This axis suggests a paired analysis of different tourist-resident relationships through social contact. It pioneers in establishing a linked framework between social contact and intergroup relationship in tourism. It also emphasises the importance of building a balanced and sustainable relationship from a social practices and exchange perspective. Last, the outlined future research directions raise the awareness of the current research topic within and beyond the tourism discipline, facilitate scholars with understanding this niche area, and foster more meaningful research to push forwards the progress of social contact studies.

Positioning social contact and tourist-resident relationship at the centre for quest, this research offers practical implications for different stakeholders in destinations. The overview of the tourist-resident social contact provides the government officials in charge of tourism development with a clear understanding of the causes and consequences of different types of social contacts, which could facilitate them to make proper policies and strategies to cultivate a pleasant tourists social experience, whereas maintaining a favourable community environment and wellbeing. For example, government support is needed from the destination through recognising the importance of tourism development and aligning it with the country's strategic development. Among the tourists and residents, an equal status should be presented to allow a favourable contact. Therefore, cultural competence and mutual appreciation should be promoted, whereas stereotypes and discriminations should be avoided. In addition, if tourists and residents hold comment goals, such as protecting the environment (in sustainable tourism) and cultural heritage (in cultural tourism), it is more likely that a mutually favourable contact could be formed. Furthermore, as a favourable and sustainable tourist-resident relationship could only be co-created with the joint efforts from all stakeholders involved in this process, it is essential for different parties to take their own responsibilities, rather than blaming each other for a negative outcome. For example, government led education about the cultural competence, tolerance and respect as a tourist and a host could minimise the negative emotions during tourism encounters at an individual level. Furthermore, tour operators should consider about the hosting communities' carrying capacity, attraction types, and tourists' preferences when designing their product itineraries. In addition, destinations which are already holding a negative tourist-resident relationship could diagnose itself according to the social contact axis and take out proper solutions to improve the situation.

This research should be considered with the following limitations. First, due to the conceptual and theoretical nature of this study, results are inferred from the existing literature and different destinations. Therefore, the generalisation of the proposed framework should be examined by empirical studies. Second, in reality, it is possible that one destination has several tourist markets, and residents could develop different relationships with different tourists. Thus, the observed tourist-resident relationship can be more complicated. Third, as tourists or residents could simultaneously form benefits as well as costs during social contact, the proposed contact axis and the four scenarios only reflect the salient and dominating impacts of social contact. The implicit benefits and costs as well as the offset effect between them deserve a further investigation. Fourth, the social contact axis does not include the possible tourist-resident relationship with no social contact between two groups. Last, there are many other factors that could influence the tourist-resident relationship, and social contact is only one of them. Therefore, future studies are encouraged to take other factors, such as economic structure, exchange rate and marketing approach into consideration to explore their effects on tourist-resident relationship.

Disclosure statement

No potential conflict of interest was reported by the author.

ORCID

Daisy X. F. Fan http://orcid.org/0000-0002-5247-8394

References

Agarwal, S. (1997). The resort cycle and seaside tourism: An assessment of its applicability and validity. *Tourism Management, 18*(2), 65–73. https://doi.org/10.1016/S0261-5177(96)00102-1

Agarwal, S. (2002). Restructuring seaside tourism: the resort lifecycle. *Annals of Tourism Research, 29*(1), 25–55. https://doi.org/10.1016/S0160-7383(01)00002-0

Akis, S., Peristianis, N., & Warner, J. (1996). Residents' attitudes to tourism development: The case of Cyprus. *Tourism Management, 17*(7), 481–494. https://doi.org/10.1016/S0261-5177(96)00066-0

Aleshinloye, K. D., Fu, X., Ribeiro, M. A., Woosnam, K. M., & Tasci, A. D. (2020). The influence of place attachment on social distance: Examining mediating effects of emotional solidarity and the moderating role of interaction. *Journal of Travel Research, 59*(5), 828–849. https://doi.org/10.1177/0047287519863883

Allport, G. W. (1979). *The nature of prejudice*. Addison-Wesley Pub.

Altinay, L., & Bowen, D. (2006). Politics and tourism interface: The case of Cyprus. *Annals of Tourism Research*, *33*(4), 939–956. https://doi.org/10.1016/j.annals.2006.03.020

Anson, C. (1999). Planning for peace: The role of tourism in the aftermath of violence. *Journal of Travel Research*, *38*(1), 57–61. https://doi.org/10.1177/004728759903800112

Ap, J. (1992). Residents' perceptions on tourism impacts. *Annals of Tourism Research*, *19*(4), 665–690. https://doi.org/10.1016/0160-7383(92)90060-3

Árnadóttir, K., Lolliot, S., Brown, R., & Hewstone, M. (2018). Positive and negative intergroup contact: Interaction not asymmetry. *European Journal of Social Psychology*, *48*(6), 784–800. https://doi.org/10.1002/ejsp.2365

Baum, T. (1998). Taking the exit route: Extending the tourism area life cycle model. *Current Issues in Tourism*, *1*(2), 167–175. https://doi.org/10.1080/13683509808667837

Berno, T., & Ward, C. (2005). Innocence abroad: A pocket guide to psychological research on tourism. *The American Psychologist*, *60*(6), 593–600. https://doi.org/10.1037/0003-066X.60.6.593

Bimonte, S., & Punzo, L. F. (2011). Tourism, residents' attitudes and perceived carrying capacity with an experimental study in five Tuscan destinations. *International Journal of Sustainable Development*, *14*(3/4), 242–261. https://doi.org/10.1504/IJSD.2011.041964

Bimonte, S., & Punzo, L. F. (2016). Tourist development and host–guest interaction: An economic exchange theory. *Annals of Tourism Research*, *58*, 128–139. https://doi.org/10.1016/j.annals.2016.03.004

Binkhorst, E., & Den Dekker, T. (2009). Agenda for co-creation tourism experience research. *Journal of Hospitality Marketing & Management*, *18*(2-3), 311–327.

Bochner, S. (1982). The social psychology of cross-cultural relations. In S. Bochner (Ed.), *Cultures in contact: Studies in cross-cultural interaction* (pp. 5–29). Pergamon Press Ltd.

Buhalis, D., Andreu, L., & Gnoth, J. (2020). The dark side of the sharing economy: Balancing value co-creation and value co-destruction. *Psychology & Marketing*, *37*(5), 689–704.

Butler, R. W. (1980). The concept of a tourist area cycle of evolution: implications for management of resources. *The Canadian Geographer/Le Géographe Canadien*, *24*(1), 5–12. https://doi.org/10.1111/j.1541-0064.1980.tb00970.x

Butler, R. W. (2019). Tourism carrying capacity research: A perspective article. *Tourism Review*, *75*(1), 207–211. https://doi.org/10.1108/TR-05-2019-0194

Camilleri, J., & Neuhofer, B. (2017). Value co-creation and co-destruction in the Airbnb sharing economy. *International Journal of Contemporary Hospitality Management*, *29*(9), 2322–2340. https://doi.org/10.1108/IJCHM-09-2016-0492

Carneiro, M. J., Eusébio, C., & Caldeira, A. (2018). The influence of social contact in residents' perceptions of the tourism impact on their quality of life: A structural equation model. *Journal of Quality Assurance in Hospitality & Tourism*, *19*(1), 1–30.

Cetin, G., Akova, O., & Kaya, F. (2014). Components of experiential value: Case of hospitality industry. *Procedia - Social and Behavioral Sciences*, *150*, 1040–1049. https://doi.org/10.1016/j.sbspro.2014.09.116

Chen, C. C., Lin, Y. H., & Petrick, J. F. (2013). Social biases of destination perceptions. *Journal of Travel Research*, *52*(2), 240–252. https://doi.org/10.1177/0047287512459106

Chen, Y., Cottam, E., & Lin, Z. (2020). The effect of resident-tourist value co-creation on residents' well-being. *Journal of Hospitality and Tourism Management*, *44*, 30–37. https://doi.org/10.1016/j.jhtm.2020.05.009

Cheung, K. S., & Li, L. H. (2019). Understanding visitor–resident relations in overtourism: Developing resilience for sustainable tourism. *Journal of Sustainable Tourism*, *27*(8), 1197–1216. https://doi.org/10.1080/09669582.2019.1606815

Chhabra, D., Healy, R., & Sills, E. (2003). Staged authenticity and heritage tourism. *Annals of Tourism Research*, *30*(3), 702–719. https://doi.org/10.1016/S0160-7383(03)00044-6

Choi, H. S. C., & Sirakaya, E. (2005). Measuring residents' attitude toward sustainable tourism: Development of sustainable tourism attitude scale. *Journal of Travel Research*, *43*(4), 380–394. https://doi.org/10.1177/0047287505274651

Cohen, E. (1972). Toward a sociology of international tourism. *Social Research*, *39*(1), 164–182.

Cohen, E. (1979). Rethinking the sociology of tourism. *Annals of Tourism Research*, *6*(1), 18–35. https://doi.org/10.1016/0160-7383(79)90092-6

Cohen, E. (1988). Authenticity and commoditization in tourism. *Annals of Tourism Research*, *15*(3), 371–386. https://doi.org/10.1016/0160-7383(88)90028-X

Cohen, E., & Cohen, S. A. (2012). Authentication: Hot and cool. *Annals of Tourism Research*, *39*(3), 1295–1314. https://doi.org/10.1016/j.annals.2012.03.004

Cordero, J. C. M. (2008). Residents perception of tourism: a critical theoretical and methodological review. *CIENCIA Ergo-Sum, Revista Científica Multidisciplinaria de Prospectiva*, *15*(1), 35–44.

Crawford, D. W., Jackson, E. L., & Godbey, G. (1991). A hierarchical model of leisure constraints. *Leisure Sciences*, *13*(4), 309–320. https://doi.org/10.1080/01490409109513147

Cusher, K., & Brislin, R. W. (1996). *Intercultural interactions: A practical guide*. Sage.

Dolan, R., Seo, Y., & Kemper, J. (2019). Complaining practices on social media in tourism: A value co-creation and co-destruction perspective. *Tourism Management*, *73*, 35–45. https://doi.org/10.1016/j.tourman.2019.01.017

Doxey, G. V. (1975). A causation theory of visitor-resident irritants: methodology and research inferences. In Travel and Tourism Research Associations Sixth Annual Conference Proceedings, San Diego, 8-11 September 1975, pp. 195–198. Travel Research Association.

Echeverri, P., & Skålén, P. (2011). Co-creation and co-destruction: A practice-theory based study of interactive value formation. *Marketing Theory*, *11*(3), 351–373. https://doi.org/10.1177/1470593111408181

Eusébio, C., Vieira, A. L., & Lima, S. (2018). Place attachment, host–tourist interactions, and residents' attitudes towards tourism development: The case of Boa Vista Island in Cape Verde. *Journal of Sustainable Tourism*, *26*(6), 890–909. https://doi.org/10.1080/09669582.2018.1425695

Fan, D. X., Buhalis, D., & Lin, B. (2019). A tourist typology of online and face-to-face social contact: Destination immersion and tourism encapsulation/decapsulation. *Annals of Tourism Research*, *78*, 102757. https://doi.org/10.1016/j.annals.2019.102757

Fan, D. X., Liu, A., & Qiu, R. T. (2019). Revisiting the relationship between host attitudes and tourism development: A utility maximization approach. *Tourism Economics*, *25*(2), 171–188. https://doi.org/10.1177/1354816618794088

Fan, D. X., Qiu, H., Jenkins, C. L., & Lau, C. (2020). Towards a better tourist-host relationship: the role of social contact between tourists' perceived cultural distance and travel attitude. *Journal of Sustainable Tourism*, 1–25. https://doi.org/10.1080/09669582.2020.1783275

Fan, D. X., Zhang, H. Q., Jenkins, C. L., & Lin, P. M. (2017b). Does tourist–host social contact reduce perceived cultural distance? *Journal of Travel Research*, *56*(8), 998–1010. https://doi.org/10.1177/0047287517696979

Fan, D. X., Zhang, H. Q., Jenkins, C. L., & Tavitiyaman, P. (2017a). Tourist typology in social contact: An addition to existing theories. *Tourism Management*, *60*, 357–366. https://doi.org/10.1016/j.tourman.2016.12.021

Farmaki, A. (2017). The tourism and peace nexus. *Tourism Management*, *59*, 528–540. https://doi.org/10.1016/j.tourman.2016.09.012

Foucault, M. (1977). *Discipline and punish: The birth of the prison*. Penguin.

Frochot, I., & Batat, W. (2013). *Marketing and designing the tourist experience*. Goodfellow.

Getz, D. (1992). Tourism planning and destination life cycle. *Annals of Tourism Research*, *19*(4), 752–770. https://doi.org/10.1016/0160-7383(92)90065-W

Giddens, A. (1984). *The constitution of society: Outline of the theory of structuration*. Polity.

Graf, S., Paolini, S., & Rubin, M. (2014). Negative intergroup contact is more influential, but positive intergroup contact is more common: Assessing contact prominence and contact prevalence in five Central European countries. *European Journal of Social Psychology*, *44*(6), 536–547. https://doi.org/10.1002/ejsp.2052

Grönroos, C., & Gummerus, J. (2014). The service revolution and its marketing implications: service logic vs service-dominant logic. *Managing Service Quality: An International Journal*, *24*(3), 206–229. https://doi.org/10.1108/MSQ-03-2014-0042

Gummerus, J. (2013). Value creation processes and value outcomes in marketing theory: strangers or siblings? *Marketing Theory*, *13*(1), 19–46. https://doi.org/10.1177/1470593112467267

Guo, Y., Kim, S. S., Timothy, D. J., & Wang, K. C. (2006). Tourism and reconciliation between Mainland China and Taiwan. *Tourism Management*, *27*(5), 997–1005. https://doi.org/10.1016/j.tourman.2005.08.001

Han, X., Praet, C. L., & Wang, L. (2019, June 25–27). *The role of social interaction in the tourism experience of Chinese visitors to Japan: A grounded theory approach* [Paper presentation]. Travel and Tourism Research Association: Advancing Tourism Research Globally Annual Conference, Melbourne, Australia. In

Jansson, A. (2007). A sense of tourism: New media and the dialectic of encapsulation/decapsulation. *Tourist Studies*, *7*(1), 5–24. https://doi.org/10.1177/1468797607079799

Joo, D., Tasci, A. D., Woosnam, K. M., Maruyama, N. U., Hollas, C. R., & Aleshinloye, K. D. (2018). Residents' attitude towards domestic tourists explained by contact, emotional solidarity and social distance. *Tourism Management*, *64*, 245–257. https://doi.org/10.1016/j.tourman.2017.08.012

Jurowski, C., Uysal, M., & Williams, D. R. (1997). A theoretical analysis of host community resident reactions to tourism. *Journal of Travel Research*, *36*(2), 3–11. https://doi.org/10.1177/004728759703600202

Kim, S. S., & Prideaux, B. (2003). Tourism, peace, politics and ideology: Impacts of the Mt. Gumgang tour project in the Korean Peninsula. *Tourism Management*, *24*(6), 675–685. https://doi.org/10.1016/S0261-5177(03)00047-5

Kirillova, K., & Wang, D. (2016). Smartphone (dis) connectedness and vacation recovery. *Annals of Tourism Research*, *61*, 157–169. https://doi.org/10.1016/j.annals.2016.10.005

Kotler, P. (1967). *Managerial marketing, planning, analysis, and control*. Prentice Hall.

Kwon, J., & Vogt, C. A. (2010). Identifying the role of cognitive, affective, and behavioral components in understanding residents' attitudes toward place marketing. *Journal of Travel Research*, *49*(4), 423–435. https://doi.org/10.1177/0047287509346857

Li, Y. Q., & Liu, C. H. (2020). Impact of cultural contact on satisfaction and attachment: mediating roles of creative experiences and cultural memories. *Journal of Hospitality Marketing & Management*, *29*(2), 221–245.

Lin, P. M., Fan, D. X., Zhang, H. Q., & Lau, C. (2019). Spend less and experience more: Understanding tourists' social contact in the Airbnb context. *International Journal of Hospitality Management*, *83*, 65–73. https://doi.org/10.1016/j.ijhm.2019.04.007

Lin, Z., Chen, Y., & Filieri, R. (2017). Resident-tourist value co-creation: The role of residents' perceived tourism impacts and life satisfaction. *Tourism Management*, *61*, 436–442. https://doi.org/10.1016/j.tourman.2017.02.013

Liu, A. X., Hsu, C. H., & Fan, D. X. (2020). From brand identity to brand equity: a multilevel analysis of the organization–employee bidirectional effects in upscale hotels. *International Journal of Contemporary Hospitality Management*, *32*(7), 2285–2304. https://doi.org/10.1108/IJCHM-08-2019-0680

Lovelock, C. H., & Wirtz, J. (2004). *Service marketing*. Prentice-Hall.

Luo, J. G., Wong, I. A., King, B., Liu, M. T., & Huang, G. (2019). Co-creation and co-destruction of service quality through customer-to-customer interactions. *International Journal of Contemporary Hospitality Management*, *31*(3), 1309–1329. https://doi.org/10.1108/IJCHM-12-2017-0792

Luo, Q., & Zhai, X. (2017). "I will never go to Hong Kong again!" How the secondary crisis communication of "Occupy Central" on Weibo shifted to a tourism boycott!" . *Tourism Management*, *62*, 159–172. https://doi.org/10.1016/j.tourman.2017.04.007

Ma, X. L., Dai, M. L., & Fan, D. X. (2020). Land expropriation in tourism development: Residents' attitudinal change and its influencing mechanism. *Tourism Management*, *76*, 103957. https://doi.org/10.1016/j.tourman.2019.103957

MacCannell, D. (1976). *The tourist: A new theory of the leisure class*. Schocken Books.

Maoz, D. (2006). The mutual gaze. *Annals of Tourism Research*, *33*(1), 221–239. https://doi.org/10.1016/j.annals.2005.10.010

Matatolu, I. (2019). Tourism and residents' quality of life: A critical examination. *Journal of Pacific Studies*, *39*(1), 128–164.

Moscardo, G., Konovalov, E., Murphy, L., McGehee, N. G., & Schurmann, A. (2017). Linking tourism to social capital in destination communities. *Journal of Destination Marketing & Management*, *6*(4), 286–295.

Moufakkir, O., & Kelly, I. (Eds.). (2010). *Tourism, progress and peace*. CABI.

Moyle, B., Croy, G., & Weiler, B. (2010). Tourism interaction on islands: the community and visitor social exchange. *International Journal of Culture, Tourism and Hospitality Research*, *4*(2), 96–107. https://doi.org/10.1108/17506181011045172

Neuhofer, B. (2016). Value co-creation and co-destruction in connected tourist experiences. In *Information and communication technologies in tourism 2016* (pp. 779–792). Springer.

Neuhofer, B., Buhalis, D., & Ladkin, A. (2012). Conceptualising technology enhanced destination experiences. *Journal of Destination Marketing & Management*, *1*(1-2), 36–46.

Neuhofer, B., Buhalis, D., & Ladkin, A. (2014). A typology of technology-enhanced tourism experiences. *International Journal of Tourism Research*, *16*(4), 340–350. https://doi.org/10.1002/jtr.1958

Nunkoo, R., & Ramkissoon, H. (2012). Power, trust, social exchange and community support. *Annals of Tourism Research*, *39*(2), 997–1023. https://doi.org/10.1016/j.annals.2011.11.017

Pearce, P. L. (1982). Tourists and their hosts: Some social and psychological effects of inter-cultural contact. In S. Bochner (Ed.), *Cultures in contact: Studies in cross-cultural interaction* (p. 199). Pergamon Press Ltd.

Pearce, P. L. (2005). *Tourist behaviour: Themes and conceptual schemes*. Channel View Publications.

Pizam, A., Uriely, N., & Reichel, A. (2000). The intensity of tourist–host social relationship and its effects on satisfaction and change of attitudes: The case of working tourists in Israel. *Tourism Management*, *21*(4), 395–406. https://doi.org/10.1016/S0261-5177(99)00085-0

Plé, L., & CáCeres, C. R. (2010). Not always co-creation: Introducing interactional co-destruction of value in service-dominant logic. *Journal of Services Marketing*, *24*(6), 430–437.

Plog, S. C. (1974). Why destination areas rise and fall in popularity. *Cornell Hotel and Restaurant Administration Quarterly*, *14*(4), 55–58. https://doi.org/10.1177/001088047401400409

Prahalad, C. K., & Ramaswamy, V. (2004). Co-creation experiences: The next practice in value creation. *Journal of Interactive Marketing*, *18*(3), 5–14. https://doi.org/10.1002/dir.20015

Rihova, I., Buhalis, D., Gouthro, M. B., & Moital, M. (2018). Customer-to-customer co-creation practices in tourism: Lessons from customer-dominant logic. *Tourism Management*, *67*, 362–375. https://doi.org/10.1016/j.tourman.2018.02.010

Rihova, I., Buhalis, D., Moital, M., & Gouthro, M. B. (2015). Conceptualising customer-to-customer value co-creation in tourism. *International Journal of Tourism Research*, *17*(4), 356–363. https://doi.org/10.1002/jtr.1993

Rothman, R. A. (1978). Residents and transients: community reaction to seasonal visitors. *Journal of Travel Research*, *16*(3), 8–13. https://doi.org/10.1177/004728757801600303

Saguy, T., Tausch, N., Dovidio, J. F., & Pratto, F. (2009). The irony of harmony: Intergroup contact can produce false expectations for equality. *Psychological Science*, *20*(1), 114–121. https://doi.org/10.1111/j.1467-9280.2008.02261.x

Seraphin, H., Sheeran, P., & Pilato, M. (2018). Over-tourism and the fall of Venice as a destination. *Journal of Destination Marketing & Management*, *9*, 374–376.

Sharpley, R. (2014). Host perceptions of tourism: A review of the research. *Tourism Management*, *42*, 37–49. https://doi.org/10.1016/j.tourman.2013.10.007

Shen, H., Luo, J., & Zhao, A. (2017). The sustainable tourism development in Hong Kong: An analysis of Hong Kong residents' attitude towards mainland Chinese tourist. *Journal of Quality Assurance in Hospitality & Tourism*, *18*(1), 45–68.

Smith, A. M. (2013). The value co-destruction process: a customer resource perspective. *European Journal of Marketing, 47*(11/12), 1889–1909.
Sthapit, E., & Björk, P. (2020). Towards a better understanding of interactive value formation: Three value outcomes perspective. *Current Issues in Tourism, 23*(6), 693–706. https://doi.org/10.1080/13683500.2018.1520821
Sutton, W. A. (1967). Travel and understanding: Notes on the social structure of touring. *International Journal of Comparative Sociology, 8*(2), 218–223. https://doi.org/10.1177/002071526700800206
Telegraph UK. (2019). Indian slum tour becomes country's most popular tourist attraction. https://www.telegraph.co.uk/news/2019/06/23/indian-slum-tour-becomes-countrys-popular-tourist-attraction/#:~:text=A%20tour%20of%20one%20of,site%20TripAdvisor's%20Travellers'%20Choice%20Awards.
Thibaut, J. W., & Kelley, H. (1959). *The social psychology of groups.* John Wiley & Sons, Inc.
Tomljenovic, R. (2010). Tourism and intercultural understanding or contact hypothesis revisited. In *Tourism, Progress and Peace* (pp. 17–34). CABI.
Tsaur, S. H., Yen, C. H., & Teng, H. Y. (2018). Tourist–resident conflict: A scale development and empirical study. *Journal of Destination Marketing & Management, 10*, 152–163.
Tung, V. W. S. (2020). Reducing tourist stereotyping: Effectiveness of communication messages. *Journal of Travel Research*, https://doi.org/10.1177/0047287519900002.
Maruyama, N. U., Woosnam, K. M., & Boley, B. B. (2017). Residents' attitudes toward ethnic neighborhood tourism (ENT): Perspectives of ethnicity and empowerment. *Tourism Geographies, 19*(2), 265–286.
Vargo, S. L., & Lusch, R. F. (2004). Evolving to a new dominant logic for marketing. *Journal of Marketing, 68*(1), 1–17. https://doi.org/10.1509/jmkg.68.1.1.24036
Vargo, S. L., Koskela-Huotari, K., & Vink, J. (2020). Service-dominant logic: Foundations and applications. In Bridges, E. and Fowler, K. (Eds.) The Routledge Handbook of Service Research Insights and Ideas, (p. 3–23). New York: Routledge.
Wang, N. (1999). Rethinking authenticity in tourism experience. *Annals of Tourism Research, 26*(2), 349–370. pp https://doi.org/10.1016/S0160-7383(98)00103-0
Ward, C., & Berno, T. (2011). Beyond social exchange theory: Attitudes toward tourists. *Annals of Tourism Research, 38*(4), 1556–1569. https://doi.org/10.1016/j.annals.2011.02.005
Warde, A. (2005). Consumption and theories of practice. *Journal of Consumer Culture, 5*(2), 131–153. https://doi.org/10.1177/1469540505053090
Wei, L., Crompton, J. L., & Reid, L. M. (1989). Cultural conflicts: Experiences of US visitors to China. *Tourism Management, 10*(4), 322–332. https://doi.org/10.1016/0261-5177(89)90011-3
Wey, T. W., Jordán, F., & Blumstein, D. T. (2019). Transitivity and structural balance in marmot social networks. *Behavioral Ecology and Sociobiology, 73*(6), 88. https://doi.org/10.1007/s00265-019-2699-3
Woosnam, K. M., & Aleshinloye, K. D. (2013). Can tourists experience emotional solidarity with residents? Testing Durkheim's model from a new perspective. *Journal of Travel Research, 52*(4), 494–505. https://doi.org/10.1177/0047287512467701
Woosnam, K. M., & Lee, Y. J. (2011). Applying social distance to voluntourism research. *Annals of Tourism Research, 38*(1), 309–313. https://doi.org/10.1016/j.annals.2010.06.003
Wu, C. H. J. (2007). The impact of customer-to-customer interaction and customer homogeneity on customer satisfaction in tourism service—The service encounter prospective. *Tourism Management, 28*(6), 1518–1528. https://doi.org/10.1016/j.tourman.2007.02.002
Ye, B. H., Zhang, H. Q., & Yuen, P. P. (2013). Cultural conflicts or cultural cushion? *Annals of Tourism Research, 43*, 321–349. https://doi.org/10.1016/j.annals.2013.07.003
Yilmaz, S. S., & Tasci, A. D. (2015). Circumstantial impact of contact on social distance. *Journal of Tourism and Cultural Change, 13*(2), 115–131. https://doi.org/10.1080/14766825.2014.896921
Yin, J., Qian, L., & Shen, J. (2019). From value co-creation to value co-destruction? The case of dockless bike sharing in China. *Transportation Research Part D: Transport and Environment, 71*, 169–185. https://doi.org/10.1016/j.trd.2018.12.004
Yu, C. P., Chancellor, H. C., & Cole, S. T. (2011). Measuring residents' attitudes toward sustainable tourism: A reexamination of the sustainable tourism attitude scale. *Journal of Travel Research, 50*(1), 57–63.
Yu, J., & Lee, T. J. (2014). Impact of tourists' intercultural interactions. *Journal of Travel Research, 53*(2), 225–238. https://doi.org/10.1177/0047287513496467
Zeithaml, V. A. (1988). Consumer perceptions of price, quality, and value: A means-end model and synthesis of evidence. *Journal of Marketing, 52*(3), 2–22. https://doi.org/10.1177/002224298805200302
Zhang, H., Fan, D. X., Tse, T. S., & King, B. (2017). Creating a scale for assessing socially sustainable tourism. *Journal of Sustainable Tourism, 25*(1), 61–78.
Zhang, J. J., Wong, P. P. Y., & Lai, P. C. (2018). A geographic analysis of hosts' irritation levels towards mainland Chinese cross-border day-trippers. *Tourism Management, 68*, 367–374. https://doi.org/10.1016/j.tourman.2018.03.011
Zimmermann, F. M. (1997). Future perspectives of tourism-traditional versus new destinations. In Oppermann, M. (Ed.), Pacific Rim Tourism. Wallingford: CAB International, pp. 231–239.

It's time to act! Understanding online resistance against tourism development projects

Philipp K. Wegerer and Monica Nadegger

ABSTRACT
Resistance against tourism development has become a key analytical domain among tourism researchers. Yet, little attention has been paid to understanding online resistance against tourism development as a discursive phenomenon. This inquiry provides a discourse analytical study regarding an online petition against a large-scale infrastructure project in the Austrian Alps. Employing an analytical framework of discursive objects, subjects, and concepts, the study investigates the justification strategies of activists, posted on the online petition platform. The study finds that activists' rationales are embedded within an overarching degrowth discourse. The conflict exists between the opposing subjectivities of activists and project initiators with nature as their primary discursive object. Activist rationales were found to criticize the growth imperative of capitalism in broad strokes, rather than directly addressing the project and its proponents.

Introduction

Scholars within the field of sustainable tourism research have observed an increasingly critical response from citizens concerning the negative impacts of tourism development projects (Fletcher et al., 2019). The significance, origin, and consequence of this critique has been theorized in terms of a visitor- resident dichotomy, directing analytical attention towards over-tourism, resident attitudes (Valdivielso & Moranta, 2019), locals as victims (Seraphin et al., 2020), the role of social movements (Milano et al., 2019), tourist discrimination (Tse & Tung, 2020), and the influence of the sharing economy on local citizens (Hassanli et al., 2019). Despite the apparent theoretical and empirical diversity of these accounts, many contributors have remarked on the lack of studies that treat tourism development and policymaking as a discursive phenomenon, shedding light on its unquestioned systemic and ideological characteristics (Fazito et al., 2016; Fletcher et al., 2019; Kallis & March, 2015; Valdivielso & Moranta, 2019).

Fletcher et al., (2019) critical review of research on sustainable tourism has noted that the discussion "has thus far neglected to seriously engage with the discourse of degrowth" (p. 1746). They point out that tourism development is situated within a wider capitalist ideology, as "something systemic and structural that has yet to be highlighted by existing over-tourism literature" (p. 1748). In a similar vein, Fazito et al. (2016) argue that, "what this literature lacks is a more discursive treatment of tourism development and policymaking," and that, "there is a dearth of critical literature linking discourse and representation to tourism development and policy making" (p. 2). With this study, we take up this call, and study tourism resistance as a discursive phenomenon. The empirical study investigates a grassroots online petition directed towards the planned connection of two glacier ski resorts in the Austrian Alps, by means of critical discourse analysis (Alvesson & Karreman, 2000; Fairclough & Wodak, 1997). We draw on an analytical discourse framework whose interest is uniquely focused on understanding how statements comprise distinct discursive subjects, objects, and concepts (Caruana & Crane, 2008), and how these discursive elements relate to each other. This allows us to understand how justification strategies of signers of the online petition are situated within an overarching degrowth discourse.

This paper offers a methodological and a conceptual contribution to degrowth research. By combining elements of netnography and discourse analysis it develops a methodological approach for the study of tourism resistance in online environments. The conceptual contribution extends our understanding of tourism resistance as a discursive phenomenon and offers insights into how the underlying degrowth discourse configures specific objects and subjects and how they relate to each other.

Theoretical background

In this section we discuss how tourism research and practices have been shaped by an endless growth paradigm, and how this growth paradigm is increasingly challenged by degrowth advocates in academia as well as by resistance movements. Finally, we suggest that it is more useful to understand tourism resistance in online environments as a struggle between a diverse group of actors, rather than a conflict rooted in a visitor- resident dichotomy.

Emergence of the degrowth paradigm

Constant economic growth, measured in terms of growing visitor numbers and increasing profits, has been the dominant paradigm in tourism research and practice (Fletcher et al., 2019; Panzer-Krause, 2019; World Tourism Organization [UNWTO], 2018). The key premise of the growth paradigm is that well-being and the notion of a good life is maintained through the prosperity of markets (Kallis et al., 2018; Velicu, 2019), and that this prosperity is as a key strategy for reducing poverty (Higgins-Desbiolles et al., 2019). Tourism growth is measured in indicators, such as the GDP, which are supposed to serve as an objective representation of wealth and positive development (Fletcher et al., 2019). The endless growth paradigm sustains a system of capital accumulation in which value and monetary wealth are created through the exploitation of human and natural resources (Euler, 2019). Despite the short-term economic benefits, environmental quality degrades with the economic growth fostered by tourism (Danish & Wang, 2018), and the negative effects linked to tourism growth outbalance initiatives for preservation, sustainability, and well-being (Raymond & Brown, 2007). Although sustainable tourism development lends itself to a long-term-oriented utilization of finite resources, the notion of sustainability gets criticized as being too weak (Blázquez-Salom et al., 2019; Panzer-Krause, 2019), as it merely replaces "bad" with "good" development (Latouche, 2010). Instead, a growing number of tourism scholars (Higgins-Desbiolles et al., 2019; Milano et al., 2019; Velicu, 2019) argue for degrowth as an alternative paradigm for sustainable tourism futures.

Derived from the French "décroissance" (Georgescu-Roegen, 1995; Latouche, 2003), the term degrowth has diverse roots (Sekulova et al., 2013): from the field of socio-political ecology (Kallis & March, 2015; Latouche, 2009) and theories of entropy and bioeconomics (Georgescu-Roegen, 1975), to the criticism of the technocratic development of society (Illich, 1974). As some of the earliest scholars to posit degrowth ideas, Meadows et al. (1972) discussed the inherent problem of the endless growth paradigm in capitalist societies and suggested possible paths to avoid a global crisis in their "Limits to Growth" reports. Building on their ideas, degrowth encompasses a different conceptualization of decrease, decline, or, more broadly, societal, political, and economic change. By referring to the law of entropy, Georgescu-Roegen (1975) theorized that economies are obliged to the limits of natural environments. Staying with these natural limits can (but does not have to) lead to an economic decline. As Missemer (2017, p. 503) points out, he was "probably concerned neither with growth, nor with degrowth. He was concerned with qualitative change, with development." Latouche (2009) stressed that it is not just about decline or negative economic development (such as a decreasing GDP). This can also happen through means that are unsustainable (Schneider et al., 2010), e.g. in an economic recession or a global crisis like the financial crisis in 2008 (Nyblom et al., 2019) or the COVID-19 pandemic (Barlow et al., 2020). Rather, degrowth should enable a "prosperous way down" (Martínez-Alier et al., 2010, p. 1741) by focusing on well-being, ecological sustainability, and social equity (Schneider et al., 2010).

In contrast to sustainable development or a green economy, degrowth challenges the taken-for-granted need for constant development, and frames future decisions as a question of leaving or escaping the economy as a whole (Cattaneo et al., 2012; Latouche, 2010). Thus, the overarching goal should be to change the pervasive characteristics of any form of growth (Heikkurinen et al., 2019; Kallis et al., 2018) by offering new voluntary principles based on a "just, participatory, and ecologically sustainable society" (Research & Degrowth, 2010, p. 524). The degrowth goals are also in line with Jamal and Camargo (2014, 2018) and Jamal (2019) who underscore the need to include justice, diversity and equity for "good" tourism governance . A future society without growth builds on decisions based on direct democracy, self-organizational processes of consensus, and open and free access to knowledge (Cattaneo et al., 2012). Degrowth strives for a "life-in-common that is marked by abundance, rather than defined by austerity" (Singh, 2019, p. 140). This reinforcement of the commons (Euler, 2019; Schneider et al., 2010) is related to Ivan Illich's (1974) concept of conviviality. Conviviality reorients human interaction around the spirit of social relations (Latouche, 2009) by liberating it from the inverse relationship of scale and power (Cattaneo et al., 2012), manipulative technologies, and the powerful elite controlling complex systems (Samerski, 2018).

In order to achieve these goals, degrowth advocates underline the need for radical political and societal strategies towards a 'just and good' life (Cattaneo et al., 2012; Jamal & Camargo, 2014; Muraca, 2012). Grassroots movements and oppositional activists are powerful actors who can reshape the public debate and prevailing conceptions of contemporary growth societies (Blázquez-Salom et al., 2019; Milano et al., 2019) through political acts, such as demonstrations, boycotts, and civil disobedience (Demaria et al., 2013). In the following section, we draw our attention to how social movements promote the ideas of the degrowth paradigm.

Social movements as advocates of the degrowth paradigm

Protest movements questioning the effectiveness of neoliberal growth in tourism are growing in number (Kallis & March, 2015; Milano et al., 2019). For example, Fazito et al. (2016) discuss the conflict between different representations and an increasingly-fragile sustainable tourism sector in Brazil, Jamal and Camargo (2014) underscore the (in)justice created and enforced by tourism governance in Quintana Roo in Mexico, and Navarro-Jurado et al. (2019) and Valdivielso and Moranta (2019) highlight the growing number of proposals of alternative bottom-up and participatory tourism planning in mature tourist destinations like Costa del Sol-Málaga and the Balearic Islands.

Although often not explicitly referring to the degrowth paradigm, activists tend to espouse its general idea (Gascón, 2019): the demand for the radical social, hierarchical, and organizational change of the predominant capitalist system (Navarro-Jurado et al., 2019). Often, these forms of protest are characterized by bottom-up hierarchies (Navarro-Jurado et al., 2019; Valdivielso & Moranta, 2019), their call for justice and equity (Jamal & Camargo, 2014, 2018), little formal organizational structure or institutional boundaries, and by communication and interaction via open platforms (D'Alisa et al., 2013). Several points of tension and power asymmetries characterize the relationship between social movements and dominant tourism agents. Struggles resonate around the production, creation, domination, and use of space. Tourism agents, as "growth machines" (Navarro-Jurado et al., 2019, p. 1800), tend to concentrate the political, economic, and media power in their hands, while resistance movements work with fewer resources and are sustained by collaborative and voluntary work.

It has been argued that in order to liberate the public sphere from predominant neoliberal ideas, an open public discourse is needed to give voice to all stakeholders in an equal way (D'Alisa et al., 2013; Kallis et al., 2018; Kallis & March, 2015; Milano et al., 2019). Therefore, it is necessary to shift power from dominant tourism agents to all citizens (Blázquez-Salom et al., 2019; Higgins-Desbiolles et al., 2019), in order to "reshape boundaries between spheres such as the market, reproduction, nature, and politics" (Valdivielso & Moranta, 2019, p. 1885). Liberating the public discourse from predominant neoliberal ideas, Milano et al. (2019), D'Alisa et al. (2013), Kallis and March (2015) and Kallis et al. (2018) see the power of tourism resistance and the future of the degrowth discourse in fostering the implementation of social and ecological justice, a new way of articulating and thinking about what is a considered to be a good life, and the redistribution of wealth and power. What is important for this study is that the conflict lines tend to be situated between local activists, on the one side, and tourists and their advocates on the other.

From visitor-resident dichotomy to a plenum of tourism actors

Following the established dichotomy between residents and visitors in tourism, tourism resistance is mainly studied as a local phenomenon, with the line of conflict located between local residents and visitors, or mega tourism projects on the other side (Navarro-Jurado et al., 2019). Examples would be the juxtaposition of citizen rights versus the right to travel (Gascón, 2019), the sentimental or financial bond between hosts and guests (Ribeiro et al., 2017), studies on tourism-phobic attitudes of residents (Cheung & Li, 2019; Fletcher et al., 2019), or the reframing of tourism as something defined by the rights of the local community (Higgins-Desbiolles et al., 2019).

While these studies provided useful insights for understanding local resistance, we argue that this dualism might not capture the peculiarities of tourism resistance in a globalized world or in online environments. Fletcher et al. (2019, p. 1889) observed that tourism resistance is increasingly evolving into a multi-dimensional and multinational phenomenon: protests shift from a local-oriented notion of "not in my backyard" to a more open approach of "not in anyone's backyard." This globalized perspective on tourism issues can also contribute to visitor-based resistance to travel (Yu et al., 2020). The reasons for such tourism boycotts are manifold. Tourists participate in boycotts to punish unsustainable tourism practices, such as whale watching and hunting (Parsons & Rawles, 2003) and the suppression of bottom-up democratic processes (Luo & Zhai, 2017).

While the above studies address a variety of approaches to, reasons for, and actors involved in resistance, they represent an epistemological tradition that is rooted in an ontology of hosts and guests, visitors and residents, or tourists and locals. Stepping back from a pre-defined categorization of resistance actors, we argue for a broader conceptualization of resistance actors. Locals and tourist identities and practices merge in the digital, as both are participants of the same online public, have the same rights, capabilities, and interests, can read and share content, and interact with each other through posts, shares, and likes (Arsal et al., 2010). Thus, both are actors that are capable of shaping and contributing to online resistance and protests, such as online petitions.

The following empirical analysis studies an online-mediated tourism development conflict that transcends the visitor-resident dichotomy. Applying a discourse analytical perspective, we are particularly interested in understanding how the conflict is configured by a distinct configuration of subjects, objects, and concepts, along with their relation to one another.

Research context

This study is interested in understanding the increasing public opposition to redevelopment projects in Austrian ski resorts. In Austria, the redevelopment of ski resorts is highly restricted by federal law (LGBl. Nr. 145/2018, 14th 2019). Within this tight legal framework, the merging of existing ski resorts has become a common growth strategy for many ski resorts. While the obvious options for mergers are exploited, intended projects try to push the boundaries between merging and expansion. Given this backdrop, merging projects have become highly political in nature and are coming under ever-increasing scrutiny from the public.

In 2016, the two glacier ski resorts Ötztal glacier and Pitztal glacier presented an infrastructure project with the intention of merging their resorts. The project had an investment volume of 131.6 million euros (Pitztaler Gletscherbahn & Ötztaler Gletscherbahn, 2019). The merging of the two glacier resorts comprised the redevelopment of three previously untouched glaciers, the construction of three new cable cars, the creation of 6,4 km^2 of new slopes, the removal of over 750,000 m^3 of rock, earth, and ice, as well as the leveling, backfilling, and removal of 720,000 m^2 of glacial surface (Alpenverein Österreich, 2019). Despite the support of the local conservative government and an extensive PR campaign that stressed the economic benefits for the region, the project faced extensive public criticism for its entry into a fragile high alpine ecosystem. The large scope of the project, and previously-unauthorized construction activities (Tiroler Umweltanwaltschaft, 2018), created intensive backlash in the media, and was reported in national and international newspapers (Focus Online, 2019; Mijnissen, 2020).

Locally, a grassroots citizen initiative (www.feldring.at) started an online petition against the project "Nein zur Gletscherverbauung Pitztal-Ötztal" (Estermann, 2019). Austrian NGOs, such as the World Wildlife Fund (WWF) Austria, the Austrian Alpine Association, and Friends of Nature Austria, supported the petition (Alpenverein Österreich, 2019). Within weeks, the petition reached more than 160,000 signatures. This petition marked a new milestone for civil resistance against tourism development projects in the Austrian Alps. Comparatively, an earlier petition by the same initiators that garnered 17,800 signatures in total, was considered to be highly successful, and contributed significantly to the detention of another infrastructure project. The number of signees (approx. 160,000) significantly outweighed the number of inhabitants in the local communities (Pitztal valley: 7,570 inhabitants; Ötztal valley: 21,536 inhabitants). When considered with international media coverage, this outcome indicates that the public resistance against this tourism infrastructure project transcended the local context. We therefore consider this case to be not just another online representation of a local conflict between residents and visitors, but also as an example of online resistance, that transcends regional boundaries.

In the following analysis, we are particularly interested in understanding how the motivation and justification strategies of this online petition's signees are situated within a wider degrowth discourse.

Methodology

This study combines elements of netnography (Kozinets, 2015) with critical discourse analysis (Caruana & Crane, 2008; Fairclough & Wodak, 1997). The primary research aim is concerned with understanding why participants signed the online petition "Nein zu Gletscherverbauung Pitztal-Ötztal!" (Estermann, 2019).

The data collection process followed methodological principles of netnography (Kozinets, 2015). Netnography is a methodology developed to meet the communicative modalities of social media. Rather than relying on interview data, it suggests to study human behavior enfolding on site. The close relation between the empirical material and the research interest, and the richness and representativeness of the sample served as quality criteria. We selected the comments section of the online petition as a primary data set. The comments are publicly available on the platform "Aufstehn.at." For data analysis, we downloaded the comments and imported them as a text file into software MAXQDA. In total, we collected a sample of 492 posts. This dataset represented a complete inventory count, at the point in time when the petition reached 150,000 participants. The low ratio of petition signees to comments posted is typical for an affect-driven online public sphere (Arvidsson & Caliandro, 2016). In netnography, it is important to understand how social media platforms structure interaction. The petition platform frames the interaction in the following way: After signing the petition by entering the names and confirming their signatures via email, participants were given the possibility to post a short comment in which they state their rationale for signing the petition. Participants were encouraged to finish the phrase "I signed the petition, because . . . ." Posts were typically one to three sentences long. Secondary data encompassed the monitoring and collection of online media coverage, as well as an expert interview with the petition initiator. Secondary data played a key role in identifying nature as the primary discursive object, and in understanding the role of visuals in the discursive construction of nature as the primary object of concern.

In order to understand the (re)negotiation of degrowth in the discursive practices, we approach our empirical analysis from a discourse-analytical perspective (Alvesson & Karreman, 2000; Caruana & Crane, 2008; Fairclough & Wodak, 1997; Fazito et al., 2016). We treat discourse in line with Watson (1994), who denoted discourse as "a connected set of statements, concepts, terms, and expressions, which constitutes a way of taking and writing about a particular issue, thus framing the way people understand and act with respect to that issue" (Alvesson & Karreman, 2000, p. 1131). Our analytical framework is particularly interested in understanding the dialect processes that configure particular subjects and objects, and defines how they relate to each other. With this approach, we unravel the storylines, actors, and activities unfolding in the discourse-coalition of the tourism development project in the Alps (Fazito et al., 2016).

Data analysis encompassed an iterative process of inductive categorization and abstraction (Kreiner et al., 2006; Spiggle, 1994) in order to derive major themes related to the petition. In a second step, we approached the data using a discourse analysis framework in order to identify subjects, objects and concepts, and how they relate to each other (Caruana & Crane, 2008). The two authors coded independently and reached a final consensus along with researcher triangulation in extensive rounds of discussion (Arnold & Fischer, 1994). Based on a Foucauldian understanding of discourse as consisting of subjects, objects, and concepts (Foucault, 1972), we follow the view of Oswick et al. (2000) and Caruana and Crane (2008) to understand this discursive subject, objects, and concepts as things that are entangled and interrelated, thus making them mutually constitutive for the current discursive construction of the degrowth discourse. Our analytical focus lies on the construction of objects and subjects and how human objects are transformed into different subjects, i.e. different groups of persons, as well as what they are like and how they ought to be. We also examine the distinction between *discourse* as social text and *Discourse* as a large-scale reasoning mechanism in the grand scheme of human praxis. Alvesson and Karreman (2000) allow us to differentiate between the local-situational context, the myopic dimension, and long-term interest, a more all-encompassing perspective.

Findings

This study finds that the comments posted in the online petition platform presented arguments that are based on ideals, values, and objectives of degrowth. Activists were found to locate the problem within the current growth imperative of ski tourism in the Austrian Alps. Activists urged the need for developing alternative and more sustainable forms of winter tourism to preserve natural resources for the well-being of all stakeholders, including future generations. In the following section, we present a detailed analysis of how individual accounts are situated within an overarching degrowth discourse, representing a specific configuration of subjects, objects and concepts.

Discursive subjectivities: initiators versus activists
The first part of the analysis is concerned with illustrating how the comments define two central discursive subjects: *the initiators* and *the activists*. The project initiators are seen as a non-humanistic group of elites that is emblematic of a powerful force of destruction. In the statements, there appeared no personal names, no explicit positions, such as "CEO," no company names, and no destination management organizations (DMO). Rather, the comments refer to the initiators as "the people," "the people in power," "the glacier ski-resort," "the elite," "money greedy humans," or "some money-hungry men." The responses also produced a number of labels with negative connotations, such as "village emperor," "vulture capitalists" and "greedy vultures." A significant proportion saw the subjectivity of the initiators situated on an even more abstract level as evidenced by responses including words such as: "the few," "the "project," "the monster project," "pure greed of a few insane," "money from ski tourism," "the intervention" and "mass-tourism." The subjectivity of those initiating the projects was described as "megalomania," "money grumbling," "insatiable mentality" and the "evil project."

This indicates that no direct persons are seen as responsible for the project. Agency lies within a specific elite that is unknown, inaccessible, faceless, and that has no identifiable personal name. The character of the initiators is seen as insane and greedy. They are short-term oriented and follow the primary aim of profit-maximization (see Figure 1). The decision-making process is subject to a technocratic governance, power is situated within dominant institutions, such as "tourism," "ski tourism" and "the money of ski tourism," rather than clearly-identifiable actors.

The initiators, the project, and the entire ski tourism sector seem to be driven by two primary motivations: greed and insanity. Terms used to allude to greed were "greed," "greedy," "moneygrubbing," "greed for profit," "pure greed" and "greedy entrepreneurs." These terms should not be misunderstood as character traits of specific individuals or groups, but as expressions of the growth fetishism of contemporary alpine ski tourism: "This greed for profit makes me sick!! Where is the respect for our beautiful nature!" (Gisela K. C.1140), or, "unfortunately, the greed for more and more, bigger and bigger, and more and more profit is spreading here" (Peter, R.). Greed and insanity are a significant pattern in the data and played a key role in framing the entire project. Greed involved the construction of the initiators as being primarily concerned with the unlimited accumulation of wealth through unlimited growth:

> Because the madness never ends. Just because some people just can't get their necks full, to sacrifice our nature again and again and again is just unbelievable! This madness simply has to be stopped, where else can it lead? Such projects also find imitators very quickly, and then??? (Angelica P. 1135)

Comments identified megalomania and greed as the primary causes not only of this project, but of ski tourism in broad strokes: "The megalomania of size and development in nature must come to an end. With greed and money, we are destroying our habitat irretrievably" (Herbert R.).

The focus on greed as a primary motivating factor is partially related to the rationale for the project provided by the initiators in public debate, e.g. in newspapers (Focus Online, 2019; Mijnissen, 2020) and other stakeholder outlets (Alpenverein Österreich, 2020). Here, the project is primarily justified by emphasizing the expected economic benefits for the region and the very short-term-oriented profits resulting from the construction period. Common arguments are that

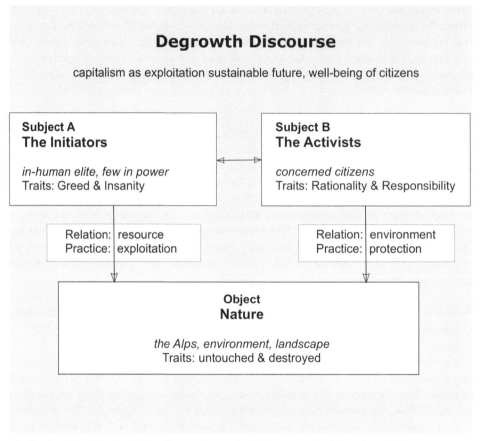

Figure 1. The discursive subjects, objects and concepts emerging in the comments of the online petition.

the local community benefits from tourism in and of itself or from employment opportunities generated from tourism, as well as from the public and private investment in tourism and tourism-related infrastructure. This is exemplified in statements that credit tourism for "every third Euro of GDP" in the region of Tyrol (Wirtschaftskammer Tirol, 2015).

In contrast to the positive self-image that the tourism industry attributes to itself, the findings reveal that an increasing number of people question the public welfare imperative of Tyrolian tourism, characterized as: "Pure greed of a few lunatics" (Karlheinz, E.). The tourism industry is seen as exploiting public resources to privatize public goods, such as glaciers and the larger alpine landscape that encompasses it: "It hurts my heart how blind the greed for profit makes [people]" (Hans-Peter K.). In the comments, the tourism industry was portrayed as a small economic elite whose primary goal was the accumulation of wealth for its own gain against the will and of the greater public: "We don't need destroyers of nature, we don't need destroyers of landscape! The greed of the tourism lobby must be stopped in favor of nature! (Astrid K.).

A significant proportion of the comments directly took up key points of degrowth, such as limiting endless growth: "We cannot leave nature to the private economic interests of the tourism industry. We have to set a limit to the greed for even more profit" (Karl, W.), or "it must finally end with more, more and bigger, bigger" (Georg, R.). The strategy of the initiators appeared to backfire. The initiators framed the project in rational economic terms and pointed out that the entire region benefits from the project economically. In contrast, the activists framed the project as an act of destruction (also for future generations): "if we continue to open up, break up, destroy more and more, how do we explain this to our children? Less is more!" (Eva-

Maria, H.) or, "In my opinion it is a megalomaniacal project of some money-hungry village emperors" (Ralf, B).

The second trait or key driver was deemed to be *insanity*. Insanity appeared in various versions, ranging from "insanity" to "megalomania," to more polemic notions such as "dementia," "ludicrous," "imbecility," "manic," "idiocy" and "bullshit." An example would be Claudia P., who said: "because it is simply madness what is being planned here … a crime against nature," or Roswith P., who added: "this proliferation of ski slopes is simply madness."

At this point, it is important to note, that the statements all appeared in an objective, serious, and respectable tone, wherein the speakers sought to make a strong, thought-through argument. Stefan, H. provides an example of this, saying: "I signed because protection of nature and landscape is a key factor of any long-term-oriented tourism policy." Polemic, offensive or insulting comments, commonly found in online platforms, were in the minority. This can perhaps be explained by the fact that activists constructed their subjectivity, in opposition to the initiators, around being the rational agents. The petition signees see themselves as the rational, altruistic, and selfless subjects. Their role is to be responsible in opposition to the perceived insanity of the initiators. Their primary aim is to be responsible and to draw a line to prevent the further destruction of nature.

Nature as the primary discursive object

The comments on the online petition identify *nature* as the primary object of concern. Nature appears as the rather abstract term "nature," as well as in a number of concrete manifestations such as "landscape," "glacier," "mountains," "mountain-landscape," "the Alps," "the Austrian Alps" and "environment." Often comments did not refer to the Pitztaler glacier or peaks directly, but made use of abstract terms, such as "mountain landscape," or simply, "landscape": "We are responsible for nature, it sustains our life, and without nature we cannot exist (…) it is time to help nature" (Lisa-Maria E.). This is perhaps rooted in the fact that many signatories of the petition did not live in the ski resorts or nearby villages and lacked detailed knowledge of the region. It can also be interpreted as an indication that the petition served as a vehicle to express a broader criticism of the environmental and social impact of ski tourism policy in the Tyrolian Alps.

The statements characterized nature as both *untouched* and *destroyed*. Nature, irrespective of its landscape, was seen by respondents as an entity that must be preserved: "intact nature in its untouched beauty is priceless and benefits everyone" (Renate, S.). The mountains and glaciers are seen as "the last paradises of untouched mountain nature" (Karin, R.). This conception of nature as an entity that is meant to remain pure of human influences presented a stark contrast to the resource-centric conception that the project initiators held in regards to nature. It can be gathered that in their view, nature is the property of the local tourism industry, a resource that can be exploited for the economic benefit of the local population. This underscored by a lobbyist's comment, published in a leading regional newspaper:

> … it is a bolt investment into a cultivated alpine landscape (…) and the co-existence of landscapes with different technological furniture would increase the sustainable attractiveness of the two alpine valleys: I am always exited from the ideology- free perspective onto bolt-placed cable cars and their stations (Tiroler Tageszeitung, 23.11.)

The strategic use of visuals played a key role in the construction of nature as the primary object in the discursive formation, with both actors using specific visuals in their communication on social media, as well as in various forms of media coverage of the debate. Figure 2 compares the graphics of the petition initiators with the project group's pictures. The visual on the left is a project visualization used and distributed by the initiators of the petition. It used bright red and yellow lines to illustrate how the slopes and planned cable cars would disrupt the alpine landscape. The picture on the right is a visualization distributed by the project group. The picture

> Original figure can be viewed in the journal article. Copyright permission could not be obtained for this figure.

was taken from a distance. The mountains appeared abstract, like a moon-like landscape. The new infrastructure was visualized in the same colors as the landscape. The slopes appeared as narrow white stripes against the backdrop of a white landscape. The cable cars were visualized with narrow, hardly-visible lines. Lift stations and other planned infrastructure were missing in this visualization.

In sum, nature was constructed as the primary object of concern, manifested as a landscape, glaciers, and mountains. While the petition signees saw it as a public good, the project initiators framed it as a resource to be exploited. We now move on to discuss how the discourse defines how two opposing subjects are relating to nature.

Relating objects, subjects, and defining actions

This section discusses how the two subjects – the activists and the project initiators - relate to the primary object nature. Here the juxtaposition between responsible activists and greedy and insane project initiators was manifested into appropriate and inappropriate relations and actions. The following quote exemplifies how the activists define an appropriate relationship to nature:

> The nature of Austria, with its mountains, glaciers and everything else must be protected to be shown to the next generations in its present splendor and beauty, so that you, too, can still experience what nature has to offer in beauty without man destroying it. (Gerhard B.)

In this statement, nature is perceived holistically, comprising a unique combination of various elements. The appropriate relationship to nature is characterized as being "preserving" and "protecting." The singular arrangement of components represents a beauty that is destroyed by any intervention from outside. The overall premise is to preserve its untouched beauty for generations to come.

The visual communication of the conflicting parties played an important role in constructing the project as an inappropriate intervention into nature. Figure 3 presents two visuals that appeared regularly on social media and in news coverage. The left picture shows the so-called *Linker Fernerkogel*. The project incorporated a plan to blast the mountain peak shaded in red in order to build a cable car station on it. This plan, and its visualization became a key target of the petition initiators and played an important role in framing the project as "insane" and as a "destruction" of an untouched peak: "Our environment needs protection" (Gabriel), "Nature conservation concerns us all" (Elfi T.); "Please protect the environment from human interference!" (Bettina O); "No more interference with nature! We must protect our habitat" (Martina K.). The picture on the right show two Caterpillars plows preparing a glacier surface for alpine skiing,

Figure 3. Visuals used by activists as promotional material. Both images: © WWF/Vincent Sufiyan.

illustrating how a mechanical actor might and deteriorate the pristine quality of the glacial surface.

Activists presented generalized ideas for an alternative path toward alpine tourism: not only in terms of dealing with scarce natural resources, but also regarding *future generations*. *Future generations* appeared alongside the terms "future," "future generations," "our children" and "our grandchildren." Quotes illustrating this include: "Let us preserve nature in its incomparable beauty for future generations," and, "I would like to leave my children an intact mountain world" (Gabriele, G.); as well as, "for the sake of our children and grandchildren" (Roland, T.). For example:

> It is a shame to see how nature and the mountains are raped and destroyed. Think of your children, grandchildren and great grandchildren, all for the sake of profit. Always only money, money, what is once destroyed is destroyed (Schwaighofer, F.)

We continue to discuss the links between the discourse surrounding the petition and degrowth ideas and concepts. The petition offers the signees the opportunity to express their general concern with environmental destruction, climate change, and the endless growth paradigm. Signing the petition, sharing the petition on social media, and leaving a comment, transforms concerned citizens – be they locals, tourists, or environmentalists – into online activists. What unites them is their concern for nature: "I was up on the glacier last summer. I could literally hear nature screaming in pain! That's enough!" (Berthold U.). The primary aim of the petition signees was to draw a line and stop the unnecessary destruction of nature, because:

> Such a project, with such a serious intervention into nature, cannot be considered good in any way. Under no circumstances should the development and the associated irreversible destruction of the last remaining mountain areas, which are still reasonably intact, be allowed (Markus, P.)

The overall rationale expressed in the comments is that enough is enough. This rationale of drawing a line and stopping the project and its exploitation of alpine landscapes for ski tourism is a central theme in the data. Quotes that indicate this call for a stop are "too much has already been destroyed" (Theodor, M.).

Overall, the petition and the project serve as a blueprint for expressing a deeper concern with a general lack of regulation as it relates to tourism development in the Alps. Activist rationales stand in stark contrast to the capitalist growth paradigm advocated by the project developers. The comments reclaimed the alpine landscape as a common, rather than as a resource at the disposal of local economic elites.

Discussion

The current study provides a discourse analytical inquiry into an online petition against a tourism development project in the Austrian Alps. This study mobilizes degrowth as an interpretative framework for understanding this online petition as part of a larger movement that is mediated by degrowth ideas. The study finds that the signatories of the petition do not see themselves as part of a degrowth movement –the term not present in the data- but their rationales, arguments and ideas are tightly aligned with ideas, values, and objective degrowth. We now set out to discuss the links in more detail.

Referring back to Latouche (2009), the key question of degrowth is, whether "productivity gains are actually fostering human well-being or undermining prospects for the future" (Milano et al., 2019, p. 1861). This is echoed in to comments posted on the platform. The project itself is seen as the manifestation of a capitalist market-force (Fletcher et al., 2019; Valdivielso & Moranta, 2019). In this sense, we can observe a clear and strong link between meaning creation on a micro-level and the ways in which the discourse incorporates larger societal phenomena and debates (Alvesson & Karreman, 2000). Productivity gains are mainly seen as increasing the wealth and well-being of a small elite, at the expense of a larger public that includes future generations. The portrayal of the elite as insane, greedy, and selfish decision-making minority for people outside their circle directly correlates to the reverse relationship of scale and democracy, as discussed by Cattaneo et al. (2012) or Samerski (2018). The online petition serves as a vehicle for grassroots activists, be it locals, tourists or environmentally conscious global citizens, to participate in the discourse of alpine tourism development and reclaim their right to democratic participation.

Resonating with the call to escape from a "one-way future of material abundance" (Kallis & March, 2015, p. 362), the activists raised vague ideas for an alternative path of alpine tourism: not only in terms of dealing with scare natural resources, but especially regarding future generations. The petition signatories demanded that sustainability and public interests, including those of future generations, should be prioritized in tourism policies. In particular, the theme, future generations points to the degrowth paradigm, which argues that, "the pace and rate of change undermine the natural endowment for future generations "(Milano et al., 2019, p. 1861). The activists frame the untouched natural glacier as common good for present and future generations. This emphasis on nature as a commons (rather than as a resource) reflects the notion of a "life-in-common" (Singh, 2019) with an abundance of possibilities for all of humanity, and the guarantee of open access (Euler, 2019) to this abundance taken in tandem with the collective responsibility of protecting such commons.

This study provides a number of contributions to research on tourism resistance. Where others have pointed out how activism has shifted from 'the local to the global' (Milano et al., 2019), we found a tourism-centered form of activism, in which a globalized macro-discourse shifted attention to a local context. In our case, a variety of "uncivil actors" (D'Alisa et al., 2013), such as residents in the valley, tourists, and concerned citizens from diverse local backgrounds, raised their voices against a local project by using online platforms for bottom-up democratic participation. We find, that for the analysis of online resistance against tourism projects, the distinction between civil and uncivil actors (D'Alisa et al., 2013) allows us to grasp the diversity of actors regardless of their location, residency or their temporal classification as tourists, especially when studying tourism degrowth activism in the digital sphere. D'Alisa et al. (2013) suggest that civil society embodies different, often competing visions of the "good life" (Adityanandana & Gerber, 2019; Velicu, 2019). On one hand, there are civil actors who benefit from the current economic growth paradigm – in our case, the project developers. On the other hand, "uncivil" actors resist the dominant vision of good citizenship in a neoliberal economy and "express unwillingness to be ruled by the growth of fetishism" (D'Alisa et al., 2013, p. 214). Critical residents, visitors, and other concerned citizens formed an *uncivil* alliance that participated in an online petition. This discursive process included a broad range of activists and rooted their emotional solidarity and collective identity in their attitude towards growth rather than linking it to their geographical location or their temporal status as locals or tourists. This study clearly shows how social movements and degrowth principles are intertwined, though not in a struggle between host community and visitor-based economic growth (Milano et al., 2019; Owens, 2008). Rather, it occurs between *uncivil* actors (D'Alisa et al., 2013) demanding tourism degrowth in alpine destinations and a small economic elite trying to sustain the current growth paradigm.

It is useful to interpret our findings and their discursive relation to degrowth in terms of *discourse* and *Discourse* as suggested by Alvesson and Karreman (2000). Whereas discourse refers to accounts on the level of 'social text,' such as the petition comments, Discourse refers to "large-scale, ordered, and integrated way of reasoning and constituting the social world" (p.1125). We found that activist accounts were situated within a wider overarching degrowth Discourse. This is indicated by the fact that the project initiators were not criticized on a personal level, nor was the project itself the object of critique, rather the critic was situated on an abstract level targeting the growth imperative of the tourism industry. Our case is an example of how activist subjectivity as rational advocates is framed by ideas, orientations, and ways of individual sense-making that are taken from a larger degrowth discourse (Kallis et al., 2018) that includes a critical stance against the idea of endless growth and endorsed debates around sustainability and the reorganization of well-being and consumption. It underlines the importance of understanding the degrowth discourse on multiple levels: as constituted and emergent in the accounts of protesters of all kinds, but also as a wider, more stable and abstract phenomenon within civil society (Milano et al., 2019; Valdivielso & Moranta, 2019). In terms of Alvesson and Karreman (2000, p. 1131), the online petition should therefore not be understood as a highly-local and context-specific phenomenon, but it shows that the infrastructure project is understood within more generalized vocabulary of degrowth. Degrowth represents a 'muscular' discourse that frames durable meanings beyond specific expressions in text towards a more stable manner driving subjectivity.

Conclusion

This study finds that the online petition serves as a vehicle for expressing concerns that current ski tourism in the Austrian Alps has reached its economic, ecological, and social limits. Activist rationales were found to share common threads relating to concerns, strategies, goals, and calls to action, which are all part of degrowth. The critique points towards the destruction of untouched and scarce alpine landscape and the jeopardization of rights and possibilities for future generations. The main concern was that current ski tourism in the Austrian Alps reached its social, economic and ecological limits, due to the scarcity and vulnerability of the alpine landscape and the lack of long-term benefits for future generations. The decision-making process was seen as being driven by a technocratic elite, lacking democratic legitimization and inclusion of a broader civil society.

Critical discourse analysis turned out to be a fruitful methodological approach for analyzing the wider political and social dynamics surrounding the connection of the two glacier ski resorts in Austria. Investigating the discourse surrounding the petition platform in terms of subjects, object, and concepts helped in understanding how activists framed their subjectivity in opposition to the project initiators. Our study finds that the activist rationale is embedded within a wider degrowth discourse. Degrowth helps concerned citizens make sense of social and economic processes while also providing arguments, meaningful subjectivity, and cues for sense-making that help in developing a critical subjectivity as activists, and identifying problems to be situated on a structural level.

This study provides a number of implications for our understanding of tourism resistance. As discussed by Velicu (2019), we find that clashing representations of well-being and sustainability underpin the conflict that exists between the two discursive subjectivities. In contrast to Velicu (2019), Higgins-Desbiolles et al. (2019), or Cheung and Li (2019), we do not see this struggle for conflict as being rooted in the visitor-residents dichotomy or as a source of tension unfolding due to the geographical location or residential characteristics of actors. Rather, the conflict lines are situated between two subjectivities: *the project initiators* as the economic profiteers and a plenum of *uncivil actors,* organized as a transnational *online public*. We argue, that a broad public positions itself as an uncivil actor (D'Alisa et al., 2013) with the aim of questioning and changing the dominant growth paradigm and articulating a vision of the good life that goes beyond endless growth. In our case, it is not local activists that protest in "their own backyard," but a plenum of civil actors that criticize the overall growth agenda in "anyone's backyard" (Fletcher et al., 2019).

Our study and its particular discourse are situated in a specific geographical and historical context with the Austrian Alps. It would be particularly interesting to compare the rationales of (online) activists and project proponents of similar projects in destinations in different stages of development and geographical locations. Historical or archival research about discussions on several platforms or media could provide deeper insights into the processual understanding of macro- and micro-discourses in various historical and geo-political contexts. As this study is only a start in understanding tourism resistance beyond the visitor-resident dichotomy, we encourage further research that re-conceptualizes tourism resistance, especially in digital environments. Such concepts could help to improve our understanding of the dynamics, similarities, and differences of tourism resistance on a local and global scale.

This study clearly shows that a concerned online public increasingly questions the growth mantra as the only way for tourism development in the valleys of Austria. Activists do not ask for a gradual reform of the project, but demand the fundamental change of a winter tourism system that is obsessed with growth. They reject the current growth imperative in ski tourism in the Austrian Alps, and urge the need for developing alternative and sustainable forms of winter tourism based on the preservation of natural resources and the well-being of guests and the local community. We see such resistance not as a threat or danger to tourism in general, but as an opportunity to rethink existing paradigms and include a variety of actors in the constitution of future paths for destinations. As a practical implication, our findings propose a reassessment of the legitimacy of tourism development projects beyond residents' perspectives and towards a broader plenum of uncivil actors (D'Alisa et al., 2013) that are characterized by their concern with an issue, as opposed to their residency status or geographical location.

Acknowledgments

We are very thankful for the helpful feedback and comments provided by the editors and the three anonymous reviewers.

Disclosure statement

No potential conflict of interest was reported by the authors.

References

Adityanandana, M., & Gerber, J. F. (2019). Post-growth in the Tropics? Contestations over Tri Hita Karana and a tourism megaproject in Bali. *Journal of Sustainable Tourism*, *27*(12), 1839–1856. https://doi.org/10.1080/09669582.2019.1666857

Alpenverein Österreich. (2019). *Nein zur Gletscherverbauung Pitztal-Ötztal*. Retrieved November 7, 2020, from https://www.alpenverein.at/portal/news/aktuelle_news/2019/2019_06_24_PK_Oettztal-Pitztal.php

Alvesson, M., & Karreman, D. (2000). Varieties of discourse: On the study of organizations through discourse analysis. *Human Relations*, *53*(9), 1125–1149. https://doi.org/10.1177/0018726700539002

Arnold, S. J., & Fischer, E. (1994). Hermeneutics and consumer research. *Journal of Consumer Research*, *21*(1), 55. https://doi.org/10.1086/209382

Arsal, I., Woosnam, K. M., Baldwin, E. D., & Backman, S. J. (2010). Residents as travel destination information providers: An online community perspective. *Journal of Travel Research*, *49*(4), 400–413. https://doi.org/10.1177/0047287509346856

Arvidsson, A., & Caliandro, A. (2016). Brand public. *Journal of Consumer Research*, *42*(5), 727–748. https://doi.org/10.1093/jcr/ucv053

Barlow, N., Chertkovskaya, E., Grebenjak, M., Liegey, V., Schneider, F., Smith, T., Bliss, S., Hepp, C., Hollweg, M., Kerschner, C., Rilović, A., Smith Kanna, P., & Saey-Volckrick, J. (2020). *More than 1,000 experts call for Degrowth as post-COVID-19 path*. Konzeptwerk Neue Ökonomie. Retrieved October 20, 2020, from https://www.degrowth.info/en/2020/05/more-than-1000-experts-call-for-degrowth-as-post-covid-19-path/

Blázquez-Salom, M., Blanco-Romero, A., Vera-Rebollo, F., & Ivars-Baidal, J. (2019). Territorial tourism planning in Spain: From boosterism to tourism degrowth? *Journal of Sustainable Tourism*, *27*(12), 1764–1785. https://doi.org/10.1080/09669582.2019.1675073

Caruana, R., & Crane, A. (2008). Constructing consumer responsibility: Exploring the role of corporate communications. *Organization Studies*, *29*(12), 1495–1519. https://doi.org/10.1177/0170840607096387

Cattaneo, C., D'Alisa, G., Kallis, G., & Zografos, C. (2012). Degrowth futures and democracy. *Futures*, *44*(6), 515–523. https://doi.org/10.1016/j.futures.2012.03.012

Cheung, K. S., & Li, L. H. (2019). Understanding visitor–resident relations in overtourism: Developing resilience for sustainable tourism. *Journal of Sustainable Tourism*, *27*(8), 1197–1216. https://doi.org/10.1080/09669582.2019.1606815

D'Alisa, G., Demaria, F., & Cattaneo, C. (2013). Civil and uncivil actors for a degrowth society. *Journal of Civil Society*, *9*(2), 212–224. https://doi.org/10.1080/17448689.2013.788935

Danish & Wang, Z. (2018). Dynamic relationship between tourism, economic growth, and environmental quality. *Journal of Sustainable Tourism*, *26*(11), 1928–1943. https://doi.org/10.1080/09669582.2018.1526293

Demaria, F., Schneider, F., Sekulova, F., & Martinez-Alier, J. (2013). What is degrowth? From an activist slogan to a social movement. *Environmental Values*, *22*(2), 191–215. https://doi.org/10.3197/096327113X13581561725194

Estermann, G. (2019). *Nein zur Gletscherverbauung Pitztal-Ötztal!: An: LH Günther Platter; LH-Stv. Ingrid Felipe; LR Johannes Tratter*. Aufstehn.at - Verein zur Förderung zivilgesellschaftlicher Partizipation. Retrieved November 15, 2020, from https://mein.aufstehn.at/petitions/nein-zur-gletscherverbauung-pitztal-otztal

Euler, J. (2019). The commons: A social form that allows for degrowth and sustainability. *Capitalism Nature Socialism*, *30*(2), 158–175. https://doi.org/10.1080/10455752.2018.1449874

Fairclough, N., & Wodak, R. (1997). Critical discourse analysis. In T. A. van Dijk (Ed.), *Discourse studies: A multidisciplinary introduction: Vol. 2. Discourse as social interaction* (pp. 258–284). SAGE.

Fazito, M., Scott, M., & Russell, P. (2016). The dynamics of tourism discourses and policy in Brazil. *Annals of Tourism Research*, *57*, 1–17. https://doi.org/10.1016/j.annals.2015.11.013

Fletcher, R., Murray Mas, I., Blanco-Romero, A., & Blázquez-Salom, M. (2019). Tourism and degrowth: An emerging agenda for research and praxis. *Journal of Sustainable Tourism*, *27*(12), 1745–1763. https://doi.org/10.1080/09669582.2019.1679822

Focus Online. (2019). *Skandal in Österreich: Tirol will für neues Skigebiet Berggipfel wegsprengen*. Retrieved November 18, 2019, from https://www.focus.de/reisen/mehr-platz-fuer-massentourismus-skandal-in-oesterreich-tirol-will-fuer-neues-skigebiet-berggipfel-wegsprengen_id_11308108.html

Foucault, M. (1972). *The archaeology of knowledge and the discourse on language*. Pantheon Books.

Gascón, J. (2019). Tourism as a right: A "frivolous claim" against degrowth? *Journal of Sustainable Tourism*, *27*(12), 1825–1838. https://doi.org/10.1080/09669582.2019.1666858

Georgescu-Roegen, N. (1975). Energy and economic myths. *Southern Economic Journal*, *41*(3), 347–381. https://doi.org/10.2307/1056148

Georgescu-Roegen, N. (1995). *La décroissance: Entropie – Écologie - Économ (1979)* (2nd ed.).

Hassanli, N., Small, J., & Darcy, S. (2019). The representation of Airbnb in newspapers: A critical discourse analysis. *Current Issues in Tourism*, *82*(1), 1–13. https://doi.org/10.1080/13683500.2019.1669540

Heikkurinen, P., Lozanoska, J., & Tosi, P. (2019). Activities of degrowth and political change. *Journal of Cleaner Production*, *211*, 555–565. https://doi.org/10.1016/j.jclepro.2018.11.119

Higgins-Desbiolles, F., Carnicelli, S., Krolikowski, C., Wijesinghe, G., & Boluk, K. (2019). Degrowing tourism: Rethinking tourism. *Journal of Sustainable Tourism*, *27*(12), 1926–1944. https://doi.org/10.1080/09669582.2019.1601732

Illich, I. (1974). *Tools for conviviality* (2nd ed.).

Jamal, T. (2019). *Justice and ethics in tourism. Tourism, environment and development series*. Routledge Taylor & Francis Group.

Jamal, T., & Camargo, B. A. (2014). Sustainable tourism, justice and an ethic of care: Toward the just destination. *Journal of Sustainable Tourism*, *22*(1), 11–30. https://doi.org/10.1080/09669582.2013.786084

Jamal, T., & Camargo, B. A. (2018). Tourism governance and policy: Whither justice? *Tourism Management Perspectives*, *25*, 205–208. https://doi.org/10.1016/j.tmp.2017.11.009

Kallis, G., Kostakis, V., Lange, S., Muraca, B., Paulson, S., & Schmelzer, M. (2018). Research on degrowth. *Annual Review of Environment and Resources*, *43*(1), 291–316. https://doi.org/10.1146/annurev-environ-102017-025941

Kallis, G., & March, H. (2015). Imaginaries of hope: The Utopianism of degrowth. *Annals of the Association of American Geographers*, *105*(2), 360–368. https://doi.org/10.1080/00045608.2014.973803

Kozinets, R. V. (2015). *Netnography: Redefined* (2nd ed.). SAGE.

Kreiner, G. E., Hollensbe, E. C., & Sheep, M. L. (2006). Where is the "me" among the "we"? Identity work and the search for optimal balance. *Academy of Management Journal*, *49*(5), 1031–1057. https://doi.org/10.5465/amj.2006.22798186

Latouche, S. (2003). Pour une société de décroissance: Absurdité du productivisme et des gaspillages. *Le Monde Diplomatique*, November, 18–19.

Latouche, S. (2009). *Farewell to growth*. Polity Press (1st ed.).

Latouche, S. (2010). Degrowth. *Journal of Cleaner Production*, *18*(6), 519–522. https://doi.org/10.1016/j.jclepro.2010.02.003

Luo, Q., & Zhai, X. (2017). "I will never go to Hong Kong again!" How the secondary crisis communication of "Occupy Central" on Weibo shifted to a tourism boycott! *Tourism Management*, *62*, 159–172. https://doi.org/10.1016/j.tourman.2017.04.007

Martínez-Alier, J., Pascual, U., Vivien, F. D., & Zaccai, E. (2010). Sustainable de-growth: Mapping the context, criticisms and future prospects of an emergent paradigm. *Ecological Economics*, *69*(9), 1741–1747. https://doi.org/10.1016/j.ecolecon.2010.04.017

Meadows, D. H., Meadows, D. L., Randers, J., & Behrens, W. W. (1972). *The limits to growth: A report for the Club of Rome's project on the predicament of mankind* (4th ed.). Universe Books.

Mijnissen, I. (2020). In Tirol soll ein namenloser Gipfel gesprengt werden, um zwei Skigebiete zu vereinigen. Viele glauben nicht daran, dass das in Zeiten der Erderwärmung die erhoffte Zukunftsperspektive bringen wird. Retrieved March 6, 2019, from https://www.nzz.ch/international/wintertourismus-tirol-sprengen-fuer-das-neue-gletscher-ski-gebiet-ld.1542333?reduced=true

Milano, C., Novelli, M., & Cheer, J. M. (2019). Overtourism and degrowth: A social movements perspective. *Journal of Sustainable Tourism*, *27*(12), 1857–1875. https://doi.org/10.1080/09669582.2019.1650054

Missemer, A. (2017). Nicholas Georgescu-Roegen and degrowth. *The European Journal of the History of Economic Thought*, *24*(3), 493–506. https://doi.org/10.1080/09672567.2016.1189945

Muraca, B. (2012). Towards a fair degrowth-society: Justice and the right to a 'good life' beyond growth. *Futures*, *44*(6), 535–545. https://doi.org/10.1016/j.futures.2012.03.014

Navarro-Jurado, E., Romero-Padilla, Y., Romero-Martínez, J. M., Serrano-Muñoz, E., Habegger, S., & Mora-Esteban, R. (2019). Growth machines and social movements in mature tourist destinations Costa del Sol-Málaga. *Journal of Sustainable Tourism*, *27*(12), 1786–1803. https://doi.org/10.1080/09669582.2019.1677676

Nyblom, Å., Isaksson, K., Sanctuary, M., Fransolet, A., & Stigson, P. (2019). Governance and degrowth. *Sustainability*, *11*(6), 1734. https://doi.org/10.3390/su11061734

Oswick, C., Keenoy, T. W., & Grant, D. (2000). Discourse, organizations and organizing: Concepts, objects and subjects. *Human Relations*, *53*(9), 1115–1123. https://doi.org/10.1177/0018726700539001

Owens, L. (2008). From tourists to anti-tourists to tourist attractions: The transformation of the Amsterdam squatters' movement. *Social Movement Studies*, *7*(1), 43–59. https://doi.org/10.1080/14742830801969340

Panzer-Krause, S. (2019). Networking towards sustainable tourism: Innovations between green growth and degrowth strategies. *Regional Studies*, *53*(7), 927–938. https://doi.org/10.1080/00343404.2018.1508873

Parsons, E., & Rawles, C. (2003). The resumption of whaling by Iceland and the potential negative impact in the Icelandic whale-watching market. *Current Issues in Tourism*, *6*(5), 444–448. https://doi.org/10.1080/13683500308667964

Pitztaler Gletscherbahn & Ötztaler Gletscherbahn. (2019). *Das Projekt - Zahlen & Fakten*. Retrieved December 17, 2019, from https://www.pitztal-oetztal.tirol/de/das-projekt/

Raymond, C., & Brown, G. (2007). A spatial method for assessing resident and visitor attitudes towards tourism growth and development. *Journal of Sustainable Tourism*, *15*(5), 520–540. https://doi.org/10.2167/jost681.0

Research & Degrowth. (2010). Degrowth declaration of the Paris 2008 conference: Notes from the field. *Journal of Cleaner Production*, *18*(6), 523–524. https://doi.org/10.1016/j.jclepro.2010.01.012

Ribeiro, M. A., Pinto, P., Silva, J. A., & Woosnam, K. M. (2017). Residents' attitudes and the adoption of pro-tourism behaviours: The case of developing island countries. *Tourism Management*, *61*, 523–537. https://doi.org/10.1016/j.tourman.2017.03.004

Samerski, S. (2018). Tools for degrowth? Ivan Illich's critique of technology revisited. *Journal of Cleaner Production*, *197*, 1637–1646. https://doi.org/10.1016/j.jclepro.2016.10.039

Schneider, F., Kallis, G., & Martinez-Alier, J. (2010). Crisis or opportunity? Economic degrowth for social equity and ecological sustainability. Introduction to this special issue. *Journal of Cleaner Production*, *18*(6), 511–518. https://doi.org/10.1016/j.jclepro.2010.01.014

Sekulova, F., Kallis, G., Rodríguez-Labajos, B., & Schneider, F. (2013). Degrowth: From theory to practice. *Journal of Cleaner Production*, *38*, 1–6. https://doi.org/10.1016/j.jclepro.2012.06.022

Seraphin, H., Ivanov, S., Dosquet, F., & Bourliataux-Lajoinie, S. (2020). Archetypes of locals in destinations victim of overtourism. *Journal of Hospitality and Tourism Management*, *43*, 283–288. https://doi.org/10.1016/j.jhtm.2019.12.001

Singh, N. M. (2019). Environmental justice, degrowth and post-capitalist futures. *Ecological Economics*, *163*, 138–142. https://doi.org/10.1016/j.ecolecon.2019.05.014

Spiggle, S. (1994). Analysis and interpretation of qualitative data in consumer research. *Journal of Consumer Research*, *21*(3), 491. https://doi.org/10.1086/209413

Tiroler Umweltanwaltschaft. (2018). *Illegale Bautätigkeit am Pitztaler Gletscher*. Retrieved December 12, 2019, from http://www.tiroler-umweltanwaltschaft.gv.at/september-2018/illegale-bautaetigkeit-am-pitztaler-gletscher/

Tse, S., & Tung, V. W. S. (2020). Residents' discrimination against tourists. *Annals of Tourism Research*, 103060. https://doi.org/10.1016/j.annals.2020.103060

Valdivielso, J., & Moranta, J. (2019). The social construction of the tourism degrowth discourse in the Balearic Islands. *Journal of Sustainable Tourism*, *27*(12), 1876–1892. https://doi.org/10.1080/09669582.2019.1660670

Velicu, I. (2019). De-growing environmental justice: Reflections from anti-mining movements in Eastern Europe. *Ecological Economics*, *159*, 271–278. https://doi.org/10.1016/j.ecolecon.2019.01.021

Watson, T. J. (1994). *In search of management: Culture, Chaos and control in managerial work*. Routledge.

Wirtschaftskammer Tirol. (2015). *Tourismus in Tirol: Die treibende Wirtschaftskraft!* Innsbruck. WKO Tirol. Retrieved December 15, 2019, from https://www.wko.at/branchen/t/tourismus-freizeitwirtschaft/Tourismusbroschuere2015_3.pdf

World Tourism Organization. (2018). *Tourism and the sustainable development goals – Journey to 2030*. World Tourism Organization (UNWTO). https://doi.org/10.18111/9789284419401

Yu, Q., McManus, R., Yen, D. A., & Li, X. (2020). Tourism boycotts and animosity: A study of seven events. *Annals of Tourism Research*, *80*, 102792. https://doi.org/10.1016/j.annals.2019.102792

Conceptualizing peer-to-peer accommodations as disruptions in the urban tourism system

Emily Yeager, B. Bynum Boley and Cari Goetcheus

ABSTRACT
In urban destinations, Peer-to-peer accommodations (P2PAs), e.g., Airbnb, HomeAway, have experienced exponential growth and are shifting the vertices of the residential and tourism landscapes. As the nodes of visitor access appear deeper within backstage places, resident non-hosts face socio-cultural impacts that can influence their attitudes towards P2PAs and subsequent P2PA success in urban destinations. Predicated upon the resident non-host stakeholder's attitudes towards P2PAs, this paper offers a conceptual model situated within socio-ecological systems and chaos theories to help guide P2PA management and planning within urban tourism destinations. The proposed model posits that P2PA density, location, and the pace of their growth can propel a destination towards its critical social carrying capacity or delay reaching this critical threshold depending on how urban destinations leverage P2PA disruptions.

Introduction

Sixty-eight percent of the world's population is expected to live in urban areas by 2050 (United Nations, 2018). Increasing population density within urban areas provide the scale, proximity, amenities, and specializations that incubate innovations, particularly those related to modes of consumption (Davidson & Infranca, 2016). Twelve years ago, in San Francisco, California, an idea to rent extra space in an apartment to tourists disrupted the international tourism industry codifying a new lodging sector – Peer to Peer Accommodations (P2PA) (Aydin, 2019; Dolnicar, 2019). For this paper, paid online P2PA is defined as 'space suitable for overnight stays sold by a non-commercial provider (the host) to an end user (the guest) for short-term use through direct interaction between host and guest' (Dolnicar, 2019, p. 248).

The disruption of P2PAs to the international lodging sector has been well documented (Guttentag, 2015; Karlsson & Dolnicar, 2016; Sigala, 2014; Tussyadiah & Pesonen, 2016; Yang & Mao, 2019). But, research has also unearthed P2PA disruptions to the urban fabric upon which P2PA depend, which are exemplified through consequences such as rent-gaps and contested place-making (Farmaki et al., 2020; Horn & Merante, 2017; Roelofsen & Minca, 2018; Wachsmuth

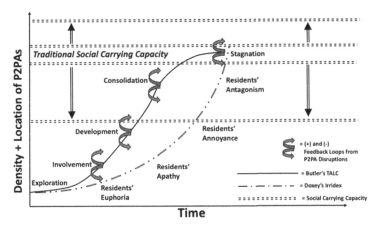

Figure 1. A conceptual P2PA management model comprised of Doxey's Irridex (1975) superimposed upon the Butler's (1980, 2008) Tourism Area Life Cycle (TALC) that posits non-host residents' attitudes towards P2PAs as a function of density and location of P2PAs. The social carrying capacity represents the threshold of residents' negative attitudes towards P2PAs that when exceeded, might result in opposing behaviors towards P2PAs. Socio-ecological systems theory supports the conceptualization of both positive and negative feedback loops induced by P2PA disruptions as opportunities to generate community benefits.

& Weisler, 2017; Yeager et al., 2020). These positive and negative disruptions are often disproportionately felt by resident non-hosts, who have emerged as the stakeholder proximal and thereby susceptible to P2PA impacts (Garau-Vadell et al., 2019; Jordan & Moore, 2017; Stergiou & Farmaki, 2020; Yeager et al., 2020). Residents' responses to P2PA development in their community can directly affect visitor satisfaction and subsequent return patronage, further elevating the vital role that non-host residents play in successful P2PA development (Ramos & Mundet, 2020). Additionally, residents can influence P2PA legislation either helping to facilitate the exchange or stifle the process (Jackson & Inbakaran, 2006).

Predicated upon the resident non-host stakeholder's attitudes towards P2PAs and the ability of P2PAs to have large-scale positive and negative effects on the urban fabric of their destinations, this paper offers a conceptual model situated within chaos and socio-ecological systems theories to help guide P2PA management and planning within urban areas (Figure 1). The proposed model posits that P2PA density, location, and pace of growth can accelerate a destination towards its critical social carrying capacity or delay reaching this critical threshold through P2PAs' ability to provide community benefits such as socially and psychologically empowering non-host residents (Boley et al., 2014; Yeager et al., 2020). Beginning with the x-axis, this paper unpacks each component of the proposed conceptual model for P2PA management and discusses future research areas to strengthen the application and expansion of this proposed model.

Timescale of tourism development with P2PAs (x-axis)

The temporal aspects of tourism development can amplify or reduce many of the impacts of tourism (Kreag, 2001). The absence of a unit of time on the x-axis is important because, according to chaos theory, change within a system can occur at any speed (McKercher, 1999). For example, in the U.S. city of Savannah, GA on May 12,017 a total of 748 Short Term Vacation Rentals (STVRs, i.e., P2PAs) were licensed to operate within the city's STVR zones (Curl, 2017). In June 2017, word spread of a potential moratorium on issuing STVR licensees until the city formed an STVR growth management plan. In fear of losing their right to host in their neighborhood, homeowners began flooding the city's Tourism Management & Ambassadorship Department with STVR license applications, regardless of their intentions to exercise their licenses (Curl, 2017). A complete moratorium never came to fruition, but the potential regulations stimulated a 53.5% (1,148 P2PAs) increase in P2PAs able to operate at any given time (City of Savannah, 2020). This rapid increase in P2PAs in Savannah presents an increasing amount of costs and benefits to the City that could influence resident attitudes.

Research on the effects of rapid tourism development within the context of the TALC has produced varying trajectories of resident attitudes. Perdue et al. (1999) findings regarding the effects of boomtown tourism on residents' attitudes reject the TALC. Rather, their findings support the social disruption hypothesis, which posits that communities enter an initial state of crisis because the disruption requires a significant increased demand for public services and infrastructure with attitudes towards tourism becoming more positive over time (England & Albrecht, 1984). Conversely, others such as Davis and Morais (2004) have found an inverse relationship between rapid tourism development and residents' attitudes within economically depressed communities that latch on to tourism as an economic savior. They found residents to initially be excited and optimistic about a large-scale tourism development planned for their community, but residents became increasingly frustrated when the economic benefits did not materialize in the community due to the enclave nature of the tourism development.

P2PAs indeed resemble a boomtown tourism phenomenon through their rapid growth and economic change to urban areas (England & Albrecht, 1984). But, unlike boomtown tourism development, in the urban front stage, P2PAs do not require a significant increased demand for public services and infrastructure to develop. If P2PA visitors do not contribute an overall net increase in tourism visitation, then P2PA visitors in the backstage simply require a redistribution of public services (e.g., recycling, sidewalk maintenance). The challenging part of this redistribution is that it could occur as a rapid event or could materialize piecemeal at varying intervals.

Future research & application of the timescale of P2PA development (x-axis)
The unitless measure of time on the x-axis suggests that changes within the urban tourism system could occur in a matter of days or take years at a time to be complete. Further documentation of distinct shifts in P2PA attributes (e.g., density, location), such as the aforementioned example from Savannah, Georgia, could help build a repository of case studies on P2PA disruptions based on varying timescales of their inception and subsequent externalities that could be explored for their application within the proposed model. Destinations may use this repository to estimate the effect of P2PA policies on the pace of tourism development in their destination.

Density & location of P2PA activity (y-axis)

The scale of tourism and the number of tourists arriving within a destination have been at the core of the sustainable tourism debate since its inception with large-scale tourism negatively connotated and small-scale tourism being considered more sustainable (Clarke, 1997). These notions of scale are evident within Butler's (1980, 2008) Tourism Area Life Cycle (TALC) and Doxey's Irridex where destinations and resident attitudes hit a critical threshold as the number of tourists exceeds the destination's ability to cope and adapt. Both Butlers TALC and Doxey's Irridex underpin the structure of the proposed conceptual model, but the is expanded upon by the replacement of the number of visitors on the y-axis with another important factor influencing a destination's stage of development and resident attitudes towards P2PAs– density and location of P2PAs. The focus on density and location over sheer numbers is qualified through an exploration of P2PA community impacts through a landscape lens.

Landscapes can be physical or socio-cultural in nature (Lewis, 1979; Sauer, 1925). They also exhibit multi-scalarity and fluid boundaries (Davis, 2005; Jackson, 2008; Massey, 2010). This fluidity results in nested landscapes that can be envisioned like a Russian Matryoshka doll. In Figure 2, the outer most layer of this 'doll' is the urban landscape containing the tourism and residential

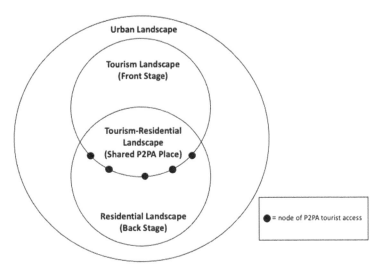

Figure 2. The tourism and residential landscapes nested within the urban landscapes. New nodes of access into the backstage produce new 'shared P2PA places' where resident non-hosts, resident P2PA hosts, and P2PA visitors re-negotiate backstage values and norms.

landscapes. Zoning laws, which regulate where certain activities may occur, solidify boundaries of sub-scapes within an urban landscape. Many of the P2PA zoning regulations across U.S. urban areas aim to balance a quality of life for all residents while also maintaining the right to pursue tourism enterprise (Lobel, 2016). It is expected then that we would find the scope of P2PA impacts in urban areas, both positive and negative, to be concentrated within the tourism and residential landscapes Visualizing the spatial dynamics of the tourism and residential landscapes as a result of P2PA development reveals non-host residents as a stakeholder whose quality of life is most jeopardized or enhanced by P2PA development.

Over time mechanisms such as formalized hospitality networks (Ikkala & Lampinen, 2015) and zoning have limited tourists' access to 'front-stage' places where tourism activity occurs (tourism landscape) leaving sheltered 'backstage' places for residents' daily lives free from the gaze of non-residents (residential landscape) (MacCannell, 1973; Urry, 1990). Nodes of tourist access at the junction of these two landscapes often manifest as mixed-use zones. In these shared places, residents and tourists enjoy leisure and engage in similar commercial activities. Moreover, the products and services consumed by tourists in these shared places are marketed specifically to them by government entities (e.g., Destination Marketing Organizations, Convention & Visitor Bureaus). However, tourists are on a quest for authenticity (Cohen, 1988), and the emergence of the experience economy and the prevailing symbolic use of travel to convey status via social media has further pushed tourists towards these 'backstage' experiences (Boley et al., 2018). Even the famous European travel guru, Rick Steves, uses "Europe through the Backdoor" as a slogan to his guidebooks (Steves, 2017).

The nodes of tourists' access penetrating further into the residential landscape generate interstitial P2PA places where stakeholder values, norms, and power become renegotiated (Farmaki et al., 2020; McKercher et al., 2015). Resident non-hosts directly feel the impacts of these negotiations because they reside proximally to P2PAs. Previous research suggests that residents' tolerance of tourism is correlated with an increasing density of tourist accommodations (Bestard & Nadal, 2007; Tokarchuk et al., 2020). However, this finding is likely moderated by where accommodations develop in the urban landscape; increased P2PA density in traditionally backstage places has garnered backlash from residents (Morris, 2015; Ramos & Mundet, 2020). To provide solutions for resident discontent, it is not enough however to simply know that landscape boundaries are shifting within the urban system. In the proposed model, resident attitudes towards

P2PAs become increasingly negative as a function of the density and location of P2PAs. But destination managers need a deeper understanding of the mechanisms driving these changes and influencing resident attitudes towards P2PAs in their community. One way to achieve this insight is to critically examine the place-making process generating these new nodes of access within the backstage.

Tourism place-making in all contexts is an iterative socio-political process through which imaged and physical images of place build upon each other (Davis, 2005; Farmaki et al., 2020; Lefebvre & Nicholson-Smith, 1991; Lew, 2017). Davis (2005) explains that there may be varying conceptualizations of a place but 'power then dictates which version of place gets to be reproduced' (p. 612). P2PA success depends on a carefully constructed narrative of a place that begins with property owners buying into the "laisse faire platform capitalism" as a form of community participation (Roelofsen & Minca, 2018, p. 172). Initiation into this newly created community requires sharing your community with others. P2PA guests perform the marketed version of the backstage. The sense of place in the urban backstage, in turn, adapts to the demands of P2PA guests (Richardson, 2015; Rickly-Boyd et al., 2016). In this process, non-host residents' agency in the marketing of their backstage neighborhood is elusive.

Further exacerbation of a skewed place narrative can be found in P2PA platform initiatives such as Airbnb's 'Neighborhoods' program (Airbnb, 2020). The intention of the 'Neighborhoods' program was to expand Airbnb's appeal beyond hosts and guests to local businesses that might struggle to market themselves otherwise (Thomas, 2012). For each neighborhood featured in a city, guests can access information curated by hosts such as the neighborhood's hand-mapped borders (Lawler, 2012) or photos virtually guiding guests through the neighborhood (Airbnb, 2020). While the 'Neighborhoods' website does offer an opportunity for general resident feedback and contributions, there is no publicly available details on the vetting process of these neighborhood curations. This lack of transparency highlights two issues potentially perpetuating mythological representations of the places featured in the 'Neighborhoods' program (Davis, 2005).

First maps are inherently power-laden because their creation requires privileging a specific group of people to present their 2-D reality of space and place (Rocheleau, 2005; Swyngedouw, 2004; Zieleniec, 2007). This power could be 'wielded in order to advocate for certain interests and perhaps even change control over space and place' (Bosak et al., 2010, p. 462; Corbett & Keller, 2003; Rocheleau, 2005). The Neighborhoods program empowers hosts to designate attractive places of the community where their P2PA is located. Residents' pride in their neighborhood is comprised in part of material elements of their backstage (e.g., local coffee shop, locally owned antique store). The abstracted Airbnb Neighborhoods map may produce a sense of place foreign to resident non-hosts thus inducing feelings of psychological disempowerment (e.g., reduced pride in their community) that could perpetuate negative attitudes towards P2PAs (Boley et al., 2014; Yeager et al., 2020).

Second, urban tourism landscape production often involves utilizing neighborhood or city-wide stereotypes in tourism marketing efforts (Shields, 2013). If non-host residents are not equitably involved in the discursive creation of their home, inauthentic neighborhood stereotypes could be reified through the platform by P2PA hosts (Stors, 2020). Also, the streamlining of marketing efforts within a P2PA platform could result in over-simplification or reinforcement of neighborhood stereotypes that may create dissonance between guests' expectations and back stage realities rendering non-host residents vulnerable to sensationalization of their local culture and being gazed upon as the 'other' (Törnberg & Chiappini, 2020; Urry, 1992).

Power struggles emerge in the commodification of the home for P2PA consumption. The 'home' is intentionally marketed to P2PA guests and consequently guests expect distinct dimensions of 'home' which can influence return patronage (Tussyadiah & Zach, 2015; Zhu et al., 2019). However, to supply this 'home' experience, P2PA hosts rely on all extensions of their 'home' (e.g., neighborhood parking, a neighbor's yard upkeep) thus requiring involuntary participation from non-host residents to supply this experience in the backstage (Roelofsen & Minca, 2018; Tuan, 1975). In fact, some P2PA guests envision interactions with neighbors as a contributing factor to their P2PA experience. In this sense, home becomes an interstitial heterotopia where the values and norms of the residential landscape are re-negotiated (Farmaki et al., 2020; Foucault & Miskowiec, 1986).

A home's transformation into a heterotopia is a paramount consequence of shifting tourism residential landscape borders because the home traditionally provides the nurturing and emotional support for residents' daily lives (Chhabra et al., 2003; Cohen, 1988; Tuan, 1975). P2PA companies such as Airbnb encourage guests to 'feel at home anywhere' (Airbnb, 2018). The curation of 'home' by P2PA company marketing campaigns potentially simplifies the true process of home making, which requires compounding experiences, values, beliefs, and norms over time (Tuan, 1975). Moreover, these attributes of home making are shaped by historical, cultural, physical, and ecological attributes of the natural and built environment (Dias et al., 2015; Tuan, 1975). The oversimplification or perhaps narrow projection of the 'home' to guests reinforces the illusion that they are only consuming an experience at the listing as advertised to them thus creating a 'myth identity' of the home (Harley, 1989).

Regardless of the scale of the place (e.g. home, neighborhood) and depending upon which stakeholder possesses the most agency in its development, places can potentially evolve into place-myths that 'enable and legitimize social practices that alter that material landscape and attempt to bring it more in line with a conceptualization that was never based on the material landscape in the first place' (Davis, 2005, p. 612; Shields, 2013).

In summary, if housed solely within the traditional front stage, the number of P2PA guests would be almost inconsequential to residents. However, the y-axis of the proposed model posits that the new nodes of backstage access for P2PA guests amplifies the direct relationship between increased density and location of P2PAs and residents' negative attitudes towards them.

Future research & application of the density and location of P2PA development (y-axis)
In Figure 2, the front stage and backstage are distinct, and it clearly demarcates the formation of new P2PA places at a neighborhood scale. Massey (2010) reminds us, however, of the multi-scalarity of landscapes. Recalling the Matryoshka doll metaphor, backstage places sometimes exist in the front stage, and vice versa. For example, an apartment building may exist within the front stage of an urban tourism destination. However, its flats are backstage places with all the attributes of "home" attached to them (Tuan, 1975). Residents' negative reactions to the conversion of flats into P2PAs is unsurprising given the particularly close quarters within apartment buildings that increase the probability of P2PA visitor and resident interaction (Apple, 2018; Gurran & Phibbs, 2017; Reyes, 2020). Future research into P2PA residential impacts should consider exploring all instances of "home" particularly in urban tourism destinations. For example, in some countries such as the United States where a third of homes are rented, cities are challenging traditional values of single-family homes in the reality of increasing urbanization and exposés of racial and economic segregation exacerbated by single-family zoning and residents (Badger & Bui, 2019;).

Urban landscapes have P2PA management options to choose from. A laissez-faire approach would likely result in P2PA activity radiating from the urban core (front stage) into "non-tourism" zones (backstage) (Nieuwaland & van Melik, 2018; Gurran & Phibbs, 2017). In destinations with well-defined property rights, Gurran and Phibbs (2018) argue that Coasian approach towards managing P2PA externalities could complement laissez-faire P2PA management strategies. Future research should explore how better to equip urban destination residents with the skills and autonomy needed for Coasian P2PA problem-solving. Perhaps these skills can ameliorate negative P2PA externalities related to their spatial distribution, reduce the overhead costs of regulatory enforcement, and strengthen community bonds.

However, Gurran and Phibbs (2017) recognize that certain externalities (e.g., public health and safety risks, traffic congestion) require regulatory intervention. Careful consideration should be made by destinations managing these 'externalities' if they rely heavily on spatial P2PA management strategies (i.e. zoning). Designating P2PA zones purely on perceived visitor demand may perpetuate not only marketing the 'place myth' of a destination, but also disenfranchising residents who feel that their community would be worth sharing and of interest to visitors. With every spatial distribution P2PA management approach, destination managers should consider who resides within and outside of the front stage and backstage whose borders are being formally delineated.

Resident attitudes towards P2PAs

Residents' pivotal role in the successful development of sustainable tourism destinations is historically recognized (Belisle & Hoy, 1980; Gursoy & Rutherford, 2004; Nunkoo & Gursoy, 2012). The discussion of factors included in the y-axis of the proposed model highlight non-host residents' exceptional vulnerability to P2PA impacts. The proposed model offers non-host resident attitudes as the most important indicator of destination change due to P2PA disruptions. Case studies reveal that residents may exercise their voting rights and leverage their local tax contributions to support or challenge future tourism development in their community (Spencer & Nsiah, 2013; Sofield & Birtles, 1996). This research is timely as residents actively engage elected officials over P2PA regulations in cities such as Beacon City, New York (Martin, 2018). In Spain, residents in destinations such as Majorca view P2PAs as an additional pressure in a burgeoning tourism industry that has ushered the city and its residents past its social carrying capacity (Minder, 2018). Residents' showed support for local regulation to curb Airbnb and overall tourism in Majorca through posters hung from balconies in the city exhibiting a woman pushing a shopping cart and brandishing a walking stick towards tourists sporting selfie sticks and carry-on luggage. The sign reads 'The city is for whoever lives in it, not whoever visits it' (Minder, 2018). Residents with enough pent-up resentment towards P2PAs may become agonistic (Stergiou & Farmaki, 2020). Research has answered Heo's (2016) call for residents' inclusion in P2PA impact assessments (Jordan & Moore, 2017) discovering that resident attitudes can affect perceived P2PA impacts and ultimately influence support for P2PA development (Garau-Vadell et al., 2019; Yeager et al., 2020).This support or protest of P2PA development can push some residents to action. In Barcelona, residents to the added pressure of P2PAs on a saturated tourism industry through vandalism of buses, hotels, and engaging in negative discourse theory signage (Ramos & Mundet, 2020).

Future research & application of resident attitudes towards P2PA development

A variety of moderating factors should be considered as destination managers assess resident attitudes towards P2PAs. For instance, research finds that prior P2PA use significantly increases a resident's emotional solidarity with guests, hosts, and perceived positive impacts of P2PAs (Suess et al., 2020; van Doorn, 2020). Destination managers may assess intangible indicators of residents' satisfaction with P2PA through subjective quality of life indicators. For example, Boley et al. (2014) describe this pride as psychological empowerment, a dimension that has shown significant statistical influence on residents' attitudes and overall support for P2PAs (Yeager et al., 2020).

Related to the previous discussion of spatial P2PA management strategies, research shows that enclaves of tourism can create a dichotomy in access to tourism benefits (Davis & Morais,

2004) which might negatively impact non-host resident attitudes across the urban landscape, particularly those that do not live within formal P2PA zones.

Destination managers and researchers alike could plot resident attitudes towards P2PAs by neighborhood along the development curve or the residential curve in the proposed model to inform tourism planning based on what future iterations of the urban landscape might materialize in the context of P2PAs.

P2PA disruptions to urban residents' social carrying capacity

For this proposed model, tourism social carrying capacity is defined as the threshold at which tourism costs residents (socially, environmentally, and economically) more than they gain from tourism in their community (Madrigal, 1993, Navarro Jurado et al., 2013). The social carrying capacity of tourism destinations is often modeled as a reverse parabola with the social carrying capacity threshold found at the peak of the curve (Tokarchuk et al., 2020). In the TALC, this threshold translates into the stagnation phase and argued as the most influential time in a destination's development (Russell & Faulkner, 2004). However, this stage of development may not uniformly arrive across an urban tourism destination. The unitless measure of time on the x-axis of the proposed model makes it possible for the potential unalignment of Butler's (1980; 2008) tourism development curve and Doxey's (1975) Irridex. Therefore, one neighborhood may reach their social carrying capacity threshold before another one. For example, P2PA development in a front stage neighborhood an urban destination that has recognized hospitality name brands and a heavy reliance on tourism dollars could classify as falling between the development and consolidation phases. If interpreted as a direct correlation, the proposed model indicates that residents might start to feel apathy or annoyance towards P2PA development if the number of P2PAs was the only factor considered in predicting their attitudes towards P2PAs. However, conversion of houses and apartments within this into P2PAs to supply visitor demand for authentic walkable neighborhood experiences could induce rent-gaps and subsequent resident displacement (Wachsmuth & Weisler, 2017). In this scenario, resident attitudes towards P2PAs may quickly escalate to antagonism, thereby lowering the neighborhood's social carrying capacity towards P2PAs, while the stage of tourism development remains located between development and consolidation. In this same neighborhood, Martin and Uysal (1990) would suggest that local government transparency in its P2PA management efforts might ameliorate negative attitudes towards P2PA development, thereby stabilizing the neighborhood's social carrying capacity. Some destinations have used Geographic Information Systems software to facilitate this transparency by creating digital interactive maps for the general public to view where P2PA activity is occurring in their community (Bozeman GIS, 2020; Chattanooga GIS, 2020; City of Dunedin, 2020; City of Savannah, 2020). In the proposed model, we might see the social carrying capacity decrease, particularly in backstage areas, if P2PA development beings in the Exploration phase where second homes are converted to P2PAs, non-host residents have very little involvement in the changing sense of place associated with P2PAs and may become annoyed with externalities such as increased pedestrian and vehicle traffic from P2PA guests. On the other hand, if a backstage within an urban tourism destination can foster P2PA development but block zoning from hospitality conglomerates residents in that backstage could avoid feeling like their community has landed in the consolidation stage. Rather, opportunities arise for small local commercial development and an increased economic multiplier. In this case, residents' Euphoria related to P2PA development might sustain.

Future research & application of the effect of P2PA activity on social carrying capacity

Tokarchuk et al. (2020) argue that by statistical inclusion of other measures of quality of life can circumvent collecting resident attitudes towards tourism to establish a destination's carrying capacity. However, reliance upon secondary data as social carrying capacity indicators may not capture the true nature of resident life in urban communities. Citing Michalos' (2003) critique of quality of life indicators, Uysal et al. (2016) explain that the inherent direct relationship between quality of life indicators and tourism development overlooks the subjective quality of life measures that are not captured through secondary data (e.g., sense of place, empowerment). Therefore, destination managers and tourism researchers aiming to develop P2PA management strategies are still encouraged to utilize resident attitudes towards P2PAs as the primary indicator for a destination's social carrying capacity with a recommendation of including the wealth of research-supported quality of life indicators (Andereck & Nyaupane, 2011;Woo et al., 2015) in resident attitude assessments for P2PA impacts in the urban landscape.

P2PAs as disruptions in the urban tourism system

The x-axis factor of time combined with a discussion of resident attitudes and social carrying capacity in the proposed model, however, indicate a spatio-temporal complexity in the proposed model that is most understood through a systems lens. Researchers critique previous systems approaches to tourism destination development (Leiper, 1990; Mill & Morrison, 1985) for their reductionist approach (McKercher, 1999). Systems, in this case the urban system, are comprised of interrelated parts e.g. P2PAs, affordable housing, and hotel development that sometimes react in unpredictable ways when changes are introduced into the system (Lee, 2016; Odum, 1985; Senge, 2000; Von Bertalanffy, 1950). Complexity and tradeoffs are key characteristics of dynamic systems (Hirsch et al., 2011; Smolka & Hienerth, 2014) and are what sophisticate the lens through which this framework views the role of P2PAs in urban tourism destinations. Socio-ecological systems theory posits that communities evolve over time much like biological systems (Ostrom, 1990). In a typical controlled system, disruptions result in negative feedback loops that dampen progress of maintains homeostasis (Costanza, 1992). Conversely, system disruptions may induce positive feedback loops that may reinforce an issue or cause destabilization in a system (Costanza, 1992). Disruptions to system homeostasis result in positive and negative feedback loops. These are traditionally interpreted as a decline in the health of a system. Costanza (1992) argues that disruptions are leverageable regardless of whether they induce a positive or negative feedback loop. In the proposed P2PA management model, these positive and negative feedback loops can increase or decrease the social carrying capacity of an urban tourism system.

P2PA negative feedback loops

The COVID-19 pandemic drastically altered the tourism industry from both the supply and demand sides (Destination Analysts, 2020; McCarthy, 2020), effectively disrupting destinations and their disruptors such as P2PA companies (Glusac, 2020; Rogoway, 2020). The sharp decline in tourism arrivals (UNWTO., 2020) left many destinations reeling and unsure of how to proceed. The compounded disruption of COVID-19 and P2PAs have induced a negative feedback loop in many urban tourism destinations. For many tourism sectors and destinations, including P2PA platforms, this threatens the "volume growth agenda" which relates tourism arrivals to benefits (Gössling et al., 2020). However, the proposed framework reveals that degrowth or stabilization of tourism arrivals could prove a transformative evolutionary pathway for some destinations that leverage negative feedback loops (Brouder, 2014). For example, in Figure 2, the number of P2PA guests is, in part, correlated to residents' dissatisfaction with their community. A negative feedback loop in the urban tourism system would reduce the number of P2PAs and subsequent P2PA guests in a neighborhood to an acceptable density. Relatedly, the decrease in tourism arrivals might increase domestic travel fueled by those within a smaller travel radius who are looking for authentic experiences with associated beneficial multiplying effects within local economies.

P2PA positive feedback loops
P2PAs can potentially induce negative feedback loops in the urban tourism system that could propel a destination towards rejuvenation. These investments into their properties can create positive impacts for the residential landscape through increased curb appeal of a neighborhood and higher property values for its homeowners. However, the higher property values associated with these home improvements and the emergence of the neighborhood as a prime newly formed node in the tourism-residential landscape might also increase property taxes within the neighborhood, in turn, potentially contributing to out-pricing and subsequent displacement of residents.

P2PA growth could promote the use of existing homes and reduce the need for land development for hotels, which might not exhibit as much multi-use. Or, hosts might feel inspired to curate their guests' stay with a personalized list of local restaurants and businesses, thus increasing their P2PA guests' multiplier effect within the community.

Another example of leveraging the compounded disruptions of P2PAs and the COVID-19 pandemic is through the explosion of virtual tourism experiences. In the growing pandemic, destinations and P2PA platforms harnessed the marketing power of virtual experiences (Airbnb, 2020; Rogers, 2020). This common thread of virtual experiences highlights an opportunity for collaboration between P2PAs and the tourism industry, two entities with a complicated and sometimes contentious past (Peltier, 2017).

Future research & application of P2PAs as disruptions in the urban tourism system
Regardless of whether P2PA disruptions induce positive or negative feedback loops, Costanza (1992) contends that either disruptions are leverageable for overall system health. To better leverage these feedback loops, destination managers might benefit from conducting a SWOT analysis of a range of P2PA management strategies at their disposal. SWOT analysis has assessed P2PA lodging market competitiveness (Lehr; Meleo et al., 2016). However, research has yet utilize SWOT analysis to assess the externalities of P2PA management strategies on residents within an urban tourism system.

Conclusion

The popularity of disruptive innovations such as P2PAs is evident in countries such as the United States, where by 2015, forty-four percent of adults claimed to have participated in sharing economy transactions, e.g., ride sharing, home sharing (Steinmetz, 2016). In 2017, the United States remained one of Airbnb's largest market shares contributing 660,000 listings out its total four million listings worldwide (Hartmans, 2017). Widener (2015) explains that in organically slow-growing cities, the visionary statement of the urban area is comprised of the aggregation of many voices. Destinations use this visionary statement to address small-scale decisions regarding community development. With predictions of continued urban growth (United Nations, 2018), Widener (2015) expects that economies of scale and advancing smart city technologies will 'usher in progressively more technocratic and frenetically paced real estate development. In this era, decisions by the administrative state might become less well-informed and increasingly ad hoc' (p. 143). With no indication from research that this trend is declining, it seems P2PAs are here to stay and that there is a need for strong conceptual and theoretical underpinnings to equip municipalities with tools to make informed and proactive decisions regarding future P2PA development, which this paper attempts to provide.

The y-axis of the proposed model is premised on a landscape perspective to conceptualize the importance of considering not only the density of P2PAs when assessing their impacts on residents but also where they exist. P2PAs create new nodes of access within the backstage which sometimes produce new places (McKercher et al., 2015; Famarki et al., 2020). Depending upon which stakeholders (P2PA host, P2PA guest, non-P2PA host resident) are involved, this place-making process could potentially produce an abstracted 'place-myth' that may not portray the true character of the community (Davis, 2005) or psychologically empower residents who feel proud of sharing their community with visitors (Boley et al., 2014; Yeager et al., 2020). The proposed model further suggests that a destination's P2PA social carrying capacity depends upon resident attitudes towards P2PAs.

The x-axis factor of time in the proposed model introduces a temporal component to the proposed model that warrants a systems perspective underpinned by socio-ecological systems theory (Costanza, 1992; Holling, 2001) and chaos theory (McKercher, 1999) to better inform the proposed model's application in destination management. The positive and negative feedback loops induced by P2PA disruptions in the urban tourism system can increase or decrease a destination's social carrying capacity for P2PA development.

The proposed framework offers a toolbox that regulatory agencies can utilize for holistic P2PA regulations that consider the current contextual and historic roots of P2PA issues and how they might evolve over time with the urban landscape. Additionally, the proposed framework focuses on residents' attitudes as an indicator of P2PA impacts and the overall health of the urban system. These attitudes function as a driving force behind future support for P2PA activity. This support, however, must be coupled with a community's capacity for adaptation to rapid innovations such as P2PAs in their communities.

Disclosure statement

No potential conflict of interest was reported by the authors.

ORCID

Emily Yeager http://orcid.org/0000-0002-1868-0230
B. Bynum Boley http://orcid.org/0000-0002-4989-3773

References

Allsop, L. (2011). Battling to keep the 'real' Venice afloat. *CNN*. http://www.cnn.com/2011/WORLD/europe/06/09/venice.under.threat/index.html
Andereck, K. L., & Nyaupane, G. P. (2011). Exploring the nature of tourism and quality of life perceptions among residents. *Journal of Travel Research*, 50(3), 248–260. https://doi.org/10.1177/0047287510362918
Apple, A. (2018, August 14). Some downtown Nashville residents upset with apartments partnering with Airbnb | WZTV. *Fox 17 WZTV Nashville*. https://fox17.com/news/local/some-downtown-nashville-residents-upset-with-apartments-partnering-with-airbnb

Aydin, R. (2019). The history of Airbnb, from air mattresses to $31 billion company. *Business Insider*. https://www.businessinsider.com/how-airbnb-was-founded-a-visual-history-2016-2

Badger, E., & Bui, Q. (2019). Cities start to question an American ideal: A house with a yard on every lot. *The New York Times*. https://www.nytimes.com/interactive/2019/06/18/upshot/cities-across-america-question-single-family-zoning.html

Bartneck, C., Duenser, A., Moltchanova, E., & Zawieska, K. (2015). Comparing the similarity of responses received from studies in Amazon's Mechanical Turk to studies conducted online and with direct recruitment. *PLOS One*, *10*(4), e0121595. https://doi.org/10.1371/journal.pone.0121595

Belisle, F. J., & Hoy, D. R. (1980). The perceived impact of tourism by residents a case study in Santa Marta, Colombia. *Annals of Tourism Research*, *7*(1), 83–101. https://doi.org/10.1016/S0160-7383(80)80008-9

Bestard, A. B., & Nadal, J. R. (2007). Attitudes toward tourism and tourism congestion. *Région et Développement*, *25*, 193–207.

Boley, B. B., Jordan, E. J., Kline, C., & Knollenberg, W. (2018). Social return and intent to travel. *Tourism Management*, *64*, 119–128. https://doi.org/10.1016/j.tourman.2017.08.008

Boley, B. B., McGehee, N. G., Perdue, R. R., & Long, P. (2014). Empowerment and resident attitudes toward tourism: Strengthening the theoretical foundation through a Weberian lens. *Annals of Tourism Research*, *49*, 33–50. https://doi.org/10.1016/j.annals.2014.08.005

Bosak, K., Boley, B., & Zaret, K. (2010). Deconstructing the 'Crown of the Continent': Power, politics and the process of creating National Geographic's Geotourism Mapguides. *Tourism Geographies*, *12*(3), 460–480. https://doi.org/10.1080/14616688.2010.494686

Bozeman GIS, B. of L. M. (2020). *Short Term Rentals (STR) | City of Bozeman*. https://www.bozeman.net/government/planning/short-term-rentals-str

Brouder, P. (2014). Evolutionary economic geography: a new path for tourism studies? *Tourism Geographies*, *16*(1), 2–7. https://doi.org/10.1080/14616688.2013.864323

Butler, R. (2008). A tourism are life cycle in the twenty-first century. In A. A. Lew, C. M. Hall, & A. M. Williams (Eds.), *A companion to tourism*. John Wiley & Sons.159-169

Butler, R. W. (1980). The concept of a tourist area cycle of evolution: implications for management of resources. *The Canadian Geographer/Le Géographe Canadien*, *24*(1), 5–12. https://doi.org/10.1111/j.1541-0064.1980.tb00970.x

Chattanooga GIS. (2020). *Short term vacation rental map*. https://pwgis.chattanooga.gov/portal/apps/webappviewer/index.html?id=708ed4e6a41546369df346151197397b

Chhabra, D., Healy, R., & Sills, E. (2003). Staged authenticity and heritage tourism. *Annals of Tourism Research*, *30*(3), 702–719. https://doi.org/10.1016/S0160-7383(03)00044-6

City of Dunedin. (2020). *City of Dunedin Basemap*. https://dunedin-gis.maps.arcgis.com/apps/webappviewer/index.html?id=5590c8f613394a9c99b83960b839ef5c

City of Savannah. (2020). *Registered STVR map | Savannah, GA - Official Website*. https://www.savannahga.gov/2329/Registered-STVR-map

Clarke, J. (1997). A framework of approaches to sustainable tourism. *Journal of Sustainable Tourism*, *5*(3), 224–233. https://doi.org/10.1080/09669589708667287

Cohen, E. (1988). Authenticity and commoditization in tourism. *Annals of Tourism Research*, *15*(3), 371–386. https://doi.org/10.1016/0160-7383(88)90028-X

Corbett, J., & Keller, C. (2003). *Speaking maps: Use of digital maps and multimedia by local communities to influence decision making in West Kutai Indonesia*. Paper presented at the Proceedings of the 21st International Cartographic Association Meeting, Durban, South Africa.

Costanza, R. (1992). Toward an operational definition of ecosystem health. In *Ecosystem health: New goals for environmental management* (pp. 239–256) Haskell B, Norton B, Costanza R editors. Island Press

Curl, E. (2017). Savannah considering temporary halt on vacation rentals. *Savannah Morning News*. http://www.savannahnow.com/news/2017-06-08/savannah-considering-temporary-halt-vacation-rentals

Davidson, N. M., & Infranca, J. J. (2016). The sharing economy as an urban phenomenon. *Yale L. & Pol'y Rev*, *34*, 215–545.

Davis, J. S. (2005). Representing place: "Deserted isles" and the reproduction of Bikini Atoll. *Annals of the Association of American Geographers*, *95*(3), 607–625. https://doi.org/10.1111/j.1467-8306.2005.00477.x

Davis, J. S., & Morais, D. B. (2004). Factions and enclaves: Small towns and socially unsustainable tourism development. *Journal of Travel Research*, *43*(1), 3–10. https://doi.org/10.1177/0047287504265501

Destination Analysts. (2020). *COVID-19 insights*. Retrieved July 2, 2020, from https://www.destinationanalysts.com/covid-19-insights/

Dias, J. A., Correia, A., & López, F. J. M. (2015). The meaning of rental second homes and places: the owners' perspectives. *Tourism Geographies*, *17*(2), 244–261. https://doi.org/10.1080/14616688.2014.959992

Dolnicar, S. (2019). A review of research into paid online peer-to-peer accommodation: Launching the Annals of Tourism Research curated collection on peer-to-peer accommodation. *Annals of Tourism Research*, *75*, 248–264. https://doi.org/10.1016/j.annals.2019.02.003

Doxey, G. V. (1975). *A causation theory of visitor-resident irritants: Methodology and research inferences*. Paper presented at the the impact of tourism sixth annual conference proc of the travel research Association.

England, J. L., & Albrecht, S. L. (1984). Boomtowns and social disruption. *Rural Sociology*, *49*(2), 230.

Farmaki, A., Stergiou, D. P., & Christou, P. (2020). Sharing economy: peer-to-peer accommodation as a foucauldian heterotopia. *Tourism Review*. https://doi.org/10.1108/TR-08-2019-0354

Foucault, M., & Miskowiec, J. (1986). Of other spaces. *Diacritics*, *16*(1), 22. https://search.proquest.com/docview/1297883411/fulltextPDF/B3B58B042F8F400FPQ/1?accountid=10639 https://doi.org/10.2307/464648

Garau-Vadell, J. B., Gutiérrez-Taño, D., & Díaz-Armas, R. (2019). Residents' support for P2P accommodation in mass tourism destinations. *Journal of Travel Research*, *58*(4), 549–565. https://doi.org/10.1177/0047287518767067

Glusac, E. (2020). Hotels vs. Airbnb: Has Covid-19 disrupted the disrupter? *New York Times*. https://www.nytimes.com/2020/05/14/travel/hotels-versus-airbnb-pandemic.html

Gössling, S., Peeters, P., Ceron, J.-P., Dubois, G., Patterson, T., & Richardson, R. B. (2005). The eco-efficiency of tourism. *Ecological Economics*, *54*(4), 417–434. https://doi.org/10.1016/j.ecolecon.2004.10.006

Gössling, S., Scott, D., & Hall, C. M. (2020). *Pandemics, tourism and global change: a rapid assessment of COVID-19*. https://doi.org/10.1080/09669582.2020.1758708

Gurran, N., & Phibbs, P. (2017). When tourists move in: how should urban planners respond to Airbnb? *Journal of the American Planning Association*, *83*(1), 80–92. https://doi.org/10.1080/01944363.2016.1249011

Gursoy, D., & Rutherford, D. G. (2004). Host attitudes toward tourism: An improved structural model. *Annals of Tourism Research*, *31*(3), 495–516. https://doi.org/10.1016/j.annals.2003.08.008

Guttentag, D. (2015). Airbnb: disruptive innovation and the rise of an informal tourism accommodation sector. *Current Issues in Tourism*, *18*(12), 1192–1217. https://doi.org/10.1080/13683500.2013.827159

Harley, J. B. (1989). Deconstructing the map. *Cartographica: The International Journal for Geographic Information and Geovisualization*, *26*(2), 1–20. https://doi.org/10.3138/E635-7827-1757-9T53

Hartmans, A. (2017, October 8). *Airbnb now has more listings worldwide than the top five hotel brands combined*. http://www.businessinsider.com/airbnb-total-worldwide-listings-2017-8

Heo, Y. (2016). Sharing economy and prospects in tourism research. *Annals of Tourism Research*, *58*, 166–170. https://doi.org/10.1016/j.annals.2016.02.002

Hirsch, P. D., Adams, W. M., Brosius, J. P., Zia, A., Bariola, N., & Dammert, J. L. (2011). Acknowledging conservation trade-offs and embracing complexity. *Conservation Biology*, *25*(2), 259–264. https://doi.org/10.1111/j.1523-1739.2010.01608.x

Holling, C. S. (2001). Understanding the complexity of economic, ecological, and social systems. *Ecosystems*, *4*(5), 390–405. https://doi.org/10.1007/s10021-001-0101-5

Horn, K., & Merante, M. (2017). Is home sharing driving up rents? Evidence from Airbnb in Boston. *Journal of Housing Economics*, *38*, 14–24. https://doi.org/10.1016/j.jhe.2017.08.002

Ikkala, T., & Lampinen, A. (2015). *Monetizing network hospitality: Hospitality and sociability in the context of airbnb*. Paper presented at the Proceedings of the 18th ACM conference on computer supported cooperative work & social computing.

Jackson, E. (2008). Whatever happened to Georgia's downtown hotels? *Georgia History Today*, 2-3.

Jordan, E. J., & Moore, J. (2017). An in-depth exploration of residents' perceived impacts of transient vacation rentals. *Journal of Travel & Tourism Marketing*, 35, 1–12.

Karlsson, L., & Dolnicar, S. (2016). Someone's been sleeping in my bed. *Annals of Tourism Research*, *58*, 159–162. https://doi.org/10.1016/j.annals.2016.02.006

Koh, K. (2002). Explaining a community touristscape: an entrepreneurism model. *International Journal of Hospitality & Tourism Administration*, *3*(2), 29–62.

Kreag, Gl. (2001). *The Impacts of Tourism – Google Books*. Minnesota Sea Grant Program. https://www.google.com/books/edition/The_Impacts_of_Tourism/SgiHHAAACAAJ?hl=en

Lawler, R. (2012). *Airbnb launches neighborhoods, providing the definitive travel guide for local neighborhoods*. https://techcrunch.com/2012/11/13/airbnb-launches-neighborhoods-providing-the-definitive-travel-guide-for-its-guests/

Lee, D. (2016). How Airbnb short-term rentals exacerbate Los Angeles's affordable housing crisis: Analysis and policy recommendations. *Harvard Law & Policy Review*, *10*, 229.

Lefebvre, H., & Nicholson-Smith, D. (1991). *The production of space* (Vol. 142). Oxford Blackwell.

Leiper, N. (1990). *Tourism systems: An interdisciplinary perspective*. Department of Management Systems, Business Studies Faculty, Massey University Palmerston North.

Lew, A. A. (2017). Tourism planning and place making: place-making or placemaking? *Tourism Geographies*, *19*(3), 448–466. https://doi.org/10.1080/14616688.2017.1282007

Lewis, P. F. (1979). Axioms for reading the landscape. *The Interpretation of Ordinary Landscapes*, *23*, 167–187.

Lobel, O. (2016). The law of the platform. *Minnesota Law Review*, 101: 16–212.

MacCannell, D. (1973). Staged authenticity: Arrangements of social space in tourist settings. *American Journal of Sociology*, *79*(3), 589–603. https://doi.org/10.1086/225585

Madrigal, R. (1993). A tale of tourism in two cities. *Annals of Tourism Research*, *20*(2), 336–353. https://doi.org/10.1016/0160-7383(93)90059-C

Martin, B. S., & Uysal, M. (1990). An examination of the relationship between carrying capacity and the tourism life-cycle: Management and policy implications. *Journal of Environmental Management, 31*(4), 327–333. https://doi.org/10.1016/S0301-4797(05)80061-1 https://doi.org/10.1016/S0301-4797(05)80061-1

Martin, K. (2018). *Beacon city council votes "no" to Airbnb type short-term rentals - Striking down their own legislation.* https://www.alittlebeaconblog.com/blog/airbnbs-fate-in-beacon-right-now-no-vote-on-short-term-rentals-from-city-council

Massey, D. (2010). *A global sense of place.* Aughty.org.

McCarthy, N. (2020, May 5). COVID-19's impact on tourism: Which countries are the most vulnerable? [Infographic]. *Forbes.* https://www.forbes.com/sites/niallmccarthy/2020/05/05/covid-19s-impact-on-tourism-which-countries-are-the-most-vulnerable-infographic/#524d9e61906a

McKercher, B. (1999). A chaos approach to tourism. *Tourism Management, 20*(4), 425–434. https://doi.org/10.1016/S0261-5177(99)00008-4

McKercher, B., Wang, D., & Park, E. (2015). Social impacts as a function of place change. *Annals of Tourism Research, 50,* 52–66. https://www.nytimes.com/2016/10/22/technology/new-york-passes-law-airbnb.html https://doi.org/10.1016/j.annals.2014.11.002

Meleo, L., Romolini, A., & De Marco, M. (2016). The sharing economy revolution and peer-to-peer online platforms. The case of Airbnb. *Lecture Notes in Business Information Processing, 247,* 561–570. https://doi.org/10.1007/978-3-319-32689-4_43

Michalos, A. (2003). *Essays on the quality of life.* Springer Science & Business Media. https://www.google.com/books/edition/Essays_on_the_Quality_of_Life/h6_sCAAAQBAJ?hl=en&gbpv=1&pg=PR7&printsec=frontcover

Mill, R. C., & Morrison, A. M. (1985). *The tourist system.* Prentice-Hall.

Minder, R. (2018, June 23). To contain tourism, one Spanish city strikes a ban, on Airbnb, Europe. *The New York Times.* https://www.nytimes.com/2018/06/23/world/europe/tourism-spain-airbnb-ban.html

Morris, S. L. (2015). Airbnb is infuriating the neighbors. Is it time for new rules? *LA Weekly.*

Navarro Jurado, E., Damian, I. M., & Fernández-Morales, A. (2013). Carrying capacity model applied in coastal destinations. *Annals of Tourism Research, 43,* 1–19. https://doi.org/10.1016/j.annals.2013.03.005

Nieuwland, S., & Van Melik, R. (2018). Current issues in tourism regulating Airbnb: How cities deal with perceived negative externalities of short-term rentals. *Current Issues in Tourism, 23*(7), 811–825. https://doi.org/10.1080/13683500.2018.1504899

Nunkoo, R., & Gursoy, D. (2012). Residents' support for tourism: An identity perspective. *Annals of Tourism Research, 39*(1), 243–268. https://doi.org/10.1016/j.annals.2011.05.006

Odum, E. P. (1985). Trends expected in stressed ecosystems. *BioScience, 35*(7), 419–422. https://doi.org/10.2307/1310021

Ostrom, E. (1990). Analyzing long-enduring, self-organized, and self-governed CPRs. In *Governing the commons. The evolution of institutions for collective action.* In: Cambridge University Press, editors. Cambridge University Press (pp. 58–102).

Peltier, D. (2017, December 29). Tourism board engagement with Airbnb is not one-size fits all. *Skift.* https://skift.com/2017/12/29/many-tourism-boards-remain-trepid-on-airbnb-but-know-its-a-force-to-be-reckoned-with/

Perdue, R. R., Long, P. T., & Kang, Y. S. (1999). Boomtown tourism and resident quality of life: The marketing of gaming to host community residents. *Journal of Business Research, 44*(3), 165–177. https://doi.org/10.1016/S0148-2963(97)00198-7

Ramos, S. P., & Mundet, L. (2020). Tourism-phobia in Barcelona: dismantling discursive strategies and power games in the construction of a sustainable tourist city. *Journal of Tourism and Cultural Change,* 1–19. https://doi.org/10.1080/14766825.2020.1752224

Reyes, E. (2020, August 9). Thousands of listings violate L.A.'s new short-term rental law. *Los Angeles Times.* https://www.latimes.com/california/story/2020-08-09/los-angeles-short-term-rental-violations

Richardson, L. (2015). Performing the sharing economy. *Geoforum, 67,* 121–129. https://doi.org/10.1016/j.geoforum.2015.11.004

Rickly-Boyd, J. M., Knudsen, D. C., & Braverman, L. C. (2016). *Tourism, performance, and place: A geographic perspective.* Routledge.

Rocheleau, D. (2005). Maps as power tools: Locating communities in space or situating. In *Communities and conservation: Histories and politics of community-based natural resource management.*In: Tsing A, Zerner C, Brosius P editors. Alta Mira Press.(p. 327).

Roelofsen, M., & Minca, C. (2018). The Superhost. Biopolitics, home and community in the Airbnb dream-world of global hospitality. *Geoforum, 91,* 170–181. https://doi.org/10.1016/j.geoforum.2018.02.021

Rogers, S. (2020, March 18). *How virtual reality could help the travel & tourism industry in the aftermath of the coronavirus outbreak.* https://www.forbes.com/sites/solrogers/2020/03/18/virtual-reality-and-tourism-whats-already-happening-is-it-the-future/#73265da728a6

Rogoway, M. (2020, March 20). Portland vacation rental giant Vacasa lays off employees, cuts pay and hours amid coronavirus outbreak - oregonlive.com. *The Oregonian/Oregon Live.* https://www.oregonlive.com/silicon-forest/

2020/03/portland-vacation-rental-giant-vasasa-lays-off-employees-cuts-pay-and-hours-amid-coronavirus-outbreak.html

Russell, R., & Faulkner, B. (2004). Entrepreneurship, chaos and the tourism area lifecycle. *Annals of Tourism Research*, *31*(3), 556–579. https://doi.org/10.1016/j.annals.2004.01.008

Sauer, C. (1925). The morphology of landscape. *University of California Publications in Geography*, *2*, 19–54.

Senge, P. M. (2000). Systems change in education. *Reflections: The SoL Journal*, *1*(3), 52–60. https://doi.org/10.1162/152417300570069

Shields, R. (2013). *Places on the margin: Alternative geographies of modernity*. Routledge.

Sigala, M. (2014). Collaborative commerce in tourism: implications for research and industry. *Current Issues in Tourism*,(20) 1–10.

Smolka, C., & Hienerth, C. (2014). *The best of both worlds: conceptualizing trade-offs between openness and closedness for sharing economy models*. Paper presented at the 12th International Open and User Innovation Conference.

Sofield, T. H. B., & Birtles, R. A. (1996). Indigenous peoples' cultural opportunity spectrum for tourism (IPCOST). *Indigenous Peoples' Cultural Opportunity Spectrum for Tourism (IPCOST)*, 396–433.

Spencer, D. M., & Nsiah, C. (2013). The economic consequences of community support for tourism: A case study of a heritage fish hatchery. *Tourism Management*, *34*, 221–230. https://doi.org/10.1016/j.tourman.2012.04.003

Steinmetz, K. (2016). Exlusive: See how big the gig economy really is. *TIME*.

Stergiou, D. P., & Farmaki, A. (2020). Resident perceptions of the impacts of P2P accommodation: Implications for neighbourhoods. *International Journal of Hospitality Management*, *91*, 102411. https://doi.org/10.1016/j.ijhm.2019.102411

Steves, R. (2017). *Rick Steves Europe through the back door: The travel skills handbook: Steves, Rick: 9,781,631,216,251: Amazon.com: Books* (37th ed.). https://www.amazon.com/Rick-Steves-Europe-Through-Back/dp/1,631,216,252

Stors, N. (2020). Constructing new urban tourism space through Airbnb. *Tourism Geographies*, 1–24. https://doi.org/10.1080/14616688.2020.1750683

Suess, C., Woosnam, K., Mody, M., Dogru, T., & Sirakaya Turk, E. (2020). Understanding how residents' emotional solidarity with Airbnb visitors influences perceptions of their impact on a community: The moderating role of prior experience staying at an Airbnb. *Journal of Travel Research*, 004728752092123. https://doi.org/10.1177/0047287520921234

Swyngedouw, E. (2004). Scaled geographies: Nature, place, and the politics of scale. Sheppard E, McMaster R, In *Scale and geographic inquiry: Nature, society, and method* (pp. 129–153) Blackwell Publishing Ltd.

Thomas, O. (2012). Airbnb is turning itself into a local-business guide. *Business Insider*. http://www.businessinsider.com/airbnb-local-business-localmind-nabewise-acquisition-2012-12

Tokarchuk, O., Gabriele, R., & Maurer, O. (2020). Estimating tourism social carrying capacity. *Annals of Tourism Research*, 102971. https://doi.org/10.1016/j.annals.2020.102971

Törnberg, P., & Chiappini, L. (2020). Selling black places on Airbnb: Colonial discourse and the marketing of black communities in New York City. *Environment and Planning A: Economy and Space*, *52*(3), 553–572. https://doi.org/10.1177/0308518X19886321

Tuan, Y.-F. (1975). Place: an experiential perspective. *Geographical Review*, *65*(2), 151–165. https://doi.org/10.2307/213970

Tussyadiah, I. P., & Pesonen, J. (2016). Impacts of peer-to-peer accommodation use on travel patterns. *Journal of Travel Research*, *55*(8), 1022–1040. https://doi.org/10.1177/0047287515608505

Tussyadiah, I. P., & Zach, F. J. (2015). Hotels vs. peer-to-peer accommodation rentals: Text analytics of consumer reviews in Portland, Oregon. *Peer-to-Peer Accommodation Rentals: Text Analytics of Consumer Reviews in Portland, Oregon (April 10, 2015)*.

United Nations. (2018). 68% of the world population projected to live in urban areas by 2050, says UN | UN DESA | United Nations Department of Economic and Social Affairs. *Department of Economic and Social Affairs News*. https://www.un.org/development/desa/en/news/population/2018-revision-of-world-urbanization-prospects.html

UNWTO. (2020, May). *Impact assessment of the COVID-19 outbreak on international tourism*. Retrieved July 2, 2020 from https://www.unwto.org/impact-assessment-of-the-covid-19-outbreak-on-international-tourism

Urry, J. (1990). Theconsumption'of tourism. *Sociology*, *24*(1), 23–35. https://doi.org/10.1177/0038038590024001004

Urry, J. (1992). The tourist gaze "revisited". *American Behavioral Scientist*, *36*(2), 172–186. https://doi.org/10.1177/0002764292036002005

Uysal, M., Sirgy, M. J., Woo, E., & Kim, H. L. (2016). Quality of life (QOL) and well-being research in tourism. *Tourism Management*, *53*, 244–261. https://doi.org/10.1016/j.tourman.2015.07.013

van Doorn, N. (2020). A new institution on the block: On platform urbanism and Airbnb citizenship. *New Media & Society*, *22*(10), 1808–1826. https://doi.org/10.1177/1461444819884377

Von Bertalanffy, L. (1950). An outline of general system theory. *British Journal for the Philosophy of Science*.

Wachsmuth, D., & Weisler, A. (2017). Airbnb and the rent gap: Gentrification through the sharing economy. *Environment and Planning A: Economy and Space*, *50*(6), 1147–1170.

Widener, M. N. (2015). Shared spatial regulating in sharing-economy districts. *Seton Hall Law Review*, *46*, 111.

Woo, E., Kim, H., & Uysal, M. (2015). Life satisfaction and support for tourism development. *Annals of Tourism Research*, *50*, 84–97. https://doi.org/10.1016/j.annals.2014.11.001

Yang, Y., & Mao, Z. (2019). Welcome to my home! An empirical analysis of Airbnb supply in US cities. *Journal of Travel Research*, *58*(8), 1274–1287. https://doi.org/10.1177/0047287518815984

Yeager, E. P., Boley, B. B., Woosnam, K. M., & Green, G. T. (2020). Modeling residents' attitudes toward short-term vacation rentals. *Journal of Travel Research*, *59*(6), 955–974. https://doi.org/10.1177/0047287519870255

Zhu, Y., Cheng, M., Wang, J., Ma, L., & Jiang, R. (2019). The construction of home feeling by Airbnb guests in the sharing economy: A semantics perspective. *Annals of Tourism Research*, *75*, 308–321. https://doi.org/10.1016/j.annals.2018.12.013

Zieleniec, A. J. (2007). *Space and social theory*. Sage.

Support for tourism: the roles of attitudes, subjective wellbeing, and emotional solidarity

Ian E. Munanura, Mark D. Needham, Kreg Lindberg, Chad Kooistra and Ladan Ghahramani

ABSTRACT
Research models applying social exchange theory to examine factors predicting residents' support for tourism have been challenged for their inability to explain support fully. Recent studies drawing from other theories indicated factors that arguably play a role in the social exchange relationship between perceptions of tourism impacts and support. One factor of interest is the cognitive appraisal process eliciting emotional solidarity with tourists (ES), which arguably predicts support. According to cognitive appraisal theory (CAT), residents' emotional feelings toward tourists result from a mental evaluation of how tourism is perceived to impact one's wellbeing. Although tourism studies applying CAT are emerging, knowledge is limited about the cognitive appraisal process that elicits ES. This article examines the nature of a cognitive appraisal process eliciting ES. Data were obtained from a random sample of 1477 residents of Oregon, United States. Results from a structural equation model, show that perceived positive tourism impacts strongly predict ES. Additionally, perceived positive tourism impacts indirectly impact ES through the expected change of wellbeing. This study also reveals that perceived negative community tourism impacts have a negative relationship with ES. Moreover, ES strongly predicts support. The article closes with a discussion of research and management implications.

Introduction

Residents' support for tourism has received substantial attention (e.g. Allen et al., 1993; Boley et al., 2014; Nunkoo & Ramkissoon, 2012). Theoretical reviews (Nunkoo et al., 2013; Sharpley, 2014) and empirical studies across multiple geographical contexts have enhanced understanding of support for tourism (McGehee & Andereck, 2004; Nunkoo et al., 2010; Ouyang et al., 2017; Phuc & Nguyen, 2020). Some research indicates that when residents perceive tourism negatively, it impacts the future security of tourism (McGehee & Andereck, 2004). In some cases, negative tourism impacts (e.g. increase in crime) cause resentment among residents and subsequently reduce their support for tourism (Woosnam, 2012). Research also associates perceived positive tourism impacts (e.g. improved community infrastructure) with support for tourism development (Nunkoo & So, 2016; Nunkoo et al., 2010).

Understanding ways to enhance resident support for tourism is critical for sustainable tourism planning and management (Nunkoo & So, 2016; Sharpley, 2014). For tourism to be sustainable, its management must have actions and strategies informed by knowledge of tourism impacts. Controlling causes of impacts may reduce actual problems or change the perceptions of the problems, and potentially enhance residents' positive emotional reactions about tourists and their overall support for tourism. Some studies explore residents' support for tourism using social exchange theory (SET) (Sharpley, 2014). However, some have criticized SET's inadequacies (e.g. emphasis on economic gains to explain the exchange), in explaining support (Boley et al., 2014; Erul et al., 2020; Nunkoo & Ramkissoon, 2012; Sharpley, 2014; Woosnam, 2012). Therefore, a need exists to examine the utility of other theories that can explain the determining factors of support for tourism, including those of an intangible nature (Joo et al., 2018; Nunkoo & So, 2016; Ouyang et al., 2017; Phuc & Nguyen, 2020; Woosnam, 2012).

Many studies highlight a need for research that addresses how residents' feelings about tourists affect perceived tourism impacts and support (Woosnam, 2011, 2012; Woosnam & Norman, 2010; Woosnam et al., 2009). Since the introduction of the emotional solidarity with tourists (ES) concept by Woosnam et al. (2009), a number of empirical studies reveal that emotional reactions play a role in determining perceived tourism impacts and support (e.g. Hasani et al., 2016; Joo et al., 2018; Maruyama et al., 2019; Moghavvemi et al., 2017; Wang et al., 2020; Woosnam, 2012; Woosnam & Aleshinloye, 2018). However, according to cognitive appraisal theory (CAT), residents' emotional feelings stem from their evaluation of how tourism benefits or harms personal wellbeing (Smith & Lazarus, 1993). Although recent studies about attitudes toward tourists apply CAT (e.g. Ouyang et al., 2017; Zheng et al., 2019a, 2019b), room exists to explore the cognitive appraisal process that elicits ES. Additionally, studies that integrate wellbeing in the relationship between perceptions of tourism impacts and ES (e.g. Lai et al., 2020) lack an integrative theory linking ES to potential determinants (e.g. wellbeing and perceptions of tourism impacts).

This study addresses this knowledge gap by examining the nature of the cognitive appraisal process involving perceptions of tourism impacts, the expected impact of tourism growth on wellbeing, ES, and tourism support. Drawing on CAT (Lazarus & Smith, 1988; Smith & Lazarus, 1993), this study considers the proposition that residents' positive emotional reactions to tourists (commonly referred to as ES) are an outcome of a cognitive appraisal process that involves a mental evaluation of how tourism benefits or harms an individual's goals and desires. Therefore, this study aims to understand the relationship between ES and support for tourism, and the cognitive appraisal-based determinants of ES (i.e. perceptions of tourism impacts and expected changes in subjective wellbeing). This article utilizes empirical data from Oregon (United States) and discusses the theoretical underpinnings of the proposition above, the methodological approach, empirical results, and implications for research and management.

Conceptual background

This article integrates CAT and the concept of ES into the SET-based conceptual model that links perceptions of tourism impacts to support for tourism. SET is applied to infer a relationship that exists between perceptions of tourism impacts and support for tourism. This study focuses on understanding the factors and processes that are involved in the SET-based relationship between perceptions of tourism impacts and support. Following Woosnam (2012), the concept of ES is applied to understand if residents' emotions about tourists predict their support for tourism. CAT is applied to understand perceptions that determine these emotions. Understanding the cognitive appraisal process that elicits positive emotional reactions to tourists should: (a) increase knowledge about how positive emotions about tourists are formed, and (b) inform management decisions concerning the investment of scarce public resources in activities likely to generate tourism support. Figure 1 illustrates the hypothesized relationships.

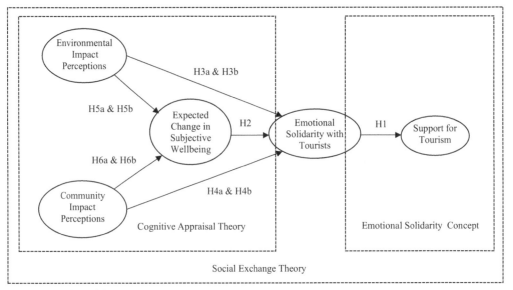

Figure 1. Research model.

Support for tourism: the SET perspective

SET, according to Ap (1992), is a sociological theory that aims to explain the exchange of resources between people through interaction. In tourism studies, SET provides a conceptual base through which "inter-relationships among perceptions of costs and benefits, positive and negative impacts, and support for tourism" are explored (Ward & Berno, 2011). Undoubtedly, SET remains a dominant lens through which researchers examine determinants of residents' support for tourism (e.g. Allen et al., 1993; Boley et al., 2014; Nunkoo & So, 2016). Studies applying SET show that perceptions of positive impacts (e.g. jobs and income) and negative tourism impacts (e.g. tourism-induced crime and pollution) often predict overall support for tourism. For example, efforts to minimize negative impacts and maximize benefits likely results in positive interactions between residents and tourists, which arguably strengthen tourism support (McGehee & Andereck, 2004). Tourism benefits are more likely than negative issues to be associated with positive support for tourism (Nunkoo & So, 2016). Similarly, residents who experience any adverse effects from tourism (e.g. overcrowding of social services) are less likely to support tourism (Andereck et al., 2005). Studies applying SET across multiple geographical contexts have sufficiently supported existence of the relationship between perceptions of tourism impacts and overall tourism support (Boley et al., 2014; Nunkoo & Ramkissoon, 2012; Nunkoo & So, 2016). However, knowledge of the cognitive process through which such an exchange-based transactional relationship occurs remains inconclusive (Nunkoo & So, 2016; Sharpley, 2014; Zheng et al., 2019a, 2019b). Therefore, given that the relationship between perceived tourism impacts and support is established knowledge, this article focuses on understanding the underlying cognitive factors (e.g. perceived impacts of tourism, perceived effect of tourism on wellbeing, and ES) likely involved in the exchange process. CAT and the ES concept are introduced next in support of the hypothesized relationships.

Emotional solidarity concept

Although many researchers apply SET in tourism attitude studies, other studies challenge SET's ability to fully explain tourism support (Boley et al., 2014; Nunkoo & So, 2016; Sharpley, 2014). Some studies indicate that the exchange relationship argument likely misses the role of intangible factors involved in the exchange. For example, one study indicates that the psychological benefits of tourism have positive relationship with tourism support (Boley et al., 2014). Another identifies how ES (i.e. welcoming nature and sympathetic understanding dimensions) significantly predicts tourism support (Woosnam, 2012). These empirical findings validate Sharpley's (2014) criticism of the utility of SET in explaining support for tourism. Remedial efforts have since emerged in the literature (e.g. Boley et al., 2014; Erul et al., 2020; Nunkoo & Ramkissoon, 2009, 2012; Nunkoo & So, 2016; Woosnam, 2012). These studies conceptually and empirically demonstrate the value of employing alternative theoretical frameworks to address the exchange process's complexity in tourism attitude studies. Among the emerging and popular alternative frameworks applied to understand support for tourism is the concept of ES (e.g. Erul et al., 2020; Joo et al., 2018; Maruyama et al., 2019; Woosnam, 2012; Woosnam et al., 2009).

The ES concept is drawn from sociology and applied in studies aimed to examine the feeling of togetherness and sense of emotional bond between people (Woosnam & Norman, 2009). The concept is rooted in Durkheim's (1915) theory of affective bonds between people formed through interactions, shared beliefs, and behaviors (Woosnam & Norman, 2010). Woosnam et al. (2009; Woosnam & Norman, 2010) introduced the ES concept to tourism studies and argued that understanding residents' feelings about tourists could enhance knowledge about residents' overall support for tourism. Tourism attitude studies that apply the ES concept argue that residents who: (a) welcome tourists, (b) feel a close bond with tourists, and (c) sympathize with tourists are typically open-minded, interested in tourism, and therefore, likely to support tourism development (Moghavvemi et al., 2017; Phuc & Nguyen, 2020; Woosnam, 2012). As a result, the following hypothesis is tested:

Hypothesis 1(H1): ES will predict support for tourism. A high level of ES will relate to greater support, whereas less ES will relate to less support.

The cognitive appraisal theory perspective

The concept of ES, as noted earlier, represents feelings of identification and bonding with tourists (Woosnam & Norman, 2010). According to cognitive psychology, feelings result from emotions emerging from the mental processing of information associated with events (e.g. tourism) or people (e.g. tourists) (Skavronskaya et al., 2017). CAT provides a framework for understanding how emotions are formed (Lazarus, 1991; Smith & Lazarus, 1993; Watson & Spence, 2007). Cognitive psychologists argue that emotions are outcomes of a cognitive appraisal process wherein individuals evaluate the positive or negative impacts of a particular stimulus (e.g. an event such as tourism or people such as tourists) on wellbeing (Lazarus, 1991). Emotions are also responses to harmful or beneficial events that trigger adaptive behavior, such as reacting positively to tourists (Smith & Lazarus, 1993). The cognitive appraisal of an event's positive and negative characteristics is defined as outcome desirability (Watson & Spence, 2007). In the tourism studies context, outcome desirability of tourism events or tourist interactions with residents is appraised by evaluating tourism impacts (Zheng et al., 2019a, 2019b). Outcome desirability represents the initial step of the appraisal, wherein individuals make determinations about event characteristics relative to the appraiser's wellbeing (Watson & Spence, 2007). Following the outcome desirability appraisal (e.g. how tourism impacts affect one's wellbeing), an emotional reaction occurs (e.g. ES), which then elicits adaptive behavioral responses that are most likely to sustain benefits from the stimuli (e.g. a decision to support for tourism or not) (Watson & Spence, 2007).

An individual's emotional reaction to tourism (as an event) or interaction with tourists is determined by how that individual's wellbeing is affected by the event or interaction (Smith & Lazarus, 1993). This effect depends on the individual's wellbeing goal relevance and congruence (Smith & Lazarus, 1993). For example, tourism may prove relevant if an individual perceives job creation role of tourism to be important. Tourism is congruent when there is a directional match between the event and wellbeing (e.g. an individual who values an increase in jobs and tourism generates the increase). In contrast, if an individual cares about environmental conservation and wants conservation to be sustained, but perceives that tourism negatively impacts conservation, that aspect would be relevant, but incongruent. Additionally, if tourism increased performing arts in the community, but the individual did not care about performing arts, that aspect would not be relevant. These examples represent one of the two critical factors underlying the cognitive appraisal process. That is, the appraised event or situation (e.g. perception of tourism impacts) ought to be relevant to one's wellbeing (e.g. expectation that the event will improve wellbeing) to produce positive emotions toward tourism or tourists (Smith & Lazarus, 1993). This argument supports emerging studies in the literature that connect perceptions of tourism impacts, wellbeing, and emotional reactions to tourism (e.g. Lai et al., 2020; Ouyang et al., 2017; Phuc & Nguyen, 2020; Zheng et al., 2020). However, empirical studies also document evidence of a direct relationship between tourism impacts and ES that is not mediated by the perceived impact on wellbeing (e.g. Phuc & Nguyen, 2020).

The second critical factor underlying the cognitive appraisal process is the efficacy-oriented adaptation behavior elicited by an emotional reaction to the outcome desirability appraisal (e.g. a decision to support tourism following the positive appraisal that tourism benefits an individual) (Smith & Lazarus, 1993). This argument supports the proposition that the outcome desirability appraisal process produces emotional reactions about tourism or tourists, potentially resulting in the decision to support tourism. Emotions may play a role in the relationship between cognitive appraisal of tourism and adaptive behavior to optimize or maintain the appraised benefits through support for tourism (Hasani et al., 2016; Nyer, 1997). Thus, the following hypotheses are tested:

> *Hypothesis 2 (H2):* Expected change in subjective wellbeing from tourism growth predicts ES. The likelihood of having positive feelings about tourists is higher when residents expect a more positive change in subjective wellbeing from tourism growth.
>
> *Hypothesis 3 (H3):* Positive (H3a) and negative (H3b) perceptions of environmental impacts from tourism predict ES. Perceived positive environmental impacts are likely to increase with residents' ES, whereas perceived negative environmental impacts are likely to decrease with ES.
>
> *Hypothesis 4 (H4):* Positive (H4a) and negative (H4b) perceptions of community impacts from tourism predict ES. Perceived positive community impacts are likely to increase with residents' ES, whereas perceived negative community impacts are likely to decrease with ES.
>
> *Hypothesis 5 (H5):* Positive (H5a) and negative (H5b) perceptions of environmental impacts from tourism predict expected changes in subjective wellbeing from tourism growth. Perceived positive environmental impacts are likely to increase with positive changes in subjective wellbeing expected from tourism, whereas perceived negative environmental impacts are likely to decrease with positive changes expected from tourism.
>
> *Hypothesis 6 (H6):* Positive (H6a) and negative (H6b) perceptions of community impacts from tourism predict expected changes in subjective wellbeing from tourism growth. Perceived positive community impacts are likely to increase with positive changes in subjective wellbeing expected from tourism, whereas perceived negative community impacts are likely to decrease with positive changes expected from tourism.

Methods

Study region

Data were obtained from a survey of residents in Oregon (USA) during the summer of 2018. Tourism is one of Oregon's critical economic sectors, with an average annual growth in tourism earnings estimated at approximately 6% over the past 10 years (Dean Runyan Associates, 2018). In 2018, travel spending in Oregon increased by approximately 4% and generated approximately $12 billion (Dean Runyan Associates, 2018). In the same year, Oregon's tourism employment increased by approximately 3% and tax revenue increased by approximately 6% (Dean Runyan Associates, 2018). Oregon policymakers, tourism management companies, marketing institutions, and the private sector hope to optimize tourism's potential to impact Oregonians positively. However, a limited understanding of the level of support for tourism and its determinants exists throughout the state.

Data collection

This study's sample included residents across all seven tourism regions in Oregon (Central, Coast, Eastern, Mt. Hood, Portland, Southern, Willamette Valley; Figure 2). Data were obtained from questionnaires administered: (a) to an online Qualtrics panel ($n = 728$; 19% response rate; complete responses from each of the seven tourism regions ranged from $n = 87$ to 124), and (b) by mixed-mode mail-based sample with paper and online completion options ($n = 749$, 18% response rate; complete responses from each of the seven regions ranged from $n = 97$ to 123). Online and mail survey data were obtained between June and September 2018. A Qualtrics panel is an online opt-in survey that is becoming increasingly popular and cost-effective for collecting data (Brandon et al., 2014). Data from the Qualtrics panel used several attention checks to minimize potential measurement bias. The mixed-mode mail survey sample was obtained using a stratified random sampling approach (e.g. a random sample of addresses from within each of the seven tourism regions). This sample was collected using a modified mixed-mode design following Dillman et al. (2014) guidelines. First, a pre-notification letter with a link to complete the questionnaire online was mailed to the sample. Two weeks later, a full packet (questionnaire, letter, postage-paid reply envelope) was mailed to potential participants. Subsequent mailings included a reminder postcard and another full packet. The obtained data from both Qualtrics panel and mixed-mode mail survey were combined to address differences in demographic characteristics and ensure that demographic distribution in the data is closely aligned to the US census data on the population of Oregon. Additionally, the data was weighted by gender, age, and education to address the remaining differences between the sample and population. The total sample size was 1477 residents. Given that about 80% of the mail survey sample did not return a completed questionnaire, a telephone nonresponse bias check was conducted with a random sample of 98 nonrespondents, asking them nine questions from the questionnaire (Vaske, 2019). There were no substantive differences between respondents and nonrespondents, as all effect size statistics were small (Cohen, 1988) with an average of 0.07 (ranging between 0.02 and 0.20), which indicates that the obtained responses were not significantly different from responses we would have obtained from nonrespondents (Vaske, 2019).

Measures

Measures utilized for this study were adapted from the available scales in the literature. Measures for the residents' support for tourism construct were adapted from Boley et al. (2014). Five statements in the questionnaire measured tourism support (e.g. "I believe tourism should be actively encouraged in my community"). Each of these statements was rated on a 5-point scale

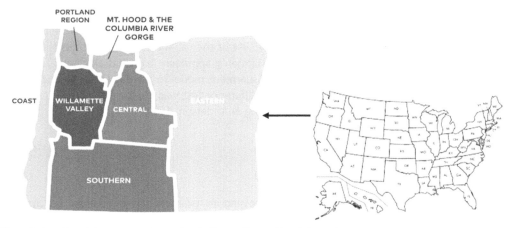

Figure 2. Location of the seven tourism regions in Oregon (Source: Travel Oregon).

ranging from 1 (strongly disagree) to 5 (strongly agree). Measures for ES were adapted from Woosnam (2012) and Moghavvemi et al. (2017). These measures encompassed items representing welcoming nature, emotional closeness, and sympathetic understanding aspects of ES, as shown in Table 2. Similarly, statements representing these items were rated on a 5-point scale ranging from 1 (strongly disagree) to 5 (strongly agree).

Measures for the perceived change of subjective wellbeing construct (i.e. the perceived change in subjective wellbeing expected from a hypothetical increase of tourism by about 20%) included five statements representing the overall evaluation of the quality of life and five dimensions of subjective wellbeing, including satisfaction with financial, social, community, recreation, and environmental conditions. These measures were adapted from Kim et al. (2013) and Organization of Economic Cooperation and Development (2013). Perceived change in subjective wellbeing perceptions expected from an increase in tourism were measured by asking participants to respond to how each of the dimensions of subjective wellbeing would change if community tourism increased by 20%. The statements shown in Table 2, representing the perceived change in subjective wellbeing, were rated on a 5-point scale that ranged from 1 (decrease a lot) to 5 (increase a lot). Finally, measures for community and environmental impacts of tourism were adapted from the literature (e.g. Nunkoo & Ramkissoon, 2011; Vargas-Sánchez et al., 2009).

Data analysis

Data analysis was conducted in the EQS software package (version 6.1). The analysis involved a two-step process. The initial process involved conducting a confirmatory factor analysis (CFA) to assess the reliability and validity of the measures for constructs in the research model. The second step involved conducting structural equation modeling (SEM) following the confirmation of reliability and validity of measures in the best fitting measurement model through CFA. Both phases followed guidelines outlined by Byrne (2006). During model estimation in CFA, missing data were imputed using the expectation-maximization (EM) procedures argued to be the most appropriate SEM approach for addressing missing data (Little & Rubin, 1989). A weighting variable accounting for differences in age, education and gender between the sample and population was included in the model specification options before running the CFA model. The initial assessment of a CFA model revealed a Mardia's coefficient that is greater than 5, which suggests multivariate non-normally distributed data (Byrne, 2006). Following Byrne's guidelines, citing Satorra and Bentler (1988), the model estimation in CFA and structural equation modeling was based on robust statistics (i.e. Satorra-Bentler scaled statistics), which adjusted for non-normal data.

Additionally, several tests were implemented to account for a common method bias (CMB) issue in social science survey instruments that can create measurement error (Podsakoff et al., 2003). First, the Harman single factor test was conducted using exploratory factor analysis without rotation. A single factor model explained 15.4% of the variance, which indicates the absence of CMB. However, given some criticisms of Harman's approach (e.g. Podsakoff et al., 2003), a common method factor was added to the measurement model to test for CMB presence using a chi-square difference test. Finally, a chi-square difference test was conducted to confirm discriminant validity of measures out of caution (Gerbing & Anderson, 1988).

Results

Measurement model

The CFA was conducted before hypotheses testing to examine the constructs' psychometric properties in the research model. Results of the initial output revealed a somewhat poor model fit (S-B $\chi2$ ($N=1474$, $df=593$) $= 1918.52$, $p < .001$, Comparative Fit Index [CFI]$=.89$, Root

Mean-Square Error of Approximation [RMSEA] = .039). Byrne's (2006) suggested procedure of identifying and addressing misfitting parameters in CFA was performed (i.e. removing significant cross-loadings, specifying significant error covariances, removing low standardized loadings below .60) (Byrne, 2006). Four items representing the ES construct with significant cross-loading on the support for tourism construct were dropped. One item, "expected change in satisfaction with the environment," was also dropped due to significant cross-loading on another factor. One significant error covariance was specified between two items, "increased opportunities for cultural activities in my community" and "creating more support for the preservation of historic buildings in my community." These changes improved the model fit (S-B $\chi2$ ($N=1474$, $df=412$) = 1008.92, $p < .001$, CFI = .946, RAMSEA = .031). A CMB test was performed out of precaution to minimize the potential effect of measurement error in hypotheses testing. A common method factor was added to the model, and a chi-square difference test was performed to compare a constrained and unconstrained model. The chi-square difference test was statistically significant, suggesting the likely presence of shared variance ($\triangle$S-B $\chi2 = 3098.39$, $\triangle df = 28$, $p < .001$) Thus, the common method factor was retained for subsequent analyses and the model fit of the measurement model was improved (S-B $\chi2$ ($N=1474$, $df=328$) = 729.57, $p < .001$, CFI = .959, RMSEA = .029) compared to the measurement model without the common method factor (S-B $\chi2$ ($N=1474$, $df=412$) = 1008.92, $p < .001$, CFI = .946, RMSEA = .031).

The retained common factor measurement model showed evidence of convergent validity, as indicated in Table 2 and 3. The standardized loadings for all construct measures were statistically significant and ranged between .70 and .93, which is at or above the recommended value of .70 (Fornell & Larcker, 1981). The amount of variance extracted (AVE) ranged between .56 and .78, above the recommended value of .50 (Hair et al., 2010). Construct reliability ranged between .84 and .95, which is above the recommended value of .70 (Hair et al., 2010). Table 1 shows that discriminant validity was violated for the positive tourism impact construct with ES, and positive environmental impact constructs. A similar discriminant validity issue for the positive tourism impact construct and other closely related constructs has been noted previously in the literature (Boley et al., 2014). Discriminant validity may not be of concern in this case given that item and construct reliability values exceeded the goal of .70, and the amount of variance extracted by these scales was substantially higher than the goal of .50 (Boley et al., 2014). Out of precaution, the chi-square difference test approach was used to verify the discriminant validity violation finding. A fully constrained measurement model (i.e. factor correlations fixed to 1) was compared to a freely estimated model (Gerbing & Anderson, 1988; Joo et al., 2019; Nunkoo & So, 2016). The latter revealed a better model fit, confirming the discriminant validity of measures used.

Structural model

Validation of the measurement model paved the way for the SEM to test hypotheses 1 through 6. The structural model revealed adequate model fit indices, according to Byrne (2006), CFI was .951, and RMSEA was .031. As shown in Table 4, most of the hypothesized relationships were

Table 1. Discriminant validity test.

	CR	AVE	1	2	3	4	5	6	7
Support for tourism	.95	.78	**.88**						
Emotional solidarity	.90	.63	.85	**.80**					
Expected change in subjective wellbeing	.89	.61	.76	.71	**.78**				
Positive environmental impacts	.87	.77	.71	.73	.65	**.88**			
Negative environmental impacts	.91	.77	−.16	.07	−.05	−.18	**.88**		
Positive community impacts	.84	.56	.76	.82	.73	.80	−.03	**.75**	
Negative community impacts	.90	.70	−.21	−.13	−.14	−.24	.76	−.08	**.84**

Note: Diagonal values are the square root of the average variance extracted (AVE), values below diagonal are factor correlations, CR: construct reliability. Correlations above the associated square-root of AVE for any two constructs violates discriminant validity (Fornell & Larcker, 1981).

Table 2. Confirmatory factor analysis (dependent variables).

Construct and associated items	Mean	SD	λ	Critical Ratio	Construct Reliability	AVE
Support for tourism					.95	.78
In general, the positive effects of tourism in my community outweigh its negative effects	3.83	1.10	.87	N/A		
I believe tourism should be actively encouraged in my community	3.89	1.12	.93	37.66		
I do not want tourism in my community[R]	3.96	1.18	.85	35.19		
My community should support the promotion of tourism	3.88	1.09	.91	30.91		
Tourism helps my community grow in the right direction	3.52	1.16	.84	32.18		
Emotional solidarity					.90	.63
I feel comfortable with some tourists I have met in my community	3.82	0.49	.79	21.72		
I feel positive about my daily encounters with tourists	3.56	0.94	.87	N/A		
I do not identify with tourists in my community[R]	3.37	1.08	.75	28.60		
I have a lot in common with tourists in my community	3.12	0.98	.78	34.54		
I feel affection towards tourists in my community	3.02	0.98	.79	30.13		
Perceived changes in subjective wellbeing[a]					.89	.61
Increase in the number of tourists in your community by 20% in the near future, with potential for both positive and negative effects would decrease, have not affected, or increase your wellbeing on ...						
Your life overall	2.91	0.87	.81	N/A		
Your financial situation	3.01	0.77	.70	17.55		
Your social life beyond family	3.14	0.78	.79	24.71		
Your community and its culture	3.27	1.04	.83	30.33		
Your recreation opportunities	3.30	1.05	.79	25.18		

Note: Scale: 1 = strongly disagree, 2 = disagree, 3 = neither, 4 = agree, 5 = strongly agree.
[a]Scale for perceived change in wellbeing construct 1 = decrease a lot, 2 = decrease a little, 3 = no effect, 4 = increase a lot, 5 = Increase a lot.
AVE: average variance extracted; λ: Standardized loading; SD: standard deviation; R: Item was reverse coded prior to analysis.

supported. Hypothesis 1 (ES predicts support for tourism) was supported ($\beta = .88$, $p < .001$). Similarly, hypothesis 2 (the expected change in subjective wellbeing from an increase in tourism predicts ES) was also supported ($\beta = .28$, $p < .001$).

Hypothesis 3 stated that perceived environmental impacts of tourism directly predicts residents' ES. Hypothesis 3a (perceived tourism's positive environmental impacts directly and strongly predict residents' ES) was supported ($\beta = .17$, $p < .01$). However, hypothesis 3b (perceived tourism's negative environmental impacts predict ES) was not supported ($\beta = -.03$, $p > .05$).

Hypothesis 4 stated that perceived community impacts of tourism predict ES. Hypothesis 4a (perceived positive community impacts from tourism predict ES) was supported ($\beta = .50$, $p < .001$). However, hypothesis 4b (perceived negative community impacts strongly predicted ES) was not supported ($\beta = -.02$, $p > .05$).

Finally, hypotheses 5 and 6 stated that perceived environmental and community impacts of tourism predict expected changes in subjective wellbeing from increased tourism. Hypothesis 5a (perceived positive environmental impacts from tourism would predict the expected changes in subjective wellbeing) was supported ($\beta = .16$, $p < .05$). However, hypothesis 5b (perceived negative environmental impacts from tourism would predict the expected changes in subjective wellbeing) was not supported ($\beta = .08$, $p > .05$). Surprisingly, however, the relationship was positive. Hypothesis 6a (the perceived positive community impacts from tourism would predict the expected changes in subjective wellbeing) was supported ($\beta = .59$, $p < .001$). Similarly,

Table 3. Confirmatory factor analysis results (predictor variables).

Construct and associated items	Mean	SD	λ	Critical ratio	Construct reliability	AVE
Positive environmental impact					.87	.77
Tourism contributed to …						
Greater protection of the natural environment in my community	2.88	1.06	.85	N/A		
Improving the natural appearance of my community	3.10	1.08	.91	35.81		
Negative environmental impact					.91	.77
Tourism has contributed to …						
Degradation of wildlife habitat in my community	2.83	1.08	.82	N/A		
Air pollution in my community	2.73	1.02	.90	23.21		
Water pollution in my community	2.69	1.03	.93	22.98		
Positive community impacts					.84	.56
Tourism has contributed to …						
Better infrastructure (e.g. roads) in my community	2.88	1.10	.71	N/A		
Greater knowledge of other cultures in my community	3.26	1.09	.76	24.27		
Increased opportunities for cultural activities in my community	3.26	1.04	.77	24.06		
Creating more support for preservation of historic buildings in my community	3.25	1.02	.75	21.73		
Negative community impacts					.90	.70
Tourism has contributed to …						
Problems of sharing resources or public spaces between residents and tourists in my community	2.91	1.09	.83	N/A		
Loss of tranquility in my community	2.82	1.10	.90	29.96		
Unpleasant overcrowding in my community	2.80	1.16	.88	31.57		
Increasing crime in my community	2.75	1.08	.74	25.58		

Note: Scale: 1 = strongly disagree, 2 = disagree, 3 = neither, 4 = agree, 5 = strongly agree.
AVE: average variance extracted; λ: standardized loading; SD: standard deviation; R: item was reverse coded prior to analysis.

Table 4. Hypothesis testing results from a structural model.

Hypotheses		Standardized coefficients	Critical ratio	Conclusion
H1	Emotional solidarity → Support for tourism	.88***	30.22	Support
H2	Expected change in subjective wellbeing → Emotional solidarity with tourists	.28***	6.29	Support
H3a	Positive environmental impact → Emotional solidarity	.17**	2.70	Support
H3b	Negative environmental impacts → Emotional solidarity	−.03	−.76	No support
H4a	Positive community impact → Emotional solidarity	.50***	6.32	Support
H4b	Negative community impacts → Emotional solidarity	−.02	−.51	No support
H5a	Positive environmental impact → Expected change in subjective wellbeing	.16*	2.28	Support
H5b	Negative environmental impacts → Expected change in subjective wellbeing	.08	1.57	No support
H6a	Positive community impact → Expected change in subjective wellbeing	.59**	7.46	Support
H6b	Negative community impacts → Expected change in subjective wellbeing	−.12*	−2.20	Support

Note: ***$p < .001$, **$p < .01$, *$p < .05$; R-square (support for tourism) = .78; R-square (emotional solidarity) = .76; R-square (perceived change in subjective wellbeing) = .55.

hypothesis 6b (perceived negative community impacts from tourism would predict the expected change in subjective wellbeing) was also supported ($\beta = -.12, p < .05$).

Discussion

This article contributes to understanding the relationship between ES and support for tourism and the links between perceived tourism impacts, effect of tourism on wellbeing, and ES. The results show that Oregon residents' ES is a strong predictor of support. This finding is consistent with previous empirical studies that show ES is strongly and positively related to support for tourism (Erul et al., 2020; Ouyang et al., 2017; Phuc & Nguyen, 2020; Woosnam, 2012). This study adds to this body of knowledge by explaining that the relationship between ES and tourism support is more substantial than previously reported in the literature (Erul et al., 2020; Woosnam, 2012). The empirical evidence that ties emotional reaction to tourism support is not surprising when considering the argument from a CAT perspective. Efficacy-based adaptive behavior (e.g. tourism support) aims to improve or sustain benefits that stimulate the emotional reactions responsible for that behavior (Smith & Lazarus, 1993). This type of self-interest preserving behavior results from an outcome desirability assessment of the stimuli (i.e. tourism impact), conceptually explained by CAT (Lazarus & Smith, 1988). Joo and Woosnam (2020), while citing Lawler's work (e.g. Lawler et al., 2000), show that emotional reactions shape perceptions and behaviors.

One of this study's primary goals was to understand the determinants of residents' positive emotional reactions to tourists. This knowledge gap has been acknowledged in the literature (Joo & Woosnam, 2020; Zheng et al., 2020). Informed by CAT, this study reveals that residents' perceived tourism impacts may affect their ES either directly or through changes in subjective wellbeing. This finding suggests that the addition of change in subjective wellbeing in the model predicting ES contributes to understanding the factors predicting ES, which arguably predicts support for tourism. The effect of positive community impacts of tourism on ES is greater in magnitude and significance than the effect of positive environmental impacts.

Furthermore, the results show that the effect of positive tourism impacts on ES is more important than negative impacts. From a CAT perspective, community impacts are more relevant than environmental impacts, whereas congruent (i.e. positive) impacts are more likely to affect ES and subjective wellbeing than incongruent (i.e. negative) impacts. These findings support the outcome desirability appraisal argument outlined in CAT, which indicates that residents' decisions to support tourism are likely stimulated by how tourism positively impacts an individual's wellbeing to elicit a positive reaction toward tourists and tourism.

The relatively weak adverse relationship between perceived negative community impacts and perceived changes in wellbeing from an increase in tourism is notable. This finding indicates that perceptions of negative impacts of tourism are less likely to predict residents' support for tourism through the appraisal processes, shaping tourism support perceptions and behaviors. As Ouyang et al. (2017) indicate, negative tourism impacts have a weaker effect on support than positive impacts and other variables (e.g. emotions). Together, these results show that perceptions of negative tourism impacts may not be critical in the cognitive process of exchange, thus, shaping decisions about supporting tourism. This finding may explain a typical weak relationship between negative perceptions of tourism impacts and tourism support, commonly seen in tourism attitude studies framed with SET (Kim et al., 2013; Nunkoo & So, 2016). A possible explanation for such a weak role of perceived negative impacts in models explaining support could be that people are more likely to cognitively minimize negative impact perceptions and amplify positive impacts while cognitively appraising tourism effects (Chancellor et al., 2011; Nunkoo & Ramkissoon, 2012; Ouyang et al., 2017).

Furthermore, the results revealed that perceived changes in subjective wellbeing expected from an increase in tourism are mainly a function of perceptions of: (a) positive community tourism impacts, (b) positive environmental tourism impacts, and (c) negative community tourism impacts. The positive community impacts of tourism have the most significant effect on perceived changes in wellbeing expected from increased tourism. Together, these results show that positive impacts of tourism on the community and environment, and the negative impacts on the community, are essential determinants of ES, either directly or through the appraisal of how such impacts affect one's wellbeing. There is support for these findings in the literature (Joo et al., 2018; Ouyang et al., 2017; Phuc & Nguyen, 2020). For example, Phuc and Nguyen (2020) show that the perceived value of tourism (e.g. income generation) directly and strongly predicts ES among residents of Ho Chi Minh City, Vietnam. Ouyang et al. (2017) also reveal that tourism costs are strong determinants of negative emotions influencing support for hosting the 2014 World Cup event in Brazil. Lai et al. (2020) reveal that perceived tourism impacts have a substantial direct effect on wellbeing. Improved wellbeing is also a strong determinant of ES among Macau residents in China.

The findings of this study and the available empirical evidence in the literature support the utility of CAT in conceptualizing and evaluating factors involved in SET-based transactional exchanges that shape residents' support for tourism. This study shows that CAT can provide an integrative theoretical framework linking perceptions of tourism impacts to support through an outcome desirability cognitive appraisal process. This integrative cognitive psychology theory may be useful in studies exploring links between tourism impacts, wellbeing, ES, and residents' support for tourism (e.g. Lai et al., 2020). Additionally, cognitive psychology theories are likely to benefit tourism researchers (Skavronskaya et al., 2017). Studies applying CAT to understand tourism attitudes are emerging (Ouyang et al., 2017; Zheng et al., 2019a, 2019b), but knowledge of its utility is more limited. Studies exploring the links between perceived tourism impacts and support can no longer ignore the role of outcome desirability cognitive appraisal processes likely responsible for the efficacy-based adaptive decision to support behavior (Zheng et al., 2019a, 2019b). Future attempts to integrate CAT into SET-based tourism attitude studies can provide better explanations of the processes involved in the exchange, thereby addressing SET's inability to fully explain residents' support for tourism (Sharpley, 2014).

Limitations and future research direction

There are several limitations to be acknowledged. First, the study was conducted in the summer when tourist numbers are generally high. Thus, the potential effect of social conflict on residents' perceptions of tourists and tourism is likely, but was not controlled for in this study. Tourism increases may create social conflict due to the overuse of environmental and social resources (Jin & Pearce, 2011). Future research may address this by ensuring that data collection occurs across all seasons. Second, online Qualtrics panel data and mail survey data were combined in the analyses. Despite efforts such as determining if statistical differences exist in responses and weighting data by age and gender, the potential effect of the difference in data collection modes is possible, but was not controlled for in the analysis. Future research may address this gap by exploring if data collection modes affect the relationships tested in this study. Third, according to the literature (Sharpley, 2014), residents' perceptions of tourism are shaped by extrinsic factors (e.g. the stage of tourism development and nature of tourism) and intrinsic factors (e.g. economic dependency on tourism and the distance from tourism areas). For example, residents with economic dependency on tourism may be relatively more supportive of tourism than residents without such dependency (Nunkoo & Ramkissoon, 2011). The potential effect of extrinsic and intrinsic factors in this study was not examined, and future research should address this issue. Fourth, a one-factor concept of ES was used in this study's model. However, ES may be a three-dimensional concept, according to Woosnam (2010). Future research could improve knowledge by examining how the three dimensions of ES are shaped by the cognitive appraisal of tourism's impact on wellbeing.

This study also revealed findings that are worth exploring in future research. For example, the perceptions of community tourism impacts and positive environmental impacts appear to be important factors in the cognitive appraisal process evaluating the effect on wellbeing and stimulating residents' emotional reaction to tourists and tourism support compared to negative environmental impacts. However, according to Schüler et al. (2009), goal incongruence (i.e. perceived negative environmental impact) is expected to have a strong adverse effect in the cognitive appraisal process eliciting ES. More research is needed to understand why environmental goal incongruence plays a minimal role in the mental appraisal of tourism's impact on wellbeing. Furthermore, this study revealed that community impacts of tourism are essential cognitions in the appraisal of tourism. However, community impacts encompass social and economic aspects (Andereck & McGehee, 2008). Future research could explore whether there are differences in how social and economic impacts of tourism influence the cognitive appraisal process that determines residents' emotional reaction and support for tourism. Finally, this research, guided by CAT, has demonstrated that subjective wellbeing and ES play a role in the exchange-based relationship between perceived tourism impacts and support for tourism. Thus, integrating SAT and CAT is likely to improve understanding of the nature of the exchange process, thereby improving understandings of what shapes residents' support for tourism. Additional empirical research that integrates both theories is needed across multiple geographical contexts to confirm the utility of integrating CAT and SET in tourism studies.

Conclusion

Sustainable tourism development and management organizations rely on residents' support in host communities (Nunkoo & Ramkissoon, 2012). A number of studies exploring the factors that determine support for tourism, conceptually framed by the SET, have advanced knowledge that perceptions of tourism impact strongly predict residents' support for tourism (e.g. Gursoy et al., 2016; Moghavvemi et al., 2017; Nunkoo & Ramkissoon, 2012; Nunkoo & So, 2016). Despite criticism of SET limitations, the literature on tourism attitudes is experiencing growth from efforts to integrate other theories aimed to understand the process of exchange producing support for tourism (e.g. Boley et al., 2014; Nunkoo & Gursoy, 2012; Nunkoo & So, 2016; Ouyang et al., 2017; Woosnam, 2012; Zheng et al., 2019a, 2019b). Across a wide range of theoretical foundations informing these studies, the focus on understanding psychological factors such as ES, trust, identity, and others, likely involved in the process of exchange, is notable. However, as Zheng et al. (2020) argue, a systematic evaluation of psychological determinants of support for tourism informed by cognitive psychological theory is lacking, yet likely to advance knowledge of tourism support.

This study, along with recent contributions (e.g. Ouyang et al., 2017; Zheng et al., 2019a, 2019b), provides empirical evidence supporting the CAT's utility in explaining the outcome desirability process of appraising the determinants of support for tourism. This study has shown that perceived change in wellbeing expected from an increase in tourism, and emotional reaction to tourists, play a role in the relationship between perceived tourism impacts and residents' support for tourism. The study also indicates that perceived positive community tourism impacts are the most impactful stimulants in the appraisal process and are likely to positively shape mental evaluation of wellbeing and the emotional reaction eliciting support for tourism. These findings raise several questions of research interest. For example, what risks exist within the outcome desirability appraisal process that may adversely affect tourism support, despite high levels of actual or perceived positive community impacts from tourism? What aspects of perceived positive community impacts from tourism are most likely to enhance support through a cognitive appraisal process? Is the pattern stable across varied geographical contexts for the outcome desirability appraisal process that elicits tourism support?

The practical implications of this study's findings are also noteworthy. The finding of a strong relationship between residents' ES and tourism support indicates that efforts to evaluate and develop actions to improve tourism support are best invested in programs that raise awareness about tourism benefits. Moreover, programs helping residents to understand the short-term and long-term positive benefits of tourism for the community are likely to improve how people feel about tourists. For example, asking residents how they feel about visitors at a local recreation site may indicate if residents are likely to support efforts to improve the site for tourism purposes.

The finding that perceptions of positive community impacts play an important role in the appraisal of tourism's impact on wellbeing shows that resources intended to enhance tourism support may be more effective if they create tourism-based wellbeing opportunities and educate residents about the value of such opportunities. Understanding residents' internal wellbeing needs and orienting tourism opportunities toward addressing such needs is essential for tourism planners and managers. Overall, based on this study's findings, sustainable tourism planning and management agencies may benefit from understanding the positive tourism impacts that residents most desire and those most likely to enhance wellbeing. Tourism agencies are likely to enhance support for tourism more efficiently when tourism impacts with most positive effect on wellbeing are understood and strengthened.

Acknowledgments

The authors wish to thank the residents of Oregon who participated in this study. The authors are grateful to Dr. Manuel A. Ribeiro and Dr. Kyle M. Woosnam for guidance on earlier drafts and the anonymous reviewers for insightful comments. Finally, the authors wish to thank Ms. Lara Jacobs for providing copy-editing services.

Disclosure statement

No potential conflict of interest was reported by the authors.

Funding

This article was prepared with funding from Travel Oregon.

References

Allen, L. R., Hafer, H. R., Long, P. T., & Perdue, R. R. (1993). Rural residents' attitudes toward recreation and tourism development. *Journal of Travel Research*, *31*(4), 27–33. https://doi.org/10.1177/004728759303100405

Andereck, K. L., & McGehee, N. G. (2008). The attitudes of community residents towards tourism. In S. F. McCool & R. N. Neil (Eds.), *Tourism* recreation and sustainability: Linking culture and the environment* (2nd ed., pp. 236–259). New York: CABI Publishing.

Andereck, K. L., Valentine, K. M., Knopf, R. C., & Vogt, C. A. (2005). Residents' perceptions of community tourism impacts. *Annals of Tourism Research*, *32*(4), 1056–1076. https://doi.org/10.1016/j.annals.2005.03.001

Ap, J. (1992). Residents' perceptions on tourism impacts. *Annals of Tourism Research*, *19*(4), 665–690. https://doi.org/10.1016/0160-7383(92)90060-3

Boley, B. B., McGehee, N. G., Perdue, R. R., & Long, P. (2014). Empowerment and resident attitudes toward tourism: Strengthening the theoretical foundation through a Weberian lens. *Annals of Tourism Research*, *49*, 33–50. https://doi.org/10.1016/j.annals.2014.08.005

Brandon, D. M., Long, J. H., Loraas, T. M., Mueller-Phillips, J., & Vansant, B. (2014). Online instrument delivery and participant recruitment services: Emerging opportunities for behavioral accounting research. *Behavioral Research in Accounting*, *26*(1), 1–23.

Byrne, B. M. (2006). *Structural equation modeling with EQS: Basic concepts, applications, and programming* (2nd ed.). Mahwah, NJ: Lawrence Erlbaum Associates.

Chancellor, C., Yu, C.-P S., & Cole, S. T. (2011). Exploring quality of life perceptions in rural midwestern (USA) communities: An application of the core-periphery concept in a tourism development context. *International Journal of Tourism Research*, *13*(5), 496–507. https://doi.org/10.1002/jtr.823

Cohen, J. (1988). *Statistical power analysis for the behavioral sciences* (2nd ed.). Hillsdale, NJ: Laurence Erlbaum Associates.

Dean Runyan Associates. (2018). "Oregon Travel Impacts: Statewide Estimates 1992–2017." June 2018.

Dillman, D. A., Smyth, J. D., & Christian, L. M. (2014). *Internet, phone, mail, and mixed-mode surveys: the tailored design method*. New York, NY: John Wiley & Sons.

Erul, E., Woosnam, K. M., & Mcintosh, W. A. (2020). Considering emotional solidarity and the theory of planned behavior in explaining behavioral intentions to support tourism development. *Journal of Sustainable Tourism*, *28*(8), 1158–1173. https://doi.org/10.1080/09669582.2020.1726935

Fornell, C., & Larcker, D. F. (1981). Evaluating structural equation models with unobservable variables and measurement error. *Journal of Marketing Research*, *18*(1), 39–50. https://doi.org/10.1177/002224378101800104

Gerbing, D. W., & Anderson, J. C. (1988). An updated paradigm for scale development incorporating unidimensionality and its assessment. *Journal of Marketing Research*, *25*(2), 186–192. https://doi.org/10.1177/002224378802500207

Hair, J., Jr., Black, W., Babin, B., Anderson, R., & Tatham, R. (2010). *Multivariate data analysis*. Pearson Education.

Hasani, A., Moghavvemi, S., & Hamzah, A. (2016). The impact of emotional solidarity on Residents' Attitude and Tourism Development. *PLoS One*, *11*(6), e0157624. https://doi.org/10.1371/journal.pone.0157624

Jin, Q., & Pearce, P. (2011). Tourist perception of crowding and management approaches at tourism sites in Xi'an. *Asia Pacific Journal of Tourism Research*, *16*(3), 325–338. https://doi.org/10.1080/10941665.2011.572667

Joo, D., Cho, H., & Woosnam, K. M. (2019). Exploring tourists' perceptions of tourism impacts. *Tourism Management Perspectives*, *31*, 231–235. https://doi.org/10.1016/j.tmp.2019.05.008

Joo, D., Tasci, A. D. A., Woosnam, K. M., Maruyama, N. U., Hollas, C. R., & Aleshinloye, K. D. (2018). Residents' attitude towards domestic tourists explained by contact, emotional solidarity and social distance. *Tourism Management*, *64*, 245–257. https://doi.org/10.1016/j.tourman.2017.08.012

Joo, D., & Woosnam, K. M. (2020). Measuring tourists' emotional solidarity with one another—A modification of the emotional solidarity scale. *Journal of Travel Research*, *59*(7), 1186–1203. https://doi.org/10.1177/0047287519878503

Kim, K., Uysal, M., & Sirgy, M. J. (2013). How does tourism in a community impact the quality of life of community residents? *Tourism Management*, *36*, 527–540. https://doi.org/10.1016/j.tourman.2012.09.005

Lai, H. K., Pinto, P., & Pintassilgo, P. (2020). Quality of life and emotional solidarity in residents' attitudes toward tourists: The case of Macau. *Journal of Travel Research*. https://doi.org/10.1177/0047287520918016.

Lawler, E. J., Thye, S. R., & Yoon, J. (2000). Emotion and group cohesion in productive exchange. *American Journal of Sociology*, *10*(3), 616–657.

Lazarus, R. S. (1991). Progress on a cognitive-motivational-relational theory of emotion. *American Psychologist*, *46*(8), 819–834. https://doi.org/10.1037/0003-066X.46.8.819

Lazarus, R. S., & Smith, C. A. (1988). Knowledge and appraisal in the cognition-emotion relationship. *Cognition & Emotion*, *2*(4), 281–300. https://doi.org/10.1080/02699938808412701

Little, R. J. A., & Rubin, D. B. (1989). The analysis of social science data with missing values. *Sociological Methods & Research*, *18*(2–3), 292–326. https://doi.org/10.1177/0049124189018002004

Maruyama, N. U., Keith, S. J., & Woosnam, K. M. (2019). Incorporating emotion into social exchange: Considering distinct resident groups' attitudes towards ethnic neighborhood tourism in Osaka, Japan. *Journal of Sustainable Tourism*, *27*(8), 1125–1141. https://doi.org/10.1080/09669582.2019.1593992

McGehee, N. G., & Andereck, K. L. (2004). Factors predicting rural residents' support of tourism. *Journal of Travel Research*, *43*(2), 131–140. https://doi.org/10.1177/0047287504268234

Moghavvemi, S., Woosnam, K. M., Paramanathan, T., Musa, G., & Hamzah, A. (2017). The effect of residents' personality, emotional solidarity, and community commitment on support for tourism development. *Tourism Management*, *63*, 242–254. https://doi.org/10.1016/j.tourman.2017.06.021

Nunkoo, R., Gursoy, D., & Juwaheer, T. D. (2010). Island residents' identities and their support for tourism: An integration of two theories. *Journal of Sustainable Tourism*, *18*(5), 675–693. https://doi.org/10.1080/09669581003602341

Nunkoo, R., & Ramkissoon, H. (2009). Applying the means-end chain theory and the laddering technique to the study of host attitudes to tourism. *Journal of Sustainable Tourism*, *17*(3), 337–355.

Nunkoo, R., & Ramkissoon, H. (2011). Residents' satisfaction with community attributes and support for tourism. *Journal of Hospitality & Tourism Research*, 35(2), 171–190. https://doi.org/10.1177/1096348010384600

Nunkoo, R., & Ramkissoon, H. (2012). Power, trust, social exchange and community support. *Annals of Tourism Research*, 39(2), 997–1023. https://doi.org/10.1016/j.annals.2011.11.017

Nunkoo, R., Smith, S. L. J., & Ramkissoon, H. (2013). Residents' attitudes to tourism: A longitudinal study of 140 articles from 1984 to 2010. *Journal of Sustainable Tourism*, 21(1), 5–25. https://doi.org/10.1080/09669582.2012.673621

Nunkoo, R., & So, K. K. F. (2016). Residents' support for tourism: Testing alternative structural models. *Journal of Travel Research*, 55(7), 847–861. https://doi.org/10.1177/0047287515592972

Nyer, P. U. (1997). A study of the relationships between cognitive appraisals and consumption emotions. *Journal of the Academy of Marketing Science*, 25(4), 296–304. https://doi.org/10.1177/0092070397254002

Organization of Economic Cooperation and Development. (2013). *OECD guidelines on measuring subjective wellbeing.* Author. https://doi.org/10.1787/9789264191655-en

Ouyang, Z., Gursoy, D., & Sharma, B. (2017). Role of trust, emotions and event attachment on residents' attitudes toward tourism. *Tourism Management*, 63, 426–438. https://doi.org/10.1016/j.tourman.2017.06.026

Phuc, H. N., & Nguyen, H. M. (2020). The importance of collaboration and emotional solidarity in residents' support for sustainable urban tourism: Case study Ho Chi Minh City. *Journal of Sustainable Tourism*, 1–20. https://doi.org/10.1080/09669582.2020.1831520.

Podsakoff, P. M., MacKenzie, S. B., Lee, J. Y., & Podsakoff, N. P. (2003). Common method biases in behavioral research: A critical review of the literature and recommended remedies. *Journal of Applied Psychology*, 88(5), 879–903. https://doi.org/10.1037/0021-9010.88.5.879

Satorra, A., & Bentler, P. M. (1988). Scaling corrections for chi square statistics in covariance structure analysis. *American Statistical Association 1988 Proceedings of the Business and Economic Statistics Section* (pp. 308–313). Alexandria, VA: American Statistical Association.

Schüler, J., Job, V., Fröhlich, S. M., & Brandstätter, V. (2009). Dealing with a 'hidden stressor': Emotional disclosure as a coping strategy to overcome the negative effects of motive incongruence on health. *Stress and Health*, 25(3), 221–233. https://doi.org/10.1002/smi.1241

Sharpley, R. (2014). Host perceptions of tourism: A review of the research. *Tourism Management*, 42, 37–49. https://doi.org/10.1016/j.tourman.2013.10.007

Skavronskaya, L., Scott, N., Moyle, B., Le, D., Hadinejad, A., Zhang, R., Gardiner, S., Coghlan, A., & Shakeela, A. (2017). Cognitive psychology and tourism research: State of the art. *Tourism Review*, 72(2), 221–237. https://doi.org/10.1108/TR-03-2017-0041

Smith, C. A., & Lazarus, R. S. (1993). Appraisal components, core relational themes, and the emotions. *Cognition & Emotion*, 7(3-4), 233–269. https://doi.org/10.1080/02699939308409189

Vargas-Sánchez, A., Plaza-Mejía, M., de los, Á., & Porras-Bueno, N. (2009). Understanding residents' attitudes toward the development of industrial tourism in a former mining community. *Journal of Travel Research*, 47(3), 373–387. https://doi.org/10.1177/0047287508322783

Vaske, J. J. (2019). *Survey research and analysis*. Sagamore-Venture.

Wang, S., Berbekova, A., & Uysal, M. (2020). Is this about feeling? The interplay of emotional well-being, solidarity, and residents' attitude. *Journal of Travel Research*. https://doi.org/10.1177/0047287520938862.

Ward, C., & Berno, T. (2011). Beyond social exchange theory: Attitudes toward tourists. *Annals of Tourism Research*, 38(4), 1556–1569. https://doi.org/10.1016/j.annals.2011.02.005

Watson, L., & Spence, M. T. (2007). Causes and consequences of emotions on consumer behavior: A review and integrative cognitive appraisal theory. *European Journal of Marketing*, 41(5/6), 487–511. https://doi.org/10.1108/03090560710737570

Woosnam, K. M. (2011). Testing a model of durkheim's theory of emotional solidarity among residents of a tourism community. *Journal of Travel Research*, 50(5), 546–558. https://doi.org/10.1177/0047287510379163

Woosnam, K. M. (2012). Using emotional solidarity to explain residents' attitudes about tourism and tourism development. *Journal of Travel Research*, 51(3), 315–327. https://doi.org/10.1177/0047287511410351

Woosnam, K. M., & Aleshinloye, K. D. (2018). Residents' emotional solidarity with tourists: Explaining perceived impacts of a cultural heritage festival. *Journal of Hospitality & Tourism Research*, 42(4), 587–605. https://doi.org/10.1177/1096348015584440

Woosnam, K. M., & Norman, W. C. (2010). Measuring residents' emotional solidarity with tourists: Scale development of durkheim's theoretical constructs. *Journal of Travel Research*, 49(3), 365–380. https://doi.org/10.1177/0047287509346858

Woosnam, K. M., Norman, W. C., & Ying, T. (2009). Exploring the theoretical framework of emotional solidarity between residents and tourists. *Journal of Travel Research*, 48(2), 245–258. https://doi.org/10.1177/0047287509332334

Zheng, D., Ritchie, B. W., Benckendorff, P. J., & Bao, J. (2019a). Emotional responses toward Tourism Performing Arts Development: A comparison of urban and rural residents in China. *Tourism Management*, 70, 238–249. https://doi.org/10.1016/j.tourman.2018.08.019

Zheng, D., Ritchie, B. W., Benckendorff, P. J., & Bao, J. (2019b). The role of cognitive appraisal, emotion and commitment in affecting resident support toward tourism performing arts development. *Journal of Sustainable Tourism*, 27(11), 1725–1744. https://doi.org/10.1080/09669582.2019.1662029

Indigenous residents, tourism knowledge exchange and situated perceptions of tourism

Tramy Ngo and Tien Pham

ABSTRACT
This study investigates how interactions with tourism knowledge varieties affect indigenous hosts' perceptions of tourism and regulate perceived tourism values. Diffusion and adult learning theories underpin the foundation of the study. Utilising a qualitative approach and a hermeneutic phenomenological methodology, this study takes Hoa Binh province (Vietnam) as the study context. Fifteen indigenous hosts from the Muong, an ethnic minority group from this province, were interviewed using life-focus, story-telling techniques. The interviewees shared their experience of judging and absorbing varied tourism know-how. They also expressed their perceptions of tourism and justified their evaluations on tourism values. The data was then analysed using interpretative phenomenological analysis. The findings suggest the role of not-for-profit supporters in informing a sustainable *expectation set* for indigenous hosts about nuanced tourism impacts, thereby positively influencing their perceptions of tourism. The potential of the hermeneutic phenomenological methodology in gauging both manifest and latent layers of indigenous hosts' perceptions of tourism is also argued. Finally, the research contributes to the ideological debates about the decolonialisation of community-based tourism development and in research with indigenous communities from an Asian context.

Introduction

Residents' perceptions of tourism are arguably one of the most intensively studied topics in the tourism social impact literature. Such perceptions are fundamental to shaping a hospitable environment for tourism activities, encouraging community engagement in tourism planning, development and policy-making, and facilitating the inclusion of residents in sustainable tourism (Nunkoo & Ramkissoon, 2011; Uysal et al., 2016). However, though extensively research, residents' perceptions of tourism are regarded as insufficiently understood. This paradox arguably stems from the dominance of research inquiries based on one-Index-fit-all quantitative hypotheses and the use of a non-cultural lens of evaluations (Sharpley, 2014). As a result, the study of residents' perceptions of tourism "tends to describe what host perceptions are but does not necessarily explain why residents choose a particular perspective(s) to understand tourism and its multi-phenomenal impacts." (Chen et al., 2020, p.1). Indeed, residents' perceptions of tourism are neither linear nor rational but intrinsically sociocultural. In these studies, how residents define tourism is equally important to how its benefits are recognised and appraised (Chen et al., 2020).

Therefore, in this study, we contest that an understanding of the complexities of embodied tourism knowledge acquisition practices is the foundational step to gauge residents' perceptions of tourism and optimise tourism's social impacts on a community.

Using the context of an ethnic minority in Vietnam, this study investigates how interactions with varied tourism knowing underpin indigenous hosts' perceptions of tourism. In accordance with this research aim, we categorise ethnic minority people under the concept of indigenous groups, defined by Pacific Asia Travel Association (PATA) and World Indigenous Tourism Alliance (WINTA),) (2014). According to PATA and WINTA (2014), indigenous groups "are typically seen to be distinct in terms of their cultural and social identities and institutions relative to dominant groups in society" (p.5). The objectives of this study are twofold: (1) explore tourism knowledge varieties exposed to indigenous hosts and (2) study how interactions with tourism knowledge varieties mould indigenous hosts' perspectives of tourism. By bringing these two facets of the inquiry on indigenous hosts' perceptions of tourism, we argue that how indigenous hosts learn from tourism knowledge varieties to which they are exposed, ultimately moderate their tourism viewpoints.

The paper is then structured as followings. The literature review will highlight the gaps in the fields of community-based tourism (CBT), indigenous hosts, knowledge exchange and learning practices. The methodology section presents the research paradigm and design. Following that, the findings section elaborates components of the tourism knowing through the lenses of indigenous hosts, and a mechanism for knowledge absorption and perception articulation is identified. The Discussion and Conclusions section details the study's contribution to the literature, and outlines the research's limitations to suggest an agenda for future research.

CBT, indigenous hosts and knowledge exchange

CBT is an alternative form of sustainable tourism development, characterized by the participation of local communities in tourism planning. This participation occurs ideally at both internal levels such as power re-distribution, and external levels, for instance, stakeholder collaboration (Okazaki, 2008). Due to its potential to deliver both economic regeneration and non-economic benefits beyond the direct impacts on a greater community (Lapeyre, 2011), CBT is commonly adopted in developing countries (Nair et al., 2020). CBT attracts most of visitors through rich cultural component in tourist offerings. As a result, CBT initiatives often flourish in indigenous communities of long-standing history and exotic culture (Espeso-Molinero et al., 2016).

Indigenous hosts play a central role in tourism activities within their communities by providing culture-based experiences to visitors, and reaping certain economic benefits while promoting positive destination images in return (Hinch & Butler, 2009). These experiences can take the form of homestays, performances, local guiding, and other services charactised by local cultural elements. Thus, indigenous hosts experience closer proximity to the tourism sector, and are more dependent on tourism activities. They are also more involved in interactions with different stakeholders and sources of knowledge.

Indeed, indigenous hosts are often targeted by various knowledge interventions for community capacity building and empowerment campaigns (Ghaderi et al., 2018; Victurine, 2000). For instance, to facilitate indigenous tourism business development in Australia, the Federal government has introduced mentoring programs to enhance the capacity building of indigenous entrepreneurs/owners (Buultjens & Gale, 2013). The government's tourism awareness campaign is another effort in boosting tourism knowledge to local communities (Cole, 2006). In their study of the learning experience of community-based ecotourism (CBET) hosts in Thailand, Regmi and Walter (2016) specified that non-governmental developmental organisations (NGDOs) offer non-formal educational programmes for CBET hosts about tourism management, environmental conservation, cross-cultural exchange and political skills.

In additions to purposive knowledge interventions for capacity building, indigenous hosts are also exposed to other tourism knowledge (Liburd, 2012; Nowotny, 2003). Indigenous hosts interact with different service providers, through which knowledge exchanges occur. For instance, community-owned tourism entrepreneurs rely on their private partners for lessons on marketing their business (Ngo et al., 2020). Networks with cohorts and with knowledge holders of different worldviews offer indigenous hosts a valuable source of knowledge. In particular, tourism networks provide knowledge exchange opportunities for membered residents (Dodds et al., 2018). Successful CBT projects act as learning centres, delivering teaching models for other projects through study tours (Walter, 2009). Additionally, collaborative works with academic researchers return knowledge advancements for involved indigenous partners, as observed in the study of Espeso-Molinero et al. (2016). Host-guest interactions provide another arena for learning opportunities (Coles, 2006).

Simultaneously, indigenous hosts possess local wisdom, which is well valued as a source of tourism knowledge. Such knowledge is culture-centralised and forms a source of indigenous hosts' assets while engaging in tourism activities. Espeso-Molinero et al. (2016) recorded the valuable understanding of Tzeltal residents about local animal and plant inventories in developing indigenous tourism products. Likewise, Travesi (2018) observed ecological knowledge and ways of knowing the land among Aboriginal tour guides in Western Australia while hosting non-indigenous domestic tourists. Walter (2009) discussed the informal ecotourism "curriculum" that residents offer based on their local expertise on tidal and marine ecosystems and other endogenous ways of knowledge about the place and the community.

Knowledge exchange occurring between indigenous hosts and knowledge holders is inherent in CBT. Fundamentally, knowledge exchange is crucial for innovations in successful tourism entrepreneurship (Carlisle et al., 2013; Hoarau & Kline, 2014). Especially in the context of CBT, knowledge exchange is imperative and inevitable for three reasons. First, CBT is well regarded as an arena of different knowledge communities holding varied interests and viewpoints (Matilainen et al., 2018). Variations among these viewpoints often trigger flows of knowledge exchange, as recorded in recent studies (Espeso-Molinero et al., 2016; Ngo et al., 2020). Second, the challenges of deficient tacit know-how are often resounded in operating CBT initiatives (Melubo & Carr, 2019; Tolkach & King, 2015). Accordingly, collaborative practices for knowledge sharing and knowledge transfer are often offered to address these challenges (Iorio & Corsale, 2014; Ngo et al., 2020). Third, continued knowledge exchange and collective learning are prerequisite for sponsored CBT projects to be sustainable in post-funded periods (Bertella & Rinaldi, 2020).

Indigenised lenses and the linkage of indigenous hosts and tourism knowledge varieties

A focus on the nexus of indigenous hosts and tourism knowledge varieties contextualises this study within the rubric of diffusion research. The concept of diffusion refers to the process of disseminating an innovation over different channels to reach the members of a social system over time (Cooper, 2006; Rogers, 2003). Under the theory of diffusion, four tenets are taken into account, i.e., the nature of the innovation, the conduit of the diffusion, time, and the social system. Innovation is identified as new and value-added knowledge from the lens of adopters (Rogers, 2003). Therefore, the transfer of knowledge underpins the diffusion of innovation (Shaw & Williams, 2009). In the tourism field, examples of diffused innovation can be changes in services and products, for instance, e-commerce or Airbnb (Guttentag & Smith, 2020). Adoption of new environmental-friendly practices (Bell & Ruhanen, 2016) and an understanding of new concepts, such as sustainable tourism development (Dabphet et al., 2012) are also associated with knowledge dissemination. With regards to the channels of knowledge transfer, interpersonal communication and mass media communication are two main themes of social networks connecting adopters and knowledge (Scott & Flores, 2015). The knowledge transfer could be facilitated at the organisational level or proceeded at the individual level (Weidenfeld et al., 2010). In terms of the social system, the role of change agents, opinion leaders, network structures, and adopters are centralised (Rogers, 2003). A substantial number of tourism studies address tourism-related diffusion processes in different contexts (see Bell & Ruhanen, 2016; Dabphet et al., 2012; Guttentag & Smith, 2020). Being framed by the diffusion theory, the present research focuses on the forms of transferred knowledge and the channels of knowledge transfer "from the eyes" of indigenous hosts – unattended domains in the theory's application.

Within the knowledge exchange canopy and through indigenised lenses, an interactice relationship between indigenous hosts and the tourism knowledge varieties emerges. Indigenised lenses are underpinned by emic viewpoints and are interpreted by local terms. Chen (2017) exemplified this endogeneity through the study about indigenous villagers in China who use the concept of *guanxi* to interpret their worldview, including tourism development. Chen's study indicates that indigenous lenses form a pre-existing reference for indigenous hosts in knowledge interactions. Indigenous lenses enable the autonomy and confidence of indigenous hosts in relationship with alien tourism knowledge varieties. Indigenous hosts might rely on their perceived effectiveness of knowledge to judge whether a form of knowledge is usable (Thomas, 2012; Xiao & Smith, 2007). This ideological process can be explained by the frame of reference concept in the adult learning theory of Mezirow (1981, 2009). According to Mezirow (1981), a frame of reference is a set of epistemological assumptions that limit or distort one's understanding of the self and others.

A frame of reference is composed of two dimensions: habits of mind and a point of view (Mezirow, 1997). In the adult's learning experience, Mezirow (1997) defines transformative learning as learning which results in transformations in the frame of reference. Examples of these transformations could be that pre-existing assumptions are questioned, and perspectives are changed. At a more common level, learning experience results in an extension of existing meanings or an establishment of new viewpoints (Mezirow, 2009). It becomes apparent that, in adult's learning processes, a frame of reference activates dual roles i.e., an assessing mechanism of knowledge absorption and a domain for perspective transformations. Determining which forms and sources of knowledge are relevant requires pre-existing assumptions established by the frame of reference. Simultaneously, such established assumptions are subject for changes through the transformative learning experience.

In tourism literature, the frame of reference in adult learning is mostly discussed in tourist studies (Coghlan & Gooch, 2011; Kirillova et al., 2017; Pung et al., 2020). The area of host learning remains sparse, with some recent exemplary works of Regmi and Walter (2016); Sen and Walter (2020); and Walter et al. (2018). However, these host learning studies mainly focus on the outputs of transformative learning. An embodied meaning interpretation construed by the frame of reference in indigenous hosts' learning practices is understudied. The present study aims to address this paucity by exploring the frame of reference among indigenous hosts that underpins their practices of knowledge judgement and learning from knowledge exchange.

The integration of the two aforementioned theories better explains the knowledge exchange of indigenous hosts and unpacks the learning practices underpinning their tourism perspectives. This incorporation empowers the role of indigenous hosts and their autonomy while interacting with knowledge varieties. Simultaneously, it highlights the complexities of residents articulating their perspectives.

The study context: the Muong ethnic minority in Hoa Binh and CBT

The selected case study for this research is in Da Bac – a mountainous district in Vietnam's Hoa Binh province. Three villages were approached for the study, namely Ke, Da Bia and Mo Hem.

Table 1. Brief information of the studied villages.

	Da Bia village	Ke village	Mo Hem village
Location	Tien Phong commune, Da Bac district 130 km from Ha Noi Can be accessed by cars or ferries	Hien Luong commune, Da Bac district 100 km from Ha Noi Can be accessed by cars or ferries	Tien Phong commune, Da Bac district 135 km from Ha Noi Can be accessed by cars or ferries
Main attributes	Is the residence of 40 Muong dwellings Villagers rely on farming and fishing as main livelihoods	Reside 112 households, nearly 100% of which are Muong ethnic people Major incomes are from afforesting, fishing and cattle farming	Inhabit 29 Muong families Fishing, followed by afforesting are the main livelihoods of Muong residents in this village
Tourism initiation	2014	2014	2019
Tourism activities	Main tourism services include: • homestay in traditional stilt houses • kayaking across the Hoa Binh lake • trekking • sightseeing • cultural performances • authentic cuisine • volunteering • interactions with local activities (fishing, shrimp catching, and other fishery and farming-related activities)		

These three villages are the residence of the Muong people, one of fifty-three ethnic minority groups in Vietnam, in addition to the ethnic majority group of King people. The village are nestled around Lake Hoa Binh – an upper stream of Da River. The villages are the new relocations for the Muong residents whose traditional lands were taken for the construction of the Hoa Binh hydroelectric dam in the lower stream of the river. Tourism initiatives in these villages were facilitated by Action on Poverty (AOP), an Australia-based NGDO specialised in community development. With focus on landscapes, indigenous culture, and local economic developments, since 2014, the organisation has supported the development of CBT projects in these villages for three years. To meet its livelihood diversification and poverty alleviation objectives, the AOP support focuses on micro-financing for homestay owners and capacity building programs. In order to sustain the CBT projects in post-funded periods, a social enterprise named CBT Da Bac was established in 2017 as a local partner of AOP, and as an agent of changes towards sustainable tourism for Da Bac. CBT Da Bac's mission is to provide tourism-related support to ethnic hosts in Da Bac. In particular, the enterprise is in charge of professionalising CBT experiences in Da Bac; marketing and promoting CBT services to potential markets, particularly the international segment; building the CBT brand of Da Bac; monitoring and driving tourism experiences in Da Bac oriented towards sustainable development (www.dabaccbt.com).

Details about these villages are presented in Table 1.

Research methodology

This study adopts a qualitative approach, with hermeneutic phenomenology driving the research paradigm. It explores the interactions with knowledge varieties from the viewpoints of indigenous hosts and interprets the concept of tourism and its values using indigenous terms. Therefore, the hermeneutic phenomenology is regarded as appropriate. A phenomenological study is an endeavour to understand and interpret research participants' experiences on their terms (Smith & Shinebourne, 2012). The hermeneutic phenomenology focuses on the experience to be interpreted, the process of interpretation and the role of the interpreter (Pernecky & Jamal, 2010). Accordingly, the co-construction of data interpretation between researchers and research participants and the reflexivity of researchers is intrinsic (Chen, 2017).

Table 2. Interview respondents' profile.

Respondents	Location	Age	Gender	Service offering
H1	Da Bia village	45	Female	Homestay
G2	Da Bia village	48	Female	Local guide
H3	Da Bia village	34	Female	Homestay
H4	Da Bia village	26	Female	Homestay
H5	Da Bia village	22	Female	Homestay
C6	Da Bia village	33	Female	Cook and local guide
P7	Da Bia village	33	Female	Cultural performer
H8	Da Bia village	36	Female	Homestay
H9	Mo Hem village	26	Female	Homestay
H10	Mo Hem village	31	Male	Homestay
G11	Mo Hem village	31	Female	Local guide
C12	Ke village	31	Female	Cook
P13	Ke village	31	Female	Cultural performer
H14	Ke village	25	Male	Homestay
P15	Ke village	31	Female	Cultural performer

In particular, the first author, who was in charge of the research design, data collection and analysis, practiced self-reflexivity along the research processes. Her educational background and academic positions in developing countries, followed by her PhD and professions in Australia informed her perspective on relationships between the researchers and research participants. Specifically, she was intrigued by how to transform research *with* indigenous communities into research *for* indigenous communities to address society-grounded problems and to improve research's social impacts. Additionally, she was an advocator of the knowledge co-construction philosophy in highly situated research enquiries. Thus, she acknowledged the issues of intellectual imperialism, the power of the self in distorting the knowledge, the impact of prior-established judgements while drawing insights raised from voices in the field (Russell-Mundine, 2012). The streams of thoughts aided her in establishing research reflexivity.

The first author had planned to visit the site in April 2020, spend time with local hosts, and invite them to participate in the project. However, the international travel bans in Australia since the end of March 2020 due to the COVID-19 pandemic interrupted the field trip. To back up the data collection plan, the research team sought assistance from the manager of CBT Da Bac to secure a list of service providers and their Facebook accounts. From the list, purposive sampling technique was used to approach suitable participants, from whom insights on a research query can be best learnt (Merriam, 1998). Through this technique, only the Muong minority ethnic hosts in the studied villages were invited for interviews. The first author sent a Facebook friend request to potential respondents. Considered that face-to-face greetings and interactions were impossible by the time of collecting data, this step of "making friends virtually" was essential to build acquaintance between the first author and potential respondents and facilitate opened sharing. Then, a message detailing the project's aim in the most readable language and requesting a "conversation" via video calls was sent to potential respondents. The term "conversation" was used to enhance the invite's acceptance, as suggested by the CBT Da Bac manager, who has experienced in working with the potential respondents in these villages since 2014. In total, 15 respondents took part in video interviews. The sample size represented hosts of all services offered in the communities. Furthermore, the diversity in terms of residence dispersion and age was balanced within the sample (see Table 2). Given that a phenomenological study prioritises the idiographic mode of inquiry (Smith & Shinebourne, 2012), the sample size is arguably sufficient as long as the experience of research participants is understood in a deep meaning of itself and a phenomenon from such experience of these individuals is forged in its richness (Creswell & Poth, 2016).

The data was collected using online, life-focus, semi-structured interviews (Chilisa, 2019; Holmes et al., 2016). Respondents were asked to recall their experience with tourism activities. The interviews were centralised around their perceptions of knowledge forms and sources, learning practices, understanding of CBT and reflecting on CBT impacts. The respondents were encouraged to share their experience through story-telling, which in turn helped to express personal viewpoints. For instance, conversations with the respondents were started with informal, non-professional questions such as "Can you share with me a bit about yourself and your major life-changing milestones as of today?" Most of the respondents addressed this question by recalling their life journey, and identifying tourism engagement as a milestone. The data collection was conducted from May to July 2020. This three-month period allowed the first author to practice reflexivity following each interview and to capture in detail the local sense of tourism stories shared before moving on to the next respondent. The interviews were conducted in Vietnamese, which both the first researcher and the respondents could fully speak and comprehend.

The interviews were transcribed verbatim. These transcripts were then analysed and interpreted using the hermeneutic circle framework (Dreyfus & Hubert, 1991; Smith & Shinebourne, 2012). In particular, each transcript was scrutinised multiple times to identify interesting or significant themes. Once all fifteen transcripts were analysed, connections among themes were identified to form theme clusters. Based on these clusters, individual transcripts were reaccessed to add or re-arrange subordinated themes into clusters. The process was repeated until the final themes were articulated and finalised. Nvivo 12 was employed to assist with theme management and forge an understanding of the respondents' experience with the topic.

Research findings

The perception of tourism as an outlandish concept among indigenous hosts

Indigenous hosts bring a different tourism know-how background from local entrepreneurs and service providers in mainstream tourist destinations. Indigenous hosts are mostly unfamiliar with the concept of tourism before their engagements in tourism activities. The modest experience of the industry either in the role of employees or tourists (Fletcher et al., 2016; Nielsen & Wilson, 2012) explains indigenous hosts' unfamiliarity with the concept of tourism. This feature was well reflected in the present study. Through their sharing, indigenous hosts had not self-identified as tourists nor had gained some tourism-related experience before initiating their business. A homestay owner shared:

> Before engaging in tourism, I had never been gone beyond my village. (P15)

> Before 2015 [when I started my homestay], I had no ideas about CBT nor thoughts of the tourism development in my village because the village's [limited] conditions were not suitable for tourism. Villagers used to live in the [Hoa Binh] lake's refugee areas. Since the Hoa Binh hydroelectric dam was built and the water level in the lake was increased, we were forced to move towards mountainous belts [surrounding the lake]. Houses were moved accordingly, with some households having to re-settle four to five times in a dryer place. Meanwhile, there were insufficient forest lands for villagers. Rice fields were submerged by water. Thus, lives in our village were very temporary and harsh. (H14)

Knowledge holders and sources of knowledge

Under the viewpoint of indigenous hosts, three major knowledge holders that mainly shaped their perception of tourism and helped them to gain tourism understanding continuously, were not-for-profit supporters, tourists and other hosts. These knowledge holders diffused different sources of knowledge to indigenous hosts.

Not-for-profit supporters

In the context of this study, not-for-profit supporters were an NGDO (AOP) and a local social enterprise (CBT Da Bac). These stakeholders' credibility in the tourism knowledge varieties was mainly justified by their access to financial and other technical support for indigenous hosts.

> For me, AOP and then CBT Da Bac most influence my current understanding of tourism because they assist us with finance. (H10)

> They [AOP] lent each homestay VND125 million [equivalent to US$5000] without interest, and we would return the loan by months within ten years to CBT Da Bac [...]. Besides, AOP coordinated with the province- and district-level tourism authorities to offer us with training courses and study tours. (H14)

Additionally, indigenous hosts appreciated these supporters for supplying knowledge that helped indigenous hosts subsidise their expertise shortage while operating tourism businesses.

> AOP supported other homestay owners and me in our first three years when we were incapable of managing our business ourselves. Until now [after five years since the CBT project was initiated in my village], if we [indigenous hosts in my village] have any issues, they [AOP and CBT Da Bac] are willing to consult even though they [finished the project in my village and] are supporting other places. (H14)

> They [AOP and CBT Da Bac] created a Facebook group and added us [homestay owners] so that they could constantly guide us about how to manage the homestay. (H5)

The not-for-profit supporters were also valued for their ability to "speak the language" and "use the eyes" of indigenous people. This capacity enabled them to successfully provide Indigenous hosts with an understanding of tourism and a mindset of being a host.

> They [AOP] visited my family, stayed with us, shared real stories and showed us the photos [...]. Altogether tremendously re-shapes my thinking of tourism. (H3)

> Consultants from these organisations [AOP and CBT Da Bac] have studied our people and local culture very well, thus, they know which tourism knowledge to be transferred and how to transfer to indigenous people. (H4)

> CBT Da Bac hired a trainer to assist us with cultural performance. This trainer is a Muong ethnic choreographer. (P13)

Both the NGDO and the social enterprise also offered both tactical know-how and ideological insights. They assisted indigenous hosts with a judgement mechanism to acquire new knowledge. To this end, they played dominant roles in shaping indigenous hosts' perspectives of tourism.

> AOP and CBT Da Bac not only enhance my knowledge of tourism but also help me to believe that I can do tourism by advancing the current resources without massive financial investment. (H3)

> Visitors, who travel a lot and have many new ideas about CBT, advised us how to improve our homestay. [In response], I asked advice from AOP before deciding on the improvements. (H14)

These not-for-profit supporters mainly disseminated tourism know-how via study trips, training and case-by-case consultations. The informal, hands-on, and localised attributes of these dissemination channels further highlighted the recognition of the not-for-profit supporters as the most influent knowledge holders in the knowledge interactions.

> I mostly learnt [my cooking skills] from training courses that AOP, in collaboration with local authorities, organised for homestay owners and other hosts. Cooking ingredients in these courses were sourced from locale [which were highly practical]. (H10).

Generally, indigenous hosts valued these knowledge holders as the most influent contributors to their perspectives of tourism. In particular, it was interpreted that the NGDO moulded the essential baseline from which indigenous perspectives of tourism were accrued. The NGDO, from the viewpoint of indigenous hosts, fundamentally shaped the initial understanding about tourism for indigenous hosts. The NGDO also propagated indigenous hosts with an *expectation set*, which delineated tourism benefits they could receive, how they could obtain these benefits, CBT pitfalls they might tackle during the engagements, and community-oriented responsibilities they should take. Meanwhile, the social enterprise was regarded as a stand-by knowledge provider for indigenous hosts, particularly in the most alien knowledge varieties such as Internet-based marketing and promotion. This organisation also monitored and updated the *expectation set* in accordance with their objectives of developing sustainable tourism in communities. The abovementioned foundational thoughts of CBT moulded and constantly reinforced by these not-for-profit stakeholders arguably helped indigenous hosts to eliminate frustration during the downturn of tourism activities due to the COVID-19 pandemic.

Other hosts
Indigenous hosts recognised other hosts as relevant knowledge holders in the knowledge exchange. Peers' knowledge values varied, depending on whether their business was pioneering or succeeding in a community. Infant or potential homestay owners tended to regard owners of the established homestays in their village as exemplary for their business and their tourism perspectives were heavily reliant on these pioneers.

> Previously, we [our family] had not thought that we would engage in tourism. As we were all peasants; thus, tourism was something exceptionally far-off to us. Later, when we saw other households initiating tourism business and doing well, we just followed. (H8)

> They [indigenous hosts in my village] observed other homestays in the [AOP funded] villages and saw these businesses gain profits and improve economic lives. This observation filled up their understanding of tourism. (G11)

Indigenous hosts regarded in-community peers differently from those out-of-the community with regards to knowledge values. The boundary was set based on the sharing of culture (Muong culture), geography (within a village or a district) and sponsors (under the support of AOP and CBT Da Bac). Accordingly, indigenous hosts valued the in-community peers' contributions to improved understanding on tourism, service offerings, and business know-how. Concurrently, indigenous hosts also learnt how to differentiate their services from these established in-community peers.

> As our homestay was after the other two homestays, I learnt housekeeping skills and guest servings from them. (H1)

> As I am planning to open homestay [in the next few years], I learn from the other homestays, but I also have to make-up things for my projected homestay. (P7)

Indigenous hosts held a scepticism regarding the knowledge values sourced from out-of-the-community peers. The cultural pride, in conjunction with the knowledge judgement mechanism propagated by not-for-profit supporters, underpinned the critical viewpoint of indigenous hosts while valuing learning benefits from out-of-the-community peers.

> I was learnt [from the AOP and CBT Da Bac] about how to operate CBT sustainably. Thus, [when I visited other villages in Mai Chau], I saw them running homestay more likely in the form of individual tourism enterprises rather than CBT with community connections. And I think that way of doing CBT is not sustainable. During the initial days when I started my homestay [which was the first homestay in the village], I was confronted with a lot of challenges, both financial difficulties and well-being issues. However, after 1-2 years [when the challenges were in better control], I shared the benefits of doing CBT to other villagers, which, in return, yield more advantages to my homestay. (H3)

> I can only learn from them [indigenous hosts in Lao Cai] the skills of hosting guests. They focus on luxurious homestays to accommodate guests, whereas, in my community, we prioritise on the connection with nature and value the available resources. [...] They have senior and children tailing visitors to sell souvenirs, which I think unsuitable for my community. Here, we have the "voluntary booth" where local farmers can freely bring their products for sale to display here, tag the products with a price and visitors can pay for what they take without the assistance of sellers. (G2)

Visitors
Host-guest interactions as an agora for learning have been widely resounded in CBT literature. In this study, indigenous hosts regarded visitors as a relevant source of knowledge exchange,

justified by the power of "being customers" and the tourism experience from these knowledge holders.

> Visitors visiting my homestay showed me how to promote my homestay via Google and Facebook. (H5)

> They [visiting travellers] advised me not to commercialise the local culture or to modernise the homestay. They also commented on using local materials such as bamboos to make the homestay's facilities [...]. I think these contributions are very relevant as they help to reduce costs and preserve cultural authenticity. (H1)

It could be observed that among the above tourism knowledge influx, expertise from not-for-profit supporters was the only planned knowledge interventions. Meanwhile, perspective building from knowledge interactions with tourists and other hosts were regarded as diverse, unplanned, and spontaneous. Additionally, pioneering indigenous hosts within a community had their perspectives fundamentally driven by the not-for-profit support. Meanwhile, the tourism perspective of succeeding indigenous hosts in the community was co-shaped by both not-for-profit supporters and the pioneers.

Forms of knowledge

Two knowledge forms emerged from the residents' experience. They include outlandish knowledge and rejuvenated knowledge. With regards to exogenous knowledge, indigenous hosts stressed the relevance of entrepreneurship, housekeeping, marketing and English.

> The housekeeping know-how [that I am inexperienced and in need] is absolutely relevant and readily practical. (H1)

> We would like to learn marketing techniques to promote our homestay. But to be honest, we are lowed educated; thus, we are still incapable of creating and running a [Facebook] page independently [for this purpose]. I hope my son can do this when he is educated in the school. (H8)

The most prevalent form of knowledge being perceived by indigenous hosts was rejuvenated knowledge. Three major facets of this form of knowledge were guest hospitality skills, cooking skills and cultural performance.

> I do have hospitality skills as I host friends and relatives to our house occasionally. However, I did not know any suitable gesture or posture to welcome visitors. (H8)

> Our cultural performance is stem from our culture [Muong]. However, I still need to learn from teachers who are experts in our culture and are experienced in understanding visitors' tastes as well. (P13)

> Cooking meals for domestic visitors do not require me to be trained a lot due to the familiarity of flavour [...]. However, I have not been trained to cook meals for international visitors. (G6)

The frame of references for knowledge absorption

Economic incentives – stabilising and improving livelihoods

The role of economic benefits in determining residents' perceptions of tourism and their attitudes is widely documented, particularly in developing countries (Ribeiro et al., 2017). Indigenous hosts indicated that they were motivated by the prospect of stabilising and enhancing livelihoods, to seek, judge and learn new knowledge. This reference point was thoroughly reflected over various indigenous hosts with different services types. Economic incentives are strongly founded on indigenous residents' daily struggles. Accordingly, the motivation of improving their standard of livings facilitated hosts' engagement with tourism knowledge varieties in which they were previously unfamiliar.

> After my high school, I started working in Ha Noi, and then, moving to Tay Nguyen [the central part of the country] to become a rubber worker. The job was so hard as I had to work during night-time. Therefore, in

2015 when my parent told me about the CBT project at my home, I decided to take the idea and this decision also initiated my first knowledge about CBT (H14).

I finished my secondary school, then married my husband and resided here [in the village] for 13 years. Our family has struggled with sources of livings. Thus, when AOP surveyed and invited us to join the CBT project, we agreed as we wished to change lives. (H3)

This framework also regulated how indigenous residents assessed new information or observations as a form of knowledge. Accordingly, indigenous hosts, being driven by these incentives, actively sought knowledge deemed to be relevant. An outstanding exemplar was the proactive manner of indigenous hosts in observing guests and learning from the observations to enhance visitor satisfaction.

I observed when I served guests. If I saw them eating just a few bites and leaving some left-over, I understood that the food did not satisfy them. (H10)

In my first-time serving guests [...], when I farewelled them, I observed them being struggled to carry stuff. Thus, I immediately gave them a bag. The visitors were so satisfied [...]. I thus understood what hospitality was. (H3)

It became apparent that indigenous hosts' tourism knowledge acquisition was motivated by economic benefits. This frame of reference regulated indigenous hosts' judgement on tourism knowledge using financial metrics. Accordingly, the active learning practices of indigenous hosts towards CBT could be explained by the capacity of this tourism activity in providing a stabilised source of income compared to farming and timber harvesting. However, economic incentives were not the sole mechanism powering indigenous hosts' learning practices. Two homestay owners' different interpretation of a single phenomenon in their study tour exemplified the multiple frames of references moulding indigenous hosts' interpretation.

[Both respondents recalled that during a study trip to Lao Cai, there was a couple of Kinh and Dao ethnics who bought a stilt house of the Thai ethnicity and accommodated as their homestay for visitors].

I observed that their facilities were very basic without huge investments, but they still can host visitors. Thus, I think I can do it too [build and run a homestay at my place]. (H3)

I think the way they did with their homestay [their homestay does not represent their local cultural traits but borrows the culture of another minority ethnic group] is problematic and should not be replicable to other CBT projects. (H4)

Additionally, indigenous hosts absorbed learning benefits from the knowledge exchange, most of which triggered by economic incentives. However, this absorption process was not automated to accrue a workable tourism perspective. The term "workable tourism perspective", from the lens of indigenous hosts, referred to a mindset that was capable of aligning with the characters of tourism service offerings (CBT and homestay).

In my village, all three homestay owners are young, and all seek livelihood improvements through tourism. They also receive similar supports from the project (AOP and CBT Da Bac). As young entrepreneurs, they are potentially opened to further developments [in their viewpoints]. However, all these tourism knowledge and intellectual interventions are just input. One of the homestay owners [whose practices to learn and adapt the new tourism ideas seem not to yield positive outcomes, thus], confront a dilemma in his tourism perspective. For instance, on his Facebook page, he still wants to host guests to his homestay [to earn income]. But, at the same time, he grazes cattle freely in the communal yard [which causes disappointments from visitors and results in unfavourite impacts on his business and other homestays] [...]. Nevertheless, I think this issue is due to his personal aspects rather than tourism-rooted factors (C12)

Self-identity – valuing tourism knowledge to make transformations

This study found that some indigenous hosts' learning practices were driven by the self-identity viewpoint. This framework of reference, which existed before tourism engagements, acted as the lens that indigenous hosts used to evaluate and absorb new tourism understanding. To this end, indigenous hosts experienced transformative learning practices and boosted the impact of such learning experience on their tourism perspectives.

> The motivation of changing my (family) life drives me to engage in tourism [...] I started hosting guests, studied their preferences and learnt how to meet their demand [...]. I used to be worried that I could not afford to build a fully-serviced homestay to host guests. But I am no longer think so. Even now if I have enough finance to modernise my homestay, I will not. My perspective on doing tourism is changed. (H3)

> As a daughter-in-law, my voice was not appreciated, and I could not make any decisions. I would like to gain more economic independence and improve gender empowerment in my family. This thought was more apparent since I engaged in tourism, interacted with visitors, with AOPs and through training courses. Currently, the homestay is still mainly managed by my husband, but my voice is empowered. I also can earn some money to afford my life and deliver some homestay-related decisions. (H5)

> The local culture (Muong) has always fascinated me since I was a little child enthusiastically listening to cultural and historical stories from seniors in the village. These stories gradually become part of my life. Before engaging in tourism, I usually told these stories to my children and nieces [but they seemed not so interested in the stories]. Then, a life-changing event came when CBT was initiated in my village. I got a chance to meet a professional from the Museum of Ethnology. He re-enlightened my passion for culture and showed me a lot of valuable resources about my culture. I was then inspired to transfer these cultural assets to the next generations via tourism. I see CBT through the cultural lens, and my tourism perspective is centralised around these cultural values. (G2)

The learning experience through tourism engagements and the expansion of tourism understanding, in turn, articulated the framework's constituents and transformed its points of view.

> I am passionate about education, particularly fundamental education for young children in my community. After five years of engaging in tourism, I now know what I am looking for through tourism activities and comprehend how tourism can articulate these goals. Being regarded as young generations compared to my grandmother, my mother and other seniors in the community, I had been grown up without acknowledging cultural bonds in the deep and genuine sense. Tourism engagements triggered the re-cohesion between the self and my culture. In conjunction with my teaching background, I can see how I would transfer this personal transformation on to the next generations through education. Through tourism activities, I would like to educate children in my community to get them developed cohesively towards the Muong culture.

Situated perception of CBT values

CBT was mostly interpreted as homestay activities. Accordingly, tourism engagements were associated with the initiation of tourism entrepreneurship and tourism values were predominantly evaluated using economic metrics.

> I do not engage much in tourism. They [homestay owners] do. I just participate in cultural performance. (P13)

> In the next few years when the situation [the COVID-19 pandemic] is in better control, and international travellers can revisit Vietnam, I would like to engage in tourism too, by running a homestay, [...] which helps to improve my livings. (P7)

The concept of *community* in CBT was interpreted as economic benefit sharing, such as sharing guests with other homestays or forming a consortium of homestays to extend service capacity. The sense of economic sharing was also reflected by rotating guests to different homestays and the formation of a community fund.

> The community fund is compulsorily funded by homestays based on their profits from visited travellers. Thus, instead of raising fund from households for public goods such as building roads, the community fund will be used. To this way, families not engaged in tourism also receive tourism benefits indirectly. (G2)

The term *community* also referred to the sense of minimising disturbance from their business to a wider community. To this end, it indicated the social responsibilities acclaimed by a business.

> In my village, all households share the water resource from the stream. Thus, the stream is a communal asset, and I cannot direct much of this resource into my homestay to fill a swimming pool. Thus, it is not suitable to open a swimming pool in my homestay like homestays in other villages. (H10)

> I am planning to expand my business, such as build another homestay and have some private rooms in addition to existing communal rooms. However, there would be a case that villagers will question how possibly I can afford such the investment and might think that it's my fortunate rewards. Thus, if I am insisted on the plan, I would also try to generate jobs for villagers and offer them some incremental incomes. (H3)

Under the viewpoint of a respondent using the lens of tourism economic impacts, the entanglement of the community into tourism activities, as in CBT, was paradoxical by nature. According to her, the heterogeneous nature of the community limited the tourism economic values to indigenous hosts, but simultaneously optimised the tourism benefits for residents as well.

> In my opinion, there always exist both supportive and discouraging perspectives within a community. Eliminating those negative viewpoints is impossible. For instance, homestay owners would like to keep the creek clean for visitors' sightseeing or swimming, but some other locals just freely feed their poultries in the creek. In the positive aspect, it is easier to run homestay hands in hands with the community as this is a win-win relationship. Homestays can offer extra services for their guests, such as harvesting cornfields or experiencing handicrafts with locals. Meanwhile, locals can earn extra income and have their local products (e.g., bamboo shoots, bananas and other agricultural products) sold to visitors with a competitive price. (C12)

To a lesser degree, the term *community* was denoted as changes that tourism activities spilled over to the quality of life of indigenous residents. These included improved natural environment, enhanced cleanliness, changed lifestyles or cultural pride among young generations.

> Since CBT has been initiated in my village, [...], it brings new and better perceptions for locals. They no longer use their stilt house's basement as stockyards. They clean up their living areas. (H14)

> For me, since I engaged in tourism, my life has been much better not only in terms of financial materials but also in other positive [non-financial] dimensions [...]. Thus, if there are things within my capacity that I can share with other villagers, I will. (H3)

Discussion and conclusions

Situated within the debates on residents' perceptions of tourism, the current research elaborates on the complexities of indigenous hosts' perceptions of tourism from the angle of situated tourism knowledge acquisition practices; therefore, responding to a call for qualitative, culturally nuanced methods of understanding residents' perceptions of tourism (Deery et al., 2012; Sharpley, 2014). Findings from this research highlights that indigenous hosts' perceptions of tourism are accumulated from interactions with varied tourism knowledge holders. Within such the knowledge exchange, not-for-profit supporters (i.e., the NGDO and its local partnered social enterprise) pave the way for indigenous hosts to engage in tourism (and economic) activities and contribute in shaping their positive perceptions of tourism. The role of NGDOs in facilitating tourism community of practices is affirmed (Kennedy & Dornan, 2009; Simpson, 2008). Similarly, the involvement of local social enterprises as knowledge brokers in the tourism field has recently advocated (Phi et al., 2017; Wang et al., 2016). These knowledge holders were also regarded as agents of change owing to the not-for-profit nature and sustainable tourism objectives embodied in their proclamations (Spenceley & Meyer, 2012). Through the findings in this study, we argue the plausibility of not-for-profit supporters in informing a sustainable *expectation set* for indigenous hosts about nuanced tourism impacts, thereby positively influencing their perceptions of tourism. This sustainable *expectation set* situates economic benefits in conjunction with other non-economic impacts that indigenous hosts should aware and consider during their tourism engagements.

CBT is an exemplary agora where criticisms on neo-colonialism are flourished, and correspondingly, where endeavours towards decolonialism are advocated. However, while the idea of decolonialised CBT initiatives is admirable, this proposal is seldom workable in practice, justified by the inevitable relationship among host communities, tourists and stakeholders (Tolkach & King, 2015) and the systemic dynamics of the tourism industry (Weaver, 2010). The current study contributes to the debate of CBT and neo- (de-) colonialism through the practices of tourism knowledge acquisition and perspectives accumulation among indigenous hosts from their vantage points.

CBT initiatives in the case study of this research were arguably framed in a decolonialism-orientated CBT development approach. In particular, power was fully in hands of indigenous communities to become a host and a business entrepreneur, external assistance was for consultative purpose only, a social enterprise and CBT networks were in place for the community empowerment, and local know-how was optimised in capacity building (Sakata & Prideaux, 2013; Tolkach & King, 2015). Nevertheless, the tourism knowledge exchange among indigenous hosts in the present study necessarily involves some forms of neo-colonialism. Specifically, CBT stakeholders, who were determinant influencers to tourism economic benefits, were also identified by indigenous hosts as the most important propagators to mould their perceptions of tourism. To this end, economic incentives remain the critical driver in knowledge exchanges between indigenous hosts and tourism knowledge varieties.

It was also found from the research findings that some indigenous hosts optimised the legitimacy of the self in the tourism knowledge exchange to increase their power in relationship to other knowledge holders. They perceived the value of their own expertise, extended their frame of reference beyond economic incentives to cover the self-identity viewpoint in learning processes and experienced transformations in their tourism perspectives. Through the learning practice of these indigenous hosts, the decolonialisation of CBT could be argued. Thus, the present study reiterates the irrelevance of a so-called universal development framework in CBT (Mayaka et al., 2019). We argue that decolonialism (or neo-colonialism) in CBT development cannot be fully articulated through models, frameworks, and best practices. Communities, heterogenous as they are, eventually determine the attainment of this ideological approach in CBT initiatives.

Methodologically, research with indigenous communities has raised heated debates regarding the non-indigenous dominance of knowledge generation – a key exemplar of neo-colonialism. Accordingly, decolonialisation of knowledge-making receives increasing advocates as a justifiable epistemic approach to conduct study with indigenous groups (Buzinde et al., 2020; Carr et al., 2016). An outstanding approach associated with this viewpoint is the Indigeneity-driven methodology, exemplified through co-authorship in research outlets. However, the application of this collaborative approach in research with indigenous communities is not without challenges. Among the challenges are language barriers hindering co-researcher collaboration (Ngo, Lohmann, & Hales, in press). Dredge et al. (2013) stress the time-consuming and community-embeddedness nature of collaborative research that hinders the alignment of this research approach in the current productivity-driven academia world. Another resoundingchallenge to the collaborative approach is the divergence of knowledge interests between practitioners and academics (Ruhanen, 2008; Thomas, 2012). Indeed, claiming the full decolonisation of knowledge generation from research with indigenous participants by non-indigenous researchers through academic platforms is rhetorical. In those cases, a decolonialism-inclined approach could possibly be achievable. In our study, we contest that the hermeneutic phenomenological analysis has potential to achieve this approach. Given the nature of a qualitative enquiry and the researchers' embeddedness in the research process, the hermeneutic circle analysis is argued to enable the data interpretation to be further away from researchers' bias and closer to the respondents' expression (Chen et al., 2020). Furthermore, insights from the analysis are argued to be meaningful and situated (Smith & Shinebourne, 2012).

Additionally, within the literature of tourism and indigenous communities, it is observed that insights rooted from works occurring in Australia, Canada and New Zealand dominate the knowledge-making (Graci et al., 2019; Ruhanen & Whitford, 2019). Accordingly, notions such as Indian, Aboriginal, Indigenous, native and First Nations tourism are mostly embraced under the abstracted concept of indigenous tourism (Hinch & Butler, 2009). Ethnic minority groups in Asian countries are still underrepresented in the literature. This observation justified a Special Issue on indigenous and ethnic communities and tourism experiences within the Asia Pacific region in the Journal of Heritage Tourism (Tham et al., 2020). In line with this trajectory, works on Asian ethnic groups, for instance, in Thailand (Husa, 2020), Taiwan (Shie, 2020), have radically boosted recognition of ethnic minority residents' involvement in the global indigenous tourism movements (Tham et al., 2020). The present study, from the best understanding of the researchers, is the first to represent voices from an ethnic minority community in Vietnam, thus, carving out a new niche in the research area. Such a development facilitates knowledge sharing across cultures and cosmologies, contributing to shape the distinguishing position of indigenous and ethnic people in the tourism knowledge system.

As for the study's limitations, respondents were engaged in tourism through a well-developed CBT model, with active involvements of the NGDO and the local social enterprise. Thus, insights from this study are unable to represent for those communities, where CBT is initiated using different CBT development approaches. For example, the frustration and tourism resentment among indigenous hosts during the COVID-19 pandemic were observed elsewhere; however, were not present in this study. Accordingly, issues associated with the violation of the *expectation set* due to unexpected disruptions were not covered in this paper. Furthermore, indigenous hosts' perceptions of tourism vary over different development stages (Lee & Jan, 2019), which were not addressed in the current study.

Therefore, the authors propose an agenda for future research to enrich the topic of CBT, indigenous hosts and perceptions of tourism. In particular, longitudinal and comparative research about the effects of different tourism knowledge propagators under different tourism models and at different development stages indigenous hosts' perceptions of tourism shaped by is recommended. Additionally, indigenous hosts' perceptions of tourism altered by external shocks could help to unlock the dynamics of community resilience building in CBT planning. Furthermore, how these varied perceptions of tourism impact indigenous hosts' quality of life and the long-term success of CBT projects warrants greater discussion.

Disclosure statement

No potential conflict of interest was reported by the authors.

References

Bell, C., & Ruhanen, L. (2016). The diffusion and adoption of eco-innovations amongst tourism businesses: the role of the social system. *Tourism Recreation Research*, *41*(3), 291–301. https://doi.org/10.1080/02508281.2016.1207881

Bertella, G., & Rinaldi, M. D. (2020). Learning communities and co-creative tourism practices in NGDO projects. *Journal of Sustainable Tourism*, *29*(4), 639–657..

Buultjens, J., & Gale, D. (2013). Facilitating the development of Australian indigenous tourism enterprises: The business ready program for indigenous tourism. *Tourism Management Perspectives*, *5*, 41–50. https://doi.org/10.1016/j.tmp.2012.09.007

Buzinde, C. N., Manuel-Navarrete, D., & Swanson, T. (2020). Co-producing sustainable solutions in indigenous communities through scientific tourism. *Journal of Sustainable Tourism*, *28*(9), 1255–1271. https://doi.org/10.1080/09669582.2020.1732993

Carlisle, S., Kunc, M., Jones, E., & Tiffin, S. (2013). Supporting innovation for tourism development through multi-stakeholder approaches: Experiences from Africa. *Tourism Management*, *35*, 59–69. https://doi.org/10.1016/j.tourman.2012.05.010

Carr, A., Ruhanen, L., & Whitford, M. (2016). Indigenous peoples and tourism: the challenges and opportunities for sustainable tourism. *Journal of Sustainable Tourism*, *24*(8–9), 1067. https://doi.org/10.1080/09669582.2016.1206112

Chen, X. (2017). A phenomenological explication of guanxi in rural tourism management: A case study of a village in China. *Tourism Management*, *63*, 383–394. https://doi.org/10.1016/j.tourman.2017.07.001

Chen, X., Zhang, C. X., Stone, T., & Lamb, J. (2020). Existentially understanding tourism in locale: A dwelling perspective. *Annals of Tourism Research*, *80*, 102828. https://doi.org/10.1016/j.annals.2019.102828

Chilisa, B. (2019). *Indigenous research methodologies*. Sage Publications.

Coghlan, A., & Gooch, M. (2011). Applying a transformative learning framework to volunteer tourism. *Journal of Sustainable Tourism*, *19*(6), 713–728. https://doi.org/10.1080/09669582.2010.542246

Cole, S. (2006). Information and empowerment: The keys to achieving sustainable tourism. *Journal of Sustainable Tourism*, *14*(6), 629–644. https://doi.org/10.2167/jost607.0

Cooper, C. (2006). Knowledge management and tourism. *Annals of Tourism Research*, *33*(1), 47–64. https://doi.org/10.1016/j.annals.2005.04.005

Creswell, J. W., & Poth, C. N. (2016). *Qualitative inquiry and research design: Choosing among five approaches*. Sage publications.

Dabphet, S., Scott, N., & Ruhanen, L. (2012). Applying diffusion theory to destination stakeholder understanding of sustainable tourism development: A case from Thailand. *Journal of Sustainable Tourism*, *20*(8), 1107–1124. https://doi.org/10.1080/09669582.2012.673618

Deery, M., Jago, L., & Fredline, L. (2012). Rethinking social impacts of tourism research: A new research agenda. *Tourism Management*, *33*(1), 64–73. https://doi.org/10.1016/j.tourman.2011.01.026

Dodds, R., Ali, A., & Galaski, K. (2018). Mobilizing knowledge: Determining key elements for success and pitfalls in developing community-based tourism. *Current Issues in Tourism*, *21*(13), 1547–1568. https://doi.org/10.1080/13683500.2016.1150257

Dredge, D., Hales, R., & Jamal, T. (2013). Community case study research: Researcher operacy, embeddedness, and making research matter. *Tourism Analysis*, *18*(1), 29–43. https://doi.org/10.3727/108354213X13613720283601

Dreyfus, H. L., & Hubert, L. (1991). *Being-in-the-world: A commentary on Heidegger's Being and Time, Division I*. The MIT Press.

Espeso-Molinero, P., Carlisle, S., & Pastor-Alfonso, M. J. (2016). Knowledge dialogue through Indigenous tourism product design: a collaborative research process with the Lacandon of Chiapas. *Journal of Sustainable Tourism*, *24*(8–9), 1331–1349. https://doi.org/10.1080/09669582.2016.1193188

Fletcher, C., Pforr, C., & Brueckner, M. (2016). Factors influencing Indigenous engagement in tourism development: an international perspective. *Journal of Sustainable Tourism*, *24*(8–9), 1100–1120. https://doi.org/10.1080/09669582.2016.1173045

Ghaderi, Z., Abooali, G., & Henderson, J. (2018). Community capacity building for tourism in a heritage village: the case of Hawraman Takht in Iran. *Journal of Sustainable Tourism*, *26*(4), 537–550. https://doi.org/10.1080/09669582.2017.1361429

Graci, S., Maher, P. T., Peterson, B., Hardy, A., & Vaugeois, N. (2019). Thoughts from the think tank: Lessons learned from the sustainable Indigenous tourism symposium. *Journal of Ecotourism*, 1–9. https://doi.org/10.1080/14724049.2019.1583754

Guttentag, D., & Smith, S. L. (2020). The diffusion of Airbnb: a comparative look at earlier adopters, later adopters, and non-adopters. *Current Issues in Tourism*, 1–20.

Hinch, T., & Butler, R. (2009). Indigenous tourism. *Tourism Analysis*, *14*(1), 15–27. https://doi.org/10.3727/108354209788970117

Hoarau, H., & Kline, C. (2014). Science and industry: Sharing knowledge for innovation. *Annals of Tourism Research*, *46*, 44–61. https://doi.org/10.1016/j.annals.2014.01.005

Holmes, A. P., Grimwood, B. S., King, L. J., & Nation, L. K. e D. F., the Lutsel K'e Dene First Nation. (2016). Creating an Indigenized visitor code of conduct: The development of Denesoline self-determination for sustainable tourism. *Journal of Sustainable Tourism*, *24*(8-9), 1177–1193. https://doi.org/10.1080/09669582.2016.1158828

Husa, L. C. (2020). The 'souvenirization' and 'touristification' of material culture in Thailand – mutual constructions of 'otherness' in the tourism and souvenir industries. *Journal of Heritage Tourism*, *15*(3), 279–293. https://doi.org/10.1080/1743873X.2019.1611835

Iorio, M., & Corsale, A. (2014). Community-based tourism and networking: Viscri. *Journal of Sustainable Tourism*, *22*(2), 234–255. https://doi.org/10.1080/09669582.2013.802327

Kennedy, K., & Dornan, D. A. (2009). An overview: Tourism non-governmental organizations and poverty reduction in developing countries. *Asia Pacific Journal of Tourism Research*, *14*(2), 183–200. https://doi.org/10.1080/10941660902847237

Kirillova, K., Lehto, X., & Cai, L. (2017). What triggers transformative tourism experiences? *Tourism Recreation Research*, *42*(4), 498–511. https://doi.org/10.1080/02508281.2017.1342349

Lapeyre, R. (2011). The Grootberg lodge partnership in Namibia: towards poverty alleviation and empowerment for long-term sustainability? *Current Issues in Tourism*, *14*(3), 221–234. https://doi.org/10.1080/13683500.2011.555521

Lee, T. H., & Jan, F.-H. (2019). Can community-based tourism contribute to sustainable development? Evidence from residents' perceptions of the sustainability. *Tourism Management, 70*, 368–380. https://doi.org/10.1016/j.tourman.2018.09.003

Liburd, J. J. (2012). Tourism research 2.0. *Annals of Tourism Research, 39*(2), 883–907. https://doi.org/10.1016/j.annals.2011.10.006

Matilainen, A., Suutari, T., Lähdesmäki, M., & Koski, P. (2018). Management by boundaries–Insights into the role of boundary objects in a community-based tourism development project. *Tourism Management, 67*, 284–296. https://doi.org/10.1016/j.tourman.2018.02.003

Mayaka, M., Croy, W. G., & Cox, J. W. (2019). A dimensional approach to community-based tourism: Recognising and differentiating form and context. *Annals of Tourism Research, 74*, 177–190. https://doi.org/10.1016/j.annals.2018.12.002

Melubo, K., & Carr, A. (2019). Developing indigenous tourism in the bomas: critiquing issues from within the Maasai community in Tanzania. *Journal of Heritage Tourism, 14*(3), 219–232. https://doi.org/10.1080/1743873X.2018.1533557

Merriam, S. B. (1998). *Qualitative Research and Case Study Applications in Education. Revised and Expanded from" Case Study Research in Education."* San Francisco: Jossey-Bass Publishers.

Mezirow, J. (1981). A critical theory of adult learning and education. *Adult Education, 32*(1), 3–24. https://doi.org/10.1177/074171368103200101

Mezirow, J. (1997). Transformative learning: Theory to practice. *New Directions for Adult and Continuing Education, 1997*(74), 5–12. https://doi.org/10.1002/ace.7401

Mezirow, J. (2009). Transformative learning theory. In J. Mezirow, & W. Taylor (Eds.), *Transformative learning in practice. Insights from community, workplace and higher education* (p. 18–32). San Francisco: Jossey-Bass.

Nair, V., Musa, G., & Hamzah, A. (2020). Conceptualizing responsible rural tourism in Asia. In V. Nair, A. Hamzah, & G. Musa (Ed.), *Responsible rural tourism in Asia* (p. 1–26). Bristol: Channel View Publications,

Ngo, T., Lohmann, G., & Hales, R. (2020). Integrating the *third way* and *third space* approaches in a post-colonial world: marketing strategies for the business sustainability of community-based tourism enterprises in Vietnam. *Current Issues in Tourism, 23*(15), 1914–1932. https://doi.org/10.1080/13683500.2019.1694494

Ngo, T., Lohmann, G., & Hales, R. (2021). Knowledge co-production in tourism and the process of knowledge development: participatory action research. In J. P. A. Pabel, & A. Anderson (Ed.), *Research paradigm considerations for emerging scholars*. Bristol: Channel View Publications.

Nielsen, N., & Wilson, E. (2012). De-marginalising tourism research: Indigenous Australians as tourists. *Journal of Hospitality and Tourism Management, 19*(1), 76–84.

Nowotny, H. (2003). Democratising expertise and socially robust knowledge. *Science and Public Policy, 30*(3), 151–156. https://doi.org/10.3152/147154303781780461

Nunkoo, R., & Ramkissoon, H. (2011). Developing a community support model for tourism. *Annals of Tourism Research, 38*(3), 964–988. https://doi.org/10.1016/j.annals.2011.01.017

Okazaki, E. (2008). A Community-based tourism model: its conception and use. *Journal of Sustainable Tourism, 16*(5), 511–529. https://doi.org/10.1080/09669580802159594

Pacific Asia Travel Association (PATA) and World Indigenous Tourism Alliance (WINTA). (2014). *Indigenous tourism and human rights in Asia and Pacific Region: Review, analysis & guidelines*. Author.

Pernecky, T., & Jamal, T. (2010). (Hermeneutic) phenomenology in tourism studies. *Annals of Tourism Research, 37*(4), 1055–1075. https://doi.org/10.1016/j.annals.2010.04.002

Phi, G. T., Whitford, M., & Dredge, D. (2017). Knowledge dynamics in the tourism-social entrepreneurship nexus. In *Social entrepreneurship and tourism* (pp. 155–172). Springer.

Pung, J. M., Gnoth, J., & Del Chiappa, G. (2020). Tourist transformation: Towards a conceptual model. *Annals of Tourism Research, 81*, 102885. https://doi.org/10.1016/j.annals.2020.102885

Regmi, K. D., & Walter, P. G. (2016). Conceptualising host learning in community-based ecotourism homestays. *Journal of Ecotourism, 15*(1), 51–63. https://doi.org/10.1080/14724049.2015.1118108

Ribeiro, M. A., Pinto, P., Silva, J. A., & Woosnam, K. M. (2017). Residents' attitudes and the adoption of pro-tourism behaviours: The case of developing island countries. *Tourism Management, 61*, 523–537. https://doi.org/10.1016/j.tourman.2017.03.004

Rogers, E. M. (2003). *Diffusion of innovations (5th ed.)*. (3rd ed.). Free Press.

Ruhanen, L. (2008). Progressing the sustainability debate: A knowledge management approach to sustainable tourism planning. *Current Issues in Tourism, 11*(5), 429–455. https://doi.org/10.1080/13683500802316030

Ruhanen, L., & Whitford, M. (2019). Cultural heritage and Indigenous tourism. *Journal of Heritage Tourism, 14*(3), 179–191. https://doi.org/10.1080/1743873X.2019.1581788

Russell-Mundine, G. (2012). Reflexivity in Indigenous research: Reframing and decolonising research? *Journal of Hospitality and Tourism Management, 19*(1), 85–90. https://doi.org/10.1017/jht.2012.8

Sakata, H., & Prideaux, B. (2013). An alternative approach to community-based ecotourism: a bottom-up locally initiated non-monetised project in Papua New Guinea. *Journal of Sustainable Tourism, 21*(6), 880–899. https://doi.org/10.1080/09669582.2012.756493

Scott, N., & Flores, A. (2015). Diffusion of tourism knowledge through stakeholder networks. In M. McLeod, & R. Vaughan(Eds), *Knowledge Networks and Tourism*, (p.93–107). London: Routledge.

Sen, V., & Walter, P. (2020). Community-based ecotourism and the transformative learning of homestay hosts in Cambodia. *Tourism Recreation Research*, *45*(3), 1–14.

Sharpley, R. (2014). Host perceptions of tourism: A review of the research. *Tourism Management*, *42*, 37–49. https://doi.org/10.1016/j.tourman.2013.10.007

Shaw, G., & Williams, A. (2009). Knowledge transfer and management in tourism organisations: An emerging research agenda. *Tourism Management*, *30*(3), 325–335. https://doi.org/10.1016/j.tourman.2008.02.023

Shie, Y.-J. (2020). Indigenous legacy for building resilience: A case study of Taiwanese mountain river ecotourism. *Tourism Management Perspectives*, *33*, 100612. https://doi.org/10.1016/j.tmp.2019.100612

Simpson, M. C. (2008). Community benefit tourism initiatives - A conceptual oxymoron? *Tourism Management*, *29*(1), 1–18. https://doi.org/10.1016/j.tourman.2007.06.005

Smith, J. A., & Shinebourne, P. (2012). *Interpretative phenomenological analysis*. American Psychological Association.

Spenceley, A., & Meyer, D. (2012). Tourism and poverty reduction: Theory and practice in less economically developed countries. *Journal of Sustainable Tourism*, *20*(3), 297–317. https://doi.org/10.1080/09669582.2012.668909

Tham, A., Ruhanen, L., & Raciti, M. (2020). Tourism with and by Indigenous and ethnic communities in the Asia Pacific region: a bricolage of people, places and partnerships. *Journal of Heritage Tourism*, *15*(3), 243–248. https://doi.org/10.1080/1743873X.2020.1751647

Thomas, R. (2012). Business elites, universities and knowledge transfer in tourism. *Tourism Management*, *33*(3), 553–561. https://doi.org/10.1016/j.tourman.2011.06.009

Tolkach, D., & King, B. (2015). Strengthening Community-Based Tourism in a new resource-based island nation: Why and how? *Tourism Management*, *48*, 386–398. https://doi.org/10.1016/j.tourman.2014.12.013

Travesi, C. (2018). Knowledge and being known: approaching Australian Indigenous tourism through Aboriginal and non-Aboriginal politics of knowledge. *Anthropological Forum*, *28* (3), 275–292. https://doi.org/10.1080/00664677.2018.1486285

Uysal, M., Sirgy, M. J., Woo, E., & Kim, H. L. (2016). Quality of life (QOL) and well-being research in tourism. *Tourism Management*, *53*, 244–261. https://doi.org/10.1016/j.tourman.2015.07.013

Victurine, R. (2000). Building tourism excellence at the community level: Capacity building for community-based entrepreneurs in Uganda. *Journal of Travel Research*, *38*(3), 221–229. https://doi.org/10.1177/004728750003800303

Walter, P. (2009). Local knowledge and adult learning in environmental adult education: Community-based ecotourism in Southern Thailand. *International Journal of Lifelong Education*, *28*(4), 513–532. https://doi.org/10.1080/02601370903031363

Walter, P., Regmi, K. D., & Khanal, P. R. (2018). Host learning in community-based ecotourism in Nepal: The case of Sirubari and Ghalegaun homestays. *Tourism Management Perspectives*, *26*, 49–58. https://doi.org/10.1016/j.tmp.2018.02.002

Wang, C., Duan, Z., & Yu, L. (2016). From nonprofit organization to social enterprise: The paths and future of a Chinese social enterprise in the tourism field. *International Journal of Contemporary Hospitality Management*, *28*(6), 1287–1306. https://doi.org/10.1108/IJCHM-05-2014-0230

Weaver, D. (2010). Community-based tourism as strategic dead-end. *Tourism Recreation Research*, *35*(2), 206–208. https://doi.org/10.1080/02508281.2010.11081635

Weidenfeld, A., Williams, A. M., & Butler, R. W. (2010). Knowledge transfer and innovation among attractions. *Annals of Tourism Research*, *37*(3), 604–626. https://doi.org/10.1016/j.annals.2009.12.001

Xiao, H., & Smith, S. L. (2007). The use of tourism knowledge: Research propositions. *Annals of Tourism Research*, *34*(2), 310–331. https://doi.org/10.1016/j.annals.2006.09.001

Exploring how perceived tourism impacts evolve over time (2009–2019) in an era of uncertainty: economic crisis, host-guest interactions, and Airbnb

Dimitrios Stylidis and Matina Terzidou

ABSTRACT
Cross sectional studies focusing on a single setting are typically not sufficient in explaining how/why residents arrive at certain perceptions of impacts and attitudes towards tourism. This study aims to explore how the impacts of tourism are perceived by local residents over time (2009–2019), potentially shaped by the transient global and local contexts (economic crisis, Airbnb expansion); and frequency of exposure to tourists, explained via the Mere Exposure Theory (MET). MET suggests that repeated exposure to a stimulus or people, is a condition for the enhancement of the attitude towards it. Targeting Kavala residents in Greece, survey data were collected in three different points in time (2009, 2011, 2019), coupled with 21 in-depth interviews with local residents conducted in 2019. Results revealed that residents' perceptions of tourism impacts are dynamic and fluid, greatly affected by the macro and micro economic environment; the rapid expansion of Airbnb in residents' living areas; and the subsequent increasing interaction with tourists. Implications for theory and practice along with limitations and future research directions are also discussed.

Introduction

Tourism largely relies on the support and goodwill of local residents for sustainable planning, development and marketing (Maruyama et al., 2019; Ribeiro et al., 2018; Stylidis et al., 2014). This is well reflected in the vast volume of studies assessing residents' perceptions of the impacts of tourism and their attitudes towards tourism (for a review see Hadinejad et al., 2019; Sharpley, 2014), commonly studied in line with the triple bottom line approach: economic, socio-cultural and environmental (Jurowski et al., 1997). Moving beyond the descriptive nature of the first wave of studies that confined themselves in documenting the various impacts of tourism (e.g., Haralambopoulos & Pizam, 1996), most recent research attempts to explain how/why residents' perceptions and attitudes develop within the tourism context (e.g., Ribeiro et al., 2013; 2018). Research focusing on the host-guest dyad to predict residents' attitudes towards tourism, in particular, includes Woosnam and colleagues' work (Maruyama et al., 2019; Woosnam, 2011; 2012; Woosnam & Aleshinloye, 2018) on the degree of emotional solidarity residents develop with tourists; Aleshinloye et al. (2020), Joo et al. (2018) work on social distance; Cheung and Li (2019) study on visitor-resident relations in developing resilience; and Eusebio et al. (2018) research on resident-tourist interactions. Implicit or explicit in such works is that the host-guest relationship and the subsequent attitudes residents develop towards tourism seem to be also linked to their level of exposure to each other.

The level of exposure to a stimulus has been identified as instrumental in influencing individuals' attitudes and perceptions towards objects or people in studies conducted in several disciplines including marketing and advertising (Janiszewski, 1993; Ruggieri & Boca, 2013), social anthropology (Flores et al., 2018), and linguistics (D'Souza et al., 2020). Exposure is defined as the extent to which we encounter a stimulus; as the Mere Exposure Theory (MET) postulates, repeated exposure to a stimulus or people, is a condition for the enhancement of our attitude towards it (Zajonc, 1968). Previous research supports that people or objects frequently encountered are more positively assessed (Flores et al., 2018; Tom et al., 2007). Flores et al. (2018), for example, who explored whether individuals' attitudes about transgender people are influenced by mere exposure to information and images of faces of transgender people, supported that mere exposure can be a source of prejudice reduction towards this group of people. Hekkert et al. (2013) also confirmed that when an individual is exposed to a stimulus, the attractiveness of an object increases with familiarity. Despite MET's merits and application in several fields, it has not been applied in the context of residents' perceptions of the impacts of tourism and attitudes towards tourism (Hadinejad et al., 2019). Exposure, engagement and interaction with visitors could result in the development of positive attitudes towards tourists and tourism, or the opposite (Eusebio et al., 2018; Raymond & Hall, 2008).

Meanwhile, new phenomena have emerged that intensify, challenge or disrupt such guest – host interactions and exposure, further determining the way the impacts of tourism are perceived, including: a) the widespread distribution of Airbnb in the accommodation sector (see Dolnicar & Talebi, 2020; Suess et al., 2021; Yeager et al., 2020); and b) the global economic crisis of 2007–2008 (considered one of the five worst financial crises) with a loss of over $2 trillion in the global economy, which caused a decrease in international tourist arrivals by 4 percent at global level, and a 6 percent decline in tourism revenues in 2009 (UNWTO. , 2013). Such crisis negatively affected tourism in many countries worldwide (see Boukas & Ziakas, 2013; Hateftabar & Chapuis, 2020; Stylidis & Terzidou, 2014). The location of transient vacation rentals (TVRs) such as Airbnb properties in residential areas rather than commercial zones intensifies residents' exposure and interaction with tourists in both public and private spheres (Jordan & Moore, 2018). Although a recently growing body of research is paying attention to TVRs, limited research exists on residents' perceived impacts of TVRs on neighbourhoods and communities (Heo, 2016; Tussyadiah & Sigala, 2018; Yeager et al., 2020). Economic crisis too has been reported to shape perceptions of tourism impacts in diverse manners; the economic, social and environmental costs of tourism are usually underestimated, whereas the corresponding benefits are overestimated (Garau-Vadell et al., 2018). Similar to TVR research, little is also known about the impact of the economic crisis on residents' attitudes towards tourism (Hateftabar & Chapuis, 2020).

In methodological terms, the vast majority of studies conducted on residents' attitudes towards tourism and the factors determining such attitudes have been cross-sectional. Case-based cross sectional studies that focus on a single setting are typically not sufficient in explaining how/why residents arrive at certain perceptions and attitudes over time (Garau-Vadell et al., 2018; Huh & Vogt, 2008). Such studies also often focus on local (e.g., state of local economy), rather than global effects like the world-wide economic crisis or Airbnb development (Sharpley, 2014). Contrary, longitudinal or repeated cross-sectional studies, as the one proposed here, allow for a better understanding of this relationship over a period of time, unpacking various factors that need to be considered.

Kavala, a city in Greece (Appendix) (estimated population 55,325), served as the study setting for the following reasons: First, international tourists' nights in the city have quadrupled from 51,998 in 2010 to 222,383 in 2018 (Hellenic Chamber of Hotels, 2018). Second, the tourism supply side has radically changed, fully reflecting the sharing economy era (see study context section 3.1). Next, in the period 2008–2017 Greece experienced a severe economic crisis, and Kavala was not an exemption, with unemployment rate, for example, exceeding 27 percent in 2012. Last but not least, the potentials for the city to attract larger volumes of visitors, along with the impacts that such developments invoke, have drastically increased as the historical site of Philippi, in the outskirts of Kavala, was declared an UNESCO world heritage site in 2016.

This study, therefore, aims by means of a mixed-methods approach to explore how: a) the impacts of tourism are perceived by local residents over time (2010–2019); and b) potentially shaped by the transient global and local contexts (economic crisis, growing accommodation supply via TVRs); and c) whether (and how) frequency of exposure to tourists determines locals' attitudes towards tourism. To address this aim, the objectives of this study are threefold: 1) identify how local residents' perceptions of tourism impacts have evolved over the last 10 years (2009–2019) via quantitative measurement over three points in time (2009, 2011, 2019); 2) investigate how the economic crisis and the subsequent growth of TVR (Airbnb) supply in the area shape residents' perceptions and attitudes towards tourism, via 21 in-depth qualitative interviews with local residents; and 3) explore how resident-tourist exposure and interactions further affect locals' attitudes, based on the results obtained in the qualitative study.

More specifically, repeated cross-sectional data based on questionnaire surveys that captured local residents' perceptions of tourism impacts and attitudes towards tourism were used. Data were collected at three points in time in Kavala: at the beginning of the economic crisis in 2009 (481 surveys); during the economic crisis in 2011 (317 surveys); and post-crisis in 2019 (321 surveys). To further explore the perceived impacts of tourism and investigate host-guest exposure and interactions, 21 in-depth qualitative interviews were conducted with local residents of Kavala in August/September 2019. Thematic analysis was used to identify the key themes that emerge from the interviews.

The study contributes to a better understanding of the perceived impacts of tourism, while also applying a new theoretical framework (MET) in the study of residents' attitudes towards tourism development, and explores the broader context within which such perceptions and attitudes develop. Both Monterrubio (2016) and Garau-Vadell et al. (2018) have recently underlined this research gap, as studies trying to explain why/how certain residents' attitudes are constructed over time are rare. Such knowledge will benefit in practice destination management organizations and other stakeholders to effectively plan for sustainable tourism development (Joo et al., 2018), as residents' disagreement can set in danger such plans (see for example the riots in Hong Kong). Findings will not be limited to the strict boundaries of Kavala or Greece, as the underlying phenomena seem to be universal; economic crisis has affected a range of countries in Europe (Spain, Portugal, Ireland) and Latin America (Argentina) (Garau-Vadell et al., 2018), while Airbnb operates on a global scale transforming the hospitality market and the tourism product (Dolnicar & Talebi, 2020; Yeager et al., 2020).

Literature review

Theoretical framework in studying residents' attitudes towards tourism

The vast majority of previous research has either been a-theoretical (Hadinejad et al., 2019), or applied social exchange theory (SET) to explain residents' attitudes towards tourism based on the benefits and costs incurred by the industry (Sharpley, 2014). In line with SET, residents are likely to support tourism development as long as they believe that the expected benefits exceed the anticipated costs (Ap, 1992; Nunkoo & Gursoy, 2012). In economic terms, such benefits include investment and employment, increased standard of living and state revenues (Dillette et al., 2017; McGehee & Andereck, 2004). Among the economic costs, inflation in prices of goods/services and/or land/houses is considered the most prominent one (Cui & Ryan, 2011).

As for socio-cultural benefits, tourism promotes inter-cultural understanding (Yilmaz & Tasci, 2015), fostering feelings of emotional solidarity among residents and tourists (Woosnam et al., 2020), and creates opportunities for shopping and recreation (Byrd et al., 2009). On the negative side, tourism disrupts everyday life and the provision of local services, and generates social issues such as crime and alcoholism (Terzidou et al., 2008). In environmental terms, tourism is often linked to pollution, noise, overcrowding, and traffic congestion (Byrd et al., 2009; Nunkoo & Ramkissoon, 2010), or is seen as catalyst for urban regeneration and preservation of the built and natural environment (Oviedo et al., 2008).

Although study results support SET - as the more positive the impacts of tourism are perceived, the more residents are willing to support tourism development (Gursoy et al., 2010; Stylidis et al., 2014) - such an approach portrays the human decision making process as being too systematic and rational (Nunkoo & Ramkissoon, 2009); often perceived as a monetary, transactional exchange, ignoring the social nature of guest-host interactions (Woosnam & Norman, 2010). It is, therefore, concluded that SET alone is not capable of explaining such complex human phenomena (Yeager et al., 2020). Other theoretical frameworks used to enlighten residents' attitudes include, among others, community attachment theory (McCool & Martin, 1994), emotional solidarity theory (Woosnam, 2012; Woosnam & Aleshinloye, 2018), and social representations theory (Fredline & Faulkner, 2000). Empirical evidence, however, on the application of these theories in tourism remain rather sporadic (Hadinejad et al., 2019).

A large volume of researchers have further argued that tourism development and residents' perceptions and attitudes are not stable, as exemplified in Doxey's (1975) Irridex and Butler's (1980) Tourism Area Life-Cycle frameworks. These models suggest that as tourism development expands, residents' attitudes will go through several stages, ranging from positive like euphoria (early stages), to apathy or antagonism (later stages). Such linear progression from positive to negative reactions is vulnerable to criticism though, as it seems to be deterministic, largely attributing change in attitudes to the increased volume of tourists.

Researchers have classified the range of factors with an effect on the formation of residents' attitudes towards tourism development as intrinsic and extrinsic (Fredline & Faulkner, 2000; Sharpley, 2014). Despite the range of potential determinants explored, some factors have received far less attention including the economic crisis (Hateftabar & Chapuis, 2020; Stylidis & Terzidou, 2014), the TVRs - best reflected in the expansion of the Airbnb (Suess et al., 2021; Yeager et al., 2020) - and guest-host interactions (Aleshinloye et al., 2020; Eusebio et al., 2018; Joo et al., 2018). Aside, past studies are largely homogenous regarding the methodological approach used. The vast majority has followed a quantitative data collection and analysis (Sharpley, 2014), varying from descriptive statistics and regression to structural equation modelling (e.g., Nunkoo & Gursoy, 2012; Ribeiro et al., 2018). As destinations are rather diverse depending on their distinctive characteristics (formed by geographic, socio-economic or tourism elements), different results are often obtained, highlighting the complexity attached to studying phenomena within the context of destinations. Sharpley (2014), Monterrubio (2016), and Jordan and Moore (2018) have criticised the overdependence on quantitative tools, as there are only few studies exploring how/why impacts are perceived by residents using qualitative or mixed methods approaches. Another methodological drawback observed is that most of previous research was cross-sectional, offering snapshots of perceptions of impacts captured on a specific timeframe (Garau-Vadell et al., 2018; Getz, 1994; Huh & Vogt, 2008). There is thus a need for new theories to supplement SET, along with greater attention to how attitudes evolve over time, and the factors that determine such attitudes including the economic crisis and Airbnb, explored using quantitative and qualitative tools. The paper now shifts its attention in presenting the application of a new theoretical framework - MET – which is capable of explaining residents' attitudes towards tourism.

Mere Exposure Theory

Responding to recent calls for additional theoretical frameworks to assist in explaining residents' attitudes towards tourism, this study applies the Mere Exposure Theory (MET) initially developed by Zajonc (1968). In his seminal work, Zajonc (1968) documented that exposure to an increasing stimulus led people to rate this stimulus more favourably, suggesting that such exposure is a condition for the enhancement of our attitude towards it. By "mere" exposure Zajonc (1968) defined a condition making the stimulus accessible to perception. What is implied is that repeat exposure enhances our learning about the stimulus, which in turn increases favourability towards it; this favourability or liking as such seems to be a result of recognition and familiarity (Montoya et al., 2017). In Zajonc's (1968) point of view, mere exposure diminishes people's uncertainty with a novel stimulus, an instinctive fear response. Overexposure, however, may also generate a negative effect and evaluation of the stimulus under consideration (Miller, 1976). Several researchers explored whether liking of a stimulus decreases after a certain number of exposures, with Bornstein's (1989) and Montoya et al. (2017) meta-analyses concluding that there is an inverted-U shaped relation for the mere exposure effect.

Studies in various fields have offered empirical support to MET. Mrkva and Van Boven (2020), for example, reported that repeated exposure to stimuli increased liking and salience, making evaluations not only stronger, but also more emotionally intense. In the context of education, Nuñez (2018) examined the application of the MET on behaviour among college students, reporting that students who are exposed to higher amounts of fictional college media are more likely to have positive attitudes towards partying and socializing in college. Similar findings were reported in fields such as consumer research (Tom et al., 2007) and tourism (Iordanova & Stylidis, 2019; Kim et al., 2019). Kim et al. (2019), for instance, concluded that mere exposure to agritourism leads tourists to change their agriproduct purchasing patterns after the experience. Similarly, frequent exposure to a brand's advertisement, was found to increase consumers' favourable perceptions/preference of it (Tom et al., 2007). Tom et al. (2007) though concluded that the mere exposure effect increased object preference but not necessarily object valuation.

Within the destination marketing context, Iordanova and Stylidis (2019) reported that the 'intensity of the visit' - measured as the volume and frequency of attractions and events visited or attended - had a positive effect on international tourists' image of Linz, Austria. However, Iordanova and Stylidis (2019) study did not consider tourists' interaction with local residents, but only with tangible assets of the destination, thereby neglecting the vital role of human interaction in shaping attitudes. Altogether, previous studies, as summarised in Bornstein's (1989) and Montoya et al. (2017) meta-analysis of 134 and 81 studies respectively, identified a reliable effect of exposure on liking, with moderators including exposure duration, stimulus type, etc.

MET, therefore, offers new opportunities for understanding how residents' attitudes are shaped as a result of increasing exposure and interactions with tourists on a personal basis. Tourists and residents do not only co-exist in or even compete for public places (as Doxey's irridex framework advocate), such as beaches, but may also develop quality relationships through such repeated interaction and exposure. Although cross-cultural understanding is an important outcome of such interactions, it is still unclear as to whether or not such exposure and interactions lead to understanding or misunderstanding among the two parties (Raymond & Hall, 2008; Simpson, 2004).

Mere exposure and guest-host interactions

The current study proposes that resident-tourist interactions can influence residents' attitudes towards tourism via two mechanisms: contact and mere exposure, which supplement well each other. Exposure, at first, does not presuppose contact, but can gradually lead to it, which is considered more deep and meaningful. The inverted-U shaped relation of the mere exposure effect identified in previous meta-analysis, in fact, suggests that after repeated exposure, favourability of the stimuli becomes more stable, while over-exposure produces a decline in its assessment (Montoya et al., 2017), which is a key difference from the principles of the contact theory.

Tourism is largely about human relationships and interactions; following Reisinger and Turner (2003, p.37) interaction is defined as "the personal encounter that takes place between a tourist and a host." Such interactions commonly are short, superficial and non-repetitive (Eusebio & Carneiro, 2012). The nature and quality of interaction are known to determine the experience of both parties (Bimonte & Punzo, 2016). In line with Luo et al. (2015), encounters between residents and tourists are a central component of the tourism experience, further determining tourists' and residents' satisfaction (Kastenholz et al., 2018), and often evolving into something less superficial and temporary.

Previous work suggests that the host-guest relationship and the subsequent attitudes residents develop towards tourism seem to be also related to their level of exposure to and contact with tourists, including the quality of time spent together (Cheung & Li, 2019; Joo et al., 2018). This can be interpreted through the Contact Theory used to understand phenomena like social distance. As this sociological framework suggests, meaningful interactions can improve intergroup relations (Allport, 1954). The Contact theory has been recently applied to explain host-guest relations in the tourism context (Aleshinloye et al., 2020; Joo et al., 2018). Yilmaz and Tasci (2015), for example, reported that perceived social distance between hosts and guests decreased due to contact and bonds with local service operators, and close friendships developed between the two parties. Similarly, exposure and interaction between residents and tourists was found in the context of volunteer tourism to be the most significant antecedent of change in cross-cultural appreciation (Kirillova et al., 2015).

Although interaction between residents and tourists has been recently reported to determine social distance (e.g., Joo et al., 2018), emotional solidarity (e.g., Joo et al., 2018) and/or place attachment (e.g., Aleshinloye et al., 2020), its role in shaping residents' perceptions of tourism impacts is thus far little understood. The few studies available include those conducted by Weaver and Lawton (2001) and Andereck et al. (2005), both reporting that residents with higher levels of contact are more likely to express supportive attitudes. Luo et al. (2015) also confirmed that the level of contact between hosts and guests influences host perceptions of backpackers' impacts. Recently, Eusebio et al. (2018) reported the positive effect of interaction on perceived benefits of tourism and attitudes towards the industry. However, these researchers operationalised interaction via three items (e.g., My interaction with tourists is positive; I make friends with tourists), predominantly focusing on interaction as an outcome. Furthermore, exposure does not necessarily presuppose any level of contact, and provides new opportunities in explaining cases where residents and tourists do no interact. There is, therefore, scope to further explore, in line with the Contact and the Mere Exposure Theories, whether increased exposure to and interaction with tourists also generates positive or negative perceptions and attitudes among residents towards tourists and tourism.

Economic crisis and residents' attitudes towards tourism

The socio-economic context in which residents' attitudes towards tourism occur is considered pivotal in understanding this complex phenomenon. Economic crisis determines people's life, often characterized by loss of income, high unemployment and reductions in investments, followed by lower standard of living and migration (Voon & Voon, 2012). Studies in various fields suggest that the economic crisis negatively affects peoples' mood (Graham et al., 2010) among others. Crisis is also known to decrease tourism demand as it reduces the available income, leading to sudden cuts in reservations and bookings from key tourist markets, thereby negatively affecting hotel occupancy (Song et al., 2011) and the local economy (Henderson, 2007). Boukas and Ziakas (2013), for example, explored the impact of the economic crisis on Cyprus and its tourism industry, highlighting a decrease in visitation and revenues, among other aspects. As a result, the communities experiencing recession undergo radical changes, which are also highly affecting residents' quality of life.

This dependability on tourism among such communities is reported to affect residents' attitudes towards tourism (Gursoy & Rutherford, 2004; McGehee & Andereck, 2004). But most of past research has adopted a micro approach focusing on the current state of the local economy (e.g., Gursoy et al., 2010; Nunkoo & Ramkissoon, 2010), rather than looking also at the broader effects of the global economic crisis, a practice criticised by Sharpley (2014). Only a few studies have explicitly focused on understanding the effects of the global economic crisis on residents' attitudes towards tourism (Garau-Vadell et al., 2018; Hateftabar & Chapuis, 2020; Stylidis & Terzidou, 2014). Stylidis and Terzidou (2014), for example, have documented that the more concerned local residents are with the state of the economy resulting from the global economic crisis, the more positively they will evaluate the economic impacts and the less negatively they will assess the environmental impacts of tourism. Garau-Vadell et al. (2018) further acknowledged that there is lack of empirical evidence in relation to how residents' perceptions of and attitudes towards tourism evolve over time, especially in a period of recession. To address this oversight, they compared data obtained in 2006 and in 2014 from two Spanish destinations (Mallorca and Tenerife), reporting that the economic downturn substantially favoured the development of positive attitudes towards tourism, while also called for further research on this direction. In response to these calls, the multiple cross-sectional design adopted here examines data obtained across three points in time, supplemented also with in-depth interviews, assisting in a greater understanding of how the broader economic environment determines perceptions of tourism impacts and attitudes towards tourism.

Airbnb and residents' attitudes towards tourism

The evolvement of the sharing accommodation sector including short vacation rentals, as envisaged mainly through Airbnb and residents' involvement in this economic activity, provides an additional angle to explore residents' attitudes and support for tourism, especially as this phenomenon intensifies over periods of economic recession (Papatheodorou et al., 2010; Smeral, 2009). Airbnb has been selected as it is the dominant sharing accommodation platform not only in Kavala (covering 93% of TVRs available in the city) but also worldwide, while it has also received the lion's share of attention in academia (Yeager et al., 2020). Notable are the changes that Airbnb generates in residents' life as a result of the increase in visitors staying in residential areas (Suess et al., 2021), including the loss of affordable housing (Lee, 2016). Such interactions can also be positive though; Farmaki and Stergiou (2019) concluded that interactions between co-habiting hosts and guests often contribute towards the alleviation of hosts' feelings of loneliness. In a recent study, Dolnicar and Talebi (2020) further highlighted some of the benefits to hosts, including the opportunity to enjoy benefits tourists themselves enjoy, an experience akin to travel itself.

In the context of residents' attitudes towards tourism, and using predominantly quantitative tools (Yeager et al., 2020) - with only a few exemptions of qualitative studies (Jordan & Moore, 2018) - researchers concluded that residents' perceptions of the positive and negative impacts of STVRs significantly influence their support for STVRs. Jordan and Moore (2018), for example, explored how residents of Oahu, Hawaii, perceive the economic, environmental, and social impacts of TVRs, reporting that the balance between positive and negative impacts is skewed towards the negative. Despite these notable developments, several researchers including Heo (2016), Suess et al. (2021), and Yeager et al. (2020) recently called for additional resident attitude research in the context of STVRs using a blended theoretical perspective, expanded qualitative approaches or longitudinal studies.

Overall, by exploring how perceptions change over time, along with the effect of TVRs, economic crisis and resident-tourist interactions on residents' attitudes towards tourism, under the prism of the MET, this study responds to recent calls for further research "in terms of how they [attitudes] are constructed- in specific contexts and within new theoretical frameworks" (Monterrubio, 2016, p. 425).

Methodology

Unlike the 80 to 90 percent of previous research on residents' attitudes that has followed a quantitative approach (Hadinejad et al., 2019), this study is using mixed-methods to address the complexity of the research objectives. The predominantly quantitative focus of past studies does not allow for a broader, in-depth understanding of residents' attitudes and community perceptions (Deery et al., 2012), and new approaches are needed to move the field forward (Campo & Turbay, 2015). Even the few studies available that have used mixed methods (Dillette et al., 2017; Lawton & Weaver, 2015) did not use a concurrent research design - as this study did in the 2019 research where questionnaires and interviews were simultaneously conducted - but the one approach commonly followed the other (i.e., qualitative followed quantitative). To allow for a better understanding of residents' fluctuating perceptions of tourism impacts, a repeated cross-sectional study was applied allowing alternative patterns to evolve over time. Data were collected at three points in time in Kavala, Greece: shortly before the economic crisis in 2009 ($n = 481$), during the crisis in 2011 ($n = 317$) and post-crisis in 2019 ($n = 321$). A series of One-Way ANOVAs with post-hoc test (Tukey) were conducted to explore for potential differences between responses across the years. The quantitative results obtained in the last data collection were supplemented by 21 in-depth interviews with local residents conducted in 2019.

Study context

The Greek economy entered a ten year recession in 2008 with the cumulative decline of the GDP for the period 2008–2017 estimated at 26.2% (World Bank Report, 2019). The unemployment rate at the national level stood at an alarming level of 27.5% in late 2013, compared to a 7.8% in 2008, and a 17.2% in 2019 (Hellenic Statistical Authority, 2020). Kavala, the setting under study, is located in the Eastern Macedonia and Thrace region. The GDP of the region decreased (in million Euro) from 9,306 in 2009, to 7,579 in 2012, to 6,838 in 2015, before slightly reverting to 7,165 in 2018 (Eurostat Regional Statistics, 2020a). Household income in Eastern Macedonia and Thrace decreased by 29% in the period 2008–2017, reported to be the second lowest in Greece. In 2012, unemployment rate in the area reached 52.6% for those aged between 15 and 24 years. Kavala's economy suffered as many manufacturing industries migrated in neighbouring countries (Bulgaria, Serbia and Romania) due to lower labour cost and taxation. As a result, one out of five people lost their jobs in the region between 2009 and 2017 (Eurostat Regional Statistics, 2020b), while one out of ten commercial businesses in Kavala closed down in 2010.

Although the hotel and rent rooms capacity in the city of Kavala has been virtually unchanged over the 2010–2018 period, the properties available at the same time in the Booking.com platform skyrocketed from 10 licensed hotel units in 2010 to 650 properties on offer in summer 2019 (as a matter of comparison, Bournemouth offers 393 properties and Munich 422). Similarly, in the Airbnb platform the number of available properties stood to 744 in the third quarter of 2019 (in Stuttgart there were 306 available), whereas two years ago the properties available were 326 and in 2011 there were none (Airdna, n.d.).

Survey design

The survey used across the three data collection stages over three points in time comprised several sections, but only the one relevant to this study is presented here. The main section focused on residents' perceived economic, socio-cultural and environmental impacts related to tourism, as well as on their level of support for tourism development. Following previous research, each impact dimension (economic, socio-cultural, environmental) was measured using between four to six items (see Table 2) (Byrd et al., 2009; Nunkoo & Ramkissoon, 2010) on a 5-point Likert scale (Andereck et al., 2005). Residents' support for tourism development was measured with three attributes (i.e., general support for tourism development, support for public funding of tourism development, increase in the volume of tourists to the city) on a five-point agreement scale (1= strongly disagree to 5= strongly agree) (McGehee & Andereck, 2004). The last section of the survey covered the demographic characteristics (gender, age, income) of Kavala residents. Prior to the 2009 study, a pilot test was conducted with 65 randomly selected Kavala residents to check the suitability of the research instrument. Only a few minor wording issues were identified and subsequently corrected. Given that all questions worked well in the 2009 study, no further revisions were required in the subsequent data collection stages in 2011 and in 2019.

Sampling and data collection

The study population was permanent residents (living over a year in Kavala) aged 18 years or over. A multi-stage cluster sampling strategy was used in all three data collection stages in 2009, 2011 and 2019. Following Woosnam and Norman (2010), the sampling strategy involved four stages: first, Kavala was clustered into five major districts based on postcodes; next, ten random streets from each of the five major districts were selected, generating a total of fifty (5 × 10) street names; and, finally, researchers systematically approached every fifth household from the pre-selected streets to complete the survey. The questionnaire survey was administered and collected over a two-month period each time alternating between weekdays and weekends to reduce sampling bias. In the 2009 study, a total of 481 usable surveys out of 650 distributed were collected with a response rate of 77 percent. Similar procedures were followed in the studies conducted in 2011 and in 2019. In the second study, which took place in November and December 2011, 317 surveys were collected and the response rate stood to 65 percent. The last study was conducted in August and September 2019, whereby 321 completed surveys were gathered and analysed with a response rate of 69 percent. Along with the distribution of the questionnaire surveys in 2019, 21 in-depth interviews were conducted with local residents of Kavala, further discussed below.

In-depth interviews

To further unpack the impacts of tourism and supplement the quantitative data, qualitative in-depth interviews were conducted with 21 local residents of Kavala in August/September 2019. The interviews aimed to further explore and understand residents' perceptions of tourism impacts through the lens/prism of the economic crisis, Airbnb development, and via locals' exposure, contact and relationship to tourists visiting the area. Participants were recruited through a combination of purposive and snowball sampling, aiming to collect insights from residents of different ages who reside in the five districts of Kavala. In the first stage, five interviewees (one from each district) were purposefully selected from researchers' acquaintances, based on their interaction with tourists using screening questions such as: *"Do you have any personal exposure to/interaction with tourists?"* Only those who responded positively were invited to take part in the interview process. After the completion of these five initial interviews, participants subsequently recommended other residents relevant to the aim of the research (e.g., coverage of the five districts, interactions with tourists, demographic characteristics), who were subsequently invited by the researchers to participate in the study. Recruitment of participants continued until the saturation point was reached.

After participants' consent was granted, interviews were conducted in public spaces and cafes, lasting on average 45-55 minutes. The interviews were digitally recorded (after permission was obtained) and were transcribed and translated (from Greek to English) retrospectively by both researchers to ensure accuracy of the data. The interview guide comprised questions related to three main areas, including participants' views on: 1) the impacts of tourism in their area; 2) the economic crisis and Airbnb development; and 3) the nature of exposure, contact and interaction to tourists experienced in their everyday life; aiming to decipher how such exposure might have overtly or covertly affected local residents. While the same backbone of questions was used in every interview, however, the two experienced interviewers followed a flexible course of questioning, allowing the research to immerse into personal experiences and views. Thematic analysis was used to identify the key themes that emerged from the interviews, while pseudonyms were used to safeguard the anonymity of the respondents.

Findings

The rich empirical data collected throughout the timespan of ten years is now used to decipher residents' perceptions of tourism impacts in Kavala. In doing this, the findings section starts with a brief presentation of respondents' profile followed by the results of the One-Way ANOVA comparing perceptions of impacts across three points in time. The quantitative results are supplemented by qualitative data obtained via 21 in-depth interviews with residents conducted in 2019 and organised under three themes: economic crisis; resident-tourist exposure and interaction; and Airbnb development, which were found to exercise an effect on residents' perceptions.

Respondents' profile

Male and female were almost equally represented in all three samples (Table 1). Residents aged over 55 years were the largest group in the 2009 sample, followed by the age group of 25-34. In the 2011 and 2019 studies, the 35-44 age group was the largest one, while the 18-24 the smallest one. In terms of income, roughly three out of four respondents across all three studies reported earning less than 30,000€. As the latest census data available are from 2011, comparisons between respondents' profile and the actual population's demographic characteristics should be conducted with caution. The chi-square test conducted did not report any significant difference in terms of respondents' gender, with its distribution being roughly equal across the three studies. Statistically significant differences were observed in age and income, similar to the

Table 1. Sample profile.

Demographic		2009 ($n = 481$)	2011 ($n = 317$)	2019 ($n = 321$)	Census 2011
Gender	Male	47.0%	45.0%	48.0%	48.0%
	Female	53.0%	55.0%	52.0%	52.0%
Age group	18-24	12.1%	14.0%	16.0%	16.9%
	25-34	18.5%	22.0%	21.0%	17.8%
	35-44	17.9%	23.0%	24.0%	17.3%
	45-54	16.4%	23.0%	19.0%	15.7%
	55+	34.8%	18.0%	22.0%	32.9%
Annual income (€)	Less than 9,999	18.0%	25.0%	30.0%	Average Annual
	10,000-19,999	35.4%	22.0%	23.0%	10200- 12650 Euro
	20,000-29,999	23.4%	24.5%	22.0%	
	30,000-39,999	12.6%	12.5%	15.0%	
	40,000+	10.6%	16.0%	10.0%	

study of Huh and Vogt (2008). Nevertheless, the median of income was reported to be '10,000-19,999' in all samples, while mode was '10,000-19,999' in 2009, and '0-9,9999' in 2011 and 2019, reflecting the sharp decrease in the net national disposable income (in Euro) from 17,409 in 2009, to 14,459 in 2011, to 14,490 in 2019, as a result of the economic crisis (Hellenic Statistical Authority, 2019). Despite some differences, the clustering sampling procedure ensured a good representation of households from the five main districts of Kavala. As for the interview participants, those were roughly equally balanced between female (52%) male (48%), mainly aged between 25 – 34 years old (24%), 35 – 44 years old (24%), and 55 years old or over (28%). The question about income was considered a sensitive one and was not asked at the interview stage.

Perceptions of tourism impacts: a transformative process over time

Overall, local residents tend to positively (mean scores exceeding 3) evaluate the economic and socio-cultural impacts of tourism in Kavala (Table 2). They also seem to acknowledge its negative impact on the environment, especially on traffic congestion and pollution. As the series of One-Way ANOVAs with post-hoc tests (Tukey) indicated, significant fluctuations are observed throughout the past decade among peoples' perceptions in ten out of fifteen impacts of tourism studied (Table 2).

In economic terms, residents' agreement with increased investment decreased in 2011 (as compared to 2009) during the recession period and increased again in 2019, which is marked by economic rejuvenation (Figure 1). Agreement with employment opportunities, and with inflation in the price of land/housing, significantly increased among the different points of measurement. Perceptions about the standard of living were rather stable in between 2009 and 2011, but

Table 2. Mean scores across three points in time.

	2009		2011		2019			
	Mean	STD Deviation	Mean	STD Deviation	Mean	STD Deviation	F ratio	Sig
Economic Impacts								
Employment opportunities*	3.51[a]	1.12	3.68[b]	1.04	4.24[c]	.89	49.82	<.000
Increase in standard of living*	3.60[a]	.94	3.49[ab]	.91	3.38[b]	1.18	4.58	.010
Investment/revenue generated*	3.73[a]	1.03	3.54[b]	1.04	3.85[a]	1.08	6.94	.001
Infrastructure development	3.51	1.09	3.50	1.03	3.60	1.07	1.00	.365
Price of land/housing*	3.33[a]	1.13	n/a	n/a	3.56[b]	1.06	124.6	<.000
Socio-Cultural Impacts								
Quality of public services	3.24	1.01	3.06	.96	3.16	1.19	2.91	.055
Community spirit	3.12	1.03	2.97	.98	3.03	1.13	2.08	.126
Opportunity to meet people*	3.74[a]	1.09	3.56[b]	1.09	3.98[c]	.86	12.99	<.000
Entertainment opportunities*	3.51[a]	1.17	3.32[b]	1.14	3.73[c]	.96	10.82	<.000
Aval. of recreational facilities*	3.42	1.10	n/a	n/a	3.24	1.21	64.33	<.000
Crime level	3.19	0.94	n/a	n/a	3.26	1.20	.963	.327
Environmental Impacts○								
Traffic congestion*	3.52[a]	1.17	3.39[a]	1.07	4.03[b]	1.04	30.44	<.000
Crowding*	3.39[a]	1.05	3.26[a]	1.02	3.10[b]	1.29	6.34	.002
Noise level*	3.18[a]	.94	3.14[a]	.86	3.34[b]	1.22	3.66	.026
Environmental pollution	3.39	1.00	3.28	.91	3.35	1.06	1.22	.297
Support for tourism								
Increase in tourists' number	3.83	1.27	3.85	1.23	3.87	.90	.157	.855
Public funding for tourism*	3.91[a]	1.24	3.52[b]	1.34	3.82[a]	1.00	10.50	<.000
Further tourism development	4.04	1.13	4.09	1.08	4.16	.84	1.24	.289

○non-favourable statements were reverse coded in the 2009 study, following Getz, 1994.
Note: F and significant level are presented for the One–Way ANOVA analysis. Significant differences in the means between pairs of the three time periods (2009, 2011, 2019) based on the Tukey test are indicated by the letters a, b or c. Pairs of means that do not have the same letter are significantly different whereas those pairs of means that have the same superscript are not significantly different.
*items where at least one significant difference was reported.
n/a: questions were not included in the 2011 survey.

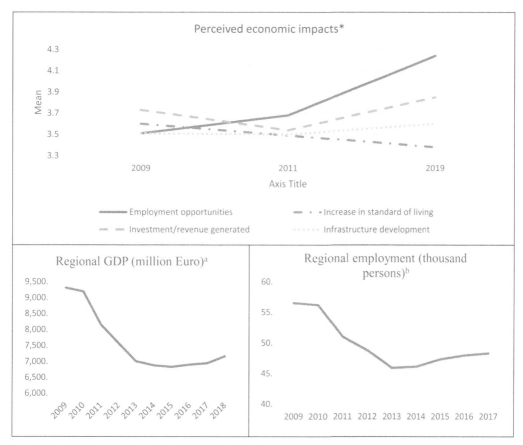

Figure 1. Perceived economic impacts, regional GDP and employment.
* No data available for price of land/housing in 2011
[a] source: https://ec.europa.eu/eurostat/databrowser/view/nama_10r_2gdp/default/table?lang=en
[b] source: https://ec.europa.eu/eurostat/databrowser/view/nama_10r_3empers/default/table?lang=en

agreement with this impact statement decreased in 2019 as compared to 2009. Lastly, infrastructure development remained virtually unchanged across the years. Inevitably, a sharp decrease in GDP and a loss of eleven thousand jobs in the region over a four year period (2009–2013) as evidenced in Figure 1, along with the immigration of several businesses to neighbouring countries, justifies why residents' perceptions on investment and standard of living decreased, inflation increased, and residents increasingly perceive tourism as an opportunity for employment.

In socio-cultural terms, opportunities to meet new people, and entertainment opportunities decreased in 2011 (as compared to 2009) over the recession period and increased again in 2019 (Table 2 and Figure 2). This trend seems to follow the fluctuations in visitor numbers observed in domestic and international tourists evidenced in Figure 3. More precisely, international and domestic tourist overnight stays experienced a downturn in 2011 and 2012 before recovering in 2013 and increasing thereof, although the domestic ones never surpassed the pre-2011 levels (Figure 3). With respect to the number of TVRs in the region (Figure 2), this skyrocketed from literally one in 2010 to 88 in 2014, to 2738 in 2018 (Athanasiou & Kotsi, 2018). The volume of Airbnb properties in Kavala also follows this trend from 326 in the third quarter of 2017 to 744 in the third quarter of 2019 (Figure 2) (Airdna, n.d.). Such increase in tourist numbers and TVRs multiplies the opportunities for interaction and exposure between hosts and guests, offering a tenable explanation to the fluctuations observed in some positive socio-cultural impacts (e.g., opportunities to meet new people). Perceptions about the recreational facilities were rather stable in between 2009 and 2011,

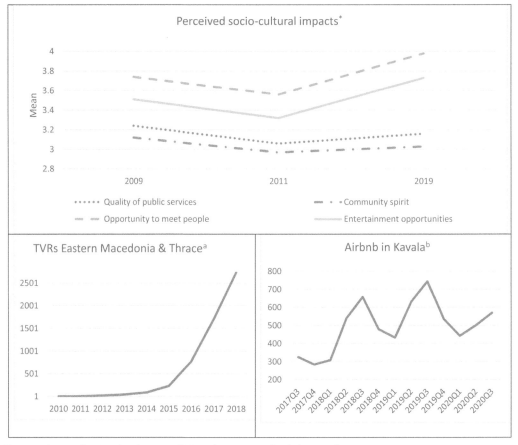

Figure 2. Perceived socio-cultural impacts, TVRs in the region, and Airbnb in Kavala.
* No data available for recreational facilities and crime in 2011
[a] Source: Athanasiou and Kotsi (2018)
[b] Source: https://www.airdna.co/vacation-rental-data/app/gr/default/kavala/overview

but agreement decreased in 2019 as compared to 2009 (Figure 2). Quality of public services and community spirit were both stable over the 10 year period of measurement.

With regards to the environmental impacts, traffic congestion and noise became more prominent in 2019 as compared to 2009 and 2011, while perceptions of crowding decreased over the same period (Table 2 and Figure 3). It is likely that the exponential increase in tourist overnight stays noticed particularly after 2012, from 51,998 international nights in 2010 to 222,383 in 2018 (Figure 3), increased the stress on the transportation system and parking availability, leading to increased traffic congestion and noise. Kavala respondents also appear generally supportive of tourism development, with their responses being rather stable across the past 10 years (Table 2). The only notable fluctuation observed was in the level of agreement for public funding invested in promoting tourism, which decreased significantly between 2009 and 2011 and started reaching the pre-crisis agreement levels in 2019.

The role of economic crisis, guest-host exposure and airbnb on residents' attitudes

Beyond the results of the quantitative studies, the in-depth interviews conducted with local residents in 2019 assisted in further understanding the role of the wider context in which tourism operates, especially focusing on the economic crisis, resident-tourist interaction and exposure, and Airbnb development.

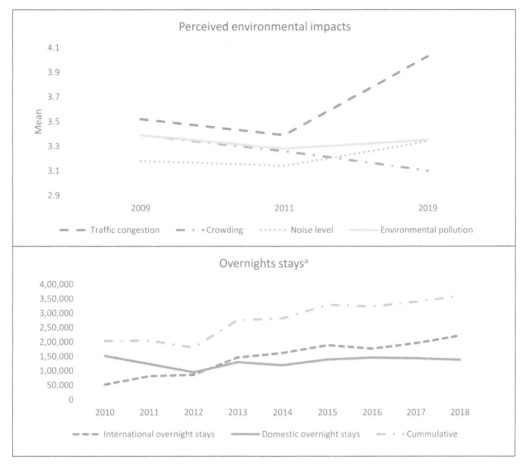

Figure 3. Perceived environmental impacts and overnight stays in Kavala.
[a]Source: Hellenic Chamber of Hotels - INSETE Intelligence 2018

Living in the era of economic crisis

The interviews with local residents further verified the results of the repeated cross sectional study. Local residents seem to hold an even more favourable perception nowadays, as compared to the past 10 years, with regards to economic impacts, such as employment opportunities and additional investment provided; the same applies to some socio-cultural ones including the increased opportunities for entertainment, and the possibility to meet people from other cultures (Dillette et al., 2017). Especially young residents seem to appreciate the employment opportunities offered as a result of the economic boost attributed to tourism development in the area, as further evidenced in the interview data; as Alex, a 25-year old male, stated, for example, "*In the last couple of years you can see a big change in the local economy… fortunately! It seems that the economy kind of restarted. We now have far more opportunities to find a job, as new restaurants, cafes, hotel establishments and shops are opening every year, both inside the city and in its suburbs.*" This was also empirically supported by the results of an independent samples t-test conducted between those aged 18-24 against the rest of the sample population, which disclosed that younger residents perceive more positively the employment opportunities (M = 4.11 vs. M = 3.63), and investment (M = 3.88 vs. M = 3.65), than those aged over 25 years old.

Tourism is widely perceived nowadays as panacea helping to heal the wounds that the long-term recession has marked. As Alex further commented: "*we went through some very dark years, recession, you know… at least one third of the shops closed down… in Omonias street (High* street) and elsewhere half of the shops were available for rent... wages and pensions were cut in half... Thankfully this has started to change now... tourists came like manna from heaven!" The significant increase in the number of tourists as evidenced in Figure 3 has resulted in residents introducing new services and opening new shops to cater for contemporary tourists' and residents' needs:

> "This place was sleepy 10-15 years ago; bars, coffee place and restaurants open up almost everywhere in these days" (Michalis, 51-years old). Another interviewee added that: "They have started offering new activities like tours, scuba-diving lessons, boat-rent, and a lots of yachting, all these things simply didn't exist in the past... it is to attract visitors you know... But as a Greek saying says 'a rising tide lifts all boats.!! [meaning that she gains also from it] [she blinks with one eye]" (Athina, early 30s).

She also added: "souvenir shops are more attractive now. not only for tourists but also for us! They do not sell the kitsch stuff anymore, but more sophisticated items that you can buy as a gift." Others, though, highlighted how expensive now everything is, which is in contradistinction with the broader economic environment in Greece: "We have suffered a lot financially, lots of reductions, wage and pension cuts, increases in VAT and taxation... and at the same time everything became more expensive... how are we supposed to live in our hometown?" (Giannis, 62-years old). This finding is in line with the significant change observed over the previous years in residents' perceptions of the economic costs of tourism.

Not only locals appreciate the positive impacts of tourism on the city's revenues and standard of living, attributed to increased tourist flows, but also acknowledge its socio-cultural benefits. Further considering the economic crisis and the impacts of tourism throughout the past 10 years, some participants stressed how the presence of tourists has positively affected their life and self-esteem: "To be honest, we felt a bit lonely in the past... Greece, you know, is a very popular tourist destination and millions of tourists have been visiting Greece for decades. however, we rarely met tourists in Kavala ... this has now changed, and it is very pleasant to meet people coming from abroad to visit our hometown, we feel proud of living here" (Giotis, 35-year old). Interview results thus also support the positive change observed across time in socio-cultural impacts like entertainment opportunities. As Vicky, 47-years old, also commented: "... especially the Cosmopolis Festival [annual summer festival] and the Air Show Festival [annual summer festival] give Kavala a cosmopolitan flair that we were not used to... Whenever they take place the city is so vivid and full of people... it is a great feeling!".

Resident–tourist interactions: Companionship vs. co-existence

Guest-host interactions and exposure, and the nature of their contact seem to play a decisive role in shaping residents' perceptions of tourism impacts. Types of interactions mentioned were similar to the ones reported in the study of Joo et al. (2018), including dining in restaurants, shopping in gift shops or grocery stores, swimming in the sea, walking around the city and participating in local festivals. In support of the quantitative data presented above, it is evident that interviewees with frequent exposure and personal relationships to tourists are more positively oriented towards visitors and their socio-cultural impacts (e.g., opportunities to meet new people). For example, Vaggelis, a 42-year old boutique hotel receptionist, who daily interacts with tourists and spends time with them, recognised how this interaction broadens his horizons and creates positive feelings. As he stated: "It is always a great pleasure to meet people coming from abroad... we exchange views about different issues, you get a better understanding of how the world operates, making you a more complete person".

The effect repeated exposure and interactions have on shaping positive perceptions of residents is further illuminated in Maria's words, a 37-year old waitress working in a hotel:

> "When you get to know them [the tourists] better you realise how many nice people exist! But also how similar we all are! With some of them we become friends over time, as they come back again and again for several years... Now we go for swimming together and spend lots of hours every time they visit us!... But also with

newcomers, you can see that after the first day of their stay, they open up to us… I mean. they are less reserved, more relaxed and happy. It is so nice to see how happy they feel when they see us in the morning!… And I feel happy as well! Every day that passes I feel we get closer. They often seek for our advice and recommendations; where to eat, where to shop, where to go for swimming… I really enjoy talking to them and spending time even outside my working hours!".

As she further added when asked about the impacts of tourists, these contain both socio-cultural and economic benefits:

"You know, the tourists in Kavala are mainly couples or families with kids… they behave well, they do not consume lots of alcohol or partying hard like other tourists do in the Greek islands… people visiting Kavala are peaceful… it is nice to have them here. Of course, there are always some people griping about tourists, but if you look at it from the other side of the coin, these people contribute a lot to the local economy. So many locals today work in this sector! They rent out their own houses, you know! I believe that we should not be ungrateful."

This seems to explain to a large extent why perceptions about crime and social issues remain rather stable across the studied period 2009–2019, despite the significant increase in tourist numbers documented over the same timeframe.

Similar to the Contact Theory (Joo et al., 2018) and Emotional Solidarity Theory (Woosnam, 2011; Woosnam et al., 2020), cultural differences and stereotyping seem to vanish when residents develop closer relationships to tourists due to their frequent exposure to them, resulting also in more positive perceptions of impacts. Increased familiarity as a result of increased exposure appear to serve as the intermediate link positively shaping attitudes as the MET advocates (Montoya et al., 2017; Zajonc, 1968). As Monterrubio (2016) suggests, relatively small differences between the two parties play a role in enjoying more favourable interactions. Such interactions and exposure do not only occur in residents' working environments but also in their spare time (Dillette et al., 2017). Giorgos, for example, a single 37-year old engineer, narrated how his opinion about Bulgarian tourists changed:

"Every day, after work, I head to the beach bar 'Friends'. EVERY [emphasis is original] day! I love this place… I know the owners and I meet my friends there in the summer… So last summer we met a couple from Bulgaria who frequented the place every day as well. they were staying in an apartment very close by. To be honest, I could never imagine having Bulgarian friends because I didn't fancy them! I thought they are so different from us… But when we started talking I realised that they were actually very cool! They stayed for a long time… we drunk beers together and went for clubbing at nights!. I reconsidered my views about Bulgarians! {he laughs} Seriously, I see them very differently now…

Interviewer: *Do you retain any contact with them?*

Giorgos: *Yes! We are friends now, I visited them in Plovdiv last winter and we chat often in Facebook. They are coming in August again with some other friends!!!"*

Not all types of exposure seem to be pleasant though; With regards to overcrowding, for example, some interviewees explained why they choose alternative supermarkets during the summer months, as they felt they had to contest their place with tourists, developing a conflict-coping strategy (Sinkovics & Penz, 2009). Christina, for example, a retired dentist, argued that:

"The place is full of tourists in the summer, full of tourists… Just imagine that I don't like to use supermarket X anymore, [which is next to the beach] as it is packed with tourists and I know that other friends and family members also prefer other supermarkets during the summer time. You know, some tourists are really rude… they think they are superior… They do not know how to behave. And have no respect. they do not even speak English, it is very hard to communicate with them."

Such an avoidance of interaction with tourists and annoyance is also noticed in Lia's, a 55-year old grocery store owner, words:

"Our place has dramatically changed because of them [the tourists]… There were beaches that only locals used to frequent, this is not the case anymore… I have stopped going there as you see masses of them [tourists], with their camping fridges, lunchboxes, they buy nothing, only leave litter behind them… terrible…

They even own beach bars where they play their own music, mainly Balkan, there is one of them in Iraklitsa bay (a summer resort)... we used to visit this place in the past, but not anymore..."

High levels of interaction in some settings and mundane activities increase the risk of irritating the locals, often creating obstacles in their daily tasks (Joo et al., 2018).

Irrespective of integration seeking or avoidance, there was an unanimous agreement among locals with regards to the negative impacts of tourism on traffic congestion and limited parking availability. This is in line with survey data comparisons revealing that Kavala residents perceive an increase in traffic congestion in 2019 as compared to 2009. *"We have been facing issues with parking in Kavala for many decades, the increase in the volume of tourists the last years has intensified the problem. You can't find a place to park your car anymore."* (Christos, mid-40s). Another relevant key issue highlighted during the interviews was the driving style of foreign tourists:

"Most of tourists in Kavala are Bulgarian, Romanian and Turkish. They reach the city by car and they often don't know the directions... they do not know where to park... how to drive here... Sometimes, they stop in the middle of the street (!), trying to locate something on their navigator/phone; sometimes they do not stop in traffic lights. And most of them drive very slowly, as they do not know the streets, causing huge traffic issues" (Andreas, 22-years old).

The rapid development of airbnb

The rapid development of Airbnb (Figure 2) has created additional opportunities for exposure and interaction between the two parties and intensified some impacts, such as social alienation, business and employment opportunities, and increased cost of living. Passive interactions have been found to sustain feelings, including suspicion, annoyance and competition, which inevitably influence residents' perceptions of impacts in a negative way. For example, the radical immersion of tourists into residents' neighbourhoods through Airbnb is causing irritation to some locals who perceive a negative effect on their sense of community (Jordan & Moore, 2018; Yeager et al., 2020): As Fotini, a 72-years old lady, for example, explained: *"Our neighbourhood used to be very quiet, we all knew each other well. nowadays, you constantly see foreign people coming and leaving, staying for one or two nights, causing trouble and then leaving... they do not show any respect... this is a residential area, you know, local people live here permanently. It affects my everyday life, you know".*

Others underlined the positive effects of tourism development, previously documented in the repeated cross-sectional study, shedding light on the changing nature of residents' occupation. Giannis, for example, argued that due to the increasing demand for tourist accommodation and the introduced tax benefits/policies, many locals have become tourist entrepreneurs themselves: *"The town has been converted into a big hotel!! [he laughs loudly]... Seriously, they have converted old houses, mansions, flats, even basements into accommodation units and they rent them out on the Airbnb platform. In every neighbourhood, in every street, even in areas and buildings that you would NEVER [emphasis given by the interviewee] imagine that people would ever consider to stay..."* (Giannis, 62-years old).

This seems to have affected the price of land and houses. As the data comparisons among the three time periods suggest, Kavala residents perceive an increase in the price of land and housing in 2019 as compared to 2009. Although a number of local residents seem to benefit from renting out their homes or second-houses through Airbnb, others feel excluded: *"People who rent out their properties or who work at hotels and restaurants are those who largely benefit from tourist numbers. The rest of the population does not get anything in return"* (Elsa, 78 years old). This practice has inflated rent prices and reduced the number of properties available for long-term rent in the market. Maria (37), one of the supportive residents of tourism in Kavala also acknowledged this claim: *"It is nearly impossible to find a good place to rent on a yearly contract, we have been looking for a place over two years now and it is still challenging. When a flat in a good condition becomes available for rent, you need to book a viewing immediately and if you don't agree to let it on the spot, it becomes unavailable after a few hours."* Lastly, some residents highlighted how the property market in the city has attracted the interest of international buyers and an increasing tourism demand, leading to power imbalance due to foreigners' superior purchasing capacity. Nikos, in his late 60s, for example, stated: *'You know what? Bulgarian, Romanian and Russian millioners buy the best houses, villas, by the sea, with garden... you cannot even think to buy a house like that nowadays, they push the prices so high... everyone is trying to sell their property to them."*

Discussion

This study aimed to explore whether residents' perceptions of tourism impacts remain stable or fluctuate over a 10-year period along with understanding the role various phenomena such as guest-host exposure and interactions, Airbnb development and the long-lasting economic crisis, play in shaping residents' perceptions and attitudes towards tourism. Results from three surveys conducted in 2009, marking the beginning of the economic crisis, in 2011, during the economic crisis, and finally in 2019, which signposted a rejuvenation of the economy in Greece, revealed that residents' perceptions of tourism impacts are very dynamic and fluid, greatly affected by the development of tourism itself but also by the broader context in which tourism operates.

The finding that perceptions of economic costs (e.g., inflation in prices) increased in Kavala, contradicts recent longitudinal research conducted in two Spanish mass tourist destinations that experienced economic crisis (Garau-Vadell et al., 2018). It also contradicts previous cross-sectional studies in rural or depressed communities (Gursoy & Rutherford, 2004; Nunkoo & Ramkissoon, 2010), which found that over periods of economic downturn, the economic costs tend to be under-estimated. This study also reported that some of the positive economic impacts increased over the years (increased investment, employment opportunities), in contrast to Huh and Vogt (2008) longitudinal study in an Alaskan community, which found economic impacts to be rather stable across two measurements conducted in 1995 and 2001.

In socio-cultural terms, some impacts (opportunities to meet new people, and entertainment opportunities) decreased in 2011, but increased again in 2019, while others remained stable. These findings only partially confirm results generated in Tenerife where a significant increase in socio-cultural perceptions was observed over the years, but contradict those produced in Mallorca, where all impacts were stable (Garau-Vadell et al., 2018). Lastly, this study indicated an increase in some negative environmental impacts (traffic, noise), with results contradicting those produced in mass tourism destinations, whereby perceptions of environmental costs remained stable (Huh & Vogt, 2008) or decreased (Garau-Vadell et al., 2018), indicating residents' willingness in other settings to sacrifice the environment for the financial benefit. Overall, the findings here differ also from Getz's (1994) longitudinal study results, between the years 1978 and 1992, which found that impacts were stable or decreased in Spey Valey, Scotland. Getz (1994) attributed this trend to the economic downturn, decline of resort facilities and failure of tourism to deliver the expected benefits.

The qualitative results also suggested that the global and local economic crisis has marked the way local residents approach tourism, with the vast majority of them recognizing the healing effect tourism had in economic and socio-cultural terms, without however undermining its negative effects on inflation, standard of living, traffic congestion and noise. These results contradict studies (Garau-Vadell et al., 2018; Gursoy & Rutherford, 2004; McGehee & Andereck, 2004), which found that in periods of economic recession residents tend to overestimate the benefits and pay less attention to the costs of tourism. Airbnb seems also to play a key role, as one the hand it offers new employment opportunities and investment, but on the other hand it increases some economic (inflation) and social costs (Lee, 2016). Jordan and Moore (2018) also reported that several interviewees in their study mentioned that their feeling of neighbourhood changed due to

TVRs. Recently Yeager et al. (2020) has also highlighted the importance of ensuring that TVRs do not infringe on residents' sense of community and reflect the values and norms of the host community. This study further advances our understanding as Airbnb provides unique opportunities for exposure and interaction, with most of them turning into meaningful engagement and cultural appreciation.

The interviews also revealed that increased exposure and interaction between the two parties leads to largely positive attitudes towards tourism (Eusebio et al., 2018), but there were also cases where such interactions produced negative outcomes, as in the case of traffic congestion and parking. Such findings confirm to a large extent that mere exposure and interaction increase familiarity and reduce social bias and prejudice as reported in other disciplines and fields (Flores et al., 2018; Iordanova & Stylidis, 2019; Tom et al., 2007). Somewhat similarly, Joo et al. (2018) have reported that frequency of interaction in the tourism context created mixed feelings of emotional solidarity with tourists, with interactions during shopping in gift shops, walking around and participation in festivals having a positive effect, while co-existence in natural areas created negative feelings. The outcome of interactions appear also to be determined by tourists' behaviour; both Tasci and Severt (2016) and Monterrubio (2016) have highlighted that the sustainable behaviour of tourists is of paramount importance for developing bonds between the two parties.

Overall, a blend of challenges and opportunities over a 10 year period of economic uncertainty, marked by austerity measures, massive development of Airbnb, and rapid expansion of tourist numbers, followed by greater opportunities for interactions between residents and tourists, comprise the various pieces of the tourism development jigsaw in the city of Kavala. The theoretical and managerial implications of the study's findings are discussed below along with the limitations of this research and opportunities for future studies.

Theoretical implications

The theoretical contributions of this study are three-fold. First, it is one of the very few studies of its kind testing the stability/fluidity of residents' perceptions of tourism impacts over a rather long period of time and at three points of measurement, as previous longitudinal research covered two points in time (e.g., Garau-Vadell et al., 2018; Getz, 1994; Huh & Vogt, 2008). Unlike the deterministic progression from positive to negative attitudes over the various development stages proposed by established models (TALC, Irridex), this study's results indicate that perceptions of impacts do change over time but not always in the predicted direction. Out of 15 impacts examined across the three dimensions (economic, socio-cultural, environmental), ten impacts exhibited significant changes over time, with perceptions turning more favourable in five of them, and less favourable in the other five. These results contradict: a) Getz's (1994) study which only reported a negative change in perceptions between 1978 and 1992, attributed to unfulfilled expectations from tourism; b) Garau-Vadell et al. (2018) longitudinal research in Mallorca and Tenerife, which found the benefits to be over-estimated and costs to be under-estimated due to the economic crisis; and c) Huh and Vogt (2008) longitudinal study, which reported the economic impacts to be stable over the two periods examined (1995 and 2001), reflecting the minor role of the industry in the small Alaskan island destination studied. Overall, the context of the study, the external forces into play, and the stage of destination's development seem to affect the stability/fluidity of residents' attitudes towards tourism.

Second, this study applies a rather new in tourism theory - MET - in understanding residents' attitudes towards tourism. An increase in the volume of tourists and the expansion of Airbnb has provided additional opportunities for interaction between the two parties. For most local residents, interactions assisted them in developing greater understanding and often bonds with visitors, and in better appreciating the impacts of tourism, helping to maintain a positive attitude towards tourists and the tourism industry (Eusebio et al., 2018). Such findings open new opportunities to interpret resident attitudes beyond a systematic, rational, quasi-transactional economic approach as advocated by SET (Nunkoo & Ramkissoon, 2009; Woosnam & Norman, 2010). In contrast, they lend credence to MET, postulating that frequent exposure to people leads to more favourable evaluations of them via increased levels of familiarity (Montoya et al., 2017), thereby expanding its application to tourism. Frequency of exposure as such seems to be a necessary condition for reduction of cultural bias and stereotypes and social distance, leading to intercultural understanding and emotional solidarity as advocated by the contact and the emotional solidarity theory (Joo et al., 2018; Woosnam et al., 2020). But exposure needs to be translated into something more meaningful, such as contact and interactions, alternatively some residents who had exposure but without interaction might develop negative feelings about tourism and tourists. In fact, for a proportion of the interviewees, superficial exposure to tourists leads to greater disturbance and a diminished experience overall, causing changes to their everyday habits and creating interaction avoidance. Such findings call for additional research on hosts-guests levels and quality of exposure to each other.

Lastly, this study contributes to a better understanding of how the broader environment such as the global economic crisis and the rapid development of Airbnb shape residents' attitudes. Results presented here differ from previous studies conducted under periods of economic uncertainty (Garau-Vadell et al., 2018; McGehee & Andereck, 2004), as Kavala residents seem to recognize beyond the economic benefits also the economic and environmental costs. Airbnb too has generated new opportunities for development and economic benefit, along with a large number of interactions between local residents and their guests, while also negatively transformed perceptions of sense of community for some locals (Jordan & Moore, 2018; Yeager et al., 2020). This study is thus unique in jointly exploring the role of economic crisis and rapid Airbnb expansion in shaping residents' attitudes towards tourism.

Managerial implications

The findings of this study provide a number of implications for destination managers and planners. Given the dynamic nature of residents' perceptions of tourism, a systematic framework and control mechanism for capturing such attitudes is much needed among various points in time. As the results of the study suggest, perceptions of impacts can vary from positive to neutral and back to positive across time. The implementation of this framework will, therefore, provide prudent knowledge for the development of tourism plans that incorporate residents' views and sustain their support, which is a passport for the sustainable development of tourism. Such framework will also monitor the various changes that take place in the local or global environment and their impact on residents' support for tourism. Next, considering the prominent role resident-tourist interactions serve in cultivating favourable perceptions for both parties (Joo et al., 2018; Woosnam et al., 2020), destination management organizations could strategically orchestrate online and offline interactions by planning activities in which residents participate hand in hand with tourists (Woosnam & Aleshinloye, 2018). For instance, it will be a good practice for the municipality of Kavala to initiate during its annual ethnic cultural festival 'Cosmopolis' sub-events that facilitate resident-tourist interaction. If meaningful interactions are achieved, locals' attitudes towards tourism will remain favourable. To this end, events promoting cultural exchange, mutual understanding, and minimizing negative stereotypes could be used (Monterrubio, 2016).

Limitations and future research directions

Like any other study, this research is vulnerable to a number of limitations. First, results are based on three studies conducted on residents living in one destination in Greece. Perceptions of individuals and their interactions with tourists can potentially be different from those living in other places in Greece or even in other countries; future research needs to continue verifying the established relationships in different contexts including mass tourism destinations. Second, this research used residents' interactions with tourists, excluding other key stakeholders such as tourism employees, or other potentially significant outcomes such as emotional solidarity (Woosnam et al., 2020). Future research will need to address these omissions by further studying the impact of interactions tourism employees have with tourists, along with the levels of emotional solidarity they develop. Further, perceptions of impacts can be influenced by political ideology, tourists' nationality and religion or other cultural factors (Kim et al., 2019). Future research should take such aspects into consideration. Additionally, one economic and two socio-cultural items were not included in the 2011 measurement, which restrains from fully understanding the variations of these three items across time. Next, given that this study was conducted prior to Covid-19 pandemic, it will be interesting to validate the results during and post-pandemic to determine potential changes in residents' attitudes. Last but not least, the MET offers strong potentials to explain an array of phenomena in tourism research including resident-tourist interactions in TVRs and inter-cultural understanding; exposure to various images, reviews, and promotional material shaping destination image and loyalty; and value co-creation among residents and tourists.

Disclosure statement

No potential conflict of interest was reported by the authors.

References

Airdna. (n.d.). Vacation rental data. Retrieved December 7, 2020, from https://www.airdna.co/vacation-rental-data/app/gr/default/kavala/overview

Aleshinloye, K., Fu, X., Ribeiro, M. A., Woosnam, K. M., & Tasci, A. D. (2020). The influence of place attachment on social distance: Examining mediating effects of emotional solidarity and the moderating role of interaction. *Journal of Travel Research*, *59*(5), 828–849. https://doi.org/10.1177/0047287519863883

Allport, G. (1954). *The nature of prejudice*. Addison-Wesley Publishing.

Andereck, K. L., Valentine, K. M., Knopf, R. C., & Vogt, C. A. (2005). Residents' perceptions of community tourism impacts. *Annals of Tourism Research*, *32*(4), 1056–1076. https://doi.org/10.1016/j.annals.2005.03.001

Ap, J. (1992). Residents' perceptions on tourism impacts. *Annals of Tourism Research*, *19*(4), 665–690. https://doi.org/10.1016/0160-7383(92)90060-3

Athanasiou, E., & Kotsi, A. (2018). Development in the TVR market in Greece. *KEPE*, *37*, 56–61.

Bimonte, S., & Punzo, L. F. (2016). Tourist development and host–guest interaction: An economic exchange theory. *Annals of Tourism Research*, *58*, 128–139. https://doi.org/10.1016/j.annals.2016.03.004

Bornstein, R. F. (1989). Exposure and affect. *Psychological Bulletin*, *106*(2), 265–289. https://doi.org/10.1037/0033-2909.106.2.265

Boukas, N., & Ziakas, V. (2013). Impacts of the global economic crisis on Cyprus tourism and policy responses. *International Journal of Tourism Research*, *15*(4), 329–345. https://doi.org/10.1002/jtr.1878

Butler, R. (1980). The concept of a tourist area life cycle of evolution: Implications for management of resources. *The Canadian Geographer/Le Géographe Canadien*, *24* (1), 5–12. https://doi.org/10.1111/j.1541-0064.1980.tb00970.x

Byrd, E. T., Bosley, H. E., & Dronberger, M. G. (2009). Comparisons of stakeholder perceptions of tourism impacts in rural eastern North Carolina. *Tourism Management*, *30*(5), 693–703. https://doi.org/10.1016/j.tourman.2008.10.021

Campo, A. R. R., & Turbay, S. (2015). The silence of the kogi in front of tourists. *Annals of Tourism Research*, *52*, 44–59. https://doi.org/10.1016/j.annals.2015.02.014

Cheung, K. S., & Li, L.-H. (2019). Understanding visitor–resident relations in overtourism: Developing resilience for sustainable tourism. *Journal of Sustainable Tourism*, *27*(8), 1197–1216. https://doi.org/10.1080/09669582.2019.1606815

Cui, X., & Ryan, C. (2011). Perceptions of place, modernity and the impacts of tourism – Differences among rural and urban residents of Ankang, China: A likelihood ratio analysis. *Tourism Management*, *32*(3), 604–615. https://doi.org/10.1016/j.tourman.2010.05.012

D'Souza, D., Brady, D., Haensel, J. X., & D'Souza, H. (2020). Is mere exposure enough? The effects of bilingual environments on infant cognitive development. *Royal Society Open Science*, *7*. https://doi.org/10.1098/rsos.180191

Deery, M., Jago, L., & Fredline, L. (2012). Rethinking social impacts of tourism research: a new research agenda. *Tourism Management*, *33*(1), 64–73. https://doi.org/10.1016/j.tourman.2011.01.026

Dillette, A., Douglas, A. C., Martin, D. S., & O'Neill, M. (2017). Resident perceptions on cross-cultural understanding as an outcome of volunteer tourism programs: the Bahamian Family Island perspective. *Journal of Sustainable Tourism*, *25*(9), 1222–1239. https://doi.org/10.1080/09669582.2016.1257631

Dolnicar, S., & Talebi, H. (2020). Does hosting on Airbnb offer hosts vacation-like benefits? Proposing a reconceptualization of peer-to-peer accommodation. *Journal of Hospitality and Tourism Management*, *43*, 111–119. https://doi.org/10.1016/j.jhtm.2020.02.010

Doxey, G. V. (1975). A causation theory of visitor-resident irritants, methodology, and research inferences. In *6th Annual Conference Proceedings of the Travel Research Association* (pp. 195–198). Travel and Tourism Research Association.

Eurostat Regional Statistics. (2020a). *Regional GDP*. Retrieved December 10, 2020, from https://ec.europa.eu/eurostat/databrowser/view/nama_10r_2gdp/default/table?lang=en

Eurostat Regional Statistics. (2020b). *Regional employment*. Retrieved December 10, 2020, from https://ec.europa.eu/eurostat/databrowser/view/nama_10r_3empers/default/table?lang=en

Eusebio, C., & Carneiro, M. J. (2012). Socio-cultural impacts of tourism in urban destinations. *Revista Portuguesa de Estudos Regionais*, *30*(1), 65–76.

Eusebio, C., Vieira, A. L., & Lima, S. (2018). Place attachment, host–tourist interactions, and residents' attitudes towards tourism development: The case of Boa Vista Island in Cape Verde. *Journal of Sustainable Tourism*, *26*(6), 890–909. https://doi.org/10.1080/09669582.2018.1425695

Farmaki, A., & Stergiou, D. P. (2019). Escaping loneliness through Airbnb host-guest interactions. *Tourism Management*, *74*, 331–333. https://doi.org/10.1016/j.tourman.2019.04.006

Flores, A. R., Haider-Markel, D. P., Lewis, D. C., Miller, P. R., Tadlock, B. L., & Taylor, J. K. (2018). Challenged expectations: Mere exposure effects on attitudes about transgender people and rights. *Political Psychology*, *39*(1), 197–216. https://doi.org/10.1111/pops.12402

Fredline, E., & Faulkner, B. (2000). Host community reactions: A cluster analysis. *Annals of Tourism Research*, *27*(3), 763–784. https://doi.org/10.1016/S0160-7383(99)00103-6

Garau-Vadell, J. B., Gutierrez-Taño, D., & Diaz-Armas, R. (2018). Economic crisis and residents' perception of the impacts of tourism in mass tourism destinations. *Journal of Destination Marketing & Management*, *7*, 68–75. https://doi.org/10.1016/j.jdmm.2016.08.008

Getz, D. (1994). Residents' attitudes towards tourism: A longitudinal study in Spey Valley. *Tourism Management*, *15*(4), 247–258. https://doi.org/10.1016/0261-5177(94)90041-8

Graham, C., Chattopadhyay, S., & Picon, M. (2010). Adapting to adversity: Happiness and the 2009 economic crisis in the United States. *Social Research: An International Quarterly*, *77*(2), 715–748.

Gursoy, D., Chi, C. G., & Dyer, P. (2010). Locals' attitudes toward mass and alternative tourism: The case of Sunshine Coast, Australia. *Journal of Travel Research*, *49*(3), 381–394. https://doi.org/10.1177/0047287509346853

Gursoy, D., & Rutherford, D. G. (2004). Host attitudes toward tourism: An improved structural model. *Annals of Tourism Research*, *31*(3), 495–516. https://doi.org/10.1016/j.annals.2003.08.008

Hadinejad, A., Moyle, B., Scott, N., Kralj, A., & Nunkoo, R. (2019). Residents' attitudes to tourism: A review. *Tourism Review*, *74*(2), 150–165. https://doi.org/10.1108/TR-01-2018-0003

Haralambopoulos, N., & Pizam, A. (1996). Perceived impacts of tourism: The case of Samos. *Annals of Tourism Research*, *23*(3), 503–526. https://doi.org/10.1016/0160-7383(95)00075-5

Hateftabar, F., & Chapuis, J. M. (2020). How resident perception of economic crisis influences their perception of tourism. *Journal of Hospitality and Tourism Management*, *43*, 157–168. https://doi.org/10.1016/j.jhtm.2020.02.009

Hekkert, P., Thurgood, C., & Whitfield, T. A. (2013). The mere exposure effect for consumer products as a consequence of existing familiarity and controlled exposure. *Acta Psychologica*, *144*(2), 411–417. https://doi.org/10.1016/j.actpsy.2013.07.015

Hellenic Chamber of Hotels – INSETE Intelligence. (2018). *Tourism regional statistics: Eastern Macedonia and Thrace*. Hellenic Chamber of Hotels.

Hellenic Statistical Authority. (2019). *Per capita figures: GDP and national income*. Retrieved December 5, 2020, from https://www.statistics.gr/en/statistics/-/publication/SEL33/-

Hellenic Statistical Authority. (2020). *Labour force report*. Retrieved December 5, 2020, from https://www.statistics.gr/en/statistics/-/publication/SJO02/-

Henderson, J. C. (2007). *Tourism crises: Causes, consequences & management*. Elsevier.

Heo, Y. (2016). Sharing economy and prospects in tourism research. *Annals of Tourism Research*, *58*, 166–170. https://doi.org/10.1016/j.annals.2016.02.002

Huh, C., & Vogt, C. A. (2008). Changes in residents' attitudes toward tourism over time: A cohort analytical approach. *Journal of Travel Research*, *46*(4), 446–455. https://doi.org/10.1177/0047287507308327

Iordanova, E., & Stylidis, D. (2019). The impact of visitors' experience intensity on in-situ destination image formation. *Tourism Review*, *74*(4), 841–860. https://doi.org/10.1108/TR-12-2018-0178

Janiszewski, C. (1993). Preattentive mere exposure effects. *Journal of Consumer Research*, *20*(3), 376–392. https://doi.org/10.1086/209356

Joo, D., Tasci, A. D., Woosnam, K. M., Maruyama, N. U., Hollas, C. R., & Aleshinloye, K. D. (2018). Residents' attitude towards domestic tourists explained by contact, emotional solidarity and social distance. *Tourism Management*, *64*, 245–257. https://doi.org/10.1016/j.tourman.2017.08.012

Jordan, E. J., & Moore, J. (2018). An in-depth exploration of residents' perceived impacts of transient vacation rentals. *Journal of Travel & Tourism Marketing*, *35*(1), 90–101. https://doi.org/10.1080/10548408.2017.1315844

Jurowski, C., Uysal, M., & Williams, D. R. (1997). A theoretical analysis of host community resident reactions to tourism. *Journal of Travel Research*, *36*(2), 3–11. https://doi.org/10.1177/004728759703600202

Kastenholz, E., Carneiro, M. J., & Eusebio, C. (2018). Diverse socializing patterns in rural tourist experiences – A segmentation analysis. *Current Issues in Tourism*, *21*(4), 401–421. https://doi.org/10.1080/13683500.2015.1087477

Kim, S., Lee, S. K., Lee, D., Jeong, J., & Moon, J. (2019). The effect of agritourism experience on consumers' future food purchase patterns. *Tourism Management*, *70*, 144–152. https://doi.org/10.1016/j.tourman.2018.08.003

Kim, S., Stylidis, D., & Oh, M. (2019). Is perception of destination image stable or does it fluctuate? A measurement of three points in time. *International Journal of Tourism Research*, *21*(4), 447–461. https://doi.org/10.1002/jtr.2273

Kirillova, K., Lehto, X., & Cai, L. (2015). Volunteer tourism and intercultural sensitivity: The role of interaction with host communities. *Journal of Travel & Tourism Marketing*, *32*(4), 382–400. https://doi.org/10.1080/10548408.2014.897300

Lawton, L. J., & Weaver, D. B. (2015). Using residents' perceptions research to inform planning and management for sustainable tourism: a study of the gold coast schoolies week, a contentious tourism event. *Journal of Sustainable Tourism*, *23*(5), 660–682. https://doi.org/10.1080/09669582.2014.991398

Lee, D. (2016). How Airbnb short-term rentals exacerbate Los Angeles's affordable housing crisis: analysis and policy recommendations. *Harvard Law & Policy Review*, *10*, 229.

Luo, X., Brown, G., & Huang, S. (2015). Host perceptions of backpackers: Examining the influence of intergroup contact. *Tourism Management*, *50*, 292–305. https://doi.org/10.1016/j.tourman.2015.03.009

Maruyama, N., Keith, S., & Woosnam, K. M. (2019). Incorporating emotion into social exchange: considering distinct resident groups' attitudes towards ethnic neighborhood tourism in Osaka, Japan. *Journal of Sustainable Tourism*, *27*(8), 1125–1141. https://doi.org/10.1080/09669582.2019.1593992

McCool, S. F., & Martin, S. T. (1994). Community attachment and attitudes toward tourism development. *Journal of Travel Research*, *32*(3), 29–34. https://doi.org/10.1177/004728759403200305

McGehee, N., & Andereck, K. (2004). Factors predicting rural residents' support of tourism. *Journal of Travel Research*, *43*(2), 131–140. https://doi.org/10.1177/0047287504268234

Miller, R. L. (1976). Mere exposure, psychological reactance and attitude change. *Public Opinion Quarterly*, *40*(2), 229–233. https://doi.org/10.1086/268290

Monterrubio, C. (2016). The impact of spring break behaviour: an integrated threat theory analysis of residents' prejudice. *Tourism Management*, *54*, 418–427. https://doi.org/10.1016/j.tourman.2015.12.004

Montoya, R. M., Horton, R. S., Vevea, J. L., Citkowicz, M., & Lauber, E. A. (2017). A re-examination of the mere exposure effect: The influence of repeated exposure on recognition, familiarity, and liking. *Psychological Bulletin*, *143*(5), 459–498. https://doi.org/10.1037/bul0000085

Mrkva, K., & Van Boven, L. (2020). Salience theory of mere exposure: Relative exposure increases liking, extremity, and emotional intensity. *Journal of Personality and Social Psychology*, *118*(6), 1118–1145. https://doi.org/10.1037/pspa0000184

Nuñez, R. (2018). College in the media: the relationship between repeated exposure and college expectations. *Educational Media International*, *55*(1), 1–14. https://doi.org/10.1080/09523987.2018.1439706

Nunkoo, R., & Gursoy, D. (2012). Residents' support for tourism: An identity perspective. *Annals of Tourism Research*, *39*(1), 243–268.

Nunkoo, R., & Ramkissoon, H. (2009). Applying the means-end chain theory and the laddering technique to the study of host attitudes to tourism. *Journal of Sustainable Tourism*, *17*(3), 337–355. https://doi.org/10.1080/09669580802159735

Nunkoo, R., & Ramkissoon, H. (2010). Modeling community support for a proposed integrated resort project. *Journal of Sustainable Tourism*, *18*(2), 257–277. https://doi.org/10.1080/09669580903290991

Oviedo, M. A., Castellanos, M., & Martin, D. (2008). Gaining residents' support for tourism and planning. *International Journal of Tourism Research*, *10*, 95–109.

Papatheodorou, A., Rossello, J., & Xiao, H. (2010). Global economic crisis and tourism: Consequences and perspectives. *Journal of Travel Research*, *49*(1), 39–45. https://doi.org/10.1177/0047287509355327

Raymond, E. M., & Hall, C. M. (2008). The development of cross-cultural (mis) understanding through volunteer tourism. *Journal of Sustainable Tourism*, *16*(5), 530–543. https://doi.org/10.1080/09669580802159610

Reisinger, Y., & Turner, L. W. (2003). *Cross-cultural behavior in tourism*. Elsevier.

Ribeiro, M. A., Pinto, P., Silva, J. A., & Woosnam, K. M. (2018). Examining the predictive validity of SUS-TAS with maximum parsimony in developing island countries. *Journal of Sustainable Tourism*, *26*(3), 379–398. https://doi.org/10.1080/09669582.2017.1355918

Ribeiro, M., Valle, P., & Silva, J. (2013). Residents' attitudes towards tourism development in Cape Verde Islands. *Tourism Geographies*, *15*(4), 654–679. https://doi.org/10.1080/14616688.2013.769022

Ruggieri, S., & Boca, S. (2013). At the roots of product placement: The mere exposure effect. *Europe's Journal of Psychology*, *9*(2), 246–258. https://doi.org/10.5964/ejop.v9i2.522

Sharpley, R. (2014). Host perceptions of tourism: A review of the research. *Tourism Management*, *42*, 37–49. https://doi.org/10.1016/j.tourman.2013.10.007

Simpson, K. (2004). Doing development: The gap year, volunteer-tourists and a popular practice of development. *Journal of International Development*, *16*(5), 681–692. https://doi.org/10.1002/jid.1120

Sinkovics, R. R., & Penz, E. (2009). Social distance between residents and international tourists: Implications for international business. *International Business Review*, *18*, 457–459.

Smeral, E. (2009). The impact of the financial and economic crisis on European tourism. *Journal of Travel Research*, *48*(1), 3–13. https://doi.org/10.1177/0047287509336332

Song, H., Lin, S., Witt, S., & Zhang, X. (2011). Impact of financial/economic crisis on demand for hotel rooms in Hong Kong. *Tourism Management*, *32*(1), 172–186. https://doi.org/10.1016/j.tourman.2010.05.006

Stylidis, D., Biran, A., Sit, J., & Szivas, E. M. (2014). Residents' support for tourism development: the role of residents' place image and perceived tourism impacts. *Tourism Management*, *45*, 260–274. https://doi.org/10.1016/j.tourman.2014.05.006

Stylidis, D., & Terzidou, M. (2014). Tourism and the economic crisis in Kavala, Greece. *Annals of Tourism Research*, *44*, 210–226. https://doi.org/10.1016/j.annals.2013.10.004

Suess, C., Woosnam, K., Mody, M., Dogru, T., & Sirakaya Turk, E. (2021). Understanding how residents' emotional solidarity with Airbnb visitors influences perceptions of their impact on a community: The moderating role of prior experience staying at an Airbnb. *Journal of Travel Research*, *60*(5), 1039–1060. https://doi.org/10.1177/0047287520921234

Tasci, A. D., & Severt, D. (2016). A triple lens measurement of host–guest perceptions for sustainable gaze in tourism. *Journal of Sustainable Tourism*, *25*(6), 711–731.

Terzidou, M., Stylidis, D., & Szivas, E. (2008). Residents' perceptions of religious tourism and its socio-economic impacts on the island of Tinos. *Tourism and Hospitality Planning & Development*, *5*(2), 113–129. https://doi.org/10.1080/14790530802252784

Tom, G., Nelson, C., Srzentic, T., & King, R. (2007). Mere exposure and the endowment effect of consumer decision making. *The Journal of Psychology*, *141*(2), 117–125. https://doi.org/10.3200/JRLP.141.2.117-126

Tussyadiah, I. P., & Sigala, M. (2018). Shareable tourism: Tourism marketing in the sharing economy. *Journal of Travel & Tourism Marketing*, *35*(1), 1–4. https://doi.org/10.1080/10548408.2018.1410938

UNWTO. (2013). *Economic crisis, international tourism decline and its impact on the poor*. World Tourism Organization.

Voon, J. P., & Voon, J. C. (2012). A structural model of consumption: An application to China during the global financial crisis. *The Journal of Socio-Economics*, *41*(3), 284–288. https://doi.org/10.1016/j.socec.2012.01.003

Weaver, D. B., & Lawton, L. J. (2001). Resident perceptions in the urban-rural fringe. *Annals of Tourism Research*, *28*(2), 439–458. https://doi.org/10.1016/S0160-7383(00)00052-9

Woosnam, K. M. (2011). Testing a model of Durkheim's theory of emotional solidarity among residents of a tourism community. *Journal of Travel Research*, *50*(5), 546–558. https://doi.org/10.1177/0047287510379163

Woosnam, K. M. (2012). Using emotional solidarity to explain residents' attitudes about tourism and tourism development. *Journal of Travel Research*, *51*(3), 315–327. https://doi.org/10.1177/0047287511410351

Woosnam, K. M., & Aleshinloye, K. D. (2018). Residents' emotional solidarity with tourists: Explaining perceived impacts of a cultural heritage festival. *Journal of Hospitality & Tourism Research*, *42*(4), 587–605. https://doi.org/10.1177/1096348015584440

Woosnam, K. M., & Norman, W. C. (2010). Measuring residents' emotional solidarity with tourists: Scale development of Durkheim's theoretical constructs. *Journal of Travel Research*, *49*(3), 365–380. https://doi.org/10.1177/0047287509346858

Woosnam, K. M., Stylidis, D., & Ivkov, M. (2020). Explaining conative destination image through cognitive and affective destination image and emotional solidarity with residents. *Journal of Sustainable Tourism*, *28*(6), 917–935. https://doi.org/10.1080/09669582.2019.1708920

World Bank Report. (2019). *Data on Greece*. Retrieved December 7, 2020, from https://data.worldbank.org/country/greece

Yeager, E. P., Boley, B. B., Woosnam, K. M., & Green, G. T. (2020). Modeling residents' attitudes toward short-term vacation rentals. *Journal of Travel Research*, *59*(6), 955–974. https://doi.org/10.1177/0047287519870255

Yilmaz, S. S., & Tasci, A. D. A. (2015). Circumstantial impact of contact on social distance. *Journal of Tourism and Cultural Change*, *13*(2), 115–131. https://doi.org/10.1080/14766825.2014.896921

Zajonc, R. B. (1968). Attitudinal effects of mere exposure. *Journal of Personality and Social Psychology*, *9*(2), 1–27. https://doi.org/10.1037/h0025848

Index

Page numbers in **bold** refer to tables and those in *italic* refer to figures.

Action on Poverty (AOP) 226
affect theory of social exchange 43–4, *44*, 142
Airbnb's 'Neighborhoods' program 194
Airbnb/STVRs: collaborative consumption 93; data collection 85–6, **86**; Foucault's power, knowledge and governmentality 82–3; measurement of constructs 86–7, *87*; positive and negative impacts and support for tourism 83, *84*; resident attitudes 78–80, *80*; Weber's formal and substantive rationality 80–1
Aleshinloye, K. D. 149, 240
Allen, L. 2
Allport, G. W. 7, 18, 30, 156, 157, 160, 166
alternative model *84*, 84–5, *88*
Alvesson, M. 185
American Hotel and Lodging Association (AH&LA) 77
amount of variance extracted (AVE) 213
Andereck, K. L. 3, 4, 245
Ap, J. 3, 208
"Aufstehn.at" platform 178

Back, K. J. 61
Becken, S. 125
Belisle, F. J. 2
Belletti, G. 58
Bentler, P. M. 212
Berno, T. 5, 41, 43, 50, 52, 150
Bobina, N. 82–3
Boley, B. B. 8, 80, 196, 211
bootstrapping 22
Bornstein, R. F. 244
bottom-up spillover theory 6
Boukas, N. 246
Bramwell, B. 10
Buda, D. M. 140
Buhalis, D. 162
Butler, R. W. 1, 159, 160, 162, 192, 243
Byrne, B. M. 212

Cacioppo, J. T. 126
Camargo, B. A. 175
Caruana, R. 178

Cattaneo, C. 184
Cheng, M. 79
Chen, X. 225
Cherayi, S. 104
Cheung, K. S. 185, 240
Cho, H. 128
Choi, H. S. C. 3, 4
Chow, B. 18
Churchill, G. A. Jr. 52
Clement, F. 104
cognitive appraisal theory (CAT): data analysis 212; data collection 211; emotional solidarity concept 208–9; measurement model 212–13, **213**, **214**; measures 211–12; perspective 209–10; positive emotional reactions 207; research model *208*; SET perspective 208; structural model 213–16, **215**; study region 210
cognitive psychologists 209
Cohen, E. 15, 32
collaboration, residents' perceived value 59–60
collective intelligence 124
Collins, R. 140–4, 146, 147, 149, 150
common method bias (CMB) 46, 212
community-based ecotourism (CBET) 223
community-based tourism (CBT) 223; hermeneutic phenomenology 226; indigenous hosts 223, 224; interview respondents' profile **227**, 227–8; knowledge exchange 224; local communities, tourism planning 223; Muong ethnic minority, Hoa Binh 225–6, **226**; perception of tourism 228; and tourism knowledge 224–5; universal development framework 235; *see also* knowledge holders
Comparative fit index (CFI) 48, 212–13
confirmatory factor analysis (CFA) 22, 61, 63–4, **65**, *66*, 87–8
contact theory 160, 245
conviviality 175
correlation matrix **66**
Costanza, R. 198
covariance-based Structural Equation Modeling (CB-SEM) procedure 87
co-variance structural equation modeling (CB-SEM) 46

Crane, A. 178
Crompton, J. L. 3
cultural distance: defined 16, 17; Hofstede's cultural dimensions theory 16
cultural heritage 100, 101
customer-domain (C-D) logic 161
cyber troops 124

D'Alisa, G. 176, 184
Davis, D. 82
Davis, J. S. 192, 194
Davison, W. P. 127
decroissance 174
Deery, M. 1
destination marketing organizations (DMOs) 93, 179
Dillman, D. A. 211
discriminant validity 48, **49**
discursive subjectivities: initiators *vs.* activists 179–81, *180*; nature as, primary discursive object 181–2, *183*; objects, subjects and defining actions 182–3
diverse methodological approaches 2
Dolnicar, S. 246
Doorn, N. V. 78
Doxey, G. V. 1, 145, 148, 157, 159, 163, 243
Dredge, D. 235
Durkheim, E. 6, 142, 143, 145, 147, 150, 209
Dwivedi, Y. K. 7–8

Echeverri, P. 161
economic empowerment 110–11, *111*
educational empowerment 103, 111–12
elaboration likelihood model (ELM) 122, 126–7
electrodermal analysis (EDA) 146
emotional solidarity 6, 7, 139, 145–6, 145–8, *148*, 208–9; affect theory of exchange 43–4, *44*; defined 58; demographic profile 45–6, **46**; dimensions of 68; local attitudes and perceptions 57; measurement and structural models 46–9, **47–9**; promotional campaigns 51; residents' attitudes, tourism development 41–2; sampling and data collection 45; study site 44–5; survey instrument 45; *see also* Ho Chi Minh City (HCMC)
Emotional Solidarity Scale (ESS) 3–4, 45, 50, 147
engagement of rural women: dimensions of 100; empowerment of women 102–4, *104*; intangible cultural heritage for tourism 99–100; *see also* Hui embroidery of Haiyuan County
Erul, E. 7
Espeso-Molinero, P. 224
Eusebio, C. 241, 245
Eveland, W. P., Jr. 128
exploratory factor analysis (EFA) 46, 61–3, **64**
exposure, defined 241

Fan, D. X. 7, 17, 18, 20, 30, 155, 157
Farmaki, A. 79, 157, 246

Farrell, B. H. 2
Fazito, M. 173, 175
Fesenmaier, D. R. 146
Fletcher, R. 173, 176
Flores, A. R. 241
formal (extrinsic) motivations 80
Fornara, F. 127
Fornell, C. 48
Fornell-Larcker method 51
future tourism development (FTD) 44, 45
fuzzy set Qualitative Comparative Analysis (fsQCA) 82

Garau-Vadell, J. B. 79, 92, 242, 246, 258
Gavilyan, Y. 82, 91, 92
gendered cultural practices and tourism 114
geographical expansion 2
Georgescu-Roegen, N. 175
Getz, D. 257, 258
Goeldner, C. R. 17
Goetcheus, C. 8
good-domain (G-D) logic 161
Gordon, K. O. 145
Gretzel, U. 122
grid-group cultural theory 16
guest-host interactions 244–5
Gunther, A. C. 127
Gurran, N. 195, 196
Gursoy, D. 4–8, 42, 43, 57, 83, 91
Gutierrez-Tano, D. 82, 92
Guttentag, D. 78

Hadinejad, A. 5, 6
Hair, J. F. 48
Haiyuan County Intangible Cultural Heritage Incubation Centre 106–7; Hui embroidery 107; research methods 107–8; tourism Hui embroidery 108–10, *109*, *110*
Handapangoda, W. S. 101
Han, X. 157
Harman's one-factor test 46
Hasani, A. 43
Hekkert, P. 241
Henseler, J. 48
Heo, Y. 246
heterotrait-monotrait ratio of correlations (HTMT) 24, 48
Higgins-Desbiolles, F. 185
Hills, T. T. 124
Hitchcock, M. 43
Ho Chi Minh City (HCMC): collaboration 58; data analysis 61; data collection 61; descriptive statistics 62, **62**; location and map of *60*; research space 60–1; residents' tourism perceptions 57–8; scale reliability tests 62, **63**; service provision 57
Homans, G. 42
Hong Kong Census and Statistics Department (2015) 23
Ho, S. S. 128

Howard, D. R. 3, 42, 45
Hoy, D. R. 2
Hsieh, H. P. 57
Hsu, C. H. 18, 140
Huang, J. 18, 140
Huh, C. 257, 258

Illich, I. 175
Incremental Fit Index (IFI) 48
incremental model fit indices 48
indigenous groups 223
influence of presumed influence model (IPIM) 122, 127–30
information and communication technology (ICT) 161–2
institutionalized tourists 159
Intangible Cultural Heritage Incubation Centre (ICHIC) 100, *106*; and women's participation 100–2
integrated threat theory 6
interaction, defined 245
interaction ritual theory: application of theory, tourism research 144–6; empirical use of theory 143–4; methods of measuring emotions 146–7; overview of 142–3, *143*; residents' reaction research 148–9
intergroup contact theory 6
interpersonal barriers 156
intrapersonal barriers 156, *158*
Iordanova, E. 244
Irridex Model 157, 159, 160, 163

Jaafar, M. 61
Jaakson, R. 15, 32
Jabreel, M. 125
Jacobs, J. 140
Jamal, T. 175
Joo, D. 5, 7, 16, 51, 216, 240, 254, 258
Jordan, E. J. 79, 243, 246, 257
Jose, J. P. 104
Jurowski, C. 4

Kaell, H. 140
Kallis, G. 176
Kapera, I. 61
Karreman, D. 185
Keith, S. J. 5
Kelley, H. 158
Khazaei, A. 78
Kim, J. 146
Kim, K. 212
Kim, S. 244
knowledge holders: economic incentives 231–2; forms of knowledge 231; indigenous hosts 230; not-for-profit supporters 228–30; self-identity 232–3; situated perception, CBT values 233–4; visitors 230–1
Ko, D.-W. 3

Lai, H. K. 217
Lai, I. K. W. 43
Lankford, S. V. 3, 42, 45
Larker, D. 48
Laszlo, S. 104
Latouche, S. 175, 184
Lawler, E. J. 41, 50
Lawton, L. J. 245
Lee, C. H. 17
Lee, C. K. 61
Lee, T. H. 57
Levy, P. 124
Liao, Y. 129–30
Li, L. H. 185, 240
Liu, J. C. 2, 57
Li, X. 43, 149
local residents 56
Long, P. T. 2
Lum, C. S. 145
Luo, X. 245
Lu, Q. 129
Lusch, R. F. 161

Manca, S. 127
March, H. 176
Martin, B. S. 197
Martin, W. J. 123
Maruyama, N. U. 5
Massey, D. 195
Mathieson, A. 1
Mcdonald, M. 82
McGehee, N. G. 4
Mckercher, B. 18
McLeod, D. M. 128
Meadows, D. H. 174
measurement model 23–4, **25**, **26**, 212–13, **213**, **214**
Mere Exposure Theory (MET): Airbnb and residents' attitudes 246–7; consumer research and tourism 244; description 241; economic crisis and residents' attitudes 245–6; and guest-host interactions 244–5; in-depth interviews 248–9; mixed-methods approach 242; overexposure 244; residents' attitudes 242–3; respondents' profile **249**, 249–50; sampling and data collection 248; study context 247; survey design 248, **250**; tourists and residents 244; transformative process over time 250–2, *251*, *252*
Mermet, A. 91
Mezirow, J. 225
Michalos, A. 198
Milano, C. 176
Millennium Development Goals (MDGs) 102
Milman, A. 2
Missemer, A. 175
model comparison procedures 89–90, **90**
moderation testing 85, **90**, 90–1
Mody, M. 8

Moghavvemi, S. 212
Monterrubio, C. 242, 243, 255, 258
Montoya, R. M. 244
Moore, J. 79, 243, 246, 257
Morais, D. B. 192
Moscovici, S. 5
Mrkva, K. 244
multivariate normality 88
Munanura, I. E. 4, 7
Mundet, L. 83, 91
Muong ethnic minority, Hoa Binh 225–6, **226**
Murray, I. 4

Nadegger, M. 8
Navarro-Jurado, E. 175
near-venturers 160
negative emotional energy 142
netnography 178
Neuhofer, B. 161
news internalizing 128
Ngo, T. 8
Ng, S. I. 17
Nguyen, H. M. 4, 7
non-governmental developmental organisations (NGDOs) 223
non-hosting residents 77
non-institutionalized tourists 159
Norman, W. C. 3, 61, 248
not-for-profit supporters 228–30
Nunez, R. 244
Nunkoo, R. 5–8, 43, 58, 82, 83, 85, 91
NVivo 11 Software 22

O'Hara, C. 104
Olya, H. G. T. 82, 91, 92
Organization of Economic Cooperation and Development 212
Oswick, C. 178
Ouyang, Z. 83, 217

Pacific Asia Travel Association (PATA) 223
paired tourist-resident social contact 167
partial least squares structural equation modelling (PLS-SEM) 22
peer-to-peer accommodations (P2PAs) 78; defined 190; management and planning 190, *191*; rent-gaps and contested place-making 190; urban residents' social carrying capacity 197–8; urban tourism system 198–9; x-axis 191–2; y-axis 192–6, *193*
perceived cultural distance 19, 30
perceived peer expression 128
Perdue, R. R. 2, 192
Petty, R. E. 126
Pfister, R. E. 42, 61
Pham, T. 8
Phibbs, P. 195, 196
Phuc, H. N. 4, 7

Picard, D. 145
Pizam, A. 2
platform urbanism 78
Plog, S. C. 159, 163
Plog's tourist psychographics 159
political empowerment 103, 113–14
positive emotional energy 142
P2PA negative feedback loops 198
P2PA positive feedback loops 199
predictor variables identification 2
Prince, S. 102
productivity gains 184
psychological empowerment 113

qualitative data analysis 27, 29
quality of life (QOL) 84
Qualtrics panel, online opt-in survey 211
quantile-quantile (QQ) plots 88

Ramkissoon, H. 85
Ramos, S. P. 83, 91
Rasoolimanesh, S. M. 61, 81, 82
Regmi, K. D. 223, 225
Reisinger, Y. 17, 245
residents' attitudes: Airbnb 246–7, 256–7; Airbnb/STVRs 78–80, *80*; categories 159; economic crisis, guest-host exposure and airbnb 252–7; impacts of tourism 123; online information society 123–5; P2PAs 196–7; and social impacts 7–8; social media platforms 122; tourism 78
residents' empowerment and overtourism 8
resident–tourist interactions 7, 254–6
Ribeiro, M. A. 4, 43, 140
Richards, S. 79
Ritchie, B. W. 129
Ritchie, J. R. 17
Rocha, E. M. 104
Root Mean-Square Error of Approximation (RMSEA) 212–13
Rosenberg, M. J. 17
Rossel, J. 144
Rothman, R. A. 1

Samerski, S. 184
Satorra, A. 212
Scheyvens, R. 10, 103
S-D logic perceives value 161
Sen, V. 225
service-domain (S-D) logic 161
service-oriented social contact 33
Severt, D. 258
Shakeela, A. 125
Sharma, B. 57
Sharpley, R. 79, 209, 243, 246
short-term vacation rentals (STVRs) 77, 191
Shoval, N. 149
Simone, L. 104
Sirakaya, E. 3

Skalen, P. 161
Smith, L. 100
Smith, S. L. 140, 150
social contact: cultural distance and 16; data analysis 22; demographics of samples 22, **23**; description 16; favourable and unfavourable experiences *162*; impacts of 157; practice theory 154; questionnaire and interview protocol development 20–1; research context 20; role of 19–20, *20*; sampling and data collection 21–2; types of 154–5; *see also* sustainable tourist-resident relationship; tourist-host social contact; tourist-resident social contact research
social dilemma theory 6
social emotions: positive perceptions and behaviors 139; segregated and conflicting groups 140; socially undesirable/senseless behaviors 139; theory of planned behavior 141
social empowerment 103, 104, 112–13
social exchange theory (SET) 4, 5, 41–3, 78, 121–2, 130, 141, 207, 208, 242
social identity theory 6
social learning theory 129
social media users: direct and indirect effects 129–30; knowledge advancement 122; public opinion 122; tourism discourses 125–6, **126**
social representations theory (SRT) 5, 122
socio-ecological systems theory 198
Soderstrom, O. 91
So, K. K. F. 82
Sørensen, A. 145
Speier, E. 83
Stergiou, D. P. 79, 246
Stewart, W. P. 3
Stienmetz, J. L. 79
Storey, J. D. 127
structural barriers 156
structural equation modeling (SEM) 46, 61, 87–9, 212; model goodness of fit and hypotheses 65, *67*; SEM model 65, **67**
structural model 24, 27, **27**, **28**, *29*, 213–16, **215**
Strzelecka, M. 81
Stylidis, D. 8, 85, 244, 246
substantive (intrinsic) motivations 80
Suess, C. 79, 246
Su, M. M. 8
sustainable development goals (SDGs) 10, 102
Sustainable Tourism Attitude Scale (SUS-TAS) 3
sustainable tourism development: description 56–7; residents' perception 58–9, *59*; stakeholders 57
sustainable tourist-resident relationship: contact theory 157–8, 160; cultural backgrounds 157; SET and 158–60; value co-creation and co-destruction 160–2

Talebi, H. 246
Tasci, A. D. A. 16, 258
Terzidou, M. 8, 246

theory of planned behavior (TPB) 5, 17, 122
theory of reasoned action (TRA) 5, 17, 122
Thibaut, J. W. 158
Tilaki, M. J. M. 4
Tokarchuk, O. 197
Tom, G. 244
tourism area life cycle (TALC) framework 159, 160, 192, 243
Tourism Impact Attitude Scale (TIAS) 3, 42, 43, 45
tourism research development stages: social impacts 2
tourism resistance, online environments: Austrian ski resorts 177; degrowth paradigm, emergence of 174–5; netnography 178; social movements 175–6; visitor-resident dichotomy to tourism actors 176–7; *see also* discursive subjectivities
tourist area life cycle 122
tourist-host social contact 18–19, 30–2
tourist-resident social contact research: co-creating relationship 162–3; co-destruction relationship 164–5; conditions 166; definitions 155; diversity of 166; egotistical relationship 163–4; intrapersonal, interpersonal and structural barriers 155–6, *158*; paired 167; scripted relationship 164; social contact, types of 156–7; value co-creation *vs.* co-destruction 166
transient vacation rentals (TVRs) 241
travel attitude: affective and behavioural component 17; cultural differences 17; and tourist-host social contact 18–19; travel motivation 17–18
Travesi, C. 224
Tucker-Lewis index (TLI) 48
Turkey Ministry of Culture and Tourism (TMCT) 41
Turner, L. W. 17, 245

urban tourism system: complexity and tradeoffs 198; P2PA negative feedback loops 198; P2PA positive feedback loops 199; system disruptions 198
Uysal, M. 197, 198

value co-creation and co-destruction 160–2
Van Boven, L. 244
Vargo, S. L. 161
Velicu, I. 185
Vetitnev, A. M. 82–3
Vogt, C. A. 257

Wall, G. 1
Walter, P. G. 223–5
Wan, Y. K. P. 42, 43, 61, 149
Ward, C. 5, 41, 43, 50, 52, 150
Wearing, S. L. 82, 83
Weaver, D. B. 125, 245
Weberian and Foucauldian framework *80*

Weber's theory 80–1
Wegerer, P. K. 8
Wei, L. 16
Widener, M. N. 199
women empowerment 102–4, *104*; economic empowerment 110–11, *111*; educational empowerment 111–12; political empowerment 113–14; psychological empowerment 113; social empowerment 112–13; through tourism participation 114; tourism and 105
Woosnam, K. M. 3–5, 41–3, 45, 51, 58, 61, 148, 149, 207, 209, 212, 216, 240, 248
World Indigenous Tourism Alliance (WINTA) 223
World Wildlife Fund (WWF) 177

x-axis, tourism development with P2PAs 191–2

Yang, B. 129
y-axis, density and location of P2PA activity 192–6, *193*
Yeager, E. P. 8, 77, 79–82, 91–3, 246, 258
Yoo, W. 128, 129

Zajonc, R. B. 244
Zhao, X. 129
Zheng, D. 141, 218
Ziakas, V. 246
Zimmermann, F. M. 160
Zuev, D. 145
Zuo, B. 81, 91